Critical Reflection

Critical Reflection

A Textbook for Critical Thinking

Malcolm Murray
Nebojsa Kujundzic

McGill-Queen's University Press
Montreal & Kingston · London · Ithaca

© McGill-Queen's University Press 2005
ISBN 0-7735-2879-2 (cloth)
ISBN 0-7735-2880-6 (paper)

Legal deposit second quarter 2005
Bibliothèque nationale du Québec

Printed in Canada on acid-free paper

McGill-Queen's University Press acknowledges the support of the Canada Council for the Arts for our publishing program. We also acknowledge the financial support of the Government of Canada through the Book Publishing Industry Development Program (BPIDP) for our publishing activities.

Library and Archives Canada Cataloguing in Publication

Murray, R. Malcolm (Robert Malcolm), 1959–
    Critical reflection : a textbook for critical thinking /
Malcolm Murray, Nebojsa Kujundzic.

Includes bibliographical references and index.
ISBN 0-7735-2879-2 (bound).—ISBN 0-7735-2880-6 (pbk.)

    1. Critical thinking – Textbooks.   2. Reasoning – Textbooks.
I. Kujundzic, Nebojsa, 1959–.   II. Title.

B809.2.M87 2005   160   C2005-900999-3

Typeset in 10/12 Baskerville with Futura Book display by True to Type

Contents

Part Two   Meaning

Part Three   Truth

Part Four   Logic

Appendices

Preface

Note to Students

One of the major motives behind your decision to become a university student is your desire to think in a more sophisticated and educated manner, and to express your thoughts more clearly. This book offers the tools to help you do that. *Critical Reflection* is an ideal textbook for use in first and second year university and college critical thinking classes. It offers the means to analyse arguments. Students are invited to study elementary formal logic; various forms of inductive arguments such as causal reasoning and analogical arguments; informal fallacies; when to accept and when to reject premises; and problems with language including bias, vested interest, slanting, emotive terms, ambiguity, vagueness, and obfuscation. As well, elementary principles of probability reasoning and scientific method are introduced. Our goal is to help you sharpen reasoning skills used in everyday life. We aim to help students think more clearly, critically, and competently: in short, to distinguish good arguments from bad arguments.

Apart from offering you the tools for critical reflection, our aim is to provide a clearly written, well organised, easily accessible, and engaging book. We offer a wide range of illustrations and examples drawn from newspapers and magazines, as well as classic philosophical texts. The wealth of examples taken from contemporary discussion and debate reinforces the wide applicability of critical thinking. We also offer a large number of questions as well as fairly elaborate answers to a healthy selection of those questions. As in many facets of life, doing is often better than merely thinking about.

In the wake of the Internet and advanced communication technologies, the need to develop the means to critically evaluate the growing flood of information has never been greater. *Critical Reflection* seeks to be a showcase of the role of reason in the confusing world of media persuasion and technological jargon. Whatever your professional and intellectual goals in life may be, critical reflection will help you enhance autonomous thinking.

Note to Instructors

There are fourteen chapters in this text book, too many for half-semester courses. Chapter 1 (Overview) and chapter 2 (Argument Components) provide good basics, but can be covered quickly. The section on suppressed propositions and assumptions (2.6) may give more trouble than it's worth, however, and there may be no loss in skipping this. Chapter 3 (Diagramming) is our introduction to diagramming arguments. Some feel that to best understand diagramming – and especially the nature of missing premises – students must first understand logic. And, once the student understands logic, discussion of diagramming is idle. For those who share this view, chapter 3 may be omitted.

A preliminary chapter on diagramming, however, offers the beginning student the basic concept that arguments have form and shape. This concept is sorely needed for a segment of the student population, and it helps ease their feet into the sometimes daunting waters of formal logic. Understanding the basic pattern of an argument will help inform students about what sort of criticism is required, or what sort of criticism is off the mark. (For example, one has not necessarily refuted a convergent argument by rightly rejecting a premise or its link to the conclusion, since other arms of the argument remain, whereas one's task is complete by rejecting a single premise of a linked argument.) The introduction of counter-considerations is also helpful for recognizing that arguments are often accepted on an "all things considered" sense, rather than an "all-or-nothing" sense. In sum, we view this chapter as a stepping stone to *both* deductive and inductive arguments that are to be introduced later.

Chapter 4 (Language Use) and chapter 5 (Definitions) focus on meaning, which is an integral part of critical reflection. Students of English may find these chapters optional. Chapter 6 (Acceptability) focuses on ways of assessing premises. This, too, is a central concern of any critical thinking course.

One may choose either chapters 7 and 8 (Categorical logic) or chapters 9 and 10 (Propositional Logic), but one needn't study both to get a good sense of the role of logic. Which one is preferable, should one be unable to study both, is a contentious issue. On one side of the debate, categorical logic is, after all, a dated system. When students take advanced logic courses, they study propositional logic, not categorical logic. Still, contradiction and the null set problem are fascinating topics and have more import in the context of categorical logic, and it is an open question whether propositional logic can capture categorical arguments. The introduction of advanced modal logic, for example, is best understood in terms of categorical logic, not propositional logic. Our solution to this problem is not to make the choice. We have presented both, and have made efforts to make the readings on propositional logic independent of the readings on categorical logic.

Chapter 11 (Causation and Probability) and chapter 12 (Science) offer a glimpse of scientific method and probability reasoning, too often ignored in standard critical thinking texts. These chapters provide a backbone for understanding probability reasoning and scientific method, as well as raising the philosophical criticisms of the scientific method. Chapter 13 (Analogical Arguments) assesses the most prevalent type of philosophical argument: arguments by analogy. Lastly, chapter 14 (Fallacies) introduces the student to some of the more common informal fallacies. These are found in almost any critical thinking textbook, but texts differ in how they organize them and to what extent they call them serious infractions. For example, no other text book (with which we're familiar) shows how a slippery slope and false dichotomy are logically equivalent infractions. But their infraction concerns our acceptance of a key premise, not the rejection of the *form* of the argument itself.

Answers to select questions are provided in the appendices. Many of these answers are provided in detail, noting where common errors may have occurred and explaining why the suggested answer is preferable. Despite this, it is possible that, particularly under differently assumed contexts, alternative answers may be permissible. Also found in the appendices is a bad essay, entitled "Vegetarianism and Moral Duty." It is written to commit as many fallacies as possible. It may serve as a ready-made assignment, or exercise. Also provided in the appendices is "Hints for Writing Philosophy Papers," which may serve students' interests.

Malcolm Murray
Nebojsa Kujundzic

Acknowledgments

We owe thanks to our students who suffered through earlier incarnations of this work, and who offered many insights, corrections, and illustrations. We are especially grateful to Kate Merriman for her detailed editorial work. We also owe much gratitude to Matthew Dorrell, Sandra Reddin, Kelly Miles, and Carl Hahn. We are also indebted to Meaghan Enright and Jeremy Livingston who pored over newspapers and magazines looking for examples of flawed reasoning for us. Not surprisingly, they did not come up empty-handed. Many of their results constitute our exercises. Dan Ryan deserves many thanks as well for his help with our discussion on probability. We are also very much indebted to the Webster's Foundation for their generous support.

M.M.
N.K.

Part One
Argument Structure

1

Overview

Philosophy and Critical Thinking • Autonomy
What Is an Argument? • Premises and
Conclusions • Assessing Arguments • Cogency

1.1 Philosophy and Critical Thinking

Philosophy is concerned primarily with concepts. What is truth? Is what we perceive an accurate account of reality or is reality something beyond perceptions? When can we legitimately say we "know" something? How can we convince ourselves that we're not merely brains in a vat? What is the moral thing to do? Is there a universal moral principle? What reason, if any, do we have to be moral, if we can prosper without being moral? What justification, if any, is there for political force? Are there any good arguments for the existence of God?

These are all fun questions, and courses in philosophy typically focus on classical and/or modern answers to these fundamental questions. A course in critical thinking, however, does not. In one important sense, therefore, critical thinking is very different from other philosophy courses. Other philosophy courses focus on content, while Critical Thinking could be described as a course without content. Critical thinking may be seen as meta-philosophy, i.e., the subject of a course *about* philosophy, as opposed to actually *being* philosophy. More accurately, critical thinking is about the methods philosophers use when they tackle fundamental questions. Analogously, then, Critical Thinking is akin to a course in statistics. Psychologists and scientists use statistics to help them assess their subjects, but the actual statistics aren't typically thought to be the subject itself. Likewise, we'll be studying the tools philosophers use when tackling their vexing problems, but not those problems themselves.

All this acts as a warning that the subject matter of this course is not typical of philosophy courses in general. On the other hand, the methods taught are applicable in every facet of life. The knowledge and skills gleaned here are not restricted to philosophy. Critical Thinking teaches reasoning skills that we can use in everyday life. No matter what the program, no matter what the discipline, no matter what our goals are in life, a better understanding of the skills of critical thinking will enhance our chances of autonomous thinking. To be autonomous means that we have escaped the snares of dogma; we hold beliefs that are justified, and not merely those thrust upon us.

1.2   Autonomy

Critical thinking assists us in becoming autonomous. Being autonomous means more than merely being free to choose based on our desires; it also means freely endorsing those desires. A cigarette smoker, for example, is free to satisfy her desire to smoke but might prefer if she did not have that desire. She is not autonomous if she does not freely endorse her desire to smoke.

What we hope to do is to provide the tools to better assess arguments. To see why the ability to better assess arguments is a good thing, worthy of study, compare shopping behaviours. Assessing an argument is a little like shopping. We are constantly bombarded by merchants trying to sell us their wares. We want to assess whether these are the sorts of wares we want to purchase. Is the item worth it? Will it last? Will I later regret my decision? Similarly, everywhere we go people are attempting to convince us to accept their particular argument. We should be asking ourselves the same sorts of questions when judging arguments as we do when deciding whether to buy a specific product or service. Is it worth it? Is the argument convincing or not?

Critical thinking has practical relevance; it can increase our intellectual independence, increase our tolerance for different points of view, and free us from the snares of dogmatism. We may agree with what our parents, our pastors, our friends, our teachers, our politicians, and our scientists tell us, but surely not *merely* on the basis of their telling us. They may be wrong, after all, however well-intentioned. This is the appeal of being autonomous. Critical Thinking invites us to call the bluff of accepted dogmas.

1.3   What Is an Argument?

So just what exactly *is* an argument? The word "argument" employed in ordinary language is oftentimes synonymous with "fight," as in "I had an argument with my father." This is not what we mean by argument. For our purposes here, an argument will mean simply *providing reasons for a belief.* Having an argument with one's father in this sense is very civil.

1.3.1 A History of the Argument

Aristotle (384–322 BC) talked about three basic activities of the mind: *representing, judging,* and *inferring.* For him, an argument involved only the latter activity. Here is a brief account of the three processes.

When a child draws an image of the moon, then we see a *representation* of that particular object. The child is not making any judgments about the represented object (i.e., this representation is not intended to be "true" or "false" of the moon). That is to say, no argument occurs here.

When an observer of the moon claims that the moon appears larger when it is just over the horizon than when it is high in the sky, he or she makes a *judgment* about the size of the moon. (Incidentally, it is true that the moon appears larger when it hangs low over the horizon, but it is false that the actual size of the moon's image varies according to its position. That is an illusion.) A judgment itself is not an argument. Certain judgments may *require* an argument. That is, we might reasonably *expect* an argument, and we are sometimes disappointed when one is not forthcoming. For example, someone might offer the following judgment, or opinion: "Homosexuality is immoral." This is not an argument. This is just a belief, or opinion, or judgment. An argument is the providing of reasons *for* that belief.

When Jane looks up in the middle of the night from her backyard and does not see the moon or any stars, she *infers* that the sky is cloudy. The process of argumentation goes on only in this last case. Therefore, we should recognize that inference-making plays an important part in argumentation. When we are giving reasons for a belief, we are making an *inference* from the reasons to the belief. Argumentation involves these inferences.

Immanuel Kant (1724–1804) referred to inferences as "indirect judgments." For Kant, an inference was a form of judgement deduced indirectly by way of the stated reasons. For example, "Human beings are living creatures. Living creatures procreate. Therefore, human beings procreate." That human beings procreate is thereby a judgment deduced *indirectly* on the basis of the offered facts that human beings are living creatures and living creatures procreate. In this text, we will stick with Aristotle's understanding and forgo Kant's. That is, we will refer to arguments as inferences as opposed to indirect judgments.

In any event, it should be noted that grasping an inference is not like understanding a sentence. Sentences are given. Inferences are made. Further, we can understand an argument without understanding its constituent sentences, and we can understand a set of sentences without recognizing its argument form.

Consider the following argument:

The entity gamma is either anisotropic or isotropic. The entity gamma is not isotropic. Therefore, it is anisotropic.

We do not need to understand the terms "isotropic" and "anisotropic" in order to recognize the basic argument pattern. Notice that the above example is a single argument comprising three sentences. A sentence is not an argument, nor is any bunch of sentences an argument. An argument entails an *inference* that links sentences in a particular way. These points show that grasping an inference is a different process than grasping a sentence.

Still, the inference process itself is perhaps little understood. To complicate matters, anthropologists have documented that there are cultures unable to recognize argument structures in speech while understanding perfectly well the claims that are being made.

So what is the process of inference? It is all very well to say an argument is a process of inference, but we are no further ahead if we fail to understand this process. Consider an analogical case, that of the inviolability of reason. The assertion that reason triumphs emotion has been much doubted in post-modern thought. Reason isn't all there is to life, some may say. Of course, no one need pretend it is, and it is a clear mis-inference to say supporters of reason in human encounters demand that human encounters ought to be *nothing but* reason. Clearly the emotions play a crucial role as well. But more than this, people may doubt the trustworthiness of reason. But on what basis can this inference be made? Do we use reason to demonstrate that reason is untrustworthy? Doing so is obviously incoherent. What then? Non-reason? Do we appeal to irrational arguments to show that reason is problematic? But if we are appealing to non-reason, what reason do we have to give such a demonstration any credence? We are at an impasse.

1.3.2 Defining the Argument

The concept of an inference remains unsatisfactorily metaphysical. We must almost accept it on faith. It is a concept we use. It is not a concept we can jettison without peril. This text is aimed at elucidating the *use* of this concept. Thus, for our purposes, we shall define an argument in the following (really rather typical) way:

An argument is the presentation of reasons offered in support of a claim.

The reasons are called *premises*. The claim they back is called the *conclusion*. An argument, then, is a conclusion backed by reason(s).

A *simple argument* has one conclusion supported by one or more premises. An *extended argument* has a main conclusion supported by premises, some of which are themselves conclusions of subsidiary arguments.

1.4   Premises and Conclusions

It is a common mistake to ignore premises and reasoning and to evaluate the conclusion alone. Consider the following argument:

Certain drugs like marijuana, hashish, and magic mushrooms are natural. Since anything that is natural can't be bad, there is no need to make these drugs illegal.

Now, we might challenge such an argument by pointing out natural substances that in fact are bad for us – poison ivy, for example. But imagine if instead someone says, "I can't refute this argument because I think drugs should be made legal." Now, this is odd. We may agree with the conclusion, but we can nevertheless point out that we don't agree with the conclusion for *those reasons*!

Too often we are tempted to respond positively whenever we agree with the conclusion, and negatively whenever we don't. But having a true or acceptable conclusion is not enough to constitute a good argument. We must have true or acceptable premises and correct reasoning from those premises to the conclusion before we can say the argument is a good one.

It is not enough to reject an argument because we do not like the conclusion, or for that matter accept an argument simply because we agree with the conclusion. To reject an argument, we must find something wrong with the premise(s) or the link between the premise(s) and the conclusion – or both.

Granted, there may be occasions where the mere implausibility of the conclusion should alert us that something may be wrong with the argument that birthed such an implausible result, *even though we may be unable to pinpoint where the argument went astray*! Consider, for example, Zeno's Paradox of Motion. In this argument, Zeno attempts to prove the impossibility of motion. One wouldn't normally think such a proof has a hope of being successful, but it appears to have acceptable premises and, furthermore, that the truth of the premises appears to support the conclusion. Yet it *can't* be right, we might like to shout.

Zeno's Paradox

No matter how fast Achilles is, he can never win a race, for wherever the finish line is, he will never reach it. Suppose Achilles is to run from the starting point S to the goal G. To do this, he must first cross the halfway point between S and G (H1). But before he can do this, he needs to cross the halfway point between S and H1 (H2). Before he can do this, however, he needs to reach the halfway point between H2 and S (H3). Yet he can't hope to do that until he first passes the halfway point between S and H3 (H4) etc., etc., etc. ad infinitum. It appears Achilles will never make it to G, since for any two points, there is an infinite amount of divisible space between them. Since one cannot hope to traverse infinity, Achilles cannot even lift his foot.

Can you see where the argument goes astray? Even if you can't quite, are you convinced that it must go astray somewhere?

One response is along the following lines. Once we incorporate the concept of infinite space in our premises, why not also incorporate the concept of infinite time? We cannot traverse infinite space in finite time. We can clearly concede this. But is it really the case that we cannot traverse infinite space in infinite time? At least we can no longer say we cannot.

Opinion

Now that we know an argument has at least one premise and a conclusion, we can distinguish arguments from *opinion*. An opinion is simply a conclusion without support. Opinions lack any inference. Not so arguments. Only when we provide support for an opinion are we confronted with an argument. Opinions, therefore, are cheap. Arguments are not.

1.5   Assessing Arguments

It is one thing to recognize an argument. It is another to assess one. How do we assess an argument? In assessing arguments, we arm ourselves with two simple questions:

1 What do the constituent parts of the argument mean?
2 Why should I believe it?

The first question concerns clarity. We want to understand the meaning of the claims before we assess the argument. The second question addresses whether the argument is sufficiently supported by good reasons. Only after we understand what is meant by each of the component parts of a particular argument can we begin to assess its merit.

1.5.1 Clarity

An argument should be clear. To be clear is to avoid using *vague, ambiguous,* or *obscure* language. We should also be wary of language that is excessively *emotive,* that is, words that elicit strong emotions in the audience. For purposes of rhetoric and persuasion, emotive language is prudent; but if it obscures an otherwise weak argument, it is something of which critical thinkers ought to be wary. Lastly, we want to detect any *bias* that may skew a proper understanding of the issues being discussed. These concepts are discussed in Part 2.

1.5.2 Reason

Once we understand what an argument means we can begin to assess its claim. We need to demand some evidence, justification, and/or support before we accept the claim. *It should be backed up.*

   To assess whether an argument is sufficiently backed up, there are two issues we need to address:

1 Are the reasons given themselves true or likely to be true? Are they plausible?
2 Are the reasons given, even if true, sufficient for us to accept the conclusion?

1 Acceptability In simple terms, the first question concerns issues of truth. We want to know if the reasons given to justify a particular claim are themselves true. Unfortunately, there are many types of claims where we may be unable to verify whether or not they are true. This may be because they are predictions of future events. We do not now know whether the predictions will come about or not, although we may now know whether they are plausible or not. Likewise, claims about events that happened in the distant past also have uncertain *truth values*. (A truth value is the value – true or false – we assign a particular statement of fact. Something's having "an uncertain truth value," then, means simply that we do not know whether the statement is true or false. The concept of a truth value will come in handy when we examine propositional logic in chapters 9 and 10.) Of course, whether there was a great flood in 1500 BC in the Baltic region is something that is either true or false, and something that would be known as true or false by Baltic citizens of the time, but we may not now know whether it is true or false. Still, we can now speak of the historical claim as being likely or unlikely.

Other claims involve specialized knowledge. We may feel unqualified to assess their truth because we lack such knowledge, although we are willing to admit others may have it. Whether the furcula muscle of the honey bee's stinging apparatus continues to contract rhythmically, forcing venom down the sting core, long after the bee has flown away, is not something we may happen to know as true. We might defer such claims to ethologists. But in the meantime, should we hold that an argument containing such a premise ought to be rejected on the grounds that we know no such thing? That would seem a bit restrictive.

Furthermore, there are other sorts of claims that can't ever rightly be termed "True" or "False." For example, "burning cats is immoral," is not, properly speaking, true or false. (Saying "It is true that we call burning cats immoral" is not the same as saying "Burning cats is immoral" unless what is moral is merely what one's culture dictates. A difficulty here is that we would not be able to critically reflect upon our own culture's mores if this were true. The fact that such reflection is possible, as moral reformers attest, indicates that morality is independent of (or at least not totally dependent on) what one's culture dictates. That is, when we say "burning cats is immoral" we might add without hesitation "... and this is so whatever one's culture happens to think." Truth and falsehood relate to facts. It may be a fact that Bob burned a cat, and it may be immoral that he did so, but the immorality is a judgment we make about the fact, and therefore is not itself a fact (other than that it is a fact that a particular judgment was made

– which is not the same thing). Likewise, aesthetic judgments are not properly speaking true or false.

The above reflections indicate that we severely limit ourselves if we will accept only those claims we know to be true. We will be unable to accept arguments that contain historical claims, future predictions, moral and aesthetic claims, and many scientific claims we cannot personally ascertain at the moment the argument is presented to us. Yet many of these claims ought to be acceptable to us. For example, merely because the immorality of burning a cat is not properly speaking "true," it hardly follows that one should reject the claim should it occur in an argument!

To avoid these problems we need to relax our criteria concerning the truth of claims. We need not demand that a claim is true before we accept it, but that it is at least *acceptable*. In Part 3, we explore various tricks of the trade to help us distinguish acceptable from unacceptable claims.

2 Grounds Even if all the propositions used to justify a claim are deemed acceptable, we still need to assess whether they in fact relate to the conclusion. We shall see in the coming chapters that our means of answering this question will differ depending on what kind of an argument has been given. Arguments come in two basic forms: *deductive* and *inductive*. We will test the *validity* of deductive arguments using *logic* (which itself comes in two forms: *categorical* and *propositional*). Inductive arguments (*probabilistic generalizations, causal arguments,* and *analogical arguments)* require different tools. We will learn how to assess both deductive (Part 4) and inductive arguments (Part 5).

All this is to better equip students to find answers to our two questions: What does it mean and why should I believe it? Of course, we shouldn't issue this challenge at every assertion. For example, "There's ice cream in the freezer," should not normally be met with "Yeah, well prove it to me!" or "What's *that* supposed to mean?" So, part of being good critical thinkers is also to recognize when and *when not* to bother assessing arguments. Not all human discourse is correctly interpreted as an argument. The composition of arguments is the subject matter of our next chapter (chapter 2).

1.6   Cogency

Obviously it is important to be able to determine what makes a good argument. When speaking of arguments in general, whether inductive or deductive, we shall call good only those arguments that are *cogent*. A cogent argument will be either

1 a valid deductive argument with acceptable premises,

or

2 an inductive argument with acceptable premises in which the
  reasoning from the premises to the conclusion is legitimate and sensible.

So, rather than saying a good argument is one in which the premises are true and the conclusion validly follows from them, we say:

A cogent argument is one in which

A. The premises are *acceptable*,

and

B. The conclusion is sufficiently *grounded* by the premises.

Practice

Let's be sure we understand the difference between acceptability conditions and grounds conditions. Assess the following three simple arguments:

(1) 1 All people are immortal.
    2 Wally is a person.
    3 Therefore, Wally is immortal.
(2) 1 Pat is either male or female.
    2 Therefore, Pat is a teacher.
(3) 1 Toronto is north of Mexico City.
    2 Mexico City is north of Buenos Aires.
    3 Therefore, Toronto is north of Buenos Aires.

Argument (1) has at least one premise that is not acceptable. We currently do not accept the claim that people are immortal. (Perhaps we could find an interpretation of the claim that would gain it some proponents, but let's keep things simple and say that the premise "All people are immortal" is unacceptable.)

Notice that the conclusion of this argument follows logically from its premises. Therefore, despite the argument's satisfying condition B (Grounds), it fails condition A (acceptability of premises) and so is not *cogent*.

Argument (2) satisfies the *Acceptability* condition (A). (One possible objection may apply, however, concerning the "either/or" phrasing. It is conceivable that the "either/or" condition is not exhaustive. It may sometimes be the case that a person is neither male nor female. Or we may complain that the "either/or" condition applies only so long as we assume Pat is human. If Pat is a computer, like Hal in *2001: A Space Odyssey*, then the male-female dichotomy fails. But let us, once again, keep things simple and say that this premise is acceptable.)

The real problem with this argument is that its conclusion does not follow from its premise. So, this argument fails the *grounds* condition (B).

Argument (3), meanwhile, satisfies both conditions. Its premises are clearly acceptable and its conclusion follows from the premises. It alone is *cogent*.

Exercise 1.1

Assess the following arguments. Say whether they are cogent arguments. If not, state which condition(s) is violated (clarity, grounds, or acceptability) and briefly explain why. (Answers to select questions are provided in Appendix 1.)

☞ 1 Animals are not human beings. Animals do not speak language as humans do, nor do animals have the same advanced cultures and technologies as humans. Therefore, animals have no moral significance and do not have any moral rights. (Govier, *A Practical Study of Argument*, 4th ed., 86.)

2 People have given children war-related toys for many centuries. Children have often enjoyed playing cowboys and Indians and using toy soldiers and related toys. Not all children who play with war toys become soldiers. Therefore, war toys have no tendency whatsoever to make children less sensitive to violence.

3 If had Hitler died at age ten, Nazism would not have developed in Germany in the way that it did. If Woodrow Wilson had never existed, there would be no League of Nations. And without Mao Zedong, who knows what would have come of the revolutionary movement in China during the 1930s and 1940s? From these facts, we can prove that great men change the course of History.

☞ 4 Since the free sale of marijuana would greatly reduce various forms of drug abuse, and we should do whatever would help reduce drug abuse in Canada, we should allow marijuana to be sold freely.

☞ 5 Homosexuality is immoral because, for one, it's unnatural. Anything unnatural should be banned. That should be obvious, but in case you forget, it's also spelled out as wrong in the Bible.

6 Phillips is in favour of privatized health care. She's also in support of euthanasia. Therefore anyone in favour of euthanasia should pay for it out of their own pockets.

☞ 7 In regards to Barbara MacLeod's statement that her "spritzers" are carbonated fruit juices and not pop ('In defence of the spritzer,' *Guardian*, 18 July 2001). The law is the law and I don't care if it is distilled by monks in the Himalayas and blessed by a voodoo priestess, if it's carbonated and in a can, according to the law, it's pop. There are a variety of natural fruit juices available for purchase at many Island stores, including hers. Add a shot of 'bottled' soda water and voilà ...

carbonated fruit juice with no extra sugar added. Of course there is the other alternative to pop that our mothers have been pushing at us for years ... water. The line has to be drawn somewhere, and carbonated beverages happens to be that line. (George Stewart, letter to the editor, *Guardian*, 30 July 2001)

8 A common objection to ethical utilitarianism is, not that it is morally wrong, but that it is an irremediably vacuous ethic since no specific meaning can be attached to "the maximization of utility" inasmuch as this presupposes the possibility in principle of comparing two alternatively attainable states of affairs from the point of view of overall utility and yet no such comparison is, in principle, possible. (D. Goldstick, "Assessing Utilities," 531)

9 Today's generation of seniors has contributed much to Canada. But what they get out of entitlement programs is more than fair. In the early days of the Canada Pension Plan, payroll deductions were smaller than they are now. Most of today's retirees paid premiums less than half as large as would have been required to fund public pensions at their current levels. No senior should go without the medication he or she needs because he lacks the means to pay for it. But then, no politician is suggesting that. People are living longer and pharmaceutical remedies are becoming more common and more expensive; it is time to recognize and acknowledge, as only a few politicians are doing, that the public purse cannot, and should not, pay for it all. ("Drug money," *National Post*, 14 June 2001, A19)

10 Editor: The headline in *The Guardian* May 23, 2001 "No Gays No B&B" prompts this writer to defend the operator. The prophet Amos wrote between 793–753 BC that there would be a famine of hearing the words of God. That day is upon us. The Christian minority today has no protection from the Human Rights Commission. Christian bashing is allowed. Sodom and Gomorrah was a cakewalk compared to society today. The Human Rights Commission should ban the Bible because it is a book of discrimination that offends. The Bible tells us about heaven and hell, God's blessings and God's curses. Presently our nation is under God's curse because of our immoral practices. (Ron Jenkins, letter to the editor, *Guardian*, 26 May 2001, A7)

11 One thing we Canadians have that we would never want to give up is our freedom of choice. This freedom has allowed for many diverse lifestyles which should be a good thing. It should help us all to grow in maturity. Individually we are different – short, tall, light, heavy, big, small, and we speak other languages, etc. Many are also challenged either physically, mentally, emotionally, and even sexually; and yes, God loves us, everyone. By sexually challenged, I mean some have biological mismatches which might help explain why some of us

choose a same-sex partner to go through life with. As intelligent human beings we should be able to live and let live without judging. God, in his infinite wisdom, is the only one qualified to judge fairly. We, in our limited wisdom, should be able to accept this fact and take the necessary steps in the right direction to promote harmony among our fellow humans. There are some who feel that they need a parade day and perhaps wave a special flag to gain recognition concerning that fact that they are different. In my mind, maybe it's high time that we get on with our individual lives and leave well enough alone. When the time is right, our good Lord, in his infinite fairness and love, will make the final call. In the meantime, let's live, love, and enjoy life while we can. (George Chisholm, letter to the editor, *Guardian*, 10 July 2001, A7)

☞12 Canadian Alliance MP Rob Anders faced a barrage of criticism yesterday after blocking a resolution to declare Nelson Mandela an honorary Canadian citizen ... He told Mr. McCallum [the Liberal MP who introduced the motion] he would not support it because Mr. Mandela was a "Communist and a terrorist," but also told reporters he was paying back the Liberals because they blocked a celebration of the Queen's 50th wedding anniversary. (Campbell Clark, "All sides blast MP for 'insult' to Mandela," *Globe and Mail*, 8 June 2001, A1, A5)

13 This letter is in regard to the recent national and provincial topic of the notorious tar ponds toxic site and possible resettlement of those wanting it. In a world where money speaks very loudly (too loudly, some would say), I believe our current government [of John Hamm] will only act when it realizes how great the cost to tax-payers will be in the not-too-distant future for medical and social costs of related illnesses caused by the toxic chemicals and waste in the Sydney, especially Whitney Pier, region (where I originally came from, by the way). The healthy children and young adults of today will soon become the sick adults of tomorrow, if we don't do something soon enough. (Phillip McLean, letter to the editor, *Chronicle-Herald*, 26 May 2001, C4)

14 David Marshall believes Mi'kmaq should be exempt from paying the $3.50 toll on Highway 104 because natives are the rightful owners of all property in Nova Scotia. "There's no treaty that suggests we ever gave up our claim to property rights," Mr. Marshall said Monday. "Why should I have to pay to travel from one point to another on my people's property?" (Steve Proctor, "Make 104 toll-free for Mi'kmaq," *Chronicle-Herald*, 17 July 2001, A1)

☞15 All this crying the blues about cruelty to animals and the rodeo (letters – July 9–10)! Rodeo is one of the things that North Americans share as a heritage – you know, before barbed-wire fence changed everything. World-class athletes competing in a dangerous sport reminding us [of] a day gone by isn't wrong. It's a reminder of our history. Aboriginal communities can defend their hunting rights to the bitter end, yet rodeo should be stopped? It's reminding us of the roots that created the greatest agricultural system in the entire world, something we should be proud of every day at the dinner table. As sports go, this one is a lot more important than golf. Sing it, Garth. (Rainer Behmer, letter to the editor, *Globe and Mail*, 11 July 2001, A12)

16 Kissing is definitely cheating [March – Is Cheating Kissing?]. If a woman feels she needs to boost her marital passion by kissing someone other than her husband, then she lacks imagination and creativity. It is much smarter and safer to add fertilizer to your own lawn than to graze elsewhere. Let's talk about how women should honour their marital commitment rather than indulge in self-centered whims. Keep your energy, attention and lips on your own husband. (Barbara Duteau, letter to the editor, *Flare*, June 2001, 16)

☞ 17 Re: the letter from a Canadian defending the actions of protestors in Quebec City during the Summit of the Americas (May 21): The rights to information, free speech and all the other ingredients of democracy are undisputed. But what if those protestors are a relatively small group of rioters who more or less represent only themselves and have no better ideas than the ones they oppose? And what if the demonstrators would use more than just rubber bullets against their opponents given the chance? (Peter Bohmer, letter to the editor, *Time* (Canadian edition), 18 June 2001, 5.

18 Suppose, tomorrow, Stockwell Day decides to step down, a leadership review is held, a new Alliance leader is selected before the end of the summer, and then the dissident dozen decide they don't like the cut of the jib of this new leader. What then? More anguished calls from the unhappy campers for yet another leadership review? How long does this procedure go on? Until there are just 12 Alliance party members left? All with gold-plated pensions. (Donna Procher, letter to the editor, *National Post*, 6 July 2001, A15)

19 The Four Noble Truths of Buddhism are
1 Suffering exists
2 Suffering is caused by insatiable, irrational craving
3 Suffering ceases when the cause disappears
4 Following the Eightfold Noble Path will cause craving to disappear

Therefore, one should follow the eightfold path to negate suffering.

Argument Components

Premises and Conclusions • Propositions and Sentences • Inference Indicators • Explanations Modalities • Suppressed Propositions and Assumptions

2.1 Premises and Conclusions

We have seen in chapter 1 that an argument is a group of sentences that offers reasons in support of a claim. These reasons are called *premises*. The claim they back is called the *conclusion*. A *simple argument* has one conclusion supported by one or more premises, while an *extended argument* has a main conclusion supported by premises, some of which are conclusions of subsidiary arguments.

It is important that we are able to identify the conclusion and the premises which lead up to it within any argument. Consider, for example, the following argument:

Since anything affecting only parties to a fully informed, voluntary agreement is moral, prostitution among fully informed, voluntary parties is moral.

The conclusion is, "Prostitution (among fully informed, voluntary parties) is moral." The premise is, "Anything that affects only parties to a fully informed, voluntary agreement is moral."

In this case, we might also detect an added or assumed premise, something like the following: "Prostitution affects only those party to a fully informed, voluntary agreement."

The order in which conclusions and premises occur in an argument does not matter for logical purposes. It may matter for oratorical or aesthetic purposes (that is, it may make the argument sound better), but that is another matter. Nevertheless, when logicians analyse arguments, they always rearrange the argument so that the conclusion occurs last, and the premise or premises first. Thus, the short argument above, from the logician's point of view, looks like this:

1 The outcomes of voluntary, fully informed agreements are moral.
2 Prostitution is (typically) an outcome of fully informed agreements.
3 Therefore prostitution is (typically) moral.

Assessing the argument is another matter. With the above argument, we might ask the following sort of questions:

i. Do prostitutes really *voluntarily* agree? What is our definition of "voluntary"?
ii. Could there be other concerned parties affected by prostitution that aren't part of that agreement? Is it impossible to imagine that women in general may be adversely affected by a patriarchal society's condoning prostitution?
iii. Is it really the case that morality is simply the outcome of agreement? Or is this too bizarre a concept of morality? Aren't some things morally heinous regardless of whether some morally insensitive people happen to agree to them? Is selling one's body for remuneration an example of such an agreement?

Of course, merely raising these questions does not defeat the argument. We have to assess the likely answers as well. For example, someone may be intent on answering "Yes" to the initial question in (i), "No," to the initial question in (ii), and "Yes," to the initial question in (iii). Such answers will require support. For our purposes here, it is sufficient to establish that it *is* an argument, and to have a glimpse at the relevant ways to question the merits of an argument.

2.2 Propositions and Sentences

Concerning the argument for prostitution, notice that the logician has broken the original sentence into three separate sentences. Why? Well, the logician isn't concerned with sentences as much as with *propositions*. A proposition is a simple assertion. A sentence may be made up of a number of simple assertions. In the prostitution argument, although only one sentence is used, there are three propositions within that sentence.

A general rule is that the more premises used to support the conclusion, the stronger the argument. But merely repeating the same thing over and over again in different sentences does not count as actually strengthening the argument. Children might make this mistake. In the argument, "It's mine. I saw it first. I saw it first. I saw it first," there is only one premise supporting the conclusion and not three separate premises.

As we grow older, we are less prone to repeating the same sentence as our method of argumentation. Still, it is surprising to see how often people repeat the same *proposition* in the belief that this benefits their case.

They won't utter the same sentence, but they might express the same idea using different words. For example:

> Prostitutes are immoral. More than that, selling one's body for sex is completely unethical.

Despite the difference in wording, no new idea is divulged. Since being a prostitute *means* selling (or renting, perhaps) one's body for sex, and something that is immoral *means* (or means sufficiently) that it is unethical, saying "prostitutes are immoral" is the *same* as saying "selling one's body for sex is unethical."

We can see, then, that any number of sentences may make the same assertion. Consider the following student response to the question, "What is a problem for epistemological relativity?"

> The theory of epistemological relativity is false. There is only one right answer. If two factual claims are given that contradict one another, it is necessary that at least one is wrong. There is only one truth, not many.

In this example, we have many different sentences, and while no key word is repeated, it should be clear that there is only one proposition uttered; everything else is merely synonymous.

Seeing this requires some understanding of epistemological relativism. Epistemological relativism asserts that there are no absolute truths. Since a "right answer" presupposes a truth that is the same for all, if epistemological relativism is accepted, there can be no "right" answers. As a result, saying that there is only one right answer is the same as saying that the theory of epistemological relativity is false. The theory of epistemological relativity may also be understood as denying the law of contradiction. Admitting contradictions is not a problem for epistemological relativists, since to contradict something means at least one of the claims is false. But if there are no right answers, there can be no wrong answers, and so a contradiction cannot matter. But that means that to say contradictions imply at least one false answer is to claim that epistemological relativism is false. Lastly, a "right" answer is synonymous with an answer that is "true." So the last line is the same as the second, which has already been demonstrated to be the same as the first, and, it turns out, the third as well. The theory of epistemological relativity denies the assertion that there is only one truth. So to deny this (the denial of there being only one truth) is equivalent to denying the theory of epistemological relativity. What the "argument" amounts to, then, is very similar to the repetition of the child's argument we have already dismissed: "The theory of epistemological relativism is false because it is false. It is false. Furthermore, it is false." In fact, the argument as stated doesn't even qualify as an argument, since an argument requires at least *two* propositions, one a premise and the other a conclusion. In this

case the whole set of sentences amounts to a single proposition. It fails
even to qualify as an argument, let alone a bad argument.

This example serves to highlight an important difference between a sentence and a proposition. And what we (as critical thinkers) want to hone
in on are propositions, not sentences. So what is the difference between a
proposition and a sentence? A sentence is a grammatical form, while a
proposition asserts a claim. Also, a sentence is not properly thought of as
either true or false, but a proposition must be either *true* or *false*. That is
why we speak of propositions as being *truth-functional*.

2.2.1 Unbreakable Propositions

The distinction between propositions and sentences might incline one to
think that logicians break complex sentences into simple sentences. This
isn't quite so. Some complex or compound sentences (i.e., sentences composed of simple sentences and a conjunction) are in fact one proposition
and ought never to be severed.

Here are two common types:

1 *If ... then* statements are always one proposition. Never split them.

Consider the following two sentences:

(1) If a fetus were a person, abortion would be immoral.
(2) Since a fetus is a person, abortion is immoral.

The first sentence is a single proposition, while the second sentence has
two propositions. The first is a *conditional* or *hypothetical* sentence. There is
no assertion, as given, that a fetus is a person, for that would be to ignore
the little word *if*. The import of the *if* is to note that the second component
of the assertion (that abortion is immoral) would follow from the condition that a fetus is a person, but nothing is asserted about the truth of the
first component of the statement (that a fetus is a person) in this instance.
We call the first component of a conditional proposition the *antecedent*. We
call the second component of a conditional proposition the *consequent*. To
assert the antecedent all by itself would require a separate premise. The
point is that the separate premise cannot be assumed on the basis of the
conditional statement presented. After all, it is not inconsistent to assert
both that a fetus is not a person and that, if it were, abortion would be
immoral. Compare the following proposition:

(3) If I leap off the top of the CN tower, I will be killed.

Obviously nothing about accepting this proposition commits us to leaping
off the top of the CN tower.

In sentence (2), however, the claim that a fetus is a person is plainly asserted. It is on the basis of that assertion that the speaker infers that abortion is immoral (as the premise indicator *since* suggests). Notice, then, that the second statement contains an argument, while the first does not. Although we might *expect* an argument for (1), by itself, it is merely an assertion.

2 *Either/or* statements are always one proposition. Never split them.

Consider, for example, the following two statements:

(1) Either the stock will rise and not drop further, or I'm selling.
(2) The stock dropped even further, so I'm bailing.

The first sentence is one single proposition; the second, two. The first is not an argument; the second is. The logic for this is the same as the logic for not splitting conditional statements. In either/or statements (or *disjunctive* propositions), we are asserting that at least one of these *disjuncts* is true. It is possible that both are true, but the proposition is asserting that at least both are not false. But the claim that at least one of these disjuncts is true does not specify *which* disjunct is true. For that reason we cannot treat a disjunctive proposition as asserting *each* disjunct.

In fact, conditional statements can be logically converted into disjunctive statements, and vice versa. If I say I'll have blueberry pie or apple pie, I'm asserting that at least one of these disjuncts is true (perhaps both are). But if this is so, then it follows that if I do not have the blueberry pie, I will have the apple. Thus, the disjunctive proposition

(3) I will have either the blueberry or the apple pie,

gets converted into the conditional proposition,

(4) If I don't have the blueberry pie, I will have the apple pie.

Since conditionals are logically equivalent to disjunctives, if we cannot split one, we cannot split the other.

Conjunctives

"And" statements are referred to as *conjunctive* statements. Statements with ... *and* ... may be split into two propositions or kept together as two units of one proposition. Unlike conditionals and disjunctives, conjunctive statements are not unbreakable. In some cases they may and should be split; it others, they should not be. Therefore, we might offer the following general recommendation: *split if necessary, otherwise keep them together*. But what constitutes "necessary"? We will better understand when splitting is necessary after we have examined logical proofs in chapter 10. For now, we shall have to resort to the following general rule for conjunctives:

Split if both conjuncts offer independent support to a conclusion; otherwise don't.
This amounts to the following general appraisal: Split conjuncts if you think doing so strengthens the argument; otherwise don't bother.

Do not be fooled into thinking "and" statements offer anything further than conjunction. Generally this warning is idle. If I say, "I watched TV and ate dinner," we are not typically tempted to think an inference or causal connection is being made between the two conjuncts. I'm not eating dinner *because* I'm watching TV, or the reverse. Fine. But consider the following conjunctive proposition:

The Body Shop supported environmental policies and their profits increased.

Might we be tempted to assume a causal relation between the two conjuncts? The fact that the events are *correlated,* that is, occur together in time, does not by itself prove a *causal* relation. If it did, consider the bizarre prophylactic result of the otherwise sensible claim, "I have a toaster and no children."

The result of the preceding speculation is this: Don't assume any causal or logical inference between two or more conjuncts unless explicitly stated.

Opinion Revisited

Recall our earlier distinction between opinion and argument (1.4). There we said that opinion is an unsupported "conclusion." Technically this is incorrect, since a conclusion by definition is supported. That's like saying a cancelled concert is still a concert. With new understanding of the concept of propositions, we can be more precise in our definition of opinion. *Opinion is an uninferenced proposition, or series of uninferenced propositions.* An argument, on the other hand, provides an inferenced proposition.

2.3 Inference Indicators

We need to be able to recognize arguments and their component parts, because we treat them differently than we do mere statements. With arguments, we are being asked to accept the conclusion on the basis of one or more inferences. Judging the merits of an inference is a different task from judging the merits of the propositions themselves. Of course, we'll have to learn how to do both. But before we apply our critical arts, we have to first make sure that we are confronted with an argument. As mentioned in chapter 1, asking "Why should I believe that?" is inappropriate when confronted with a non-argument, like a joke, or a marriage proposal, or an instructional manual.

So, are there any ready rules that distinguish an argument from a non-argument? *Intent* is important, of course. If there is intent to convince us of something – especially something about which we're not presently convinced – we should expect an argument. Unfortunately, expecting an argument doesn't mean we will be confronted with one. Too often we find ourselves in situations where we would expect an argument and find ourselves disappointed. We meet mere opinion instead.

Context matters in determining intent, but the reliance on context by itself, does not provide a clear rule. Another way to distinguish arguments from non-arguments is by *inference-indicators*.

2.3.1 Premise and Conclusion Indicators

An *inference* is the process in which a conclusion is arrived at and affirmed on the basis of one or more premises. An *inference indicator* alerts us to the fact that an inference is being assumed. Wherever there is an inference, there is also an argument of sorts. Since an argument is a claim based on reasons, the reasons are the premises and the claim is the conclusion. And when we say that the conclusion *follows from* the premises or reasons given we mean that an inference is to be made here. There happen to be a number of words that alert us to inferences.

Consider, for example, the following argument:

Since the free sale of marijuana would greatly reduce various forms of drug abuse, and we should do whatever would help reduce drug abuse in Canada, we should allow marijuana to be sold freely.

In this argument, let us highlight the first word, *since*. "Since" acts as a premise indicator. That is, what follows the word "since" is a premise. Since it is a premise, it cannot possibly be a conclusion (although a conclusion may also act as a premise to a further conclusion).

Here is a partial list of other premise indicators:

Premise Indicators

since	as shown by	may be inferred from
because	inasmuch as	may be deduced from
for	as indicated by	in view of the fact that
as	the reason is that	given that
follow from	for the reason that	granted that

A *conclusion indicator* indicates that what follows is the conclusion. Consider the following argument:

Every part of God's creation is there for a reason. Therefore, everything and

everyone deserves to be treated with respect, including the crows.
(Gail McKenzie, letter to the editor, *National Post*, 30 June 2001,
A15.2.6.4)

The word "therefore" in this argument acts as a conclusion indicator. It
claims that our needing to respect crows is a legitimate inference from
recognition of God's efficient design. Whether we agree with the inference, let alone the premise upon which the inference hinges, is another
matter. Here is a partial list of conclusion indicators:

Conclusion Indicators

therefore	which shows that	accordingly
hence	which means that	then
thus	which entails that	consequently
so	which implies that	we may infer that
ergo	which allows us to infer	I conclude that

2.3.2 Absent Indicators

Notice, however, that the absence of any inference indicator does not necessarily mean that we are not faced with an argument. In less negative
terms, we may be confronted with an argument despite the absence of
inference indicators.

Consider the following:

It's going to rain. Last time I wanted to play golf, it rained. The time before
that, it rained as well.

If we interpret the first proposition, "It's going to rain," as a conclusion,
and the specious reasons for such an inference as the small sampled correlation between raining and the desire to golf, we have the structure of an
argument. Yet no inference indicators are present.

Something similar happens with the following argument:

Joe should not go out wearing only his T-shirt and shorts. It is snowing
heavily.

There are no inference indicators, but we are nevertheless confronted
with an argument. But which direction does the inference go? Obviously,
it is not snowing *because* Joe should not go out wearing only his T-shirt and
shorts. Rather, the structure of this inference is the following:

Premise = It is snowing heavily
Conclusion = Joe should not go out wearing only his T-shirt and shorts

It is on the basis of the premise that we infer the conclusion. So, it is on the basis of the heavy snowfall that we make normative demands on Joe's outerwear.

A "normative demand," by the way, tells us what we ought to do. Normative claims are contrasted with *descriptive* claims. A descriptive claim tells us what *is*. *Normative* claims tell us what *ought to be*. Descriptive claims describe the state of affairs as they are or as they were, and by themselves make no judgments on that state, whereas normative claims are made for the purpose of judgment or to incite action. For example, "Bill put his cat in the microwave," is a descriptive claim, whereas "Bill ought not to have put his cat in the microwave" is a normative claim. Normative claims are not thereby contingent on descriptive claims. The fact that Bill put his cat in the microwave is irrelevant to what Bill ought to have done with his cat. Notice, too, that this particular normative claim is also a moral claim. All moral claims are normative; but not all normative claims are moral. For example, "Use a Bodum or at least a cloth filter for a richer, oilier coffee," is a normative albeit non-moral claim. (Note, lastly, that a non-moral claim is certainly different from an immoral claim, but we will stop the digression here.)

Consider, next, the following argument:

> Mr. Day was the one who began to drag the party down. But the rebels are the ones who have effectively killed the Canadian Alliance. They had in place a democratic and constitutional means for replacing their leader. They chose to ignore this legitimate leadership-review process in favour of a blood-soaked, premature and precipitous insurgency which tore to pieces what they had spent years building. When they began hand-grenading the leader's office, the Alliance was close to 20% in the polls. Now it is at 6%. (Lawrence Martin, "More than one guilty party," *National Post*, 17 July 2001, A15)

Again, we should be fairly adept at detecting that this is an argument, yet no inference indicators are present. Distinguishing the conclusion from the premises requires paying attention to the *intent* of the speaker. It should be clear to newspaper readers that the second proposition (the rebels have effectively killed the Alliance party) is the conclusion. The propositions that follow are offered in support of that. (We may also notice that the language used is fairly *emotive*. That is to say, the language is carefully crafted to elicit strong, and in this case negative, emotions. We will complain about this in chapters 4, 5, & 6.)

Consider next the following argument:

> He did not intend to kill her. The knife stroke was delivered with only moderate force.

There are no inference indicators to help us distinguish which proposition is the premise and which the conclusion, but this should not make it impossible for us to discern the direction of the inference. Presumably we will agree that it makes sense to say that the second proposition implies the first. That is, the conclusion comes first; the premise second. We can imagine that the force of the knife stroke is used as support of the accused's innocence. Whether it necessarily follows is certainly another matter. His intent to kill her may merely have been thwarted by his impotence.

Admittedly, this example often troubles students. The direction of inference from the second to the first proposition is frequently challenged. The *causal* connection, if true, moves from the first to the second. It is because he didn't intend to kill her that his knife thrusts were "only moderate." (What a sweet guy.) This we can admit. Does this admission show that the conclusion is the second, and not the first? Not quite. For we have to remind ourselves that the conclusion of an argument is that proposition which we're asked to believe. We wouldn't be asked to believe it if we already did. In the likely context for this argument, the evidence in front of us is the depth of the knife-blade thrusts, and not the intentional state of the accused. We are not asking for the causal direction; we are asking for the inferential direction.

Consider one more example:

> An eighty-year-old man backed out of a driveway and ran over a five-year-old girl on a bike. The girl fell under the back wheel of the car as it backed out and her head was crushed. We should prevent people over seventy from driving.

It begins like a report, rather than an argument. The last line, however makes an inference based on the stated information. It is therefore an argument, despite the absence of inference indicators. We are asked to accept the last proposition on the basis of the first propositions. The second line, notice, is not really an addition in factual content to what we have already gleaned from the first line. Therefore, we should notice that there is one premise here.

2.3.3 Decoy Indicators

We have seen that arguments may be present in the absence of any inference indicators. When this occurs, our ability to distinguish conclusions from premises is made more difficult, but not impossible. More troubling, however, is the fact that there exist *decoy indicators*. Finding an inference indicator does not guarantee that an argument is being presented. Some of the terms we have labelled "inference indicators" may in fact be *decoys*. Consider the inference indicator "since" in the example below:

> Since all men are mortal and Socrates is a man, Socrates is mortal.

The "since" indicates that what follows is premise. On the other hand, "I have had buck teeth since I was five years old," does not mean that being five years old is offered as a *reason* for having buck teeth. This "since" merely indicates the passage of time.

Our point, then, is to beware. There is no hard-and-fast rule for recognizing an argument when we are confronted with one, but this does not mean such recognition is impossible. Context usually plays a key role. Remember: If someone is trying to get us to believe something, we should expect an argument.

Even this last claim needs qualification. Advertisers often try to get us to believe something, such as that Canadian beer is great. But often we are not presented with any argument for the claim. Rather we are bombarded with intriguing images, and somehow these are supposed to help convince us to buy Canadian beer. Such advertising schemes are very successful, so we cannot say the advertisers are unaware of what they're doing. We can say, however, that the success of such advertising is predicated on the general lack of awareness of consumers. Although we can't change everyone, our hope is to at least curb the tendency to nonautonomous acceptance in ourselves and our readers.

When we expect an argument yet do not find one, or do not find an adequate one, *we should not be convinced.* The fact that many of us are convinced only reveals something that we have known all along: we are not, by and large, as rational as we think we are.

Other words that sometimes act as inference indicators, and sometimes serve other purposes, are *for, because, as.* Compare the following uses:

Arguments	Non-Arguments
You should be careful, *as* it's slippery out.	*As* Gregor Samson awoke one morning from uneasy dreams he found himself transformed into a gigantic insect. Kafka, "The Metamorphosis"
Beware, *for* we are sinners all.	Use a Phillips head *for* those screws.
Take the asparagus juice off the shelf, *because* it isn't selling.	The Titanic sank *because* it hit an iceberg.

2.4 Explanations

Sometimes people are trying to convince us of something about which we are already convinced. Then, in one sense, they are not presenting an argument. They may instead be giving an *explanation.* For example,

The car crashed because the driver slammed on the brakes to miss the pedestrian and lost control on the ice.

Here we have the premise indicator "because," and what appears *in form* to be an argument. But, if the person being addressed already knows that the car crashed, there is no reason to convince her that the car indeed crashed. An argument, don't forget, is intended to convince us to accept the conclusion on the basis of the premises. If we already accept the conclusion, and the speaker knows this, the intent must be something other than an argument. In this case, the intent seems to be an *explanation*. As an explanation is being offered for why the car crashed, not an argument that the car crashed. Thus the propositions "braked," "avoid the lady," and "lost control on the ice" are not mustered to support the conclusion, since the conclusion needs no support, but to explain why the crash happened.

Let's consider another example:

> Tension was especially high ahead of Monday's opening of the Maccabiah Games, an Olympic-style event for Jewish athletes. Two Palestinians were killed in Jerusalem early Monday while trying to assemble a bomb near the stadium ... The two apparently were killed while a bomb they were preparing exploded prematurely. ("Israeli tanks move into Hebron," *Chronicle-Herald*, 17 July 2001, A8)

In this example, we are not confronted with an argument. There is no inference we are being asked to accept. What is given is simply a description. There is a set of facts, or putative facts, and we are not asked to accept any inference from those facts. Argument, therefore, is more than a bundle of facts, just as a house is more than a bundle of bricks.

Here is a good rule of thumb for distinguishing arguments from explanations:

> *If the reasons provided are less obvious than the claim for which they are given, the passage is probably an explanation.*

Practice 1

Identify whether the following are arguments or explanations. Be prepared to justify your position.

(1) It is useful to study philosophy because it enables one to become a more sophisticated reasoner.
(2) I have decided to take philosophy because I need a credit in general arts.
(3) World Vision Canada, an aid organization that has shipped medicine to Iraq with great difficulty because of the UN trade ban, also welcomed a lifting of sanctions, which would make it easier to send humanitarian supplies, spokeswoman Kathy Vandergrift said. (Jeff Sallot, "Ottawa backs plan to ease Iraqi sanctions," *Globe and Mail*, 19 May 2001, A9)

The first example is an argument because it puts forth the conclusion "It is useful to study philosophy," and does so on the basis of the particular reason of becoming a sophisticated reasoner. Of course, this presumes that being a sophisticated reasoner is useful, but we shall let that pass for present purposes. The whole drift of the argument, as it were, is headed towards the following: "It is reasonable to conclude that studying philosophy is useful."

In contrast, (2) is not an argument. It is an explanation offered to clarify one's personal decision. It is not appropriate to translate (2) as: "It is reasonable to conclude that I've decided to take philosophy." In other words, my decision to take philosophy is not put forth for consideration – it is simply stated.

Likewise, (3) is not an argument. We are not being asked to accept anything beyond what is baldly stated.

The point of this short exercise is to warn us that terms such as "because," "so," "hence," "since," "for," etc. cannot be taken to guarantee argumentative contexts. Speakers have a wide variety of intents other than argumentation. Utterances have to be carefully examined in light of their broader context and intent.

Exercise 2.1

Determine whether each of the following passages is an argument, explanation, or neither. If they constitute arguments, state what the main conclusion is. (Answers to selected questions provided in Appendix 1.)

☞ 1 Schools often define learning as an independent activity – learning is supposed to be done quietly, by students working alone. However, since most adult work is carried out in groups, school does not prepare children for their future learning styles.

2 The "zero-tolerance" policy on violence in schools (students are expelled at once for violent behaviour) will lead to more violence, not less. There are no special schools for children who have been expelled for violent behaviour. That means that these children will have no alternatives for education, and with no education will have little likelihood of finding a job. The resulting poverty, unemployment, and lack of opportunities are likely to lead to more violence.

☞ 3 Often, accidents in the workplace occur because machine safety devices have been removed to improve productivity, or because workers have been given inadequate training or inadequate safety equipment.

4 You should buy or sell your house with a professional realtor, rather than trying to do it yourself. Realtors know how to market and sell houses, and you do not. Ninety-nine percent of people buy and sell with professional realtors for a reason. Are you going to try

to do your own dental work? That could also save you thousands of dollars.

☞ 5 The use of marijuana and other drugs is on the rise among young adults after years of decline. Drug and alcohol use tend to increase when young people leave home to go to college. Later, with marriage and family responsibilities, people often cut down or even quit; but in times of stress they are likely to fall back on their old habits.

6 Gregor Mendel did his genetic experiments with pea plants. Around 1900, scientists wanted to perform his experiments on animals. They needed small, easy-to-keep animals that also had distinct and variable characteristics that could be traced from generation to generation. The animals also needed to be easily breedable, so scientists didn't have to wait years to see the results. That's how the mouse became such a common lab animal.

☞ 7 Supermarkets are designed to maximize the likelihood of buying. The most-visited departments are placed furthest from the entrance. For example, someone who just wants a loaf of bread is forced to travel through the whole store, ideally passing many high-profit items. Market research has shown that impulse buys are most likely to occur early in the shopping trip. Thus, the items with the highest profit margins are located near the entrances. The seductive appearance of the food is accomplished by lighting – bright fluorescent lighting makes the cans sparkle, whereas in the produce department lower-level track lighting makes the vegetables and fruits look vibrantly coloured.

☞ 8 Colchester Regional Hospital will once again have fewer staff available this summer because of vacations, says Krista Burrill, director of public relations for the District 4 health authority. (Mary Ellen MacIntyre, "Vacations to leave Truro hospital short-staffed," *Chronicle-Herald*, 22 May 2001, A5)

9 Septuplets born last week to a couple from Saudi Arabia have a 95 per cent chance of survival, their doctor said Monday ... The father, Fahad Qahtani, who currently lives in nearby Falls Church, Va., said he and his wife are overjoyed by the births because they want a large family and have lost two of their three children to illness over the last five years. ("Septuplets likely to live, doctors say," *Chronicle-Herald*, 17 July 2001, A8)

☞10 "Since ecosystems are interconnected networks of biotic and abiotic components, they cannot be delimited by specific boundaries," Dr. Joseph Gerrath, president of the Canadian Botanical Association, wrote in a letter to Dave Lipton, superintendent of the P.E.I. National Park. "This is why particular attention should be given to those adjacent areas around the park that have potential to be developed," Gerrath said in the letter.(Gauthier, Mike, "Potential development near Greenwich dunes worries P.E.I. botanists," *The Guardian*, May 22, 2001, A2)

11 Problems stemming from sea trials will force the second of Canada's new submarines to be delivered a month later than planned. HMCS Windsor was scheduled to leave a British shipyard this week but "a few challenges have arisen which have caused some delays," said the man leading the effort to acquire the subs. "The delay is not entirely unexpected, as these boats were out of service for a few years before Canada agreed to acquire them," said Cpt. Mike Williamson. ("Second of new subs to be delayed till August," *Chronicle-Herald*, 17 July 2001, A3)

Exercise 2.2

Distinguish conclusions and premises in the following arguments and highlight any inference indicators. (Answers to select questions provided in Appendix 1.)

1 Climate models suggest that during the next century the average values of temperature and precipitation are likely to change over large areas of the globe. As a result, widespread adjustments are likely to occur in the distribution of terrestrial vegetation. (Schlesinger et al., "Biological Feedbacks in Global Desertification," 1043)

☞ 2 The evidence of sexologists strongly indicates that women whose partners are aggressively uncommunicative have little chance of experiencing sexual pleasure. But it is not reasonable for women to consent to what they have little chance of enjoying. Hence it is not reasonable for women to consent to aggressive non-communicative sex. (Lois Pineau, "Date Rape: A Feminist Analysis," 239)

3 Good sense is of all things in the world the most equally distributed, for everybody thinks himself so abundantly provided with it, that even those most difficult to please in other matters do not commonly desire more of it than they already possess. (Descartes, *Discourse on Method*)

☞ 4 A computer cannot deliberately break rules. We should be able to see, then, that a computer cannot cheat.

5 Women generally do not have confidence in themselves, or else they find it difficult to maintain confidence. Therefore, if we are to achieve true equality, hiring preference should be given to women in cases where men outnumber women. To some people this might at first appear to be unfair to men, but I think that on reflection they will change their minds.

☞ 6 He that loveth not knoweth not God; for God is love. I John 4:8 (King James Version)

7 I knew you came from Afghanistan. The train of reasoning ran,

"Here is a gentleman of a medical type, but with the air of a military man. Clearly an army doctor, then. He has just come from the tropics, for his face is dark, and that is not the natural tint of his skin, for his wrists are fair. He has undergone hardship and sickness, as his haggard face says clearly. His left arm has been injured. He holds it in a stiff and unnatural manner. Where in the tropics could an English army doctor have seen much hardship and got his arm wounded? Clearly in Afghanistan." (Sir Arthur Conan Doyle, *A Study in Scarlet*)

☞ 8 That today's parents are under an increasing strain in bringing up children is shown by the rapid and horrible rise in the incidence of child abuse. Obviously the government must provide substantial help to the family, which means there should be a broad system of day-care centres for children of working parents. The number of working mothers is constantly increasing, so certainly small children will be even more neglected unless there are day-care centres. Moreover, we now know how important it is for children to be stimulated and given the chance to learn at the earliest ages, and this need can best be filled by such centres. (Adapted from Beardsley, *Thinking Straight: Principles of Reasoning for Readers and Writers*)

9 Animals are not human beings. Animals do not speak language as humans do, nor do animals have the same advanced cultures and technologies as humans. Therefore, animals have no moral significance and do not have any moral rights.

10 People have given children war-related toys for many centuries. Children have often enjoyed playing cowboys and Indians and using toy soldiers and related toys. Not all children who play with war toys become soldiers. Therefore, war toys have no tendency whatsoever to make children less sensitive to violence.

☞11 We should abolish the minimum wage. The burden of helping the unfortunate is placed on businessmen, and most minimum-wage earners would be happy to work for less, anyway.

12 Mr. Day has every right to insist on a role in picking his interim replacement. He has every right to ensure his party not be turned over to those who sought and plotted his destruction, since there are tens of thousands of CA [Conservative Alliance] members whose views and desires are not represented by these dissidents, and because there is reason to believe the dissidents would take 30 pieces of silver for delivering the CA to Mr. Clark. (Lorne Gunter, "Summertime, and the leader's uneasy," *National Post*, 9 July 2001, A14)

13 "We think the current slump in the telecom sector will be prolonged, due to a decline in telecom operator spending, a glut of network capacity and the absence of compelling new network technologies," agreed analysts at UBS Warburg. (Michael Higgins, "Analysts expect prolonged tech slump," *National Post*, 25 July 2001, A8)

2.5 Modalities

Apart from inference indicators, which help us distinguish arguments from nonarguments and premises from conclusions, there are other signals we do well to recognize. One such signal is called a *modality*. Modalities involve two factors: *Scope* and *Degrees of Certainty*.

Scope concerns the breadth of the conclusion, that is whether we are talking about "All," "Most," "Many," or "Some" of a certain thing. Whether all abortion is immoral, or some abortions are immoral, or no abortion is immoral will very much affect your decision to have an abortion.

Certainty concerns the degree of belief with which the arguer holds (or asserts) the proposition to be true, with what certainty he takes it to follow from the premise(s). This will range from 100 per cent to 0 per cent. Notice, for example, the differences reflected in the following terms: absolutely, probably, and possibly. Compare the following two claims. "It is obvious she didn't intend to kill him, judging by the moderate force of the knife thrust." "It is likely that she didn't intend to kill him, judging by the moderate force of the knife thrust." Between the two, which is the stronger argument?

Perhaps we've noticed an ambiguity in the question. The *strong* claim is the one that is more certain. One's degree of confidence or conviction is stronger. At the same time, however, the stronger our conviction, the easier for critics to cast doubt. We might want to say, therefore, that the stronger argument is the one more able to withstand critique. If this were so, we should see that the second provides the stronger argument, not the first. Since our main goal is to know whether we should accept a conclusion on the basis of the given premises, we'll understand strong arguments as offering conclusions we have more reason to accept. Given this, the second argument is better than the first. The only difference between the two is the difference in modalities – and this should give insight into why we should pay attention to modalities.

Here is a partial list of words or phrases that indicate varying degrees of certainty:

must be	this implies that	probably	suggest
necessarily	this entails that	apparently	supports
it seems	this proves that	evidently	we may deduce
likely	it follows that	it is certain that	I bet that
possibly	definitely	it might be	may

We'll come back to these concepts when we begin assessing arguments. The general rule is that an argument is stronger the weaker the conclusion. A weaker conclusion means it is smaller in scope (some rather than all) and stated less categorically (probably rather than certainly). For example, imagine if we answer the claim, "All birds fly south for the winter," with the statement, "A chicken is a bird, but it doesn't fly south." This single instance is sufficient to refute the entire claim. Had the argument been "Most birds fly south for the winter," the observation that a chicken doesn't fly south for the winter would not refute the claim.

In our diagramming and standardizing of arguments, then, it will be important to make note of any modality. Be prepared to point them out.

2.6 Suppressed Propositions and Assumptions

Sometimes a stated conclusion does not follow from the premises unless we assume some other *unstated* premise. We have already seen a case of this in the argument in support of prostitution (2.1):

> Since anything affecting only parties to a fully informed, voluntary agreement is moral, prostitution among fully informed, voluntary parties is moral.

The missing premise is that prostitution is a case of voluntary agreement among fully informed concerned parties. In some arguments, the conclusion itself is suppressed and we are required to supply it. For example,

> In "China Fears U.S. Could Spoil Games Bid" (May 17), Miro Cernetig notes that, of the three countries vying for the 2008 Olympic Games, China is the only one that jails political dissidents. He must have forgotten Jaggi Singh. (Steve Gowens, letter to the editor, *Globe and Mail*, 18 May 2001, A12)

In Canada, Jaggi Singh was jailed for being a political dissident. Let us treat the last line as stating that proposition. What's missing, then, is the conclusion, which amounts to something like "Cernetig is mistaken."

With a better understanding of the logical structure or form of arguments we can more quickly identify suppressed propositions. So part of this skill will be enhanced after examining part 4. In the meantime, we can get a general idea of how to detect missing propositions.

2.6.1 Suppressed Premises

Unstated premises which need to be added to form a coherent argument are called *suppressed premises*. Consider, for example, the following argument:

> (1) All mammals are warm-blooded, so all whales are warm-blooded.

The problem is, (1) has the same form as (2):

> (2) All mammals are warm-blooded, so all snakes are warm-blooded.

What makes the first cogent and not the second is a missing premise that
we need to supply. In the first argument we need to add

(1') All whales are mammals.

This suppressed or missing premise, once added, makes the argument
complete. Of course, we could add,

(2') All snakes are mammals

to make (2) complete, but we're more likely to accept (1') than (2').

Admittedly, some propositions are generally so well known that they
don't need stating. Usually this is precisely why they weren't mentioned in
the first place. Still, for critical reflection, we should make explicit these
implicit steps. This is important, not so much to reveal the obvious, such
as that whales are mammals, but to be better equipped to reveal *problematic*
assumptions. When arguments rely on contentious unstated premises,
these propositions need to be made explicit. For example, presuming the
false claim that snakes are mammals would make the snake argument a
good one.

This points out an important lesson:

The premises should be less problematic than the conclusion they aim to
support.

Remember, the whole point of an argument is to convince someone that
she should accept the conclusion. But if the premises offered to convince
her are as problematic as the conclusion she is being asked to accept, one
should expect failure. After all, it would be unlikely that an agreement on
the conclusion can be reached if there can't be any agreement on the
premises.

One common error is the unnecessary addition of missing premises. If
the added premises cohere with common sense, or if they are irrelevant to
the logical structure of the argument they are not needed.

When should suppressed premises or hidden assumptions be added?
Only when they are logically required and contentious – otherwise what's
the point? Thus, if the missing proposition is needed, that is, logically
required to make the inference, *but not itself problematic*, then we needn't
bother asserting it. Likewise, if a problematic proposition *is not logically*
required for the inference, then we should not add it. In both cases, making explicit the missing premise is idle. It will have no bearing on our
assessment.

Consider one more case:

Kicking a cat is wrong, since kicking a human is wrong.

The missing link needed to make the inference from the premise to the conclusion is that cats are relevantly like humans. Those who think this suppressed premise problematic are presumably the very ones we want to convince. So pointing out this missing link gives us a clue as to what further argumentation is required to make our case against those who think it not immoral to kick cats.

2.6.2 Suppressed Conclusions

In some arguments, the conclusion is suppressed, and we will be required to fill it in. Always be careful not to fill in a conclusion that is unwarranted by the context and the stated premise(s).

Most often the conclusion is left out because it should be obvious. For example,

> If he's smart, he isn't going to go around shooting one of them, and he's smart. (*Murdock v. Commonwealth of Pennsylvania*, 319 U.S. 105, 1943)

The missing conclusion here is simply that he isn't going to go around shooting people. This should be straightforward.

At other times, a conclusion may be suppressed because there is something woefully inadequate about it, and this becomes apparent when the conclusion is made explicit. Consider, for example, the following argument:

> Morality places restrictions on people only, and corporations are not themselves persons.

Spelled out, the conclusion states that corporations ought to have no moral restrictions. They can do anything they want with impunity. Spelling this out reveals that something has gone astray. In this case, the first premise is questionable, but even if it were true, the second premise may be debated, for it hinges on how we define a "person."

2.6.3 Missing Premises and Conclusion

Occasionally, we'll find an argument with a missing premise *and* a missing conclusion. Still, the context must be sufficient for us to detect that an implicit argument is being made, as opposed to the mere utterance of an opinion. (Recall, an opinion is not an argument; it is simply a belief. An argument involves providing reasons for the belief.) For example,

> If matters of justice and retribution were simple, society would have settled them as easily as it has settled on the advantages of paved roads.

Here, it is common knowledge that society has not easily settled matters of justice and retribution, so we can add that as a permissible missing premise. Once the missing premise is added, we must also add the conclusion "Matters of justice and retribution are not simple."

Consider, next, the following implicit argument.

> To date, diplomacy isn't doing the job. The Iraqis won't evacuate Kuwait because the United Nations' secretary-general – or even the garrulous Jesse Jackson – lays on the unction of sweet reason. If Saddam Hussein were reasonable, he wouldn't have invaded Kuwait in the first place.

Before reading further, answer for yourself what the *main* conclusion is here.

The answer is stated in the first line: Diplomacy isn't doing the job. Since it's stated, it obviously doesn't count as a suppressed conclusion. But there is a suppressed conclusion here. To see this, let's first ask why diplomacy isn't doing the job. What is the premise for this conclusion? Presumably, diplomacy isn't doing the job because diplomacy requires reasonable participation. But, alas, Hussein is not a reasonable participant. Notice that this isn't stated anywhere, but it may be inferred on the basis of the stated premise ("If Saddam Hussein were reasonable, he wouldn't have invaded Kuwait in the first place") and a missing premise that Hussein did invade Kuwait. (Of course, whether he invaded may be challenged by Hussein apologists. Perhaps he "liberated" Kuwait instead.) Now, since we are entitled to infer that Hussein is not reasonable from the stated and suppressed premise, we have unearthed a suppressed conclusion. This suppressed conclusion now acts as a premise that works in tandem with the premise concerning the unction of sweet reason and entitles us to infer the main conclusion.

The argument, then, takes the following form (with missing propositions indicated by {bracketing}):

1 Anyone who invades Kuwait is unreasonable.
2 {Hussein invaded Kuwait.}
3 {Hussein is unreasonable.}
4 Reason is required in all participants for diplomacy to work.*
5 Therefore, diplomacy isn't working in this case.

2.6.4 Assumptions

An assumption is simply an unstated proposition. Usually assumptions are *assumed truths.* If they are assumed, they are not stated. But they need not be assumed to be true even for the speaker. That is, when spelled out, the

---

*This is a modification of the line about "the unction of sweet reason."

speaker herself may recognize the inadequacy of the assumption. Typically, the difference between an assumption and an unstated premise is *where* they occur in the argument. If an unstated premise exists between the stated premise and conclusion (stated or suppressed), we tend to speak of a suppressed premise. If the unstated premise resides *prior* to the stated premises, we speak in terms of an assumption. For example, consider the following argument:

> You should not steal because it says so in the Bible.

Now the mere fact that it says something in a book is not sufficient grounds to believe it. What makes this particular argument so persuasive are the unstated propositions:

> The Bible authoritatively indicates God's will.

and

> You should obey God's will.

Both occur prior to, or antecedently to, the stated premises. We may logically infer the belief structure or assumptions of the arguer. The listener, on the other hand, may not share these assumptions, and failing that, will not be convinced.

For our purposes, however, the difference between assumptions and suppressed premises is unimportant, except to highlight the following crucial point. If we speak of a problematic assumption, we are speaking about a proposition that is not itself explicitly stated and which is problematic. This should strike one as obvious, and thus not worth stating here, but remarkably it is a common fault among students.

In the Hussein example, a student might reply in the following manner:

> This argument assumes that anyone who invades Kuwait is unreasonable, whereas surely there are grounds where it may be reasonable to invade a country.

There are a few things we can note about this. For one, the student should say "The arguer assumes ...," since an argument does not have the requisite mental state to "assume" anything. Secondly, we might wonder what definition of "reasonable" this student is employing. Is it reasonable to invade another country if one has good odds of success? If the aggression is in self-defence, we don't usually say they "invade." Of course, what constitutes self-defence is left open here. Is self-defence warranted to preserve one's uninfluenced culture?

Our main worry, however, is that *we cannot call an assumption that which is explicitly stated.* Recall that propositions are not to be confused with sentences. To say, "If Saddam Hussein were reasonable, he wouldn't have invaded Kuwait in the first place," is the same as asserting that "anyone who invades Kuwait is unreasonable." Therefore, it cannot count as an assumption. For our purposes, assumptions and suppressed premises are synonymous.

Recap
There are two points to remember about assumptions and suppressed propositions.

1 Unearthing hidden assumptions doesn't further discussion, *unless* the assumptions are themselves contentious. Only then do we have reason to reject a premise on the grounds that it requires accepting a *problematic claim* which we have independent reasons for rejecting.

2 Assumptions are to be made only if necessarily thrust upon us. As long as they are not *necessitated*, we ought not make them. Consider again the following argument:

He did not intend to kill her. The knife stroke was delivered with only moderate force.

Should we assume that she was in fact killed? Did you assume that? Is it a necessary inference? The answer is no.

Practice 2

Consider the following arguments. What underlying assumptions are being made and are they themselves acceptable?

1 Abortion is wrong because murder is wrong.
2 We should never allow capital punishment because we can never be 100 per cent certain that the accused really committed the crime.
3 I refuse to have a blood transfusion because it is God's law not to ingest human blood.

In the first argument, the unstated assumption is "killing a fetus is murder." Typically murder is the willful killing of a sentient being. It is questionable whether a fetus, at least in the very early stages of pregnancy, counts as sentient. Nor is the intent of the abortion aimed at harming the fetus. The harm may be viewed more as a side-effect. Thus, there may be reason to reject the unstated assumption, but since the stated premise requires our accepting the unstated assumption, the argument would fail the acceptability condition.

In the second, the missing and contentious assumption is "We cannot act unless we are 100 per cent certain." Such a belief is extremely limiting.

In reality, we can't be 100 per cent certain of anything. Since we would reject this extreme assumption, we must reject the premise that presupposes it. Hence, the argument fails.

There are two hidden assumptions in the third argument: "God exists," and "God understands blood transfusions as an act of cannibalism." If both are deemed uncontentious, then go ahead and accept the premise; otherwise reject it.

Guidelines for Identifying Argument Components

Here is a quick checklist for identifying argument components:

1 Identify inference indicators
2 Identify modalities
3 Identify all propositions (Do not splice or conjoin propositions. Omit background, non-essentials, and repeated propositions.)
4 Insert relevant missing propositions

Exercise 2.3

Supply relevant missing premises, assumptions, and/or conclusions to the following arguments. (Answers to indicated questions provided in appendix 1.)

   1 Let me join the cries of righteous outrage against the foolish audacity of Rob Anders, who dares go against the moral certitude of us smart people. What does he think this is, a democracy? (Boris DeWiel, letter to the editor, *Globe and Mail*, 8 June 2001, A15)
☞ 2 To favour the anti-terrorist bill is as reasonable as being so against civil liberties that one would prefer to sell oneself into slavery.
   3 Everyone is entitled to use deadly force to defend himself or his loved ones from death or grievous bodily harm. The death penalty is the citizen's right of self-defense ceded to the state when he can no longer defend himself. I can't think of anything more barbaric (or destructive of the social contract) than a state serving notice on its citizens that their lives – along with the lives of their parents, spouses, siblings or children – cannot possibly be worth the life of any other person who has taken their lives from them. (George Jonas, "Capital Punishment – In favour: A value on citizens' lives," *National Post*, 12 June 2001, A18)
   4 While I share E.J. Adams' negative appraisal of Picasso, it should be remembered that he was able, as a young man, to draw the human figure to perfection. He learned his craft thoroughly before deciding to dispense with it and look in new directions. Modern artists have

learned the wrong lesson from him, and show no evidence of having learned their craft before starting their careers. The result? Modern art is really about the loss, within less than a century, of time-tested skills such as the casting of bronze. It seems to be one long lament for when art sought to portray the good, the true and the beautiful; bad and ugly were just that, and not the only options open to the buying public. (Don Campbell, letter to the editor, *National Post*, 18 June 2001, A15)

5 It is with great dismay and shock that I read last Saturday's *Guardian* to see that the gay pride flag will be flown at City Hall and that Attorney General Jeff Lantz plans to proclaim a gay pride week. Have we really sunk this low that we honour the sin of sodomy with its own special week? May God forgive us for allowing it to happen. (Paul Chandler, letter to the editor, *Guardian*, 25 June 2001, A7)

☞ 6 Scientists argue research on fetal stem cells that can develop into muscles, nerves and blood could help find cures for diseases such as Alzheimer's and Parkinson's. Republican leaders say Mr. Bush should not give in to "an industry of death." Nonetheless, some Republicans who are strongly opposed to abortion, such as Senator Orrin Hatch, have come out in favour of the research. Mr. Hatch has said, "Stem cell research facilitates life. Abortion destroys life. This is about saving lives." ... But leading conservatives have said any compromise on the issue would be untenable. "There should be a non-negotiable principle that says innocent human life is sacrosanct," said Ken Connor, president of the Family Research Council. (Toby Harnden, "Nancy Reagan backs stem cell research," *National Post*, 14 July 2001, A12)

7 If there were an honest tribunal in The Hague, Mr. Milosevic would not be the only government leader on trial. NATO's leaders, from Bill Clinton and Jean Chrétien to Tony Blair and José Maria Aznar committed what the Nuremberg judgement called "the supreme international crime" – resorting to war. (Michael Mandel, "Milosevic has a point," *Globe and Mail*, 6 July 2001, A15)

8 Every part of God's creation is there for a reason. Therefore, everything and everyone deserves to be treated with respect, including the crows. (Gail McKenzie, letter to the editor, *National Post*, 30 June 2001, A15.2.6.4)

☞ 9 Allan Rock, the Minister of Health, is again attempting to prove he is the master of sophistry. As Minister of Justice he introduced gun registration that he said would cost no more than $85-million over five years. Already it has cost $600-million. Now he is "cracking down" on cigarette packaging. At the same time, he is moving inexorably towards the legalization of marijuana. Mr. Rock obviously operates on the principle that if two wrongs don't make a right – try three. (Michael Stevenson, letter to the editor, *National Post*, 14 August 2001, A15)

10 To expect entertainment moguls to stop peddling lucrative scum is just about as realistic as to expect hyenas to become vegetarians. (Groarke et al., *Good Reasoning Matters*, 41)

11 It seems high school graduates are being herded toward academic university education. How can we allow this to continue, to load debts onto students? This very day the cost of courses is rising by six per cent. What is behind it all? Who is benefiting? Is it society, is it big business? It certainly isn't marriage and the family. (Mrs. Ray Brown, letter to the editor, *Guardian*, 3 June 2004, A7)

Mapping an Argument

Diagramming • Serial, Convergent, and Linked Arguments • Diagramming Arguments with Missing Propositions • Visual Arguments Counter-Considerations

3.1 Diagramming

So far, we've learned to distinguish arguments from non-arguments, propositions from sentences, and premises from conclusions. We will now pay attention to the relation of the various premises to each other and to the conclusion. By doing so, we will learn how to recognize the *structure* of an argument.

Understanding the structure, or *form*, of an argument will help us to understand the argument. Better understanding the argument structure also helps to inform us *where* we should challenge it should that be our desire. Why this is the case will become more apparent as we progress. For now, the following metaphor will have to do. A surgeon's knowledge of the structure of the human body enables her to know where to cut. Focussing on a hangnail when the problem is kidney failure is honing in on the wrong part of the body.

To better visualize the structure of the argument, we will start with two steps:

1 We will replace the relevant propositions with numbers. (Our ability to distinguish sentences from propositions will help us here.)
2 We will draw inference arrows between the numbers. (Our ability to recognize inference indicators and to tell conclusions from premises will help us here.)

The arrows that we draw will pictorially represent the direction of the inferences. That is, an arrow will lead from the premise to the conclusion.

In order to number all the relevant propositions, we must, of course, be able to detect propositions. As we learned in chapter 2, we can pay attention to inference indicators, and recognize that no single proposition can contain an inference indicator. Inference indicators remain outside of propositions. They will be represented by arrows. We'll also need to recall the discussion concerning conditional (if ... then), disjunctive (... or ...), and conjunctive (... and ...) propositions. Only the last may be broken into two propositions.

So, in any argument, a first step is to detect all inference indicators. Take, for example, the following argument:

The motel business will be very bad this summer due to the current recession.

Our first task is to note the premise indicator "due to." Let us note this by placing double brackets around it:

The motel business will be very bad this summer ((due to)) the current recession.

Because it is a premise indicator, we now know the proposition *following* it stands as the premise to the proposition that *precedes* it. Since our arrows will always move from the premise to the conclusion, we now know we may replace the "due to" with an arrow that will point from the current recession to the poor state of the motel business. But we're getting ahead of ourselves. Our next task is to number all the propositions as they occur in the stated argument. Using square brackets to indicate the scope of the proposition, we get the following result:

(1) [The motel business will be very bad this summer] ((due to)) (2) [the current recession].

Notice that, as put, "the current recession" is not itself a sentence. It does indicate a proposition, however, which might be cashed out in the following grammatically correct form: "There is a current recession."

Since we know that "due to" is a premise indicator, we now know that (2) is the premise. In this case, since there are no other propositions to worry about, by the process of elimination, we likewise know (1) is the conclusion. That is to say, (1) is asserted on the basis of (2). Or, if you prefer, (2) is given as support for (1). Since the direction of our arrow will always lead from the premise to the conclusion, we now know that we will place an arrow leading from (2) to (1).

One last bit of information is needed to complete the necessary steps to diagramming arguments. You may recall, from the previous chapter, that logicians like to rearrange arguments so that the conclusion is placed at the bottom, no matter where it occurs in the argument itself. In our argument above, the conclusion is placed ahead of the premise. In our diagram of that argument, we shall place the conclusion at the bottom. Thus, when we say arrows always lead from premises to conclusions, we can now also say that arrows always lead downward.

Thus, we diagram the argument

$$2$$
$$\downarrow$$
$$1$$

This says that (2) is the premise that supports the conclusion (1). Sometimes the conclusion is stated second in the argument, as in the following case:

(1) [People have given children war-related toys for centuries]. ((Therefore))
(2) [war toys have no tendency whatsoever to make children less sensitive to violence.] (Govier, *A Practical Study of Argument*, 155)

We would diagram this argument in the following manner:

$$1$$
$$\downarrow$$
$$2$$

When we visualize an argument in this way, we can better see that there are *two* ways we can object to it. We may either challenge the likelihood of the premise being true, or challenge the inference itself. In the first case, we may doubt that we are in a recession, although we may accept that *if* there were a recession, this would indeed impact on the motel business. Alternatively, we may accept the premise that we're in a recession, but doubt that this *leads* to the conclusion. After all, our recession may signal to foreigners that we're a cheap vacation spot, in which case the motel business may increase.

3.2 Serial, Convergent, and Linked Arguments

Arguments tend to come with more than one premise, however, and these premises can interrelate in different ways. Arguments with more than one premise can be divided into three categories: *serial, convergent,* or *linked.**

---

* A further category is logically possible: divergent arguments. This is when, on the basis of a single premise, we may infer two independent conclusions. Thus we get the following form:

This is rarely seen in arguments, however, because our usual task is to convince someone of *one main* thing. We shall focus on serial, convergent, and linked arguments only.

3.2.1 Serial Arguments

Let us say that we want to bolster our argument above. Someone is not convinced. So we claim the following.

(1) [The motel business will be very bad this summer] (due to) (2) [the current recession], (since) among other things (3) [the government is intent on taking money out of our pockets to send armies to interfere in others' disputes.]

Diagramming the above argument will take the following form:

$$3$$
$$\downarrow$$
$$2$$
$$\downarrow$$
$$1$$

This argument is in serial form. (3) supports (2) which supports (1). Serial arguments are diagrammed in a straight line.

Since (3) is offered in support of (2), which in turn supports (1), we can see that to challenge either premise (2) or premise (3) will be sufficient to undermine the entire argument. As an analogy, consider the prospect of bungee jumping. Whether the rope breaks at the top or in the middle, the results are the same.

One caveat may need mentioning. Perhaps we accept (2) on its own, although not for the reason cited by (3). In this case, we could reject the stated support to (2), yet nevertheless accept (2). In this case, unlike the bungee cord, the conclusion may survive. Of course, this would be so only because we recognize what is not stated, that (2) has independent support other than (3). But *as stated*, the argument would collapse.

3.2.2 Convergent Arguments

Alternatively, we could have given a further independent reason why the resort industry will decline this summer. Consider

(1) [The local resort business will be very bad this summer] (due to) (2) [the current recession]. Also (3) [it is predicted to be a cold, rainy summer].

We would diagram this argument

$$2 \quad\quad 3$$
$$\searrow \quad \swarrow$$
$$1$$

The two premises converge independently on the conclusion. If we reject (3), or the arrow between (3) and (1), (1) still has the support of (2). Admittedly, the argument may be *weakened* in cases of challenging one prong of a convergent argument, but not refuted as in the case of a serial argument, or, as we shall see presently, in the case of a linked argument.

Certain words or phrases often accompany convergent arguments that may help us distinguish convergent arguments from serial or linked arguments. These are terms such as *moreover, secondly, furthermore, not only that,* and *also*. These terms indicate that another set of independent premises is now to be employed to help support the conclusion. These are terms that are inappropriate in linked and serial arguments.

3.2.3 Linked Arguments

Often we are faced with arguments in which the premises work together to support the conclusion. For example, astute readers may have detected a missing premise in the argument above. The fact that it is a cold, rainy summer does not directly support the claim that the motel business will be bad unless we supply the obvious conditional bridge: "If it is a cold rainy summer, the local resort business will be bad." By itself this is fairly innocuous, we may guess, but how would we diagram the argument if we made this explicit? The answer is that we need a way of *linking* premises that is not shown by an arrow. Consider the following argument:

> (1) [The local resort business will be very bad this summer]. (2) [It is predicted to be a cold, rainy summer] and (3) [whenever the summer is poor, people tend to go elsewhere for their vacations].

Here, (2) and (3) work in tandem. (3) clearly doesn't support (1) *all by itself,* for it may be true even when the summer is gorgeous. Further, (2) doesn't support (1) *unless* we assume (3). Thus we cannot technically draw an arrow to (1) from (2) by itself, nor (3) by itself, yet clearly the inference from (2) and (3) provides warrant for asserting (1). We shall therefore diagram such mediated premises by placing a "+" sign between the two premises to show their *linked* connection.

The above argument, thus, looks like this

$$\frac{2 + 3}{}$$
$$\downarrow$$
$$1$$

Here is another case (favoured by logicians for some reason) demanding linked premises:

(1) [All men are mortal]. (2) [Socrates is a man]. ((Therefore)) (3) [Socrates is mortal].

Assuming that Socrates is a man, the fact that we need convincing that he's a mortal demands an unlikely context. Thus, given our skills at differentiating arguments from explanations, we might complain that this doesn't even *count* as an argument. Still, treating it as an argument (where we are for some reason forbidden to assume ahead of time that Socrates is a man, much less is mortal, or that all men are mortal) demands a *linked* structure

$$\frac{1 + 2}{\downarrow}$$
$$3$$

We have already indicated that linked premises stand or fall together. Unlike the case for convergent arguments, to challenge one of the links in a linked premise argument is to challenge the *whole* argument. That means that in assessing a linked argument, we don't have to dispute *both* premises, we need merely focus on one (or the inference).

A common error is confusing linked with convergent arguments. Sometimes the confusion is due to the arguer herself. There is a lack of clarity in the wording. Sometimes it is due to insufficient general knowledge on the part of the audience. But often it is because students fail to grasp the point being made here. Some premises can lend support directly to the conclusion, and others only indirectly, through the mediated support of another stated premise.

Notice that we say another *stated* premise. Confusions arise when we throw in the prospect of suppressed premises and assumptions. To make things clearer, let's focus on the difference between convergent and linked premises using only those propositions stated. In such a case, how can we tell whether an argument is linked or not?

A good rule is to ask ourselves this: If we blocked one of the premises completely out of our minds, would we see why the first gave a reason for the conclusion? If yes, then the premises are either convergent or serial. If not then they are linked. The argument is convergent if both premises give independent reasons for accepting the conclusion. It is serial if only one does. It is linked if neither do. For example,

Linked:
(1) [Pizza delivery drivers love to drive 80 km/hr through parking lots].
(2) [Mario is a pizza driver], ((so)) (3) [Mario loves to drive 80 km/hr through parking lots.]

$$\frac{1 + 2}{\downarrow}$$
$$3$$

Here, we can see that (1) by itself does not yield (3), and nor does (2) by itself lead to (3) (and, by the way, (1) does not yield (2), and nor does (2) support (1)). Together they do lead to (3), however, and that's what the diagram reveals.

Convergent:
(1) [Socialized medicine is bad]. When market pressure is taken off the health-care industry, (2) [it removes the competitive incentive for a doctor to provide the best care he possibly can]. Also, (3) [it's harder to get good equipment], and (4) [waits are longer for diseases which are better treated quickly]. As a result, socialized medicine is only the most efficient way of distributing the most death to the greatest number of people.

$$2 \quad 3 \quad 4$$
$$\searrow \quad \downarrow \quad \swarrow$$
$$1$$

Notice that in our diagramming of this argument, we ignored two things. We treated the phrase, "when market pressure is taken off the health-care industry" as synonymous with "socialized medicine," which is what is being referred to by the pronoun "it" starting our premise (2). The last line is deemed a rhetorical flourish repeating the main proposition already indicated by proposition (1). The conclusion indicator "as a result" is thus left off. Admittedly, one might claim this last to be the conclusion. If so, three premises (1), (2), and (3) would converge on the conclusion (4).

Notice the words "also" and "and." In this case, they help tell us we're confronted with a convergent argument.

As far as recognizing that this is a convergent argument, rather than linked or serial, we may ask whether (2) by itself lends some support to (1), and the answer is yes. Likewise, we may ask whether (3) by itself lends support to (1), and the answer is yes, again. The same applies to (4). Each of these premises provides some support independently of the others. Whether any of the support is sufficient to make this a *cogent* argument is another matter. At least we know what type of argument it is. Because it is a convergent argument, it will not be sufficient to dismiss merely one strand of support. This would admittedly weaken the argument, but it would not refute the argument.

3.2.4 Mixed Arguments

Most arguments we face contain a mixture of these three types. To demonstrate, let us combine our previous arguments about the resort business into the following complex argument:

(1) [The local resort business will be very bad this summer] ((due to)) (2) [the current recession], ((since)) (3) [the government is intent on taking money out

of our pockets to send armies to interfere in others' disputes.] Of course, it need hardly be said that (4) [the current recession will prevent people from travelling as much]. Also, (5) [it is predicted to be a cold, rainy summer] and (6) [if the summer is poor here, people who can afford to travel will go elsewhere for their vacations].

We would diagram this argument

$$
\begin{array}{cc}
3 & \\
\downarrow & \\
\underline{2 + 4} & \underline{5 + 6} \\
\searrow & \swarrow \\
& 1
\end{array}
$$

Notice that the two linked arguments converge on the main conclusion. The word "also" helps inform us of this intent. Meanwhile, a serial argument is provided in support of (2). In this case, we can see that (2) acts both as a premise and as a sub-conclusion. When we speak of the conclusion, we generally mean the *main* conclusion, unless otherwise stated. That is, if we ask what the conclusion is in this argument, the intended answer is (1), and not (2).

Following is another complex argument. How should we go about diagramming this one?

Socialized medicine is good. When market pressure is taken off the health-care industry, people will more readily go to the doctor, since they will not have to pay for it. If one goes to the doctor more regularly, more illnesses may be detected sooner. The sooner illnesses are detected, the greater the chances of successful intervention. Meanwhile, the doctor can prescribe whatever tests or procedures he professionally feels are best for the patient (rather than most profitable for him), which means that expensive illnesses are prevented. As a result, more people will be healthy and most will, in general, live longer and lead more productive lives.

The standardization of the preceding argument is as follows:

(1) [Socialized medicine is good]. When market pressure is taken off the health-care industry, (2) [people will more readily go to the doctor], ((since)) (3) [they will not have to pay for it]. (4) [If one goes to the doctor more regularly, more illnesses may be detected sooner]. (5) [The sooner illnesses are detected, the greater the chances of successful intervention]. Meanwhile (6) [the doctor can prescribe whatever tests or procedures he professionally feels are best for the patient (rather than most profitable for him)], ((which means that)) (7) [expensive illnesses are prevented]. As a result, more people will be healthy and most will, in general, live longer and lead more productive lives.

Again, we shall treat the last line as sufficiently synonymous with (1). Our diagram of this argument is as follows:

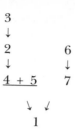

Practice

Let's exercise our ability to recognize the structure of arguments (linked, serial or convergent).

1 All enterprising people support an open global market. You are enterprising. Therefore I conclude that you support an open global market.
Standardization:
(1) [All enterprising people support an open global market]. (2) [You are enterprising]. ((Therefore)) (3) [You support an open global market].
Diagram:

$$\underline{1 + 2}$$
$$\downarrow$$
$$3$$

2 John Doe supports an open global market, and he is an enterprising person. Jane Doe supports an open global market, and she is an enterprising person. Enterprising people support an open global market.
Standardization:
(1) [John Doe supports an open global market, and he is an enterprising person.] (2) [Jane Doe supports an open global market, and she is an enterprising person]. (3) [Enterprising people support an open global market.]
Diagram:

$$1 \qquad 2$$
$$\searrow \quad \swarrow$$
$$3$$

If we separated the propositions on either side of the "ands" in the two premises above, we would have to link these components together in our diagram. This would present the following pattern:

(1) [John Doe supports an open global market] and (2) [John Doe is an enterprising person.] (3) [Jane Doe supports an open global market] and (4) [Jane

doe is an enterprising person]. (5) [Enterprising people support an open global market.]
Diagram:

$$\underline{1 + 2} \qquad \underline{3 + 4}$$
$$\searrow \qquad \swarrow$$
$$5$$

Both would be deemed correct.

Exercise 3.1

Diagram the following arguments. (Answers to selected questions are provided in Appendix 1.)

☞ 1 Surrogacy is really another form of prostitution. Prostitutes "rent" out their bodies and are remunerated. So too do surrogates. Since prostitution is outlawed, surrogacy should be outlawed, too.

2 The death penalty does not deter criminals because at the time the crime is committed they do not expect to be arrested. Also, since many offenders are mentally unbalanced, they do not consider the rational consequences of their irrational activities.

3 Men generally have difficulty expressing their emotions. If it is desirable for our society to consist of fully developed human beings, then people who do find it easier to express their emotions should make a special effort to draw out those who do not. Generally this means that women should make a special effort to encourage men to express their inner feelings.

☞ 4 The signnatories to the Declaration of Independence did not intend to claim that men and women should be considered equal. For one thing, they used the word *men* in the statement, "All men are created equal." For another, it is a historical fact that men and women were not considered equal in 1776. Women were not even guaranteed the right to vote in the United States until 1920.

5 So, the city is planning to spend millions of hard-earned tax payers' money on a youth centre. I don't know why we think we have money to burn. There are plenty of things to do in Charlottetown for youth. There are many parking lots where they can park their cars and watch pizza delivery drivers, and there are a host of good television shows they can watch.

☞ 6 Desert mountaintops make good sites for astronomy. Being high, they sit above a portion of the atmosphere, enabling a star's light to reach a telescope without having to swim through the entire depth of the atmosphere. Being dry, the desert is also relatively cloud-free. The merest veil of haze or cloud can render a sky useless for many astronomical measures.

7 Bodies become heavier with increasing speed, thus requiring more force to accelerate them further; in the end an infinitely strong force would be required to make them reach the speed of light. Therefore no object can be accelerated to that speed, let alone beyond.

8 If we cannot safely dispose of waste products from nuclear power plants, then we should not allow the plants to operate. At present, there is no way to safely dispose of such nuclear wastes. Hence, we should not allow nuclear power plants to operate. But from this, it follows that current nuclear plants should be shut down and new ones should not be allowed to start operating.

☞ 9 Don't go to the hospital unless you have absolutely no choice. The director of the Centre for Disease Control says two million of the people who enter hospitals each year catch infections unrelated to their original conditions. Eighty thousand die from these infections. This makes hospitals more lethal than highways, and that's not even counting victims of botched surgery. (Charles Peters, "Tilting at Windmills," *The Washington Monthly* 14, no. 3, May 1982: 5)

10 I knew you came from Afghanistan. From long habit the train of thoughts ran so swiftly through my mind that I arrived at the conclusion without being conscious of intermediate steps. There were such steps, however. The train of reasoning ran, 'Here is a gentleman of a medical type, but with the air of a military man. Clearly an army doctor, then. He has just come from the tropics, for his face is dark, and that is not the natural tint of his skin, for his wrists are fair. He has undergone hardship and sickness, as his haggard face says clearly. His left arm has been injured. He holds it in a stiff and unnatural manner. Where in the tropics could an English army doctor have seen much hardship and got his arm wounded? Clearly in Afghanistan.' The whole train of thought did not occupy a second. I then remarked that you came from Afghanistan, and you were astonished. (Conan Doyle, *A Study in Scarlet*)

☞11 Autumn comes, and the ubiquitous green of summer briefly explodes into autumn's warm golds and russets. Autumn comes, and while the harvest of the summer field is gathered, another crop – a repulsive one – is revealed by the receding roadside vegetation. Covered by the summer's green, but now exposed to the recoiling senses, are countless littered beer bottles and soft drink cans. There is a solution to this disgrace: A so-called "bottle bill" – a bill requiring beer and soft drink to be sold only in returnable bottles and requiring a refundable deposit on each bottle. If you give people a monetary incentive to return the bottles, then they will. But if people return the bottles, then they will not be discarded as litter. But a monetary incentive is precisely what the bottle bill provides. Hence the bottle bill would remove a major source of litter. Thus, I repeat, a bottle bill would remove this disgraceful blight on our landscape. (N.K., *Sunday Star-Ledger*, Newark, NJ, 28 November 1982)

12 This letter is in regard to the recent national and provincial topic of the notorious tar ponds toxic site and possible resettlement of those wanting it. In a world where money speaks very loudly (too loudly, some would say), I believe our current government (of John Hamm) will only act when it realizes how great the cost to tax-payers will be in the not-too-distant future for medical and social costs of related illnesses caused by the toxic chemicals and waste in the Sydney, especially Whitney Pier, region (where I originally came from, by the way). The healthy children and young adults of today will soon become the sick adults of tomorrow, if we don't do something soon enough.(Phillip McLean, letter to the editor, *Chronicle-Herald*, 26 May 2001, C4)

☞13 A strong case can be made for amending the sanctions [on Iraq]. First, as with most embargoes, they leak like a sieve. Smuggled oil is pouring across Iraq's borders, most notably into Turkey, Syria and Jordan. Second, the sanctions clearly worsen the plight of Iraq's 22 million captive people, notwithstanding the 1997 oil-for-food program, which allows the regime to sell a portion of its oil output to buy food, medicine and other humanitarian goods. Third, the sanctions provide Baghdad with its most powerful ammunition in portraying itself as a victim of Western aggression. ("Relaxed sanctions? Not on Iraq's terms," *Globe and Mail*, 26 May 2001, A14)

14 Dear editor: I am writing to encourage people to attend the Moscow State Circus that is currently touring the Maritimes. The Moscow State Circus is one of a growing number of animal-free circuses that deserve community support. In contrast to animal-free circuses, circuses that choose to exploit animals for human entertainment generally maintain performing animals in small, barren transport cages (four to five feet wide by eight to 10 feet long), or keep them chained or tethered for the majority of their lives. Circus animals are denied the opportunity to engage in instinctive behaviours and as a consequence of their continued confinement, often exhibit unnatural, stereotyped and harmful behaviours. I would therefore hope that Maritimers going to the circus this year choose an animal-free circus such as the Moscow State Circus, rather than one in which animals are being abused and used as objects of amusement. (Wendy Turner, letter to the editor, *Chronicle-Herald*, 19 May 2001, C3)

15 A world in which people receive a leg up solely because of their skin colour is also a world in which visible minority individuals who accomplish impressive feats under their own steam risk having these achievements dismissed as unmerited. Affirmative action encourages racism by prompting suspicion that minorities in high-powered jobs, or occupying coveted positions, are there not because of their

achievements but because of their skin colour or sex. ("Talk about racism," *National Post*, 27 July 2001, A15)

☞16 "We think the current slump in the telecom sector will be prolonged, due to a decline in telecom operator spending, a glut of network capacity, and the absence of compelling new network technologies," agreed analysts at UBS Warburg. (Michael Higgins, "Analysts expect prolonged tech slump," *National Post*, 25 July 2001, A8)

17 One argument for vegetarianism is its effect on other humans. It can take up to 21 pounds of grain protein fed to feedlot calf to produce a single pound of meat protein for humans. In a world where millions are starving, this is a colossally inefficient approach to agriculture. If North Americans reduced their meat consumption by 10 percent for one year, this would free enough grain to feed 65 million people. (Hurka, *Principles: Short Essays on Ethics*, 41–2)

18 A second argument [for vegetarianism] concerns the suffering inflicted on animals by modern factory farming. A veal calf spends its entire life in a stall less than two feet wide, unable to move or even adopt its natural sleeping position. To keep its meat light-coloured – something unrelated to its taste – the calf is denied nutrients such as iron. Craving these nutrients, it licks any metal fittings on its stall. In the most intensive operations, broiler chickens are confined in cages whose wire floors cut their feet. They spend their entire lives in a space no bigger than a single piece of typing paper. Stressed by overcrowding, the birds peck at and even kill each other. (The farmer's solution to this problem: cut off their beaks when they're young.) (Ibid., 42)

19 Climate models suggest that during the next century the average values of temperature and precipitation are likely to change over large areas of the globe. As a result, widespread adjustments are likely to occur in the distribution of terrestrial vegetation. (Schlesinger et al., "Biological Feedbacks in Global Desertification," 1043)

3.3 Diagramming Arguments with Missing Propositions

It is very important to recognize that, in everyday discourse, we typically do not encounter whole and complete arguments. Most of our conversations are guided by the principle of *economy* – we omit everything that is not absolutely necessary to make our point. This tendency is also recognizable in writing. All we have to do is to check our favourite magazine's letters to the editor. We will see that, in most cases, it takes careful reconstruction to fill in the gaps in the writer's reasoning. (Admittedly much of this may be due to editorial butchering, and limited available media space.)

In most situations, we seem able to automatically, and without much effort, reconstruct missing argument parts. In fact, it becomes so automatic that it is difficult to recognize this process of tacit argument reconstruction. This is not surprising – think about some other skills that we may possess. Take, for example, riding a bike. As soon as riding becomes second nature to us, we "internalize" the skill. Once this happens, however, it becomes difficult, if not impossible, to formulate just what it is that we need to do in order to ride a bike. Still, that's precisely what we need to do if we wish to improve our skills, as any coach will tell us.

Consider the following example:

January 9, 2000. As if you needed any more evidence that astrology works, today is the shared birthday of Richard Nixon (1913) and Joan Baez (1941).

The form of this argument appears to be in favour of astrology. It appears that *evidence* is being given in its support. It is not obviously cogent evidence, but if our first task is to make sense of what it is we're being asked to accept here, the form alone seems to point toward an argument that is pro-astrology. But clearly, the intent is the opposite. How do we know? We need certain background information. Importantly, Nixon and Baez are not alike. Richard Nixon played a pivotal role in the Vietnam war, while Joan Baez was an active pacifist fighting against the war. Nixon was a politician, Baez a folk singer. Also, we need to remember that astrology works on the assumption that people born under the same sign share certain common characteristics. If we now put these bits of information together, the argument is asserting that one needs no further evidence to see that astrology does *not* work.

That is, we can restructure the above utterance as an argument. To do this, we need to insert the appropriate missing premises and assumptions. At the same time, we need to distinguish these added components from the stated components. We will add an "H" to our proposition numbers to reveal when we're adding an unstated or Hidden proposition (which may be or may not be the conclusion).

Standardization:
(1) [January 9th is the shared birthday of Richard Nixon and Joan Baez]. (H2) [Richard Nixon's and Joan Baez's characters are dissimilar]. (H3) [If astrology were to work, then people born under the same sign would share certain common characteristics.] (H4) [Astrology does not work].
Diagram:

$$\underline{1 + H2 + H3}$$
$$\downarrow$$
$$H4$$

As we see in this example, only the first premise (1) was explicitly stated. We needed to "build" our argument around that premise. Our construction, of course, must be consistent with the original intent.

The process of building arguments is very significant for the art of critical thought. We need to become proficient in doing this in order to

recognize condensed arguments in all forms of media. Building arguments helps us reveal important assumptions in reasoning. Very often, hidden premises contain value assumptions and other interesting presupposi-
tions that may well be contentious. For example,

(1) [Automobile accidents are the prime cause of deaths among teenagers,]
(so) (2) [high schools should teach students good driving skills.]

Upon careful examination, it turns out that the following assumption is
required:

(H3) [Poor driving skills cause teenage automobile accidents.]

Our diagram reveals the following structure:

$$\frac{1 + H3}{} \\ \downarrow \\ 2$$

We can imagine drawing an entirely different conclusion from (1) (Automobile accidents are the prime cause of deaths among teenagers) if we
were to make a different assumption about the cause of teenage automobile accidents. For example,

(1) = Automobile accidents are the prime cause of deaths among teenagers.
(H3) = Drinking and driving leads to most teenage automobile accidents.
(2) = High schools should intensify their campaigns against drinking and
driving.

This argument would have the same diagram as the previous one. Both
arguments are centred around their respective assumptions: in the first it
was assumed that poor driving skills cause teenage automobile accidents,
and in the second that drinking and driving leads to teenage automobile
accidents.

Recall the following argument from chapter 2:

Since anything affecting only parties to a fully informed, voluntary agreement
is moral, prostitution among fully informed, voluntary parties is moral.

The missing premise in this argument is "Prostitution is a case of voluntary
agreement among all fully informed concerned parties." Thus, the mapping of this argument is as follows:

((Since)) (1) [anything affecting only parties to a fully informed, voluntary
agreement is moral], (2) [prostitution among fully informed, voluntary parties

is moral]. (H3) [Prostitution is a case of voluntary agreement among all fully informed concerned parties].

$$\frac{1 + H3}{\downarrow}$$
$$2$$

Caution: Do not fall into a trap of uncovering each and every assumption that can be revealed in reasoning. Obviously, some of those assumptions are quite trivial. Instead, attempt to focus on *controversial* assumptions. Notice, for example, that we did not need to discuss some obvious assumptions in the student driving example (e.g., "Young people's lives should be saved").

Longer Arguments

We are often confronted with longer arguments. They shouldn't intimidate us. The skills gleaned so far may be applied to an argument of any length. Consider the following longer argument:

> Let me suggest a few reasons why we ought to take the allegations about the US President's behaviour more seriously. First, the President is a powerful man in possession of important secrets. If he does things he will be ashamed to admit to his family and his neighbours, he is open to blackmail. If he has no self-control or conscience, he is open to bribery. And, even if his behaviour is spotless in reality but he fails to guard his reputation, he is open to character assassination. Second, and no less important, no one demands a "paragon of virtue." But citizens do expect political leaders to exhibit ordinary human decency, which is all that is required for a man to place a higher priority on the feelings of his wife and child than on his momentary physical pleasure. If he is unable to muster this level of concern for those he loves, how can we trust him to make decisions that will affect the well-being of millions of citizens that he does not know and love?

It turns out that the then president of the USA had become involved in a sex scandal with Monica Lewinski. We might therefore conclude that he *did* do things he was ashamed to admit to his family and neighbours, that he *did* lose self-control and conscience, and that he *did* fail to guard his reputation, and that thereby he *did* fail to exhibit the ordinary human decency which is all that is required for a man to place higher priority on the feelings of his wife and child than on his momentary physical pleasure.

There is a further missing premise here, for otherwise the second line hangs uselessly. Presumably it is not intended as a useless utterance. Therefore, we should make explicit the lurking assumption that people in power are more prone to blackmail. But this isn't sufficient for us to be concerned about, we can guess, unless we have the President's best interests at heart. We need to make clear why being open to blackmail is a bad thing for us. Thus, we might also make explicit the claim that people who are blackmailed will be tempted not to perform their proper duties. We might further add the otherwise innocuous, though unstated, assertion that if the president fails to perform his duties, this is a bad thing for us, the citizens.

Thus, the standardization of the preceding argument becomes a bit larger than its original. It takes the following form:

Let me suggest a few reasons why (1) [we ought to take the allegations about the US President's behaviour more seriously]. First, (2) [the President is a powerful man in possession of important secrets]. (3) [If he does things he will be ashamed to admit to his family and his neighbours, he is open to blackmail]. (4) [If he has no self-control or conscience, he is open to bribery]. And, (5) [even if his behaviour is spotless in reality but he fails to guard his reputation, he is open to character assassination]. Second, and no less important, no one demands a "paragon of virtue." But (6) [citizens do expect political leaders to exhibit ordinary human decency, which is all that is required for a man to place a higher priority on the feelings of his wife and child than on his momentary physical pleasure]. (7) [If he is unable to muster this level of concern for those he loves, how can we trust him to make decisions that will affect the well-being of millions of citizens that he does not know and love?] (H8) [Powerful persons are more open to manipulation than regular folk]. (H9) [People who are manipulated will be tempted not to perform their proper duties]. (H10) [If the president fails to perform his duties, this is a bad thing for us, the citizens]. (H11) [The president got involved in a sex scandal with Monica Lewinski]. ((We might therefore, conclude that)) (H12) [he *did* do things he was ashamed to admit to his family and neighbours, that he *did* lose self-control and conscience, and that he *did* fail to guard his reputation], and that ((thereby)) (H13) [he *did* fail to exhibit the ordinary human decency which is all that is required for a man to place higher priority on the feelings of his wife and child than on his momentary physical pleasure].

Given the clues noted by the phrases "first" and "second," we know a part of this argument, anyway, is convergent. The two convergent arguments each turn out to be linked. The (plausible) structure is

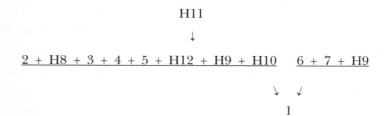

Exercise 3.2

Provide relevant missing propositions and diagram the following arguments. (Answers to selected questions are provided in Appendix 1.)

☞ 1 To date, diplomacy isn't doing the job. The Iraqis won't evacuate Kuwait because the United Nations' secretary-general – or even the garrulous Jesse Jackson – lays on the unction of sweet reason. If Saddam Hussein were reasonable, he wouldn't have invaded Kuwait in the first place.

2 If matters of justice and retribution were simple, society would have settled them as easily as it has settled on the advantages of paved roads.

3 To favour the anti-terrorist bill is as reasonable as being so against civil liberties that one would prefer to sell oneself into slavery.

☞ 4 How can you be so inconsistent? You argue against capital punishment and say you are opposed to the taking of human life. Yet you argue for a pro-choice stand on abortion.

5 No machine is more intimate with you than your phone. It listens – patiently – to everything you say. It hears things your best friend never hears. It brings you good news and bad news, and it isn't offended when you neglect it.

6 How then could individuals possibly replace government? In a democracy they are the government. This myth of the triumphant, unattached individual is pure romanticism and, I repeat, romanticism is a handmaiden of ideology. (John Ralston Saul, *The Unconscious Civilization*, 73.)

☞ 7 The administration's economic program is unwise, because it takes significant benefits away from the poor. Furthermore, its environmental impact is enormous. Twelve million hectares of environmentally sensitive swamp lands are zoned for a silicone parkland.

8 It is very characteristic of friendship that friends live together. Now that one cannot live with many people and divide oneself up among them is plain. Further, a person's friends must be friends of one another, if they are all to spend their days together ... It is found difficult, too, to rejoice and to grieve in an intimate way with many people, for it may happen that one has at once to be happy with one friend and mourn with another. Hence, apparently, it is impossible to be a great friend to many people. Presumably, then, it is well not to seek to have as many friends as possible, but as many as are enough for the purpose of living together. (Aristotle, *Nichomachean Ethics*, Book 1, IX, 10, 1091)

9 We should not build nuclear power plants to generate electricity if better means to generate sufficient electricity are available. Even without building any more dams, there are now 48,000 dams across

the US. These dams can be adapted to hydroelectric generation cheaper than building equivalent nuclear or even fossil fuel generating stations, and with far less health risk to both the environment and humans. Further, these water dams can provide so much electricity that we do not need even the existing nuclear generating plants. They can produce 30 million kilowatts per hour compared to existing nuclear energy providing only 20 million kilowatts per hour. (Adapted from Freeman, *Thinking Critically*, 201)

☞10 The claim that family-planning programs have contributed to the decline of sexual mores is not supported by the evidence. Family planning first came onto the scene in the 70s. In the 50s and 60s, more than half of all teenage women entering marriage were pregnant, and many others who became pregnant escaped notice by obtaining illegal abortions.

3.4 Visual Arguments

Visual arguments appear, among other places in magazine ads. We already know that these ads are very carefully designed. We will also find that they frequently employ quite clever and intricate visual arguments. Consider the following advertisement for Volkswagen.

Pictured is a man at a gas station holding the pump nozzle to his head as if he were about to commit suicide. We can present the visual argument's structure in the following way:

(H1) [Either you commit financial suicide by pouring too much gas in your vehicle or you buy a Volkswagen]. (H2) [You should not commit financial suicide by pouring too much gas in your vehicle]. (H3) [You should buy a Volkswagen].
Diagram:

$$\frac{H1 + H2}{}$$
$$\downarrow$$
$$H3$$

The analysis of visual arguments makes it apparent that they frequently contain many suppressed premises. Sometimes the conclusion is itself suppressed. This should not come as a surprise because that is how reasoning based on images works: the images can be set up to suggest an inference or to entice the reader to make a whole nexus of inferences.

In most cases, it is not necessary to diagram the entire set of possible inferences and present them as suppressed premises. Many suppressed premises can be left out since we can assume they are common knowledge. We should diagram only the premises which provide direct support to the conclusion in a relevant and informative manner. Perhaps another example is in order.

There is an ad which features a manual typewriter with the following caption: *If you took typing in high school, it's time to see an internist.* This visual argument obviously attempts to persuade readers to see an internist. The most important, and arguably pressing, reason to see an internist is the risk of certain types of health problems which begin to arise in the middle-aged population. What is of special interest in this case is the clever way in which this visual argument "packs in" the inference that those who took type-writer-based typing in high school must be middle-aged by now. What can count as common knowledge is the further inference that those who took that kind of typing in high school must have graduated (in North America) from high school at least twenty years ago. As well, it is common knowledge that people in the so-called middle age bracket are at least (shall we say?) forty years old. Of course, there are many more such inferences. Yet, our analysis of arguments should strive to attain simplicity. We should diagram this argument in the following manner:

(H1) [If you took typing in high school then you must be middle-aged].
(H2) [If you are middle-aged then you should see an internist]. (H3) [If you took typing in high school then you should see an internist].
Diagram:

$$\underline{H1 \; + \; H2}$$
$$\downarrow$$
$$H3$$

3.5 Counter-Considerations

There is one last point about diagramming worth making. In argumentation, persons may often mention countervailing claims to their own position. Although this may seem self-defeating, it is a necessary feature of good critical thinking. Our challenge is not merely to convince others we're right, but to hold beliefs that are more likely right than wrong. To do this, we need to be honest about our own arguments. Noting their weaknesses, and especially responding to those weaknesses, is a sign, therefore, of integrity.

Negatively relevant points are called *counter-considerations.*

Rarely is any issue simply right or wrong. There are almost always various pros and cons to either side. Our audience is not unaware of that. Just as we realize that thinking up relevant counter-considerations to someone else's argument is an excellent way to refute it, so too, does our audience. To ward off someone else refuting our argument, it is always a good idea to consider relevant counter-considerations yourself ahead of time. If we note these in our argument, *and respond to them,* we show that we are sincere, have considered the issue thoroughly, and have alleviated any fears or reservations our audience may have. If we can show reason to maintain our position despite these counter-considerations, we have strengthened our argument far more than by trying to conceal our argument's potential problems.

Just as with inference indicators and modalities, there exist common words which may act as signals to us about the existence of counter-considerations. Words which indicate the existence of a counter-consideration include

although	notwithstanding	despite
nevertheless	but	admittedly

To diagram counter-considerations, we need a different symbol than our inference arrows, since what we're diagramming is the *denial* of an inference. For present purposes, let us use the following marks: ⌇ (for serial counter-considerations) ⌇ (for right side convergent counter-considerations) and ⌇ (for left side convergent counter-considerations).

Counter-considerations may focus on premises or inferences, and we should be clear about this difference.

3.5.1 Premises

Consider, the following arguments as a demonstration of the use of counter-considerations aimed at premises.

1. Notwithstanding that the sun is shining brightly now, it will be raining by this afternoon. The Weather Channel said so. So, we had better postpone our golf game.

((Notwithstanding that)) (1) [the sun is shining brightly now], (2) [it will be raining by this afternoon]. (3) [The Weather Channel said so]. (So), (4) [we had better postpone our golf game].

$$
\begin{array}{cc}
3 & 1 \\
\downarrow & \zeta \\
2 & \zeta \\
\downarrow & \\
4 &
\end{array}
$$

2. Although it is surely difficult to kill a loved one, euthanasia is the only humane and moral choice under appropriate circumstances, since the death otherwise would be much more painful.

((Although)) (1) [it is surely difficult to kill a loved one], (2) [euthanasia is the only humane and moral choice under appropriate circumstances,] ((since)) (3) [the death otherwise would be much more painful.]

3. Admittedly the proposed sports grounds site takes up existing gardens, but these gardens are poorly located anyway, and furthermore, they can be moved to the top of the hill. And although the proposed site is not centrally located, it does mean fewer neighbours will be bothered by the noise. Moreover, there will be less landscaping work required, compared to the other sites, and this alone will save us nearly a $1000.

((Admittedly)) (1) [the proposed site takes up existing gardens], ((but)) (2) [these gardens are poor], and (3) [can be moved to the top of the hill]. And (although) (4) [the proposed site is not centrally located], (5) [it does mean fewer neighbours will be bothered by the noise]. Moreover, (6) [there will be less landscaping work required, compared to the other sites], and (7) [this alone will save us nearly a $1000]. {8} [We should put the sports grounds on the proposed site].

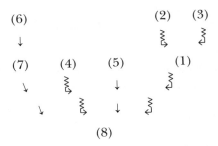

You may recall from chapter 2 the following argument:

In "China Fears U.S. Could Spoil Games Bid" (May 17), Miro Cernetig notes that, of the three countries vying for the 2008 Olympic Games, China is the only one that jails political dissidents. He must have forgotten Jaggi Singh. (Steve Gowens, letter to the editor, *Globe and Mail*, 18 May 2001, A12)

A missing ingredient in the last premise of the second argument is that Jaggi Singh was jailed in Canada for being a political dissident. Given this, we now know the argument is missing the following conclusion: Cernetig is mistaken. But claiming that Cernetig is mistaken is the same as denying the claim that of the three countries vying for the 2008 Olympic Games, China is the only one that jails political dissidents. But how is this to be diagrammed? Since we can now see that the main point of the argument is to reject Cernetig's claim, Cernetig's claim may be placed *as the conclusion*, and have the counter-consideration aimed at denying it. Thus, we could diagram the argument in the following way:

> In "China Fears U.S. Could Spoil Games Bid" (May 17), Miro Cernetig notes that, (1) [of the three countries vying for the 2008 Olympic Games, China is the only one that jails political dissidents]. (2) [He must have forgotten Jaggi Singh].

2

↯

1

3.5.2 Inferences

Recall that our goal of assessing a clearly stated argument is to question two things, the merit of the premises, and the merit of the inferences. Thus, we should also be able to distinguish in our diagrams when counter-considerations are aimed at the premises, and when they are aimed at the inferences. The following examples raise challenges to the inferences, and not the premises. Thus, our counter-consideration symbols must reflect this difference. For the purposes of our diagramming, let us use the following symbols: ⇒ and ⇐ , indicating counter-considerations that challenge an inference from the left side, and counterconsiderations that challenge an inference from the right side, respectively, in our argument map.

As an illustration, consider the following arguments:

> Although marijuana use may not relieve all types of suffering, it has been clearly documented to relieve some. Therefore the decriminalization of marijuana use is essential if we take health-care issues seriously.

The first line challenges the inference from the claim that marijuana use helps relieve suffering to the claim that we should therefore legalize it, because it points out that *some* is not sufficient to yield *all*. The arguer notes this truism, but suggests the argument may stand notwithstanding this counter-consideration. Notice that we need to provide some missing propositions here as well. The standardization and map proceeds thus

> ((Although)) (1) [marijuana use may not relieve all types of suffering], (2) [it has been clearly documented to relieve some]. ((Therefore)) (3) [the decriminalization of marijuana use is essential if we take health-care issues seriously]. (H4) [We take (or ought to take) health care seriously]. ((Therefore)) (H5) [The decriminalization of marijuana use is essential].

$$2 \qquad \underline{3 + H4}$$

$$\begin{array}{c} \zeta \\ \hookrightarrow \end{array} 1 \Rightarrow \text{--} \Rightarrow \text{--} \Rightarrow \text{--} \downarrow$$

$$H5$$

(2) refutes (1), which refutes the link between (3 + H4) and the unstated conclusion (H5). Here is another example:

Genetic manipulation should be prevented, since it's patently unnatural and anything unnatural should be prevented. Someone might object that being unnatural is not sufficient grounds to prevent something, after all, art is unnatural yet we don't prevent that, but when we focus on mucking with nature, this is where the problem occurs.

(1) [Genetic manipulation should be prevented], ((since)) (2) [it's patently unnatural] and (3) [anything unnatural should be prevented]. ((Someone might object that)) (4) [being unnatural is not sufficient grounds to prevent something], after all, (5) [art is unnatural] yet (6) [we don't prevent that], ((but)) (7) [when we focus on mucking with nature, this is where the problem occurs].

$$7 \qquad \underline{5 + 6}$$

$$\underline{2 + 3} \qquad \begin{array}{c} \zeta \\ \downarrow \end{array} \qquad \downarrow$$

$$\downarrow \ \text{--}\subset \ \text{--}\subset \ \text{--}\subset 4$$

$$1$$

Here we have two counterconsiderations, both focussed on an inference, and not a proposition. (4) challenges the link from (2) and (3) to (1), while (7) challenges *that* inference. Whether (7) can withstand reflection is certainly up for discussion. Suffice it to say here, that if it cannot, the argument crumbles.

Lastly, consider the following:

Some claim that breeding animals for human consumption is wrong. If we developed a taste for babies' flesh, we couldn't justify breeding and killing them on the ground that otherwise they wouldn't be born. True enough, but animals, though they have some moral standing, don't have all the standing of humans. What's wrong to do to humans isn't wrong to do to beings that have no autonomy.

Here the objection is not to any premise. The speaker isn't suggesting that it *is* ok to eat babies. Quite the contrary. What the speaker is doing is arguing against the inference. The argument structure looks like this

(1) [Some claim that breeding animals for human consumption is wrong.] (2) [If we developed a taste for babies' flesh, we couldn't justify breeding and killing them on the ground that otherwise they wouldn't be born]. ((True enough, but)) (3) [animals, though they have some moral standing, don't have all the standing of humans]. (4) [What's wrong to do to humans isn't wrong to do to beings that have no autonomy].

<pre>
                3

                ↓   2

            4 ➤ ➤ ➤ ➤↓

                               1
</pre>

Exercise 3.3

Diagram the following arguments. Pay attention to counter-considerations. (Answers to selected questions provided in Appendix 1.)

☞ 1 A second argument [for vegetarianism] concerns the suffering inflicted on animals by modern factory farming ... Sometimes suffering is justified by later benefits, but here the benefits are morally trivial. Unlike wolves or lions, we humans don't need meat for a healthy diet. And the pleasures of the table surely don't justify torturing animals throughout their lives. (Hurka, *Principles: Short Essays on Ethics*, 42)

☞ 2 The National Rifle Association (NRA) argues that having guns in the home will lessen violent attacks in the home. Even if this were true, it is not to the point. A substantial majority of the nation's gun victims are felled by relatives or friends, not by criminals, often in the heat of anger or passion, using readily available handguns. If a gun were not so handy, it is possible a less deadly weapon would suffice to release the momentary surge of aggression. (Editorial, adapted, *Sunday Star Ledger*, 5 April 1981)

   3 The moral relativist might argue that our language should be reformed. We should talk differently. At one time people used to talk and act as if the world were flat. Now they don't. The relativist could suggest that we can change our ethical language in the same way. But consider how radical the relativists' response is. Since most, if not all, cultures speak and act as if there were universal moral principles, the

relativist can be right only if almost everyone else is wrong. How plausible is that? (Bowie, "Relativism and the Moral Obligations of Multinational Corporations," in *Ethical Theory and Business,* 6th ed., 539)

☞ 4   The Ontario Ministry of the Environment is not criminally responsible for allowing dangerous pollutants to flow from an abandoned mine into a tiny village's water because the government was working to fix the problem, a judge ruled yesterday. Justice Celynne Dorval conceded ministry officials allowed some liquid contaminated with metals to flow into the water surrounding Deloro, Ont., but said the government is not at fault because it had taken significant steps to remedy the discharge. (Michael Friscolanti, "Judge rules in ministry's favour in pollution case," *National Post,* 28 June 2001, A4)

5 What this means is that the province must be more vigilant in the governing of elder care. It's arguable that tightening restrictions on small establishments may force some to close, but that doesn't justify a hands-off approach toward small operators. Such operators are, after all, in the business of caring for the elderly and should be subject to regulations and inspection. Government doesn't have to lower the boom so heavily that it drives operators out of business; surely it can come up with a moderate form of regulation and inspection that would respect financial restraints of small operators, but still require them to meet certain standards and submit to routine inspections. Our frail elderly are citizens who have given their time, talents and energy toward building up the communities we enjoy today. They deserve our respect in the form of protection in their vulnerable years. ("Seniors deserve both respect and protection," *Guardian,* 6 June 2001, A6)

6 There are sound, even compelling, arguments to support special status for aboriginals. First and foremost, there are binding treaties already in place that establish them as a separate people within the Canadian state. That is why, for example, the courts have upheld their right to fish and hunt in apparent violation of existing laws. Beyond the treaties, there is shame. The record of government stewardship of aboriginal peoples has been less than impressive. Current thinking among most politicians, bureaucrats and academics is that the best way to lift Indians, Inuit and Metis from the squalor in which so many of them live is to grant them the natural and legal resources to take charge of their own destiny, to create states within the state. But the Canadian social contract rests on the bedrock principle of equality before the law. Transcending in importance even freedom of speech and multiparty elections, liberal democracies embrace the rule of law, applied equitably to all regardless of stature, as the surest safeguard of individual and collective liberty. (John Ibbitson, "Get set for B.C. referendum ride," *Globe and Mail,* 18 May 2001, A5)

☞ 7 The report does not deny the accomplishments for which Yale presumably chose its honorees – prominent politicians, philosophers
and inventors. It objects, however, to Yale, even now, making no mention of these men's more questionable positions and activities in support of slavery, which might have made them more controversial
choices when the campus's most prominent honorees were named ...
"Yale is far from being the only or the worst in this regard," said Gerald Horne, a professor of African and Afro-American studies at the
University of North Carolina, "but on the other hand, Yale purports
to be, and is, a leading force in higher education in the United
States, and it's important for Yale to set an example." (Kate Zernike,
"The taint of slavery," *National Post*, 14 August 2001, A11)

8 Simply put, smoking a joint – illegal since the 1920s – is no longer
viewed with the repugnance the public has for other criminal
offences. It makes sense to change the law so that violators will be
ticketed, rather than charged criminally. The Canadian Police Association, which represents rank-and-file officers, claims decriminaliz-
ing marijuana will weaken moral disapproval of drug use. The reality
is that the public attitude about marijuana has already made the
shift. ("Feds must realize smoking a joint no longer as repugnant,"
Guardian, 25 July 2001, A7)

9 Contingency fees, in which lawyers are paid a percentage of the
award if they are successful but receive no compensation if the case
fails, allow people to retain a lawyer without making a large financial
commitment. Ontario is the only province that does not permit
them. Mr. Krishna says he intends to approach the Ontario government this fall about changing the law. Previous treasurers have
approached the attorney-general of the day and been told it was not
politically expedient. "The great problem the public has with contingency fees is the perception that lawyers will gouge you. That's why
we want a structure. We are concerned that there should be some
protection," he said. "The contingency fees could be capped, they
could be subject to judicial approval, there would be a system for pre-
registering the fees before the matter is actively undertaken." (Sandra Rubin, "Passion for justice," *National Post*, 27 July 2001, A13)

10 The federal government's decision to test all immigrants and
refugees for HIV, the virus that causes AIDS, is wise. Like tuberculosis
and hepatitis B, the other diseases for which new arrivals are tested,
AIDS is deadly and communicable. The drugs required to medicate
full-blown AIDS typically cost tens of thousands of dollars per year per
patient ... Some AIDS activists argue that testing stigmatizes AIDS sufferers and leads to discrimination against gays and immigrants from
high-risk countries. But these arguments are weak. AIDS has been
with us for 20 years and the phobic attitude toward sufferers that
manifested itself in the early stages of the epidemic is largely a thing

of the past. Moreover, the new policy will actually lessen the risk of discrimination. Under the old system, only those prospective arrivals whom doctors suspected might be suffering from HIV were tested. Obviously, such a policy lent itself to arbitrary discrimination far more than one in which testing is mandatory. ("Immigrants and AIDS," *National Post*, 14 June 2001, A19)

11 Now that delegates are in Charlottetown to discuss the future of British North America, inhabitants of all the represented regions are asking themselves: Should the remaining British Colonies in North America form a federation? On the one hand, the Maritime Provinces have rich economies, and are currently benefiting from independence from Upper and Lower Canada. In particular, Prince Edward Island's shipbuilding economy is particularly strong, and while Islanders might benefit from a federation with New Brunswick and Nova Scotia, and maybe even Newfoundland, it's difficult to tell whether they'd benefit from a union with territories further east and inland. On the other hand, a federation would improve trade, mitigating regional tariffs that interfere with mutual economic improvement. It would permit the opportunity for a railway connecting Montreal and York to the sea during the winter, and the railway could one day be extended to Red River and even British Columbia. Furthermore, federation would provide a basis for common defence. None of the colonies can rely on the Imperial government to provide troops in the event of an invasion from either the United States or the Confederate States. Also, the Fenians (a group of Irish separatist terrorists) have failed to start a war in Ireland, and would think nothing of starting one in the Maritimes. Finally, federation appeals to many British North Americans on a patriotic level; although many are taken with regional rivalries, we are all united under one crown on one continent. For these reasons, British North Americans should definitely consider consolidating their power into one state.

Part Two
Meaning

4

Language Use

Euphemism and Doublespeak • Form and Intent Reading Between the Lines • Biases and Vested Interests • Recognizing a Slanted Argument Weasel Words • Obfuscation • Different Kinds of Disagreements

4.1   Euphemism and Doublespeak

In part I, we learned the basic structure of argumentation. In part II, we shall explore in more depth the question of meaning. Language use can clarify ideas, but it can also obscure them. For critical reflection, we need to become better acquainted with the wily ways of language.

   In this chapter, we will talk about the importance of using words precisely. In particular, we will address the problems associated with euphemisms and doublespeak, vagueness, and ambiguity. In the following chapter, we will discuss definitions.

Euphemisms are expressions that substitute mild and indirect ways of speaking for those that are blunt or harsh. We live in a society where euphemisms abound; they flourish especially, but not exclusively, in the discourse of politics, bureaucracy, the military, and advertising.

   Here is a small list of examples:

euphemism	translation
to take out	to kill or destroy (used by the military or the police)
to downsize	to lay off (used by corporations)
comfort women	women of conquered countries forced to work as prostitutes "servicing" soldiers

Sexual intercourse is a ripe topic for the invention of euphemisms. Consider the following news item:

> Friday, July 6: Rep. Gary Condit had admitted to Washington, D.C., police that he had a romantic relationship with missing intern Chandra Levy, a police source told Fox News.

Robert Fulford, a well-known Canadian journalist, was quick to note the loaded euphemism lurking here:

> Romantic? In some contexts, "romantic" might have meant they read Keats and Shelley to each other or played soft music during dinner while candles flickered. But that's not what the writer was trying to convey. "Romantic" has become one of the words we use in place of "sexual" because we remain nervous about a subject that everybody decided, 30-some years ago, not to be nervous about any more. (Robert Fulford, "How 'intern' became a dirty word," *National Post*, 24 July 2001, B1)

Similarly, persons don't have sex, they "see" each other, or perhaps "sleep with" each other. The Bible suggests they "knew" each other. Notice, too, that the word "intercourse," though more direct than "seeing," is still a euphemism. Intercourse occurs in conversation, and we know both that conversation alone does not constitute sex, and that sex may occur without conversation. Still, when these terms are uttered, the audience is sufficiently aware of the overarching conventions governing language to know what is meant.

Death is another taboo topic typically closeted away by euphemisms. Granny did not die, she "went to sleep," inculcating in our children poor sleeping habits.

"Defecation" and "urination" are other terms rarely used in public. Euphemisms usually take their place. Thus one may "visit the lavatory," or "go to the bathroom," both of which can be done without voiding, itself a euphemism. Also popular is the expression "to go powder one's nose." Honey, the young woman guest at the dinner party in *Who's Afraid of Virginia Woolf?* says she would like to powder her nose. George, the host, turns to his wife and says, "Martha, won't you show her where we keep the euphemism?"

We don't wish to suggest we never use euphemisms, or always object to another's argument if it contains a euphemism. Euphemism may be appropriate in certain contexts. Language, like mode of dress, should fit the occasion. Our intention is to highlight the vagaries of language. We don't wish to be beguiled.

Sometimes euphemisms backfire. Consider the following account by Robert Fulford:

> In Laurence Sterne's novel *The Life and Opinions of Tristram Shandy, Gentleman*, Tristram tells us how he figured out the precise date he was conceived. He says his father was a man of regular habits in all spheres of

life, and he made it a rule always to wind the great house-clock on the first Sunday night of every month. Gradually, he "brought some other little family concernments to the same period, in order, as he would often say to my uncle Toby, to get them all out of the way at one time, and be no more plagued and pestered with them the rest of the month." Tristram tells us that "my poor mother," upon hearing the winding of the clock, knew that something else was about to happen. In this way, Tristram dates "my geniture" to Nov. 5, 1718.

Tristram Shandy was the great best-seller of 1760 in England, and this passage created a euphemism that was apparently used by both the gentry and the masses. Soon, streetwalkers took to asking potential clients, "Sir, will you have your clock wound up?" Before the year was out, an aggrieved craftsman published anonymously a pamphlet called *The Clockmaker's Outcry Against the Author*, claiming Sterne had ruined his business. He reported that women who had commissioned him to make clocks for them had cancelled their orders "because no modest lady now dares to mention a word about winding up a clock, without exposing herself to the sly jeers and jokes of the family." The clockmaker claimed that virtuous matrons were even hiding their clocks in storage rooms, to keep the sight of them from exciting family and guests "to acts of carnality." (Ibid.)

Emotive terms exert great power. A new political party being formed somewhere in the world will now tend to define itself as "democratic" or "progressive," and *not* (except for a few throw-back groups like the Taliban) as "hard-line" or "fundamentalist." Employers in the United States who want to pay employees less than the minimum wage or escape contractual obligations to provide health benefits for employees need only call them *subcontractors* instead of *employees*. Minimum wage laws in the United States apply to employees but not to subcontractors.

Euphemisms, used to soften, diminish, or obscure the real meaning of words are just one side of the coin. Words can also be used to make the ordinary seem extraordinary, and to make everyday things seem impressive. This is sometimes achieved by overwhelming the audience with buzz words. Politicians seem especially adept at this, although academics also fall prey to it. Sometimes, this kind of language abuse is called *doublespeak* (a term first used by George Orwell in his novel *1984*).

Here are some examples of doublespeak:

Doublespeak	Translation
automotive internists	car mechanics
pre-owned vehicles	used cars
involuntary conversion	loss of property

Sometimes, euphemisms and doublespeak can be combined (what a feat!):

Doublespeak/Euphemism	Translation
negative patient care outcome	the patient died
pre-emptive counterattack	we attack first

As this brief series illustrates, language is ripe for obfuscation and manipulation. A critical thinker should pay special attention to both substance and style in language.

4.2 Form and Intent

If someone asks, "Do you have the time?" it would be inappropriate to answer simply "Yes," and pass by. But the literal structure (or *form*) of the question clearly permits a simple affirmative. Compare, for example, asking "Do you have the remote?" or "Did you watch the game last night?" Answering "Yes" to both these questions is only the beginning of the conversation. As with wanting to know the time, someone might really want us to pass the remote, or to share the speaker's emotional fervour toward last night's game. Still, answering "Yes" to these latter questions and waiting for more will not contravene convention, as it would with the first question.

Something similar is going on when we note that the appropriate response to the question, "How's it going?" is "Fine." This is so even when things are not going particularly well. The form of the utterance appears to belie in the speaker a real interest in knowing what's going on in our lives. Telling him, however, will generally be met with a certain degree of discomfort and impatience. That is to say, the *intent* of the question is not captured by its form. The intent in this case is ritual. It is a formal pleasantry, like saying *"en garde"* or "check" in a game of chess, or tipping one's hat, or applauding at the end of a performance. Admittedly there are occasions when speakers really are interested in how we're doing. In such cases they will provide clues that they are not speaking merely ritually. One might add, for example, "I mean *really*" after the initial question. This may also be accompanied by a gentler tone, perhaps even a hand on a shoulder, or at least actually making eye contact. Sometimes the context alone may qualify treating the intent as matching the form, when, for example, the questioner sees that we're crying. Saying "Fine" in that case can only be understood as sarcasm. This may result from noting the inanity of the question in such a case. Asking whether it is raining when the speaker and audience are both standing out in the rain unprotected may parallel the peculiarity of the question.

The important point here is to show that language use consists of at least two things: *form* and *intent*. The form of the utterance is the grammatical structure. The intent of the utterance is what the speaker means. Often the two overlap, but as we've already seen, this is not always the case. The form of the language may not match the intent.

For further demonstration, imagine if your boss tells you: "You won't make that mistake again." The form of the statement is a *prediction*, like "It's going to rain." Mere prediction is unlikely to be the boss's intent, however. It is more likely intended as a threat. "Thank you," as a response should strike us as wildly inappropriate, a confusion of intent and form.

If someone says "I would like you to pass me the remote," the form of the statement is a description of the speaker's desires. Compare, for example, "I hope Catriona Le May Doan wins," or "I'm afraid of flying." Such utterances don't normally require us to do anything, save provide some form of ritualistic response indicating that at least we heard what the speaker said. "That's nice," or "Me too." Neither response would be fitting to the statement "I would like you to pass me the remote." Such a response confuses the form of the utterance for the intent.

Few will misconstrue the form for the intent in these examples. We're quite adept from early on at correctly making such distinctions with ease. This is a remarkable feat in its own right, and how our brains are configured to be able to do this is a fascinating topic of study, given the enormity of different types of language use.

Here is a partial list:

Questions: "Was it the *Timaeus* where Plato mentioned Atlantis?"
Commands: "Get out!"
Directives: "Add milk and, stirring continuously, bring to a boil."
Rituals: "Nice weather we're having." "Hot enough for you?"
Expressives: "Wow!" "Yech!"
Predictions: "Team Canada will lose."
Performatives: "I promise to clean my room tomorrow."
Jokes: "Why did the turkey cross the road? Cuz he wasn't chicken."
Information: "Joe is a mechanic."
Arguments: "Forbear to judge, for we are sinners all."

Notice that with *performatives*, we are doing something with words. We are not merely *describing* what we're doing, or making a prediction about what we will do, but by the very uttering of the words we do the thing in question. The groom's saying "I do" at the right moment in the wedding ceremony commits him. And it is the saying that makes it official. It isn't official prior to his saying it, although of course he intends to be so committed in order for him to say so. In any event, he cannot get out of the marriage merely by claiming that his "I do" was not intended as a performative, but merely as a string of words he happened to say. The same may be said for the act of promising. When we say we promise, that is what commits us. We cannot get out of our promise by claiming that we didn't mean it when we said we promised. Performatives, then, are treated very differently from other language use. For performatives, the intent is the form, and we reject the possibility of it being otherwise.

Expressives are an interesting use of language as well. All swear words, for example, are expressives. Expressives can only be understood as form. They are contentless utterances expressing nothing in and of themselves. Cries of pain and cries of joy, whether put in language form or in mere sound, utter no content. They are pure form. Asking whether they are true or false, therefore, makes no sense.

Of course, it may be true that someone is in pain, or in ecstasy, or feels disgusted, and the expressives or expletives used may help outsiders understand the emotional state of the agent, but we would not describe the ejaculation itself as true or false. Compare the following two utterances:

(A) "Descartes said 'Cogito ergo sum'."
(B) "Yahoo!"

We can sensibly say of (A) that it is a true statement in a way that we cannot of (B). Of course, we could say of (B) that it is true that the agent uttered "Yahoo!". That is, it is true that the speaker uttered something. But *what* the speaker uttered in the case of (B) is *neither* true nor false, any more than a sneeze is true (although it may be true that someone sneezed).

Typically the form (grammatical structure) of our language matches our intent, but not always. Rhetorical questions, for example, look like questions, but are really statements. Consider:

"Can anyone seriously maintain that infanticide is morally permissible?"

The form of the utterance is a question. The intent is more likely to be translated as the following statement:

"No one seriously maintains that infanticide is morally permissible."

This could be presented yet more strongly:

"Infanticide is clearly immoral."

Sometimes, a few stages of unpacking the intent from the form are needed. Consider, for example, the following utterance.

"How can anyone with any degree of intelligence vote Reform?"

The form is a mere question, but most will see that it is rhetorical. Thus, we might translate the intent in the following manner:

"No one with intelligence will vote Reform."

As put, this takes the form of providing information. But this is unlikely to be the intent of the speaker either. Rather, it is conceivable that something more is going on here: particularly, a directive.

"Don't vote Reform."

The complexity of language is subtle, and our advice to writers of arguments is to match form with intent. For example, avoid rhetorical questions in argumentation. Since an argument is designed to convince our audience about that which we take to be true, confusing the audience by mismatching form and intent won't achieve the goal. Concerning the ability to distinguish intent from form in others' writings, read on.

4.3 Reading between the Lines

The ability to see the intent beneath the form is sometimes called "reading between the lines." Consider the following exchange:

Ms. Wormwood:	You have a question Calvin?
Calvin:	I just want to say that education is our most important investment in the future, and it's scandalous how little our educators are paid!
Ms. Wormwood:	Ok. Hands up. Who ELSE didn't do the homework for today? (Bill Watterson, *Calvin and Hobbes*, 1992)

Ms. Wormwood is adept at reading between the lines. Part of her success is due to her experience with the speaker in question. We may also rely on context. Sometimes reading between the lines requires a bit more effort. Consider the following ads:

No regular aspirin product reduces headaches better!
Nothing outlasts Energizer!
Nothing gets clothes whiter!

On the not unreasonable assumption that advertisers are out to make the strongest claim truthfully possible, we begin to realize how weak the above claims really are. Reading between the lines reveals that they merely say their products are as good as any other product out there. Each slogan is consistent with the claim that the products are *no better* than their competitors. Assuming that advertisers have spent a great deal of time and money to come up with these very slogans, and that they are motivated to make the *strongest claim possible*, we can now reasonably deduce that the products therefore *are* in fact no better than their competitors; otherwise the advertisements would have said so.

A Note on Headaches

Concerning the first advertisement above, notice that the nonprescription pain-reliever market involves just three drugs: aspirin, acetaminophen, and ibuprofen. This market is dominated by four major pharmaceutical companies. Sterling Drug controls a major share of the aspirin market with its product, Bayer Aspirin. Johnson & Johnson produces an acetaminophen (Tylenol) and an ibuprofen product (Mediprin). American Home Products makes an aspirin (Anacin), an acetaminophen (Anacin-3), and an ibuprofen (Advil). Bristol-Meyers also produces aspirin (Bufferin and Excedrin), an acetaminophen (Datril), and an ibuprofen (Nuprin).

Since there is no chemical, and therefore no medicinal, difference between brands of acetaminophen and ibuprofen, and no significant difference between aspirins (Anacin has caffeine), these companies have two basic choices for succeeding in the marketplace: they can compete over price, or they can rely on advertising. They have tended to favour the second choice.

In the 1940s, Anacin claimed that its "combination of highly proven and active ingredients" was superior to and different from Aspirin. This was straightforwardly false, however, since no evidence exists to support the claim that caffeine, the only difference between Anacin and Aspirin, improves Anacin's analgesic effect. In the 1960s, television ads claimed that Anacin offered "fast, fast relief," Bufferin was "twice as fast as aspirin," St. Joseph's aspirin was "faster than other leading pain relief tablets," and Bayer offered the "fastest relief of pain." Anacin also cited surveys that showed "three out of four doctors recommend the ingredients in Anacin" and called Anacin's ingredients the "greatest pain fighter ever discovered." These ads did not disclose that this "ingredient" was plain aspirin.

The popularity of acetaminophen increased in the 1970s and brought with it similar specious claims. Johnson & Johnson supplied hospitals with Tylenol at costs well below what consumers were paying, and then advertised the following: "Last year hospitals dispensed ten times as much Tylenol as the next four brands combined." While American Home Products sued Johnson & Johnson for the misleading advertising, they provided the following advertising campaign for their acetaminophen, Anacin-3: "Hospitals recommend acetaminophen, the aspirin-free pain reliever in Anacin-3, more than any other pain reliever." The acetaminophen recommended by hospitals, of course, was Tylenol. (Boatright, *Ethics and the Conduct of Business*, 274)

Sometimes we need to do some math to read between the lines. Examine the following:

Consider the state of agriculture between the Civil War and World War I, a period of immense growth in the American economy. Agriculture shared in that growth: The number of farms tripled, the number of acres of farmland doubled, the net farm income increased more than fourfold. Despite this growth, two stark figures stand out. Farm population decreased from 60 per cent to 35 per cent of the national population, and agriculture's share of the national income dropped from 31 per cent to 22 per cent. In other words, agriculture did not keep pace with the rest of the economy.

Two other facts can be deduced by reading between the lines. Can you see what they may be? (Answer provided at the end of this chapter.)

4.4 Biases and Vested Interests

Biases are something external to the argument that influences one's commitments. *Vested interests* are present when the outcome of accepting A's proposal will benefit A herself.

Imagine a study showing no effects between smoking and lung cancer. This outcome ought to be surprising given the general understanding that there is a clear positive correlation between smoking and lung cancer. In fact, the surprise would likely be so great that, despite the results of the study, we would be inclined to look elsewhere for the explanation of the results. By elsewhere, we mean that on the basis that we will not accept that smoking does not cause lung cancer, we seek another explanation for the counter-intuitive result. Perhaps we discover that the study was funded by a cigarette manufacturer. This sponsorship would be a clear case of vested interest, and would greatly impact on the degree of our accepting the results. We would quite reasonably be content in our belief that we had now discovered the explanation for the skewed results. We need look no further.

A protest group is depicted on the front page of the 20 February 2002 edition of the Charlottetown *Guardian* newspaper. Their slogan reads: "Keep the Farm Green!" The story line concerns a group's disappointment with the selling off of part of the Canadian government's experimental farm. On closer inspection, we learn that the protesters have something in common beyond their wanting to keep the farm green: they all come from a small subdivision adjacent to the parcel of land in question. They aren't known environmental activists, nor had they joined other environmental protests – against pesticide use on farms, against pesticide use on urban lawns, in favour of the protection of swamp lands or the dunes, in favour of a recycling program for Islanders, for example. These facts belie the true motive of their complaint: self-interest. The city was purchasing the land from the experimental farm to put up a community swimming pool. This would certainly cause traffic and hubbub that these residents are not used to, and do not particularly desire. Who would? But the fact that they feel uneasy about complaining primarily on the grounds of self-interest motivates them to find some other reason (than what really motivates their complaint) for stopping the project. Always popular are appeals to environmental protection. The move is transparent, however. It does not conceal that their main motive entails straightforward vested interests.

A similar pattern occurred in a community's protest against placing a recycling plant beside them. Although everyone may be in favour of a recycling plant, few want it next door. Afraid that straightforward appeals to their self-interest would not outweigh the interest of the community, the residents mounted a safety-issue campaign, alleging that the increased truck traffic would cause accidents. Again, the move was transparent. The campaign could not hide the fact that the motive entailed vested interests.

A charge of vested interest involves a claim that the arguer *intended* to skew the results, or the reporting. As a result of the intentional manipulation of data, vested interest involves a moral failure. Accusations of bias, however, do not carry such a degree of condemnation. Bias is *unintentional.* A psychology professor who urges you to become a psychology major is probably showing bias. She will not likely gain in any way by your becoming a psychology major, and her advice may indeed be sincere. But if it is predicated mainly on your academic ability, you may be well suited for any number of academic careers, and her thinking of psychology in particular is likely due to her bias in favour of psychology.

Although bias creates an unintentional contamination, it is still a contamination. Therefore, it behooves critical thinkers to weed out as much bias as possible and to seriously reflect on whether they are biased at present in unconscious ways. In chapter 12 we will examine ways scientists try to manage bias. For now, we will examine ways to detect bias and vested interests in arguments and reports.

Consider the following two reports. Can you correctly identify whether the culprits may be accused of bias or vested interest?

(1) In 1996, ABC devoted the entire two hours of *Good Morning America* to a show on Disney World. They ran a special program on "Disney's Most Unlikely Heroes," and featured footage from the Disney film *The Hunchback of Notre Dame* as well as a special program on that film. Not surprisingly, Disney owns ABC.

(2) "Do cigarettes have a future?" a *Weekly Reader* cover asked on a 1994 sixth-grade students edition, illustrated by tobacco workers carrying signs: "No more Taxes" and "Freedom of Choice." "Taxes and bans have caused many tobacco growers and workers to lose their jobs," the cover noted. The article inside played down the health risks of smoking – and didn't mention that the demonstration pictured had been organized by the tobacco industry. Nor did it mention that the *Weekly Reader* is owned by K-III Communications – a division of Kohlberg Kravis Roberts and Co., which is the largest investor in tobacco giant RJR Nabisco.

There is a clear case of vested interest in both examples. Bias will also be rampant in cases of vested interest, but not necessarily the reverse. That I will benefit greatly from your accepting X will greatly impact on my bias, even if I am not immorally motivated.

This is important. Merely pointing out vested interest or bias is not sufficient to show the argument to be poor. Arguments stand or fall on their own merits, and not because of who made them. If a doctor encourages us to come back for more appointments, this may be a case of vested interest. Notwithstanding that she may benefit, we may have good reasons to take up her suggestion!

For that matter, there are cases where our bias counts as a proper tool. Of course, this is when we are engaged in criticizing someone else's report, study, or argument. If the findings run counter to our own bias, we may be prompted to suspect the study is itself biased (in this case, biased against our position). By itself this is insufficient to undermine the study, report, or argument, but it may help guide us in our search for the contamination. In fact, we did precisely this in the cigarette example at the outset of this section. The result went against our bias, that cigarettes are bad for us, and this prompted us to seek some explanation to debunk the results. Notice that we cannot simply use our bias as a definitive tool. In no way can I say, "That goes against my biases, therefore it is wrong." That would be the complete antithesis of what critical reflection is about.

Consider another example where bias was used as a helpful guide to criticize a study. For some reason, many scientists have consumed their time with "proving" cognitive differences between men and women. One wonders whether such zeal is not predicated on an attempt to *justify* discrimination against women by men. Of course, this will work only as long as men "win" the cognitive games. When women are discovered to do better, the study tends to be quickly dismissed as contaminated. When men win, the studies are trumpeted as sound science. The whole game reeks of bias, and perhaps, even vested interests. But women are scientists too, and just as a man is allowed to use his bias as a *prima facie* tool to debunk studies giving women the cognitive edge, a woman has every reason to use her own biases to debunk studies giving the cognitive edge to men. Please note, if the studies are debunked, this is for scientifically valid reasons, and not merely because of bias. Case in point: A study was done in which men and women, university students all, were placed individually into a darkened room with the male experimenter. A white line was flashed on the black wall, and the participants were asked to say when the line reached the perpendicular. Given the complete darkness of the room, the ability to distinguish the perpendicular must be done absent any other markers. Evidently, men scored significantly better than women on this task, and the logical conclusion from this was that men were cognitively superior to women on spatial orientation tasks. Finally we have a scientific backing for why men don't ask for directions as frequently as women do: men don't have to. (Their getting lost more often is to be explained by some other factor).

A woman scientist admitted she had a strong bias to doubt the results. This bias led her to seek other factors to explain such counter-intuitive results. (Again, it was not her mere bias that "proved" the result mistaken!) The answer was not far to be found. Male experimenters would be less likely than female experimenters to see what was wrong with the methodology of that particular study. Sitting alone in a darkened room with an unknown man will create quite different mental states in women than men. Quite likely, she thought, the women were terrified, and their ability to sufficiently concentrate on when a line was perpendicular would be seriously undermined. To test this hypothesis, the scientist duplicated the experiment, but this time used a brightly lit, white room with a female experimenter and a black line. The claim was that the ability to detect a perpendicular line absent any other indicators was still maintained. In this study, no difference between men's and women's cognitive abilities was found. (Fausto-Sterling, *Myths of Gender*, 32)

This is not to say that bias is good. Far from it. But we may avail ourselves of our own bias to detect the likely bias in others' arguments. Importantly, this is not enough. Once we detect bias, we must show that this indeed undermines our acceptance of the claim.

4.5 Recognizing a Slanted Argument

Bias is often detectable by language use. Consider these two news stories from otherwise reputable sources reporting on the same Reagan economic plan:

(1) President Reagan is launching the nation on a dramatic and unexplored course that reverses decades-old policies in Washington ... his revolutionary program ... the economy should start to shake off its doldrums this summer and shoot up next year ... Firms will pour cash into new buildings and equipment. Defence contractors will enjoy a boom in orders. (*U.S. News & World Report*, 2 March 1981)

(2) The President is taking a whole series of high-risk gambles. He is betting ... That is at least questionable ... and there is something in his plan to offend just about every lobby in Washington ... taking a long chance ... [that] could instead deepen deficits ... or make inflation worse. (*Time*, 2 March 1981)

Compare the different adjectives used to describe Reagan's plans in the two reports: "dramatic" and "revolutionary" versus "high-risk gamble" and "questionable." What is really interesting about these articles is that we aren't given anything that would justify these choices. We are given merely the *attitudes* of the writers, and no information at all. That is the sad part. We may have thought that the role of the media was to report the facts, and nothing but the facts, and let us form our own attitudes and opinions about those facts. But in reality, we are more often than not provided ready-made attitudes and opinions in the guise of a report.

We shall call arguments that are unduly biased or affected by vested interest *slanted arguments*. People will slant an argument, sometimes unconsciously, in an effort to make it appear stronger than it is, or in an attempt to say things indirectly that they couldn't get away with saying explicitly. Pay attention to the different *slants* of the following two "reports."

In a pair of cases to be heard today, the Supreme Court will be the final arbiter on whether the federal government can deport refugees to countries that impose beatings, electric shock and death on their citizens. At issue is whether two Toronto men in their mid-30s – Manickavasagam Suresh of Sri Lanka and Mansour Ahani of Iran – have the constitutional right to remain in Canada, despite being classified as security threats. The two men have been fighting their deportation for years in Canada's courts.

(Janice Tibbetts, "Supreme Court to decide whether to deport 'threats'," *National Post*, 22 May 2001, A11)

A misguided defence of the rights and privileges of terrorists and spies by Canadian courts is making our country, as well as the rest of the world, a more dangerous place to live. It is time to recognize that Canada's famous welcome mat cannot be extended to the globe's most undesirable people. This week the Supreme Court will hear arguments on the cases of Manickavasagam Suresh and Mansour Ahani. Both men have well-documented pasts as members of terrorist organizations in Sri Lanka and Iran respectively. Extraordinarily, the fact that they have been engaged in global terror campaigns has not been enough to allow the federal government to expel them.

(Editorial, "Terrorists welcome," *National Post*, 22 May 2001, A19)

One interesting difference between the two reports is that the left hand column uses the word "alleged" to describe the charges against the two men. They are "alleged" criminals – that is, they haven't gone to trial, and haven't been convicted of any crime. So far, they've only been accused, and therefore their crimes are "alleged," i.e., stated but not determined. The threats to life and limb they face in their home countries, though, are presented as being very real.

In the editorial on the right-hand column, the use of the word "alleged" is reversed. The men are referred to as "terrorists" – but the threats they face back home are "alleged."

There are several ways to slant an argument. Here are four:

1 selection or omission
2 presentation

3 distortion or innuendo
4 emotive terms

4.5.1 Omission or Selection

We cannot possibly present all pertinent information, especially in the media, when the attention span of the audience is usually less than a minute. We have to edit. Of course, editing is generally a good thing, but it may involve bias. What is cut out and what is left may be significant. Slanting by omission occurs when key information is cut out. Slanting by selection occurs when the material that is selected reveals bias. Of course, selecting one thing over another means we're omitting one thing in favour of another, so slanting by omission will also tend to concern slanting by selection, and vice versa. For example, telling us how the men did in a non-major golf tournament, but not how the women did in a major championship, reveals bias by both selection and omission.

Still, we can generally focus on whether slanting occurs mainly by selection, or mainly by omission. In slanting by omission, the speaker tells the truth, but not the whole truth. The charge is best levied when what is left out of the argument is precisely that which works against the speaker's bias. Recall the ads for headache tablets, batteries, and clothes detergents? They may be accused of omission. Telling us that no products are better than these omits the information that these products are not better than their competitors.

Recognizing a case of slanting by omission is more difficult than recognizing a case of slanting by selection because we have to know what is being omitted. For example, nothing seems problematic with the following report:

> Dr. Phillips, a professor at the University of Toronto, spoke in favour of the proposed legislation.

But if no mention is made of Drs. Thierault, Ferdinand, and Hendrickson, also professors at the University of Toronto, speaking *against* the proposed legislation, this would be a clear case of slanting by omission.

Consider, again, the deportation case mentioned in the columns above. In neither piece is it entirely clear to what extent Mr. Suresh was involved with the Tamil Tigers, or what charges he faces in Sri Lanka. But in the second piece, there's a glaring omission: the author (who is one of the editors of the *Post,* though the article is unsigned) doesn't mention the charges Mr. Ahani faces. The problem isn't simply that Mr. Ahani was a member of a terrorist organization (which is the ruling party of the state of Iran), but that he defected from that organization when he balked at brutal orders to massacre civilians. This fact is an extremely important consideration in deciding whether to be merciful.

But how would unsuspecting readers know that bias occurs without knowing more about what's being reported than the report itself? Few of us may have such additional information. Recognizing ways of slanting by selection may help provide hints for us. Consider the following case.

In 1999, there was a protest against the World Trade Organization (WTO) in Seattle. One national television news station showed damage to buildings followed by glimpses of a variety of disreputable-looking youths. They had spiked black hair, and were wearing leather jackets adorned with thick chains. They stared pithily at the camera. The announcer spoke of the damage the protesters had done to local businesses. The announcer said the protest was also aimed against Clinton's policies. The scene shifted to Clinton disembarking from a plane and smiling. At the same time, the announcer claimed that one of Clinton's agendas at the WTO meeting was to stop trade with countries using child labour. What could be wrong with this report?

The answer is bias by selection. Selecting only a tough gang of youths as being representative of the protestors is a distortion. The protestors represented a wide range of socio-economic backgrounds. Also, telling us that Clinton is in favour of abolishing child labour selects one feature of Clinton's platform, and omits the others. By such selective reporting, we are led to believe that the protestors are a bunch of punks, intent on wilful damage of property, because they are in favour of child labour. Without relying on anything but our own understanding of life, of politics, and of the media, it is less miraculous to suspect a skewed report.

Of course, sometimes merely pointing out a case of omission is not sufficient. Consider the following article:

Video footage depicting Fisheries and Oceans Canada officers striking native lobster fishermen with batons and fists last summer is being distributed around the world as Mi'kmaq natives try to gain public sympathy in the East Coast fishing dispute. The film, titled *Who Will Sing for Us?*, includes an edited version of footage shot by fisheries officers during a dispute last July 26 between the department and members of the Indian Brook band at St. Mary's Bay, N.S. The clip has been called misleading by fisheries officials because it leaves on the cutting room floor what preceded the confrontation. What it shows is native fishermen standing on their boat at a wharf in New Edinburgh when they are surrounded by fisheries officers in boats and RCMP officers on the wharf behind them. One fisherman is seen jumping from his trawler into a boat operated by fisheries officers wearing helmets and padded vests and holding truncheons. Officers strike him several times with batons and closed fists on the head and back before he lands in the water and swims to another boat. The altercation is shown more than once from different angles ... But *Who Will sing for Us?* does not show the actions of the native fishermen directly before the clash. Edited out of the film are scenes showing the native fishermen angrily raising pieces of wood and poles to fend off

fisheries officers announcing they intend to board their boat. The natives yell
obscenities and gesture as if to taunt the officers. (Louise Elliott, "Government
calls native film 'misleading'," *National Post,* 30 July 2001, A7)

The charge of slanting by omission against the video is correct, but clearly
not sufficient. Obscenities and gestures do not normally warrant beatings.

4.5.2 Presentation

In presenting news reports, one must choose which story gets prominence
and which gets delegated to the rear. This is inevitable, just as editing is,
since we can't report stories simultaneously, obviously. Paying attention to
the location of stories, however, can help reveal bias. An article buried in
the middle of the paper is usually viewed as less important than the article
which is emblazoned on the front page. That the Liberal government lost
billions of taxpayers' dollars seems like an important piece of information,
but finding the report buried somewhere in the middle or back of a newspaper, or sandwiched between local interest stories in a newscast, might
give us the idea that it isn't really that big a deal. Perhaps it is routine for
all governments to lose such sums of money, just as we may be prone to
misplace our wallet now and then. At least, that is what Liberal supporters
may want us to believe (if they can't flatly deny that it happened).

The presentation, selection, and omission of stories may reveal not so
much the bias of the local media, as that of the intended audience. People
from Prince Edward Island would be more thrilled to see stories about
Suzanne Gaudet, the repeat Canadian junior curling champion from Summerside, PEI, than would audiences in Red Deer, let alone Missouri. Likewise it is misplaced to complain that American media coverage of the
Olympics tends to focus too heavily on American athletes.

4.5.3 Innuendo

Innuendo is a form of implying something without making it explicit. We
ought to be suspicious, for if the charge really can be made, we would
expect it to be made explicitly, without fear. Innuendos are mere vague suggestions. We should treat them as such. Recall the difference between mere
opinion and argument? Opinion is cheap. Arguments back up one's claims.
Likewise, innuendo is cheap. It should fail to be convincing on its own.

Consider the following. Jones accuses Smith of lying. Williams points out
that no lie occurred in what Smith said. Jones replies, "Well, ok, he didn't
lie *this time.*" The innuendo is clear: Despite lack of evidence, Jones is a liar.
But since we ought to conform our beliefs as much as possible to the evidence, mere innuendo ought to be seen for what it is – empty. Insincere
apologies often suffer this defect.

Sometimes the innuendo is less subtle, and this is when we must be most
wary. Consider the following headline in the *San Francisco Chronicle:*

"Chiapas peasants start big land grab."

The article beneath this headline is about how the Chiapas won a court case proving that the land was illegally taken from them, and were now granted the legal right to reclaim it. Notice the words used, however: "Big Land Grab," leads us to think that the Chiapas are greedy opportunists. Even if the subsequent article is fairly presented, most people read only the headlines of newspaper articles. The headline can indicate a bias that may influence thousands.

Here is another newspaper headline in which innuendo reveals bias:

"Spunky Sheila Copps tries to defend her new proposal."

Sheila Copps is "spunky," is she? And notice also that she merely "tries" to defend her proposal. We may presume that's why she's "spunky," since the insinuation is that her proposal cannot possibly be defended, but good ol' spunky Sheila tries anyway. Given that it is unlikely that similar language would be used for male politicians, we are not wrong to suspect sexism.

Can you detect the distorting innuendo in the following headline?

"Bush defends his son's 'honor'." (*USA Today*, July 1990)

Compare this to the following:

"Bush defends his son's honor."

The use of quotation marks adds a special flavour. Reading the two headlines aloud will likely reveal differences in both tone and tempo. When words or phrases are highlighted by scare-quotes, the meaning of the terms is altered. The basic message in the first headline is that Bush's son really has no honour to defend. This sarcasm is completely absent in the second headline.

Consider a few other examples:

Professor Smith has adopted Rebecca as his "protégée."
Here is a clear case where the "cure" is worse than the ailment.
For some reason, many scientists have consumed their time with "proving" cognitive differences between men and women.
So, she's sober now, is she?
Well, he hasn't been imprisoned, yet.

Alienans Adjectives

The quotation marks around *honor* operate much like *alienans* adjectives, a term coined by medieval philosophers. An *alienans* adjective may be viewed as a negative adjective. When attached to a noun, it renders the referent remarkably non-existent. This is quite a feat. For example, the adjectives "forgery" and "cancelled" may be *alienans*. We understand what a hundred dollar bill is. And we also understand what a torn, or wet hundred dollar bill is. It is a hundred dollar bill that is torn and wet. But is a *forged* hundred dollar bill still a hundred dollar bill? The answer is No. Any more than a forged Renoir is a Renoir. Likewise, we understand what a concert is. We also know what a loud concert is, or a jam-packed concert. These are still concerts, obviously. But is a *cancelled* concert still a concert? The answer is No. Quotation marks operate in ways similar to *alienans* adjectives. They insinuate that the audience is not to treat the word or phrase in its normal sense, and usually innuendo is lurking.

4.5.4 Emotive Terms

Emotive terms are terms or phrases that elicit strong emotional responses in the audience. We need to be wary of such terms. But this warning may be misunderstood.

Emotions count as reasons. That I pity the stray cat is a reason to take him in. That I'm afraid to fly is a reason not to fly. That A loves B is a reason for A to do something nice for B. That I hate mushrooms is a reason for me not to eat them. Of course in all such cases, we need to qualify the claims by adding the following rider: *all things considered*. That I hate needles, say, may be overridden by the benefit of the inoculation. My fear of flying may be deemed too restricting on my life, so that I may have a reason to undergo some form of therapy to get rid of that particular emotional facet of my life. My desire for a cigarette may be outweighed by my greater preference for health. Despite A's love for B, B may have made it perfectly clear that what A considers nice, B finds contemptuous.

Emotions count, then, as *prima facie* reasons for action. A *prima facie* reason is a reason considered on its own, not against the backdrop of other considerations. A *prima facie* reason may be distinguished from a *considered* reason. A considered reason is an all-things-considered sort of reflection. Notice that *prima facie* reasons may become considered reasons. Even though I may lose out on zinc intake from avoiding mushrooms, I could take zinc supplements and still avoid mushrooms. So my *prima facie* reason not to eat mushrooms can become a considered reason not to eat mushrooms.

So, absent any countervailing reasons, emotions do count as reasons for actions. They are good motivators. It is false to say emotions cannot count as reasons, or that reason and emotion necessarily conflict, as science fiction pretends. Admitting this, however, does not lead to the opposite folly: the supposition that emotions will always count as considered reasons for action. Instead, they are *prima facie* reasons, and more is needed before we ascertain whether they also count as a considered reason for the case at hand.

Arguments that rely solely on tweaking our emotions are therefore suspect. They are doubly so because we are psychologically prone to react on emotions without checking to see if other considerations should come into play. The power of the stray cat's cuteness may well overpower any other consideration, such as vet and food costs, one's own allergies, and the condition of one's leather couches, china, and Persian rugs.

Generally, *the more emotive the language, the less it is factual and the more it is interpretive: hence the fewer grounds we have to accept the conclusion.* Sometimes, if we're not aware, we can get caught up in the emotive flavour of terms and lose sight of the fact that the argument is simply unconvincing. More often, frighteningly enough, the emotive terms are used in place of an argument altogether. Although we expect an argument, we don't find one. All we get are emotive terms designed to coerce us into accepting others' beliefs.

The power of emotive terms should not be underestimated. Consider Bertrand Russell's famous "conjugation" of the word "obstinate":

> I am firm.
> You are obstinate.
> He is pig-headed. (Copi and Burgess-Jackson, *Informal Logic*, 97)

While all three sentences express the same thought applied to different people, clearly there is a difference in the way we read each of those sentences. By claiming that I am firm, while he is pig-headed, I make the same trait look positive when I possess it, and negative when it is possessed by someone else.

Another example is found in a comic by Thomas Szasz, describing the distinction between the analyst and her patient:

> "... the patient is narcissistic, the analyst has self-esteem; the patient is inhibited, the analyst has self-control; the patient is promiscuous, the analyst is liberated ..." (Szasz, *Heresies*, 137–8)

Similarly, we may say Jake is rude, while Tom is uncompromisingly honest. Phyllis is dynamic, while Gretchen is aggressive. Jones is careful; Smith is picky. He's worldly; she's a tramp.

These examples reveal an important fact about language. There are two basic types of meaning: *cognitive* and *emotive*. The cognitive meaning of a term concerns the term's literal meaning. It is sometimes referred to as the *denotative* meaning. The term is used to denote an object in the world. The word "cat" denotes the object cat. But so does the word "chat" denote the object cat (in French). Likewise, "kitty." Thus different terms may have the same denotation, or cognitive meaning.

The *emotive* meaning of a term is less attached to its literal meaning than to the subjective emotions, flavours, or values that are associated with the term. Grammatically, these are referred to as offering the *connotation* of a term. "Kitty" has a different connotation than "cat," although they both have the same (roughly speaking) denotation. Consider the many terms to describe women: "girl," "chick," "fox," "broad," "lady." Although all have the same cognitive meaning, they differ according to the emotive flavour they elicit. Even identical words may elicit different emotive content depending on *who* utters them. Likewise, observe the difference between the terms "homosexual" and "faggot." They have the same cognitive meaning, but offer clearly different emotive meanings: they elicit different emotions, or values. The first may be said to be neutral, the second carries with it generally a negative connotation. Admittedly, the emotive flavours may vary depending on the context in which they are used. The connotation of "faggot" when uttered by someone who's gay has a different flavour than when uttered by someone who isn't.

Pay attention to the emotive terms in the following report:

> Ferraro has a striking gift for tart political rhetoric, needling Ronald Reagan on the fairness issue and twitting the Reagan-Bush campaign for its reluctance to let Bush debate her.

Readers may not know who Ferraro is, but chances are, from the above report, they can guess Ferraro's sex, even absent the final pronoun.

When we write, we often have a choice about which words to use. So when we look at a claim, we should ask ourselves, why were *those* words used rather than others? In the report above, we might ask, why was the word "tart" used, when it might also refer to women of low virtue. It is not used to describe men. And why did the writer say she "needled" Reagan? Of course, one who "needles" is a sewer of sorts, and sewing is generally associated with women rather than men. Worse, though, we tend to think of "needlers" as "bitches." Again, "bitch" is not deemed fitting applied to a man. "Twitting" is another form of "needling," but notice also that it has the root "twit" embedded in it. A twit is someone of low intelligence. Are these words used deliberately? Given that journalists are professional writers, one could scarcely imagine otherwise. In any event, the word choice reveals a bias, a bias not necessarily aimed specifically at Ferraro, but possibly at women being in politics at all.

Here is a subtle example taken from a plaque atop Beacon Hill Park in Victoria, British Columbia:

> Before the arrival of white men, this was the site of an ancient fortified Indian village. A battery of two 64 pound wrought iron rifled guns stood here 1878–1892 for protection against an expected Russian invasion.

Can you detect the emotive terms which reveal bias? Pay close attention to the language used in the plaque. Ask yourself why some words were used instead of others. Hint: it is not the fact that the plaque uses the term

"Indian" rather than "Native." It was written before the euphemism took hold. (Answer below.*)

Political talk is rife with emotive language. When speaking about one's own party, it is best to employ *positive* emotive terms. When speaking about another party, *negative* emotive terms are to be used. We may refer to these as political buzz words. A classic illustration of both the power of words and the recognition by propagandists of the power of words is illustrated by the following excerpt. It is taken from a pamphlet sent in 1990 to Republican candidates running for office, reprinted in *Harper's* (November 1990). The pamphlet was produced by a conservative group called Gopac. It reads as follows:

This list is prepared so that you might have a directory of words to use in writing literature and letters, in preparing speeches, and in producing material for the electronic media. The words and phrases are powerful.

Optimistic Positive Governing Words

courage	freedom	precious	rights
crusade	hard work	pride	strength
dream	liberty	principle(d)	truth
duty	moral	pro-environment	vision
fair	peace	prosperity	common sense
family	pioneer	reform	empower(ment)

Often we search for words to define our opponents. Sometimes we are hesitant to use contrast. These are powerful words that can create a clear and easily understood contrast. Apply these to the opponent, his record, proposals, and party.

Contrasting Words

anti-child	disgrace	lie	shallow
anti-flag	excuses	obsolete	status-quo
betray	failure	pathetic	steal
cheat	greed	radical	taxes
collapse	hypocrisy	red tape	traitors
corruption	incompetent	self-serving	welfare
	liberal	sensationalists	

---

* Answer: The plaque describes the white man as merely arriving on Indian territory. "Arrival" is a fairly neutral term. The Russians, however, are described as invading. Which term applies depends on a biased perspective.

4.6 Weasel Words

Weasel words are words that weaken a claim or conclusion in order to lessen the chances of being refuted. They're so named because of the behaviour of weasels. Weasels like to eat eggs, but rather than smashing the egg-shell and leaving evidence of their crime, they make tiny holes in the egg and suck out the contents. The egg-shell remains intact and the birds think their precious contents still survive. Similarly, weasel words suck out the meaning of a claim, but do so surreptitiously so that most people aren't aware that the content has been removed. We have seen a weasel word in the Sheila Copps headline. By indicating that she "tries" to defend her proposal, the headline makes it clear that she doesn't actually defend her proposal without saying so outright.

Weasel words can be used very cleverly indeed. Advertisements are rife with them, where they often serve to avoid lawsuits. Consider the ad for Nicorette, a product designed to help people quit smoking. The ad implies that Nicorette will help us quit, but does it actually say such a thing? No. Instead it says "If you have the will, Nicorette may help you quit smoking."

We applaud the honesty, but anyone picking up on the weasel words should be wary of the product's effectiveness. For one, if we have the will already, we should be able to quit on our own. And two, Nicorette merely *may* help us quit. Of course this means that it also may not. This avoids any lawsuit, since the statement is consistent with the possibility that Nicorette doesn't do a thing. The advertisers admit as much.

Consider, also, the famous use of "up to" in the following sort of claim:

Brand names on sale up to 50% off.

Because this is often announced in an excited voice, we naturally think of the famous "brand names" – the Calvin Kleins, Tommy Hilfigers, and Nikes. And when we see up to 50 per cent off, we think we can get these fine products for half price. What we typically find, however, when we make our way to the store, is that, at best, some never-before-heard-of brand is on sale for 50 per cent of a marked-up price. Can we complain? No, this never-before-heard-of brand is still a brand name. Look, there's the brand name right there. What about the Nike brand? Well, it's on sale for 5 per cent off. That's within the range stated in the promotion, as is a 0 per cent off sale.

Weasel words can trick the unsuspecting audience, and we should be wary of them. They are analogous to the fine print that one finds at the bottom of advertisements or warranties. They retract, or qualify, claims in ways we're not intended to detect.

Of course, it is misleading to say we should reject claims with weasel words in them. Consider, for example,

If a large enough meteor hit the earth, this may explain the extinction of the dinosaurs.

Such a proposition seems acceptable, but precisely because it really isn't saying very much. That a meteor *may* explain the extinction of the dinosaurs does not commit us to believing it *is* the cause of their extinction.

Next time you peruse the horoscopes, see how many weasel words you can find. Consider, for example, the following warnings and advice:

Virgo:	You could be seeking attention in all the wrong places.
Leo:	A trip might be very appealing.
Gemini:	In some sense you cheer someone toward a long-term goal.
Capricorn:	Love can happen in a split second.
Scorpio:	You might be more inspired to stay home and get into a project rather than run around aimlessly. You also might opt to do both.

In each of these cases, the prophecy is cleverly qualified to accommodate nothing of the sort happening. It is also sufficiently vague to accommodate even extremely diverse events as "verifying" the portent. (We shall learn more about vagueness in chapter 5.)

Weasel words also occur in arguments. Consider the following:

Since paying a worker the current minimum wage is arguably the same as having a slave, and since slavery is illegal under the Constitution, the current minimum wage ought to be outlawed.

All this seems fairly straightforward until we look closer at the little weasel word "arguably." To give an argument is not necessarily to give a *good* argument. That someone might argue for something hardly shows that the argument is cogent.

Sometimes we wish to retract a weasel word, as the following note indicates was the case with a former prime minister:

Asked about the ubiquitous Mr. Wappel's infamous letter to a constituent, Mr. Chrétien was either more or less critical of his party member, depending on which version you got. In the Hansard official record – released about two hours after Question Period – our noble leader said "The letter was written and it was unfortunate." Close, but that's not exactly what he said. The tape shows a word was strangely omitted. He actually said: "The letter was written and *probably* it was unfortunate." ("Political Notebook," *Globe and Mail*, 12 May 2001, A7)

Just as with inference indicators and modalities, there are a number of terms that are often (but not necessarily) used as weasel terms. They include

arguably	may	possibly
basically	might	practically
conceivably	nearly	supposedly
could be	perhaps	virtually

4.7 Obfuscation

Obfuscation is using language obscurely. For an argument to be effective the words used must be precise. If the argument lacks precision it can be confusing. To obfuscate is not merely to offer a bewildering onslaught of words, but to do so with the intention of confusing the audience or lulling them into submission. One of the psychological downfalls endemic to being human is the fear of appearing stupid. Obfuscation plays on that fear. The use of contorted language will confuse the audience. Afraid of being taken for chumps, we are reluctant to admit our confusion. As a result, we accept whatever the author doles out to us. But to do so is the real sign of ignorance!

Observe the following illustrations:

- History can be totalized when being reified only if it moves into the absence of the real, since the shift from experience to structural totality cannot ground mediation. (Alex Heard, *The New Republic*, 29 January 1990)

- Reports that say something hasn't happened are always interesting to me, because as we know, there are known knowns, there are things we know we know. We also know there are known unknowns: that is to say we know there are some things we do not know. But there are also unknown unknowns – the ones we don't know we don't know. (Donald Rumsfeld, US Defense Secretary, at a news briefing on Iraq, *Guardian*, 2 December 2003, B5)

- Abstraction is by its nature an undervalue aporia, inserting doubt into the aesthetic discourse. This aporia appears as various lacunae demanding embraces, demanding contradictions, demanding rejections, but always impelling a reinscription that must rupture and collapse. (Harvard University art exhibition handout in Kahane and Cavendar, *Logic and Contemporary Rhetoric*, 138)

- If the apparent menace of the akrates as unredescribed to the soundness of Aristotle's construction has nothing to do with reductive commensurability in the *Protagoras* sense and everything to do with such formal requirements as the self-sufficiency of eudaimonia, and with the special prospect of having just about nothing to regret that eudaimonia holds out to rational intelligence, then it will be timely to review the question whether Aristotle could not have contrived to accommodate together both akrasia as pretheoretically described and eudaimonia as theoretically described (still appealing solely to reason). (Wiggins, *Needs, Values, Truth*, 59)

The language above is so confusing it is nearly impossible to attach any meaning to the sentences presented. As Goethe says, "Where an idea is wanting, a word can always be found to take its place."

Why do people obfuscate? There are at least four possible reasons:

1 Insincerity: The speaker is be afraid that if she says what she means, people will reject the idea, so she attempts to kick dust in the audience's eyes hoping they will fail to see the paucity of her claims.

2 Pomposity: The speaker imagines himself to be better than, or superior to, others, and feels that this is proved by their not being able to follow his talk. Our suspicion is that this is the most common motivation to obfuscate.

3 Ignorance: People are led to believe they're *supposed* to talk this way. This is especially troubling since academia is rife with obfuscation, and students quickly learn to imitate it.

4 Inclusion: By our talking a certain way, we reveal that we belong to an in-group. Obfuscation functions like a badge or uniform. After all, it isn't just academics and students who obfuscate; many people obfuscate. Kids use pig Latin, truckers have c.b. jargon, and mechanics use shop talk. Each generation forms its own talk, like its own style of clothing or hair.

Admittedly, technical terms may help make things more precise. Telling a police officer that the suspect "was pretty big, and he had sort of longish hair, but not too long, the colour of brownish," may benefit from more specific terms. And more technical discourse does require more technical terminology. As long as the audience is also part of the in-group, such language use cannot be criticized. Likewise, it is possible that the author has earlier defined some of the more obscure terminology, and this, too, is therefore permissible. The danger occurs when the obfuscation is clearly unwarranted and when plainer language would suffice. We must distinguish the use of technical terms *when required* from their use when not required.

Exercise 4.1

Check for bias and slanting in the following arguments and reports. Avail yourself of all of the material gleaned from this chapter. (Answers to selected questions are provided in Appendix 1.)

1 Another of Clinton's diversionary tactics following the Lewinsky sex scandal included the orders to bomb Iraq.

2 Arguably, the reason people are in favour of euthanasia is because of their still strong desires toward ethnic cleansing. After all, the Nazis were in favour of euthanasia.

☞ 3 China has more immediate fears that even a limited missile defence could nullify its far smaller number of long-range missiles. These concerns are legitimate.

4 If you reject affirmative action, then you're buying into the paternalistic oppression of a master-slave race.

☞ 5 Throughout history, crimes of ignorance and greed have been beset upon us by government, and now corporations are jumping on the gravy train. The recent use of Franken-Foods, foods genetically altered, may well cause unnamed defects in us or our children, and yet these unnatural mutations are being crammed down our throats without our consent. Put a stop to genetically altered foods!

6 Anyone pushing affirmative action is endorsing discriminatory policies themselves, fuelled merely by man-hatred much like the anti-Semite laws of the Nazis.

☞ 7 Populated by deer, alligators, wild turkeys, and a tribe of Indians who annually perform a rite known as the Green Corn Dance, the track of land could suredly accommodate a super jetport twice the size of Kennedy International in New York and still have a one mile buffer on every side to minimize intrusion in the lives of any eventual resident. (*New York Times,* 30 November 1968)

8 A United Nations conference in New York City aimed at controlling the proliferation of small arms ran into withering fire from the United States on its opening day. In a statement echoing the position of the National Rifle Association – a major Bush campaign contributor – the United States announced it would not support the draft agreement because it threatened legitimate arms manufacturers and infringed on citizens' rights to bear arms. The United Nations estimates there are up to 300 million small arms illicitly owned worldwide. ("Unfriendly fire," *Maclean's,* July 23, 2001, 12–13.)

9 A recent study by the environmentalist Pembina Institute found that of Canada's 15 biggest polluters, nine of them saw emission increases between 1990 and 1997. And that's according to unaudited voluntary reporting by the companies in question. (Mark MacKinnon, "We're getting warmer," *Globe and Mail,* 26 July 2001, A13)

☞10 Gordon Campbell's new British Columbia government was greeted yesterday by two Oppositions. Across from Mr. Campbell in the Legislature during the Throne Speech were Joy MacPhail and Jenny Kwan, all that's left of the NDP caucus, demurely dressed in mauve and olive suits respectively. The Official Opposition, too small to form a recognized party and, on this day at least, awfully quiet. (Paul Wells, "Nipping at Gordon Campbell's heels: Opposition to B.C. Throne Speech merely half-hearted," *National Post,* 25 July 2001 A1, A6)

11 Gulf Canada Resources Ltd. agreed yesterday to be bought by Conoco Inc. of Houston for $9.8-billion in cash and debt in the largest takeover ever of a Canadian energy company. With the

friendly deal, Gulf joins the growing list of Canadian oil patch firms that have recently fallen into U.S. hands, weakened by low Canadian currency, an unfavourable tax regime and low share prices relative to their U.S. rivals, despite strong demand for their oil and gas and concerns of an energy crisis in the United States.(Claudia Cattaneo, "Gulf sale biggest oil patch deal," *National Post*, 30 May 2001, A1)

☞12 This cereal is low in fat and is a source of fibre. Emphasizing grain products such as cereals and increasing fibre intake are components of healthy eating. Cheerios financially supports the Health Check education program of the Heart and Stroke Foundation. This is not an endorsement. Health Check ... tells you it's a healthy choice. The Heart and Stroke Foundation of Canada has developed a program to help you make healthy food choices when you shop for groceries. It is called Health Check and it's your assurance that foods meet specific nutritional criteria. Cheerios is proud to be the first cereal in Canada to participate in the Health Check program. When you see the Health Check logo, you can be confident that you are making a healthy choice. Find out more at www.healthcheck.org or call the Heart and Stroke Foundation toll-free at 1–888–HSF-INFO. (Box of Cheerios)

13 Staunch Senate liberals like Edward Kennedy and relative moderates like Joseph Biden will replace hawkish right-wingers like Jesse Helms and conservative Republicans like Orrin Hatch as chairs of the powerful Senate committees.(Paul Koring, "Bush's agenda buckles as Sen. Jafford buckles," *Globe and Mail*, 25 May 2001, A1)

14 One day after Bridgestone/Firestone Corp's U.S. subsidiary severed its 100-year old relationship with Ford, the automaker said an internal investigation has forced it to question the safety of Wilderness AT tires on the road, including tires made at a plant in Joliette, Que ... "We feel it's our responsibility to act immediately," said Jacques Nasser, Ford's president and chief executive. He said the company does not have enough confidence "in the future performance of these tires keeping our customers safe." ... This time, however, Firestone does not support the recall. It says replacing additional Wilderness tires is just a desperate public relations move by Ford, which refuses to acknowledge the role its Explorer may have played in the controversial crashes. (Thomas Watson, "Ford forced to replace 13 million more tires," *National Post*, 23 May 2001, A1, A9)

☞15 The federal government describes Mr. Suresh as a "dedicated and trusted leader" of the Liberation Tigers of Tamil Eelam, an organization for Sri Lanka's ethnic minority that engages in torture, executions, ethnic cleansing of Muslims, kidnapping and forcible conscription of children. (Janice Tibbetts, "Supreme Court to decide whether to deport 'threats'," *National Post*, 22 May 2001, A11)

16 It should be easy and natural for Romanow to debunk the idea that health care is just another commodity to be sold to the highest bidder. Despite the socially destructive braying from the far right, Canadians understand that a progressive health-care system is as much about values as it is about services. (James Travers, "Romanow musn't be fooled," *Charlottetown Guardian,* 4 July 2001, A6)

☞17 The findings come as provinces offer an increasing amount of school choice – a move welcomed by parents and critics who say there are too many underperforming and unaccountable schools but opposed by teachers' unions and school boards. A number of provinces partially fund private schools and Ontario plans to introduce a tax credit for independent schooling. (Julie Smyth, "Choice of schools boosts students' marks: study," *National Post,* 22 June 2001, A5)

18 "Is it criminal to smoke marijuana in the confines of your own home, arguably doing no harm to anyone but yourself?" Mr. Johnson [Gary Johnson, Governor of New Mexico] asks. (Jan Cienski, "Pot's U.S. poster boy," *National Post,* 30 May 2001, A13)

19 The Sierra Club of Canada, the World Wildlife Fund and the Toronto Environmental Alliance have succeeded in steering this issue from the path of sound science to a political terror campaign. Their strategy of hijacking municipal councils into adopting bans [on pesticides for cosmetic purposes] has been well-orchestrated and successful.(Daniel Passmore, letter to the editor, *National Post,* 9 July 2001, A15)

☞20 Those tests [on blood and hair from residents of the area around the Sydney tar ponds, as well as extensive soil testing to determine whether there are levels of arsenic and lead that would pose a long term risk to the people living in the area] are expected to take six to eight weeks to complete. If they show a risk to human health, then people could be relocated, Donald Ferguson, regional director-general of Health Canada, told the meeting. (Kevin Cox, "Tar-pond families skeptical," *Globe and Mail,* 24 May 2001, A7)

21 Despite tiresome complaints that having the private sector compete with public sector in health care is contrary to the interests of Canadians, this new proposal offers only positive possibilities. If the existence of private PET facilities spurs the public system to adopt this new technology sooner than it otherwise would have, then the private clinics have benefited all Canadians. If, on the other hand, the public systems choose not to buy more PET scanners, then the private clinics will be providing a service that would otherwise have been unavailable. ("Health care pursuit," *National Post,* 9 July 2001, A15)

22 It is important for informed citizens to oppose Canada's participation in the Kyoto Protocol, and I am glad to see that Petro-Canada CEO Ron Brenneman has had the guts to do so. Kyoto is the brainchild of the same gang of haters of capitalism, Green freaks and eco-

terrorists whose followers recently staged their street theatre in Genoa and Quebec City (and will be opening soon in a town near you). The science they put forward is suspect and politically motivated. A fully implemented Kyoto Protocol would be ruinous to Canada's economy, and cede our autonomy further to decisions of international and highly politicized tribunals. To its great credit, the U.S. government has recently withdrawn from Kyoto, and will set its own course. Canada must do the same. (Robert Wilson, letter to the editor, *National Post*, 30 July 2001, C15)

☞23 There is no better mandate for the tyranny of the majority than the concept of vox populi vox dei (the voice of the people is the voice of God). Therefore the freedom and the rights of minorities and individuals are protected best by vesting sovereignty in a monarch who is deemed to rule Dei Gratis (by the grace of God). (Joseph Kenneth Malone, "The monarchy: a necessary tradition for a stable democracy," *Guardian*, 24 May 2001, A7)

24 Your editorial about celebrities such as Sarah Polley or Robert Redford trading on their fame to promote half-baked causes is about as saccharine and smarmy as a respectable newspaper can get (Star Light, Star Might – May 24). Instead of mooning, starstruck, over the blatherings of these clay-footed idols, whose opinions are no more informed than any other dilettante's, you should have told them to stick to what we pay them for: their entertainment value. When the plumber comes to fix my drain, his opinions on the state of Arctic wilderness are his own business. I couldn't care less. (Don Campbell, letter to the editor, *Globe and Mail*, 26 May 2001, A14)

☞25 Women's experience, informed by feminist theory, provides a potential grounding for more complete and less distorted knowledge claims than do men's. (Harding, *Feminism and Methodology*, 183)

4.8 Different Kinds of Disagreement

There are three kinds of disagreement: Disagreements about facts, disagreements in attitude, and *verbal disagreements*. Our concern in this chapter is with the last.

In *factual disputes* people disagree about questions of fact. They hold conflicting beliefs. "He thinks the toilet seat was down. She thinks it was left up," or "He thinks Critical Thinking is a required course for business students, while she doesn't."

Sometimes factual disputes cannot be resolved. There were no other witnesses, no pictures, no records, etc. If the dispute continues anyway, it is no longer a philosophical argument. It may be an argument in the colloquial sense, but since it is recognized that no evidence can settle the issue, it is best to put it off for the time being (perhaps indefinitely), and not carry on fruitlessly. For example,

"If Quebec separates, other provinces will follow."
"No, they won't."

In *attitudinal disputes* one person gives a key word or phrase a different *value* than the other person gives it. The dispute reveals a genuine disagreement in attitude. For example,

"It's great that I'm taking a philosophy course."
"Great?! Are you kidding? Philosophy is the worst course ever!"

(Of course, one might utter the same sentence sarcastically: "Oh great, I have to take philosophy." If so, it would be inappropriate to utter "Yeah, isn't it just!")

Imagine someone uttering, "The crisis in Russia is deserved." To disagree is not (necessarily) to counter that there *is no* crisis in Russia. We may all be in agreement about that. The disagreement may be in our attitudes toward Russia, or to people in general.

In *verbal disputes*, the presence of an ambiguous or differently interpreted vague term in the disputants' formulations of their beliefs conceals the fact that there is no *substantive* disagreement between them. Resolving the ambiguity or vagueness may well resolve the dispute. For example,

"The Titanic sank because it hit an iceberg."
"No it didn't. It sank because of hubris."

This example may seem like a factual disagreement, but it would be unlikely that the second speaker really doubts that icebergs played a definitive role in the sinking of the Titanic. The two disputants are more likely interpreting the little word "because" differently. The first is looking at the very last cause of the sinking in a long series of precipitating causes when he interprets the word "because." The second speaker, however, is less interested in this final cause. She is more interested in the factors leading up to that isolated event. In this case, she's looking at the fact that the Titanic wouldn't have sunk if it had hit the iceberg at a slower speed, and that the captain would have given the order for a slower speed when he heard about the ice fields, had he not been suffering from hubris: an overconfidence in the Titanic's being unsinkable. We would expect agreement between the disputants once they agree on their interpretation of "because."

In summary, verbal disagreements are due to the disputants' failure to see that they are using terms in different ways.

We would be remiss not to mention that it is often the case that verbal and attitudinal debates will overlap. For example,

"Pornography is despicable."

"How can you say that? Some of it is very good."

The above dispute appears to be a debate about attitude. The second person likes (some) pornography, while the first doesn't like any. But their different attitudes may be driven by their different interpretations of what pornography is. A may be thinking of clearly despicable stuff, perhaps even associating it with child pornography. B, on the other hand, may be thinking of the more sensuous erotica, where all partners participate willingly and equally. What B calls pornography, A may not.

Exercise 4.2

For the following, decide whether the disputes concern factual, attitudinal, or verbal matters. (Answers to selected questions are provided in Appendix 1.)

☞ 1 Huck: Injun' Joe did it of his own free will. No pressure was brought to bear on him; no threats were made; no inducements were offered; there was no hint of force. He deliberated about it and made up his own mind.

    Tom: That is impossible. Nobody has free will, because everything anyone does is inevitably determined by heredity and environment in accord with inexorable causal laws of nature. (Adapted from Copi and Burgess-Jackson, *Informal Logic*, 154)

  2 Veronica: Retired people have a right to collect Social Security even if they're wealthy, provided they paid into the system during their working years.

    Archie: I disagree; it's not right to draw government funds when you don't need them. (Ibid., 153)

☞ 3 Sporty Spice: There are fewer than 8 million unemployed persons in this country, according to the Bureau of Labour Statistics.

    Scary Spice: Oh no, there are more than fifteen times that number of unemployed. The President's Economic Report states that there are 99 million employed in this country, and the Census Bureau reports a total population of 250 million. So the government's figures reveal that there are more than 150 million unemployed persons in this country. (Ibid., 155)

  4 Groucho: Mrs. Tinsdale shot an elephant in her pyjamas. How it got in her pyjamas I'll never know.

    Harpo: ♫♪♪

    Chico: No, they were Mr. Tinsdale's pyjamas.

☞ 5 Aquinas: Sex without the possibility of procreation is immoral.

    Hefner: No it isn't. Sex is a beautiful thing in its own right.

6 Huey: Socrates argues against Callicles's hedonism in the *Gorgias*,
            yet argues from a hedonist perspective in the *Protagoras*. So,
            he's inconsistent.
   Louie: You're wrong. He rejects hedonism in the *Protagoras*.
   Dewey: You're both wrong. Socrates is in favour of hedonism in the
            Protagoras, an early work of Plato, but the later *Gorgias*, takes
            on more of Plato's philosophy, leaving behind the beliefs of
            his old, long since dead master.
☞ 7 Alice: Being in favour of free speech at the same time as wishing to
              control violence in the media is inconsistent.
     Queen: No it isn't. Every right, including free speech, has bound-
              aries against harming others that must be respected.
     Alice: I agree, but violence in the media hasn't been shown to
              harm anyone.
     Queen: Ah, but there you're wrong!
☞ 8 Rudolph: A tree falling in a wilderness with nobody around to hear
               will produce no sound. There can be no auditory sensa-
               tion unless someone senses it.
     Dasher: No, whether anyone is there to hear it or not, the crash of
               a falling tree will cause vibrations in the air and therefore
               will produce a sound in any event. (Adapted from Copi
               and Keith Burgess-Jackson, *Informal Logic*, 155)

Exercise 4.3

Discuss what sort of disagreements are occurring in the following.
(Answers to selected questions provided in Appendix 1.)

1 When I have raised the issue of smoking in shelters previously with
   Metro Transit, the stock reply has been that the no-smoking "policy"
   cannot be enforced, and that it's not Metro Transit's job or place to
   enforce this "policy." This is not a "policy"; it's the law, a law made for
   good reason – to protect people like that small child from the toxic
   effects of second-hand smoke. It's clearly stated on the HRM web site
   that it is the responsibility of HRM staff to enforce the anti-smoking
   law. That means Metro Transit folks, or don't they work for HRM?
   (Peggy McCann, letter to the editor, *Chronicle-Herald*, 19 May 2001,
   C4)
2 A judge has dismissed demands by members of an alleged drug gang
   for their own barber shop and a personal librarian. Lawyers for the
   Trang family also requested that seven of the 30 accused be released
   or given private cells on their own floor, their own phones, TVs with
   cable hookup and guards who will treat them with integrity and
   humanity. Lawyer Tom Engel argued the accused are suffering
   irreparable harm and psychological damage. But the judge said he

doesn't really believe they are suffering. ("Accused want cable, barber," *National Post*, 30 June 2001, A16)

3 He [David McFarlane] said the government has done its best to starve Ontario's cultural life. In the same piece he wrote, "I've been racking my brains trying to think of something that the Harris government hasn't ruined." How about theatre, opera, the visual arts, films, television and literature? Harris-haters may find this astonishing or even impossible to believe, but the truth is that culture has actually flourished in the capital of Ontario since Harris came to office in 1995. (Robert Fulford, "Don't blame him, he's just the premier," *National Post*, 10 July 2001, B1)

4. In "Calling Doctor Wilt Chamberlain," Terence Corcoran makes an interesting statement about user fees: "Since there are no user fees in existence in Canada, there can't be much empirical data around to prove any point, one way or another." This makes me wonder where Mr. Corcoran has been living; it certainly can't be Canada. Health care in Canada has never been completely without user fees. Furthermore, with recent cutbacks to health care budgets, many provinces have extended the list of services for which a fee is charged to include services which can be considered necessary – in clear violation of the Canada Health Act. User fees definitely are in existence in Canada, and even if they weren't, there are plenty of other countries we could look at to see the effect of user fees. Statements by people like Robert Evans and Michael Rachlis that the poor have trouble paying user fees, that they sometimes have to go without services, and that overall costs will rise, are not "arbitrary conclusions" but statements of fact about what we really do see when user fees are imposed, not only in Canada, but in just about any country you could name. (Mark Hendriks, letter to the editor, *National Post*, 9 July 2001, A15)

5 Advocates of the hunting ban say it is necessary to protect international whale populations, depleted from decades of widespread hunting, against possible extinction. Opponents say whale stocks are strong enough to withstand limited hunts. ("Commercial whaling ban at stake as meeting opens," *Guardian*, 24 July 2001, B5)

6 The notion that tax cuts pay for themselves has never been supported by the evidence, and now the [B.C.] Liberals will have to rely on other, equally dubious justifications. They talk a lot about the brain drain, and about being competitive in Alberta and the state of Washington. But if they rely on the available evidence, they will go zero for three on these arguments as well. The brain drain myth dies hard despite overwhelming evidence that high tech employees and other professionals do not leave Canada because of taxes. A study done by PricewaterhouseCoopers and ComputerWorld Canada in 1999 asked high tech workers to rank the factors they used to judge

their jobs. They listed take-home pay eighteenth. The top five factors involved how they were treated by management and whether or not they had access to the latest technology. By far the largest exodus of professionals to the United States is actually in the public health-care sector. Why? Because governments laid off thousands of nurses and now won't pay the market price to get them back. What about the so-called "Alberta Advantage" that the Liberals whine about for years? It doesn't exist either. According to the CCPA, a two-income B.C. family of four earning $90,000 paid $830 more in taxes than their counter-part in Alberta last year. But if that Albertan family sent just one child to university, the advantage would all but disappear in higher tuition fees. Add in higher private health-care expenses and other user fees, and you have the Alberta disadvantage. If all of B.C.'s direct taxes were considered, they would be the second lowest in the country, after Alberta, except for the top 4% of income earners. As for being tax-competitive with Washington, the average family in B.C. does pay almost $1,700 more a year in provincial taxes than their Washington counterpart. But a recent CCPA study comparing B.C. and Washing-ton, *In Search of the Good Life* (www.policyalternatives.ca), revealed that university students in Washington pay almost $1,700 a year more in tuition fees. Families spend $763 a year more for health care, and $540 more for water, electricity and home heating fuel. They spend $2,300 more per year for life insurance, public pensions and UI. But all of this is just so much factual chaff in the ideological grain as far as the Campbell Liberals are concerned. They are committed to gov-ern for the rich and powerful, not for the province, and certainly not for the vast majority of its citizens. No matter how you cut it, ordinary British Columbians will be sacrificing – through higher debt or slashed services – so the wealthy can get even wealthier. (Dobbin, Murray, "Liberal British Columbia: Open for business, closed to rea-son," *National Post,* July 24, 2001, C15.)

Reading between the Lines Answer:
1 The average farm, contrary to what one might think, seems to have decreased in size during this period.
2 Although many farmers went broke, those who remained improved financially more than their non-farmer counterparts.
Why?
1 The number of farms tripled, while the overall acreage use of farms only doubled.
2 The decrease in farm population is from 60 per cent to 35 per cent (i.e., by 25 per cent), while the decrease in the overall income for farm-ers is from 31 per cent to 22 per cent (only 9 per cent).

Definitions

Verbal Disputes • Purposes of Definition
Types of Definition • Types of Meaning
Evaluating Genus and Species Definitions

5.1 Verbal Disputes

Definitions play an important role in critical reflection. Let us briefly examine two common ethical debates, one on pornography and the other on abortion.

Is Pornography Art?

We generally agree that art is not something that should be censored. But if we entertain the position that pornography should be censored, then we might feel impelled to claim that pornography is not art.

One argument for censoring pornography is that it depicts immoral sexual activity. Permissible sexual activity is limited to marriage. Sex in general is taboo, off limits, restricted within firm and clear boundaries. Engaging in sexual activity outside marriage is immoral, especially for women – perhaps solely for women. Men may be exempt from this prohibition. Since pornography depicts women as unchaste and immoral, men are led to conclude that they may sexually exploit women. Women who allow themselves to be exploited do not deserve to be treated with respect anyway. Pornography, therefore, undermines the respect men have for women.

On the other hand, one could argue that permissible sexual activity should not be so narrowly defined. The double standard should be rejected: there is one standard of moral behaviour for men and women. Sexual activity can be responsibly engaged in and enjoyed by women as well as men. Therefore, pornography should not be censored.

Some (not all) feminists oppose pornography because it denigrates women and endorses such degradation of women, not because sex is taboo. In fact, for many such feminists, pornography is *defined* as involving the denigration of women. Erotica that does not denigrate women is not considered pornography. Pornography, then, is always offensive.

Even if we accept that pornography is offensive, does that rule out our calling pornography art? This question leads to a new worry: what is art? Must art have lofty goals to make it art? Or is art any artificial representation that can be appreciated by some people? The resolution of this debate requires an agreement on definition of terms.

Is abortion morally permissible?

Here is one argument for why abortion is morally wrong:

1 Murder is wrong.
2 Murder entails the killing of innocent persons.
3 Abortion entails the killing of fetuses.
4 Fetuses are innocent persons.
5 Hence, abortion is murder.
6 Hence abortion is wrong.

This argument would be diagrammed

$$\underline{2 + 3 + 4}$$
$$\downarrow$$
$$\underline{5 + 1}$$
$$\downarrow$$
$$6$$

The logic is impeccable, but this does not mean the argument cannot be challenged. Premise (4) can be rejected, for example. Fetuses, it might be argued, are not persons.

Who is right? It depends, obviously, on how "person" is defined.* Anti-abortionists often say that "person" has a biological definition: anything born of persons are persons. The counter is that being a "person" is more than having the requisite biological structure; it is also having conscious-ness or sentience, something that fetuses in the early stages, at least, don't have. A response to this objection is to expand the meaning of persons to include anything that has the *potential* of being a person. Of course, this admits that fetuses aren't persons *now*, and when rights conflict we would expect the rights of *actual* persons to trump the rights of *potential* persons, an admission which will not likely help the pro-life side.

---

* Actually the issue revolves around the criterion of "having rights." A cat is not a person yet has rights, we may presume. If whatever criterion we adopt of being a rights-holder perfectly encompasses all humans, then deciding whether a fetus is a human may be sufficient, but only contingently so.

Who is right? How does one decide? Do we resolve these sorts of debates by looking up words in the dictionary?

Our concern here is not to resolve the moral status of abortion and pornography, however interesting we might find these questions. Rather, our concern is to recognize that the disagreements above rest on definitions, and that this kind of disagreement is not usually resolved by turning to the dictionary. Sometimes the *disputants must come to an agreed understanding of the terms on their own*. This doesn't mean that they can define terms in any way. For it to be accepted by the other player in the dispute game, the proposed definition must satisfy a number of criteria of reasonableness. There are *reasons* for defining terms one way rather than another, and these reasons *can* be evaluated.

In this chapter, we explore different types of definitions and the different ways to appraise them.

But Is It Verbal Quibbling?

It is sometimes asserted that philosophy is little more than quibbling over words. The debates above partly revolve around how we define "person," "pornography," and "art." Different philosophers define the terms in different ways, not coincidentally in ways that support their own antecedently held views.

Hence, the debates appear to be about the definitions each employs, and there seems no rational resolution if we rule out appeals to the dictionary. The solution seems to depend *merely* on how we define our terms.

The answer to such skepticism is "Of course it all depends on how we define our terms. But that isn't a trivial matter by any means."

5.2 Purposes of Definition

There are at least four purposes we hope to serve when we define our terms: to increase vocabulary, to eliminate ambiguity, to reduce vagueness, and to minimize (or possibly promote) emotively provocative attitudes.

5.2.1 Increasing Vocabulary

"An apodictic claim should always be accepted." Before we accept this assertion, however, we may need to look up the word "apodictic." Once we do, we will be less reluctant to accept the claim.

Some people think that dictionaries are just for kids, that adults are supposed to have a good grasp of their mother tongue. Consequently, we might feel embarrassed to have to resort to looking a word up. This is another instance of our fear of appearing stupid. Even the most literate, however, know only a fraction of the words in the dictionary, and it is never a bad thing to try to improve that proportion. A good habit, far too often unheeded, is to have a good dictionary handy.

Verbal disputes, however, are not always so easily resolved. More is required than increasing our vocabulary when the issue is a conceptual matter. We aren't concerned with how a term is defined, but with how it *ought* to be defined. That debate is not resolved by a simple appeal to a dictionary. Furthermore, dictionary definitions come after use, and our debate may revolve around current usage. Specialized fields develop their own terms and these won't be found (yet) in the dictionary. To understand what a term means in these cases, we'll need to consult someone in the field. Moreover, definitions are fluid. What a word meant in 500 BC is not necessarily what it meant in AD 500, let alone in 1500, or in 2002. What Descartes meant by rationality or knowledge, or Plato by the concept of "spirit," or Aristotle by what was translated as "happiness" may not be what we mean by these terms today. However much we may complain that dictionaries are not used enough, dictionary use alone is not sufficient.

5.2.2 Reducing Ambiguity

Ambiguity stands for the use of words or expressions that have two or more distinct meanings. The word "bank," for example, has different meanings in different contexts. A "mud *bank*" is different from a "*bank* teller." Typically the context is sufficiently determinate for us to tell which meaning is intended. Sometimes, however, it is less clear.

For example, the term "end" may be used to indicate a boundary, as in "there is a bug at the end of my finger." Conversely, it may be used synonymously with "goal," as in, "My end in life is to make money." But which meaning are we to assume in the following claim?

Staying out of trouble is my end.

The statement, as put, is ambiguous. Does the speaker intend to say that if he stays out of trouble, that will be the end for him? In other words, is he saying a boring life is not worth living? Or is the opposite meant, that getting into trouble would be awful?

Looking up "end" in the dictionary will not help resolve the ambiguity, since the ambiguity is caused precisely by the multiple dictionary definitions.

In many cases we can resolve the ambiguity by paying closer attention to context. As Wittgenstein noted, language is best understood *in use*. Usually, in fact, the context makes the intended meaning so clear we may not even notice the possibility of an ambiguity lurking beneath statements. Neither statement below, for example, is ambiguous, yet together they reveal a subtle switch in our understanding of the verb "to have."

Mary had a little lamb; he followed her to school.
Mary had a little lamb, and then a little broccoli. (Fogelin, *Understanding Arguments*, 79)

In our own arguments, it is a good idea to anticipate potential ambiguities and make a concerted effort to avoid them. We will need to define those terms which could be viewed as ambiguous to reduce the possibility of fallacious inferences.

In other people's arguments we must challenge any ambiguous terms that context cannot resolve. Ask others to define what they mean. Of course, sometimes we are reading the argument, and so we can't ask the author to define her terms. A good exercise then is to interpret the argument using both senses and see which one is the most defensible.

Semantic and Syntactic Ambiguity

We can divide ambiguities into two sorts: *semantic* and *syntactic*. Semantic (or word) ambiguities are ambiguities inherent in the words themselves. Syntactic (or sentence) ambiguities are caused by an ambiguous arrangement of otherwise unambiguous words in a sentence. The example, "Staying out of trouble is my end," is a *semantic* ambiguity.

The following also suffers from semantic ambiguity:

Homosexuality is not normal.

What is meant by "normal" here? Does it mean a statistical average? If all that is meant is that less than 50 per cent of the population is homosexual, this is probably true. If, on the other hand, "normal" in this context is meant to be synonymous with "natural," then this is questionable, since the very fact that there are homosexuals is good evidence that it *is* natural.

Sometimes a sentence can be ambiguous, even though all its component words are perfectly understood. In such cases, the sentence suffers from *syntactic* ambiguity. Consider this title of a famous book:

The Conquest of the Persians

Does this mean that the Persians were conquered, or that the Persians conquered someone else? Consider the seemingly sensible remark

I only drive in daylight.

Presumably the speaker means that she does not drive at night. The little word "only" is misplaced, however. What the sentence says instead is that she does nothing other than drive in daylight. She doesn't eat, she doesn't walk, she doesn't take a shower – nothing at all except drive. Even day-time taxi drivers don't *only* drive in daylight. What she meant to say is that she drives only in daylight (or drives in daylight only).

Newspaper headlines are a rich source of ambiguities. When seemingly "unnecessary" components are removed to fit the limited space, the results are often hilarious. Take, for example, the following headlines:

MILK DRINKERS TURN TO POWDER
ANTI-BUSING RIDER KILLED BY SENATE
GHANDI STONED IN RALLY IN INDIA
COLLEGE GRADUATES BLIND SENIOR CITIZEN
TUNA BITING OFF WASHINGTON COAST
POLICE KILL MAN WITH AX

(Columbia Journalism Review, *Squad Helps Dog Bite Victim*)

That these ambiguities strike us as at least mildly amusing shows that a good portion of humour plays on ambiguity. Imagine the caption, "She finally consented to his drawing her in the nude," accompanying a cartoon of a naked artist painting a woman fully clothed. (Mike Baldwin, *cornered* ©2000 Mike Baldwin) Groucho Marx's notorious quips play on ambiguities. For example "I once shot an elephant in my pyjamas ... how he got in my pyjamas I'll never know."

Children's riddles also rely on rudimentary ambiguities, as in these classics: "Have you ever seen a house fly?" "Excuse me, is your fridge running?"

Ambiguity is sometimes intentional. Newspaper headlines are written by professional writers, after all, and it is unlikely that they would not notice ambiguity. Simon Blackburn makes clever use of ambiguity in the title of his book *Ruling Passions*. The topic is ethics, but the focus is the debate between empiricists and rationalists. Rationalists will say that reason ought to rule the passions, whereas empiricists will claim the reverse, that reason is and ought to be the slave of the passions. With Blackburn's title, we may ask, Are passions that which do the ruling (empiricism) or are we to rule over the passions (rationalism)? The title plays nicely on this ambiguity, spelling out for the initiates precisely the debate at issue.

Exercise 5.1 A

Among the examples listed below, can you determine which are semantic ambiguities and which are syntactic ambiguities? (Answers provided in Appendix 1.)

1 Milk Drinkers Turn to Powder
2 Anti-busing Rider Killed by Senate
3 Ghandi Stoned in Rally in India
4 College Graduates Blind Senior Citizen
5 Tuna Biting Off Washington Coast
6 Police Kill Man with Ax
7 Squad Helps Dog Bite Victim
8 Prostitutes Appeal to Pope
9 Teenage Prostitution Problem Is Mounting
10 Scientists Are at a Loss Due to Brain-Eating Amoeba (*The Arizona Republic*, 5 October 1978)

Exercise 5.1 B

Search your local paper for ambiguities in the headlines.

5.2.3 Reducing Vagueness

Sometimes we know the meaning of a term, we know there is no ambiguity present, but we may nevertheless still be confused as to the *full* or *precise* meaning of the term. If this is the case the term is *vague*. We require a decision about the scope of a term's applicability in the given situation.

Relative terms, such as tall, healthy, rich, wise, ruthless, good, are vague in the sense that although we have a good idea of whether extreme cases apply (Socrates is wise, Homer Simpson is not), we are less sure of the much larger set of cases in between.

One particularly noteworthy phrase in Canadian politics is "distinct society." An idea put forward by the Bloc Québecois, it is used as a justification for Québec's separation, or at least special mention in the Constitution. Unfortunately, it's difficult to find a definition that would make Québec a "distinct society" and some other groups in Canada *not* "distinct." Québec's French heritage and language isn't unique; all three of the Maritime provinces, particularly New Brunswick, have (proportionately) large Francophone populations and have strong connections to a French heritage. While Québec's culture differs in many ways from that of the rest of Canada, so does Newfoundland's, or Nunavut's. Above all, it's difficult to see exactly *what* makes a society "distinct" and why it warrants mention in the Constitution.

Perhaps the most obvious case of vagueness in the media is language employed by horoscopes. Horoscopes rely on vagueness to be successful – they seek to apply to as many people as possible, and this cannot happen if the words and phrases used are too specific.

Here are some typical horoscope phrases:

Scorpio:	This evening, you go on cruise control.
Sagittarius:	Your imagination comes out this afternoon.
Aries:	If single, you will meet many people this year.
Pisces:	Share a favourite pastime with a loved one.

Many of these cases are bound to apply. Ought we to be convinced about the powers of the horoscope if they do? Think about the vast number of possible interpretations suggested by the above passages! Phrases like "someone has a distorted view" are dangerous because they *look* like expressions that mean something (especially if we are not paying attention). The fact that they are true is not the issue. The problem is that they are *too easily* true, and as a result say little. Certainly *someone* has a distorted view. But will that impinge on us? Of course we'll meet many people this year. Don't we always? Sharing a favourite pastime with a loved one is excellent. No one will say that this is poor advice. Criticizing the concept of horoscopes is certainly not a denial that we should spend quality time with loved ones, any more than rejecting the concept of God entails that we must also reject love or morality.

Popular advertising slogans are another good example of vagueness in the media. Consider the following illustrations:

"Just do it" (Nike)
"A better way" (Liberal Party campaign slogan)
"Be a part of it" (Canadian Club)
"Coke adds life" (Coke)
"I am" (Canadian beer)

"Just do what?" we are likely to ask. "A better way compared to what?" we are apt to wonder. The answers are not forthcoming. Vague slogans provide no information. One would expect that the defining function of advertising is to provide information to consumers. But these slogans are a far cry from that. A 1984 study found that more than half of all television ads contained NO consumer information about the advertised product. And only about half of all magazine ads contained more than one informational cue. (Velasquez, *Business Ethics: Concepts and Cases*, 342)

Advertisers and political pundits may defend their slogans by denying that they had intended to provide any information. If they did not intend to provide information, they certainly cannot be charged with providing *false* or *misleading* information. Still, providing no information at all (other than the information that the product exists) is somewhat odd, since we would expect advertisers to do more than this. We expect them to convince us to buy their product instead of the competitors'. The fact that no or little information is provided, and yet advertising is successful, shows that consumers purchase on the basis of name recognition only – a sad commentary on the degree of our autonomy, and a clear disincentive for quality production.

Slogans are useful in reaching vast audiences, but they are clearly useless as vehicles of rational persuasion (i.e., they do not attempt to persuade people using any particular reasons or evidence). For example, we all want to be good; unfortunately we disagree on what that implies. Or we may agree that it's a good idea to respect others, yet our agreement may still belie an underlying disagreement on how to cash out such a sentiment. For example, does my respecting you mean I have to oblige your desires, wishes, and ideas? Or does it mean, more weakly, that I must not denigrate your ideas, wishes, desires, though I can ignore them in my actions and policies? Political speech is rife with vague buzz terms – "Fairness," "Family Values," "The Right," "Respect" – none of which politicians bother to define, for it is in making these vague terms more precise that the trouble begins.

We call a definition or concept vague if, in a given context, it leaves open too wide a range of borderline cases for the successful use of that concept in that context.

Vagueness is typically removed by adopting a more precise definition. "By light, I mean someone under 120 pounds." "By smart, I mean someone with at least a high-school education." "By sexual relation, I mean the intended mutual genital stimulation of two or more persons." "By a good act, I mean one in which no concerned party is adversely affected without her informed, competent, voluntary consent." Whether these definitions are satisfactory is another matter.

Remember: Vagueness and ambiguity are different things.

A term is *ambiguous* if it has more than one possible meaning and the context does not make clear which meaning is intended.
A term is *vague* if there is only one meaning, but the number of disparate items that satisfy that meaning is too large and dissimilar to be helpful.

Exercise 5.2

Are the following claims vague, ambiguous, or both? If vague, explain why. If ambiguous, state at least two alternative meanings. (Answers to selected questions provided in Appendix 1.)

   1 Democracy is government by the people.
☞ 2 Universities should choose among applicants on the basis of their academic ability. (Adapted from Christopher Jencks and James Crouse, "Aptitude vs. Achievement: Should We Replace the SAT?" *The Public Interest*, Sprint 1982, 21)
☞ 3 Visiting professors can be boring.
   4 What you never thought possible. – advertisement slogan
   5 Tammy said that the chicken was ready to eat.
   6 I love philosophy more than my wife.
☞ 7 Kevin told James that he wouldn't be able to go to the game.
   8 A good politician is one who appeals to the people.
   9 Farm Expansion Causes Stink (Headline in the *Guardian*, 25 May 2001, A1)
  10 Army lovers who went AWOL demoted, jailed (Headline in *National Post*, 17 July 2001, A10)
  11 Cheating Time (Headline in *Maclean's*, 9 July 2001, 14)
  12 Vatican Orders Rebel Archbishop to Leave Wife and Moon Church. (Headline in the *Guardian*, 18 July 2001, B7)
☞13 Wanted: Mature person for home deliveries.
☞14 We strive for excellence in the production of quality products.
  15 Sarah gave Cheryl's notes to her sister.
  16 Headline: Elderly Often Burn Victims.

☞17 We're making exciting changes in our Malpeque plant to streamline operations. It's just part of our attempt to be more responsible to our shareholders.

18 Russia had said missile defence would upset the strategic balance and could trigger a new arms race that could suck in China. (Robert Fife, "U.S., Russia reach arms truce," *National Post*, 23 July 2001, A1)

19 Time for Football and Meatball Stew. (Columbia Journalism Review, *Squad Helps Dog Bite Victim*)

20 Crisis Held Over at Nuclear Plant. (Ibid.)

21 Aging Expert Joins University Faculty. (Ibid.

☞22 Woman Better After Being Thrown from High-Rise. (Ibid.)

23 Ford, Reagan Neck and Neck in Presidential Primary. (*Ethiopian Herald*, 16 February 1976)

24 Mauling by Bear Leaves Woman Grateful for Life. (*Herald-Dispatch*, 8 September 1977)

25 Bathing suits 40 per cent off. (Engel, *Analyzing Informal Fallacies*, 3)

26 Nude Patrol ok'd for Muir Beach. (Ibid.)

☞27 FOR SALE: Antique desk suitable for lady with curved legs and large drawers. (Ibid.)

28 Yes, we serve crabs here.

29 Fine for Littering (Engel, 36.)

30 The patient has chest pains if she lies on her left side for over a year.

31 The patient has been depressed since she began seeing me in 1993.

5.2.4 Minimizing Emotively Provocative Attitudes

Compare the lexical definitions in A with the "*pseudo-definitions*" offered in B.

(A) A net is an interstitial vacuity.
    A griffin is a fabulous creature with eagle's head and wings and lion's body.
    An eidolon is another name for a spectre or phantom.
    A weasel is a small, nimble reddish-brown, white-bellied, slender-bodied, carnivorous quadruped.
(B) Abortion is murder.
    Affirmative action is reverse discrimination.
    Homosexual sex is immoral.
    Active euthanasia is state-sanctioned execution.

The examples in B appear in grammatical form exactly like the lexical definitions in A. They both offer two terms or phrases separated by the copula "is." The similarity ends there. The form of the B statements has the look of the reportive, lexical definitions of A. But they are not reportive definitions. The list in group B reveals the speaker's attitude about the concept, and does not define the concept itself. Our ability to see this distinction is crucial if we are to avoid being fooled.

If abortion is a form of murder, and murder is wrong, then abortion too must be wrong. But such an argument is uninteresting. The conclusion depends on the initial definition. Yet it is precisely whether the definition is apt that is at issue in the debate about abortion. The debate is whether or not to accept this "definition." Since the focus is on whether to accept the definition, we cannot appeal to the definition itself. So, the attempt to "solve" the debate by such a definition simply cheats.

Likewise, if discrimination is wrong, whether forward or in reverse, and affirmative action is a form of discrimination, then affirmative action is wrong. But the conclusion follows merely from the definition. In this case, we may accept the definition, as long as we do not treat "reverse discrimination" in a negative light. Since the negative emotive connotation is precisely the intention of this definition, we have grounds to reject it as a definition. Since the discussion focuses on whether we should accept the definition, appealing to the definition itself will not further matters any more than simply thumping one's chest furthers debate.

The definition of homosexual encounters the same problem. It appears to be a definition, but on closer inspection cannot be, at least not in the normal sense (to be clarified further in section 5.3). At any rate, it is a definition we can easily reject. All that is required is a counterexample. Let's use theft. Theft is immoral, but can hardly be understood in terms of homosexuality. Therefore, to "define" homosexual sex as immoral misses the mark.

Part of the problem is that these are the sorts of claims for which we would expect an argument. Instead, we are presented with the definition as if it is fact, as if no argument is warranted, since this is the definition. Definitions, however, are not necessarily facts. They may be proposals, proposals which we may have reasons to reject. The claims in B are examples *where definitions are being stipulated under the guise of being reported.*

There are reasons to object to such sleight-of-hand definitions.

5.3 Types of Definitions

There are two main types of definitions: *reports* and *proposals.* Reports are often referred to as *lexical* definitions. Proposals, meanwhile, may be further separated into stipulative, precising, and persuasive definitions.

The distinction between reports and proposals will help clarify the difference between the claims made in A and those made in B. In arguments, claims have to be defended. An exception occurs if the claim is a lexical definition. Lexical definitions are defended by appealing to a good dictionary. But not all definitions are lexical in this sense. Some are *proposals.* Proposal definitions *do* have to be defended. And this is where the confusion lies. People often provide a definition proposal and believe, since it is a definition, it doesn't need to be itself defended. That is where they go astray. Definition *reports* don't have to be defended, but definition *proposals* do. The definitions in A are reports, those in B are proposals. The arguments in which the latter pseudo-definitions occur are plausible only if we mistake the pseudo-definitions for lexical reportive definitions.

5.3.1 Reportive Definitions

A *reportive definition*, also called a *lexical definition*, reports an established meaning of the term. Thus, reportive definitions may be deemed true or false, depending on how well they accord with the dictionary use.

A definition report intends to mimic the standard definition of a term. We judge the report by how well it accords with established use, and we settle disagreements or uncertainties about the established use by appeal to reputable dictionaries. If someone says "My vacation was great. I went to the woods. It was very peaceful and restive," this might confuse the listener. Either the speaker is schizophrenic, or has confused the word "restive" with the word "restful." The listener can check this by pointing out the dictionary definition of "restive" (an antonym of restful, not a synonym!).

Sometimes terms are best defined within specific disciplines. For example, biological terms may be clarified in a dictionary of biology, rather than a regular dictionary. Consider the following oft-made mistake:

> Danny Hendricken, a vocal opponent of Genetically Modified seeds, said, "It flies in the face of evolution. We have a plant that has evolved over millions of years and because Monsanto has inverted one gene, that changes some of the traits of the plant, they get to claim ownership of the plant." (Wayne Thibodeau, "Island Farmers Divided over GMO decision in favour of Monsanto," *Guardian*, 22 May 2004) A3)

But evolution *is* change in genes found in a population. "When a new gene is introduced or an old one disappears or when the mix of genes changes, the population is said to have evolved." (Sober, *Philosophy of Biology*, 5)

Sometimes, however, going to either a specialized or a general dictionary does not help. There is often more than one standard definition of a term, and disputants need to be clear about which one each intends. This cannot be done by a mere report of the dictionary use. Disputants must first agree on which standard definition should be applied, and this cannot be settled merely by the dictionary, since there is more than one use of the term in these cases. Nevertheless, we can consider this sort of disagreement resolved by reporting on one of the standard uses of the term.

Whether we ought to use the method of casuistry in biomedical ethics, for example, may depend on what component of the lexical definition of casuistry we intend. On the one hand, casuistry involves applying principles to cases, which is a sensible thing to do. Another component of the lexical use of casuistry, however, points to the connotation of the term. It is sometimes used derogatorily and associated with the art of sophistry – the ability to dupe listeners through rhetoric into believing what isn't so. The term "rationalization," in its negative sense, matches what is meant by sophistry. Thus, casuistry would be interpreted as a process of an after-the-fact rationalization of a decision that was actually made for reasons entirely different from those stated. This would hardly count as a commendable practice for bioethical decisions.

5.3.2 Definition Proposals

A *Definition Proposal* suggests, rather than reports, a definition for a word or idea. We may find ourselves, or have found ourselves, wondering whether someone loves us or not. Let's imagine they have in fact said so, but we wonder. We might set up a criterion to decide. If so, we set up a *proposed definition* of "love." Perhaps we suggest the following: "Look, what I mean by love is having a heart rate of sixty beats per minute in my presence, and I measured your heart rate this morning and it was forty-eight." This would be a definition proposal of love – not one we'd recommend, mind you.

Definition proposals are assessed in a different way than definition reports. A definition report is evaluated by looking up the word in a good dictionary. It is in this way that we may say of a lexical definition that it is true or false. A definition proposal, on the other hand, is not assessed this way. It cannot be deemed true or false, for it is a suggestion, or proposal, and not a report. We want to better understand the assessment of definitions, and as usual, this depends on what type of definition we are looking at.

Definition proposals can be subdivided into three separate types: *stipulative, persuasive* and *precising*.

i. Stipulative Definitions   When we introduce a new symbol or a new word, we have complete freedom to stipulate what meaning it is to be given. For example, the university has stipulated that the mark that looks like this "A" means 85 per cent correct. For the purposes of this course, your professor could stipulate that the mark "#" means 85 per cent. Nothing is wrong with that as long as she translates the marks to coincide with the university's when she transcribes them.

More than merely stipulating a meaning for a new symbol, she may stipulate a new meaning to a familiar symbol. For example, in your course, the mark "A" will mean 55 per cent and the mark "F" will mean 85 per cent. Or, whenever she uses the word "dog" she means "very good."

As long as the new definition is consistently used *within the proper context,* (in this case, not sent to the transcript office untranslated) nothing is wrong with this.

In fact, stipulative definitions are created all the time. Acronyms, where we use just the initials of a longer string of words to represent that long string of words are one example. Shop talk often stipulates new symbols to act as shorthand for something else. Stipulated definitions may serve the purpose of economy, or may help to indicate inclusion in an in-group. "Hey, he knows the lingo, he's one of us." Inclusion, like it or not, is a strong psychological motivator. Why else would advertisements tweak that psychological need so often?

Another use of stipulative definitions is to remove the emotive suggestions of familiar words. Logicians do this all the time. If interested in the form of the argument, they let certain arbitrary letters stand for the propositions in the argument. That way they can examine the logical connections free of emotive bias. Consider, for example, the following argument: "Students pay too much in tuition. Students aren't responsible for the deficit. Those responsible for the deficit should foot the bill, not the students." Now, assuming we interpret this *as* an argument, and not simply a string of unconnected opinions, we will learn (in part 4) that the argument is invalid, despite its emotive force for chronically poor students. Lawyers, scientists, police investigators, also remove much of the emotively persuasive component of claims in order to examine the facts independent of interpretation. Whether they succeed at this entirely is an important question, but this doesn't prevent them from trying to remove as much emotive bias as is possible. Apparently obscure legal and scientific texts are that way mainly to avoid emotive bias.

Stipulative definitions are neither true nor false. It may be true that that's how I define a term, but to say the definition is itself true is to misspeak. Stipulative definitions can be judged good or bad, however, and this judgment will depend on the purpose being served. For example, there seems little point in altering the meaning of the familiar letter grades, as the current system is easily understood and widely used. Any changes made would likely lead to pointless confusion.

If the intent is to reduce emotively charged terms, then the stipulative definition can be appraised on how well it accomplishes this. For example, altering "bureaucrat" to "public official" will work only if the negative connotation attached to bureaucrat is absent in the case of public official – a claim many might flatly deny. Euphemisms and "politically correct" alterations may likewise be judged.

ii. Precising Definitions   While stipulative definitions are useful for removing ambiguity, precising definitions are used to reduce vagueness. Precising definitions, while remaining true to ordinary use of a dictionary definition, delimit the range of cases that apply.

If Jones says, "By smart, I mean having an IQ of 120 or higher," Jones has made the relative term "smart" less vague, more precise. The more precise a term is, the less vague, and vice versa.

Truth and falsity don't apply to precising definitions as they do to lexical definitions, but precising definitions have closer affinities to lexical definitions than do stipulative definitions. Although precising definitions cut out some of the cases that lexical definitions allow, some consistency with lexical definitions still applies. If Smith said, "By 'smart' I mean someone having an IQ below 120," this can no longer be viewed as a precising definition, since it veers from standard usage too drastically. We would have to understand Smith's proposal as a stipulative definition, while Jones offers a precising definition. While stipulative definitions need not conform with dictionary use, precising definitions do.

iii. Persuasive Definitions. Persuasive definitions are used to influence attitudes. Their function is *expressive*. The danger is that they are disguised as stipulative definitions, and often work only if undetected. If detected, we see that they bespeak merely the speaker's attitudes toward a concept, not a definition of the term. So these are at best *pseudo-definitions*.

The following list provides terms often used which reveal persuasive definitions:

true/truly	genuine(ly)	correct(ly)
real(ly)	authentic(ally)	honest(ly)
	proper(ly)	

Persuasive definitions may occur absent these terms, of course, but whenever we see these words, we should suspect a persuasive definition is being used. When confronted with persuasive definitions, check to see if there has been any argument given to support such claims. If not, don't be fooled!

Consider these definitions

True freedom is willing subjection to God
No proper feminist is heterosexual.
No one has genuine free will.

In the first case, we must recognize that normally being subjugated to something is not typically what we mean by "freedom." The use of the word "true" makes us realize the meaning of "freedom" being employed here is different from our normal concept. In the last case, we must recognize that the distinction we typically make between being bound and gagged, or held at gun point, and not being externally coerced in these manners is supposed to be irrelevant. This, again, digresses from our normal understanding of being free and not being free. We are really being given a choice about how to define "free will": the normal way or this very different, obscure way. We might wonder whether any other argument is forthcoming that might convince us to switch our meanings so drastically. The bald assertion that this is the proper definition of free will is hardly going to be convincing by itself. In the feminist case, it is crucial to recognize that feminism is not one thing, any more than philosophy is one thing. Philosophers can disagree with each other on many facets: so too feminists. Claiming that only one view is "properly" feminist is being a bit dictatorial, typically believed to be a patriarchal character trait.

Nothing is necessarily wrong with redefining terms, as long as we aren't later fooled into thinking there is any relation to the normal meaning of the term – at least not without further argument.

5.3.3 Combining Types of Definitions

Of course, some definitions may involve more than one type. For example, "Abortion is the unfair killing of a human fetus" is partly reportive or lexical, since the definition accords with what abortion is, but it is also partly persuasive, since it adds the emotive term "unfair."

The type of definition we employ will vary according to our purpose for defining the term in the first place. The following table shows the match between the purpose of the definition and the type of definition to be used.

Purpose	Types
vocabulary	lexical
ambiguity	stipulative
vagueness	precising
attitude	persuasive

Exercise 5.3

State what sort of definitions are being employed in the following illustrations (lexical, stipulative, precising, or emotively persuasive). (Answers to selected questions are provided in Appendix 1.)

☞ 1 Back in Montreal, the Rockers offered Mr. Simard a spot on their "football team." (The "baseball team" merely beat up people, the "footballers" killed.) [Background: Mr. Simard is one of the "bisexual biker hit men" and the Rockers are a gang of bikers in Montreal who "undertook muscle jobs for the Angels."] (Tu Thanh Ha, "Bisexual biker hit men helped bust the Hells Angels," *Globe and Mail,* 26 May 2001, A3)

2 A couple of weeks ago, I had a run-in with a Lurper ... He is a North American full of contradictory hatreds and hungers, almost invariably youngish, white and male. A Lurper is angry, sometimes clever, and full of a terrible, mind-warping envy. He hates other people for having the many things he lacks – success, confidence, fame, money,

sex, charm, recognition, art, conversational ease, style, respect, drugs, a sense of wonder ... I came across the name of this post-grunge subspecies a couple of years ago, in the last paragraph of a dreadfully overwritten letter to the editor, which appeared in this newspaper. "I know not in which drearily savvy and opulent College Street halls this 'new creed' is uttered, but you can leave me out," a Lurper with Literary Aspirations sniffed in response to an article about successful young authors. "I'll be lurping up a veal sandwich on one of the side streets, dripping sauce on my more hopeful poems." The verb "lurp" doesn't actually exist, of course. The letter writer's use of it was either a pretentious poeticism or typo on "slurp." I still can't decide which is more perfectly lurperish ... The Lurper is a profoundly cynical creature. He believes that life is a game in which good guys finish last, and he's fond of expressing this sentiment in constipated prose. (Leah McLaren, "Lurpers: the 21st century's angry young men," *Globe and Mail*, 19 May 2001, L3)

☞ 3   The protestors at last week's G8 meeting in Genoa, Italy, would have us believe the violence there reflected a battle of ideas, and that Carlo Giuliani, the protester killed by Italian police, martyred him-self to a noble ideology. But if this is the case, then Mr. Giuliani's compatriots must now be packing their black hoods and paving stones and winging their way to Zanzibar, an island off the east coast of Africa. Anyone who is truly worried about free trade and its impli-cations should be far more concerned with meetings attended by trade ministers from the world's 49 least developed nations than last week's G8 confab. ("After Genoa, Zanzibar?" *National Post*, 24 July 2001, A19)

4   While every individual has the right to his or her own views, a true believer in conservatism wants to decrease the role and influence of government. Hence, believing in fiscal conservatism is a must. Social conservatism, on the other hand, implies increased government con-trol and absolutely contradicts the goal of fiscal conservatism. No party that truly believes in smaller government and the so-called grassroots would believe it has the right to force its social views upon every citizen. (Doug Fawcett, letter to the editor, *National Post*, 17 July 2001, A15)

☞ 5   One popular encyclopaedia defines stereotypes as "a prejudicial set of notions, gained secondhand, and used to define other ethnic, gen-der or social groups in simplistic and erroneous ways." That's non-sense. In fact, stereotypes are the result of the collective observation of generations. They're shorthand expressions of common charac-teristics, or of frequent phenomena. They're the simplified results of shared experiences that give us, as the writer Henry James put it, "the power to guess the unseen from the seen." Stereotypes may be trite and banal. As clichés, they may be shopworn and boring. They may not fit individuals, and they've certainly no place in the legal system. But, contrary to current beliefs, they aren't untrue or inaccurate by definition. The problem with "myths" and stereotypes isn't that they're baseless, but that they're poor substitutes for open-minded inquiries into particular cases. If one wants to discover what actually happened in a given instance, myths are of limited help. Even valid statistics have little use. Aviation accidents or incidents involve individuals, not statistics. Things that may be generally or statistically true can easily be false in the example at hand. Unfortunately, people regularly invoke fables and stereotypes to support their prejudices or politics. Feminists have their own twist. They've not only insisted that stereotypes are unreliable for the judgement of individual women – which is quite true – but turned the word "stereotype" into a synonym for falsehood. They've declared that stereotypes are altogether unfounded, which isn't true at all. (George Jonas, "Stereotypes not always false," *Guardian,* 6 July 2001, A6)

6 The perfect government is "an oligarchy tempered by assassination." (Malcolm Muggeridge, reported in Peter C. Newman, "Lord of his realm," *Maclean's,* 4 June 2001, 14)

☞ 7 The current state of the Canadian Alliance and Tory parties is understandable. Canadians have lost the ideological and philosophical understanding of what it means to be a true conservative. Conservatives believe the role of government should be minimal in such areas as taxation, social services, health and education, and that competition and the free market are the best avenues for the delivery of goods and services. The failing of the so-called right-wing parties is not just a question of unity or leadership. It is the continuous blending of liberal ideals and moving to the left on every issue. Give us a real conservative party and we, the people, will vote for it. (Joe Berglis, letter to the editor, *National Post,* 22 August 2001, A15)

☞ 8 [C]onsider "megacity." Instead of using the word to mean a large city, a more appropriate Canadian usage might be to pronounce the word something like mendacity. A suitable definition could then be "the arrogance of an elected official to pursue a policy, contemptuous of the opinions of the overwhelming majority of the electorate affected by such a policy." (Dave Morgan, letter to the editor, *Globe and Mail,* 19 June 2001, A12)

9 A Canadian "gaffe" at the United Nations has identified abortion as one of the social "services" people worldwide should expect as a right. Officially, the United Nations does not fund abortion, but in defining a reference to UN-agreed "services" in the declaration, a Canadian delegate said abortion was included. This was in reply to a United States request for "somebody" to explain the meaning of "services," defined as including "education, nutrition [and] health care" in a draft of the declaration titled A World Fit for Children. "I

do not understand why the distinguished delegate asks the question because he knows the answer," responded Andras Vamos-Goldman, legal affairs counsellor at the Canadian mission to the United Nations. "But of course it includes – and I hate to say the word – but it includes abortion." His remark prompted immediate protests from the United States, the Vatican and Chile, which spoke for the 10-nation Rio Group of Latin American countries, whose populations are predominantly Catholic. Several Muslim countries protested later. They all demanded the word "services" be at least qualified because Canada's linking of "services" and "abortion" had created a precedent. "Never before have we heard that 'services' included abortion," said the Chilean delegate. "In our country, this is illegal and we are ready to delete it. For us, it does not mean abortion." Msg. James Reinert of the Vatican said, "I am shocked. I can't believe that I heard what I just heard. If this conference agrees to this definition of the word services, we will have to go through this entire document and all future documents where this word is used." Mr. Vamos-Goldman said he was surprised his interpretation had caused a "firestorm" and added countries could place their own interpretation on the word ... Carl Schwenger, a spokesman for the Department of Foreign Affairs, said Mr. Vamos-Goldman meant abortion is one of the services available to women in some countries. "The word abortion isn't normally used in formal negotiations at the UN, but it was used by a member of the Canadian delegation in a late-night meeting to illustrate [that] point," he said. "Words are everything at the UN," he added. The incident highlights the ambiguity of UN statements, declarations and treaties. "What's the use of even negotiating a declaration if it means different things to different people," said Tanya Granic, spokeswoman for the Campaign Life Coalition, an Ontario anti-abortion group. (Steven Edwards, "Canadian gaffe ignites UN abortion debate," *National Post*, 18 June 2001, A2)

5.4 Types of Meaning

We have learned that definitions come in four varieties: lexical, stipulative, precising, and persuasive. But we are not yet finished with our classification of definitions. Across each of these four types of definitions there is a further demarcation. A definition tells us the *meaning* of a term. The meaning of terms can be understood in at least two ways, however: extensionally and intensionally.

Definitions deal with classes of objects. A class stands for the total number of objects which correctly belong to it. A definition, then, does two things: (i) it defines the classes, and (ii) it denotes the various individual objects which belong to that class. The collection of these objects constitutes the *extension* of the term. For example, John, Paul, George, and Ringo are the extension of the term "the Beatles."

In order to know how to apply a general term correctly, it is not always necessary to know *all the objects* to which it may be correctly applied. If we know the *meaning* of a general term then we know the common attributes that guide us in using that general term. The set of attributes shared by all and only those objects to which the term refers is called the *intension* of that term. For example, we can define an "Olympian" as a person who has been a competitor in the Olympic games. Note that we do not need to know the extension of this term (quite a few people would belong there) in order to do this. Yet we have produced a criterion for deciding, for any given object, whether or not it falls within the extension of the term "Olympian."

To understand an intension of a term, then, is to think of drawing a circle. The circle sets a boundary. The purpose of the boundary is to divide things that are included in the circle from those that are excluded. The intensional definition *is the circle itself.* The extension of the term, however, is the *items that are included in the circle.* A good definition of a horse will have only horses inside the circle, and things like sawhorses and sea horses, cows and pigs, yachts and kumquats, will remain outside the circle.

5.4.1 Extensional Definitions

When we use *extensional definitions*, we clarify the meaning of a term by identifying members of the class of things named by that term. For example,

1 By "Spice Girls" I mean Baby, Posh, Scary, Ginger, and Sporty.
2 Blues musicians include Muddy Waters, Taj Mahal, and Etta James.
3 Golf club manufacturers include Mizuno, Callaway, Tommy Armour, and Cleveland.

In the extensional sense, the meaning of a term consists of the class of objects to which the term may be applied. This is its "referential" sense. In other words, we point out what the term refers to. The word "dog" refers to German shepherds, collies, huskies, etc. It also refers to this particular dog and that particular dog.

Listing all or some of the things a word refers to is giving the *extension* of the term. The term *extends* to cover all these things.

Listing all or some of the referents of a term is also giving the term's *denotational* meaning, since it tells the listener some or all of the things which the word *denotes.*

The collection or class of objects referred to by the word constitutes that term's extension or denotation. We may refer to the extensional class of objects in two ways, however: by listing a subset of objects which belong to the class, or by simply pointing at objects in the world which count as mem-

bers of the designated set. Pointing at objects as members of the extensional set is called providing an *ostensive definition.*

i. Ostensive Definitions.   If we go around pointing at things, this is
called giving an *ostensive definition.*

> This is a line: ————————.
> That is a cat (said when pointing at a cat).
> That is a *chat* (said when teaching French and pointing at a cat).
> This is a true proposition.
> That is yellow (said when pointing at something that is yellow).
> This sentence commits, three erors.

Ostensive definitions are useful at the early stages of language acquisition.
The act of pointing at objects transcends language barriers, and so serves
as an immediate teaching device. Some things may be defined *only* by
ostension – the colour red, for example. We feel unable to define red to
those unable to *experience* red, to see it. Pointing at red objects seems to be
our only hope. We could say that red is the result of 700-nanometre wave-
lengths striking intact eyes. Some have argued that the notions of good
and bad are similarly limited to ostensive definitions (G. E. Moore, most
famously, but this idea would be welcomed by Aristotle). They claim that
whenever we try to define "good" in relation to other things, like happiness, or self-interest, or pleasure, we seem to miss the mark. Instead, they
argue, we can only point to good or bad acts while we say "This is good.
That is bad."

There are problems with ostensive definitions, however. The act of
pointing itself presupposes a custom of pointing, a custom that may itself
need to be learned. The concept of pointing itself cannot be taught by
ostension. For example, some dogs and cats learn the concept of pointing,
and move their focus of attention in the direction of the point, but other
cats and dogs simply stare at the hand. They do not seem to grasp the concept of pointing. Likewise, infants must first develop their cognitive capacity before pointing is understood, before ostensive language acquisition
will work. Pointing, then, may itself be understood as a language. We cannot, therefore, suggest that ostensive definitions are a *pre-language* device.
The basis on which we learn the concept of ostensive definitions remains
a puzzle.

Another concern is that ostensive definitions are problematically
ambiguous. To give an ostensive definition of book, a teacher may point at
the student's red book. How will the student know the teacher is not giving an ostensive definition of red, or rectangle, or things purchased in the
course of getting an education, or things on a table, or things that obey the
law of gravity? For that matter, how can the student even be sure the
teacher is pointing at the book at all, rather than the desk upon which the

book happens to be lying, or the molecules that hover in the air above the book?

Extensional definitions are broader in scope than ostensive definitions, for they can appeal to more objects than those immediately present, and so will escape some of the unwieldy interpretation woes of ostensive definitions, but not by much. Extensional lists do not always fare much better than ostensive definitions. Few terms can have their extensions completely enumerated. A limited extension may create ambiguities as to what is being referred to, yet an exhaustive list is tedious. Given that we usually rest content with enumerating only a few of the extensions, we will not be able to distinguish the intension of the word, and ambiguity may result. A particular individual, John Doe, can be given as an extensional example in defining "man," "animal," "husband," "taxpayer," "father," "son," "things having mass," "things extended," etc. Therefore, mentioning or pointing at John Doe will not help to distinguish one's intensional meaning.

Likewise, definitions by partial enumeration cannot serve to distinguish terms that have different extensions. If you point out all red-haired people on a bus, you have also pointed out people with hair, people riding a bus, things over two feet, things without guck on their faces – none of which, presumably, is what you *mean*.

Lastly, two terms with different intensions may nevertheless share the same extension. A featherless biped and a human happen to have exactly the same extension (assuming there are no bald chickens), although presumably different intentions.

ii. Contextual Definitions.   Sometimes, we may provide a *contextual definition*. We may be tempted to do so when a term lacks both extension and intension. Words like "when" and symbols like "?" are best explained when *used*. In this sense, contextual definitions are a form of ostensive definition, for we don't give a definition, we simply *use* the term, and hope that by understanding how the term is used, we now sufficiently know the meaning of the term. Placing the terms in context may satisfactorily provide them with a meaning. For example,

1 "When" is an interrogative adverb asking what time something will or has occurred, as in "When did (shall) you meet him?" or "When did I suggest such a thing?" or "The time when such things could happen is gone."
2 "Aha" is an expression of surprise, or triumph, as in "Aha, I knew she was lying!" or "Aha, there you are!"
3 The question mark "?" is a grammatical punctuation used after a question, as in "How far is it to Wawa?" or "How do you pronounce 'Souris' in this part of the country?"

The contextual component of the preceding definitions occurs in the examples with the term in context. Notice that the first part of the definition is not contextual. Usually contextual definitions do not come unadulterated.

5.4.2 *Intensional Definitions*

Intensional definitions are greatly superior to extensional definitions. They provide the criteria for determine the extensional set, as opposed to provide a partial extensional list. There are three different kinds of intensional definitions: *Synonymous definition, Operational definition,* and *Genus and Difference definition.*

i. Synonyms. Two words that have the same intensional meaning are called synonymous. Giving a synonym for a word is giving a *synonymous definition.* This is helpful if our concern is mainly lexical, as opposed to conceptual, and if we understand the synonym but not the original.

Its applicability is limited, however, as many terms do not have exact synonyms, and so a synonymous definition for these terms may be misleading – especially with respect to the emotive connotation. Notice also that synonyms will be as vague as the original term, so synonymous definitions are useless for precising definitions.

ii. Operational Definitions. Used in conjunction with scientific definitions, they specify for the limited scope of an experiment what will count as an instance of a theoretical definition. If I want to measure *pain,* I might record the decibels of someone's screaming and claim the higher the decibels the more pain sensation. In this case the relative volume of the scream is my operational definition of pain.

This may work very well in an experimental situation where I am giving shocks to people, but it doesn't serve, nor is it intended to serve, as a general definition of pain, since we would then be led to say that many rock stars are in a great deal of pain. Confusing operational definitions with lexical definitions may be one of the faults of Skinnerian behaviourism.* We have not observed a particular mental state like pain, we have observed

---

* B.F. Skinner's aim in *The Behaviour of Organisms* (New York, 1938) was to eliminate mental states (like yearnings and aversions) from the range of phenomena with which psychology is properly concerned. Intentions and pains, for example, are defined in terms of functional relations that refer exclusively to environmental input stimuli and mechanistic output motions of the body. Talk of the mind can be reduced without remainder to talk about behaviour. The concept of the mind that initiates the behaviour is seen as a useless theoretical appendage that goes the way of other myths, fantasies, delusions, and chimeras. One may be a behaviourist without endorsing such reductionism, however. *Methodological* behaviourists maintain merely that there is no scientific way to study the immaterial mind through the effects of observable, bodily motions. They are not averse to inferring a mind on the basis of such observable behaviour. *Eliminativist* behaviourists, like Skinner, deem such inferences idle.

merely our operational definition of a particular mental state, but it does not follow from this alone that we do not have mental states.

Operational definitions focus on what can be observed and measured, and are limited to empirical use. They have great applicability for that use, as long as they are not understood to be doing anything more than that.

iii. Genus and Difference.   By far the most important and common type of definition is *genus and difference.*

Classes can be divided into subclasses. Consider the class of fish. Subclasses of fish include cod, haddock, trout, tuna. The overarching class of fish is called the genus; the subclass is called the species.

Since a class is a collection of entities having some common characteristic, all the members of a given genus will have some characteristics in common. All fish have gills, are cold-blooded, and live in water.

Now, if we distinguish among this class a subclass which, although sharing the characteristics common to all fish, have certain other characteristics that are unique among fish, for example live in fresh water, or have no scales, are predators, or eat plankton, etc., then we have isolated a *specific difference* of this subclass among the overarching class. We can say of a trout, therefore, that it is a kind of freshwater fish esteemed as food and game.

A genus and difference definition that lists the genus (class) and difference (subclass) is an effective way to define in fairly precise terms.

A common genus and difference definition of "human" is "rational animal." "Animal" is the genus, and "rational" is the difference belonging to this subclass which distinguishes it from the other members of its class, i.e., the nonrational animals. Such a definition may warrant criticism, however. Just as there exist freshwater fish other than trout we like to eat, we may complain that humans are not the only rational animals. We may even complain that we are not as rational as we imagine, and our survival so far has more to do with luck than skill. Conversely, we may point out that our survival has occurred *despite* our general irrationality. Still, it is an excellent example of a genus and difference definition.

The method of definition by genus and difference has two limitations:

1 It cannot apply to *universal* attributes, attributes for which no member of the genus can be differentiated from any other member (for example, "being," "thing," "entity," "substance," "property," "universe," etc.). (How could we define "being" : "A thing that is not a non-being, but which differs from other non-beings in the sense that … ???") These things are defined by being precisely the largest class of things, and so cannot be differentiated from a yet larger class.

2 The difference cited may be merely accidental. For example, the genus and difference intentional definition of human as "featherless biped" will include humans, to be sure, but we might like to think that this difference (featherlessness) and the genus (bipededness) are accidental,

or non-essential, traits of being human. We feel (rightly or wrongly) that the correct definition should do more than accurately capture the extension; it should somehow do so for the right reasons. A correct definition should focus on *essential* differences, and *essential* genuses. We are apt, therefore, to think something like "rational animal" is a better definition, even though it may bring into our extensional set more creatures than we had otherwise thought. (Notice, a "rational, featherless biped" may exclude dolphins, but not orangutans and Macaw monkeys.) Our concern at present, however, is to provide the structure of a genus and difference definition. We will learn how to evaluate them in section 5.5.

Meno's Definition of Virtue

In Plato's dialogue, *Meno*, Meno and Socrates engage in a discussion on virtue. Before the discussion can proceed, Socrates asks Meno for a definition of virtue, for how can they converse on the merits of virtue if they are not certain they are referring to the same concept? Meno thinks this is a simple enough task, but quickly discovers otherwise. Here is Meno's first attempt:

> First, if you want the virtue of a man, it is easy to say that a man's virtue consists of being able to manage public affairs and in so doing to benefit his friends and harm his enemies and to be careful that no harm comes to himself; if you want the virtue of a woman, it is not difficult to describe: she must manage the home well, preserve its possessions, be submissive to her husband; the virtue of a child, whether male or female, is different again, and so is that of an elderly man if you want that or if you want that of a free man or a slave. And there are many other virtues, so that one is not at a loss to say what virtue is. (Plato, *Meno*, 71e)

Not surprisingly, this definition will not satisfy Socrates. All Meno has provided here is a catalogue of examples, an *extensional* definition, whereas Socrates is looking for an *intensional* definition. Furthermore, we can certainly wonder whether Meno has even supplied us with a good extensional set. Is it really a virtue to manage public affairs in such a way as to harm one's enemies? Is the virtue of a woman to be submissive to her husband and do household chores? Socrates's concern is not with the latter. Instead, he replies,

> Even if they are many and various, all of them have one and the same form which makes them virtues and it is right to look to this when one is asked to make clear what virtue is. (*Meno*, 72c)

In other words, although the virtues of these various groups are different, if we're content in nevertheless calling them all "virtues," there must be something which they all share in common. It is this commonality that Socrates wants. The commonality is what the *intensional* definition is after.

Exercise 5.4

Give a genus and difference intensional definition and an extensional definition of the following words.

☞1 dog   4 delicacies   ☞7 cartoon
  2 game   5 snow   8 feminist
  3 kindergarten   6 eggplant   9 unicorn

Pay special attention to question 9 in exercise 5.4. Certain terms, like "unicorn," or "the set of all prime numbers between but not including five and seven" have empty extensional sets. This is of vital importance. One of Kant's criticisms of St. Anselm's *ontological proof of the existence of God* is based on the recognition that there can be intension without extension. (*Critique of Pure Reason*) That is, Anselm insufficiently appreciated the fact that there may be empty or *null sets*.

Anselm's Ontological Argument

  1 God is that than which nothing greater can be conceived.
  2 Existence is greater than non-existence.
  3 A God existing in reality is obviously greater than a god existing merely in the imagination or concept alone.
  4 Therefore, God must exist. (*Proslogium*)

This is a very clever argument. Unfortunately Anselm fails to sufficiently appreciate the difference between intensional and extensional definitions. He fails to recognize that the intensional meaning does not by itself necessitate any corresponding extensional meaning.

The intensional meaning of "God" is that than which nothing greater can be conceived, and if existence is greater than non-existence (something suicide, euthanasia, and the interest in horror movies tend to challenge), then part of the intensional meaning of God is that He exists. All very fine, but it doesn't speak at all to the *extensional* meaning. Whether there is anything that satisfies this intensional meaning cannot be presumed from this argument. Just as we have to go to the empirical sciences to see whether there are any horned horses, we have to go to the empirical sciences to see whether anything satisfies this specific intensional definition of "God."

In other words, Anselm provides an intensional meaning of God, and presumes this alone guarantees an extensional set: a real God that satisfies the intentional definition. As long as the possibility of a null set exists, we are not entitled to make this inference – a lesson we are better able to understand once we clearly distinguish extensional from intensional meanings.

5.5 Evaluating Genus and Difference Definitions

Definitions may be good or bad, better or worse. We assess definitions by how well the intension captures the proper extensional set. Genus and difference definitions will tend to do this better than the others, but even they can go astray. Here are five rules for evaluating genus and difference definitions:

1 A definition should not be circular
2 A definition should not be too broad
3 A definition should not be too narrow
4 A definition should be clear
5 A definition should be emotively neutral

5.5.1 Circular Definitions

If the term needing to be defined appears in the definition itself, the definition is circular. By circular, we mean we are put in a loop. To know a term, we need to know the term in order to know the term. For example, "father" means "a person who is a father." Or "A politician is someone who does politics."

A definition may involve an extended circle. For example, if we define dog by canine and then later define canine extensionally by saying dog, we are put in a loop; and the series of definitions is circular. Consider also "economics" defined as "the science which treats of the phenomena arising out of economic activities of men in free society," coupled with "economic activity" as "the activities studied by the science of economics." (J.M. Keynes, *Scope and Methods of Political Economy*, 1)

Earlier, we defined an Olympian as a competitor in the Olympic games. If we follow that with saying an Olympic game is one in which Olympians compete, we have offered a circular definition.

Recall Meno's attempt at defining virtue? Socrates presses him, and Meno continues with a variety of further attempts. The last attempt he makes before giving up in disgust – as happened to many of Socrates' interlocutors – is the following:

Virtue is to be able to secure good things with justice (Plato, *Meno*, 79b)

This should strike one as not bad, particularly compared to his earlier attempts. Unfortunately, in his earlier catalogue of virtues, Meno has included justice *as a virtue* (Plato, Meno, 78e, 79b). But in that case, he cannot define virtue by appealing to justice without circularity.

A Worry

The charge of circularity may be applied to all definitions if we extend the circle far enough. After all, to define a term, we need words other than the term being defined. And if these new terms require definitions, we cannot resort to any term already used. To define a term (term 1), we require a new set of terms (term 2). These new terms have definitions, and to avoid the charge of circularity, none of the definitions can invoke term 1. So we require a third set (term 3) to define term 2. The process continues. To avoid the charge of circularity, none of the new sets can be defined in terms of the preceding sets. But since the number of words in any given language is finite, at some point this condition must fail.

Another problem ensues. A proper definition will set up an equivalency between the term being defined (the *definiendum*) and the terms doing the defining (the *definiens*). For example, a bachelor is an adult unmarried male. A triangle is any three-sided enclosed plane figure. But since the denotations are the same between the *definiendum* and the *definiens*, we are entitled to replace one with the other wherever they occur. For example, given the definition of bachelor, the following two sentences are equivalent:

(1) The car ran over the bachelor.
(2) The car ran over the adult unmarried male.

(1) and (2) are equivalent because we can replace "adult unmarried male" wherever we see "bachelor." This should make perfect sense, but here's the problem. Consider the following claim:

(3) A bachelor is an adult unmarried male.

Given the replacement rule noted above, we are entitled to translate (3) in the following manner:

(4) A bachelor is a bachelor.

(4) is the epitome of a circular definition. Since it follows from a good definition, we can begin to see that all definitions are circular.

So, in our accusation of circularity, we need to be careful. We want to point out only the more obvious short extended loops.

5.5.2 Broad Definitions

Intensional definitions should include neither more nor less than the intended extension. A definition is *too broad* if the extensional set includes things that are not intended in the intensional definition. In other words, there are things inside the circle that don't belong there.

If someone says "a cat is an animal that has four legs," however true that is, it is much too *broad* a definition. It means that dogs, monkeys and horses are cats. Our circle would include them, rather than exclude them. Think of a fishing net. We want to catch haddock, say, but not dolphin. Catching dolphins in our net, particularly if they die as a result, is seen as a tragedy we wish to avoid. Similarly, definitions that are cast so widely they ensnare other innocent creatures are seen as problematic.

Saying "A father is a parent" is too broad, since the definition includes mothers in the extensional set. Or take the following definition: "A car is a motor vehicle used for transportation." This definition is too broad because the intension (a motor vehicle used for transportation) includes things like trucks and trains that are not supposed to be found in the extension. The intensional net is cast too widely, too indiscriminately, too broadly.

Meno's second attempt at a definition of virtue is the following:

> Virtue is to desire beautiful things and to have the power to provide them.
> (Plato, *Meno*, 77b)

A difficulty lurks here, which Socrates is quick to point out to Meno. All men *always* desire what is, or seems, good or beautiful to them. That is, what they believe will make them happy is what motivates them. This makes the definition *too broad*, since we will end up calling the vicious (those who also pursue what they take to be good or beautiful) virtuous. So something must be added to the definition to exclude this group from the extension of the virtuous.

Meno tries again, the trooper that he is.

> [Virtue is] the power of securing good things. (Plato, *Meno*, 78b)

This is one of the drawbacks of writing philosophical treatises in dialogue form. The temptation to bolster one's own position by making complete dolts out of the "bad guys" may be too strong. "Good things" may be secured by evil means, so this definition is still too broad a definition of virtue.

5.5.3 Narrow Definitions

A definition is *too narrow* if the intensional set *excludes* things that properly belong in the extension. If I say a cat is a furry feline that is a good pet, this is too *narrow,* for some cats are not all that furry, and my cat, anyway, is not really a good pet. It scratches the furniture, eats the telephone cord, and claws and bites my hand. Saying, "A parent is a father," is also too narrow, since it excludes mothers. Saying, "A car is a four-door motor vehicle" is too narrow because the intension (a four-door motor vehicle) excludes two-, three-, and six-door cars that should be found in the extension.

When we define terms, we already know what's supposed to be in the extensional set and what's supposed to be excluded. We therefore can

appraise our own or someone else's definitions on the basis of this knowledge. We judge our definitions by how well they accord with the intended
extensional set. We don't provide definitions in the dark and see what falls
from them, like dealing cards, or rolling dice. We don't say, "Well, then, I
guess you don't have a cat after all, but something else." We don't say,
"Well, I guess you don't have a car." Such responses get the order backward. Instead, we start with the extensional set, of cats say, and we try to
derive an intensional definition that best captures that external set. And
this is why we are able to criticize definitions according to how well they
achieve their goal.

Too Broad and Too Narrow.   Often, definitions may be too broad and
too narrow at the same time (though in different respects). The idea is
that the definition offered should denote no more things and no fewer
things than are denoted by the original term.

If I say a cat is a feline animal that likes tuna, that is both too narrow and
too broad at the same time. It rules out cats that don't like tuna (inessen-
tial to being a cat, so it is too narrow), and at the same time it includes
cougars, leopards, tigers, and lions (so it is too broad).

Or, if you prefer, consider the following definition: "Hockey is a game
played on ice in Canada." This definition is too narrow because the intension (a game played on ice in Canada) excludes other countries in which
hockey is played (Sweden, Czech Republic, USA, Belarus). It is at the same
time too broad because the intension includes some other sports (curling,
speed skating, luge, ice dancing).

Admittedly, arriving at a definition that is neither too narrow nor too
broad is not always an easy task. Thus definitions may be deemed good or
bad, as opposed to wrong or right. We try to provide as accurate a definition as possible while realizing that the ideal is unrealizable. This doesn't
mean any definition is as good as any other on the grounds that no
supremely good definition exists, or because each definition is as infinitely
removed from an impossible ideal as any other definition. We can still
detect better or worse by how much of the extensional set is included, and
how much of the non-extensional set is excluded.

5.5.4 Unclear Definitions

Definitions should be perspicuous and non-sesquipedalian.* Enough said?
To rephrase this, definitions should be clear and concise. Wherever possible, we should avoid expressing claims that are ambiguous, vague, or
obscure.

---

* *Perspicuous*: Easily understood, clearly expressed. *Sesquipedalian*: Of words and
  expressions having many syllables. Hence *sesquipedalianism*, style characterized by
  the use of long words; lengthiness. Notice that the second term is *onomatopoeic*,
  while the first is not.

Our earlier discussion about the need to reduce vagueness, ambiguity, and obfuscation should suffice to show the importance of clear and precise definitions. If we are offering a definition, the intent is to clarify something. Using obscure, ambiguous, or vague terms will not assist this. Consider the following vague definitions:

> The President of a country is the pilot of the ship of state.
> Harmonica: name of several musical instruments.
> Poetry is the liquid silver of language.

A variation on vague definitions are downright obscure definitions. Definitions are intended to *clarify* matters, and when things are made more opaque, we may complain. Consider the following definitions:

> *Network.* Any thing reticulated, or decussated, at equal distances, with interstices between the intersections. (Samuel Johnson, *A Dictionary of the English Language*, 1755)
> *Thridace.* Inspissated juice of lettuce. (The *Concise Oxford English Dictionary*, 1959)
> *Nasturtium.* Genus of pungent-tasted cruciferous plants. (The *Concise Oxford English Dictionary*, 1959)

As already discussed in 4.7, academics are among the worst offenders. Consider the following "clarification" (note the innuendo!):

> If the apparent menace of the akrates as unredescribed to the soundness of Aristotle's construction has nothing to do with reductive commensurability in the *Protagoras* sense and everything to do with such formal requirements as the self-sufficiency of eudaimonia, and with the special prospect of having just about nothing to regret that eudaimonia holds out to rational intelligence, then it will be timely to review the question whether Aristotle could not have contrived to accommodate together both akrasia as pretheoretically described and eudaimonia as theoretically described (still appealing solely to reason). (Wiggins, *Needs, Values, Truth*, 59)

Despite Wiggins's brilliance in other respects, this is an excellent example of how *not* to write. Please do not emulate such style in your academic aspirations.

5.5.5 Emotively Loaded Definitions

We have seen the problem with persuasive pseudo-definitions. Genus and difference definitions may give rise to the same worries. Plainly, we should not try to dupe our listeners with emotively loaded language in the guise of a reportive definition. Likewise, we should not be duped ourselves by emotively loaded pseudo-definitions. Consider, for example, the following claim:

Taxation is a form of theft.

Here, the intentional definition imbues its terms with heavily charged emotive tone. The term "theft" carries with it an emotive force that will strike most readers. It has a negative connotation. Theft is bad. If we aren't careful, we will associate that negative connotation with taxation without further ado. That is precisely the intent of this pseudo-definition. But notice, the association requires backing. If nothing further is claimed, we have merely an emotively loaded pseudo-definition. We discover more about the speaker's attitude than about taxation. We would expect the claim as a conclusion to an argument, not as a bare definition. Or consider

A politician is a professional liar and scoundrel.

Again, we should see that this pseudo-definition tells us more about the person who defined politicians (at least about what that person's feelings and attitudes are towards politicians) than about politicians themselves.

Samuel Johnson, who provided one of the first English dictionaries, was accused of inserting some of his own biases into the work. Consider the following droll selections:

Oats. A grain which in England is generally given to horses, but in Scotland supports the people. (Samuel Johnson, *A Dictionary of the English Language*, 1755)

Lexicographer. A writer of dictionaries; a harmless drudge, that busies himself in tracing the original, and detailing the signification of words.

Patron. A wretch who supports with indolence, and is paid with flattery.

There is a tale behind this last definition. During the ten years in which Samuel Johnson amassed his dictionary, Philip Dormer Stanhope, the fourth earl of Chesterfield, was to act as patron. To Johnson's chagrin, Lord Chesterfield provided a paltry (even for then) sum of ten pounds, yet took all of the credit. Of Lord Chesterfield, Johnson later said that he taught "the morals of a whore and the manners of a dancing-master." (Winchester, *The Professor and the Madman*, 93–4)

Definition Assumptions. Sometimes no definitions are given, but we can see by the terms used that an assumed definition lurks. If we detect these assumed definitions, and find them problematic in one of the five ways, we may rightly complain. Consider the following

A letter published on June 7, 2001 written by Suzanne Norris stated that one "can be religious and be gay." If the ultimate goal of someone's life is to become "religious" they will miss salvation by a country mile. Being religious can be a very dangerous thing. The people who frustrated Christ the most were the religious leaders. Time and again Jesus ridiculed them because they were the ones to whom people looked for guidance, yet they were the ones who refused to recognize Christ as their saviour and hand over control of their lives to him. (Alvin Jay, "Standing up for what is right," *Guardian*, 29 June 2001, A7)

Pointing out the danger of being overly zealous, or inconsistent, or hypo-critical, or fundamentalist are all good things, but in order for Alvin Jay's point to succeed, he needs to *define* being religious as being overzealous, inconsistent, and hypocritical. It is this definition assumption that we may challenge, either in terms of its being emotively loaded, or in terms of its being excessively narrow.

Exercise 5.5

Criticize the following definitions according to whether they are circular, too broad, too narrow, ambiguous, vague, obscure, or emotively loaded. (Answers to selected questions are provided in Appendix 1.)

☞ 1 "They have to respect democracy. Democracy is those who gave all their lives to public affairs – it's not an easy life for any of us to do these jobs." (Jean Chrétien quoted in Justine Hunter, "PM laments hectic travel schedule," *National Post*, 22, June 2001, A6)

2 "Base" means that which serves as a base. (Ch'eng Wei-Shih Lun, *A History of Chinese Philosophy*)

3 Alteration is the combination of contradictorily opposed determina-tions in the existence of one and the same thing. (Kant, *Critique of Pure Reason*)

☞ 4 To sneeze is to emit wind audibly by the nose. (Samuel Johnson, *A Dictionary of the English Language*, 1755)

5 A bore is a person who talks when you want him to listen. (Ambrose Bierce, *The Devil's Dictionary*)

6 Art is a human activity having for its purpose the transmission to oth-ers of the highest and best feelings to which men have risen. (Count Leo Tolstoy, *What is Art?*)

☞ 7 Freedom of choice: The human capacity to choose freely between two or more genuine alternatives or possibilities, such choosing being always limited both by the past and by the circumstances of the immediate present. (Corliss Lamont, *Freedom of Choice Affirmed.*)

☞ 8 Faith may be defined briefly as an illogical belief in the occurrence of the improbable. (H.L. Mencken in Copi and Burgess-Jackson, *Informal Logic*, 181)

9 True art is reverent imitation of God. (Tyron Edwards, *The New Dic-tionary of Thoughts: A Cyclopedia of Quotations*, 30)

10 Intercourse remains a means or the means of physiologically making a woman inferior. (Andrea Dworkin, "Intercourse," 93)

☞11 Knowledge is true belief. (Plato)

12 Poetry is the record of the best and happiest moments of the happiest and best minds. (Percy Bysshe Shelley, *A Defence of Poetry.*)

13 Religion is the opiate of the masses (Karl Marx and Friedrich Engels, *The Communist Manifesto.*)

14 A chair is a wooden piece of furniture designed for sitting.

☞15 A lesbian is a woman who wants to have sex with any other woman.

16 Surrogacy is a fancy word for baby-selling.

17 A circle is a geometric plane figure.

☞18 Health is a state of complete physical, mental, and social well-being and not merely the absence of disease or infirmity. (World Health Organization, *Basic Documents*, 1–2)

19 Science is a groping in the dark, forever unable to reveal the true nature of things.

☞20 A self-interested act is any act motivated by some desire of the acting agent.

21 A stereo is what you use to play music.

22 Pornography is a display of nude bodies with the intent to satisfy sinful lust.

☞23 If you're a liberal, you can't support the teaching of values in school, not merely religious values, but also moral values, like "It's wrong to steal," or "It's wrong to murder." If you do teach such values to children, you're interfering with their freedom, and as a liberal, you must believe in freedom above all else.

24 Coffee is a drink made from beans that you have in the morning.

25 The Internet is a bad thing. It claims to enable widespread communication, free speech, and a worldwide community, but actually it prevents people from real communication, which takes place face to face in a real physical community.

☞26 Opera is merciless shrieking that appeals to those who confuse pain for pleasure.

27 Money is a germ-ridden token to be exchanged for cigarettes, booze, and heroin.

☞28 A protagonist is one who gets the girl.

29 A proper coiffure is a beacon to the nocturnal void.

30 A motorcycle is a motorized vehicle that is not a car or a truck.

31 Myron's: One of Canada's premier entertainment facilities.

☞32 Cheers: Where good friends meet.

33 Smitty's: The place where breakfast was born.

34 By fair, I mean the outcome that ensues from proper procedures.

☞35 Acts satisfying one's self-interest properly speaking are only those which aspire to a virtuous or contemplative life.

☞36 By morally good, I mean that which is useful to us.

37 Cutlery: knives and similar utensils.

☞38 Creativity is imaginative, motivated, transformative, and productive thinking and activity within a particular context of framework of knowledge, inquiry and skills – a process that generates outcomes which are original, significant, effective and of value or use (or both) to the community. (Symposium on Creativity and Innovation in the Arts and Sciences, Edmonton, May 2000, reported in Robert Fulford, "Whose bright idea was this?" *National Post,* 30 May 2001 A14)

☞39 To know something is to believe it sincerely and strongly.

40 A hazard is anything that is dangerous.

☞41 Art is that which has aesthetic value.

42 The meaning of a word is what is explained by the explanation of the meaning. (Ludwig Wittgenstein, *Philosophical Investigations.*)

43 Political power, properly so called, is merely the organized power of one class for oppressing the other. (Karl Marx and Friedrich Engels, *The Communist Manifesto.*)

☞44 Phenomenology emphasizes the intentionality of consciousness. (Unfairly excerpted from the glossary in John Perry and Michael Bratman (eds.), *Introduction to Philosophy: Classical and Contemporary Readings,* 862)

45 *Commotrix.* A maid that makes ready and unready her mistress. (Henry Cockeram, *The English Dictionarie,* 1623)

46 *Shrew.* A kind of Field Mouse, which if he ever goes over a beast's back, will make him lame in the shin; and if he bite, the beast swells to the heart, and dies. (Thomas Blount, *Glossographia,* 1630s)

☞47 *Masturbate.* To practise self-abuse. (*Concise Oxford English Dictionary,* 1959)

48 *Murder.* The unlawful killing of a human being with malice afore-thought. (*Concise Oxford English Dictionary,* 1959)

Part Three

Truth

$\frac{6}{e}$

Acceptability Conditions

Truth and Acceptability • A Few Preliminaries
Acceptance Criteria • Rejection Criteria

6.1 Truth and Acceptability

Generally speaking, critical thinkers want to believe propositions that are true rather than those that are false. We say "generally speaking" because there may be exceptions to this rule. If a placebo works only as long as we're deluded into thinking it has medicinal properties, perhaps it is better to falsely believe that the placebo has medicinal properties. Likewise in sports. It is often reported that confidence in one's abilities (within limits) must precede the ability itself.

But even for the general case, the adage "believe true beliefs, not false beliefs" cannot get us far. Consider the distinction between "a belief that is true" and "a belief that is likely true." Holding a belief that is likely true is not done on the basis of its being known to be true. (If it were, we wouldn't insert the adjective "likely.") If we were to hold *only* true beliefs, we would have to abandon all beliefs that we don't know for sure to be true. Since most (some say all) of our beliefs fall short of the indubitability that Descartes, for example, demanded, those who follow the adage "hold only true beliefs" hold very few beliefs indeed. This is wildly impractical, if not downright unreasonable. We want a more forgiving adage, one that will allow us to *accept* beliefs that are more probable than not. We want to hold beliefs more likely true than false.

Of course, this supposes we understand what truth is.

Jesus was on this earth to bear witness to the truth. At least that is what we are told Jesus told Pontius Pilate (John 18: 36). Pilate did not ask the accused, "What is that truth?" He asked, instead, "What is Truth?" (John 18: 37). The first question is a practical question concerning facts about the world in which we live. The second concerns the concept of truth itself.

The conceptual puzzle about truth concerns the relation between truth and knowledge. Is something true because we know it, or do we know it only when it is true? Consider, for example, the number of calories in a serving of pork. Whatever that number is, it will remain the same whether anyone knows it or not. If people say at a particular time that there are forty-three calories in a serving, and then later recant, and say "No sorry, fifty-six," we do not say "There *were* forty-three calories in that pork, but *now* there are fifty-six." We say, "We *thought* there were forty-three, but we were wrong. There are really fifty-six." Similarly, we say people *thought* the world was flat (even though at the time they would have said they *knew* the world was flat), but that they were mistaken. Given these sorts of reflection, it seems sensible to say that our knowledge depends on what's true, and not the other way around. In fact, a common definition of knowing something is to have a justified *true* belief. That is, our concept of truth must be independent of our beliefs, of our knowledge. But how can a concept of truth be so divorced from what we can know? What is the point of a concept of truth that remains forever disassociated from what we may know? How would we ever *come to know* things as true if truth has no bearing on how we come to know things? We can certainly never say that something is true if we don't know it to be so. As a result, some schools of thought have it that truth *must* be dependent on what we happen to *take as true*.

We are in a quandary. If we define knowing in connection to our concept of truth, and truth in connection to our concept of knowing, we are no further ahead. But if we separate truth from what we know or can know, the concept of truth hovers in some inaccessible metaphysical void. Neither view seems palatable. What are we to do? Well, our focus in this chapter is on the question Pilate *might* have asked, not the one he *did* ask (according to John).

We can avoid the debate at the conceptual level by recognizing the simple fact that it may well be in our interest to accept some claims and reject other claims on grounds that remain independent of our knowledge about the truth of those claims. That is to say, our admitting being puzzled by the concept of truth need not interfere with the *practical* issue at hand: whether a given claim is *acceptable* to us or not.

Sometimes our concern is not merely that we don't *know* whether a given claim is true, but that we know a given claim can *only* be spoken of as plausible or not. Take, for example, *conditionals*. Conditional propositions take the form "If ..., then ..." For example, imagine that someone utters the following conditional

If Jones had evaded the tackle, he would have made a touchdown.

The fact is that Jones did not evade the tackle. So how can we know whether he *would* have run for a touchdown had he avoided the tackle? We can appraise the claim as plausible, or possible, or improbable, or impossible, but to say of the claim that it is "True," or "False" seems to misspeak. Consider the following claim:

The extinction of the dinosaurs was caused by a large meteor striking the earth.

"Is this true?" and "Is this plausible?" are two very distinct questions. Answering the first may be beyond our abilities, but answering the second will prove much easier. It is only the second question that need concern us. The first question we will leave to others.

6.2 A Few Preliminaries

6.2.1 Vagueness, Ambiguity, and Obscurity

Recall, from chapter 5, that if a premise is vague, ambiguous, or obscure, we haven't enough information to judge whether it is acceptable. We cannot know what sort of evidence will establish its plausibility, or worse, what sort of evidence will count against it. A premise that is vague is similar to a definition that is too broad. We don't quite want to accept a claim if it includes components that we would want to reject. For example, if Liam rejects the claim that pornography should be banned, he likely doesn't wish to be met with "What?! You think child pornography is acceptable?" Liam's definition of pornography may well exclude child pornography. He might retort, in fact, that the mere naming of that insidious practice with the compound name, "child pornography," is evidence that the meaning of pornography by itself does not necessitate the use of children.

Premises that are ambiguous, recall, will give rise to two or more distinct claims. My accepting one needn't commit me to accepting the other, but if I am unclear which one the author intended, I can rightly resist accepting it. "Only men are rational" may be rejected on the grounds that some animals are also rational, but perhaps more problematic is the possibility that the speaker may be sexist. Perhaps he really intends us to accept the antiquated notion that women cannot be rational. Clearly we wouldn't want to align ourselves with him by frivolously accepting such an ambiguous proposition.

This acts as a reminder. If we cannot clearly understand the meaning of a claim, we cannot properly accept it. But assuming that we can understand the meaning of a claim, we can avail ourselves of a few criteria to help us decide whether we should accept or reject a given premise.

6.2.2 Acceptable to Whom?

In a good argument, the premises need to be acceptable. But acceptable to whom? Should they be acceptable to an omniscient observer? That would be nice, but difficult to ascertain. Should they be acceptable to the scientific community? It would be a good idea to accept premises that the scientific community would accept, but that doesn't exhaust the sort of premises we might also want to accept. In the end, the only persons that matter are ourselves. We're the ones judging whether or not we should be convinced.

Our acceptance of *others'* premises is what matters to us. When we are presenting an argument to someone else, however, our mere acceptance of the premises is not enough. In pitching our arguments to others, our task will not be to provide premises we alone would accept. This would not work in our favour. Recall, our goal is to convince our audience of something they do not already accept. To provide premises that we *alone* accept will clearly fail to do this job. Knowing who our audience is will certainly help in determining what premises to provide. If we are preaching to Catholics, we are free to provide Catholic premises. These same premises may be inappropriate to non-Catholic audiences, though, and if they, too, are members of our audience, a failure ensues.

In order for premises to be geared to our audience, it is important to know who our audience is. This is easy if we are physically in front of our audience, or are presenting an argument in a letter to someone we know. Essays, articles, reports, letters to the editors, however, are different. Our audience is both anonymous and diverse. To write well, we need to have a specific audience in mind, and our premises should be geared to them. Who we pick as our audience will greatly impact the merit of our argument. If we pick an audience member that shares all our beliefs, we will fail to convince those who do not, plus bore members who already believe what we think. We have wasted everyone's time. Good writers and arguers have a skill apart from grammar and syntax; they can also correctly identify the appropriate audience.

How can we gain this skill ourselves? Recall that the purpose of argumentation is to convince people of something they don't already believe. This helps us identify our audience. Our audience should be someone who will not be convinced by our uttering the conclusion alone. Thus, we will need to find premises she will accept and which lead to the conclusion. Consider, most argument positions take sides. Whatever side we're on, we should address our argument to reasonable agents who endorse the other side. This will force us to find good, solid premises that reasonable agents should accept.

Of course, telling someone how to assess the adequacy of premises in general is peculiar, since much relies on what we know. We may know how to assess premises that lie within our limited experience. How do we assess claims that lie beyond our experience, though? Should we simply ask "Why?" for every premise we confront? After all, isn't it up to the arguer to back up his claims with further premises until some of these premises are familiar to us? But this is impossible when we're reading arguments, or listening to arguments from the media. Moreover, it is a good way to lose friends.

Although it is important to ask "What does it mean?" and "Why should I believe it?" we should not assume we should ask those questions all the time. At some point, statements must be acceptable without further support. We simply don't have enough time or stamina to research every bit of information. For reasons of economy, we often accept as true many sorts of claims that we have not researched ourselves. Surely this strategy makes sense. If we tried to research everything, we wouldn't have the time to do anything else.

But our sources may be wrong. So what should we do? There are two things. We must accept that our knowledge claims are fallible. This will help us keep an open mind, plus tolerate false beliefs over indecision. An open mind may also make us more tolerant of others' ideas. A danger exists, however. One may have too open a mind. Persons willing to accept *every* claim that comes their way are not tolerant: they're wishy-washy or indiscriminate. So, we need some criteria to distinguish good from bad premises. What follows are some guidelines for when to accept premises. Later, we shall explore when *not* to accept premises.

6.2.3 Common Knowledge

Should we accept a claim that is common knowledge? It seems foolish to say "No," but let's take a closer look.

What do we mean by "common knowledge"? If it is really "knowledge," then we have grounds to accept it. To know something entails that it is true. Knowledge is justified true belief. If it weren't a true belief, we couldn't properly be said to "know" it. So if we treat "knowledge" in "common knowledge" literally, the answer to our question will be "Yes." Unfortunately, the knowledge in "common knowledge" is metaphorical at best. What is meant by "common knowledge" is simply, here is a belief that is commonly held.

We know beliefs commonly held that turned out to be false. It was commonly held that the earth was flat, that the sun revolved around the earth, that women shouldn't be allowed to vote or enter prestige careers. On the other hand, a commonly held belief is more likely true than false. Although we admit errors, can't we generally do well by accepting common beliefs? Quite likely, but there are further worries.

Basically, if a premise is very widely accepted, *and* there is no known evidence against it, it is often appropriate to allow it as acceptable. Notice, however, we are not accepting it *because* it is commonly held. As our mothers may have reminded us, we would not jump off a cliff (without water below, bungee cords attached to our feet, a parachute or a hang glider, etc.) merely because others were. It is quite possible that a premise we find acceptable because it matches common knowledge may in fact be false.

For example, not long ago, people accepted it as common knowledge that the world was flat. But if we have no good grounds ourselves to think that which is common knowledge is false, we are justified in accepting it. To think otherwise is to soon lose friends.

If a belief is deemed "common knowledge," then there must exist independent grounds to believe it as true other than the mere fact that others – commoners like us – believe it. It can't be the case that each member of the common group believes it on the basis of the group's believing it – for how could the first or subsequent members ever come to believe it by such means? This suggests there are independent grounds for believing "common knowledge" to be true.

Common knowledge is not knowledge based on authority. Authoritative knowledge is not based on the reasoning of commoners. But common knowledge is. So, although many acceptable beliefs will be common knowledge, the mere fact that they're common knowledge cannot be the *reason* for you to accept them.

Let's take an example. It is common knowledge that it snows in Winnipeg. Do we believe this *because* it's common knowledge? Or can we appeal to our experience with snow in Canadian climates?

A further problem with common knowledge is that it is too vague. How do we know what is "common"? What constitutes "commonly held"? A number of local people believe it? A majority of local people believe it? A majority of people in general, wherever they live, hold it? Or is it simply one's group that holds it, one's friends, or peers, or those in power? Who decides that a belief is commonly held? Are surveys done, or are these appraisals merely anecdotal? A majority of people may find curling boring. Should that outweigh what curlers think? The curlers may be biased, but the non-curlers may be uninformed. Does the concept of common knowledge preclude the prospect that the specific commoners are either biased or uninformed? A worry connected to defining our groups leads into the problems of racism, sexism, and any other of the countless forms of prejudice.

6.3 Acceptance Criteria

What follows are five criteria which, if met, give us reason to accept an understandable premise. They involve *Textual Support, A Priori Truths, Perceptual Evidence, Adequate Testimony,* and *Proper Authority.*

6.3.1 Textual Support

Textual support refers to the support of stated premises in writing. This support may occur either elsewhere in the argument itself, or it may be cited. If it is cited, it may be the author's own argument, or someone else's argument.

i. Cogent Sub-Arguments. If a premise is not acceptable to us, we have no reason to accept the conclusion. Before we dismiss the argument on that basis, however, we should check to see if the argument provides some reason to accept the presently unacceptable premise. It would be bad form to look no further in an argument to see if the premise is in fact defended elsewhere.

ii. Premises Defended Elsewhere. We often can't write or say everything we want. The attention span of our audience, as teachers in particular are well aware, is limited. So it is often a permissible strategy to merely refer the interested reader to arguments we or someone else have given for the acceptability of the otherwise questionable premise. In such a case, the audience may elect to *conditionally* accept the questionable premise, and move on with assessing the rest of the argument. If the argument is sufficiently important to them, and every other part of the stated argument seems sound, they'll know where to go to assess the acceptability of the questionable premise.

6.3.2 A Priori True

Claims that are known to be *a priori* true are those known to be true by logical relations or by definition. The truth of the claim is known independently of experience. That is to say, we needn't go out into the world to discover whether it is so or not. What is true follows from the relation of ideas, and not from distinguishing whether any objects satisfy the extensional set (to use language learned in chapter 5).

For example, given the definition of "a bachelor," and the truth of the claim that Chris is a bachelor, we know it to be true, without knowing anything else about Chris, that he is an adult unmarried male. Likewise, although you don't (presumably) know the colour of your professor's car, you do know that either it is green or it isn't green; whatever colour it is, it can't be both green and not green at the same time in the same respects. It may be partly green and partly some other colour, of course, but even then it is true that the car is green. We aren't saying the car is *entirely* green, necessarily. Nor is it likely we would say of any car that it is *entirely* one colour (except maybe cars belonging to the middle order of Mennonites who paint even the hubcaps black).

We can also deduce by *a priori* means that if he gave her the book, she did not steal it. We can make such a grand claim because we know that the definition of stealing entails the transaction of property without permission, while the definition of "giving" is a transaction of property *with* permission.

In contrast to *a priori* truths are *a posteriori* truths. These are claims we know to be true by experience. That is to say, we must go out into the real world to see whether the claim is so or not so. For example, to discover whether Chris really is a bachelor, we have to do more than look up the meaning of "bachelor" in the dictionary. To know whether your professor's car is green, you have to do more than understand the inadmissibility of contradictions. Likewise, to discover whether he in fact gave her the book, you have to do something more than understand the meaning of "stealing."

You can see that most of our knowledge comes to us by *a posteriori* means. Consider

Abortion involves the premature termination of pregnancy.

Should we accept this claim on *a priori* grounds? It might depend on what we mean by "premature." One interpretation is simply "not full term." As such, the claim appears to be merely part of the definition of abortion. As put, it is too broad. Miscarriage is not an abortion, yet would satisfy the definition. For that matter, premature delivery is also a termination of a pregnancy, but not a case of abortion.

Alternatively, "premature" is a matter of individual judgment. What is premature for one, may be overdue for another. A woman might terminate a pregnancy by abortion and not consider it "premature" at all. In fact, she may have had to wait longer than she would have preferred.

6.3.3 Sensory Evidence

Normally, when we see a shooting star, others needn't demand proof of this *other* than the fact that we saw it. Appeals to sensory data therefore constitute good grounds for accepting a claim. If I say, "It is raining," you may look outside and see rain. Your sensory evidence supports your accepting my claim. Perhaps you cannot see outside for one reason or another, but you can hear the rain on the roof, or on the road, or hear the drone of wet car tires on wet roads. Your sensory evidence supports the claim. Perhaps you cannot see outside, or hear outside, yet you witness people coming inside with wet umbrellas. Sensory evidence constitutes good reason to accept the claim that it is raining.

An epistemological problem may rear its head, however. Can we trust our sensory organs? After all, our sensory organs are not foolproof. We've mistaken people we know for strangers and vice versa. Mirages, dreams, hallucinations, random noises in one's ear, all show that we can be mistaken about our sense observations. Therefore, we need independent evidence to be able to trust our sensory apparatus. But this is a problem, for we have no sources *other* than our senses to use to test the reliability of our senses. One sense can be used to test another sense. "It sounds like rain, but I don't see anything; maybe it's only the wind." But what could test all our sense at once? This is to ask someone to prove that the cup is on the table without using any of the senses. We are apt to think the request is improper. Yet this is the impossible task we face if we wish to confirm the reliability of sense perception.

The impossibility of checking the veracity of our senses can actually help us out of the problem. It seems that we are so constituted that all of our knowledge of the empirical world comes to us through our senses, and so we cannot help but generally trust them. If we are wrong about this, that is something we can never know. Since we can never *know* it, it is not worth worrying about. We will simply call our knowledge of the empirical world that which our senses provide.

We are on firm footing, therefore, in asserting that sensory observation generally provides good grounds for accepting claims. We may be wrong in a more mundane sense, but as long as the probability of our being right is greater than the probability of our being wrong, it is reasonable to believe claims on the basis of sensory evidence. Obviously, the more serious the claim, the more we should double-check our sensory observations. We may do so not merely by checking with our other senses, but also by appealing to the senses of others. My grandmother once asked me whether the wording on a bread bag wavered for me too.

Generally, if a claim is supported by our own sensory evidence, we have reason to accept it. We may be wrong. We do make mistakes, but as long as we are well situated to observe the phenomena, we have reason to accept them as received.

6.3.4 Adequate Testimony

Quite often we accept someone's word for something. If a witness says he saw that it was a blue cab that hit the pedestrian and drove away, we have grounds to believe that a blue cab hit the pedestrian and drove away. People generally tell the truth. To doubt that people generally tell the truth is to abandon the concept of communication itself: a hard sell.

Not every testimony is worth believing, however, and so we need to distinguish times when we should accept someone's testimony from times when we should not. There are two basic factors to consider before taking someone's word: *external factors* and *internal factors*. External factors are those factors that we should pay attention to, but that have nothing to do with the character of the witness herself. They involve the plausibility of the claim, the number and agreement of witnesses, and the position and ability of the witness. These latter obviously affect the witness, but are external to her control. Internal factors concern what the witness herself can control. They involve the reputation of the witness, the manner of presentation, and the degree of interpretation embedded in the claim. Each of these criteria is discussed more fully below.

External Factors

External factors refer to factors that impinge on the accuracy of the testimony that are external to the agent. These include our judgment about the plausibility of the claim itself, the agreement of other witnesses, the position of the witness in relation to the event witnessed, and the perceptual abilities of the witness at the time of the event in question.

i. The Plausibility of the Claim.   The witness claimed the car that hit the pedestrian was a blue taxi cab. If there were no blue cabs in the city, this should count against the testimony.

David Hume, a famous atheist, was confronted with a choice between believing in someone's testimony about a miracle, or believing that the person was deluded in some respects. He deemed it required less adjustment to his understanding of known physics to disbelieve the testimony than to believe it. *When everything else is equal, always choose the lesser miracle.*

> When anyone tells me that he saw a dead man restored to life, I immediately consider with myself whether it be more probable that this person would either deceive or be deceived, or that the fact, which he relates, should really have happened. I weigh the one miracle against the other ... and always reject the greater miracle. (David Hume: *Of Miracles*)

Likewise, we might find it easier to believe someone was deluded than that she really saw a flying saucer. Although it is more than probable that life exists elsewhere, it is less probable that these other life forms have machines that could travel vast distances through the universe, and even less probable that such life forms would travel to this remote, uninteresting corner of the universe.

In either case, we need not doubt the *sincerity* of the witness. The people who saw Jesus's face on a Tim Horton's wall in Sydney, Cape Breton, were sincere and moved by the experience. Still, the plausibility of the claim seemed so remote we felt impelled to search for an alternative account. In this case a splattered moth on the light bulb was the more plausible explanation. (Or did the visage depart after the skeptics contaminated the sacred ground when they changed the light bulb?)

Problems with Probability

Distinguishing the plausibility of a claim may sometimes require familiarity with probability theory. Consider the following incident:

The Taxi Cab Incident
A hit and run accident occurred late last night. A witness, standing nearby, reported that it was a taxi cab that caused the accident and then fled the scene. When asked which of the two cab companies (blue and green) the taxi was from, the witness reported that it was a blue taxi. 15 per cent of the city

taxi cabs are blue; 85 per cent are green. The witness was tested under night conditions and correctly distinguished blue from green 80 per cent of the time.

Question:

Should we accept the witnesses's testimony, assuming there is no reason to doubt his reputation? In other words, what is the probability that the cab is in fact blue? (Answer is provided at the end of section 6.3.)

A: 85–100%   C: 50–69%

B: 70–84%   D: Below 50%

ii. Number and Agreement of Witnesses.   If the witness's testimony is contradicted by other witnesses equally situated, this should count against the claim. If a variety of witnesses each report similar or compatible claims, this should count in favour of the claim.

iii. Position and Ability.   The *perceptual abilities* of the witness also matter. Is she blind, or colour blind, or hard of hearing? Ability is a relative concept, of course. Someone may be too weak to lift two hundred pounds, but strong enough to lift fifty pounds. Likewise, someone who's colour blind might have a hard time distinguishing red from green, but may have no problem distinguishing yellow from beige. Being hard of hearing does not necessarily rule out the ability to hear screams.

Even if the witness is not colour blind, has 20–20 vision and perfect hearing, other factors may impinge on her abilities as a witness. Was she standing too far away? Was it at night? Was the sun in her eyes? Were other noises occurring that may have affected her proper hearing? What else was happening in the vicinity that might have distracted her? These factors impinge on our assessment of the testimony.

Absent any evidence to the contrary, we shall assume witnesses were in good position and were sufficiently able to properly observe the event. Our trusting the witness' perceptual abilities is the *default* position.

Internal Factors

Internal factors are conditions owing to the witness herself that undermine or support the believability of the testimony. They include the reputation of the witness or source, manner of presentation, and the degree of interpretation embedded in the testimony.

i. Reputation   Generally speaking, if the person who claims to have seen the flying saucer is a known drunk, or drug addict, or suffers from hallucinations or paranoid delusions, these would be reasons to doubt the testimony. Likewise, if the testifier was known to lie and cheat, we should be more reluctant to take him at his word. Even though the boy who cries wolf speaks the truth on the *third* time, we are not unreasonable to disbelieve him.

Of course, any witnesses *might* have lied. Notice the weight of the weasel word "might" here. Everyone *might* lie and if the force of this might is sufficient to cast doubt on one witness, it is sufficient to cast doubt on *all* witnesses. We would be unable to reasonably rely on testimony at all. This result seems worse than permitting the prospect of being led astray periodically by witnesses. Absent any evidence to the contrary, we shall assume witnesses are reputable. Trusting witnesses is the *default* position, just as one is innocent until proven guilty in courts of law.

Conversely, our rejecting a witness's testimony on the basis that she was drunk risks our discounting a true report. A drunkard's report that "A cat meowed," for example, shouldn't be dismissed merely on the grounds that the witness was drunk. The more improbable the putatively witnessed event and the poorer the reputation of the witness, the more reason we have to doubt the testimony.

The believability of testimony when given through the media will depend on the reputation of the media source. A report in the *National Enguirer* should be less convincing than the same report in the *Globe and Mail.*

ii. Manner of Presentation   Testimony may be delivered hesitantly or with great bravado. Eye contact may be made, or it may be avoided. Nervous hand movements may occur or they may not. These gestures and mannerisms act as cues concerning the witness' conviction. If the witness herself is less assured about her testimony, we have more reason to doubt it ourselves.

Admittedly, psychological differences among people weaken this criterion. Some people are inordinately shy. Others are excessively bold. A shy witness may state even what she is absolutely convinced of more hesitantly than an extroverted witness uttering a claim about which he's uncertain. Good poker players, for example, are adept at hiding their own insecurities. So this criterion needs to be treated delicately.

Ideally, we need a base-rate measure with which to compare. A shy person may still fluctuate in her presentation between claims she is assured about and claims she is less assured about. Likewise with those who utter all claims with the utmost degree of conviction: we can predict some slight variation. Still, as a general rule of thumb, paying attention to the manner of presentation itself can act as a cue to the degree with which we should accept, doubt, or reject testimony.

iii. Report, Not Interpretation   The more an interpretation is given, the less reason we have to accept the testimony. The more it is a description, the more reason we have to accept the testimony. The idea here is if we're to accept a claim, we're accepting the whole package, that is, every component of that claim. But the more interpretation, the more we're being asked to accept the speaker's subjective slant. Although we may accept the bare facts, we may have reasons to doubt the interpretation of those facts. For example, compare the following two versions of what we shall assume to be the same event:

The car deliberately swerved toward the pedestrian, ran over him in cold blood, and then escaped the scene of the accident.	The car unfortunately lurched out of control and could not stop in time before hitting the pedestrian. It appeared that the driver at any rate prevented the car from hitting a child that was also near by. He must have driven off in an anguished panic due to shock.

We are adept enough readers now to detect the emotive flavour in each. The emotive flavouring is being used to emphasize the *interpretation* of the report. If we were asked to single out what is common between the two testaments, we would get something like the following:

The car hit the pedestrian, and then drove off.

It is this last testimony we wish to call the report. The first two involve too much interpretation for us to accept at face value. The more the testament is a report the more acceptable it should be, assuming it passes the other criteria.

Compare the following reports of a subjective experience:

I had a mystical experience. Everything turned white, and quiet, and I felt that I was the ocean and the ocean was me.	I had a mystical experience. I understood the nature of the universe and communed with God.

Should we view these as different *interpretations* of the same event, or different reports of different events? Admittedly, this is a contentious issue. Part of our debate may be precisely about whether the two experiences were in fact the same. On the other hand, how can we know? Should we treat all subjective avowals as reports? That would seem a bit too lax. For those who wish to treat these as reports of different events, and not two interpretations of identical events, there is an underlying assumption that needs to be aired. One might claim that they can't possibly be the same experience, since otherwise we would expect the same interpretation. The assumption here is that same events cannot possibly have different interpretations, or at least that same subjective events cannot possibly have different interpretations. We know this assumption is false in other cases, so we have no reason to believe it is true when dealing with subjective experiences. If anything, we have more reason to doubt it.

In any event, the more we can detect interpretation in a witness, the less reason we have to accept him at his word. The less interpretation is presented, the more plausible the testimony should appear. When police detectives interrupt babbling witnesses with the comment, "Nothing but the facts, Ma'am," this is the criterion they're employing.

Sense-data?

One worry is worth noting. Some have claimed that everything we experience is inevitably an interpretation, and not a report. If we're walking in the woods we might casually remark that we've just heard a bird. For the more discriminate, we might say we heard a robin. But did we really hear a robin, or did we instead hear a "tweet tweet" and from that datum of noise triggering various receptors in our auditory canals infer, or interpret "Bird"?

Even if we see a bird, we're not off the hook. The same applies. Do we really see a bird? Or do we instead, see redness and brownness and somewhat of an oval shape with a slightly feathery texture? From the various bits of sense data received, we construct or interpret "Bird." Sensation may be similar to dreaming. By some theories, we do not dream in sequence, but have simply a pandemonium of imagery that confronts the brain. In waking, the brain, resistant to chaos, arranges the imagery into a random linear pattern, and that's what we "see." Perhaps it is the same with perception of "reality." Perhaps all perception of "facts" and "events" and "objects" is merely an arbitrary interpretation imposed on us in the reconstruction of sensory imagery in our brains, and not a report.

No doubt this takes things too far. Even if such sense-data talk were true, we can still distinguish the sort of bare interpretation of "That's a bird," from the more elaborate interpretation in "That's a full-throated thrasher giving out its danger alarm call," or "That bird's jeering at me."

Right interpretations?

One last point on this discussion of interpretation is warranted. Some interpretations may be right. Perhaps the driver did run over the pedestrian intentionally. That interpretation occurs doesn't mean that it can't be backed up. Nothing is more frustrating than, after having carefully laid out our argument, receiving the repy "Well, that's your interpretation," as if that defeats all argumentation.

Bias and interpretation are inevitable, as we've already admitted in chapter 4. But we needn't imagine interpretation or bias is to be understood as an all-or-nothing matter. There are degrees of interpretation, and our message here is to try to reduce that degree in giving testimony, and to beware of excessive degrees of interpretation in others' testimony.

6.3.5 Proper Authority

Most of our knowledge comes to us second-hand. We have neither the expertise, nor the time, nor the stamina, nor even the motive to check all reports firsthand. We rely very much on the testimony of experts. As long as they are experts, it is expedient to defer our judgements to them.

People can manipulate our gullibility on this score, however. When people are referred to as authorities in fields that have no relevance to the particular argument, we ought to be prepared to call their bluff.

If Dr. Q says "X," and Dr. Q is a recognized authority on X, we have good grounds to accept X ourselves. It is also fortuitous that there are experts out there. If we had to personally verify the plausibility of every claim before we accept it, we simply wouldn't have time to get on with our lives. We all have more important things to do, surely, and if we can rely on the experts, this is clearly a time-saver for us. Besides, given that they're the experts and not us, it would be more prudent to believe them than to rely on our understanding anyway.

Still, we should be wary not to be duped by faulty "appeals to authority." To arm ourselves against such chicanery, there are three factors we should take into account before we appeal to authority:

(i)   Within field – Dr. Q is an authority *on X*
(ii) Agreement – other authorities on X do not disagree with Dr. Q about X
(iii) Recognizable field – X admits authorities

i. Within Field   Concerning the first restriction, however authoritative Dr. Q may be on X, this doesn't mean he is also an authority on Y. Accepting Dr. Q's testimony on a province outside his field of expertise simply because he is an expert in *some* field is a poor reason to accept Dr. Q's claims. Advertisements are rife with people in lab coats telling us about our hygiene or hair colour. The implicit message is that these people are authorities. But notice that they often don't tell you what they're an authority *on*. A podiatrist is really not an authority on headache tablets. Nor is a sports personality an authority on shampoos.

Sometimes the boundaries of the area of expertise are difficult to determine. For example, we know that a doctor knows how to perform an abortion. If she says, "abortions are morally wrong," should her testimony have greater weight than a housewife's? No. A medical degree cannot grant this woman a licence in ethical decision-making, however much she may pretend it does.

Sometimes, detecting the "within field problem" requires extra care. Consider the following letter to the editor, from the *Arizona Republic* of 3 June 1987:

The solution to teen-age pregnancy depends on related segments of society: family, church, schools, government, economy. In focussing on the "too-soon parent," we must not abandon her "too-soon child" to the quick fix of abortion.
William V. Dolan, MD

Can you see how we might complain about a faulty appeal to authority here?

Answer: The problem is the two initials after the writer's name. That he is a medical doctor may have the effect of giving his words more weight. But such an inference would be a faulty appeal to authority, for though Dr. Dolan may be an authority on *how* to give an abortion (although we can't even be sure of this), he is not an authority on the social ills of abortion, let alone the social solution to abortion.

ii. Agreement   The second condition is too often overlooked. Accepting a premise on the basis of Scientist Q's avowal won't be sufficient if other scientists within Q's field disagree with Q. Appeals to authority in such cases will yield conflicting claims (You cite Q, but I cite V). Such disputes can't be settled by merely telling us what Q said within her field, since V and W, also experts within the field, disagree with Q.

Often there is disagreement within specialized fields. This is probably the norm, not the exception. How does this fact affect our ability to appeal to authority? As long as the authority we appeal to is at least representative of the majority of experts within that field (and she's speaking about something within her field!), we have good reason to accept the claim.

For a case of disagreement within one's field, consider the following news article:

Ronald Mallett, a theoretical physics professor at the University of Connecticut, thinks he has figured out a more practical way to fulfill the old science-fiction fantasy of time travel – by slowing down light. No one will be going back to witness the War of 1812 any time soon, but Mallett thinks we are at least close to achieving time travel at the atomic level ... Don Page, a professor of physics at the University of Alberta, is skeptical of the whole proposition. He estimated a mass-energy of 100,000 times the sun would be necessary to give a significantly large space-time curvature – a feat that will not be attained in the foreseeable future, he said. "It seems likely to me that one would need an enormous energy for limited energy density to give enough space-time warpage to get anywhere near time travel, and even then we are highly uncertain whether it can be achieved," he said. Many physicists would not even comment on Mallett's theory, dismissing the whole notion of time travel as fantasy. "I should say that the idea of time travel is certainly not accepted by the community of theoretical physicists working on the problems of space and time – at least, not among the ones I talk to," said one California-based theoretical physicist who asked not to be named. (Jason Chow, "Slowing down time travel," *National Post*, 8 August 2001, A12)

Failing to appreciate the criterion concerning agreement within the field is the cause of many a poor student research paper. Finding one published author supporting X should not end our research. Keep digging. Perhaps others in the field have refuted that author's position. Merely getting something in print does not sanctify the utterance.

iii. Recognizable Field   There are some fields that really can't boast of any "authority" at all. Citing an "expert psychic" or "noted numerologist" is simply playing with language. The same may legitimately be said about morality. It is doubtful that there exist any "moral" experts. There may be some experts about what moral philosophers have said, but whether that alone makes these individuals moral experts is another matter entirely. Nor do priests have copyright on moral pronouncements. Admittedly, the priest will be an authority on what morality means within a Judeo-Christian framework, but whether we should accept that framework for our moral decision-making is not settled by appealing to the authority of a priest, let alone the Pope. The field of morality *contains*, is not *contained by*, the Judeo-Christian framework, just as it contains utilitarian, Kantian, virtue-theory, feminist, relativist, emotivist, and contractarian frameworks, among others.

6.3.6 Accepting Premises Provisionally

Sometimes we just can't decide whether a given premise should be accepted or not. Then what? One good option is to accept the premise(s) provisionally. This means we simply move on to examine the other premises, and/or the grounds conditions.

If we accept a premise provisionally, and all the other conditions of the argument satisfy the conditions of grounds and acceptability, we are not entitled to accept the argument as cogent. Instead, we must recognize that we have merely accepted the argument as a whole under the condition that our *provisionally* accepted premise really is acceptable (i.e., IF the premise is acceptable, then the argument is cogent).

Until we know whether we should or should not accept the premise, we must grant only provisional acceptance of the argument (as long as the other conditions are met, otherwise we can reject the argument, notwithstanding the status of the provisionally accepted premise).

Answer to the Taxi Cab Problem:
The answer is D: Less than 50 per cent. Why? We have independent grounds for rejecting the plausibility of the witness's claim. It is still more probable that the cab was green. Basically this can be seen by recognizing that the witness's night vision accuracy (80 per cent) is less than the base-rate probability that the cab is green (85 per cent).

Formula:
(prob.blue)(prob.right) / (prob.blue)(prob.right) + (prob.green)(prob.wrong)*
= (.15)(.8) / (.15)(.8) + (.85)(.2)
= .12 / (.12 + .17)
= .12/.29
= 0.41

Most people overemphasize the witness's identification and underemphasize the base rate, or prior probability, that the cab is blue.

Many studies have shown that people emphasize anecdotal accounts over statistical probabilities. Nevertheless, scientific theories rely on statistical or probabilistic reasoning. This is partly why scientific claims are ripe for misapplication in the everyday world. (For a fuller account of probability, see 11.3.)

Exercise 6.1 A

For each of the following claims, state why you think it is acceptable. (Answers to selected questions provided in Appendix 1.)

    1 Every living creature has some kind of reproductive system.
☞ 2 Having a previous life would require surviving as a soul during the time interval between the several different bodily existences.
    3 Fishing is an important industry in Atlantic Canada.
    4 As the impoverished father of three sons, I can say that it is hard not to buy expensive sports equipment for children when there are a lot of pressures for such purchases from schools. (Govier, *A Practical Study of Argument*, 144)
☞ 5 As a professional therapist, I would say that a primary cause of divorce today is problems with money. (Ibid.)
    6 Either God exists or He doesn't.
    7 Every pentagon has five straight sides.
    8 Everyone is a relative of someone who has died.
☞ 9 As indicated by S. Omura (*Chinese Painters*), the emperor Hui Tsung was himself a painter and a great collector.
  10 According to Beth, Joe's sister, Joe has smoked since he was fourteen. Therefore he'll probably get cancer.

Exercise 6.1 B

Do the following discussions appeal mainly to testimony, or authority? Is there a good case for accepting or rejecting these appeals? If not, which criterion (or criteria) is violated?

---

* This formula concerns Bayesian inference for conditional probability.

1 Although other veterinarians have resisted Dr. Hamill's finding, the veterinarian, Dr. Rudolph Hamill, argues that animals are not merely able to feel pain, they can suffer psychological distress as well from being cooped up in barns or pens or stalls.

2 According to Dr. Rizzaro, a leading physicist, meat-eating dulls one's intellectual capabilities.

☞ 3 Wally claimed to have seen a cat without a tail. This confirms Ben's story that he saw two teenagers chop off a stray cat's tail.

☞ 4 Look, she claimed the accused maliciously and gleefully drove the nail into the victim's hand and she was standing right there. That clearly is all the jury needs to hear to convict the accused.

☞ 5 Jean Chrétien will back the fledgling campaign to expunge the "sons" from *O Canada*, says the wife of one of the Prime Minister's closest advisors. "The Prime Minister has a daughter, a granddaughter and of course a very loving wife and I am sure he would want to include them in the national anthem," Jeanne d'Arc Sharp said yesterday. Her husband, Mitchell Sharp, is a close advisor of Jean Chrétien. "My husband is very supportive. The Prime Minister has not been briefed on this issue but if we need to, we will meet him and I know that we are going to be well received." (Mohammed Adam, "PM will want to delete 'sons' from anthem," *National Post*, 31 July 2001, A7)

☞ 6 Donald Zenert was viciously gored by a 300-pound buck deer but he survived with only his wits and a penknife by grabbing the animal's antlers and holding on for a wild 90-minute ride. The 33-year-old construction worker was attacked this past February 4 while video-taping deer in Alberta, Canada. *(National Enquirer, 3 July 1990)*

7 During the World Series of Golf in 1995, [Greg] Norman accused [Mark] McCumber of violating a rule that prohibits repairing spike marks or touching the line of your putt. McCumber maintained he was removing a small insect from his line ... "I saw what I saw," said Norman. The tour ruled that it was one player's word against another's with inconclusive proof and didn't take action. (Bob Verdi, *Golf Digest*, April 2002, 218)

8 But can you doubt that air has weight when you have the clear testimony of Aristotle that all the elements have weight including air, and excepting only fire? (Galileo Galilei, *Dialogues Concerning Two New Sciences.*)

9 Rewarding students – at home or in the classroom – is controversial and the effect on academic achievement has been widely debated in academic circles. A number of studies, mainly in the United States, have suggested financial incentives do not motivate children and are a poor substitute for good teaching and parenting. However, a new study by the University of Alberta has contradicted that belief and vindicated what critics would label bribery as a useful teaching tool.

Judy Cameron, professor of educational psychology at the University of Alberta, and her colleague, David Pierce, professor of sociology, found students who are paid for doing well on tests perform better and are more motivated than those who are not given a financial incentive. The study of about 140 university students concluded a nominal payment of $10 encouraged them to excel at problem-solving tests. Students who were paid for succeeding at increasingly difficult tests performed the best and maintained interest even when the rewards were taken away. (Julie Smyth, "When it pays to get good marks," *National Post*, 29 June 2001, A13)

10   Photographs of bacteria found in space could be the most explosive scientific discovery of the age, proving the existence of extraterrestrial life. Or the bacteria could have floated up from Earth. Professor Chandra Wickramasinghe, a renowned astronomer, believes the photographs show two extraterrestrial bugs on the edge of the Earth's atmosphere. The images resemble bacteria found on Earth, but Mr. Wickramasinghe, from the Centre for Astrobiology at Cardiff University in Britain, says that because of the height at which they were found, and their distribution, it strongly indicates they were not swept up in air currents, but fell from space ... If Mr. Wickramasinghe is correct, the pictures show life that originated from somewhere other than Earth. However, other astrobiologists are not so sure. Dr. Bruce Jakosky, director of the Center for Astrobiology at Colorado University, said: "It would be a truly spectacular result, but I'm skeptical. I'm skeptical about the theory. Why can't they have been swept up from Earth?" Dr. Michael Myer, NASA astrobiologist, said he was skeptical for the same reason. "I'm sure that Prof. Wickramasinghe has been working on this and I had heard a rumour about it. I would just say that if bacteria was found in the upper atmosphere, why wouldn't it have come from Earth? If it's been swept up in the atmosphere, then it must have been swept from somewhere and the planet closest with life seems the most likely. This is something presented as an abstract. It would be good to have a thorough review by his peers." (Michael Higgins, "Photos spark debate over space bacteria," *National Post*, 31 July 2001, A2)

6.4 Rejection Criteria

Except for the two conditions of *Testimony* and *Authority*, if premises fail to meet the acceptability conditions, it does not follow that we should reject them. That it snows in Canada is not an *a priori* claim, nor a claim for which textual support is necessarily provided, yet it is not one we wish to reject. If a testimonial fails to meet our four criteria of acceptable testimony, then we can reject the claim. Likewise, if an appeal to authority fails our three conditions for acceptable appeals to authority, then we may reject the appeal. Apart from shoddy testimonials and improper appeals to author-ity, there are seven other criteria we may use to help us recognize when premises should be rejected.

6.4.1 Claim Known a priori to Be False

Just as we can know the truth of some premises by *a priori* means, we can safely and swiftly reject claims that contradict a priori truths. Consider the following claim:

"Everything I say is a lie.

We need not know anything about the person uttering the claim (although we might make some inferences: "Here is a person to avoid asking direc-tions," etc.), to nevertheless tell that the claim has to be false. Let us con-sider that the claim is true, that the speaker always tells a lie. But then the speaker is uttering a truth at least in this case. But then it is false that *every-thing* the speaker says is a lie, for here is one truth. If the claim is itself a lie, then it indicates that not everything the speaker says is a lie. In any case, the claim must be understood to be false.

One cautionary note – we need to recognize that sometimes evident *a priori* impossibilities are not dismissible for that reason. Saying something like, "Although he was a bachelor, he wasn't really a bachelor," seems at face value incoherent. Either he's a bachelor or he isn't, so the utterance as put is *a priori* false. But perhaps something else is meant. Surely the speaker isn't trying to get us to accept an *a priori* falsehood. It is more likely that the speaker is using two different senses of "bachelor." The first is the lexical definition. The second is the emotive connotation of the term; someone who has a variety of sexual partners, or at least someone who accepts no moral strictures on the number of different sexual partners, or something like that. In such a case, the seemingly *a priori* false claim is asserting that although a bachelor, he doesn't act like a bachelor, and this is no longer an *a priori* falsehood.

6.4.2 Internal Inconsistency

Another way to reject premises is to see if two or more premises clash. If they do, we have reason to reject at least one of them. We may not be sure *which* one to reject, but as long as the argument requires both, we have all the evidence we need to reject the argument. Consider the following argument:

Although we as a society should tolerate homosexuals, I'm against their being allowed to adopt children, since the children may themselves become homo-sexuals when they're older.

Perhaps you can see the inconsistency right away, but if not, compare the following similarly structured argument:

> Although I believe it's morally permissible to be a philosopher, I'm against their being able to adopt children, since the children may themselves grow up to be philosophers.

The inconsistency lies in holding both of the following claims:

(1) allowing an *X*
(2) disallowing something's becoming an *X*

If we allow an *X*, we shouldn't mind something's becoming an *X*. Likewise, if we disallow something's becoming an *X*, then this must be on the basis that we do not allow *X*s.

Consider this condensed version of St. Thomas Aquinas's famous *Cosmological Argument* for the existence of God:

1 Everything has a cause.
2 But we can't trace this causal chain back to infinity (since otherwise there would be no initial cause to get the whole chain started, but the chain did start, obviously).
3 So there must be a first cause.
4 We call that first cause "God."

What do you think of the argument? If it is problematic, where would you indicate the problem lies? Bertrand Russell objects in the following way:

> But, if everything has a cause (from premise 1), then it can't be the case that there will ever be a first cause (inconsistent with premise 3). Conversely, if something does not have a cause (from premise 2), then it is false that every-thing must have a cause (denies premise 1).

Even if we are unsure which premise to reject (though 2 may be rejected for independent reasons), we still have a reason to reject at least one of them. Because of this internal inconsistency the argument fails to be convincing.

By the way, our rejection of the cosmological argument as stated does not entitle us to now claim that God does not exist. Recall (from chapter 1) that to object to an argument is not necessarily to dismiss its conclusion. There may be other arguments for the same conclusion, and one of them may be cogent. Of course, if no known argument is cogent for a particular claim, and we are aware of a number (and have accurately represented them) we may at that point reasonably decide the conclusion is false.

The fact that one argument fails to support a conclusion does not guarantee that there are *no* cogent arguments for the conclusion. Bad arguments are non-partisan. They are not something used only by our opponents. On the other hand, neither is it the case that the existence of bad arguments for a specific claim guarantees that there exist good arguments. Bad arguments greatly outnumber good arguments. At some point we should be entitled to recognize this. On the basis that, among many arguments presented for *X*, none of them succeed in establishing *X*, we may reasonably conclude *X* is false. After all, that may be the best explanation for why we have failed to support *X*.

In summary, if there are inconsistencies in the premises, they cannot all be acceptable. So merely pointing out an inconsistency is sufficient to say the premises are unacceptable – even if we do not know which is the unacceptable one!

6.4.3 Non-Falsifiability

We may also reject claims when they are *non-falsifiable*. Something that is non-falsifiable cannot be falsified in principle. It may seem odd to introduce non-falsifiability as a criterion of acceptability. If we don't know what would count against a claim, some might infer that the claim should then be accepted. This is not so. A claim should be *falsifiable*: that is, we ought to be able to know what would count against it, *at least in theory*. Failing this condition would make the claim non-falsifiable. Why would this be a bad thing?

Suppose A goes to the doctor about a rash on her hand. The doctor claims that the rash is caused by stress. As put, the claim that A's rash is caused by stress does not sound vague all by itself, but imagine how A can respond. She can say, "Yes, I am under stress." Or she can say, "No, I'm not under any stress." The first reply would certainly not show the doctor's stress theory to be false. What about the second? "Ah," the doctor might say, "that proves my point. It is because you are in denial about your stress, you are suppressing it deep within your psyche, and that in turn is causing the manifestation of stress in the form of your rash," or any similar Freudian reply. The problem is, if *that's* the explanation, admitting one was under stress should count against the theory; but alas, it never does. The problem here is that both of A's replies work in favour of the claim. There is nothing even in principle that can count against the claim. This violates the falsifiability condition, and, as a result, gives us a reason to reject the claim.

Note that sometimes we can't imagine a premise being false. A *priori* premises, for example, such as "A bachelor is an unmarried adult male," or *a posteriori* claims that seem absolutely uncontroversial, such as "It snows in parts of Canada during part of the year," are statements which we can't conceive of as false.

But not imagining the claim to be false is different from not allowing the possibility that the claim can be false in principle. We know what would make the bachelor claim to be false, that the definition has changed. Likewise we know what would make the snow claim false, a shift of the hemispheres or global warming, or something of that sort. The fact that these things won't likely occur during our lifetime is not to the point. They are still "falsifiable" claims, and thus pass the acceptability test, at least on that score.

Thrasymachus's Account of Justice

Plato's *Republic* is a dialogue between Socrates and a variety of others engaged in discovering what justice is. One disputant named Thrasymachus is portrayed by Plato as an overbearing surly oaf. There existed a real Thrasymachus, and whether Plato could be accused of libel is a likely possibility. Still, Plato's Thrasymachus provides us with an excellent illustration of non-falsifiability in action.

Thrasymachus claims that justice is whatever is in the interests of the stronger party. "[I]f one reasons rightly, it works out that the just is the same thing everywhere, the advantage of the stronger" (Plato, *Republic*, I, 339 a). Since the stronger party will also become the ruler, the stronger and ruler will be synonymous. Socrates asks whether it is possible the stronger or the ruler will make a mistake and Thrasymachus agrees (Plato, *Republic*, I, 339 b). The snare is set. Socrates continues:

> Let us consider it more closely. Have we not agreed that the rulers in giving orders to the ruled sometimes mistake their own advantage, and that whatever the rulers enjoin it is just for the subjects to perform? Was that not admitted? [Thrasymachus agrees.] Then you will have to think that to do what is disadvantageous to the rulers and the stronger has been admitted by you to be just in the case when the rulers unwittingly enjoin what is bad for themselves, while you affirm that it is just for the others to do what they enjoined. In that way does not this conclusion inevitably follow, my most sapient Thrasymachus, that it is just to do the very opposite of what you say? For it is in that case surely the disadvantage of the stronger or superior that the inferior are commanded to perform. (Plato, *Republic*, I, 339 d–e.)

In other words, consider a weakling is walking along a road with rat poison in an unmarked bottle. A stronger person mistakes the rat poison for wine and demands the weakling hand it over. According to Thrasymachus it is just to hand the poison over, even though this can't be to the advantage of the stronger party. But if it is to the advantage of the stronger party not to hand over the bottle, it is just not to do so. Socrates's question thereby points out a weakness in Thrasymachus's definition of justice: it demands that we obey and disobey the stronger party at the same time – not particularly helpful.

Thrasymachus responds to Socrates's objection by altering what he means by a stronger party:

> Why, to take the nearest example, do you call one who is mistaken about the sick a physician in respect of his mistake or one who goes wrong in a calculation a calculator when he goes wrong and in respect of this error? Yet that is what we say literally – we say that the physician erred, and the calculator and the schoolmaster. But the truth, I take it, is that each of these in so far as he is that which we entitle him never errs, so that, speaking precisely, since you are such a stickler for precision, no craftsman errs. For it is when his knowledge abandons him that he who goes wrong goes wrong – when he is not a craftsman. So that no craftsman, wise man, or ruler makes a mistake then when he is a ruler, though everybody would use the expression that the physician made a mistake and the ruler erred. It is in this loose way of speaking, then, that you must take the answer I gave you a little while ago. But the most precise statement is that other, that the ruler in so far forth as ruler does not err, and not erring he enacts what is best for himself, and this the subject must do. (Plato, *Republic*, I, 340d-341a.)

We can see that Thrasymachus has avoided the charge of inconsistency by providing a non-falsifiable account of justice. If we say, "Here is a ruler or strong person who makes a mistake," then he replies, "But that's not who I mean." So, he has set up his definition in such a way that it is *impossible to refute in principle*. It is non-falsifiable. As such, it should count as an unacceptable premise. Notice that the problem of non-falsifiability shades into persuasive definitions.

Illusions and Dreams

Another classic non-falsifiable position is the following sort of claim:

> Everything is an illusion.

Such an utterance seems to be saying something rather than nothing. On closer inspection, we may begin to doubt that. If the utterance is true, as taken, then we have been deluded all our lives, since we have assumed that not everything is an illusion. In fact, we have tended to live our lives as if most things are not illusions, although we may tolerate some delusions. That is, we tend to think our perceptions are veridical. Alas, this claim denies that and it strikes at the very core of our world view. But it is a non-falsifiable utterance, and should therefore be rejected. Can you see why?

To see why this is non-falsifiable, let us ask the following simple question: "What evidence could we muster to discount the claim that everything is an illusion?" Can *anything* count against it? Perhaps we are presently sitting in a chair and reading a book. The chair and the book *seem* real to us. Can the seeming reality of the book and the chair be offered as a counter to the claim that everything is an illusion? No! That this book and this chair seem real to us is consistent with they're being an illusion nonetheless. The result is that no empirical evidence can count against the claim that every-thing is an illusion. This doesn't make it true that everything is an illusion: it makes the utterance that everything is an illusion a non-falsifiable claim. We may reject it for *that* reason.

The issue is the same as the dreaming question. "Am I awake or dream-ing?" Periodically we may experience this uncertainty. I seem to be awake, one might say, but I've seemed to be awake when in reality I was dreaming. Seeming to be awake, then, cannot by itself distinguish dreaming from being awake. If I pinch myself, I will feel pain. This works as a test case only as long as one is unable to pinch oneself in one's dream and dream that one is experiencing pinch pain. But, alas, surely we are able to dream this. As long as I'm wondering whether I'm dreaming or not, can't I also won-der whether I'm merely dreaming I'm pinching myself and dreaming that I'm in pain?

As soon as we recognize that, in principle, no evidence could count against the claim that everything is an illusion, we also realize the claim is non-falsifiable, and therefore worthy of rejection.

To summarize, if we can't understand what would count against the premise then we have no reason to accept it as plausible. (For a brief review of some of the objections to the falsifiability principle, however, see 12.2.)

6.4.4 Questionable Assumptions

As we have seen before (chapter 2), sometimes an argument can make sense only if we assume something unstated. Remember, if this underlying assumption is unacceptable, then so too is the premise that relies on it.

Recall: an assumption is *not* what is stated. We might question what is *stated*, but that wouldn't count as violating the criterion of questionable assumptions. Often, we might complain that someone is simply asserting a claim, and not backing it up. So, in this sense, the person is merely *assum-ing* its truth, not demonstrating it. This isn't what we mean here, though. Any claim asserted is, by definition, *not* an assumption. An assumption is something *not stated*. In pointing out that a speaker's assumption is prob-lematic or faulty, we have to do three things:

1 Say what that assumption is,
2 Clearly demonstrate that the *stated* premises require that assumption, and
3 Show why the revealed assumption is problematic

For example, if I claim that pornography should be banned because I can cite cases where scenes of rape are portrayed, I am assuming (though I didn't state it anywhere) two things. (1) Depiction of rape causes or condones rape. The claim that violent pornography *causes* rape is unfounded, but being sexually aroused by rape scenes and selling violent pornography precisely for sexual arousal does seem to be a case of *condoning* rape, and perhaps should be forbidden. Still, there is a further assumption that gets in the way. (2) Rape and violence are typical of pornography, an assumption that is overstated. Some studies indicate that violence in pornography, however bad this may be, represents only 8 per cent of pornography. (Steinberg, "The Roots of Pornography," 397)

6.4.5 Premises Less Certain than the Conclusion

The primary purpose of an argument is to convince our audience to accept our conclusion. If they already accept our conclusion, then there's little point in arguing for it. If they don't accept our conclusion, and we want them to, then we should support it with premises that they are likely to accept. For if they don't accept our premises either, they aren't going to accept the conclusion.

This is simply part of what we do when we argue. We try to give acceptable premises to support our conclusion. Thus, if the premises we give are less acceptable than the conclusion, or as questionable as the conclusion, we just aren't doing our job.

To test this, we must always ask, Is this premise I'm being given (or am giving to someone else) more believable than the conclusion, or less believable?

Moore's Hand
G.E. Moore, an early 20th century British philosopher, understood well the criterion of having premises be more certain than the conclusion. A classic philosophical conundrum is whether we can know if objects really are as they appear to us, or further, whether any objects actually exist at all independently of our perceiving them. Now, admittedly, this isn't necessarily the sort of problem we might have. It does, however, challenge our concept of "knowledge." When asked, "How do you know this page exists?" We'd likely answer "Because I see it," or "Because I can feel it," or "Because I hear it when I crumple it up in frustration." But all of these otherwise sensible replies rely on our *perception* of the page. This doesn't answer the fundamental question, which can be worded as, how do we know that our perceptions are veridical?* To answer this question, it appears we have to step outside our perceptions to see if the objects appear the same or not. *But that's precisely what we cannot do!* We can't do it since all of our knowledge of

---

* Technically, a perception can be neither true nor false. It can accurately picture what is true, though, and if so, the perception is *veridical.*

objects is filtered through our perceptions. So the question puts us in a quandary.

Moore, who understands that all premises should be less contentious than the conclusion they aim to support, simply raised his hand (the one that touched the paper) and asked, "What could be more obvious to me than that my hand exists?" His point, at least for our purposes, is that no argument can possibly get off the ground at this point, since to prove the veridical nature of his hand, he requires a premise *more certain* than his hand, and this he recognizes to be an impossible request. ("A Defense of Common Sense" in Muirhead, *Contemporary British Philosophy*)

Impossible requests are illegitimate requests. This is another way of dismissing the claim that everything is an illusion, and that oft-quoted puzzle about whether, if a tree falls in the forest, it makes a noise if no auditory apparatus is present.

6.4.6 Excessive Modalities

Recall, from chapter 2, our desire to recognize modalities of *scope* (all, none, some) and *certainty* (definitely, probably, possibly)? Variations in scope and certainty can affect our decision as to whether to accept or reject claims.

i. Scope   When premises are sweeping in scope, it is easier to challenge them than when they are more reserved in scope.

Saying, "Abortion is always wrong," is more contentious than saying, "Abortion is generally wrong," which is turn more contentious than saying, "Abortion is wrong in specific instances." Similarly, saying, "All humans are nice at heart," is more contentious than saying, "Most humans are nice at heart," which in turn is less defensible than saying, "Some humans are nice at heart."

The reason for this is that for "All" statements, all we require is one counter-example to refute the premise, whereas for "Most" statements, we need to do more than this, for one counter-example is compatible with the "most" claim. Pointing out one smoker who did not get lung cancer is compatible with the claim that most smokers get lung cancer.

Consider the following claim: "Most dentists recommend regular dental visits." It won't do to cite a dentist who does not recommend such a policy. Nor will we refute the claim by showing twenty dentists who disagree with it, since the twenty dentists do not numerically represent most dentists. If there are 1000 dentists, we would require at least 500 dentists who do not recommend regular dental visits (good luck!) before we could call it unacceptable. Were the claim "All dentists recommend regular dental visits," all we would need is one dentist who says otherwise to make the claim unacceptable.

It is even more challenging to refute "Some" claims. Consider the claim, "There is at least one dentist who does not recommend regular checkups."

In one sense, this seems a very weak claim. To call this claim weak, we would have to mean by "weak," that it doesn't say much, or that our accepting this claim does not commit us to much. It is an innocuous claim to accept. There is another sense of "weak," however. A *weak claim* is one which is easily toppled, or refuted, just as a weakling is someone who is easily knocked down. Innocuous claims are not easily knocked down in this sense. In fact, just the opposite. For us, "Some" claims will be *stronger*, not weaker, than "All" claims precisely because they will be more difficult to refute. The task of refuting them, that is to say, will be greater. The claim, "There is at least one dentist who does not recommend regular check-ups," is a *strong claim* in the sense that this claim is harder to reject than the previous claims. If there are 1000 dentists, and we want to refute the claim that there is at least one dentist who does not recommend regular check-ups, we would need to interview all 1000 dentists until we found one who was against regular checkups. It won't do to stop at 500 or 900, because the claim is *compatible* with 999 dentists who *do* recommend regular checkups.

ii. Certainty   The other sort of modality concerns the degree of certainty with which the claim is made. Statements such as "It is indubitably the case that ... " or "It is certain that ... " are easier to reject than claims that appear more wishy-washy, like "It might be the case that ... " or even "I would bet that ... " The more certain the premise is asserted to be, the easier it is to refute.

Why? Because we need not refute the claim itself to discredit the premise. We can merely cast some doubt on it, and doing this rejects the "certainty" of the claim. Since the certainty was built into the premise, by rejecting or casting doubt on the certainty, we reject the entire premise *as stated*.

Of course, we don't want to be misleading. It doesn't follow from this discussion that all universal or categorical claims should be rejected. Think, instead, of a small warning bell going off that alerts us to be wary of strong modalities, while recognizing that not all "all" statements are necessarily false. For example, the claim, "It is definitely the case that all mammals have lungs" should be accepted despite the universal and categorical wording.

Critical thinking skills are useless without a good dose of common sense.

Exercise 6.2

Assess the acceptability of the premises in the following arguments. Note: a common error is to assess the *grounds* condition, that is, to see whether the conclusion is warranted on the basis of the premises. Our concern here is not with the strength of the argument as a whole, just with the strength of the premises. That is, we may have perfectly acceptable premises in a perfectly awful argument. So, don't be fooled. (Answers to selected questions provided in Appendix 1.)

☞ 1 All meat-eaters are too dim-witted to realize that meat-eating is wrong. Of course, some meat-eaters recognize it is wrong, but are too weak-willed to do anything about it.

2 We should abolish minimum wage, since anyone who works for any amount is happy just to be working.

☞ 3 Everyone alive today has experienced innumerable past lives. That is why you are having troubled dreams.

4 Anyone who has the capacity to kill should avoid keeping guns around the house. Actually, when you think about it, we all have the capacity to kill. So no one should keep a gun around the house. (Govier, *A Practical Study of Argument*, 155.)

5 If a law is so vague that it is difficult to know what counts as a violation of it, and if there is really no distinct and clear harm that this law could prevent, then the law should be abolished. Laws that prohibit obscenity have both of these defects. The conclusion to which we are driven is obvious: laws against obscenity should be abolished. (Ibid.)

6 Certain drugs like marijuana, hashish, and magic mushrooms are natural. Since anything that is natural can't be bad, there is no need to make these drugs illegal.

7 A great leader is infallible and can never be wrong. Hitler was clearly a great leader, because he could really inspire people to follow him. Yet, anyone advocating genocide is clearly wrong, and since Hitler did advocate genocide, Hitler could not have been infallible. (Ibid.)

☞ 8 Say No to Sunday shopping. Without restrictions, workers would be forced to work seven days a week.

9 He [David MacFarlane] said the government has done its best to starve Ontario's cultural life. In the same piece he wrote, "I've been racking my brains trying to think of something that the Harris government hasn't ruined." How about theatre, opera, the visual arts, films, television and literature? Harris-haters may find this astonishing or even impossible to believe, but the truth is that culture has actually flourished in the capital of Ontario since Harris came to office in 1995. (Robert Fulford, "Don't blame him, he's just the premier," *National Post*, 10 July 2001, B1)

☞10 [Background: In response to a court ruling, the Cepicas closed their bed and breakfast rather than allow homosexuals to stay there.] While Olson said she would not turn gays and lesbians away from her establishment ... she said she would "prefer if the world was minus that kind of thing." "Why should [the Cepicas] have to give up on their own beliefs?" asked Olson, who describes herself as having strong Christian beliefs. "B&B's are our homes. Say for instance there was a young couple who had kids running around and here they see what's going on. Do these people really want to have them in their home? Because you don't want to compromise your beliefs, you have to shut your doors. And that's what happened to [the Cepicas]."

Olson said there should be some sort of protection for bed and breakfast owners. "I don't object to [homosexuals] being what they are, but why should they come and make me accept what they are in my home?" (Wayne Thibodeau, "Tourist lodgings open to gays: minister," *Guardian*, 24 May 2001, A2)

11 If private companies get involved, then the motive becomes profit. If the motive is profit, then costs need to be cut. If costs need to be cut, then quality goes down. (Maude Barlow, *Compass*, 6 July 2001)

12 In short, President Bush has a choice to make. He can make further "progress" on missile defense by heeding the advice and respecting the sensibilities of those who have kept this nation defenseless against missile attack to this point. Or he can make the only kind of progress that matters – by initiating deployments forthwith, first from the sea (as he intimated in his address last Friday at Annapolis was his intention), and pursuing thereafter whatever co-operation makes sense with the Russians and whatever dialogue is constructive with allies and congressional Democrats. The difference between the two approaches may determine whether the United States deploys effective anti-missile systems before we need them, or only after we do. (Frank J. Gaffney, Jr, "Stop playing footsies with the Russians," *National Post*, 30 May 2001, A14)

☞13 In response to the Irish electorate's rejection of the Treaty [of Nice], the EU announced it had no plans to change so much as a comma, and therefore the Irish could hold a second referendum and get onside or just be ignored. Peter Hain, Britain's new Minister for Europe, maintained that the Irish hadn't really rejected the Nice Treaty: They obviously didn't understand what they were voting about, he said, because if they had, they would have voted in favour rather than against it. (Mark Steyn, "Fantasyland in Europe," *National Post*, 18 June 2001, A14)

14 Every part of God's creation is there for a reason. Therefore, everything and everyone deserves to be treated with respect, including the crows. (Gail McKenzie, letter to the editor, *National Post*, 30, June 2001, A15)

☞15 For many years now, Canada has enjoyed recognition as one of the world's leaders. A lot of this recognition came as a direct result of the premise that we were a Christian country. (Rebecca Matheson, letter to the editor, *Guardian*, 29, June 2001, A7)

16 It is with great dismay and shock that I read last Saturday's *Guardian* to see that the gay pride flag will be flown at City Hall and that Attorney General Jeff Lantz plans to proclaim a gay pride week. Have we really sunk this low that we honour the sin of sodomy with its own special week? May God forgive us for allowing it to happen. The question needs to be asked, where are the teachings of the churches as represented by bishops, priests and ministers that allow this to take

place unchallenged? This is a sinful act and should be rejected, not respected, and the teaching of this falls into the domain of our ever-silent church leaders. Unless God has changed his mind on this since Sodom and Gomorrah, then sodomy is still not a natural act. Make no mistake about it, this is an issue about sexual orientation and sexual acts; if it were not then it would be known as a friendship of two people of the same sex. These people are our brothers and sisters and need our love and respect as people, but, to publicly recognize that sin is to be respected is too much to ask. As children of God, we are called to reject the sin and love the sinner. (Paul R. Chandler, letter to the editor, *Guardian*, 25 June 2001, A7)

Review

Criteria for Accepting Premises
1 Textual support
2 A priori true
3 Sensory evidence
4 Testimony
 – plausibility
 – reputation
 – ability and position
 – report, not interpretation
5 Proper authority
 – speaking within field
 – no disagreement within field
 – field admits authority
6 Accepting premises provisionally

Criteria for Rejecting Premises
1 Inadequate testimony
2 Improper authority
3 Claims known to be *a priori* false
4 Internal inconsistency
5 Non-falsifiability
6 Dependence on questionable assumptions
7 Premises less certain than the conclusion
8 Excessive modalities

Part Four

Logic

$$\frac{7}{\text{\large\char"2144}}$$

Categorical Logic: Translation

Logic and Validity • Categorical Propositions
Natural Language • Syllogisms
Venn Diagramming

7.1 Logic and Validity

Recall from chapter 1 that our task in assessing an argument is to look at three things: meaning, truth, and logic. In part 2, we examined the issue of meaning. We want to understand what is being offered. In our own arguments, we want to state our case in ways our intended audience can understand. In part 3, we examined the concept of truth. The reasons we provide to support our conclusion must themselves be acceptable to our audience. In assessing others' arguments, we need to be sure the premises they offer are acceptable to us. Arguments that have under-standable and acceptable premises are not necessarily worth accepting, however. The third component is needed: logic. That is the theme of part 4.

Logic concerns the relations of the premises to the conclusion. If the premises do not relate to the conclusion, no matter how clear and accept-able they may be, we have grounds to dismiss the argument. For example, consider the following two premises: "Turnips are vegetables," and "Some cats make nice pets for some people." These are clear enough, and pre-sumably acceptable. But what can we conclude from these two premises? Can we conclude that Bin Laden is a terrorist? Even if this last proposition is true, it hardly follows from the two premises. The propositions, despite being acceptable and clear, are *unrelated*. There is no logical relation here.

Sometimes the lack of relation is less obvious. Consider the following argument:

All pregnant persons are women. Some women have hyphenated names.
Therefore some pregnant persons have hyphenated names.

All propositions (both premises and conclusion) may indeed be true, and understandable, but the logical relation between the premises and the conclusion is just as poor as in the Bin Laden argument above. We might not notice this, however, since there is an overlap in subject matter or *terms* between the propositions. Nonetheless, this argument is not logical, because the premises may be true while the conclusion is false. That is, whether or not the conclusion is false, the fact that it *could* be false while the premises are true shows us that the conclusion does not follow from the premises. The conclusion is not *forced* upon us from our accepting the premises.

To see why the hyphenated name argument is invalid, let's compare an argument with an identical structure that should strike us as more obviously faulty. Try this:

All pregnant persons are women. Radcliffe-Richards is a woman. Therefore Radcliffe-Richards is pregnant.

We hope it's not this easy to become pregnant!

Logic concerns the relations between the premises and the conclusion. If an argument is valid, the conclusion must necessarily follow from the premises; otherwise the argument is invalid. Notice the reliance on the word "necessarily." That the conclusion *happens* to be true is not sufficient.

The term "logic" is narrowly used here. For logical relations, the conclusion must necessarily follow from the premise(s). But we also want to speak about arguments which claim less than necessity. Some arguments claim merely that there is a *good bet* that the conclusion will follow from the premise(s). Such arguments are called *inductive arguments* and will be the subject of part 5.

Deductive arguments, on the other hand, do deal in terms of necessity. *A deductive argument is one whose premises are claimed to provide conclusive grounds for the truth of its conclusion.* They are the subject of this part. Deductive arguments come in two forms: *categorical* and *propositional.* Categorical logic deals in terms of objects, sets and classes. Propositional logic is translated in terms of simpler propositional units. In one sense, categorical logic deals with real entities in the world, whereas propositional logic deals with propositions about things, but not the things themselves. The method of testing validity differs between the two systems. The subject of this chapter is categorical logic. Chapters 9 and 10 will examine propositional logic.

Validity

As noted above, part 3 focuses on deductive arguments. A deductive argument is one in which the conclusion is asserted to follow *necessarily* from the premises. This gives us a clue concerning how to test validity. We need merely ask whether the conclusion does indeed follow from the premises. That is, we wonder whether it is *possible* for the conclusion to be false while the premises are true. If yes, the argument is invalid. If no, the argument is valid.

Validity is an all-or-nothing affair. One cannot claim that an argument is partly valid, or partly logical, any more than one can claim to be only partly pregnant. An argument is valid if it is impossible for the conclusion to be false while the premises are true. For valid arguments, the conclusion is forced upon us by the premises.

Even if the premises are false, an argument can be valid. We decide by asking whether the conclusion necessarily follows from *those* premises. If yes, the argument is valid. If the premises are in fact untrue, or unacceptable, then we have reason to reject the argument as stated, but not because it is invalid. Assessing validity is only *part* of the process. Often people say of arguments that they're valid, *as if* that's all there is to be said. There is nothing inconsistent in rejecting a perfectly valid argument, as long as we're doing so on the basis of the acceptability conditions.

In testing validity, we are not concerned with whether premises are *in fact* true. Our focus is strictly on the logical relations. The truth of the premises is irrelevant to the validity of the argument. It is critical that we hone in on the *relations* of the ideas, or the *structure* of the argument, and not the content.

For example, the following argument contains false propositions, yet is perfectly valid:

All people fly. All things that fly have wheels. Therefore all people have wheels.

It is valid because if the premises were true, the conclusion would also have to be true. This relation still holds when we point out that, in fact, all propositions are false.

Whether propositions are true in fact is irrelevant to our understanding validity. The acceptability of premises is obviously important in our assessment of the argument as a whole, but not in our assessment of the argument's validity. A good deductive argument will need to be clear, have acceptable premises, and be valid. All three conditions need to be met. All three are necessary, but none is sufficient. Logic concerns only the last condition.

7.2 Categorical Propositions

Apart from asking whether the premises are true, we ask whether a deductive argument is *valid*, or logical. We ask this question by wondering whether it is conceivable that the conclusion is false while the premises are true. If it is a valid argument, it is *impossible* for the conclusion to be false while the premises are true.

As noted in section 7.1, there are two types of deductive arguments: categorical and propositional. In this chapter we will focus on categorical logic. A categorical argument is one in which all propositions are put in categorical form. A *categorical proposition* asserts that one class, in whole or in part, is either included or excluded from another class.

A *class* is a collection of objects that have some specified characteristic in common. The class of insects, the class of good business deals, the class of prime numbers, the class of previous lovers, the class of classes, ... Class can be applied to anything.

Categorical propositions are *subject-predicate* statements expressing relationships between classes of things. The class of previous lovers, for example, may intersect with the class of things that are contrite. The claim, "All ex-lovers are contrite," therefore, is an example of a categorical statement. The subject is ex-lovers. Contrite qualifies the subject and is therefore the predicate. The subject class is included in the predicate class. In this case, the class of ex-lovers is included in the class of things that are contrite. The predicate class may be larger than the subject class: that is, there may well be more things that are contrite than ex-lovers. This shows that saying "All ex-lovers are contrite" is not the same as saying "All contrite things are ex-lovers."

Except for passive statements, the subject is what occurs first, and the predicate is what follows. The subject of a sentence is what we are talking about, or what is doing the action. Technically, it is that member of a proposition about which something is predicated. The predicate of a sentence is what modifies our subject. Perhaps we want to ridicule an acquaintance. The acquaintance is the subject, the person we're talking about. The ridiculing is what we're saying *of* the subject, and that represents the predicate, or attribute of the subject.

The definition of a passive statement, by the way, is that the subject-predicate order is reversed. Usually we like to place the subject first in the grammatical order, but when it follows the predicate, or object, this is deemed a passive sentence. "The ball was thrown by Bobby," is passive. "Bobby threw the ball" is active. Here the subject is Bobby, and the predicate is his throwing of the ball. This shows that the grammatical order alone does not determine the subject.

Saying "All things that are ex-lovers are things that are contrite," is fairly cumbersome and it veers from natural language. Still, we can translate any subject-predicate sentence into a categorical proposition. For example, we might hear a disillusioned student say "School sucks." In terms of categorical reasoning, this student has related the subject class of his expression ("school") with the predicate class of the expression ("things that suck"). Furthermore, this student did not mean to say that "A school sucks." He meant, rather, that schools (in general) suck. So, his statement amounts to the following:

"All schools are things that suck."

Of course, telling him this won't likely help matters.

Quantity and Quality

In order to test the validity of arguments using categorical logic, we will need to be reasonably proficient in recognizing categorical statements in natural language. It is helpful to recognize that categorical statements have two determining properties: *quality* and *quantity*.

In terms of quantity, categorical statements can be either *universal* or *particular*. Propositions that are universal speak about the entire set of things. Propositions that are particular speak only about some members of that set, and make no allusions to the rest of the members. Saying "All ravens are ..." speaks about the entire set of ravens, and so is a universal proposition. Saying "Some ravens are ..." speaks only about particular ravens.

In terms of quality, categorical statements can be either *affirmative* or *negative*. Affirmative propositions assert something about a set, whereas negative propositions deny something about a set. We might say either that a cat is a good pet, or that a cat is not a good pet. The subject in the first proposition is *included* in the predicate class of things that are good pets, and the statement is therefore affirmative. The subject class in the second is *excluded* from the predicate set of things that are good pets and the statement is therefore a negative proposition.

Given that there are two types of quantity (universal or particular) and two types of quality (affirmative or negative), there will be four types of categorical propositions in all. These four types of categorical propositions may be derived by recognizing that we're combining the two variables of quantity and quality: whether a proposition is affirmative or negative, and whether a proposition is universal or particular. Combining these two variables in a two by two matrix provides us with the following four categorical statements.

	AFFIRMATIVE	NEGATIVE
UNIVERSAL	All A are B	No A are B
PARTICULAR	Some A are B	Some A are not B

Thus we have either Universal Affirmative propositions (UA), Universal Negative propositions (UN), Particular Affirmative propositions (PA), or Particular Negative propositions (PN). For example,

All statistics are lies. (Universal Affirmative (UA))
No statistics are lies. (Universal Negative (UN))
Some statistics are lies. (Particular Affirmative (PA))
Some statistics are not lies. (Particular Negative (PM))

7.3 Natural Language

What we shall next examine are tips to help the student translate natural language into categorical language. For example, how would you translate the following statement?

"People who live in glass houses should not throw stones."

Answer: "No G are S" (UN) where G = people who live in glass houses, and S = things that should throw stones. How did we do this? Are there any translation rules that can help us correctly translate natural language into categorical form? Yes.

Earlier we mentioned the peculiar nature of categorical reasoning. All natural language must be translated into the confines of our four categorical propositions, and sometimes this process seems unnatural. A graver danger, however, is mistranslation. The following act as guides for translation.

7.3.1 UA: Universal Affirmative

The universal affirmative begins with the word "All." The word all is followed by a noun or noun phrase specifying a category of things. This category of things is the subject. The subject category is followed by the word "are" or "is" which in turn is followed by another noun or noun phrase specifying a category of things. This second category is the predicate. Strictly speaking, the sentence "All crocodiles are fast" is not in categorical form, because the predicate is only an adjective. To put that sentence into categorical form, we would have to rewrite it as "All crocodiles are things that are fast."

Similarly, many sentences in natural language can be put into Universal affirmative form with slight linguistic alterations.

The following statements, for example, are all verbal variations of "All S are P."

Any S is P
Every single S is a P
Whatever S you look at it's a P.
Each S is a P.
S's are P's.
If it's an S, it's a P.

Very often, sentences are not explicit about whether we're confronted with a universal affirmative or a particular affirmative. For example,

Zebras have stripes.
Wars lead to pillage and rape.
Politicians are crooks.

In these cases it is permissible to assume the speaker is intending the entire set of zebras, wars, and politicians.

Under certain conditions, even indefinite articles may be best translated as universal, rather than particular.

A monkey has a tail = All monkeys are things with tails.

but,

A man is fat = Some men are fat things.

In such cases, we need to take the context into consideration. Depending on the context, we may translate these sorts of claims as either "Some" statements or "All" statements. For example, "A woman gave birth last night" should not commit us to believing all women gave birth last night.

Only
Whenever we see the word "only" we're dealing with a universal. There is a catch, however. In such cases, we need to reverse the subject and predicate; otherwise we are saying something other than what is meant.

"Only cats are nimble" means "All things which are nimble are cats." It does not mean "All cats are nimble," since some cats may not be nimble. Compare,

Only women are pregnant.

Surely we cannot plausibly translate this as saying "All women are pregnant"! Rather, we should reverse the subject and predicate and translate it as "All Pregnant persons are women."

To translate "Only" claims,
1 Change the "only" to an "all."
2 Reverse the subject and predicate.

Natural Language	Categorical Form
Only the lonely come to this saloon.	All persons who come to this saloon are lonely.
Only ticket holders are allowed.	All persons allowed are ticket holders.
Only adults are allowed behind the curtain.	All persons allowed behind the curtain are adults.

Names
Harry met Sally. How should we translate this? Should we try "Some H are S"? This might seem fine, at first. When we say Harry met Sally, however, we are referring specifically to Harry, and not someone else. But if we translated that as saying someone met Sally, this is a different thing. Likewise, if the witness says "Phillips committed the crime!" she is not making the banal statement that *someone* committed the crime. Presumably we're well enough aware of *that*. What she's stating is something different: that it

wasn't just anyone that committed the crime, it was Phillips. Saying "Some
H ..." is peculiar in another respect. Harry would be both an intension and
an extension; that is, both a set of things (all things that are Hs), and a
member of that set (a particular H) – a paradoxical feat.

The solution is to translate names as universals. "Harry met Sally"
becomes "All things equivalent with Harry are things that met Sally."
Granted, this may seem excessively unnatural, but for purposes of logic it
is a perfectly apt translation.

Notice this isn't saying all Harrys *are* Sally. If it were, S would be defined
as a set of things identical with Sally, i.e., Harry *is* Sally, which is hardly a
good translation. Of course the confusion is avoided when we recognize
that "S" does not stand for "Sally," but for "things which have met Sally."

Point: Treat subject names as universals.

An Exception

All names which appear as subjects must be treated as universals, *but a
name need not always be treated as a universal set identical with itself.* We've seen
what happens when we try to treat names in the predicate as universals. We
would not be able to say that Harry *met* Sally; we could only say that Harry
was identical with Sally – a grave limitation. But this rule cannot be indiscriminately applied. Consider this relatively straightforward argument:

> Joseph plays the saxophone better than Frank. Frank, at least, plays it better
> than Morris, though. So, Joseph plays the saxophone better than Morris.

Most of us should be able to recognize that this is a perfectly valid argument. Minimally, this helps show that we cannot treat names as particulars,
for then we would read

> Some J are F
> Some F are M
> Therefore Some J are M.

This is not only a poor translation, it is invalid. The whole is undetermined.
Are the some Js that are F also the Fs that are Ms? Nothing forces this conclusion in this translation. (Compare: Some women are red-headed. Some
red-headed persons are men. Therefore some women are men.) But, if we
treat all names as universals, a problem still lingers. Consider:

> All J are F
> All F are M
> Therefore All J are M.

Clearly the argument is valid. Just as, if A is taller than B, and B taller than
C, we are logically entitled to infer that A is taller than C. The problem is

not that this is an invalid form, and nor that this is a good translation of the argument. In fact, this is precisely how we recommend you translate it. The problem is that the set of things that play the saxophone better than Frank cannot be identical with the set of things of which Frank is a member.

The set of things which play the saxophone better than Frank in the first premise cannot possibly be the same as the set of things identical with Frank in the second. If we treat "Frank" in the first premise (as we did with Sally above) as "things which play better than Frank"," and "Frank" in the second premise as a name ("things identical with Frank"), we end up with too many terms. That is, if we treat "F" in the first premise as "things that play better than Frank," we cannot treat "F" in the second premise as "Things identical with Frank." For then, clearly, we are introducing different terms, and the argument would be invalid.

The solution here is to treat "F" in the second premise, not as a name, but as the set of things which play better than Frank. And we must do this, despite the natural language argument clearly giving us a name. Without this shift, the argument would be invalid. Thus, although our categorical form looks as above, the premises are to be treated as

1 All things identical with Joseph are things which play better than Frank.
2 All things which play better than Frank are things which play better than Morris.
3 So, all things identical with Joseph are things which play better than Morris.

This is the correct translation. We have treated only "Joseph" as a name. This is why we must qualify our rule above. Treat subject names as universals only as long as they do not also occur as predicates.

7.3.2 UN: Universal Negative

Consider the following ways of uttering a universal negative:

Not a single whale can fly.
Whales can't fly.
None of the beings who are whales can fly.
There never was a whale that could fly.
No whales can fly.
Whales are not able to fly.
All whales are flightless mammals.
All whales are things that cannot fly.

All these are variants of "No whales are creatures that can fly" (No W are F).
Notice that "All A are not B" will be translated as "No A are B." We are speaking of the entire set of A, and claiming that B is not part of that.

Hence, No A are B is the correct categorical translation. "All babies aren't cute," is to be translated as "No babies are cute."

Notice, next, that "Not all ..." *does not* mean "None ..." "Not all soldiers in the war died" does not mean that no soldiers died in the war. Saying "not all" means that we're not speaking about the entire set of something. We are speaking of particular members of that set. This shows we cannot treat "not all" statements as universals. Rather, we will treat "not all" claims as PN statements: "Some ... are not ..."

As another illustration of how the placement of our "nots" is important, consider the difference between saying "Not obviously ..." and "Obviously not ..." If we say the first, we're challenging the use of the modality "obviously." By casting doubt on a claim, we can say it is no longer obvious. It still may be true. We needn't doubt that. Simply, we're challenging the *obviousness* of the truth. Whereas, if we say the second, we're clearly denying the truth of the claim, and we're adding a strong modality to help illustrate how assured we are in our thinking it false. Saying, "That's not obviously a wig," is different from saying, "That's obviously not a wig." In the first, the speaker takes it to be a wig, but this is denied in the second.

7.3.3 PA: Particular Affirmative

"Some" can mean "only one," "at least one," "more than one," "quite a bit more than one," "many," "most," or even "virtually all." In essence, it covers the wide range of possibilities between (but not including) none and all. For logical purposes, every "Some" statement will be translated as "at least one." Oddly enough, this will include claims beginning with "Most."

The inability to make the distinction between one and many shows one of the limitations of categorical logic. By contrast, the concern of inductive arguments is precisely the distinction between some and most. Consider, for example, how peculiar it would be to try to translate into categorical form the following sort of generalized probability statements: "A woman gives birth every seven seconds," or "Someone dies every second." We don't want to misinterpret this statistical claim as uttering the following PA statement: "There is at least one woman who gives birth once every seven seconds," or "There is at least one man who dies sixty times a minute." And neither, of course, can we say "All women give birth every seven seconds," nor "All men die every second." Categorical language cannot deal with these claims without convoluted re-translation. For example, "For all seven seconds, a woman gives birth." The woman giving birth becomes the predicate, the thing qualifying the true subject of the sentence: the time slice. This is obviously strained.

But for purposes of categorical logic, "Some" means simply: "At least one." Hence:

Most of the good-looking people were at the party.

Quite a number of good-looking people were at the party.
There were many good-looking people at the party.
Nearly everyone at the party was good-looking.
A few good-looking people were at the party.
A good-looking person was at the party.

All variations are translated exactly the same: "There was at least one person at the party who was good-looking." (Some P are G).

Conversely, we may say instead "There was at least one good-looking person at the party." (Some G are P). As we shall see presently, these are logically equivalent.

7.3.4 PN: Particular Negative

"Not all" asserts a *particular negative*. For example,

"Not all fish are pleasant to look at."
= Some fish are not things that are pleasant to look at.
= Some F are not P.

Note: we do not translate it as "All F are not P." That is not in proper or "legal" categorical form. A proper translation of "All F are not P" is "No F are P" (see the discussion in 7.3.2 PN). But "Not all fish are pleasant to look at" is not equivalent to "No fish are pleasant to look at."

A person who says "Some readers of science fiction are not computer hackers" is likely to be interpreted as saying, in addition, that some readers of science fiction *are* computer hackers. Strictly speaking, however, we cannot make such an inference. At any rate, it is not *deductively entailed*. For otherwise, merely on the grounds that some people are not able to fly, we would be able to infer that therefore some people are able to fly. Since the inference is to be forbidden in the latter example, logicians recognize we must forbid it in all cases. This may seem excessively severe. Logicians are concerned with the *structure* of arguments, though. If an inference is denied, every identical inference is always denied. Recall, logic entails necessary connections, not merely plausible or contingent connections. If the inference is faulty in one argument structure, the same inference will always be faulty in identical argument structures.

Exercise 7.1

Translate the following into categorical form. (Answers to selected questions provided in Appendix 1.)

☞ 1 A dog is man's best friend.
  2 Politicians are crooks.

   3 Only monkeys eat grubs.

   4 No pets allowed.

☞ 5 Not all prostitutes are pretty.

   6 All dogs aren't tame.

☞ 7 A fly found its way into a flybottle.

   8 Not all plants are poisonous.

☞ 9 Jones could not get a date.

  10 Some hookers play rugby.

  11 All plants are not edible.

☞12 White boys can't jump.

  13 A Hindu widow may choose to be burned alive on her husband's pyre.

  14 A ship sank in Cuban waters.

☞15 Most lobster men are poor.

  16 A stitch in time saves nine.

☞17 My cousin went to a homeopath down the street in the old Gym.

☞18 Only the qualified need apply.

  19 No walking on the grass.

  20 Diamonds are a girl's best friend.

  21 The late frost destroyed the crop.

  22 Not a single student failed the required course for economics.

☞23 The average salary for a professional baseball player is $2,383,235.

  24 Only Edmund is allowed into the fort.

7.4 Syllogisms

So far, we have learned how to translate natural language into categorical form. What we want to do now is determine whether categorical arguments are valid. To test the validity of categorical arguments, a restriction applies: we can only test the validity on *categorical syllogisms*.

A categorical syllogism is a specific argument form having exactly two premises and one conclusion, all in categorical form. As put, however, this is too broad. Compare the following two arguments:

(1) All apples are fruit.   (2) All apples are fruit.
      No kumquats are poisonous.   No fruit is poisonous.
      No carrots need peeling.   No apples are poisonous.

In both cases, we have two premises and one conclusion, all in categorical form, but (1) does not count as a syllogism. Only (2) is a syllogism. The difference is that categorical syllogisms, or simply syllogisms, need to have interconnected propositions.

Let's be more specific. Recall that a categorical proposition has a subject and a predicate. We shall refer to these as *terms*. The subject of a categorical proposition is a term. Likewise, the predicate of a categorical proposi-

tion is a term. The proposition, "All apples are fruit" contains two terms (apples and fruit.) Since all categorical propositions are defined in subject-predicate terms, we now see that every categorical proposition has precisely two terms: never more, never less.

The number of distinct terms in a syllogism is three. Of course, we might expect six, since there are three lines and two terms per line, but the issue here concerns *distinct terms*. Notice that the term "apple" in argument (2) occurs twice. So does the term "things that are poisonous," as well as the term "fruit." In argument (2), there are only three distinct terms. In any syllogism, there will never be more, or less than three distinct terms. Otherwise we are no longer confronted with a syllogism. If we are not confronted with a syllogism, we will be unable to test the argument's validity using categorical logic.

The three terms in a syllogism can be further identified as *major, minor,* and *middle* terms (Aristotle's use). The major term is the subject of the conclusion. The minor term is the predicate of the conclusion. The middle term is the term that does not occur in the conclusion. It acts as the inference bridge between the major and minor terms. In our translations from natural language into categorical language, we place the subject first, and the predicate second. Given the grammatical restrictions of our four categorical forms (UA, UN, PA, and PN), we cannot have any passive sentences. Therefore the major, minor, and middle terms should be easily identifiable. The major term is the subject of the conclusion. The subject of the conclusion is the term that occurs first in the conclusion. The minor term is the predicate of the conclusion. The predicate of the conclusion occurs second in the conclusion. The middle term is that which does not appear in the conclusion.

The major term, apart from appearing as the subject of the conclusion, must also occur once in either premise, as either subject or predicate.

The minor term, apart from appearing as the predicate of the conclusion, must also appear once in the premises, either as a subject or a predicate. The minor term can never occur in the same premise as the major term. They will occur together in the *conclusion,* but never in a premise. Another way of putting this rule is to prohibit any single term from occurring twice in a single proposition. For example, "All apples are apples," however true, cannot count as a proposition in a syllogism. If the major and middle terms occur together *both* in the conclusion and one of the premises, then the middle term would have to occur twice in the remaining premise: a violation.

The middle term will occur in the leftover places, once in the first premise, either as subject or predicate, and once in the second premise, either as subject or predicate.

In argument (2), the major term is apples (the subject of the conclusion), and apples occurs once as the subject in the first premise. The minor term is poisonous things, and this occurs as a predicate in the second premise. The middle term is fruit. This occurs as the predicate of the first premise, and as the subject of the second premise, and does not occur in the conclusion. Argument (2) satisfies the conditions of a syllogism.

Our definition of a syllogism, then, is this:

> *A syllogism is a deductive argument having two premises and one conclusion, all in categorical form, in which the major, minor, and middle terms each occur twice on separate lines.*

Consider the following syllogism.

> All socialists are in favour of redistributed wealth.
> All those in favour of redistributed wealth can tolerate violations of property rights.
> Therefore, all socialists can tolerate violation of property rights.

Assigning S to stand for things that are socialists, W, for things that are in favour of redistributed wealth, and V, for things that can tolerate violation of property rights, we can translate this argument into the following notation:

> All S are W
> All W are V
> All S are V

What are the major, middle, and minor terms? Looking at the conclusion we discover S is the subject and V is the predicate. V is the attribute we're ascribing to S. This tells us that S is the major term and V is the minor term. W is the middle term. This argument is in proper syllogistic form.

What we shall next do is learn how to test the validity of categorical syllogisms using the *Venn diagram method*.

Exercise 7.2

Syllogisms do not often present themselves in pure form. Be that as it may, we can often translate arguments into proper syllogistic form. To do so, we need to hone in on the meat of the argument, to avoid the irrelevant bits, and sometimes to provide a missing ingredient. Create syllogisms out of the following arguments. (Answers to select questions are provided in Appendix 1.)

☞ 1 Euthanasia is wrong, because it's murder.
    2 The government should do all it can to protect some illegal immigrants who face criminal charges in their home countries from deportation because those countries practice torture or execution.

☞ 3 Some genetically modified foods should bear labels to warn consumers.

4 Marijuana is a drug, and should therefore remain illegal.

5 Some alternative marriage arrangements should be tolerated, since they're entered into voluntarily.

☞ 6 Students are paying too much tuition already. The problem with the deficit is the politicians', not the students. Taking it out on students is the proverbial kicking of the dog. It isn't fair and we won't stand for it.

☞ 7 "The logic being used for vitamin C supplements is that fruits, vegetables and so on contain vitamin C. These foods prevent cancer and thus vitamin C prevents cancer," Dr. Blair said. (Margaret Munro, "Highly touted since 1970s," *National Post*, 15 June 2001, A8)

8 It is unfortunate that Brian Segal (June 9) does not have contact with many young people in his daily life. If it were otherwise, he would not have compartmentalized an entire demographic into the much-touted stereotype of 16-year-old as air head. I am 16, and I can assure Mr. Segal that there are many young people who would be capable, active participants in the democratic society in which they live. An excellent example of this is the student debating tournament I have attended as a delegate for three years. The teams are composed of articulate, knowledgeable and thoughtful members of society. Awarding suffrage to younger Canadian citizens may strike fear into the heart of Mr. Segal, but one must keep in mind that "flakiness" knows no age limit. Who, in 40 years, will be living on a planet with no ozone layer, rain forests or open spaces? We do not inherit the Earth from our parents, but borrow it from our children. Therefore, who better than Canada's young people to have a say in the future of our country and our world? (Meredith Lapp, "Whose future is it?" *National Post*, 12 June 2001)

7.5 Venn Diagramming

7.5.1 Diagramming Categorical Propositions

In order to assess the validity of categorical syllogisms, we shall use the Venn diagram method. A Venn diagram pictorially represents the interconnections of sets. Since categorical propositions are defined in terms of sets, using Venn diagrams is perfectly apt. Recall that the definition of validity is that it is impossible for the conclusion to be false while the premises are true. If we can pictorially represent the premises, then, valid arguments will already have the conclusion pictorially represented. By simply drawing the premises, the conclusion should already be drawn. If it is, the argument is valid. If it isn't, the argument is invalid. That is the idea behind testing for validity using Venn diagrams.

Venn diagrams avail themselves of the following three tools: *circles, shading,* and *asterisks*:

Circles define sets of things. Shading defines the absence of things. Asterisks define the existence of at least one thing

In a categorical proposition, two circles will be required to represent the two sets – one for the subject set, and one for the predicate set. A set of all quadrupeds can be defined by a simple circle. But "All quadrupeds," or "No quadrupeds," or "Some quadrupeds," are not by themselves complete sentences. A sentence requires both subject and predicate. We have to say something about quadrupeds and this requires another circle.

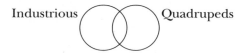

A set of all things that are both quadrupeds and industrious requires two intersecting circles. One circle represents quadrupeds, and the other circle represents things that are industrious. Notice that the two circles overlap. This is necessary, for we have to allow for the prospect that there exist some things that are both industrious and quadrupeds. All things that are industrious quadrupeds reside in the intersection. All things that are industrious but not quadrupeds reside in the industrious circle but not in the intersection. All things that are quadrupeds but not industrious reside in the quadruped circle but not in the intersection.

To diagram the UA proposition, "All A are B," we need to deny that there are any As that are not also Bs. This entails that we have to cross out all the A that does not overlap with B. So,

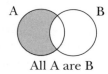
All A are B

For if all A are B, it cannot be the case that there exists any A that is not a B.

To diagram the UN proposition, "No A is B," we need to deny the existence of any A that is also a B. In other words, we have to cross out all the A that overlaps with B.

No A are B

The PA statement, "Some A are B," is clearly not saying that All A are B, nor denying the possibility that Some A are not B. We need to place an asterisk (*) in the overlap between A and B.

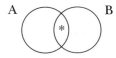

Some A are B

Lastly, in order to diagram the PN statement, "Some A is not B," we need to place an asterisk in A where it does not overlap with B.

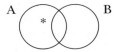

Some A are not B

Conversion

Notice, by the way, that "Some A are B" is equivalent with "Some B are A," and that "No A are B" is equivalent with "No B are A." Whether we say "No bellhops were at the union meeting" or "No one at the union meeting was a bell hop" is unimportant logically. Likewise, it doesn't matter whether we say "Some butter is fattening," or "Some fattening things are butter."

Notice, as well, that this equivalence is not maintained with UA or PN propositions. "All A are B" is not the same as "All B are A." Although it is true that all pregnant things are women, it is not true that all women are pregnant, fortunately. Similarly, "Some A are not B" is not the same as "Some B are not A." Saying "Some students do not take logic" is not the same as saying some people who take logic are not students. "Some mammals are not sheep" does not imply that some sheep are not mammals.

To reverse the subject and predicate is to convert a categorical proposition. To see the equivalence of converting UN and PA statements, we need merely to draw Venn diagrams for each conversion and compare. If the diagrams are equivalent, the conversion is equivalent. Likewise, to see how the conversions of PN and UA statements are not equivalent, a quick Venn diagram of each should suffice.

The chart below illuminates the logical equivalence of conversion.

Equivalence Chart for Conversion

Symbol	Categorical Form	Conversion	Equivalence
UA	All A are B	All B are A	no
UN	No A are B	No B are A	yes
PA	Some A are B	Some B are A	yes
PN	Some A are not B	Some B are not A	no

Reverse Shading?

Some people may have been taught to shade in sets when there is existence, rather than non-existence. To be now told to do the reverse may seem not merely confusing, but arbitrary. To shade areas where existence is, rather than where existence is not, creates a problem, however. Notice what happens to the diagram of the UN statement, "No A are B." Reverse shading would require us to shade in all of A that is outside B. But what if there is no A at all? We may want to say "No tooth fairies came to your pillow last night," but not be committed to the claim that tooth fairies exist. If A is an empty set, we can't infer there are A's merely on the grounds that no As are Bs. "No one who got 100 per cent on the test failed the course" may well be true, but to infer from this there were people who scored 100 per cent on the test is specious.

More, since we've seen that "No A are B" is equivalent to its conversion, "No B are A," we would also have to shade in all of B that is outside A. Using the reverse shading to say no tooth fairies visited your pillow last night not only would commit us to the specious claim of asserting the existence of tooth fairies, it would also commit us to the claim that things did visit your pillow last night, whereas perhaps we want to deny that as well. Or conversely, saying "Despite appearances, no teachers are alien monsters," would commit us to the claim that there do exist alien monsters, a claim we might not believe we're committed to by denying that teachers are such things.

We want to be able to diagram only that which can be logically inferred from a given statement, and nothing beyond. The reverse shading method cannot handle the prospect of null sets. (For more on null sets, see section 8.2.2.)

Exercise 7.3

Diagram the following propositions. (Answers to selected questions provided in Appendix 1.)

☞ 1 All clowns are scary.
   2 Some professors are bald.

☞ 3 No hockey players are underpaid.
☞ 4 Some lawyers are trustworthy.
   5 All doughnuts are tasty.
☞ 6 Some television shows are not boring.
☞ 7 Teletubbies are creepy.
☞ 8 Some classes never end.
   9 No philosophy classes are boring.
☞10 Not all jokes are funny.
  11 John is lazy.
☞12 Only babies cry.
  13 A lot of politicians don't lie.
  14 A dime is worth ten cents.
  15 Murder is not allowed around here.
☞16 Most of the guests became sick.
  17 Truth telling can still mislead.
  18 Thermostats contain mercury.
  19 Microwaves are bad for your health.
  20 Some examples are not interesting.
☞21 You can't castle in this case.
  22 The garbage needs to be taken out.
  23 Few hockey players are underpaid.
☞24 A tooth fairy visited my pillow.
  25 Suffering is bad.
  26 Animals have rights too.
  27 The mind is simply a part of the body.
☞28 All killers should not be executed.

7.5.2 Diagramming Categorical Syllogisms

We have so far shown only how to diagram subject-predicate propositions. What we want to do, however, is diagram categorical syllogisms. Recall that a syllogism is an argument with three terms evenly distributed over three categorical propositions. Since we are dealing with three terms, and a given circle represents one term, we will need to introduce a third circle in our Venn diagram.

Custom has it that we place the third circle below and overlapping the first two circles, like this

Labelling Convention

It is also customary to label the circles in a standard way. The standard is that the major term (the subject set of the conclusion) is represented by the top left circle, and the minor term (the predicate of the conclusion) is represented by the top right circle, while the middle term (the remaining term that does not occur in the conclusion) is represented by the bottom circle. Consider the following argument:

> Taxation is theft, plain and simple. Taxation takes from your paycheck by force, for to resist is to be arrested. Meanwhile, as any idiot knows, taking from paycheques or wallets are synonymous, and taking from one's wallet by force is theft.

To translate this argument into a categorical syllogism we remove some of the supporting premises, focussing instead on the two main premises and the main conclusion. We also place the conclusion at the bottom in standard form, thus:

> Taxation is taking from one's paycheque by force.
> Taking from one's paycheque by force is theft.
> Taxation is theft.

These propositions aren't quite in categorical form. Properly speaking, our argument will look like so:

> All things that are taxation are things that are taken by force.
> All things that take by force are things that are theft.
> All things that are taxation are things that are theft.

Admittedly, this doesn't read as nicely as the original, but we are interested in logic, not prose. If we assign X for the set of things that are taxation, F for the set of things that take by force, and T for things that are theft (notice that we chose X for taxation rather than T, since we already have a "T" representing a different set of objects), we can portray the argument as

> All X are F
> All F are T
> All X are T

Now that we know the conclusion, we are ready to properly label our three circles. Recall the labelling convention: the subject of the conclusion (the major term) is the top left hand circle, while the predicate of the conclusion (the minor term) is the top right circle. The conclusion contains the subject "Taxation" and the predicate "things that are theft," so we will label our top left circle, X and our top right circle will be labelled T. The set that is left over (called the middle term) is the bottom middle circle. In this case, the set of things left over is the set of things that take by force, which we've labelled F. Thus, to follow our labelling convention of the tax-is-theft argument, we have

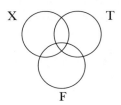

Designating the subject of the conclusion to be the top left circle, the predicate of the conclusion the top right circle, and the middle term the bottom circle is not necessary to assessing validity: it is merely a convention. It helps to the extent that our diagrams will look the same, and errors will be more readily noted.

Diagramming with Three Circles

To diagram categorical syllogisms, we diagram one premise, and then the next on the same three circles. To diagram one premise is to focus on only two circles, and to ignore the circle defining the third set. For example, in our taxation-is-theft argument, to draw the first premise, we will only focus on the sets labelled X and F, and ignore the set labelled T. To ignore T is to pretend it isn't there, at least for universal propositions. Particular propositions pose a difficulty when the third set is introduced, but we will take this up in 8.2.2. Since we know that "All X are F" is diagrammed as

we will not be fooled when we add in the third circle:

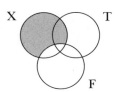

Notice that to diagram "All X are F" we are shading out anything that exists in X that is outside of F. To do this, as can be seen in the three circle diagram above, we enter into part of T. A common error is to stay out of T, but since some X (that are not F) are in T, we must shade that section in as well. Notice that this doesn't preclude the possibility of some X's being T, since that is still allowed by the opening in the very middle, the overlap of all three sets, XTF.

So far we have incorporated one premise in our Venn diagram. We now need to diagram the second premise. Keeping our three circle Venn diagram, "All F are T" is diagrammed like so:

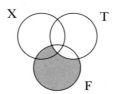

Combining the first and second premises of the tax-is-theft argument gives us the following result.

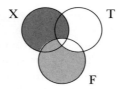

Fine. Is the argument valid? That's what we want to know. Turn to the following chapter to see how we can distinguish valid from invalid argument forms using the Venn diagram method.

$$\frac{8}{8}$$

Categorical Logic: Validity

Testing Validity • Extended Categorical Arguments • More on Translation A Non-Venn Test

8.1 Testing Validity

8.1.1 The Basic Pattern

An argument is valid if after diagramming the first two categorical propositions, the conclusion *is already sufficiently diagrammed*. Otherwise the argument is invalid.

In the tax-is-theft argument, we can see that the conclusion "All X are T" is *already* sufficiently illustrated in our Venn diagram after drawing in the first two premises. That is, if we *were* to draw in the conclusion, we would cross out everything in X that is outside of T. This is already done for us by having previously drawn in the premises. Therefore, the argument is valid. The Venn diagram method *visually shows* that if the premises are true, the conclusion must be true. That is the definition of validity. It is impossible for an X to exist without it also being a T.

Notice that some X-T intersection is also crossed out, and if we were drawing in just the conclusion, we wouldn't have crossed this section out. This is irrelevant. The conclusion is *sufficiently* illustrated, and that is all that matters. We can clearly see that if we were to put an asterisk in the X, it would necessarily have to be inside T. That is precisely what the conclusion claims. Hence the argument is valid.

That the argument is valid is not to say it is cogent. Perhaps we may reject one or both of the premises. But that is not our concern when we are examining the logical relation of the premises to the conclusion. If an argument is valid, then we know that the premises necessarily yield the conclusion; we don't know whether the premises are acceptable or not. That is an altogether different matter.

Let's try again. Consider the following categorical argument:

All Ontarians are Canadian.
Some Ontarians smoke.
Therefore some Canadians smoke.

First, using our labelling convention, we have

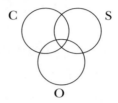

Diagramming the first premise (a UA proposition) gives us

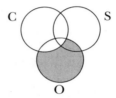

Diagramming the second premise (a PA proposition) presents this final picture:

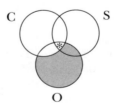

To see whether this argument is valid or not, we do not do any more diagramming. Instead, we ask, "Is the conclusion already sufficiently diagrammed?" If we were to draw in the conclusion, is our work already sufficiently done for us? In this case, our conclusion (a PA proposition) is shown as an asterisk *somewhere* in the C and S overlap. So we ask, is there already an asterisk in the C and S overlap? If so, the argument is valid. If not, the argument is invalid. In this case, as you should be able to see, we already have an asterisk somewhere in the C and S overlap. Hence the argument is valid.

The idea here is to provide a *pictorial* representation showing that if the premises are true, the conclusion is necessarily true.

An invalid argument will be one in which the conclusion is not suffi-ciently drawn after drawing our two premises. Examine the results of the following invalid argument.

No British Columbians smoke
All British Columbians are Canadians
Therefore no Canadians smoke

Following our labelling convention, we have

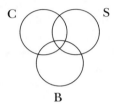

The first UN premise is diagrammed

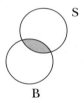

The second UA premise is diagrammed

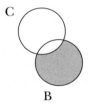

Putting the two premises together gives us the following diagram:

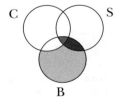

Notice how in our second premise we are crossing out a section already crossed out. The first premise rules out everything in the intersection of S and B. This includes a little bit of C. This is as it should be. Had we left that spot open, there would exist the possibility of an S being a B, precisely the state of affairs denied in the first premise, which we assume to be true. The same logic applies with our second premise. Our crossing out everything in B that is outside of C continues into a bit of the S circle. Notice, also that given the first premise this is a bit redundant (notice the overlapping lines). That's fine; in fact, it is recommended. It is good advice to cross everything out that the premise tells us to cross out, even in cases where the other premise has already done so. It helps train us to focus only on what a given proposition entitles us to claim, and in that focus, we ignore what other propositions have already provided. This advice may seem idle, but it will help us avoid the common mistake of letting the third circle interfere in our diagramming.

Is the Canadian-smokers argument valid? If so, the conclusion should *already* be sufficiently diagrammed by the two premises. In other words, if we were to diagram the conclusion, would we find that our work has been done for us?

The conclusion states that no C are S, and for that to be diagrammed, we would have to cross out the entire intersection of C and S. Notice however, that this is not satisfied here. There is still the prospect of a C being an S. The conclusion is not represented by the two premises alone; hence the argument is invalid.

A Common Error

Some students have a tendency to draw the conclusion onto their Venn diagrams. Don't. The conclusion is supposed to be *already* diagrammed by merely diagramming the premises alone. If the conclusion is sufficiently pictured, the argument is valid; otherwise it is invalid. After all, our definition of validity claims that the conclusion necessarily follows from the premises. Venn diagrams provide a pictorial representation of that process.

What we're looking for is the mere possibility that the conclusion is false while the premise is true. Recall, we're analysing deductive arguments and logical validity, not the truth or acceptability of premises.

Exercise 8.1 A

Test the validity of the following arguments using Venn diagrams. (Answers to selected exercises provided in Appendix 1.)

☞ 1 All Ontarians are Canadians. Some Ontarians are not sports fans. Therefore, some Canadians are not sports fans.

☞ 2 No Canadians want Quebec to separate. All Quebecers want Quebec to separate. Therefore no Quebecer is Canadian.

3 All optophones are cellular. All oracles are optophones. Thus, all oracles are cellular.

☞ 4 All coyotes are animals that love to howl at the moon. All kids are animals that love to howl at the moon. Hence all kids are coyotes

☞ 5 No ministers are cigarette smokers. Some cigarette smokers are persons who will succumb to cancer. Therefore, some ministers are not persons who will succumb to cancer.

6 No Kurd is a resident of Summerside. All Kurds are citizens of Kurdistan. Consequently, no citizen of Kurdistan is a resident of Summerside.

7 No platypus is native to Canada. Some platypuses are not wild animals. It follows that some wild animals are not native to Canada.

8 Some academic textbooks are expensive. No philosophy textbook is expensive. Some philosophy textbooks are not academic textbooks.

☞ 9 No true Islander was in favour of the bridge. Some Islanders were in favour of the bridge. Some Islanders are not true Islanders.

10 All fortunate people have good hearts. Some fortunate people are wealthy. Some people with good hearts are wealthy.

Exercise 8.1 B

Once we understand the logical structure of arguments, we can begin to assess the validity of arguments *without even knowing what the arguments are about*! To demonstrate, test the validity of the following "arguments" using the Venn Diagram method.

1 No G are Y.
Some Y are not L.
Some L are not G.

☞ 2 All R are H.
No F are H
No R are F.

☞ 3 No T are A.
No A are N.
No N are T.

4 All W are S.
All W are Q.
All Q are S.

5 No Y are J.
Some J are not L.
Some L are Y.

6 No D are C.
All C are G.
No G are D.

☞ 7 All Z are M.
All M are V.
All Z are V.

☞ 8 No E are O.
Some O are U.
Some U are not E.

8.1.2 Two Further Complications

1. The Asterisk Problem Sometimes we are confronted with an ambiguity about where to put the asterisk. In such cases, we are not given specific enough information. Consider

All goats eat cans.
Some worms are in cans.
Therefore some goats eat worms.

It is common to view this argument as valid. The conclusion seems to fol-low from the premises. It is invalid, however. The second premise does not provide us with sufficient information. Where are we to put the asterisk, in the intersection of only CW or in the intersection of all three circles GCW? Notice how our decision impinges on the conclusion. Only if it goes in GCW will the argument be valid. But since it is POSSIBLE that the asterisk goes into CW, we must proclaim the argument invalid. Remember, validity entails that it is *impossible* for the conclusion to be false while the premises are true. Since in this case we can imagine a case where the conclusion is false despite the premises being true, the argument fails our test for valid-ity.

In diagramming this asterisk problem, we must place the asterisk ON THE LINE (in this case inside the intersection of W and C, but on the G line).

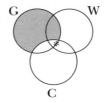

Universals First!

So far when we've been diagramming, we start with the first premise. There is no rule to do so. In fact, a better rule is to *start with the universal premise.* Consider the following argument:

Some Alliance members have uttered racist comments.
No one who utters racist comments should be voted into office.
Therefore, some Alliance members should not be voted into office.

Let us assume the following translation: "Some A are R," "No R are V," therefore "Some A are not R." If we wish to start with the first premise, we would be forced to put the asterisk on the V line within the AR intersec-tion. The second premise corrects the ambiguity, however, since it denies the existence of anything that is both an R and a V. So, if we start with the universal premise first, we resolve that ambiguity. Given this new rule (to diagram universals first), we must modify slightly the observation stated above. We said whenever an asterisk goes on a line, the argument is invari-ably invalid. But this presupposes we have diagrammed the universals first. In other words, we don't want to start with a particular proposition, place the asterisk on the line and call the argument invalid without first checking to see if the second premise is a universal statement which might resolve the ambiguity (as is the case with the racist Alliance example above).

Notice, by the way, that if both propositions are particular, both asterisks will be forced to go on a line, and the argument will invariably be invalid.

2. Null Sets   From the claim, "All S are P," it would seem to follow that we can infer that some "S are P." Consider, for example, the claim that all librarians have glasses (All L are G). From this it seems correct to assert that some librarians have glasses (Some L are G). After all, if "All L are G" is true, pick any L and it must also be a G, and if this doesn't mean "Some L are G," what does? Of course, we won't assume the reverse, that since some librarians have glasses, all do.

We are not allowed to make this seemingly sensible inference, however. If we do allow the inference from All to Some, a glaring peculiarity arises. Consider

All Martians have big eyes.

Given this, can we infer that

Some Martians have big eyes?

When we say "some," we mean at least one. To assert such a thing is to assert *the existence* of a Martian, something no logician wishes to be committed to. What if there were no Martians at all? Contemplating this prospect, we should see that by permitting the "Some-from-All" inference, we are denying the prospect of empty or *null* sets. That is, surely we can define a set of things without supposing anything actually exists in that set. (Refer back to chapter 5, where we discussed the difference between extensional and intensional definitions.) For example, I might speak about the set of all whole prime numbers between, but not including, 5 and 7. Since it is possible (in fact true) that no such prime numbers exist in such a set, we cannot blithely assume there exists a whole prime number between 5 and 7. A null set is one where the statement "All A are B" is asserted although, in fact, there are no As. There is an intension without an extension. Given the prospect of null sets, we must forbid the otherwise sensible sounding inference that "All A are B" implies there are at least some As. A sign reading "All trespassers will be shot" does not imply that any trespassers have indeed been shot. If the sign is successful, the set of trespassers will be empty.

Another way of illustrating this point is to translate "All A are B" statements as meaning "IF there are any As, they are Bs." Here we should see that nothing in this statement implies that there are any As. Telling the child that she may go to the movie only if she completes her homework does not guarantee that she's going to the movie. We must resist sticking asterisks into universes unless expressly told to do so.

Consider the following argument:

God is benevolent
Nothing benevolent will tolerate sin.
Therefore there is a God who will not tolerate sin.

To diagram this argument, and treating names as universals, we get the following:

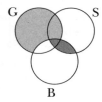

Is this argument valid? It depends on how we treat the conclusion, as a PN statement, or as a UN statement. A particular negative seems more to the point. We might feel we're being impelled to believe there is a particular G we're asserting, that we're denying that the set of G is empty. That is, it strikes us that the author of the argument, at any rate, is not talking merely about a set of things that are gods, but a particular being within that set, God himself. Notice, too, that if there were any G's, they would have to be outside of the S circle.

The question, though, is whether there are any G's. If we forbid the some-from-all inference, we must deem this argument invalid. In plain English, it is logically possible that there is no such thing as God. (Notice, by the way, that saying it is logically possible there is no God is not to be confused with saying therefore it is impossible there is a God. To make such an inference would be to misunderstand what is meant by logical possibility.)

If we treat the conclusion as a PN, the argument is invalid. The existence of something can not be inferred from universal propositions unless we assume the set is not empty. But that inference is not forced on us by the premises themselves. Perhaps, then, we wish to translate the conclusion as a universal statement as opposed to a particular statement. If so, the argument is valid. The UN statement is already sufficiently diagrammed by having diagrammed the premises alone. This translation will hardly satisfy theists, however, precisely because All statements do not imply existence. You may recall our earlier discussion of Anselm's ontological argument (chapter 5).

In pragmatic terms, if an asterisk is demanded in the conclusion, there must be an asterisk in one of the premises. (Note: for arguments to be valid, there can only be one asterisk in the premises. Two asterisks create on-the-line problems.)

More on Names and Null Sets

Consider the following valid argument:

> All the dancers had a good time.
> Cedric did not have a good time.
> Cedric must not have been dancing.

We've already seen that we cannot translate the second premise as "Some C are not G" since this means that Cedric is himself an intension and extension, that is, both the set and an instance of that set, which is a little too bizarre. If we were to treat Cedric as an instance of a third set, we'll notice immediately that we're in fact missing a third set of which Cedric is a member. After all, it certainly isn't the set of things that had a good time, and nor is it the set of dancers. Nothing prevents us, however, from inventing a third set to suit our purposes. We might choose something like "Persons at the night-club (or dance, or party, etc.)" Then, we would translate the argument above as All D are G; Some N are not G; Therefore, Some N are not D. Notice that this is perfectly valid (as it would also be if we translate Cedric as an All statement throughout). The trouble is that it seems a poor translation to say that someone at the night club wasn't dancing if what we meant was that it was specifically Cedric who wasn't dancing.

If treating names as particulars were an adequate translation, then we might be able to elude our debts. "Yes, I owe the bank, $100,000, but this merely means *someone* owes the bank $100,000. Why they should be after me is a little unfair, no?"

Another problem looms, however, concerning null sets. Our reluctance to assert particulars from universals seems even more strained when we treat names as universals. It is odd to treat names as universals and at the same time resist inferring particulars from universals. If we say Cedric was at the night club, we are not entitled to claim that at least one person was at the night club. The oddity of this has not gone unnoticed. Admittedly, we are limited in our ability to neatly translate natural language into categorical form.

Exercise 8.2

Test the validity of the following arguments using Venn diagrams. Pay special attention to the null set and asterisk problems.(Answers to selected questions provided in Appendix 1.)

☞ 1 All vitamins are taxed. Some taxed things are not found in closets. I conclude that some things found in closets are not taxed.

☞ 2 No mice are psychologically distraught. Some mice are not found in heroic tales. Hence, some animals found in heroic tales are psychologically distraught.

☞ 3 Some jacks are diamonds. All jacks are two-dimensional. So some two-dimensional things are diamonds.

☞ 4 Some cancer-causing agents are not addictive. All cancer-causing agents are hurtful. Thus, some hurtful things are not addictive.

☞ 5 All Martians have gills. Things with gills are torpid. So, some Martians are torpid.

6 Only white moves first. Those who move first are usually victorious. White is usually victorious.

7 Some coffee filters are carcinogenic. Most carcinogens affect normal cell division. Some coffee filters affect normal cell division.

8 All cataclysms are foretold. Nothing foretold can be avoided. No cataclysm can be avoided.

9 Genetically modified foods risk annihilating current life-sustaining crops. We certainly should not tolerate the annihilation of life-sustaining crops. We should not tolerate genetically modified foods.

10 Connor survived the terrorist attack of New York's Trade Centre. No one who survived that terrorist attack avoided psychological distress. There is one person, anyway, who suffered psychological distress.

8.2 Extended Categorical Arguments

Often we are confronted with arguments with more than three terms. The Venn diagram method, limited to testing syllogisms, then, seems poorly fitted to handle real-life arguments. The problem is not insurmountable. All we have to do is run a number of connected tests on the larger argument. That is, we break the argument down into a number of distinct syllogisms. We run our Venn tests on each one. If they are all valid, the whole argument is valid. If only one syllogism is invalid, the whole is invalid. Consider the following argument:

> Only informed, rational adults can engage in consensual acts. Fetuses are not informed rational adults. Some fetuses are aborted. Only consensual acts are moral acts. Therefore, some abortions are immoral.

Let's translate this argument. We'll use R to represent the set of things that are informed, rational adults. We'll assign C for the set of all things that are consensual acts. We'll use F to stand for the set of things that are fetuses. A we'll assign to things that are abortions, and M will represent things that are moral. Given that notation, and paying attention to the two occurrences of "only," and the "All ... are not ..." formation of the second premise, the above argument is translated

All C are R
No R are F
Some F are A
All M are C
Therefore, some A are not M.

There are five terms and four premises in this argument. The restriction of doing Venn diagrams on only syllogisms seems to prevent us from proceeding further. Yet the argument is valid, and the extended use of categorical logic can demonstrate this. To do so, we need to divide the argument into three separate syllogisms. To do this, we'll need to incorporate a few extra propositions that may legitimately be inferred from the stated (or derived) propositions.

Let's start with the first two premises. Here we have three terms: C, R, and F. R occurs twice, while C and F each occur once. If we can infer a conclusion based on these two premises alone, the conclusion will entail the C and the F. By diagramming the first two premises, we'll be able to pictorially represent the conclusion we're entitled to infer.

1 All C are R
2 No R are F.

By drawing a Venn diagram on these two premises, another proposition will be become visible. (Notice that we'll have to abandon the labelling convention here, since that is predicated on our knowing what the conclusion is. We can see that R is the middle term, but without knowing the conclusion, we can't tell what the major or minor terms are. Here, we're using the Venn diagram to *see what the conclusion will be.*)

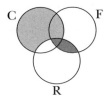

By studying this diagram, we should be able to see what other proposition we're entitled to infer. Given the truth of the two premises, what logically follows?

The answer is "No C are F." (Or, the converse, "No F are C." Since these are logically equivalent, it won't matter to us.)

This is not the conclusion of the argument, so our work is far from being done. But we can use this new derived proposition as a further premise in the argument. Let us see what develops from diagramming this new proposition along with the next stated premise ("Some F are A").

3 No C are F
4 Some F are A.

Again, we can run our Venn diagram on these two premises, and rather than *test* if a particular stated conclusion can be validly derived, we see what conclusion is validly derivable. Our Venn diagram will look like this

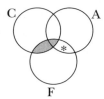

Given premises 3 and 4, we are entitled to infer that "Some A are not C." As we did above, we can now add this new line and run a third Venn diagram test on the last premise ("All M are C"), and now see whether the stated conclusion ("Some A are not M") can be validly deduced from the stated premises. We get

5 Some A are not C
6 All M are C
7 Therefore some A are not M

Doing universals first, and reinstating our labelling convention, we get

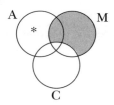

The conclusion is indeed already diagrammed merely by diagramming the premises (and valid derivations from the stated premises). Since each separate syllogism is valid, and each separate syllogism is based either on the stated premises or the valid derivations from the stated premises, the whole argument is valid.

Although for testing purposes categorical logic is restricted to syllogisms, it does not follow that we cannot run a number of tests on interconnected syllogisms.

Exercise 8.3

Test the validity of the following extended arguments. (Answers to selected questions provided in Appendix 1.)

☞ 1 Jones was at the party. No one at the party could have been in the alley at midnight. The murder happened in the alley at midnight. Therefore, Jones is not the murderer.

2 The thief entered by the window. The window was eleven feet above the ground. My client is only five feet five inches. No one five feet could reach a height of eleven feet. Therefore, my client is not the thief.

☞ 3 Some K are F. All H are F. All K are P. Therefore, some P are not H.

4 No A are B. All C are B. All D are A. Some E are C. Therefore, some E are not D.

5 No Y are T. All N are T. All K are N. Some K are S. Therefore, some S are not Y.

☞ 6 All F are G. No G are P. Some P are L. All L are O. All O are M. Therefore, some M are not F.

7 All E are T. Some E are R. No J are R. All J are V. No S are V. All V are B. Therefore, some B are not S.

8 No P are Y. All S are P. All T are Y. Some S are W. All W are B. Therefore, some B are not T.

8.3 More on Translation

Natural language comes in still more convoluted forms than those we've seen above, and we need help in translating these cumbersome patterns into our proper categorical forms if we want to test validity. Here we shall examine the rules of contraposition, obversion, and contradiction.

8.3.1 Contraposition

Sometimes we say things like "Non-smokers are intolerant." How should we translate this? We cannot translate it as "No S are I," let alone "No S are T," since the subject is things who don't smoke, not things that do smoke. A more plausible (though still poor) suggestion is "All N are I." If so, how would we translate the statement "All smokers are tolerant"? To keep the same terms, this would have to be "All non-N are not-I." Not only is this seemingly backward, we have not avoided the difficulty of having to translate this into proper categorical form.

The solution is to turn to the rule of contraposition. The contraposition of a categorical proposition has two steps:

1 We convert the statement (reverse the subject-predicate ordering), and
2 We negate each category (subject and predicate).

Consider the statement above: "Non-smokers are intolerant." We must first recognize that we're talking about the entire set of non-smokers, and we're denying that that set belongs in the tolerant set (as opposed to being included in the intolerant set). Thus

"All non-S are not-T"

The rule of contraposition allows us to translate this into a proper UA categorical form:

Step 1 conversion: "All not-T are non-S"
Step 2 negation: "All T are S"

Notice that step 2 really yields the rather more cumbersome statement

All non not-T are not non-S

We availed ourselves of the rule of *double negation* (where two negatives equal a positive). The two negatives preceding T are removed, and the two negatives preceding the S are likewise removed. Thus, "All T are S." In verbal form, this means "All Tolerant people are Smokers."

We may disagree with this statement. That is not to the point. If we disagree with this statement, we disagree also with the original formulation, since the two are equivalent.

Contraposition, please note, helps us translate cumbersome natural language into proper categorical form. We certainly do not want to take our simple categorical statements and contrapose them into cumbersome natural language.

We cannot legitimately contrapose every natural language form into an equivalent categorical form, however. As the chart below shows, we are entitled to contrapose natural language forms into categorical forms for only UA and PN statements, precisely the two that we were unable to convert. This follows since contraposition is the negation of conversion. (For the conversion chart, see section 8.5.1).

Equivalence Chart for Contraposition

Symbol	Categorical Form	Contraposition	Equivalence
UA	All A are B	All non-B are non-A	yes
UN	No A are B	No non-B are non-A	no
PA	Some A are B	Some non-B are non-A	no
PN	Some A are not B	Some non-B are not non-A	yes

From the chart above, we notice that only the contraposition of UA and PN is a logical equivalence. UN's contraposition says what is outside the S category does not intersect at all with what is outside the P category. For example,

"no non-mountains are non-valleys" ≠ "no mountains are valleys"

What the contraposition equals is that the only thing in the universe is either a mountain or a valley. To say that is to assert that nothing else exists. We should be able to see that the contraposition of UN statements are bound to be false. For example, a piece of cheese is neither a mountain nor a valley. Of course as long as the universe can be divided into only two sets, the contraposition of a UN statement may be true; for example, no non-living things are non-dead. The contraposition of a UN statement will be true only in cases where S and P encompass the universe. Anything outside the universe of existing things just doesn't exist, obviously.

Practice 1

Draw a Venn diagram of the contraposition of a UN statement. (Answer provided at the end of section 8.3).

8.3.2 Obversion

Perhaps someone might claim, "No rapists are non-pornography viewers." How should we translate this to see whether an argument in which this premise is embedded is valid? Following our discussion above, a general rule is to recognize negatives as logical relations. To do this, we cannot embed them in our subject or predicate terms. That is, we cannot treat this claim as "No R are N." Instead, we would have to give the following preliminary translation: "No R are non-P." We can see that this is not one of our proper categorical forms. So which form is equivalent?

The answer is that we are really saying "All rapists view pornography." Likewise, if we say "No babies are not cute," we are saying, "All babies are cute." (Whether this is true or not may depend on who's looking, of course.) The translation rule we're appealing to here is called obversion.

To know when we can use the rule of obversion to translate natural language into categorical form, it is helpful to see how the process goes in reverse. To obvert a categorical proposition, we require two steps.

1 Add a "non" to the predicate category.
2 Change the statement from negative to affirmative, or vice versa.

To illustrate, let's obvert the claim "All hillbillies are marksmen"

Step 1 "All hillbillies are not marksmen"
Step 2 "No hillbillies are non-marksmen."

Notice, by the way, we are treating "... not marksmen" as synonymous with "... non-marksmen." This may be contentious when we contemplate translating the negative prefix "ex," as in "my ex-lover," an "ex-smoker," or even a "recovering alcoholic." Is a recovering alcoholic a non-alcoholic? Is an ex-lover a non-lover? As put, such inferences seem specious, but the context of the proposition will clear up such ambiguities. For example, if we're talking about the set of my current lovers, the ex-lover will be excluded, and the terms "not" and "non" do this equally well.

It turns out that the obversion of each of our categorical forms will be logically equivalent. This means we are entitled to translate natural language that takes the form of the obverse of categorical propositions into the corresponding categorical form (see the chart below).

Equivalence Chart for Obversion

Symbol	Categorical Form	Obversion	Equivalence
UA	All A are B	No A are non-B	yes
UN	No A are B	All A are non-B	yes
PA	Some A are B	Some A are not non-B	yes
PN	Some A are not B	Some A are not non-non-B	yes

All obversions are logically equivalent.

The rule of double negation (where two negatives make a positive) is sufficient when we're dealing with negations in the predicate. Two negatives in the subject, however, are not so simply resolved. "No non A are not B" (the non-equivalent contraposition of the UN statement) does not mean "All A are not B" (which becomes "No A are B" by obversion.)

Notice the similarity between the obverse of UA and our earlier explanation of diagramming UA statements (section 8.5.1). Basically, in explaining how to diagram UA statements with negative shading, we appealed to the obversion of UA statements. We are able to do so, given their logical equivalence.

8.3.3 Contradiction

If asked to produce a statement that contradicts the claim "All politicians are honest," most people would say "No politicians are honest." This fails to do the trick, however, since it could be the case that "Some politicians are honest." If it is true that "Some politicians are honest" then "All P are H" and "No P are H" are both false at the same time.

Contradiction demands something more. If A contradicts B, then B has to be false whenever A is true, and B has to be true whenever A is false.

(For more on contradiction, see 10.6). The only statement that contradicts "All politicians and honest" is "Some politicians are not honest."

The definition of contradiction, therefore, is the following:

Two statements are contradictory if (i) they cannot both be true, and (ii) they cannot both be false, at the same time in the same respects.

What we want to know is how to properly translate a contradiction of a claim into categorical form. For example, what is the categorical translation of the following?

"It is false that all horses are black"

Recall, categorical propositions have a subject and a predicate, or speak about two classes of things, in terms of inclusion and exclusion and negative and positive. But in this statement ("It is false that all horses are black") we have, evidently, three sets of things: horses, things that are black, and things that are false.

The solution is to avail ourselves of the rule of contradiction. If it is false that all horses are black, the contradiction of "All horses are black" must be true. From the discussion above, we now know the contradiction is not merely the contrary "No horses are black," since it is conceivable that both propositions ("All H are B" and "No H are B") are *both* false. The answer is that "Some horses are not black."

Aristotle devised what he called the *Square of Opposition*. This helps show us which categorical form counts as the contradiction of another categorical proposition. The square of opposition (below) tells us that the contradictions follow the diagonal lines. Thus, the PA statement is the denial of the UN statement and *vice versa*. The PN statement is the denial of the UA statement and *vice versa*.

Square of Opposition

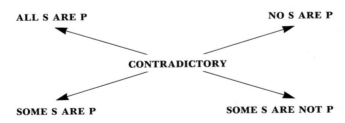

The square of opposition shows which categorical forms contradict each other, by following the diagonal line. UA and PN are contradictory, and UN and PA are contradictory. This means that if someone claims "It is false that school sucks," we can translate this as claiming "Some schools don't suck."

Likewise, if a premise in an argument is "In no way is it the case that some Alliance Party members are racist," we would translate that as an affirmation of the contradiction of "Some A are R" which, following our diagonal in the square of opposition, is "No A are R." Whether the claim is true is another matter.

In translating contradictions into categorical form, it is helpful to use the following two-step guideline:

1 Bracket the embedded statement that is being denied and place a negative sign on the outside of the bracket.

For example, if we want to translate the claim "It is false that all horses are black," our first step is to translate the claim denied into proper categorical form, bracket that claim, and place a negative sign on the left outside of the bracket. In this case, we shall use the tilde, ~, to represent our negative sign. (We needn't, but since this is the symbol we'll be using in the next chapter on propositional logic, we might as well employ it here, too.) Thus, our first step is

Step 1 ~[All H are B]

2 Now focussing only on the categorical proposition inside the bracket, we follow the diagonal inside Aristotle's Square of Opposition to see what counts as its contradiction.

In this case, that will be the PN statement "Some H are not B." This is the correct translation of the complex proposition "It is false that all horses are black." Hence

Step 2 Some H are not B.

This procedure may seem overly rigid. The help it provides is more obvious when the embedded statement (the statement being contradicted) itself requires translation. For example, how would we translate the following claim:

"It is false that only non-gays don't get AIDS"?
Step 1 ~[Only Non-G are not A] (preliminary step)
Step 2 ~[All non-A are non-G] (rule of only)
Step 3 ~[All G are A] (contraposition)
Step 4 Some G are not A. (contradiction)

Claiming "It is false that only non-gays don't get AIDS" is logically equivalent to claiming that some gays do not have AIDS. Was that your translation?

Other Logical Inferences?

Apart from contradiction, Aristotle believed there existed other logical inferences: contraries, subcontraries, and subalteration. The definitions of these terms are as follows:

> *Contraries*: Two statements are said to be contraries if they cannot both be true. If they cannot both be true, the truth of one entails that the other is false. "All A are B" and "No A are B" are contraries. They cannot both be true, although they may both be false.
>
> *Subcontraries*: Two statements are subcontraries if they cannot both be false, although they may both be true. "Some A are B" and "Some A are not B" are subcontraries. It is conceivable that they are both true, although inconceivable that they are both false.
>
> *Subalteration*: Two statements with the same subject and the same predicate and the same quality but different in quantity are subalterated. That is, "All A are B" and "Some A are B" are subalterations of each other. Likewise, "No A are B" and "Some A are not B" are also subalterations. According to Aristotle, we are entitled to infer the subalteration of universal propositions, but not the subalteration of particular propositions. That is, we may infer "Some A are B" from the proposition "All A are B," but we are not entitled to infer the reverse.

We can draw these inferences on the square of opposition if we wish. Aristotle did. If we draw a box around the square, subalteration will follow the vertical lines of the "square." The contraries will be along the top horizontal line. The subcontraries will be along the bottom horizontal line of the "square." Aristotle is wrong on these matters, though.

The rule of subalteration is in express contradiction to our null set problem since it rejects the assumption that null sets may exist. The rule of subalteration permits particular statements to be derived from universal statements, precisely what we disallowed earlier. Once we admit the possibility of null sets, we can no longer tolerate subalteration.

The rule of subcontraries is also problematic for the same reason. If we allow the inference from PA statements to PN statements, or the reverse, we would be able to infer PA statements from UA statements, a move we expressly disallowed.

Consider, if "All A are B" is true, it follows that "Some A are not B" is false, since that is what the rule of contradiction informs us. Meanwhile, since subcontraries cannot both be false, it follows that "Some A are B" must be true. This means we can infer existence from All statements. What went wrong?

Here is the problem in steps:

1 "All A are B" is true   (premise, accepted as true)
2 "Some A is not B" is false   (follows from 1, by law of contradiction)

3 "Some A is B" is true   (follows from 2 by rule of subcontraries which asserts two subcontraries can't both be false)

In fact, the problem gets worse. Often when we utter a PA, people tend to make conversational inferences from it. Imagine, for example, the prospect of a gluttonous child eating all of the cookies. The parent asks the child, "Did you eat all the cookies?" A resourceful child might reply, "I ate some of the cookies." She has not lied, since in order to eat all of the cookies it must be the case that she ate at least one of the cookies. Of course, she isn't uttering this half-truth idly; she's counting on her parent making the inference that therefore she didn't eat *all* the cookies, otherwise she would have said so. But since it follows from eating all the cookies that she ate *some* of the cookies, now it seems to follow that therefore she *didn't* eat all the cookies. By allowing loose inferences, we end up in a contradiction. From the truth of a UA statement, and appealing to the laws of contradiction and subcontraries, we seem entitled to assert its negation.

Here is this problem in steps:

1 "Some A are B" is true   (stated premise, accepted as given)
2 "Some A is not B" is true   (from 1 by conversational implication)
3 "All A is B" is false   (from 2 and law of contradiction)

Thus, in our first derivation, we deduced "Some A are B" from "All A are B," but by this second derivation, we are entitled to infer that "All A are B" is false by the assertion of "Some A are B." This means that from "'All are B' is true" we are entitled to infer "'All A are B' is false." Logical relations have broken down.

Admittedly Aristotle would not permit the second derivation. We present this to highlight the sort of loose logic that people employ "on the streets," if you will. But the problem with both derivations stems from Aristotle's rule of subcontraries. We must reject it.

Plainly the rule itself cannot tolerate null sets. What we want to maintain is that it *is* possible for both subcontraries to be false. We have already seen such examples when we were speaking about null sets. Consider the following subcontraries:

At least one King of Canada was obese.
At least one King of Canada was not obese.

If one is false, does this mean the other must be true? We want to answer that *both* statements are false. They are both false because there never was a King of Canada (saving Mackenzie King, of course).

The inference of contraries fares no better. If "All A are B" is true, the rule of contraries entitles us to infer that "No A are B" is false, because although both contraries may be false, they can't both be true. So if one is true, the other must be false. But if the PN is false, the rule of contradiction entitles us to infer that the PA is true. But then here's another way of deriving PA from UA statements, a move the contemplation of the null set expressly rejects.

The steps of this problem ensue as follows:

1 "All A are B" is true.	(premise, accepted as given)
2 "No A are B" is false	(from 1 by the rule of contraries. If both UA and UN can't be true, and UA is true, UN must be false)
3 "Some A are B" is true	(from 2 by the rule of contradiction. If UN is false, PA is true)

Again, we've moved from a universal to a particular, a move we expressly disallow if we are to tolerate the prospect of empty sets.

Despite his genius in other respects, Aristotle failed to consider the prospect of null sets. Once we admit the prospect of null sets, we must reject the rules of subalteration, contraries, and subcontraries. Thus, the only inference from Aristotle's Square of Opposition we will admit as valid is the rule of contradiction.

Exercise 8.4 A

What are we entitled to infer from the following claims? (Answers to selected questions provided in Appendix 1.)

☞ 1 No loitering allowed.
   a. It is false that some loitering is allowed.
   b. It is false that loitering is allowed.
   c. Some loitering is not allowed.
   d. All of the above.

2 It is false that some old dogs are not teachable
   a. All old dogs are teachable.
   b. No old dogs are teachable.
   c. Some old dogs are not teachable.
   d. Some old dogs are teachable.

3 It is incorrect to surmise that some true Canadians are terrorists.
   a. No terrorists are true Canadians.
   b. No true Canadians are non-terrorists.
   c. Some non-terrorists are not non-true Canadians
   d. All true Canadians are terrorists.

4 Some peanuts have come in contact with the chocolate.
   a. Some peanuts have not come into contact with the chocolate.
   b. No peanuts have come into contact with the peanuts.
   c. Only peanuts have come into contact with the chocolate.
   d. It is false that no chocolate has come into contact with peanuts.

☞ 5 All non-fattening foods are not tasty.
    a. All fattening foods are tasty.
    b. No fattening foods are tasty.
    c. It is false that some tasty foods are non-fattening.
    d. Some tasty foods are fattening.
  6 Only by spanking can we teach good manners.
    a. It is false that some spanking does not teach good manners.
    b. No spanking can teach good manners.
    c. Some good manners can be taught by spanking.
    d. It is not wrong to say that good manners is taught by spanking.

Exercise 8.4 B

Translate the following sentences into categorical form.

☞ 1 People who are going to be punished are immoral.
☞ 2 Not all professors are impractical
☞ 3 The only thing we have to fear is fear itself.
☞ 4. Man is the only creature that consumes without producing.
☞ 5. Any product that is not better than any other like product is not worth buying if it costs more than another similar brand.
  6 No debts are to be unpaid.
☞ 7 Lonely people are prone to exploitation by others.
☞ 8 Every dog has his day.
  9 Satan scores for Buffalo.
 10 No expert knows everything.
 11 Some conflicts are not resolvable by negotiation.
 12 Not all rapists are avid pornography viewers.
☞13 It is false that white boys can't jump.
 14 All people who don't pay taxes are not responsible for the deficit.
☞15 It absolutely wrong to suppose that some non-persons are not non-fetuses.
 16 Only mothers who risk death if they go full term should be allowed to have abortions.
 17 It is wrong to believe that only logicians are socially inept.
☞18 No shoes, no service.
 19 Not all men consume without producing.
 20 It is false to believe that those who suffer deserve it.

Exercise 8.4 C

Using Venn diagrams, prove the validity or invalidity of the following arguments.

☞ 1 You'll gladly admit that suicide is permissible, and since euthanasia is simply assisted suicide, euthanasia is obviously permissible as well.

2 I've watched a couple of British sitcoms and found them funny. But I read that most British sitcoms are sexist. Therefore sexist sitcoms are funny.

☞ 3 Nothing valuable is free. Drugs and alcohol are not free. Therefore drugs and alcohol are valuable.

4 No one benefits who has cheated. Some people who cheat have never been caught. Therefore some people who have been caught do not benefit.

5 Some tv shows are educational. Some educational things are not non-boring. Therefore some tv shows are boring.

☞ 6 Some dental work is unnecessary. Everything necessary is worth paying for. Therefore some dental work is not worth paying for.

7 All brunettes are not things that have fun. Almost all blondes are really brunettes. Therefore, some blondes do not have fun.

8 Not all sycophants have had disreputable childhoods. Many sycophants have attained high offices. Therefore, some people who have attained high offices have had disreputable childhoods.

9 Only if they are quick and capable readers can students easily master the books required for the English courses here. Unfortunately many students are poor readers and so will have problems.

☞10 Emma likes chocolate ice cream and since some chocolate ice cream has nuts she likes nuts.

11 Advertisements using deception are immoral even though people buy things if they are deceived, so it appears immoral things sell.

☞12 Some non-taxable items are not non-perishable and all non-perishables are not healthy. You can see that no taxable items are healthy.

☞13 Only non-females are non-sensitive. All sensitive creatures are not good business partners. One good business partner, anyway, is male.

☞14 It is not the case that some entrepreneurs are unfamiliar with the law of supply and demand. Nor is it true that most people familiar with the law of supply and demand are Marxists. Hence, Marxists are not entrepreneurs.

☞15 Harry loves Sally. Anyone loving Sally does not love Lucy. Harry doesn't love Lucy.

16 It is false to assert that all correlations are causal relations. CFC use and ozone depletion are correlates only. Therefore it is false to assert that some CFCs cause the depletion of the ozone layer.

Answer to Practice 1:

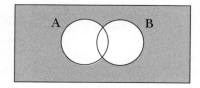

The Contraposition of No A are B

8.4 A Non-Venn Test for Validity

We can test for validity without using the Venn diagram method. Some people find this approach easier. To use it, however, we need to be familiar with whether terms are *negative* or *positive, universal* or *particular, distributed* or *undistributed,* and whether terms count as the *major, minor,* or *middle* term.

We are already familiar with whether terms are negative, positive, universal or particular, since these are what determine whether we're dealing with a UA (universal affirmative, or positive), a UN (a universal negative), a PA (particular affirmative, or positive), or a PN (a particular negative).

Likewise, we've already introduced the meaning of the major, minor, and middle terms when discussing the definition of syllogisms (8.4) and when introducing the labelling convention of our Venn diagrams (8.5.2). The following should act as a quick and easy reminder:

Major term   the subject in the conclusion
Minor term   the predicate in the conclusion
Middle term   the term that does not appear in the conclusion

We have not, however, discussed the concept of the distribution of terms.

8.4.1 Distributed and Undistributed Terms

A term is distributed if its scope includes the entire set; undistributed otherwise.

UA: All S is P. The subject S is distributed, since it speaks of the entire set of S ("All S ... "). But the predicate P isn't distributed. We don't know if other things can be P as well. That is, UA statements do not speak about the entire set of P.

UN: No S are P. S is distributed since, again, it is universal. When we say "No S ..." we're speaking of the entire set of S. But note that P is distributed too since the UN statement refers to the entire set of P. We may not know much about things that are P, but we know that we will never find any

Ss in P. This follows once we know that the conversion of UN statements are equivalent. Recall from our chart for conversion (section 8.5.1) that "No S are P" and "No P are S" are logically equivalent. In cases where conversions are equivalent, if the subject is distributed, so too is the predicate.

PA: Some S are P. Neither the subject S, nor the predicate P are distributed. When we are speaking of merely *some* S, we are not speaking of the entire set of S. What is true of this subset of S may or may not be true of the remainder of S. Some S may not be P. Likewise, some P may not be S. We don't know. There is not enough information. This shows that the predicate is not distributed either. PA statements are not speaking about the entire set of P, let alone the entire set of S. Just as the conversion of UN statements are equivalent, so are the conversions for PA statements equivalent. This shows that whatever we can say of the subject, we can equally say of the predicate. This is why both the subject and the predicate are equally not distributed in PA statements.

PN: Some S are not P. S is not distributed, since some S may be P, or it may not, we don't know. But note, the predicate term, P *is* distributed. Why? because at least for those Ss, they can't be P. Of the whole category of Ps, some Ss are not in it. If we say, "Some pigs are not pretty," we can see that among the entire set of pretty things, some pigs aren't included.

Distribution Chart

	Predicate not distributed	Predicate distributed
Subject distributed	ALL S ARE P	NO S ARE P
Subject Not distributed	SOME S ARE P	SOME S ARE NOT P

The subject is distributed in universals, but not particulars. The predicate is distributed in negative statements, but not affirmative ones.

Practice 2

Examine the following syllogism.

> No A are B
> Some B are C
> Some C are not A

Now answer the following questions. (Answers are provided below.)

1 Is the middle term distributed in the second premise?
2 Is the middle term distributed in the first premise?
3 Is the major term distributed in the conclusion?
4 Is the minor term distributed in the conclusion?
5 Is the minor term distributed in the premise?

6 Is the major term distributed in the premise?
7 Are there two negative premises?
8 Is the conclusion negative?
9 Is there a negative premise?
10 Is the conclusion universal?
11 Is the first premise universal?
12 Is the second premise universal?

8.4.2 Five Rules for Validity

Given our new understanding of distribution and a reminder about universals, particulars, positives (or affirmatives), negatives, and major, minor, and middle terms, we are ready to apply the following five rules to test the validity of categorical syllogisms without drawing Venn diagrams. All of the following five rules must be met if the syllogism is to be valid. If any one rule is violated, the argument is invalid.

Rule # 1 The middle term must be distributed in at least one premise.
Rule # 2 No term is distributed in the conclusion that is not distributed in at least one of the premises.
Rule # 3 A valid syllogism cannot have two negative premises.
Rule # 4 If the conclusion is negative, one of the premises must be negative. Likewise, if one premise is negative, the conclusion must also be negative.
Rule # 5 If there are two universal premises, the conclusion must be a universal. Otherwise, we would be violating the null set criteria.

Answers to Practice 2
Let's see how you did.

1 No.	4 Yes.	7 No.	10 No.
2 Yes.	5 Yes.	8 Yes.	11 Yes.
3 No.	6 No.	9 Yes.	12 No.

Practice 3

Now that we're familiar with major, minor, and middle terms, as well as with universal and particular propositions, and whether terms are distributed or not, let's use the five rules of validity on the following argument:

No A are B
Some B are C
Some C are not A

Rule #1 Is the middle term distributed in at least one premise?

Yes. The middle term is B. B is distributed in the first premise.

Rule #2 (a) Is there a distributed term in the conclusion?

Yes. The minor term (predicate) A is distributed in the conclusion.

(b) If so, is it also distributed in at least one premise?

Yes. A is distributed in the UN first premise.

Rule #3 Are there two negative premises?

No.

Rule #4 (a) Is the conclusion negative?

Yes. It is a PN, particular negative.

(b) If yes, is there at least one negative premise?

Yes. The first premise is negative (a UN statement.)

Rule #5 (a) Are there two universal premises?

No.

(b) If yes, is the conclusion universal?

N/A

So, is the argument valid? Yes. All rules are satisfied. No rules are violated.

Here are a few more illustrations. The numbers below the arguments indicate the rule numbers. A ✓ represents satisfaction of the rule. An ✗ indicates violation of the rule. In cases where rules are inapplicable, as when the first condition is not met, we will treat that as satisfying the rule. When any ✗ occurs in any rule, the argument as a whole is invalid.

1.	2.	3.
All K are F.	All O are J.	No E are G.
Some C are F.	Some C are not O.	Some G are not L.
Some K are C.	Some C are not J.	Some L are not E.
#1. ✗	#1. ✓	#1. ✓
#2. ✓	#2. ✗	#2. ✓
#3. ✓	#3. ✓	#3. ✗
#4. ✓	#4. ✓	#4. ✓
#5. ✓ Invalid	#5. ✓ Invalid	#5. ✓ Invalid

4.	5.	6.
All D are V.	All J are W.	All G are H
All M are D.	No J are K.	All H are Y
No M are V.	Some W are not K.	All G are Y
#1. ✓	#1. ✓	#1. ✓
#2. ✓	#2. ✓	#2. ✓
#3. ✓	#3. ✓	#3. ✓
#4. ✗	#4. ✓	#4. ✓
#5. ✓ Invalid	#5. ✗ Invalid	#5. ✓ Valid

Exercise 8.5

Prove the validity or invalidity of the following categorical syllogisms using the above 5 rules. (Answers to selected questions provided in Appendix 1.)

☞ 1 Some bats are scary. All scary things love to stare at the moon. Hence some bats love to stare at the moon.

☞ 2 No volleyball player is a resident of Red Deer. Some residents of Red Deer do not drive noisy trucks. Hence, some people who drive noisy trucks are not volleyball players.

3 Some people who wear jackets and ties are trustworthy. All trustworthy people can take books out of the library. It follows that some people who wear jackets and ties cannot take books out of the library.

☞ 4 Nothing man-made is safe to humans. Some flowers are not man-made. Therefore, some flowers are safe to humans.

5 Some cacti are not good house plants. Some aloe plants are cacti. Some aloe plants are not good house plants.

6 All redecorated houses take time. Anything that takes time is not worth doing. No redecorated houses are worth doing.

7 All veiled images are terrifying things. Some terrifying things are not found in closets. I conclude that some things found in closets are not veiled images.

☞ 8 Some lawn pesticides are not toxic to pets. All products toxic to pets have restrictions in place. It follows that some lawn pesticides have no restrictions.

9 Some jet planes are conducive to meditation. All jet planes are good places to do metaphysics. So, some good places to do metaphysics are conducive to meditation.

10 Some cancer-causing agents are not additives. All cancer-causing agents are chemicals. Thus, some chemicals are not additives.

☞11 All Martians are people with green skin. All people with green skin are terrifying to look upon. So, some Martians are terrifying to look upon.

12 Only white moves first. Those who move first are usually victorious. White is usually victorious.

13 Some coffee filters are carcinogenic. Most carcinogens affect normal cell division. Some coffee filters affect normal cell division.

☞14 All cataclysms are foretold. Nothing foretold can be avoided. No cataclysm can be avoided.

15 Genetically modified foods risk annihilating current life-sustaining crops. We certainly should not tolerate the annihilation of life-sustaining crops. We should not tolerate genetically modified foods.

16 No one benefits who has cheated. Some people who cheat have never been caught. Therefore some people who have been caught do not benefit.

☞17 You'll gladly admit that suicide is permissible, and since euthanasia is simply assisted suicide, euthanasia is obviously permissible as well.

18 I've watched a couple of British sitcoms and found them funny. But I read that most British sitcoms are sexist. Therefore sexist sitcoms are funny.

☞19 Nothing valuable is free. Drugs and alcohol are not free. Therefore drugs and alcohol are valuable.

20 Connor survived the terrorist attack of New York's Trade Centre. No one who survived that terrorist attack avoided psychological distress. There is one person, anyway, who suffered psychological distress.

☞21 Some TV shows are educational. Some educational things are not non-boring. Therefore some TV shows are boring.

22 Some dental work is unnecessary. Everything necessary is worth paying for. Therefore some dental work is not worth paying for.

23 All brunettes are not things that have fun. Almost all blondes are really brunettes. Therefore, some blondes do not have fun.

☞24 Not all sycophants have had disreputable childhoods. Many sycophants have attained high offices. Therefore, some people who have attained high offices have had disreputable childhoods.

25 Cults require non-autonomous persons. Cults provide a sense of belonging. Therefore some autonomous persons do not have a sense of belonging.

9
∂

Propositional Logic: Translation

Preliminaries • Translation • Truth Values

9.1 Preliminaries

9.1.1 Logic and Validity (Again)

There are two common kinds of mistakes about logic. One is to assume that validity is a *sufficient* condition for accepting an argument. It is not. We may have a perfectly valid argument that deserves rejection. Validity concerns the *relations* between propositions only, and says nothing at all about whether the propositions are true, or acceptable. That is why we may have a valid argument with false or unacceptable premises. To determine validity we ask, *if the premises were true, would the conclusion necessarily follow?* This condition can be met by false propositions as well as true propositions. When we examine an argument, as long as we can make sense of it, we look to *two* things: acceptability and logic. Looking at only one will be *insufficient.* For example, the following argument contains false propositions, yet is perfectly valid:

> Canada is a leader in the world economy. If a country is a leader in world economy, it needn't worry about toxic waste or world hunger. Canada needn't worry about toxic waste or world hunger.

However deplorable its sentiments, the argument is valid because if the premises were true, the conclusion would also have to be true. This relation holds even after we point out that no proposition is acceptable. That is, we may have reason to reject the argument despite its being valid.

The second common mistake is to pretend that validity is not even a necessary condition for a good argument. For deductive arguments, at least, validity is a necessary condition. And as long as we interpret validity more broadly as providing good grounds for the conclusion, then validity is a necessary condition for inductive arguments as well. To pretend that validity doesn't matter is to flatly deny that reason matters, that there is no connection between one's premises and one's conclusion. But if that were so, there is no reason to accept one's conclusions – ever. (For the argument concerning why, see 10.6.)

Presumably critics of logic mean to point out that there is more to life than logic alone, that those who focus *only* on logic are missing something. We agree. For example, some persons may be outraged that we can say that the toxic argument above is perfectly valid. The outrage is misplaced. To be sure, we have every reason to reject the conclusion. We may agree that the argument is problematic, but its problem does not lie in its logic. To pretend that logic has *no* role is to simply misunderstand the role logic does play. Logic is a necessary, but not sufficient condition for good argumentation.

It is worth reiterating a few observations made in the last chapter about logic and validity. Our task in assessing an argument is to look at three things: meaning, truth, and logic. In part 2, we examined the issue of meaning. We want to understand what is being offered. In our own arguments, we want to state our case in ways our intended audience can understand. In part 3, we examined the concept of truth. The reasons we provide to support our conclusion must themselves be acceptable to our audience. In assessing others' arguments, we need to be sure that the premises they offer are acceptable to us. Arguments that have understandable and acceptable premises are not necessarily worth accepting, however. The third component is needed: logic. That is the theme of part 4.

Logic concerns the relations of the premises to the conclusion. If the premises do not relate to the conclusion, no matter how clear and acceptable they may be, we have grounds to dismiss the argument. For an argument to be valid, the conclusion must necessarily follow from the premises; otherwise the argument is invalid. Notice the reliance on the word "necessarily." That the conclusion *happens* to be true is not sufficient in deductive logic.

The fact that, in deductive arguments, the conclusion is asserted to follow necessarily from the premises gives us a clue about how to test validity. We need merely ask whether the conclusion indeed follows from the premises. That is, we wonder whether it is possible for the conclusion to be false while the premises are true. If yes, the argument is invalid. If no, the argument is valid.

Validity is an all-or-nothing affair. One cannot claim that an argument is partly valid, just as one cannot claim to be partly pregnant. An argument is valid if it is impossible for the conclusion to be false while the premises are true. For valid arguments, the conclusion is forced upon us by the premises.

In testing validity, we are not concerned about whether premises are in fact true. Whether they are or not is irrelevant when testing validity. Of course the acceptability of the premises is not irrelevant when judging the merits of the argument as a whole. That is, to repeat ourselves, validity is not a sufficient condition of good argumentation. It is a necessary condition, however. Because it is a necessary condition, we need to examine logic in more depth. Logic focusses on the relations of the ideas, or the structure of the argument, and not the content. For this reason, as we will shortly see, the content of the argument will be completely stripped away.

9.1.2 Categorical vs. Propositional

Deductive arguments come in two forms: *categorical* and *propositional*. Categorical logic deals in terms of objects, sets and classes. Propositional logic is translated in terms of simpler propositional units. The method of testing validity differs between the two systems. The subject of the last chapter was categorical logic. This chapter will examine propositional logic.

There are three positions to take concerning categorical and propositional logic: (1) We only need categorical logic. That is, all propositional logic can be recast in categorical form, but not all categorical logic can be recast into propositional form. (2) We only need propositional logic. That is, all categorical logic can be recast into propositional form, but not *vice versa*. (3) We need both. A good part of categorical logic cannot be translated into propositional logic, and a good part of propositional logic cannot be translated into categorical form. We shall not decide this controversial issue here except to note that most advanced courses in logic focus on propositional logic with existential and universal quantifiers. Some interpret this as logic that partly combines both forms.

Two clear advantages of propositional logic over categorical logic, if nothing else, are that it permits easier translation from natural language and it can more readily handle arguments with more than two premises and three terms. In fact, there is no limit to the number of terms or premises, and since most arguments do come in an extended form, this may seem to be a clear advantage.

A disadvantage of propositional logic is that it requires more skill in determining validity than does categorical logic. Although translation is simpler, the testing of validity is more difficult for most students. Validity and invalidity are visually apparent in Venn diagrams. This is not the case with propositional logic. Still, the skills are basic and can be easily mastered if we proceed step by step. Although more difficult to learn than categorical logic, once students have mastered it, most tend to prefer it. It can offer a much quicker glimpse at logical structure.

9.2 Translation

Logic is about the *form* or *structure* of arguments. It has nothing to do with content. To examine validity, then, logicians symbolize arguments to better see the logical structure, or the *form* of the argument. There are two things to symbolize: the *proposition units* and their *relations*.

9.2.1 Proposition Units

We can symbolize a proposition unit with a capital letter A, B, C ... The letter we choose doesn't matter, as long as we retain that letter for subsequent occurrences of the same proposition unit elsewhere in the argument. The convention is to use the first letter of either the subject or the predicate of the proposition we're intending to denote. Usually the predicate is the more descriptive letter. For example, if I want to symbolize the proposition, "The abortion that occurred is not moral," it would be potentially misleading to interpret that as the negation of "A" (the subject) as opposed to the negation of "M" (the predicate). After all, we aren't saying the abortion *did not* happen; we're instead denying that the abortion has the particular predicate of being moral.

Sometimes, however, using the first letter of the subject of the proposition unit is more salient. For example, we might want to assert that both Detroit and Colorado will make it into the playoffs. Here, we want to say that Detroit will make it into the playoffs, and that Colorado will make it into the playoffs. Both propositions share the same predicate, so it wouldn't do to label the different propositions with the same letter "P" for playoffs. In this case, labelling the propositions by the first letter of the subject term is preferable.

Note, using the first letter of the subject or the predicate is a convention. Sometimes we will have to veer from that convention. Consider, for example, an argument with the following propositions:

Ants infested the walls.
Water damage destroyed the attic.
The window was covered with algae.

If we choose A to represent the first proposition, and W to represent the second, what shall we use for the third? Besides, might we confuse A for "attic" or "algae" and W for "walls" or "window"? In such cases, we are entitled to select less ambiguous letters. In this case, perhaps we might choose I for the first, D for the second, and C for the third.

For that matter, using letters at all is a mere convention. We could just as easily use iconic symbols, or geometric shapes, or names of fish. The main object is to keep the same symbol for repeated instances of the same proposition.

If the proposition unit is "A fetus is a person" we can symbolize that with a "P." That would constitute an adequate translation into propositional form. That is, some propositions are single units. A single unit is any proposition which takes a subject-predicate grammatical form without any logical relations. Another proposition may be "Abortion is morally wrong." For the time being, we can symbolize that with the letter "W." (Really, we want to treat this as the negation of M, but we'll hold that off for the moment.)

P and W may fit together in a wide range of ways, however. We cannot symbolize the connections between the two proposition units with the letters P and W all by themselves, since that won't tell us the *relation* between these two proposition units. Consider the following (non-exhaustive list) of what might be said with these two proposition units:

1 A fetus is a person and abortion is immoral.
2 A fetus is a person or abortion is moral.
3 If a fetus is a person, then abortion is immoral.
4 A fetus is not a person, but abortion is immoral anyway.
5 Although a fetus is a person, abortion is moral.
6 A fetus is not a person or abortion is immoral.
7 Abortion is moral if a fetus is not a person.
8 Unless abortion is immoral, a fetus is not a person.

In order to distinguish these from each other, we need more than the symbols for the propositions. We need to also symbolize the *relations* of proposition units. Therefore, apart from capital letters indicating proposition units, we require some symbols to tell us what the intended relation is between these propositions.

9.2.2 Logical Relations

Propositional logic limits itself to four types of logical relations: *negation, conjunction, disjunction,* and *conditional.*

The relation of *negation* is indicated by words and phrases such as *not, false, no way, wrong, incorrect, untrue,* and prefixes such as: *non, ex, dis, un, im, de,* and the like. The effect of a negation is to alter the truth value of a proposition. If a proposition A is true, then not-A is false. Conversely, if a proposition A is false, then not-A is true.* For simplicity's sake, we will

---

* One might object. Can't there be an indeterminate category between truth and falsehood? Within that category, presumably, we'd imagine degrees of certainty. For example, although I don't know for sure I'm not going to die tomorrow, I bet I won't. But my not knowing I won't die tomorrow hardly entails I think I will die tomorrow. All this is true: but notice it concerns my *belief about what's true and false,* not my concept of truth and falsehood itself. We need to distinguish our concept of *knowing* from our concept of *truth.* A proposition is true or false, whatever our beliefs are about that.

translate all negations as "*not.*" A rule of thumb is to symbolize all proposition units in their positive form, even if only the negations of that proposition unit occur throughout the argument. Thus, above, we suggested calling things that are morally wrong "W." But really, we should be treating the proposition unit as things that are moral, and thereby, rather than "W," we want to say "not-M."

The relation of *conjunction* joins propositions. Conjunctions are indicated in English by the following partial list: *and, but, although, notwithstanding, however, as well as, also, despite,* and the like. A conjunctive proposition asserts that all proposition units are independently true. If any one is false, the conjunctive is false. For simplicity's sake, we will refer to all conjuncts as "*and.*"

Grammatically, conditionals and disjunctives are types of conjunctives. This fact may tend to confuse some readers. Conjunctions are any word or phrase that links terms or phrases together one way or another. By this definition, premise indicators and conclusion indicators are also conjunctives. Such an all-encompassing account is too sweeping for our purposes, however. For us, a conjunction will be limited to the "and" relation.

The logical relation of *disjunctives* indicates that at least one of two or more proposition units is true. Disjunctives are indicated in English by *or* and *either/or.* We will refer to disjunctives as "*or.*"

Our last logical relation concerns *conditionals.* These indicate a more dependent relation between the proposition units than the relations of disjunctives and conjunctives. Conditional relations assert that one proposition is true on the condition that the other is true. Conditional phrases in English include *if, if … then, in case, provided, as long as, whenever, wherever,* and such. Conditionals may also be indicated by subjunctives, such as *should,* or *would.* For example, "Had I been there, I would have saved you," or "Should you be passing this way, please visit," or "I would have been here on time, but for a flat tire." For simplicity's sake, we will refer to all conditionals as "*if … then.*"

Sometimes we may refer to conditional propositions as *hypothetical* propositions. In proposition 3 above (If a fetus is a person, then abortion is immoral), we may say that abortion is immoral *on the condition that* a fetus is a person. Conversely we may say that abortion is immoral *on the hypothesis* that a fetus is a person.

For "or" and "and" statements, it will make no difference whether we reverse the A and the B. "A or B" is logically equivalent with "B or A." Likewise, "A and B" is logically equivalent with "B and A." Saying "Apples and oranges are fruit" or saying "Oranges and apples are fruit" will not make any difference in meaning. For "if … then" statements, however, the ordering matters. "If A then B" is not the same as "If B then A." Saying "If you're pregnant, then you're a woman," *does not mean* the same as saying "If you're a woman, you're pregnant," luckily.

The proposition unit that occurs after an unadulterated "if" is referred to as the *antecedent*. The proposition unit that occurs after the "then" is called the *consequent*. In proposition 3 above, the antecedent is "A fetus is a person." The consequent is "Abortion is immoral." Conditional propositions assert that the consequent will be true as long as the antecedent is true.

Notice that in English the "if" clause needn't occur first. In the proposition, "Pigs could fly if they had wings," the antecedent occurs second, and the consequent first. This shows that we don't mean that the antecedent is simply defined as whatever occurs first in a conditional proposition. The antecedent always occurs after an unadulterated "if," or the "if" substitute. For example, in the proposition, "I would have been on time but for a flat," the "if" substitute in this case is the term "but." "But" coupled with the subjunctive "would" acts as a negative conditional. Thus we can translate this as "I would have been here on time if not for a flat tire." By placing the antecedent first, this gets converted to the following: "If not for a flat, I would have been on time." *For purposes of translation, we will always place the antecedent first.*

"Only If" and "If Only"

Above we noted that the antecedent always occurs after an unadulterated "if" or "if" substitute. Why did we say "unadulterated"? The reason is that there is an exception to this rule. When using the phrase "*only if*" this rule fails. Saying "There is fire only if there is oxygen" does not mean "If there is oxygen, there is fire," fortunately. It means, instead "If there is fire, there is oxygen." (In natural language, one might express the proposition in the following ways: "Whenever there's fire, there's oxygen" or "You can't have fire without oxygen.") Notice that in this case the antecedent *does not* follow the "if." The modifier "only" placed in front of the "if" affects that rule. "A only if B" simply translates to "If A then B." Thus, "There is fire only if there is oxygen" becomes "If there is fire, there is oxygen." So when "if" is not followed by an "only," the antecedent follows the "if" wherever the "if" occurs in the proposition. When an "only" follows the "if," the consequent is what follows the "only if."

Notice that "only if" does not equal "if only." "*If only*" is used to highlight a negative conditional. "If only I hadn't eaten the second helping, I wouldn't be in such pain now," is translated simply by removing the "only." The modifier "only" is redundant when placed after the "if." It alters the order of the antecedent and consequent when placed before the "if."

Negative Conjunctives, Disjunctives, and Conditionals

There exist negative forms of conjuncts, disjuncts, and conditionals. A negative conjunct is in fact a disjunctive, and a negative disjunct is in fact a conjunct. The words *nor, neither,* or the phrase, *neither ... nor* indicate the negation of a conjunct, not a disjunct. "Neither A nor B," indicates that both A and B are false. So it is a conjunct of two negations "Not A and not

B." If we say neither the Flames nor the Oilers will make the playoffs, we are saying more than that at least one of those teams will not make the playoffs. We are saying both will not.

Meanwhile, to deny a conjunct is to affirm a disjunct. If we say, "It is false that the Flames and Oilers will make the playoffs," we needn't be asserting that *both* will not make the playoffs. All that can logically be inferred is that at least one will not make the playoffs. Thus the negation of a conjunct is translated as a disjunct: "Either the Flames will not make the playoffs or the Oilers will not make the playoffs." This has a habit of confusing people in conversation. Consider the following conversation, overheard at a canteen. "I'll have the fries." "Do you want gravy and fries?" "No, thank you." "What? You don't want fries then?" The question reveals a failure to recognize that the negation of a conjunct is simply a disjunct. Saying, "It is false that A and B" *does not* say "Not A and not B."

Negative conditionals will use terms such as *unless,* and, when coupled with subjunctives (*would, could, should*), terms such as *but, except, if only, had,* and such.

9 You won't get dessert unless you eat your vegetables.
10 Unless you hear from me first, don't call.
11 I'd have been here on time, but for a flat tire.
12 Had I not had an aversion to waking up in the dark, I would have made the tee time.
13 Should you ever need help, don't hesitate to call.
14 I made an excellent first impression, except for the egg salad incident.
15 If only I hadn't eaten the second helping, I wouldn't be in such pain now.

When we recast these conditionals with "if ... then," and make sure we place the antecedent first, and the consequent second, we'll see that we'll sometimes need to add in negation. For example, the term "*unless,*" will be translated as "If not." The proposition "Unless a fetus is a person, abortion is moral," becomes "If a fetus is not a person, abortion is moral." Conversely, the proposition, "Unless a fetus is not a person, abortion is immoral," becomes, by double negation, "If a fetus is a person, abortion is immoral."

Notice that what follows the phrase "unless" is the antecedent. Thus (9) above becomes "If you do not eat your vegetables, you will not get dessert." Some might be tempted to translate that in the positive form, "If you eat your vegetables, you will get dessert." We could happily do so if the term "unless" was a *bi-conditional.* A bi-conditional is a conditional proposition in which the antecedent and consequent are interchangeable. Bi-conditionals are designated by "*if and only if*" clauses (often shortened to *iff*) to distinguish them from unidirectional conditionals. The claim, "A if and only if B" asserts two conditional propositions: (1) "If A, then B," and (2) "If B, then A." Consider the definition of the correspondence theory of truth: "A proposition is true if and only if it corresponds to facts in the world." This is to be read as asserting two separate conditionals: (1) "A proposition is true *if* it corresponds to facts of the world" and (2) "A proposition is true *only if* it corresponds to facts in the world." From the discussion above, we can see the difference between these two statements. In (1), the antecedent is the correspondence to facts in the world. In (2), the antecedent is a proposition's being true. Thus, this offers us a bi-conditional statement.

We will not concern ourselves with bi-conditionals *except* to point out that unless indicated explicitly, we will assume all conditionals are unidirectional. On that note, "unless" is not a biconditional. To see more clearly why not, contrast (9) with the following claim:

16 You won't get pregnant unless you have intercourse.

We can translate this as "If you don't have intercourse, you won't get pregnant." But while we may accept this claim, we will likely reject the following rendition: "If you have intercourse, you will get pregnant." Learning from this, we must resist inferring from (9) that you *will* get dessert if you eat your vegetables. Perhaps you took so long, there is no dessert left. Perhaps judging by your track record of vegetable eating, dessert was not even made. All we can infer from the conditional statement is the negative form: no way are you getting dessert without eating your vegetables. After all, we might utter the similarly structured claim: "No way are you going to be immortal if you don't eat your vegetables." It turns out, even if you do eat your vegetables, you're not going to be immortal.

Note: the phrase *even if* is not a conditional. It is best read as a conjunction. When we say, "Buckminster is a good guy *even if* he's guilty of robbing the store," we really mean "*Although* Buckminster robbed the store, he's a good guy." In propositional logic, this will be further translated as "Buckminster robbed the store and Buckminster is a good guy." Admittedly, the logical translation misses something, but nothing *logically relevant*.

Transposition

For unidirectional conditionals, we are allowed to reverse the antecedent and consequent *only as long as* we also negate each term. Let's look again at the following two forms of the same conditional proposition:

There's oxygen if there's fire.
There's fire only if there's oxygen.

Both are translated as:

If there's fire, there's oxygen.

But we are also entitled to infer that

If there's no oxygen, there can't be fire.

That is, we can reverse the antecedent and consequent and negate each term. Likewise, the claim, "If you're pregnant, you're a woman," is equivalent to "If you're not a woman, you're not pregnant." Likewise (12) "Had I not had an aversion to waking up in the dark, I would have made the tee time" becomes, "If I did not have an aversion to waking up in the dark, I would have made the tee time," which is equivalent to "If I did not make the tee time, then I have an aversion to waking up in the dark."

The rule to reverse the antecedent and consequent and to negate each term is called *transposition*. (We will learn more about transposition in 10.4.)

Symbols

We are now acquainted with the four logical relations of negation, conjunction, disjunction, and conditional propositions. We also know that all negations will be translated as "*not*," all conjunctions translated as "*and*," all disjuncts translated as "*or*," and all conditionals translated as "*if... then*." We shall now proceed to assign symbols for these four logical relations. They are as follows:

not = ~
and = •
or = v
if ... then = ⊃

Review

There are two steps to translating natural language into propositional form.

(1) We will choose a capital letter to symbolize a proposition unit, A, B, C ... Concerning this step, there are three things to note: (i) We shall tend to choose either the predicate or the subject of the proposition unit, depending on salience. (ii) In choosing our letters, we will always symbolize the positive form of the proposition unit. In other words, we will not embed any logical relations in our proposition units, and we shall remember that all negative forms, including prefixes, are logical relations. This means that something that is morally wrong would not be translated as W. Rather, we recognize that the positive form of the concept are things that are moral. Thus, to say that something is morally wrong, is to say that it is *not* moral. Thus, rather than symbolizing the proposition "Abortion is morally wrong" as W (as we suggested earlier), we should symbolize this as ~M. (iii) Some proposition units are themselves complete propositions. That is, not all propositions have logical relations.

(2) We insert the appropriate symbols for any logical relations – ~, •, v, ⊃. "~" will cover all negations (not, false that, no way that, wrong that, incorrect, untrue, non, ex, dis, un, ...). "•" will cover all logical (not grammatical) conjunctions (and, but, although, notwithstanding, however, as well as, also, despite, neither/nor). "v" will cover all disjuncts (or, either/or, not both). "⊃" will cover all unidirectional conditionals in which the antecedent occurs left of the horseshoe and the consequent right of the horseshoe (if, if ... then, in case, provided, as long as, whenever, wherever, should, would, only if, if and only if, unless, but, except, if only).

We are now ready to translate.

9.2.3 Translation

Using our four logical symbols (~, •, v, ⊃) and capital letters (A, B, C, ...), we may now translate any natural language proposition. Let us start with providing the complete translations for the numbered examples above.

1 A fetus is a person and abortion is immoral . . . . .P • ~M
2 A fetus is a person or abortion is moral . . . . .P v M
3 If a fetus is a person, then abortion is immoral . . . . .P ⊃ ~M
4 A fetus is not a person, but abortion is immoral anyway . . .~P • ~M
5 Although a fetus is a person, abortion is moral . . . . .P • M
6 A fetus is not a person or abortion is immoral . . . .~P v ~M
7 Abortion is moral if a fetus is not a person . . . .~P ⊃ M
8 Unless abortion is immoral, a fetus is not a person . . . . .M ⊃ ~P
9 You won't get dessert unless you eat your vegetables . . . . . .~V ⊃ ~D
10 Unless you hear from me first, don't call . . . .~H ⊃ ~C
11 I'd have been here on time, but for a flat tire . . . .~F ⊃ T
12 Had I not had an aversion to waking up in the dark, I would
    have made the tee time . . . .~A ⊃ T
13 Should you ever need help, don't hesitate to call . . . . .N ⊃ ~H
14 I made an excellent first impression, except for the egg
    salad incident . . . .~E ⊃ F
15 If only I hadn't eaten the second helping, I wouldn't be in such
    pain now . . . .~S ⊃ ~P
16 You won't get pregnant unless you have intercourse . . . .~I ⊃ ~P

Now you try.

Exercise 9.1

Translate the following into proper propositional form. (Answers to selected questions provided in Appendix 1.)

☞ 1 If the astrophysicists are right about the age of the universe, the Bible cannot be interpreted literally.

2 If it's raining tomorrow, then I'll go bowling.

3 I'm going to go bowling or study.

☞ 4 Unless the test is cancelled, I don't have a chance

5 Both the Alliance and NDP have little chance of winning the election.

6 If I don't pass this test, I'm not going to law school.

☞ 7 Ethics are impractical.

8 Notwithstanding my asseverations to the contrary, Janice started her own tannery.

9 Milton Acorn tasted his own blood.

☞10 Although the roads were icy, driving was fine.

11 Elephants have burial grounds.

12 Interpreters have to translate quickly or find other employment.

☞13 Had I been there, I would have saved you.

14 Should you be passing this way, please visit.

15 I would have played the blues, but I couldn't afford a guitar.

☞16 Pigs could fly if they had wings.

17 There is fire only if there is oxygen.

18 If only I won the lottery, I wouldn't be in debt anymore.

☞19 Except in cases of emergencies, do not pull cord.

20 Wretches hang that jurymen may dine.

21 The Ontario Municipal Employees Retirement Board, a major institutional investor in Canada, would consider investing in native-backed bonds if they had at least a single-A rating. (Steven Chase, "Native-band bonds interest European investors," *Globe and Mail,* 15 August 2001, A7)

9.2.4 Bracketing

There is one further detail to consider before we complete our discussion of translation. Consider the ambiguity of the following statement:

2 + 3 x 2.

This could mean either "(2 + 3) x 2" or "2 + (3 x 2)," Without bracketing (or some other convention, like the rule "Do addition first!") we aren't sure whether the sum is 10 or 8. Bracketing is also important in propositional logic. The statement,

A v B ⊃ C,

is similarly ambiguous. It could mean either "(A v B) ⊃ C," or "A v (B ⊃ C)." The statements are not equivalent. When translating, we need to match the bracketing to the speaker's intention.

For the purposes of testing validity, it is crucial that every proposition has no more than one main logical relation. Nevertheless, propositions in the real world can become quite complex, involving numerous proposition units and numerous logical relations. We can simplify such propositions by bracketing.

For example, someone might say, "If Fred and Nancy come, Hector will leave." Here we have two logical relations, "and" and "if ... then." The main logical relation in this case is the "if ... then." The conjunct "Fred and Nancy" is the antecedent condition. On the basis of this proposition, we cannot assume that Hector will leave. We can only do so *on the condition* that Fred and Nancy come, a matter that we can't make any inferences about, given the stated information. To translate this, we must place brackets around Fred and Nancy:

$(F \bullet N) \supset H$

The main logical relation here is the "$\supset$." We read the $(F \bullet N)$ inside the bracket as a *single* proposition unit, for the time being. Notice, too, that this is not equivalent to $[F \bullet (N \supset H)]$. To fully see this, we require an understanding of the truth values of our logical relations (see 9.3.1). For present purposes, consider the structure of water. Water is the composite of two parts hydrogen and one part oxygen. We could translate this chemical fact into propositional logic as $[(H \bullet O) \supset W]$, where H stands for H^2. Notice this isn't saying $[H \bullet (O \supset W)]$, because O by itself does not give us W; rather, O with H is required. Consider the following translations:

1 It is false that if a fetus were not a person, abortion would be moral.
   $\sim(\sim P \supset M)$
2 If it's raining tomorrow, then I'll go bowling or study.
   $R \supset (B \lor S)$
3 If she is rich or famous, she will not get to heaven.
   $(R \lor F) \supset \sim H$
4 If pornography is either harmful to women, or degrading to women, it should not be allowed.
   $(H \lor D) \supset \sim A$

Sometimes, ambiguity may exist. Consider the following proposition:

5 Either I will go home and watch TV or I will think about the election.

What is the main logical connection here? Is it the "or," or is it the "and"? It will depend on whether or not the speaker will think about the election *at home.* If the speaker will either think about the election wherever she is, *or* go home and watch TV, then the main logical connection is the disjunctive. Thus, our translation will be

(H • W) v E

Alternatively, the speaker is intending to go home in any event, and what she does at home is what's undecided. If this is the intention, the conjunctive is the main logical connection. To represent this intention, our translation would be

H • (W v E)

Does this shift in bracket placement matter logically? Absolutely. In the second case, unlike in the first case, we can infer that, whatever she did, she went home. We can't make any such inferences in the first.

Ambiguity may be unresolvable without having some contextual information. Consider the following pronouncement:

6 The balls were red and yellow and green and blue.

How many balls are we speaking about? There may be four solid-coloured balls, or there may be two bi-coloured balls, or there may be two solid-colour balls and one bi-coloured ball, or one solid-coloured ball and one tri-coloured ball. Of course, as long as we are dealing with only one type of logical relation (excluding the hypothetical relation ⊃), the placement of the brackets is less crucial. "(A • B) • (C • D)" is logically equivalent to "A • (B • C) • D," and since, as we've already noted, the ordering of the letters is also irrelevant for conjunctives and disjunctives, the above formations are also logically equivalent to "(B • D) • (C • A)," or "(A • D) • (C • B)."

{[(More brackets)]}

Propositions can get more complex. If so, we may need more brackets. The general convention is after (round brackets), we next use [square brackets], and should we need further distinguishing of proposition units, we next use {squiggly brackets}. For example,

7 If the person is not coerced, or is suffering unendurably without hope of relief, euthanasia should be permissible, or we should simply admit that persons in hospitals have no autonomy whatsoever.
    {[~C v (S • ~R)] ⊃ E} v ~A

Notice, too, that we might negate the entire bracket. For example,

> 8 It is false that Betty or Mary went to the party.
>
>   ~(B v M)
>
> 9 Neither the Oilers nor the Flames will make the playoffs.
>
>   ~(O v F)
>
>   10 It is incorrect to surmise that if the Toronto Maple Leafs make the playoffs they will win the Stanley cup.
>
>   ~(T ⊃ W)
>
>   11 You are wrong to suppose Linda is a bank teller and a feminist.
>
>   ~(B • F)

Given what we've already noted when speaking about negative conjunctives and disjunctives, (8) and (9) may also be translated as two negative proposition units joined by an "and." (8) will become "~B • ~M." (9) will become "~O • ~F." Meanwhile, (11) may be translated as two negative propositions joined by an *or* "~B v ~F." We will later refer to this rule as *DeMorgan's Law* (9.7.6).

Exercise 9.2 A

Among the options provided, what can you infer from the following propositions?

☞ 1 ~(A v S)
    a. ~A v ~S
    b. A • S
    c. ~A • ~ S
    d. A v S

2 ~(L • ~B)
    a. L • ~B
    b. ~L • B
    c. L v ~B
    d. ~L v B

☞ 3 ~Y ⊃ Q
    a. ~Q ⊃ Y
    b. Y ⊃ ~Q
    c. Q ⊃ ~Y
    d. Q

4 B ⊃ F
    a. F ⊃ B
    b. F v ~B
    c. ~F • ~B
    d. ~B ⊃ ~F

☞ 5 M v ~O
    a. ~(M • ~O)
    b. ~(~M ⊃ O)
    c. ~(~M • O)
    d. O v ~M

☞ 6 ~D • N
    a. N ⊃ D
    b. ~(D v ~N)
    c. ~(D • ~N)
    d. ~N • D

7 R v I
    a. ~I v ~R
    b. I v R
    c. I • R
    d. ~I • ~R

8 K ⊃ ~G
    a. G • K
    b. ~G
    c. G ⊃ ~K
    d. ~G ⊃ K

☞ 9 ~(C ⊃ J)
    a. ~C ⊃ ~J
    b. ~(~J ⊃ ~C)
    c. ~C v ~J
    d. ~C • ~J

10 ~(D v ~W)
    a. W • ~D
    b. W v ~D
    c. D • ~W
    d. D v ~W

11 T v K
    a. K v T
    b. ~K v ~T
    c. ~K • ~T
    d. ~(~K v ~T)

☞12 Z • ~G
    a. ~(~Z v ~G)
    b. ~(~Z • G)
    c. ~(Z v ~G)
    d. ~(~Z v G)

Exercise 9.2 B

Translate the following propositions. (Answers to selected questions provided in Appendix 1.)

☞ 1 It is false that if the soul is not connected to the body, it is possible we can survive death.

2 If construction of the bridge will damage the breeding grounds of lobster, or merely lure in Walmart, we should halt its construction.

3 Most students did not pass the test unless the professor adjusts the scores.

☞ 4 Although the Canadiens made the playoffs, they will be eliminated in the first or second round, and not win the coveted Stanley Cup.

5 If you do the dishes and clean your room, you can go to the movies.

6 If you master calculus and vastly improve your English grammar, plus learn logic, you will not have any difficulty with the SATs.

☞ 7 If you don't buy free-range chickens nor eat veal, you're guilty of cruelty to animals.

8 Whether Ulysses chose Charybdis or Scylla, he would lose a number of his crew.

☞ 9 It is never the case that one can be too logical.

10 It is not the case that the antecedent condition is what occurs on the right of the horseshoe, nor that the consequent is what occurs on the left.

11 If the election is called shortly after Trudeau's death, it is a blatant political ploy and shows disrespect to Trudeau.

12 In this riding, either the Liberals or the Alliance will win, but it won't be the NDP or the Conservatives.

☞13 Sometimes readers of Homer experience events in their lives that coincide with Ulysses's plight, and if this happens it is a case of serendipity.

14 If we abolish minimum wage laws, employment figures will rise, and this will in turn help the disenfranchised.

☞15 If it is neither the case that miracles attest to the existence of God nor that the people who testify are liars, it must be the case that those who so testify are somehow deluded.

16 If I can translate this properly into propositional form and I can master logical proofs, I should do well in the upcoming assignment.

17 If you believe that money makes the world go `round, then you either don't believe in the magnanimity of the human spirit, or you're simply observing the diseased state of contemporary society.

☞18 Scientists claim that we evolved from apes or the primordial slime, but they're just wrong.

19 Whatever occurs on the left of the horseshoe is the antecedent, while it is the consequent if it occurs on the right.

9.2.5 Arguments

We can now translate natural language into propositional form. Our main concern is to assess the validity of arguments, of course. Arguments are comprised of propositions, all of which may be translated into propositional form. Symbolizing argument structure requires nothing further except to note that (i) we will designate whole propositions on separate lines, and that (ii) we will number these lines, and that, in order to distinguish the conclusion from the premises, (iii) we will always place the conclusion of the argument on the last line. Otherwise, we will number the propositions as they are presented to us in the argument.

Let us see this in practice. Consider the following argument:

1 If we had no free will, deliberation would be a useless exercise. Since evolution tends to weed out the useless, we are not loathe to suspect we have free will.

Given our new-found skill at translating, we will discover that the first premise is translated "~F ⊃ U." The second premise is translated as a denial of the consequent of the first premise "~U." The conclusion, somewhat awkwardly put, is translated simply as the negation of the antecedent of the first premise. By double-negation, this becomes "F." To represent this in full argument form, we separate each of these propositions out on their own lines, we number each line, and we make sure we put the conclusion, wherever it occurs in the argument, on the last line. Thus we get

1 ~F ⊃ U
2 ~U
3 F

Here, we placed a dividing line between the last premise and the conclusion to highlight the fact that line 3 is the conclusion. Line 3 is claimed to be a valid derivation of the premises above it. Whether it is or not is what we're here to learn. Numbering our lines, by the way, is a step needed to prove the validity of arguments. The line separating the premises from the conclusion will drop out of our proofs, but until then, we shall use it to help demonstrate what argument forms or translation inferences are valid.

Before that, here is another argument, followed by its translation. Notice that the conclusion occurs first here, but we place it at the bottom of our symbolized structure.

2 It is clear the one-eyed prisoner did not see two red hats. If the one-eyed prisoner saw two red hats, then he could tell the colour of the hat on his

own head. But the one-eyed prisoner could not tell the colour of the hat on his own head.

1 R ⊃ C
2 ~C
3 ~R

As a preliminary test for what's coming, can you see that arguments 1 and 2, despite minor differences, have an identical structure?

Exercise 9.3

Translate the following arguments into propositional form. (Answers to selected questions provided in Appendix 1.)

☞ 1 Truth is either independent of belief, or dependent on belief. If truth were independent of belief, we could never know it, so truth must be dependent on belief.

2 If I have a hole in my bucket, I will stop it with lumber. If I stop it with lumber, I'll need to sharpen my axe. If I sharpen my axe, I'll need to fetch water. If I fetch water, I'll need my bucket.

3 Either the Liberals or the Conservatives will win. If the Conservatives win, there goes any chance of improved health care. Since people want improved health care, I suspect the Liberals will win.

☞ 4 If morality were culturally relative, then we would not be able to criticize a culture's inhumane treatment of a minority group. Yet surely, a bare minimum understanding of morality is to prevent inhumane treatment to persons. Therefore morality cannot be culturally relative.

5 Put into natural language the following: "S ⊃ C, C ⊃ P: therefore S ⊃ P," where S = there is a snowstorm; C = school is cancelled; and P = parents will be scrambling for babysitters.

6 Anyone who isn't blind can see the artistry in Modigliani is far superior to that of Turner, yet our esteemed art director chose Turner over Modigliani, and I must therefore regretfully submit that our director is blind.

7 Mystics are typically very sincere about their religious experiences, and since a true belief is simply that which is sincerely held, religious experiences are veridical.

☞ 8 If abortion is allowed merely on the woman's wishes, next we'll have to allow infanticide should the woman wish it, and if we allow that, why not next permit women to kill their husbands merely on the basis of their so desiring. I needn't point out that we clearly want to reject such a consequent, so it is obvious that we ought to reject abortion.

9 Use Scope or let bad breath ruin your date. You don't want bad breath to ruin your date, do you? So use Scope!

10 If government is based on lies and deceit, welfare policies cannot be for the benefit of the poor. But clearly welfare policies are for the benefit of the poor, so the government must be based on lies and deceit.

☞11 If government is not based on lies and deceit, welfare policies must be for the benefit of the poor. But clearly welfare policies are for the benefit of the poor, so the government must not be based on lies and deceit.

12 If government is based on lies and deceit, welfare policies cannot be for the benefit of the poor. But the government is based on lies and deceit, so clearly welfare policies cannot be for the benefit of the poor.

☞13 If government is based on lies and deceit, welfare policies cannot be for the benefit of the poor. But the government is not based on lies and deceit, so clearly welfare policies are for the benefit of the poor.

14 If it's raining, she'll take her umbrella. She's taking her umbrella. Therefore it must be raining.

☞15 If it's raining, she will take her umbrella. She doesn't have her umbrella. Therefore it must not be raining.

16 If it's raining, she will take her umbrella. It isn't raining. Therefore, she won't take her umbrella.

17 If it's not raining, she won't take her umbrella. It is raining. Therefore, she'll take her umbrella.

☞18 It's either raining or she doesn't have her umbrella. Look, she has her umbrella, so it must be raining.

9.3 Truth Values

9.3.1 Truth Tables

Truth Tables will reveal how logical relations affect the truth value of a proposition. For our purposes, there are only two possible *truth values* of a proposition: True (T) or False (F). That is to say, a proposition is either T or F and never neither T nor F. This assumption is called (following Aristotle) *the Law of the Excluded Middle.* The law (or better, the assumption) excludes the prospect of something's being neither T nor F. Admittedly we may not know whether a proposition is T or F, but that alone doesn't mean it isn't either T or F.

Another assumption, familiar to readers of chapter 8, is the *Law of Non-Contradiction.* This asserts that propositions *cannot be both T and F.*

Although the law of non-contradiction is not one logicians are willing (yet) to abandon, there is much worry about the law of excluded middle. In fact, our preference for the use of term "acceptability" of premises rather than truth of premises has already admitted that many meaningful propositions are not, properly speaking, true or false. Admittedly a large portion of these are merely those in which *we* are unable to determine truth value with any degree nearing certainty. We can admit this much without abandoning the law of the excluded middle. Our not knowing whether P is true or false does not mean P is neither true nor false. But we have also suggested that some propositions are not, properly speaking, true or false, for example, moral claims. It is true that people around here think murder is immoral, but we might nevertheless feel reluctant to place a truth value on moral claims themselves.

We needn't get bogged down with such worries, however. For purposes of logic, we needn't be frugal in assigning the truth value T to claims. What we're really interested in is not whether a proposition is true *in fact*. Instead, we're interested in whether, if the various propositions are true, they invariably entail the conclusion's being true. To test this out, we can gratuitously assert premises are true, by virtue of their merely being presented. If this seems too gratuitous, recall, we're only testing validity. Validity is only part of the puzzle. For this test, we can happily adopt the law of the excluded middle without committing ourselves to any grand metaphysical doctrine.

i. Negation   Truth tables will show us how the various logical relations affect the truth values of propositions. Consider, first, the truth table of the logical relation not. If a proposition P is true, then ~P is false. Likewise, if P is false, then ~P is true. The table below demonstrates this.

NOT

P	~P
T	F
F	T

We can see that P is either T or F. Given the law of the excluded middle, there is no other option. Given the law of non-contradiction, if it is T, it cannot be F, and vice versa. Meanwhile, ~P is the negation of P.

ii. Conjunction   To see the truth table for the conjunctive logical relation (as well as for disjunction and conditional), we must first introduce a second proposition Q. Now, since P may be T or F, and Q likewise will be T or F, it follows that there are four permutations of P being T or F and Q being T or F. Either both are true, neither are true, or P is true while Q is false, or P is false while Q is true. This is demonstrated in the four-line truth table below.

P	Q
T	T
T	F
F	T
F	F

Previously we saw the truth value for the "not" logical relation. Here is the truth table for the "and" logical relation.

	AND		
	P	Q	P • Q
1	T	T	T
2	T	F	F
3	F	T	F
4	F	F	F

Here we can see that the proposition "P • Q" asserts that both P and Q must be true, and this condition is met only in the first line, and nowhere else. In the second row, although P is true, Q is false. If this condition occurs, the statement "P • Q" is false. The third row represents a case where although Q is true, P is false. Again, the conjunct "P • Q" is false. Row 4 represents a case where both P and Q are individually false. Here is a case where two wrongs do not make a right. The conjunct "P • Q" is false in such cases.

iii. Disjunction   A disjunctive proposition asserts that at least one of the disjuncts is true. Thus the disjunct (P v Q) will be deemed true so long as either P or Q is true. The truth table for the "or" condition is

	OR		
	P	Q	P v Q
1	T	T	T
2	T	F	T
3	F	T	T
4	F	F	F

What the proposition "P v Q" asserts is that at least one of these propositions is true. We place a "T" in the row where at least P or Q registers a "T." We can see that only in the case where P is F and Q is also F (the fourth row of our truth table) is the "or" statement deemed false. This shows that an "or" statement is more likely to be true than an "and" statement. That is, "or" is a more permissive relation than "and." For the "and" condition to be true, all proposition units must be true, whereas, for an *or* relation, only one proposition unit need be true. Therefore, the odds of a disjunct being true are better than the odds of a conjunct being true.

The Conjunction Fallacy

Failing to recognize that the odds of a disjunct being true are better than the odds of a conjunct being true sets one up for losses in gambling. People erroneously assume that pairs of events will be more likely than single events. When they do so, they have committed the *Conjunction Fallacy.* Amos Tversky and Daniel Kahneman, for example, neatly demonstrated this by providing eighty-eight college students with the following scenario:

> Linda is thirty-one years old, single, outspoken, and very bright. She majored in philosophy. As a student she was deeply concerned with issues of discrimination and social justice and also participated in anti-nuclear demonstrations. How likely is it that
> - Linda is a teacher in an elementary school.
> - Linda works in a bookstore and takes yoga classes.
> - Linda is active in the feminist movement.
> - Linda is a psychiatric social worker.
> - Linda is a member of the League of Women Voters.
> - Linda is a bank teller.
> - Linda is an insurance salesperson.
> - Linda is a bank teller and is active in the feminist movement. (Tversky and Kahneman, "Extensional versus Intuitive Reasoning," 293–315)

Eighty-six per cent of the respondents believed it more likely that Linda is a bank teller *and* active in the feminist movement than that Linda is a bank teller. This is implausible. How can it be *more* likely she is a bank teller *and* a feminist than bank teller or a feminist? This is like thinking rolling five sixes in a row is more probable than rolling two sixes in a row.

College students are not unique in committing the conjunction fallacy. Kahneman and Tversky gave thirty-two medical internists the following scenario:

> A fifty-five-year-old woman had a pulmonary embolism (blood clot in the lung). How likely is it that she also experiences
> - dyspnea [shortness of breath] and hemiparesis [partial paralysis]
> - calf pain
> - pleuritic chest pain
> - syncope [fainting] and techycardia [accelerated heart beat]
> - hemiparesis
> - hemoptysis [coughing blood]

Of the internists questioned 91 per cent believed that the combination of a probable symptom (in this case dyspnea) and an improbable one (in this case hemiparesis) was more likely than the improbable symptom alone.

Another example may be called for. How many seven-letter English words have the following form?

(1) _ _ _ _ _ n _

Not many? Are there more instances of seven-letter English words having the following form?

(2) _ _ _ _ i n g

Most people say, "Of course!" but all instances recorded in (2) will also be recorded in (1), whereas not all cases satisfying (1) will satisfy (2). Thus, despite most people's claims, the probability of (1) is greater than the probability of (2).

The fallacy committed above is similar to preferring to bet that a fair coin will come up heads on the first throw and tails on the second, rather than heads or tails on the first throw and heads or tails on the second throw as well. The odds of the first are .25 (.5 x .5), whereas the occurrence of the second bet is certain [(.5 + .5) x (.5 + .5)].

iv. Conditional   The truth tables for negation, conjunction and disjunction should strike the reader as fairly straightforward. The truth table for the conditional proposition is less so. Here it is:

	IF ... THEN		
	P	Q	$P \supset Q$
1	T	T	T
2	T	F	F
3	F	T	T
4	F	F	T

Pay close attention to the above distribution of truth values. Most people find something implausible about the distribution of truth values in this table. Can you see why?

Take for example, the fourth row. In this case, both the antecedent and consequent are false, yet the whole proposition is necessarily true. How is this possible? Imagine my saying, "If Trudeau were alive today, he would run for the Conservative Party." The antecedent and presumably the consequent are both false propositions, so what would possess us to call the proposition, as a whole, true? What's going on?

Of course, that the whole proposition is true *does not* mean Trudeau would run for the Conservative Party. It doesn't say that, so we shouldn't be misled by it. The truth of a conditional does not commit us to inferring the truth of any of its parts. Saying "If you were a god, you'd be immortal" hardly commits us to believing that you are therefore immortal. Still, why do we call the proposition, as a whole, true?

The case represented by line 3 is no better. Consider the following ludicrous proposition: "If elephants flew, some mammals swim." In this case, the antecedent is false, though the consequent is true. Why would we call the proposition as a whole true in such cases? Whether elephants fly or not has no connection to whether some mammals swim. The antecedent in this case is totally *irrelevant* to the consequent. Since it is irrelevant, shouldn't we *deny* the truth of the conditional?

Even in the case of the first row, we can imagine two totally irrelevant claims. Despite their being true, we wouldn't necessarily want to call the conditional claim linking them true. The simple proposition, "you have a nose" is true, as well as the simple proposition, "water is wet." But it doesn't seem obvious that we would *therefore* say, "If you have a nose, water is wet," since the two seem wildly unrelated.

The truth table for conditional propositions is a problem for logicians. It makes many wonder whether Aristotle's law of the excluded middle is something we really want to keep. Perhaps we really do need another value other than *T* and *F*: an *indeterminate* that is neither T nor F.

We shall leave this debate for advanced studies in logic. Here, we can do well enough by explaining the reasoning for assigning the truth values for conditional propositions in the manner above. The reasoning is analogous to our North American legal system, where we like to imagine that everyone is assumed innocent until proven guilty. In such cases, the default is that the person is innocent. Absent any evidence to the contrary, we assert his innocence.

Similarly, the default of any proposition unit is T, and we change that to an F only reluctantly, only on the condition that we know for sure it has to be F. Given this ploy, we can see that the only condition in which we know for sure that the conditional is false is represented by the second line. The conditional "P ⊃ Q" asserts that whenever we have P, we will necessarily have Q. That is, we can never have P without Q. But in line 2, here is a case where we have P, but not Q. So in this instance, we know that "P ⊃ Q" is F.

In no other situation can we make such an assertion. In the lines 3 and 4, the antecedent isn't met. Consider how odd it would be to respond "You're wrong, because I'm not injured," to the following prediction: "If you jump off the roof you'll be injured." Since you did not jump off the roof, the antecedent condition is not met: therefore, we are not in a position to say the conditional is false. Thereby we fall back to the default position: T.

In the first case, both conditions are met, and so, again, we cannot say that the conditional is false. For that reason alone, we fall back to the default position of T.

This is to say that we needn't be confident that the conditional is true in cases 1, 3, and 4. All that we need assert is that we are not confident the conditional is false in those cases. If we are not confident that the suspect is guilty, we deem him innocent. (The Scottish legal system permits an intermediary position between guilty and innocent, and thus is analogous to a logic that permits an intermediary between truth and falsehood.)

The horseshoe ($\supset$) represents, in logic, a minimal condition. The intended claim is this: provided the antecedent is true, the consequent must be true. If the antecedent is false, the speaker hasn't made any claims about that. Nor does this show that what he did say is false. The only case in which we can prove for sure that the conditional relation is false is when the antecedent (the "if" clause) is true, while the consequent (the "then" clause) is false. Why? Because the claim asserts precisely that this would not be the case. We may read a "P $\supset$ Q" proposition as asserting, "if P is true, then Q will necessarily be true," and this condition is clearly not met in the second row. Concerning the other rows, we don't have enough information. Since we're charitable, we give them the benefit of the doubt.

Complex Propositions

Truth tables can be performed on more complex propositions as well. Since all complex propositions are comprised of these four logical relations and simple propositions, we need only extend our table to incorporate the complex. For example, let us say we wanted to deny a disjunctive statement. "It's not the case that P or Q." This would be symbolized as "~(P v Q)." The truth table of this is therefore the negation of the truth value for "(P v Q)," which we derived by examining the truth values of P and Q separately. Hence, our truth table will be this:

	~P V Q			
	P	Q	P v Q	~(P v Q)
1	T	T	T	F
2	T	F	T	F
3	F	T	T	F
4	F	F	F	T

The truth table for "~(~P • ~Q)" is

	~(~P • ~Q)					
	P	Q	~P	~Q	~P • ~Q	~(~P • ~Q)
1	T	T	F	F	F	T
2	T	F	F	T	F	T
3	F	T	T	F	F	T
4	F	F	T	T	T	F

Notice that the truth values for the final column are identical to the truth value for "P v Q." This is as it should be, given our discussion of the negation of conjunctives.

Truth tables may be constructed for yet more complex propositions. The process is always the same. To determine the truth value of a complex proposition, we need to determine the truth values of each of its constituent proposition units. The truth table for the complex "(~P v ~Q) $\supset$ P" will look like this:

$[(\sim P \vee \sim Q) \supset P]$

	P	Q	~P	~Q	~P v ~Q	(~P.v ~Q) ⊃ P
1	T	T	F	F	F	T
2	T	F	F	T	T	T
3	F	T	T	F	T	F
4	F	F	T	T	T	F

In the above, the complex "~P v ~Q" is the antecedent in the yet larger complex "(~P v ~Q) ⊃ P." P is the consequent. Therefore, we look to see in what case (or row) the antecedent is true while the consequent is false, and only in that case do we call the conditional complex "(~P v ~Q) ⊃ P" false; otherwise we call it true. In this case, "F" occurs twice, in rows 3 and 4. This is because although the antecedent ("~P v ~Q") is true in both those cases, the consequent ("P") is false.

Exercise 9.4

Provide truth tables for the following complex propositions. (Answers to selected questions provided in Appendix 1.)

☞ 1 (F v R) ~F   5 U • ~(T v U)   ☞ 9 F v (H • ~F)
☞ 2 (T • E) T   6 (D • ~S) ~D   10 ~(C N) C
☞ 3 ~(G • ~W) v W   7 (C v ~C) ~B   11 ~(M • B) • ~M
   4 ~K ~(Y v K)   ☞ 8 (J • ~L) v ~J   ☞12 (~O v O) G

9.3.2 Validity by Truth Table

The truth table can show us whether arguments are valid or invalid. Recall what validity is: *For a deductive argument to be valid, the conclusion must already be contained in the premises.* We saw that diagrammatically with Venn diagrams; we can also "see" it in truth tables.

How? If the argument is valid, it *cannot* be the case that the premises are true while the conclusion is false. Thus, when we look at the lines of a truth table, we should be able to see cases where the premises are true yet the conclusion is false. If so, we know that argument to be invalid. Conversely, if in every case, or row, where all premises are true, the conclusion is also true, we know the argument to be valid. Consider the following argument (translated on the right):

If it's raining, she'll take her umbrella.	1 R ⊃ U
Look, she's taking her umbrella	2 U
I guess it's raining.	3 R

This argument has two simple propositions and one logical relation. So we can perform a truth table on it in the same way we can perform a truth table on any complex proposition.

	R	U	R ⊃ U
1	T	T	T
2	T	F	F
3	F	T	T
4	F	F	T

Notice that this is the identical truth table for the conditional "if ... then" proposition. To test for validity, though, we need to do more. First, we need to distinguish which propositions are the premises, and which the conclusion. So, we put a small "c" above the column representing the conclusion, and a small "p" above the columns representing each premise. Thus,

	c. R	p. U	p. R ⊃ U
1	T	T	T
2	T	F	F
3	F	T	T
4	F	F	T

Now, given our understanding of validity, we check to see the rows where all the premises are true. All arguments will always have at least one such row, though they may have more. In this argument, two such rows meet the requirement, rows 1 and 3. Rows 2 and 4 do not meet the requirement and we can therefore ignore them. Next, in all cases where all premises are true, (in this case rows 1 and 3), we check to see if the conclusion is also true in all those cases. (Sometimes there may be only one such case, but there will never be no such case.) In row 1, when both premises are true, notice that the conclusion is also true. So far so good. But look at row 3. Although both premises are true in row 3, the conclusion is false. The truth table reveals that it is possible for the premises to be true while the conclusion is false. This shows that the argument is invalid. Let's highlight row 3:

	c. R	p. U	p. R ⊃ U	
1	T	T	T	
2	T	F	F	
3	*F**	*T**	*T**	both premises T, but conclusion is F, so
4	F	F	T	*invalid.*

Consider the following valid argument and its truth table:

Argument: 1 A v B
               2 ~A
               3 B

Truth Table:	c.	p.	p.
	A	B	~A	A v B
1	T	T	F	T
2	T	F	F	T
3	F	*T**	*T**	*T**
4	F	F	T	F

This argument is valid, since in all cases where all premises are true, the conclusion is also true. Notice that in this case, the only occurrence where all premises are true is line 3. Notice next, that the conclusion is true in this instance as well. This truth table reveals that it is impossible for the conclusion to be false while the premises are true. This is the definition of validity.

It is important to note that there may be more than two premises in an argument, and there may be more lines than one where all the premises are true. In any event, we can ignore the other cases where at least one of the premises is false, since that has no bearing on our determination of validity. Recall our definition of validity: If the premises are true, the conclusion must necessarily be true. But in cases where the premises are not all true, the antecedent condition is not met, and so they are of no interest to us.

9.3.3 Larger Truth Tables

So far, we've seen truth tables constructed for arguments or propositions with two terms only. Arguments often come with more than two terms, and our truth tables need to accommodate those as well. Both the number of rows and the number of columns we'll need to determine validity may increase dramatically. We can determine in advance how many rows and how many columns we'll need for any argument. As the rows increase, we will also need a method to determine how we assign truth values to the capital letters.

Rows
If we add a third proposition, the permutations of three propositions being true or false increases from four to eight. If an argument has four terms, we shall need sixteen lines to accommodate all the permutations of those four propositions being true or false. If there are five terms, we shall need thirty-two lines in our truth table. A six-term argument requires sixty-four lines, etc.

The formula for determining how many rows our truth table requires is 2^n, where n = the number of distinct simple propositions and 2 is the number of truth values for each simple proposition. (With logic incorporating an indeterminate truth value, the number of rows for a truth table will need to be 3^n.) Thus, if we have four terms, we require 2^4 ($2\times2\times2\times2 = 16$) rows.

Columns

We can also determine in advance how many columns are needed for any argument. We need the truth values for the premises and the conclusion, obviously. In order to get the truth values for these propositions, we need the truth values for all components for each premise and the conclusion. This may be determined in advance by counting all the single occurrences of the capital letters, plus all the single occurrences of each logical relation.

For example, "A v B" contains three components: A, B, and the relation 'v'. Hence we will need three columns. "A v ~B" contains four components: A and B, and the two logical relations, '~' and 'v'. Hence we will need four columns. "(A v ~B) ⊃ (C • ~D)" contains nine components: A, B, C, D, two '~'s, 'v', '•', and '⊃'. Hence, we will need nine columns. The argument,

    1 (A • ~B) ⊃ ~C
    2 A
    3 ~B
    4 Therefore ~C,

contains seven components: A, B, C, two '~'s, •, and ⊃. We will therefore need seven columns. The argument,

    1 ~A ⊃ B
    2 B ⊃ ~C
    3 ~C ⊃ D
    4 ~A
    5 Therefore D,

requires nine columns: A, B, C, D, two instances of '~', and three instances of '⊃'. Notice that we're only including two instances of the negation sign, even though we can count four negation signs in that argument. The second two uses of the negation sign are repeats of our first uses. Likewise each letter occurs twice, but we only need one column to adequately represent them. Thus, we count only *unique* proposition units and *unique* logical relations.

Truth Value Assignment

T and F placements for logical relations follow the logical rules noted above. That is, if A is T, then ~A is F. And if A is T, and B is F, then A v B is T, etc. Still, you might wonder whether there is a pattern for the initial placing of Ts and Fs for the bare proposition units represented by the capital letters A, B, C ... The answer is Yes. Any pattern will do, of course, as long as we exhaust all and only the various permutations of each of the proposition units being true and false. With only four rows, this is relatively easy to do, but as the number of rows increases, it is helpful to appeal to a pattern to make sure we are covering all the various logical permutations only once. The pattern we offer here is a convention.

first term, top half all Ts, bottom half all Fs.
second term, top quarter all Ts, second quarter all Fs, repeat.
third term, top eighth all Ts, second eighth all Fs, repeat.
fourth term, top sixteenth all Ts, second sixteenths all Fs, repeat

To follow this convention, we first must know how many rows we need. If there are two terms, we will need four rows. The column representing the first term will begin with two Ts, followed by two Fs. The second column, representing the second term, will begin with a T, followed by an F, and this pattern will be repeated once more. If there are three terms, we will need eight rows. The first column will have four Ts followed by four Fs. The second column will have two Ts, followed by two Fs, followed by two Ts, followed by two Fs. The third column will alternate between T and F starting with T.

The benefit of this convention is that we can assign the truth values to our tables in auto-pilot mode. Plus, for purposes of teaching, all truth tables should look alike, which will make things easier for discussion. Admittedly, coming up with a different pattern will not affect the test for validity, as long as we have not missed any permutation. Following this convention will prevent that from happening.

Meanwhile, the size of our truth table will not affect the basic process for testing validity. We will still need to designate all the premises and the conclusion. We also need to check all rows where all premises are true. And we need to check to see if in every such instance, the conclusion is also true. If yes, the argument is VALID; if no, the argument is INVALID.

Let's see the test for validity of a larger argument in practice. Let's try the following argument:

1 H ⊃ F
2 F ⊃ L
3 H ⊃ L

For this argument, since there are three terms, we require 2^3 rows (2 x 2 x 2 = 8). Apart from the three terms, there are three distinct logical relations. Thus we need six columns. Let us assign the first term we come across to our first column, the second term to our second column, and the third term to our third column. Since there are eight rows, the first four rows of the first column will be given a T. The second four rows of the first column will be given an F. The first two rows of the second column will be given a T, while the third and fourth rows of the second column will be given an F. This pattern is repeated in the next four rows of the second column. The first row of the third column will have a T. The second row of the third column will have an F. This pattern is repeated for the next six rows. The remaining truth values will be assigned according to the truth tables of the conditional logical relation. Our result is

					p.	p.	c.
	H	F	L		H ⊃ F	F ⊃ L	H ⊃ L
1	T	T	T		T^*	T^*	T^*
2	T	T	F		F	F	F
3	T	F	T		T^*	T^*	T^*
4	T	F	F		F	T	F
5	F	T	T		T^*	T^*	T^*
6	F	T	F		T	F	T
7	F	F	T		T^*	T^*	T^*
8	F	F	F		T^*	T^*	T^*

In the preceding argument, since the conclusion is true whenever all the premises are true, the argument is valid. In this truth table, there are five cases where all premises are true. But in each of these cases, the conclusion is also true. There is no case where, despite all the premises being true, the conclusion is false, and that is why we claim the argument is valid. This shouldn't be surprising. If Heather is a better soccer player than Franco, and Franco is a better soccer player than Louise, Heather is a better soccer player than Louise.

Let's try another. Consider the following argument:

1 J v ~G.
2 ~G ⊃ K.
3 ~J.
Therefore K.

For this one, we shall need eight rows, since there are three terms. The truth value assignment of the first three terms will be identical to the truth table above, except the first column will be for J, the second G, and the third K. We'll need seven columns, since apart from the three terms, there are four distinct logical relations (two '~'s, one 'v', and one '⊃'). The truth table is

			c.	p.		p.	p.
	J	G	K	~J	~G	J v ~G	~G ⊃ K
1	T	T	T	F	F	T	T
2	T	T	F	F	F	T	T
3	T	F	T	F	T	T	T
4	T	F	F	F	T	T	F
5	F	T	T	T	F	F	T
6	F	T	F	T	F	F	T
7	F	F	T^*	T^*	T	T^*	T^*
8	F	F	F	T	T	T	F

All conclusions true when all premises true, hence valid.

In this case, there is only one instance where all premises are all true, and that occurs on line 7. In this instance, the conclusion is also true. Therefore, it is impossible for the premises to be true while the conclusion is false. Ergo, the argument is valid.

Ok, your turn.

Exercise 9.5

Prove the validity (or invalidity) of the following arguments using the truth table method. (Answers to selected questions provided in Appendix 1.)

☞ 1 If we engage in misleading advertisement, our profits will increase. We want to increase our profits, obviously, so we should engage in misleading advertisement.

2 We can either cut production costs, or be beaten by our competitors. We clearly do not want to be beaten by our competitors: therefore we'll have to cut production costs.

☞ 3 In order to know that this chair exists, we have to trust that our perceptions are veridical. But since that is precisely what is in doubt, we cannot know that this chair exists.

4 If you become a sycophant, you will rise in administration. If you rise in administration, the number of your friends will increase. So, if you want friends, be a sycophant.

☞ 5 Martyrs were given the choice of renouncing their faith or having their faith tested. Having their faith tested invariably meant being killed. Martyrs are known for refusing to give up their faith: so, they were invariably killed.

6 If abortion is allowed merely on the woman's wishes, next we'll have to allow infanticide should the woman wish it, and if we allow that, why not next permit women to kill their husbands merely on the basis of their so desiring. I needn't point out that we clearly want to reject such a consequent, so it is obvious that we ought to reject abortion.

☞ 7 (H • O) ⊃ W. Therefore H • (O ⊃ W).

9.3.4 Two Problems with the Truth Table Method

There are two problems with the truth table method: cumbersomeness and redundancy.

i. Cumbersomeness The truth table method is a little problematic, unfortunately. This method of diagramming arguments is much too cumbersome. It is like using the slide ruler when we have a calculator handy. For example, consider this otherwise simple argument made monstrous by the truth table technique:

If I have a hole in my bucket, I will have to fix it. (H ⊃ F)
If I have to fix it, I will stop it with lumber. (F ⊃ L)
If I stop it with lumber, I'll need to sharpen my axe. (L ⊃ A)
If I sharpen my axe, I'll need to fetch water. (A ⊃ W)
If I fetch water, I'll need my bucket. (W ⊃ B)
So, If I have a hole in my bucket, I'll need my bucket. (H ⊃ B)

How many rows and how many columns are required to perform the test for validity on this argument? Well, there are six proposition units and six separate logical relations, so we will need twelve columns. That's not as bad as the number of rows we'll need. Seeing as how there are six separate proposition units, we require 2^6 rows. That's sixty-four!

ii. Redundancy If it's legitimate to go from "H ⊃ F" and "F ⊃ L" to "H ⊃ L" (which we've already demonstrated by the eight-line truth table in section 8.3.3), then, since the rest of the argument is of the same form as this valid step, the whole must be valid. And we can see that quite quickly without having to do a sixty-four-line truth-table! Even more than being simply cumbersome, then, truth tables are redundant. Consider the following two arguments:

(1) If this class gets more difficult, I think I'll drop it. (C ⊃ D)*
Hey, this class is getting more difficult. (C)
I guess I better drop it. (D)

	p. C	c. D	p. C ⊃ D	
1	T*	T*	T*	
2	T	F	F	
3	F	T	T	
4	F	F	T	Valid.

Now consider this argument:

(2) If this example looks the same as the previous example, then I wonder what's the point of another truth table. Hey, this example is like the previous example. So, what's the point of the truth-table technique? (S ⊃ P; S; therefore, P)

---

* Notice that the two predicates both start with D. Thus we used the first letter of the subject "C" to represent the proposition unit, "The class is getting more difficult," and we used the first letter of the predicate "D" to represent the proposition unit, "I think I better drop the class."

	<u>S</u>	<u>P</u>	<u>S ⊃ P</u>	
1	*T**	*T**	*T**	
2	T	F	F	
3	F	T	T	
4	F	F	T	Valid.

Notice that the two truth tables are identical. This means that the first argument is really identical in *form* to the second. Once we recognize valid forms, we'll no longer need to write out these truth tables. It is this insight that leads us to our next chapter.

Propositional Logic: Validity

Logical Forms • Complex Argument Forms
Proofs • Immediate Inferences • Invalid Forms
Contradiction • A Puzzle about Logic

10.1 Logical Forms

There is a quicker and simpler method for determining validity than using truth tables, and that's the use of *logical forms*. There are four logical forms that will concern us. A logical form is the structure, or shape of an argument. Any argument, whatever it is about, as long as it takes the shape of one of these forms, will always be valid. The four forms are *modus ponens*, *modus tollens, hypothetical syllogism*, and *disjunctive syllogism*.

10.1.1 Modus Ponens (m.p.)

An approximate translation for *modus ponens* is *Affirming the Antecedent*. The antecedent, recall, is what occurs on the left of the horseshoe in a conditional proposition. To *affirm* the antecedent means the antecedent of the conditional proposition is true. Given the two premises (a conditional and an affirmation of the antecedent of that conditional), we are entitled to conclude that the consequent of the conditional is true. For example, from the following two premises

> If its raining out, then I'll get wet.
> It is raining!

we are logically entitled to conclude that I will get wet.

The structure of the *modus ponens* (m.p.) starts off with a conditional proposition, A ⊃ B. Another premise asserts the truth of the antecedent. Hence, A. Given the truth of both these premises, we are entitled to conclude B.

In form, the argument looks like this

```
1 A ⊃ B
2 A
3 B
```

A valid argument may not be cogent. Since we can imagine the case of its raining and my not getting wet, we must claim that the first premise is false. We deny the necessary connection between its raining and my getting wet. I may have an umbrella, or I may not go outside, etc. Alternatively, it may not be raining. Still, the argument is valid, since *if* the premises were true, the conclusion would also be true. Any argument taking the *modus ponens* form (A ⊃ B; A; Therefore B) will always, for ever, invariably be valid.

Notice that the following variations are also *modus ponens*.

(i)
```
1  B
2  B ⊃ A
3  A
```

(iii)
```
1  (A v B) ⊃ (C • ~D)
2  A v B
3  (C • ~D)
```

(ii)
```
1  ~A ⊃ ~B
2  ~A
3  ~B
```

(iv)
```
1  ~(E ⊃ ~B)
2  ~(E ⊃ ~B) ⊃ (~F v J)
3  ~F v J
```

In every case, the antecedent of the conditional proposition is being affirmed, and on that basis we are entitled to conclude the consequent of the conditional. In (i), the affirmation of the antecedent occurs first in the argument. This shouldn't throw us off. Also, notice that our letters have been reversed. Since the letters are mere symbols for proposition units, this also shouldn't throw us off. The antecedent of the conditional proposition is B in this case (at line 2). This is affirmed at line 1. Therefore we are entitled to infer the consequent of the conditional proposition of line 2. (i) is a perfect *modus ponens*.

In (ii) the antecedent is ~A, and it is ~A that is being affirmed in line 2; consequently we can conclude ~B, because that is the form of consequent of the conditional proposition in line 1.

In (iii), the structure is more complex, but notice that the main logical relation is the horseshoe. Everything on the left of the horseshoe is the antecedent, and that precise object is being affirmed in line 2. Hence we are entitled to assert whatever occurs on the right of that horseshoe at line 3.

In (iv), the affirmation of the conditional occurs first, and the conditional occurs next, just as in (i). That should not fool us. The structure is still a *modus ponens*. Notice that whatever occurs at the left of the horseshoe in the second premise is being affirmed in the first premise. Hence we're entitled to infer whatever occurs on the right of the horseshoe at line 2. In this case, that's the disjunct "~F v J."

10.1.2 Modus Tollens (m.t.)

Modus tollens (m.t.) is another valid argument form. Roughly, it means *Denying the Consequent*. It starts off with a conditional proposition (A ⊃ B) just like the *modus ponens*. Unlike the *modus ponens*, however, the *modus tollens'* second premise *denies the consequent* of the conditional proposition. The second premise in a *modus tollens* argument form, thus, looks like this: ~B. What can we logically conclude from these two premises? Answer, ~A

Anything of the form

```
1 A ⊃ B
2 ~B
3 ~A
```

is called an argument in the *modus tollens* form and is *always* perfectly valid. For example

"If a benevolent God exists, we shouldn't have suffering of innocents. Innocents do suffer, however, so a benevolent God cannot exist."

Our translation is

```
1 G ⊃ ~S
2 S
3 ~G
```

Normally, being good isn't necessarily sufficient to stop suffering, but if we are good, know about suffering, and can stop the suffering, we would expect to do so. Since God's nature is often described as omniscient (all knowing), and omnipotent (all powerful), these conditions would appear to be satisfied. This simply makes the problem of uniting a belief in God with the belief that suffering of innocents occurs all the more intractable. This is called the *Problem of Evil*, and is much debated within philosophy of religion. For an excellent historical survey see John Hick's *Evil and the God of Love*.

With the *modus ponens* form, we can tolerate a number of variations among *modus ponens* arguments. As long as one premise denies the consequent of a conditional premise, we are entitled to conclude the negation of the antecedent. That entitlement rule is what we call *modus tollens*. If the antecedent is itself prefaced by a negative sign, then the conclusion will be a positive. Likewise, if the consequent is itself a negative, as in the argument above, then the premise that negates the consequent will not be a negative. Similarly, if brackets are included, we must negate the whole bracket. Below are various arguments, all in identical *modus tollens* form.

(i)
1 ~A ⊃ B
2 ~B
3 A

(iii)
1 M
2 P ⊃ ~M
3 ~P

(ii)
1 (C • ~Y)
2 (~L v D) ⊃ ~(C • ~Y)
3 ~(~L v D)

(iv)
1 ~[(A • B) v ~C] ⊃ (M ⊃ P)
2 ~(M ⊃ P)
3 (A • B) v ~C

At first glance, few will see i-iv as equivalently structured arguments, but that's because they get caught up in the *content*, not the structure. Pay closer attention to the *structure* of each argument until you recognize their similarities. What is similar about i-iv is that they are all in *modus tollens* form.

Scientific Experiments

Scientific experiments, as we'll study later (chapter 12), often follow the *modus tollens* form. We have a hypothesis that we aren't sure is true. To test whether it is true, we make predictions about what would occur *if it were* true. That is, if our theory *T* were true, then we should expect a particular event *E* to happen. So we run an experiment to see if *E* happens. If *E* does occur, we cannot say that our theory is proven, since we cannot rule out the possibility that *E* may have occurred even if *T* were false. But if *E* does not occur, and we are correct in making the conditional link between the hypothesis and the effect, then we conclude that our hypothesis is false. This may not be welcome news if *T* is our pet theory, but if *T* is someone else's theory that we're trying to disprove, then this is an important discovery. We will get the following *modus tollens* structure.

> If Stanford's theory is right, the patient ought to recover.
> See, here, though, the patient did not recover.
> This shows, as I expected all along, that Stanford's theory is bogus.

10.1.3 Hypothetical Syllogism (h.s.)

When we first introduced conditional propositions, we indicated these may also be referred to as *hypothetical propositions*. Of the proposition "A ⊃ B," we can say that B is true on the condition that A is true. Or, we can say that B is true on the hypothesis that A is true. Thus a hypothetical proposition is the same as a conditional proposition. An argument that takes the

structure of a hypothetical syllogism is an argument in which all propositions are in hypothetical or conditional form. Since the antecedent and
consequent of any conditional proposition may be referred to as *terms*, the
emphasis on *syllogism* should be familiar (see 7.4). That is, there will be a
major, minor, and middle term, each of which occurs precisely twice in the
hypothetical syllogism. The major and minor occur in the conclusion and
once each in separate premises, while the middle term occurs once in each
premise, but not in the conclusion. The pattern of a *hypothetical syllogism*
(h.s.) is this:

1 A ⊃ B
2 B ⊃ C
3 A ⊃ C

If A is bigger than B, and B is bigger than C, then it follows that A is bigger than C. Notice that we cannot conclude from this that A is big all by
itself, since big is a relative term. For example, A may be a molecule, B an
atom, and C a neutrino. We wouldn't likely assert that, since an atom is bigger than a neutrino, an atom is big. Nor can we conclude that C is small by
itself. Perhaps we claimed that a whale was bigger than an elephant, and
an elephant was bigger than a buffalo. A buffalo is still pretty big, although
quite a bit smaller than a planet.

More importantly, though, we cannot assert the truth of the proposition
unit C from this argument. C will be true on the condition that A is true,
but nothing in this argument commits us to that. To demonstrate, consider
the following conditional proposition (that might at one time have been a
platitude):

"If I won a million dollars, I'd be rich."

Each of the following variations is a hypothetical syllogism:

(i)   (iii)
1 T ⊃ S   1 D ⊃ (L v ~K)
2 L ⊃ T   2 (L v ~K) ⊃ ~F
3 L ⊃ S   3 D ⊃ ~F

(ii)   (iv)
1 ~A ⊃ ~B   1 G ⊃ (F ⊃ ~E)
2 ~B ⊃ C   2 ~L ⊃ G
3 ~A ⊃ C   3 ~L ⊃ (F ⊃ ~E)

What may fool students in (i) is the reversal of the first and second
premises. It is still a hypothetical syllogism. The complexity involved in (ii)
is the use of negatives. We shouldn't be fooled by this. (iii) introduces

brackets, and ought not throw us from recognizing a hypothetical syllogism when confronted with one. In (iv), we have brackets, negations, and a reversal in the order of the premises, but none of that should throw us off the track. In each case, we must pay attention to the basic structure: all share the identical *hypothetical syllogism* form.

10.1.4 Disjunctive Syllogism (d.s.)

The rule of *disjunctive syllogism* (*ds*) entitles you to make the following sort of inference:

> Emma played golf or rugby. She didn't play golf. Therefore, she played rugby.

The idea here is that if a disjunctive proposition (an "A or B" claim) is true, and one of those disjuncts is false, the remaining disjunct must be true. Nothing should be surprising about this. After all, this follows from what we've said about the *meaning* of a disjunctive claim. When I say, "A or B," I *mean* at least one of these is true. Given that, and that we know one of them to be false, obviously the other must be true. If the disjunctive proposition "A or B" is true, and if we also know that A is false, then by the rule of disjunctive syllogism, we are entitled to infer that B is true.

A disjunctive syllogism is an argument that has two premises – one, a disjunctive proposition, and the other a negation of one of those disjuncts. The conclusion is the remaining disjunct. "Either this drug I've been taking for years is a placebo or it would have by now provided me with eternal youth. Alas, the wrinkles tell it all. The drug must be a placebo." The argument is valid. It isn't a good argument, mind you. We might be in the position to complain about the acceptability of the disjunctive premise. Asserting an "either/or" claim is to assert that *at least one* of the disjuncts is true. If this condition is not met, the claim is unacceptable. We refer to disjunctive propositions in which neither disjunct is acceptable as a *false dichotomy*. We shall return to false dichotomies in 14.1.4. Our focus now is on the logical structure of disjunctive syllogisms.

Like the hypothetical proposition, disjunctive propositions do not assert two independent propositions. They are not conjunctive propositions. If we know "A • B" is true, we now know that A is true. Likewise, we know B is true. We can make no such inferences from our knowing that the disjunctive "A v B" is true. That is, we cannot infer from a disjunctive proposition alone that a particular disjunct is true.

It is important to understand disjunctive statements as claiming "at least one of these disjuncts is true." It is *possible* that both are true, but not necessary. It is necessary, however, that as long as the disjunct is true, it is *impossible* that both are false. So, if a disjunctive proposition (A v B) is true, then we know that at least one proposition (either A or B) is true *all by itself*. Perhaps both are, but without further help, we can't say if both are true. Nor can we say *which* one is true.

This uncertainty is resolved, however, as long as we are given another premise that denies the truth of one of the disjuncts. If we have the following two premises: 1. A v B and 2. ~A, what can we logically conclude from this? Answer, that B is therefore true. Hence the disjunctive syllogism looks like this:

(i)   (ii)
1 A v B   1 A v B
2 ~A   2 ~B
3 B   3 A

Notice that both (i) and (ii) are valid disjunctive syllogisms. Since reversing the terms around the "or" condition makes no logical difference, (ii) is equal to 1. B v A; 2. ~B: 3. Therefore A. The first term rather than the second term in the disjunctive proposition is negated, just as in (i). But whether we negate the first term or the second term is not what concerns us. A disjunctive syllogism merely requires that one term of a disjunctive proposition is negated in another premise.

Just as with *modus ponens, modus tollens,* and hypothetical syllogisms, complexities in propositions will not affect the basic disjunctive syllogism structure. Each of the following is a valid disjunctive syllogism.

(i)   (iv)
1 ~A v ~B   1 S
2 A   2 ~S v ~G
3 ~B   3 ~G

(ii)   (v)
1 (A ⊃ B) v ~D   1 ~[(N ⊃ X) v (R ⊃ ~T)] v (Q ⊃ W)
2 D   2 ~(Q ⊃ W)
3 A ⊃ B   3 ~[(N ⊃ X) v (R ⊃ ~T)]

(iii)   (vi)
1 ~K   1 {D • [(G ⊃ ~E) v (~R ⊃ O)]} v I
2 ~(P • Y) v K   2 ~{D • [(G ⊃ ~E) v (~R ⊃ O)]}
3 ~(P • Y)   3 I

Here are three disjunctive syllogisms in natural language.

1 Either the apples were shipped in the refrigerator car or they have been ruined. The apples were not shipped in the refrigerator. Therefore the apples are ruined.
2 Phyllis told me she's choosing either psychology or sociology as her major,

but I happen to have discovered she's not a major in sociology: so she must have chosen psychology.

3 Either we have free will, or everything is determined. Not everything is determined (take, for example, free radicals in physics): so we must have free will.

FOUR VALID FORMS

m.p.	m.t	h.s.	d.s.
1 P ⊃ Q	1 P ⊃ Q	1 P ⊃ Q	1 P v Q
2 P	2 ~Q	2 Q ⊃ W	2 ~P
3 Q	3 ~P	3 P ⊃ W	3 Q

Exercise 10.1 A

Translate the following arguments and state which valid argument form the main argument takes (m.p., m.t., h.s, or d.s.). (Answers to selected questions provided in Appendix 1.)

☞ 1 If we have free trade, then another country cannot impose restrictions on our goods. The US constantly imposes limitations on Canadian exports, so we do not really have free trade with the US.

2 If I don't understand logic, I will fail the assignment. If I fail the assignment, I can still pass the course, though. Therefore, if I don't understand logic, I can still pass the course.

☞ 3 Either Kant or Hume claimed we should commit to the flames anything not founded in empirical sciences or in the logical relations of ideas. Kant claimed there was a type of knowledge grounded in neither strict empiricism nor pure reason, so it must have been Hume who made the claim.

4 If Santa Claus exists, there must be some evidence of his existence. But there is no such evidence (story books, parades, and mall Santas don't count). Therefore, I am sad to say, Santa Claus is mere fiction.

5 If it doesn't rain, I won't need my umbrella. It's not raining. Therefore I won't need my umbrella.

☞ 6 If you demand labelling on all products, packaging costs are going to increase dramatically. If packaging costs increase, businesses will pass the increase on to the consumer. It follows that if you demand labelling on all products, it's the consumer who will pay in the end.

7 Anyone who isn't blind can see the artistry of Modigliani is far superior to that of Turner, yet our esteemed art director chose Turner over Modigliani, and I must therefore regretfully submit that our director is blind.

☞ 8 Mystics are typically very sincere about their religious experiences and since a true belief is simply that which is sincerely held, religious experiences are veridical.

9 If abortion is allowed merely on the woman's wishes, next we'll have to allow infanticide should the woman wish it. I needn't point out that we clearly want to reject such a consequent, so it is obvious that we ought to reject abortion.

☞10 Use Scope or let bad breath ruin your date. You don't want bad breath to ruin your date, do you? So use Scope!

11 If government is based on lies and deceit, welfare policies cannot be for the benefit of the poor. But clearly welfare policies are for the benefit of the poor, so the government is not based on lies and deceit.

12 If government is based on lies and deceit, welfare policies cannot be for the benefit of the poor. But the government is based on lies and deceit, so clearly welfare policies cannot be for the benefit of the poor.

13 If it's raining, she will take her umbrella. She doesn't have her umbrella. Therefore it must not be raining.

☞14 It's either raining or she doesn't have her umbrella. Look, she has her umbrella, so it must be raining.

Exercise 10.1 B

Using your new skills in detecting valid argument forms, provide the missing propositions for the following arguments.

☞ 1 If there were an honest tribunal in The Hague, Mr. Milosevic would not be the only government leader on trial. NATO's leaders, from Bill Clinton and Jean Chrétien to Tony Blair and José Maria Aznar committed what the Nuremberg judgement called "the supreme international crime" resorting to war. (Michael Mandel, "Milosevic has a point," *Globe and Mail,* 6 July 2001, A15)

2 If the proposed Free Trade Area of the Americas makes sense – and it does – then expanding it to include the entire EU is an even better idea. TransAtlantic free trade could thus herald a bold new era in commerce that goes beyond trading blocs to permit barrier-free trading the world over. ("TransAtlantic trade," *National Post,* 27 July 2001, A5)

☞ 3 Ivan Noonan, general manager of the Prince Edward Island Potato Board, said potato growers have been extremely anxious to have more reasonable terms negotiated for the 2001 crop, in light of extensive testing and surveillance that has turned up nothing. (Wayne Thibodeau, "Anxious potato industry awaits U.S. ruling," *Guardian,* 25 July 2001, A1)

4 If Israel truly wanted peace, it would end the military and economic blockade of the West Bank and Gaza, dismantle settlements and return confiscated lands. (Zeid Salah, letter to the editor, *National Post,* 8 August 2001, A12)

5 Aboriginal people in Atlantic Canada are being advised by their chiefs to destroy a federal questionnaire about possible changes to the Indian Act ... The chiefs are clinging to power and its perquisites, and they regard federal direct mail to their subjects as a threat rather than an opportunity for citizens to participate in an important dialogue. If the chiefs represent their people's views accurately, a questionnaire can do no harm. Of course, if the chiefs are misrepresenting their people to the federal government, a plebiscite of this sort spells trouble for the aboriginal potentates. ("Chief complaints," *National Post*, 9 July 2001, A15)

☞ 6 If private companies get involved, then the motive becomes profit. If the motive is profit, then costs need to be cut. If costs need to be cut, then quality goes down. (Maude Barlow, *Compass*. CBC, 6 July 2001)

7 Since anything affecting only parties to a fully informed, voluntary agreement is moral, prostitution among fully informed, voluntary parties is moral.

8 If matters of justice and retribution were simple, society would have settled them as easily as it has settled on the advantages of paved roads.

☞ 9 If Saddam Hussein were reasonable, he wouldn't have invaded Kuwait in the first place.

10 He did not intend to kill her. The knife stroke was delivered with only moderate force.

11 To favour the anti-terrorist bill is as reasonable as being so against civil liberties that one would prefer to sell oneself into slavery.

☞12 Every part of God's creation is there for a reason. Therefore, everything and everyone deserves to be treated with respect, including the crows. (Gail McKenzie, letter to the editor, *National Post*, 30 June 2001, A15)

10.2 Complex Argument Forms

Arguments in real life aren't so simple. Nevertheless, no matter how big the argument is, or how complicated, it can always be reduced to one or more of our four valid forms and these can be analysed individually. Consider the following hypothetical syllogism:

If Jones gets elected, then taxes will increase.
If taxes increase, then the economy will decline.
Therefore, if Jones gets elected, the economy will decline.

We can extend this argument by adding the further hypothetical proposition

If the economy declines, we will suffer.

Given this new addition, we are logically entitled to conclude that

> If Jones gets elected, we will suffer.

We are entitled to get to this conclusion, not by a single hypothetical syllogism, but by two hypothetical syllogisms. Recall that a syllogism requires exactly two premises and one conclusion, but here we have three premises, and one sub-conclusion and one main conclusion.

At this stage, notice that it seems permissible to assert the following isolated proposition:

> We don't want to suffer.

Given this new premise and our previous conclusion, we are entitled, by *modus tollens*, to make a new main conclusion, namely,

> Don't elect Jones.

Despite the limitations of mapping validity only on syllogisms, we can see that we can test the validity of larger arguments by linking together our syllogistic tests for validity without problem. As long as we can get from the premises to the conclusion with valid steps, no matter how many steps it may take, the whole argument is valid.

Here is another illustration of how complex arguments are comprised of instances of one of our four logical forms:

> If abortion is allowed merely on the woman's wishes, next we'll have to allow infanticide should the woman wish it, and if we allow that, why not next permit women to kill their husbands merely on the basis of their so desiring. I needn't point out that we clearly want to reject such a consequent, so it is obvious that we ought to reject abortion.

This is a valid argument, consisting of a hypothetical syllogism and a *modus tollens*. Thus

> 1 A ⊃ I
> 2 I ⊃ H
> {3 therefore A ⊃ H by h.s.}
> 4 ~H
> 5 Therefore ~A by m.t.

Line 3 is marked by a squiggly bracket. This is a *derived* line, not a premise. But we are entitled to derive it by hypothetical syllogism. Once we have this line, then we may couple it with line 4 to derive the intended conclusion by *modus tollens*.

This example provides insight into what it means to "prove" an argument's validity. What we shall do next is formalize our proofs for validity.

10.3 Proofs

To *prove* an argument's validity is to show that the conclusion follows logically from the premises. With complex arguments, this might take more than a few steps, but as long as each derivation is a valid inference from the previous lines and any of our four valid forms (m.p., m.t., h.s., or d.s.), then the whole is valid. Every line in our proof will therefore be either a premise or a valid derivation. For every such line, we need to say two things: (1) how we got it, and (2) where we got it.

If the proposition is a premise, then we need not worry about where we got it; we need merely indicate that it is a premise. As a premise, it is underived. To indicate that a line is a premise, we shall simply place a "p" on the right of the proposition.

Recall that in testing validity, we treat all premises as true. We are not necessarily generous in doing so, since our task in testing validity is to see merely if the conclusion necessarily follows from the premises. To do this, it hardly matters to us whether the premises are in fact true. Of course, their truth does matter to us if our task is to see whether the argument is cogent.

To illustrate, let us look at the first line of the complex proof above concerning whether we should vote for Jones. In our formal proof, we shall write it as follows:

1 J ⊃ T   p

Of course, other lines in that argument are not premises, but derivations from premises that we are entitled to infer by using one of our four rules (m.p., m.t., h.s., or d.s.). When this is so, we have to (1) state which rule we used, and (2) state which lines we used that rule on. Perhaps we have used *modus ponens*. If so, on the right of our derived proposition we shall write "m.p." *Modus ponens* requires two premises (a hypothetical and an affirmation of the antecedent of that hypothetical). So, we have to indicate on which two lines we used our *modus ponens*. It might have been from given premises on lines 1 and 2, but in larger complex arguments, it might have been from two previous derivations, or one derivation and one premise. Nor need the two lines be back to back. One might have occurred on line 3, perhaps as a premise, while the other might have occurred on line 7 as a derivation from some previous valid inference. Let us suppose, for example, that in a complex argument, line 3 claimed "Y" and line 7 claimed "Y ⊃ G." Then, we can infer G at line 8, by *modus ponens*. Writing this in our proof would give us the following:

8 G   3,7 m.p.

What line 8 tells us is that we derived G from lines 3 and 7 using the rule *modus ponens*. Of course, in this case, line 8 is an illustration only; it isn't attached to any argument stated. Now that we know how to formalize our proofs, let's demonstrate. Below is the formal proof of the complex argument against electing Jones (10.2). Notice that we place all the premises first, and then make our derivations. We stop when we arrive at the derivation of the conclusion.

```
1 J ⊃ T       p
2 T ⊃ D       p
3 D ⊃ S       p
4 ~S          p
5 J ⊃ D       1,2 h.s.
6 J ⊃ S       3,5 h.s.
7 ~J          4,6 m.t.
```

The lower case "p"s on the right of the first four lines indicate that the propositions on those lines are premises. They are part of the argument as given, and so we simply assume they are true. Our task is to see whether we can derive the stated conclusion (in this case line 7) by using our logical forms, or rules. The derivations occur in lines 5–7. On line 5, it is shown that we are entitled to infer J ⊃ D by using hypothetical syllogism on line 1 (J ⊃ T) and line 2 (T ⊃ D). Line 6 claims that we are entitled to infer J ⊃ S by line 3 (D ⊃ S) and our newly derived line 5 (J ⊃ D), also by hypothetical syllogism. Lastly, at line 7, we are entitled to infer ~J from line 4 (~S) and our previous derivation at line 6 (J ⊃ S) using our *modus tollens* rule.

Notice that we no longer require the line separating the premises from the conclusion. Our comments to the right of the line are sufficient for that purpose.

By the above method, we have given the proof of the argument's validity, and all the information we need is provided. An argument is valid if it can be shown to derive the conclusion from the premises by a sequence of valid steps, steps that use one of the logical forms (or logical inferences, which we'll introduce in 10.4).

Here is the formal proof of the abortion argument (presented in 10.2).

```
1 A ⊃ I       p
2 I ⊃ H       p
3 ~H          p
4 A ⊃ H       1,2 h.s.
5 ~A          3,4 m.t.
```

In this case, we placed premise 3 ahead of the derived line 4. In practice we shall always place the premises first, and then provide the derivations. Notice, though, that the conclusion is always at the end. This is the point where we're headed. Once we reach the conclusion by valid derivations, we have completed our proof. In this case, the ps to the right of lines 1, 2, and 3 indicate that those were the given premises. Line 4 claims that we are entitled to infer A ⊃ H from lines 1 and 2 using our rule, hypothetical syllogism. Line 5 claims that we are entitled to infer ~A, our conclusion, from lines 3 and 4.

Notice that, in the above example, we might have used a *modus tollens* at line 4, rather than a hypothetical syllogism. We would get, instead, the following:

```
4 ~I        2,3 m.t.
5 ~A        1,4 m.t.
```

This is perfectly fine. It will not matter how one proves the argument is valid, as long as each step has been independently demonstrated to be valid using one of our four valid forms.

Two Approaches

In proving an argument's validity, there are two methods of proceeding, which we shall call the *shotgun approach* and the *reverse-order approach*. The tactic of the *shotgun approach* is to make derivations where one can. Consider, for example, the argument an airline passenger might consider during turbulence:

If the plane shakes any more, I'm afraid the wing is going to be ripped off. If the wing is ripped off, we will certainly plummet to the ground. If we plummet to the ground from this height, we will certainly die. Oh, oh, the plane is shaking more. I'm afraid we're going to die.

This argument is translated

```
1 S ⊃ W       p
2 W ⊃ P       p
3 P ⊃ D       p
4 S           p
Therefore D
```

The strategy of the shotgun approach is to do whatever one can and see where it leads us. In this argument, those familiar with the four valid forms will probably see that a couple of hypothetical syllogisms are in order. Since S gives us W (from line 1), and W gives us P (from line 2), we should be entitled to infer that S gives us P (by hypothetical syllogism). Once we do that, and we see that P gives us D (from line 3) we should be entitled to infer that S gives us D (from line 3 and our newly derived line). Writing this down in our standard proof format gives us

5 S ⊃ P   1, 2 h.s.
6 S ⊃ D   3, 5 h.s.

We're not done yet. What we want is D, not the hypothetical inference, if S then D. Again, those familiar with our four forms will have no difficulty seeing that if S gives us D and we already have S (line 4), we are certainly entitled to infer D all by itself using *modus ponens*. Writing this manoeuvre in our standard proof notation becomes

7 D   4, 6 m.p.

Since D is the stated conclusion, and we arrived there from the premises and our valid inferences, the whole is valid.

The strategy of the shotgun approach is to do whatever we can and see where it leads us. For the most part this will work, but sometimes, admittedly, it will take us down dead-end alleys. The likelihood of this increases once we add immediate inferences, introduced in section 10.4.

A more directed approach is to work in reverse. The *reverse-order approach* looks first at the conclusion, and asks, "What do we need to get that?" Once we see what we need, our next task is to see whether we already have it (that would be a very simple argument if we did), or what it will take to get it. Perhaps we want Z, but to get Z we need Y; yet to get Y we need W, but we can't get W until we have X. Perhaps we already have X. Now we know we can get W, and once we have W, we know we can get Y, and Y gives us Z. Using this method on the fear-of-flying argument above, we might proceed as follows:

I want D. I can get D if I have P (line 3, using *modus ponens*). So I need P first. Hey, I can get P if I have W (line 2, m.p., again). Ok, so I need W. I can get W only if I have S (line 1 and m.p.). So, it comes down to my needing S. Hey, wait a minute, I already have S (line 4 as a premise). Now I know how to proceed. Hence,

5 W   1,4 m.p.
6 P   2,5 m.p.
7 D   3,6 m.p.

Notice that the two proofs (shotgun and reverse-order methods) are different. That's not a problem for us, since the main issue is that we have arrived at the conclusion using the premises and valid steps; hence the whole is valid. The shotgun method simply applies steps one sees; the reverse-order method works it out from the conclusion backwards. Everyone is different, and it is conceivable that the method that works for one person will not work as well for another. So we can experiment with both. Probably a mixed strategy is what most of us use. We may start with whatever we see, but at some point check with the conclusion to see where we're supposed to be going. The most important point cannot be overemphasized: *as long as we arrive at the conclusion using valid steps, the whole is valid; otherwise invalid.*

Practice 1

Nothing beats practice. To that end, here are a few further illustrations of logical proofs.

(1) The mechanics are either going to go on strike or their demands will have been satisfactorily met. If the mechanics go on strike, the safety of the plane will be in jeopardy. If the safety of the plane is in jeopardy, I will cancel my flight. I'm flying, by the way, so you can bet the mechanics' demands were met.

Translation:	1 S v M	p
	2 S ⊃ J	p
	3 J ⊃ ~F	p
	4 F	p
	Therefore M	
Derivation:	5 ~J	3,4 m.t.
	6 ~S	2,5 m.t.
	7 M	1,6 d.s.

The derivation above, notice, may have used the reverse-order or the shotgun method. The shotgun method, recall, simply jumps to any logical inference the logician first sees. Perhaps the logician sees *modus tollens* more readily than hypothetical syllogisms (which we could have performed on lines 2 and 3). Here's another example:

(2) What is in our self-interest is either subjectively determined or objectively determined. If self-interest is subjective, then we cannot be mistaken about what we take to be in our interest. So long as we can regret our choices, however, we can be mistaken about what is in our interest. We do often regret our choices, so it is clear that self-interest must be objective.

Proof:	1 S v O	p
	2 S ⊃ ~M	p
	3 R ⊃ M	p
	4 R	p
	5 M	3,4 m.p.
	6 ~S	2,5 m.t.
	7 O	1,6 d.s.

In the above example, we cannot proceed any other way (when limited so far to our four logical rules), so the shotgun method and the reverse-order method will overlap. Line 5 infers M from lines 3 and 4 using our friendly *modus ponens*. Line 6 infers ~S from the premise at line 2 and our newly derived line 5 using *modus tollens*. Finally, we are entitled to get O since line 1 asserts it is either S or O and line 6 claims it isn't S: therefore it must be O (by disjunctive syllogism).

The *shotgun* approach would look for things to do and come across m.p. at lines 3 and 4. The *reverse-order* approach will see that in order to get O, one needs ~S by d.s. To get ~S, we'll need M and m.t., on line 2. To get M, we need R and m.p. at line 3. We already have R at line 4, so the first step will be M by m.p. at lines 3 and 4.

Whether the argument is cogent or not is another matter. For example, we might complain that regretting choices does not entail that self-interest must be objective, as long as a subjective account of self-interest can account for regret and mistaken interests.

In any case, as long as each line is a premise or a legitimate derivation, and the conclusion is reached, the whole is valid.

(3) In Homer's *The Iliad*, Paris abducts Helen, the wife of King Menelaus of Lacedaemon or Sparta. This is not well received. The forces of mainland Greece thereby unite to sack Troy. Troy is not a random choice. Paris is the son of Priam, King of Troy. The Trojan war is merely a backdrop for the main storyline, the rage of Achilles, a demigod warrior, against his king, Agamemnon of Achaea (the country of Athens). Earlier, when Achilles sacked Lyrnessus, he took a woman by the name of Briseis captive. Agamemnon, Achilles' superior, in turn captured Briseis in a fit of spite. As a result, the near-invincible Achilles turns his ire from the Trojans to his own king, Agamemnon.

With Achilles against Agamemnon, the chances of sacking Troy are greatly diminished. In book 9, Agamemnon, afraid of Achilles and of losing the war to the Trojans, makes an offer to Achilles via Odysseus. Odysseus makes the following pitch to Achilles. If Achilles renounces his plans of revenge against Agamemnon, then Agamemnon will give Achilles the following dowry: seven new tripods; ten bars of gold; twenty cauldrons; twelve strong stallions; seven maidens; Briseis (with an oath that he never had relations with her); one of his own daughters and therefore status as his son-in-law; and seven citadels filled with subjects. In addition, if the Achaeans breach Troy, Achilles can have his pick of twenty Trojan women and the opportunity to kill Hector, another of Priam's sons and the greatest fighter of Troy. Furthermore, Achilles will receive the eternal gratitude of his troops. Despite the tempting offer, Achilles is not impressed. He answers in the following way. Hector can live or die. Agamemnon can have Briseis or not. He'll never marry one of Agamemnon's daughters. His honour has already been challenged, and he must defend and reaffirm it. He will have his revenge.

That is, the offer to Achilles is, if no revenge, then great gifts. But for Achilles, if he accepts these great gifts, he will lose his honour. Since his honour is more important to him than even Briseis's return, the reason for the falling-out in the first place, Achilles rejects the antecedent. The logic may be represented

```
1 ~R ⊃ G      p
2 G ⊃ ~H      p
3 H           p
4 ~R ⊃ ~H     1,2 h.s.
5 R           3,4 m.t.
```

Exercise 10.2

Prove the validity of the following arguments. (Answers to selected questions provided in Appendix 1.

1 If you allow abortions in the first trimester, next you'll allow abortions in the second. If you allow abortions in the second, why not also in the third. But if you allow abortions in the third trimester, then next you'll allow infanticide. Since infanticide is clearly wrong, we ought not allow abortions even in the first trimester.

☞ 2 If you think it's permissible to have an abortion in cases of rape, then you can't believe that the fetus has an inviolable right to life. If you don't believe that fetuses have inviolable rights to life, then you can't maintain that the rights of a fetus should trump the rights of the mother in other cases. If that is so, that the fetus's rights should not trump the mother's rights, then you should accept the fact that abortion is in general morally permissible. I see you admit that in cases of rape, abortion should be permissible, so you should also accept the fact that abortion in other cases should be permissible too.

☞ 3 A university education has either intrinsic value or purely extrinsic value. If it had a purely extrinsic value, then taking philosophy courses would help with getting a job after university. It is clearly false that philosophy has any benefit to landing jobs, so it seems that a university education must have intrinsic value.

4 If you can't master logic, you'll be easily swayed by the pretensions of others. Those who are easily swayed by the pretensions of others are, at least, not stubborn, pig-headed fools. Forgive me for pointing out that you are a stubborn, pig-headed fool, so I guess you can master logic.

5　1 A ⊃ W
　 2 D ⊃ P
　 3 ~D ⊃ A
　 4 ~P
　 Therefore W

6　1 L v D
　 2 N ⊃ ~D
　 3 ~L
　 Therefore ~N

☞ 7 1 H ⊃ F   ☞ 8 1 O ⊃ (P v ~E)
    2 L   2 Y ⊃ O
    3 F ⊃ ~L   3 E
    4 H v ~M   4 Y
    Therefore ~M   Therefore P

   9 1 Y v ~X   ☞10 1 S
      2 (Y v ~X) ⊃ I   2 W ⊃ ~T
      3 ~G ⊃ ~I   3 D v T
      Therefore G   4 S ⊃ ~D
                                       Therefore ~W

10.4 Immediate Inferences

We are not fully equipped to prove the validity of all propositional arguments. Some valid arguments will not quite fit the pattern of any of our
four valid forms. Consider, for example, the following argument:

> Barb and Sue went to the party. If Barb went, then you can be sure Mallory
> went: ergo Mallory went to the party.

This argument is clearly valid, but notice that, as put, it doesn't quite fit the
modus ponens form. In translation, the argument goes like this

   1 B • S   p
   2 B ⊃ M   p
   3 M   ?

As put, line 1 is not the antecedent of line 2, although *part* of it is. The
question is whether we are entitled to infer B by itself on the basis of line
1. When we refer to the truth table of conjunction (section 9.3.1), we
should see that the answer is "Yes." If B • S is true, then we know that B
must be true, for the only case in which B • S is true on the truth table is
when B is true (as well as S). Deriving B from B • S, however, is not permitted by our four logical forms. Thus, we need to introduce a new rule to
permit such derivations. In fact, what we shall do in this section is introduce six new inferences: *conjunction, simplification, addition, transposition,
implication,* and *DeMorgan's.*

10.4.1 Conjunction (conj)

The rule of *conjunction* entitles us to conjoin the results of two lines
together with an "and" symbol in between. After all, if A is true, and B
is true, then it follows that A • B is true. In logical form, it looks like
this

```
1 A
2 B
3 A • B          1,2 conj
```

Notice that we didn't assert that lines 1 and 2 were premises. They may have been valid derivations from premises.

Conjunction may be handy if an antecedent of a hypothetical is a conjunct. For example,

```
1 (C • ~E) ⊃ R      p
2 ~E                p
3 C                 p
4 (C • ~E)          2,3 conj
5 R                 1,4 m.p.
```

10.4.2 Simplification (simp)

The rule of simplification asserts that whenever we have two propositions conjoined by an "and," we are entitled to assert as true one of those propositions. For example, if it is true that I ate a hamburger and salad, it is true that I ate a salad. Conversely, if it's true that I ate a hamburger and salad, it is true that I ate a hamburger. This logical deduction is called the rule of simplification.

Simplification is the reverse of conjunction. That is, if the conjunct is true, the separate parts are true. It looks like this:

```
1 A • B
2 A             1, simp
```

Notice that it is this rule that solves the Barb and Sue problem above. We can also assert B by itself by the same rule on the same line.

```
3 B             1, simp
```

The truth value of conjunction shows us why both simplification and conjunction are valid inferences. If A • B is true, then A all by itself must be true. Likewise, if A is true, and B is true, then it follows that A • B will be true.

10.4.3 Addition (add)

The rule of addition is a bit less intuitive than simplification or conjunction, but perfectly valid all the same. Here we are entitled to add to any single proposition an "or" relation followed by *any other premise we want.* If it's true that I had a hamburger, then it's true that I ate a hamburger *or* a salad.

To see why this is a perfectly valid addition, we must recognize the logic of the word "or." When I say "A or B," I assert that *at least one of those propositions* (A or B) is true. I'm not making any grand claim that *both* are true, although they *may* be. But if this is the case (that "A or B" asserts merely that at least one of those propositions is true), it will then follow that since we already know A is true, we can add to A an "or" followed by *anything* we want. If it is true that you're reading this line, then it is true you're reading this line *or* snorkelling. The fact that you aren't snorkelling is irrelevant to the logical inference, since one of the disjunctives is already known to be true. That is, if A is true, then A or B is true. If Anne is Connor's sister, then Anne or Beth is Connor's sister, as well as Anne or Desdemona.

Notice, though, we can't go from the fact that Anne is Connor's sister to the claim that therefore Desdemona is Connor's sister, as if this is a matter of simplification. The rule of simplification works only on "and" statements, not "or" statements. This means that however weird the rule of addition may seem, it can't by itself create falsehoods out of truths.

More formally, addition asserts that if A is true, then A or B is true. The rule is

1 A
2 A v B   1, add

Addition may seem like cheating, but its logic can be seen by performing a truth table (9.3.1). Since the disjunctive is true as long as at least *one* disjunct is true, then as long as there is one disjunct already known to be true, it can be conjoined by an "or" condition to *any* proposition unit whatsoever, true or false. By referring back to the truth table of disjunction, we can see that, as long as A is true, A v B is true in *both* the cases where B is T (line 1) and where B is F (line 2).

For example, if it's true that you're reading this page, then it's true that you're reading this page or talking on the phone with your favourite international politician.

The rule of addition is not magic. It cannot magically make a false claim true. Inferring A v B from A by itself cannot, without further ado, entitle us to infer B by itself. *That* would be magic. On the basis of A we can assert A v B, but we cannot conclude B all by itself, for that would require the negation of A, given our understanding of disjunctive syllogism. But since we begin with the assertion that A is T, then ~A cannot itself be T; otherwise we have a contradiction. So, although the rule of addition seems like magic, it cannot get us anything we are not entitled to.

Another worry might be why we would ever use such a rule. Well, perhaps we have an antecedent condition that is itself a disjunct, while we have only one of that disjunct, in other words, something like

If you're either an environmentalist or a socialist, you'll probably vote NDP. I've seen your Green Peace bumper sticker, so you must vote NDP.

Such an argument cannot be shown to be valid without the rule of addition. The proof goes as follows:

```
1  (E v S) ⊃ N         p
2  E                   p
3  E v S               2, add
4  N                   1,3 m.p.
```

10.4.4 Transposition (trans)

Transposition reverses the antecedent and consequent, and negates each term. Doing so will yield a logical equivalent. If I say that for there to be fire, there must be oxygen, I am also saying that if there is no oxygen, there will be no fire. These are logically equivalent by the rule of transposition. Hence,

```
1  A ⊃ B
2  ~B ⊃ ~A       1, trans
```

Notice that the statement "A ⊃ ~B" becomes "B ⊃ ~A," etc.

Consider this argument:

If Jones gets elected, taxes will increase. If we don't have to work harder, our taxes won't increase. Therefore, if Jones gets elected, we'll have to work harder.

Without the rule of transposition, we would not be able to show that this argument is valid. The proof is as follows:

```
1  J ⊃ T         p
2  ~W ⊃ ~T       p
3  T ⊃ W         2, trans
4  J ⊃ W         13, h.s.
```

Notice that we can change a *modus tollens* into a *modus ponens* by the use of transposition. Doing so takes another step, and is therefore a bit redundant, but perfectly valid. Below, compare the *modus tollens* on the left and the switch to a *modus ponens* on the right.

	M.T.			M.P.	
1 A ⊃ B	p.		1 A ⊃ B	p
2 ~B	p		2 ~B	p
3 ~A	1,2 m.t.		3 ~B ⊃ ~A	1, trans
			4 ~A	2,3 m.p.

10.4.5 Implication (imp)

The rule of *implication* converts hypothetical propositions into disjunctive propositions and vice versa. Hence,

1	A ⊃ B		or	1	A v B	
2	~A v B	1, imp		2	~A ⊃ B	1, imp

The idea here is that if A gives us B, then the only way we can have B is if ~A is false. That is to say, we have a choice between ~A or B. If you prefer, consider this explanation. We have a choice between A or ~A (given the law of excluded middle, as discussed above). Since A gives us B (premise 1), we can substitute B for A in our choice: hence ~A or B.

Given the rule of implication, notice that we can turn a *modus ponens* into a disjunctive syllogism:

	M.P.				D.S.	
1	A ⊃ B	p		1	A ⊃ B	p
2	A	p		2	A	p
3	B	1,2 m.p.		3	~A v B	1, imp
				4	B	2,3 d.s.

Admittedly this is a bit redundant since we could have derived B on line 3 by m.p. (from lines 1 and 2), but since each step is valid, this proof is perfectly acceptable.

10.4.6 DeMorgan's (dem)

The rule of *DeMorgan's* changes "and"s to "or"s and vice versa. To do so, each term is negated, and the whole is bracketed and negated. That is, the logical inference of DeMorgan's (named after the logician, Augustus DeMorgan, 1806–1871), requires three steps:

1 Change "•" to "v" (or vice versa)
2 Negate each term on either side of the logical relation
3 Negate the whole proposition.

Following this procedure gives us, for example, the following derivations:

(1)	1	A • B		(4)	1	~(A v B)		
	2	~(~A v ~B)	1, dem		2	~A • ~B	1, dem
(2)	1	A v B		(5)	1	~(A • B)		
	2	~(~A • ~B)	1, dem		2	~A v ~B	1, dem
(3)	1	~(~A v B)		(6)	1	~A v B		
	2	A • ~B	1, dem		2	~(A • ~B)	1, dem

The derivations may get more complex, as in the following:

(7) 1 (A v B) • ~(~C • D)
     2 ~[~(A v B) v (~C • D)]   1, dem
(8) 1 ~(A ⊃ ~B) v [C ⊃ ~(D • ~E)]
     2 ~{(A ⊃ ~B) • ~[C ⊃ ~(D • ~E)]}   1, dem

In all cases, the DeMorgan derivations above can also go in reverse. That is, line 1 is a valid inference by DeMorgan's on line 2.

The logic of DeMorgan's can be seen by the various translations we could give to the following claim: "Neither Peterson nor Bilker ran for re-election." We could translate this as either "It is not the case that P or B" (~(P v B)), or "not P and not B" (~P • ~B). Both are equivalent. We have seen this inference before when we were looking at negative conjunctives and negative disjunctives (9.2.2), and now we have a name for that equivalence – *DeMorgan's*.

DeMorgan's Rule can be helpful in a variety of ways. For example, if we can alter the negation of a disjunctive proposition, we can get a conjunctive proposition. Once we have a conjunctive proposition, we can use the rule of simplification. This manoeuvre will be helpful in the following argument:

If Peterson or Bilker run for re-election, MacGregor won't run. If Peterson doesn't run, I think we may finally have a chance at a true democracy. I've heard that MacGregor is running for election, so we've got a shot at a true democracy.

Proof:
1 (P v B) ⊃ ~M   p
2 ~P ⊃ D   p
3 M   p
4 ~(P v B)   1,3 m.t.
5 ~P • ~B   4, dem
6 ~P   5, simp
7 D   2,6 m.p.

The standard procedure is to perform these proofs on whole lines, and never partial lines. For example, students might be tempted to perform DeMorgan's on line 1.

4 ~[(~P • ~B)] ⊃ ~M   1, dem

In fact, there is nothing wrong with this, except logical convention has it that the rules are supposed to operate on the main logical relation, and not on a subsidiary logical relation. For example, one certainly *cannot* perform simplification on the following line:

1 (A • B) ⊃ C
2 A ⊃ C   1. simp?? INVALID

To avoid such indiscretions, the standard rule of performing these logical inferences on whole lines (or on the main logical connectives) is involved.
    To show these are all valid steps, try doing truth tables on them!!

SUMMARY OF VALID INFERENCES

conj	simp	add	dem	trans	imp
A	A • B	A	A v B	A ⊃ B	A ⊃ B
B	A	A v B	~(~A• ~B)	~B ⊃ ~A	~A v B
A • B			A • B		A v B
			~(~A v ~B)		~A ⊃ B

    Except for conjunction, notice that these inferences work on only one line. Our four valid forms (m.p., m.t., h.s., d.s.) work on two lines.

Exercise 10.3

Using only our six immediate inferences, prove the validity of the following arguments. (Answers to selected questions provided in Appendix 1.)

        Sample: A v B: therefore B v A.
            Proof: 1 A v B   p
                    2 ~A ⊃ B   1, imp
                    3 ~B ⊃ A   2, trans
                    4 B v A   3, imp

Now you try.

☞ 1 R • A: therefore R v Z   6 ~S: therefore ~U ⊃ ~S
☞ 2 ~(C ⊃ J): therefore C.   7 ~(~A • T): therefore T ⊃ A
☞ 3 K: therefore B ⊃ K   ☞ 8 ~N: therefore ~(N • M)
   4 L v Y: therefore ~Y ⊃ L   9 ~(S v T): therefore ~S v T
☞ 5 K ⊃ ~G: therefore ~(K • G)   ☞10 H • ~O: therefore L ⊃ H

Translation Rules

The six rules for immediate inference are really *translation* rules. They don't act to help demonstrate validity in and of themselves. Instead, they can help us rephrase propositions, either premises or valid derivations, into a mould whereby we can use one of the four valid forms. They act as intermediary steps in a larger picture. Consider the following cases where we can employ one or more of the immediate inferences in proving validity.

(1)	1 A ⊃ (B v C)	p
	2 B ⊃ D	p
	3 D ⊃ G	p
	4 A • ~C	p
	5 A	4, simp
	6 B v C	1, 5 m.p.
	7 ~C	4, simp
	8 B	6,7 d.s.
	9 B ⊃ G	2, 3 h.s.
	10 G	8, 9 m.p. valid

Look at line 5. We have "A" and "4, simp." This means we are entitled to derive A from line 4 "A • ~C" by using the rule "Simplification." That is to say, since A and ~C are true, A must be true.

Line 6 justifies our asserting the disjunctive proposition "B v C" by using the rule of *modus ponens* on lines 1 and 5. Line 1 asserts that whenever we have A we will get B v C. Line 5 gives us A, so, by m.p. we get B v C.

Line 7 is another move by simplification. Notice that we require a step to take ~C out of line 4. Although we've already taken A out of line 4, we can't just assume that line 4 now reads simply ~C.

Line 8 uses disjunctive syllogism on lines 6 and 7. Line 6 indicates that at least B or C is true. Perhaps both of them are true, but it is certainly the case that at least one of them is true. Given that, if it is discovered that one of the disjuncts is false, the other one must be true. Line 7 claims that one of those disjuncts is false. Therefore the other one (B) must be true. That's what's going on by when we say "B ... 6,7 d.s."

Line 9 derives B ⊃ G using hypothetical syllogism on lines 2 and 3. We could have done that much earlier in our proof. That doesn't matter, as long as every step we take is a valid inference. If B gives us D and meanwhile D gives us G, then it follows that B gives us D. The logic here should be obvious: If Barbara is taller than Debbie, and Debbie is taller than Gloria, Barbara is taller than Gloria.

Line 10 gives us G by using *modus ponens* on lines 8 and 9. Line 9 asserts that whenever we have B, we will necessarily have G. If there's fire, there must be oxygen. If you're pregnant, you must be a woman. Line 8, meanwhile, asserts B. This is the antecedent condition of line 9. That is to say, the antecedent of line 9 is affirmed in line 8. This entitles us to affirm the consequent of line 9, which is G.

Since each step we took is a valid inference, and we arrived at the conclusion by using the premises and our valid inferences, the argument as a whole is valid.

Here's another:

(2)	1 ~(C v D)	p
	2 ~D ⊃ ~(H • G)	p
	3 (Q ⊃ G) • H	p

4 (Q ⊃ G)	3, simp
5 H	3, simp
6 ~C • ~D	1, dem
7 ~D	6, simp
8 ~(H • G)	2,7 m.p.
9 ~H v ~G	8, dem
10 ~G	5,9 d.s.
11 ~Q	4,10 m.t. Valid

The tricky step here is the use of DeMorgan's on line 9. Lines 4, 5 and 6 used the rule of simplification. Simplification, being a simple rule, is a good target for the shotgun method. Sometimes, however, we do better not separating the conjuncts. Consider this argument:

(3)   1 L • ~K   p
       2 P ⊃ S   p
       3 S ⊃ (~L v K)   p
       Therefore ~P

The shotgun method might start off with simplification on line 1. This would lead us astray. Looking in reverse, we can see that to get ~P, we need ~S. We can get ~S if we have the complex ~(~L v K). We can get that by performing DeMorgan's on line 1 as it is. Hence,

4 ~(~L v K)	1, dem		5 P ⊃ (~L v K)	2,3 h.s.
5 ~S	3, 4 m.t.	or	6 ~P	4,5 m.t.
6 ~P	2,5 m.t.			

Practice 2

Now you try. Provide proofs of the following arguments. They are titled by the immediate inference which is required to complete the proof. We'll supply the answers to each below.

1 DeMorgan's
1 (P • ~Q) ⊃ V
2 ~V
3 (~P v Q) ⊃ W
Therefore W

2 Transposition & Implication
1 B ⊃ Q
2 K v B
3 Z ⊃ ~Q
Therefore ~K ⊃ ~Z

3 Simplification & Conjunction
1 (N • T) ⊃ C
2 ~T ⊃L
3 ~L • N
Therefore C

4 Addition
1 (P v ~Q) ⊃ Y
2 Y ⊃ ~F
3 ~A v F
4 P
Therefore ~A

5 *All Six Immediate Inferences*
1 (M ⊃ P) ⊃ O   5 (Y • B) ⊃ K
2 ~O v N   6 (L v ~Y) ⊃ ~N
3 P   Therefore K
4 B

Answers to Practice 2

1 DeMorgan's   *2 Transposition & Implication*
1 (P • ~Q) ⊃ V   p   1 B ⊃ Q   p
2 ~V   p   2 K v B   p
3 (~P v Q) ⊃ W   p   3 Z ⊃ ~Q   p
4 ~(P • ~Q)   1,2 m.t.   4 ~K ⊃ B   2, imp
5 ~P v Q   4, dem   5 ~K ⊃ Q   1,4 h.s.
6 W   3,5 m.p.   6 Q ⊃ ~Z   3, trans
           Valid   7 ~K ⊃ ~Z   5,6 h.s.
                                            Valid

3 Simplification & Conjunction   *4 Addition*
1 (N • T) ⊃ C   p   1 (P v ~Q) ⊃ Y   p
2 ~T ⊃ L   p   2 Y ⊃ ~F   p
3 ~L • N   p   3 ~A v F   p
4 ~L   3, simp   4 P   p
5 N   3, simp   5 P v ~Q   4, add
6 T   2,4 m.t.   6 Y   1,5 m.p.
7 N • T   5,6 conj   7 ~F   2,6 m.p.
8 C   1,7 m.p.   8 ~A   3,7 d.s.
           Valid   Valid

5 All Six Immediate Inferences
1 (M ⊃ P) ⊃ O   p   10 O   1,9 m.p.
2 ~O v N   p   11 N   2,10 d.s.
3 P   p   12 ~(L v ~Y)   6,11 m.t.
4 B   p   13 ~L • Y   12, dem
5 (Y • B) ⊃ K   p   14 Y   13, simp
6 (L v ~Y) ~N   p   15 Y • B   4,14 conj
7 P v ~M   3, add   16 K   5,15 m.p.
8 ~P ⊃ ~M   7, imp   Valid
9 M ⊃ P   8, trans

Notice a couple of things in the demonstrations above. The numbers on the right indicate which line we've used to derive a particular proposition. Notice that, *except for simplification*, no line gets used more than once. Once we've used a line, we need not return to it. If we do, we've taken a redundant step somewhere. Redundancy is not a violation of logic. Simply, we could be more efficient. Particularly for those who elect the shotgun approach, the numbers on the right can help us to see what propositions are *still left*.

How did you do? With practice it gets easier. The skill is no more than *form recognition.* We have taken logic to its purely formal or abstract level. It is probably a good idea to remind ourselves every now and then that we are examining the structure, or shell, of argumentation here, and leaving out the content. The content does not matter for understanding the logical structure of arguments. Once we become familiar with detecting the logical structure in this formalistic sense, we will at the same time better recognize the form in natural language.

Exercise 10.4

Prove the validity of the following arguments (all are valid). To do so, you will need to avail yourself of all of our logical inferences (m.p., m.t., h.s., d.s., simp, conj, add, trans, imp, and dem). (Answers to selected questions are provided in Appendix 1.)

☞1   1 (W • F) ⊃ C
      2 R ⊃ W
      3 R
      4 F
      Therefore C

2   1 (K • T) ⊃ ~J
     2 T • ~W
     3 (B ⊃ W) • (~B ⊃ J)
     Therefore ~K

3   1 ~K v P
     2 P ⊃ C
     3 (K ⊃ C) ⊃ X
     Therefore X

☞4 1 (~J ⊃ ~P) ⊃ M
     2 P ⊃ J
     3 ~M v L
     Therefore L

5   1 (D ⊃ ~X) ⊃ Q
     2 ~X
     Therefore Q

☞6 1 A v R
     2 P ⊃ ~A
     3 ~P ⊃ J
     Therefore ~J ⊃ R

7   1 (~L • G) ⊃ (D v X)
     2 ~(L v ~G) • ~X
     Therefore D

☞8 1 (D ⊃ C) • (~E ⊃ ~C)
        • (~E v G)
     Therefore G v ~D

9   1 (F • ~Q) ⊃ V
     2 ~V
     3 (~F v Q) ⊃ W
     Therefore W

☞10 1 A v R
      2 R ⊃ L
      3 W ⊃ ~L
      Therefore ~A ⊃ ~W

11 1 [(W • Q) v Y] ⊃ ~(S • Z)
      2 S
      3 W
      4 Q
      Therefore ~Z

☞12 1 (M ⊃ D) ⊃ O
      2 ~O v N
      3 D
      Therefore N

13 1 L
    2 ~O ⊃ Y
    3 N
    4 ~(~L v ~N) ⊃ ~Y
    Therefore O

☞14 1 (G • ~N) ⊃ ~Y
     2 (O v G) • ~F
     3 {(K ⊃ L) v ~[I • (L v ~A)]} ⊃ ~O
     4 N ⊃ F
     5 S v ~J
     6 S ⊃ {(K ⊃ L) v ~[I • (L v ~A)]}
     7 J • ~K
     Therefore ~Y

10.5 Invalid Forms

If an argument can be shown to derive the conclusion from the premises
and any of our logical forms or immediate inferences, then the argument
is valid; otherwise the argument is invalid. This *otherwise* condition needs
clarification. If we cannot construct valid steps to reach our conclusion, it
does not *necessarily* mean we have shown the argument to be invalid. It may
instead mean the proof is more complicated than we realize.

So a limitation of propositional logic is that it requires *more skill* than
either the truth table technique or categorical logic.

Fortunately, some logical errors are so common, we can recognize them
just as easily as we can recognize the logical forms they corrupt. Here are
three invalid argument forms – called the *Fallacy of Affirming the Consequent*,
the *Fallacy of Denying the Antecedent*, and the *Disjunctive Fallacy*.

10.5.1 Affirming the Consequent (AC)

The fallacy of *Affirming the Consequent* (AC) is a misapplication of the *modus
ponens*. Recall that the form of the *modus ponens* goes like this:

    1 A ⊃ B
    2 A
    3 B   1,2 m.p.   valid

What the *modus ponens* does is affirm the antecedent. When someone
affirms the consequent and on that basis infers the antecedent, that person is making a mistake. The structure of an Affirming the Consequent
argument looks like this:

    1 A ⊃ B
    2 B
    3 A   ??? 1,2 AC   invalid

It is invalid because we can imagine cases where both A ⊃ B and B are
true and yet where A is false. Such cases are represented by line 3 of the
truth table for conditional propositions (9.3.1). Consider, for example, the

following two true claims: "If he knows his stuff, he will get the answer," and "He got the answer." We cannot conclude that he therefore knows his stuff, since it is conceivable that he merely guessed or cheated.

Likewise, recall the true proposition, "If you're pregnant, you're a woman." If it happens to be also true that you're a woman (affirming the consequent), it hardly follows that therefore you're pregnant. Put this way, the AC fallacy should strike us as an obvious error. Remarkably, it is committed with great frequency nonetheless.

Notice, by the way, that, at line 3 above, we placed some question marks after the invalid conclusion "A." We need to be clear that invalid steps are not warranted. We want to signal invalid inferences in a salient way. We certainly do not want to confuse an AC for a valid inference in an argument. So, in addition to marking it with an AC, we offset that line.

Any argument in the form of affirming the consequent is always invalid.

10.5.2 Denying the Antecedent (DA)

A misapplication of the *modus tollens* is called *Denying the Antecedent* (DA). Recall that the form of the *modus tollens* looks like this:

1 $A \supset B$
2 ~B
3 ~A   1,2 m.t.   valid

Any argument in this form is always valid.

What the *modus tollens* does is deny the consequent. On that basis we are warranted to infer the negation of the antecedent. The fallacy of Denying the Antecedent gets this backwards. It takes the following shape:

1 $A \supset B$
2 ~A
3 ~B   ??? 1,2 DA   invalid

All arguments having this form are always invalid. We can conceive of cases where the premises are true, while the conclusion is false. For example, "If it is raining I will get wet. Look, it is not raining." But we cannot *logically* conclude that I will not get wet, since it is conceivable that I will take a shower, or swim, or fall in a puddle, etc. The mere possibility of the premises being true and the conclusion being false is sufficient to show the argument is invalid. Or consider the proposition, "If you're pregnant, you're a woman." If you point out that you're not pregnant (denying the antecedent), it doesn't follow that you're not a woman. Here would be a case where both premises are true while the conclusion is false.

10.5.3 Disjunctive Fallacy (DF)

This invalid argument form corrupts the disjunctive syllogism. Compare the two forms below:

Disjunctive Syllogism				*Disjunctive Fallacy*			
1	A v B			1	A v B		
2	~A			2	A		
3	B	1,2 d.s.	Valid	3	~B ???	1,2 DF	Invalid

The *Disjunctive Fallacy* (DF) assumes that since one of the disjuncts is true, the other must be false. We can check back to our truth table (9.3.1) to see that this doesn't follow. A disjunctive proposition claims that at least one of the disjuncts is true. It permits the possibility that both are true. Line 1 of the truth table for disjunctive propositions represents such cases. This is why we cannot make any inferences concerning the remaining disjunct merely on the basis that one disjunct is true. If any of these invalid steps is needed to reach the conclusion, the whole argument in which it occurs is deemed invalid.

Practice 3

When we prove the validity of an argument, we move from the premises to the conclusion using valid inferences. When we discover that the only way to arrive at the conclusion from the premises and valid inferences is via an *invalid* step, then we have proven that the argument is invalid. To demonstrate this process, let's examine the following three arguments:

(1)	1	C ⊃ (N • T)	(2)	1	L ⊃ S	(3)	1	U v T
	2	~T ⊃ L		2	S ⊃ J		2	B ⊃ ~
	3	~L • N		3	~L		3	B • (~T ⊃ L)
		Therefore C			Therefore ~J			Therefore ~U

Answers to Practice 3
The proofs proceed as follows:

(1)			(2)			(3)		
1	C ⊃ (N • T)	p	1	L ⊃ S	p	1	U v T	p
2	~T ⊃ L	p	2	S ⊃ J	p	2	B ⊃ ~L	p
3	~L • N	p	3	~L	p	3	B • (~T ⊃ L)	p
4	~L	3, simp	4	L ⊃ J	1,2 h.s.	4	B	3, simp
5	T	2,4 m.t.	5	~J ???	3,4 DA	5	~L	2,4 m.p.
6	N	3, simp			invalid	6	~T ⊃ L	3, simp
7	N • T	5,6 conj				7	T	5,6 m.t.
8	C ???	1,7 AC				8	~U ???	1,7 DF
	invalid						invalid	

Exercise 10.5

Test the following arguments to see whether they are valid or invalid. (Answers to selected questions provided in Appendix 1.)

☞ 1 If government is based on lies and deceit, welfare policies cannot be for the benefit of the poor. But clearly welfare policies are for the benefit of the poor, so the government must not be based on lies and deceit.

☞ 2 If government is not based on lies and deceit, welfare policies must be for the benefit of the poor. But clearly welfare policies are for the benefit of the poor, so the government must not be based on lies and deceit.

3 If government is based on lies and deceit, welfare policies cannot be for the benefit of the poor. But the government is based on lies and deceit, so clearly welfare policies cannot be for the benefit of the poor.

☞ 4 If government is based on lies and deceit, welfare policies cannot be for the benefit of the poor. But the government is not based on lies and deceit, so clearly welfare policies are for the benefit of the poor.

5 If it's raining, she will take her umbrella. She's taking her umbrella. Therefore it must be raining.

6 If it's raining, she will take her umbrella. She doesn't have her umbrella. Therefore it must not be raining.

7 If it's raining, she will take her umbrella. It isn't raining. Therefore, she won't take her umbrella.

8 If it's not raining, she won't take her umbrella. It is raining. Therefore, she'll take her umbrella.

9 It's either raining or she doesn't have her umbrella. Look, she has her umbrella, so it must be raining.

☞ 10 It's either not raining or she has her umbrella. Look, it's not raining, so she must not have her umbrella.

11 We have a choice between being moral or increasing profits. If you want to remain in business, you want to increase profits. Obviously you want to remain in business, so you must choose immorality.

12 If blackmail is moral, then it must be simply a matter of payment of money for services rendered. But blackmail is simply a matter of paying someone for services rendered; therefore blackmail is perfectly moral.

☞ 13 If my period starts within two days of the regular cycle, then I'm sure I'm not pregnant. I'm already three days overdue and there's no sign of my period starting. So, I must be pregnant. (MacKinnon, *Basic Reasoning*, 290)

14 Genetically modified foods will either harm the environment or help provide alternative food sources for developing countries. They do

provide alternative food sources for developing nations, so they cannot be harmful to the environment.

☞15 Anyone who is a Communist or Communist sympathizer always opposes any expansion of American military might. Senator Cortez has consistently voted against every weapons system the Pentagon has requested. So, he must be either a Communist or a Communist sympathizer. (MacKinnon, *Basic Reasoning*, 288)

16 1 A ⊃ B
    2 ~B v C
    3 C ⊃ D
    4 ~D
    Therefore ~A

☞17 1 A v B
     2 ~B ⊃ C
     3 D v ~C
     4 ~D
     Therefore ~A

☞18 1 P • M
     2 L ⊃ ~Y
     3 O v L
     4 ~Y ⊃ ~ (P • M)
     Therefore O

19 1 (K v L) ⊃ C
    2 D ⊃ L
    3 ~K ⊃ D
    Therefore C

20 1 E v F
    2 F ⊃ G
    3 E ⊃ H
    4 G ⊃ I
    5 ~I
    Therefore H

☞21 1 (F ⊃ G) v D
     2 ~S ⊃ ~F
     3 ~G ⊃ ~S
     Therefore ~D

22 1 [(Q v Y) ⊃ X] ⊃ (Z v P)
    2 ~V ⊃ [(Q v Y) ⊃ X]
    3 ~Z • ~P
    Therefore V

☞23 1 Y • R
     2 V ⊃ (~Y v ~R)
     Therefore ~V

24 1 [(E ⊃ F) ⊃ G] • (H v I)
    2 H ⊃ (~F ⊃ ~E)
    3 [(J v K) ⊃ ~I] • J
    Therefore G

☞25 1 ~E ⊃ ~R
     2 E ⊃ ~K
     3 (L • ~Y) v F
     4 (~Y ⊃ K) • ~F
     Therefore ~R

26 1 (D v ~W) ⊃ S
    2 (C • U) ⊃ ~(~D • W)
    3 ~U ⊃ ~Z
    4 Z • C
    Therefore S

27 1 Q ⊃ S
    2 L v S
    3 Y ⊃ L
    4 Y
    Therefore ~Q

28 1 W • (U v ~P)
    2 P ⊃ ~W
    Therefore ~ U

☞29 1 B • (G ⊃ ~R)
    2 F ⊃ ~R
    3 F ⊃ ~B
    Therefore ~G.

☞30 1 A v B
    2 ~B
    3 A ⊃ C
    4 ~D ⊃ C
    Therefore ~D

31 1 E • [(E v D) ⊃ ~X]
    Therefore ~X

32 1 L ⊃ J
    2 H ⊃ L
    3 I
    4 ~O v ~I
    5 ~H ⊃ O
    Therefore J

☞33 1 M ⊃ G
    2 (I v ~E) ⊃ ~H
    3 ~T v H
    4 G ⊃ T
    5 M
    Therefore E

10.6 Contradiction

We are now in a position, by the way, to show why the law of contradiction is required. Earlier, we noted that the law of the excluded middle hinges on our acceptance of the law of contradiction, but why should we accept that? For example, logic may be understood a good thing so long as contradiction is bad, but *is* contradiction so bad? Do we have independent means to claim that contradictions are bad, without simply presupposing that they are? Some might argue otherwise, Walt Whitman, for example:

> Do I contradict myself?
> Very well, then I contradict myself,
> (I am large, I contain multitudes.)
>   - Song of Myself, verse 51, *Leaves of Grass*

Others take a slightly narrower stance, allowing contradiction in only children and saints. (Henry Adams, *Mont St. Michel and Chartres*) In any event, logic *requires* the *law of non-contradiction*.

    The law of non-contradiction asserts

Two contradicting propositions cannot both be true, and nor can they both be false.

If we dismiss the law of non-contradiction, then *everything* would be true: nothing could be false. But if nothing can be false, the concept of truth dissolves as well. To demonstrate this, we need to know three rules of logic: the *rule of simplification*, the *rule of addition*, and the *rule of disjunc-*

tive syllogism. The explanation for these rules may be found in 10.1 and 10.4.

Allowing only our three rules of simplification, addition, and disjunctive syllogism, we are ready to show what happens if we – like poets, children, and saints – tolerate contradictions. Let us imagine, then, that contradictions are permitted. A contradiction, recall, will be the following sort of claim: "There is gum on your shoe and there is no gum on your shoe." For brevity's sake, let us represent the contradictory claim about gum on your shoe as follows:

1 G • ~G,

where "G" represents the proposition "There is gum on your shoe," and "~G" represents the denial of that claim. What can we infer from this premise? Well, the answer is *anything we want!* But how so? Let's take the specious claim that you are really a brain in a vat. We'll represent that proposition by the letter "V." The formal presentation of the argument, therefore, looks like this

1 G • ~G
Therefore V

How can the statement, "There is gum on your shoe and there is no gum on your shoe," logically imply that you are a brain in a vat? The derivation is easy. How so?

1 G • ~G   p
2 G   1, simp
3 G v V   2, add
4 ~G   1, simp
5 V   3,4 d.s.

At line 2, we inferred G from line 1, using the rule of simplification. After all, if "A and B" is true, "A" is true. So likewise, if "G and not-G" is true, "G" is true. Ok. Where to from here? Can we really get from V to G? Easily. The rule of addition, recall, asserts that if any claim is true, that claim coupled by an "or" and *any other claim at all* will also be true. Hence, at line 3, we have added " ... or V" to line 2, using the rule of addition. We added "V," by the way, rather than any other letter, because that was our goal: to infer "V" from "G and not-G." Of course, "G or V" is not the same as "V," any more than that you are either reading this proof or snorkelling shows that you're really snorkelling. That's fine. The proof is not finished yet. Another two steps are needed, but these too are simple. Recall at line 2 we inferred "G" from line 1 by simplification? We are entitled to go back to line 1 and infer by simplification "~G." After all, if it's true that I ate a hamburger and salad, it's not merely true that I ate a hamburger, it's also true that I ate a salad. Ok, fine, you might say, but what does this do? It does all that we need. We now can derive our V by using the rule of disjunctive syllogism on lines 3 and 4.

This demonstration shows that *once we admit contradiction*, all sense of truth evaporates. Using the logical rules of simplification, addition, and disjunctive syllogism, we can "prove" anything we want as long as we tolerate contradictions. What this reveals is that if we do not accept the law of non-contradiction, nothing can be false! If nothing can be false, what possible meaning could the concept of truth have? None. There would be no point learning how to argue. Argument and critical thinking presuppose we can convince someone of something they don't already believe. If we tolerate contradiction, such "convincing" will be useless. In fact, education itself would be useless. Think of all the taxpayers' money we could save by wiping out education merely by tolerating contradictions. Education, argument, and critical thinking are all predicated on the belief that there are wrong and right beliefs. Education and critical thinking are designed to better equip us to endorse the right beliefs, rather than the wrong ones. But if we tolerate contradictions, we can no longer distinguish between right and wrong beliefs. They will all be right. If everything is right, the very meaning of "right" vanishes as well.

10.7 A Puzzle about Logic

The following demonstrates a puzzle for logic. We have been hubristically asserting our logical rules. But *should* you accept them? This is the question that Lewis Carroll asks in an article published in the philosophical journal, *Mind*, in 1895.

Achilles had overtaken the Tortoise, and had seated himself comfortably on its back. "So you've got to the end of our race-course?" said the Tortoise. "Even though it DOES consist of an infinite series of distances? I thought some wiseacre or other had proved that the thing couldn't be done?"

"It CAN be done," said Achilles. "It HAS been done! *Solvitur ambulando.* You see the distances were constantly DIMINISHING; and so –"

"But if they had been constantly INCREASING?" the Tortoise interrupted. "How then?"

"Then I shouldn't be here," Achilles modestly replied; "and YOU would have got several times round the world, by this time!"

"You flatter me – FLATTEN, I mean," said the Tortoise; "for you ARE a heavy weight, and NO mistake! Well now, would you like to hear of a race-course, that most people fancy they can get to the end of in two or three steps, while it REALLY consists of an infinite number of distances, each one longer than the previous one?"

"Very much indeed!" said the Grecian warrior, as he drew from his helmet (few Grecian warriors possessed POCKETS in those days) an enormous note-book and pencil. "Proceed! And speak SLOWLY, please! SHORTHAND isn't invented yet!"

"That beautiful First Proposition by Euclid!" the Tortoise murmured dreamily. "You admire Euclid?"

"Passionately! So far, at least, as one CAN admire a treatise that won't be published for some centuries to come!"

"Well, now, let's take a little bit of the argument in that First Proposition – just TWO steps, and the conclusion drawn from them. Kindly enter them in your note-book. And in order to refer to them conveniently, let's call them A, B, and Z:

"*(A) Things that are equal to the same are equal to each other.*
"*(B) The two sides of this Triangle are things that are equal to the same.*
"*(Z) The two sides of this Triangle are equal to each other.*

"Readers of Euclid will grant, I suppose, that Z follows logically from A and B, so that any one who accepts A and B as true, MUST accept Z as true?"

"Undoubtedly! The youngest child in a High School – as soon as High Schools are invented, which will not be till some two thousand years later – will grant THAT."

"And if some reader had NOT yet accepted A and B as true, he might still accept the SEQUENCE as a VALID one, I suppose?"

"No doubt such a reader might exist. He might say, 'I accept as true the Hypothetical Proposition that, if A and B be true, Z must be true; but I DON'T accept A and B as true.' Such a reader would do wisely in abandoning Euclid, and taking to football."

"And might there not ALSO be some reader who would say 'I accept A and B as true, but I DON'T accept the Hypothetical'?"

"Certainly there might. HE, also, had better take to football."

"And NEITHER of these readers," the Tortoise continued, "is AS YET under any logical necessity to accept Z as true?"

"Quite so," Achilles assented. "Well, now, I want you to consider ME as a reader of the SECOND kind, and to force me, logically, to accept Z as true."

"A tortoise playing football would be –" Achilles was beginning.

"– an anomaly, of course," the Tortoise hastily interrupted. "Don't wander from the point. Let's have Z first, and football afterwards!"

"I'm to force you to accept Z, am I?" Achilles said musingly. "And your present position is that you accept A and B, but you DON'T accept the Hypothetical –"

"Let's call it C," said the Tortoise.

"– but you DON'T accept

"(C) If A and B are true, Z must be true."

"That is my present position," said the Tortoise.

"Then I must ask you to accept C."

"I'll do so," said the Tortoise, "as soon as you've entered it in that notebook of yours. What else have you got in it?"

"Only a few memoranda," said Achilles, nervously fluttering the leaves: "a few memoranda of – of the battles in which I have distinguished myself!"

"Plenty of blank leaves, I see!" the Tortoise cheerily remarked. "We shall need them ALL!" (Achilles shuddered.) "Now write as I dictate: –

"(A) Things that are equal to the same are equal to each other.
"(B) The two sides of this Triangle are things that are equal to the same.
"(C) If A and B are true, Z must be true.
"(Z) The two sides of this Triangle are equal to each other."

"You should call it D, not Z," said Achilles. "It comes NEXT to the other three. If you accept A and B and C, you MUST accept Z."

"And why must I?"

"Because it follows LOGICALLY from them. If A and B and C are true, Z MUST be true. You can't dispute THAT, I imagine?"

"If A and B and C are true, Z MUST be true," the Tortoise thoughtfully repeated. "That's ANOTHER Hypothetical, isn't it? And, if I failed to see its truth, I might accept A and B and C, and STILL not accept Z, mightn't I?"

"You might," the candid hero admitted; "though such obtuseness would certainly be phenomenal. Still, the event is POSSIBLE. So I must ask you to grant ONE more Hypothetical."

"Very good, I'm quite willing to grant it, as soon as you've written it down. We will call it

"(D) If A and B and C are true, Z must be true.

"Have you entered that in your note-book?"

"I HAVE!" Achilles joyfully exclaimed, as he ran the pencil into its sheath. "And at last we've got to the end of this ideal race-course! Now that you accept A and B and C and D, OF COURSE you accept Z."

"Do I?" said the Tortoise innocently. "Let's make that quite clear. I accept A and B and C and D. Suppose I STILL refused to accept Z?"

"Then Logic would take you by the throat, and FORCE you to do it!" Achilles triumphantly replied. "Logic would tell you, 'You can't help yourself. Now that you've accepted A and B and C and D, you MUST accept Z.' So you've no choice, you see."

"Whatever LOGIC is good enough to tell me is worth WRITING DOWN," said the Tortoise. "So enter it in your book, please. We will call it

"*(E) If A and B and C and D are true, Z must be true.*

"Until I've granted THAT, of course I needn't grant Z. So it's quite a NECESSARY step, you see?"

"I see," said Achilles; and there was a touch of sadness in his tone.

Here the narrator, having pressing business at the Bank, was obliged to leave the happy pair, and did not again pass the spot until some months afterwards. When he did so, Achilles was still seated on the back of the much-enduring Tortoise, and was writing in his notebook, which appeared to be nearly full. The Tortoise was saying, "Have you got that last step written down? Unless I've lost count, that makes a thousand and one. There are several millions more to come. And WOULD you mind, as a personal favour, considering what a lot of instruction this colloquy of ours will provide for the Logicians of the Nineteenth Century – WOULD you mind adopting a pun that my cousin the Mock-Turtle will then make, and allowing yourself to be renamed TAUGHT-US?"

"As you please," replied the weary warrior, in the hollow tones of despair, as he buried his face in his hands. "Provided that YOU, for YOUR part, will adopt a pun the Mock-Turtle never made, and allow yourself to be re-named A-KILL-EASE!"

Part Five

Induction

11

Causation and Probability

Inductive Generalizations • Causation
Probabilistic Reasoning

11.1 Inductive Generalizations

A *deductive* argument asserts that the conclusion necessarily follows from the premises. If it does, we call the argument *valid*; if not, *invalid*. A deductive argument is either valid or invalid; there is no other option. The method of assessment we employ in testing validity is logic – either *propositional* (chapters 9 and 10) or *categorical* (chapters 7 and 8).

An *inductive* argument, on the other hand, asserts that there is (merely) a good chance that the conclusion follows from the premises. Typically this is on the basis of generalizing from a sample to claims about members of a group outside that sample. The greater the chance of the conclusion following on the basis of the given premises, the better. The less chance, the worse. An inductive argument, then, may be better or worse, and there is a whole range of possibilities in between. Our method of assessing inductive arguments is *probabilistic* reasoning. We test probabilistic reasoning by checking the size of the sample used to make the generalization, and assessing how unbiased the selection of the sample was.

An inductive generalization makes inferences to a target population on the basis of a sample. On the basis of discovering that 1,000 swans are white, the argument concludes that *all* swans are white. That is, on the basis of examining a sample of a certain class or population, swans in this case, a claim is made about the entire class or population. In other words, we proceed from the *particular* to the *general*. Our premises make statements about particular members of a class, and the conclusion makes a claim about all members of that class based on that sample.

Inductive generalizations do not need to make categorical claims (i.e., all, none, etc.). One could make *statistical* or *probabilistic* inductive generalizations as well. For example, if thirty-eight out of fifty people surveyed say they would vote Liberal in the next election, we cannot conclude that everyone will vote Liberal, but we can conclude that about 75 per cent of people will vote Liberal – as long as the sample is sufficiently representative of Canadians.

11.2 Causation

11.2.1 Correlation and Causation

Correlational claims are based on observations of two distinct objects or events (event A and event B, let us say). A may be *positively* correlated with B, *negatively* correlated with B, or show *no* correlation with B. A is positively correlated with B when an increase in As is accompanied by an increase in Bs. That is, if there are more As, there are more Bs. A is negatively correlated if the reverse holds, such that the more As there are, the less Bs. If however many As there are has no bearing on how many Bs there are, we say there is no correlation; the two are unrelated.

The purpose of statistical testing is to see if any correlation is *significant*. Significance involves a mathematical formula to determine whether differences are due to chance. Only with a significant difference can we generalize from our sample to our target population. So we have to distinguish between correlation and no correlation, between positive and negative correlation, and also between significant and insignificant correlations. There is much room to go astray.

Correlation does not equal causation. Just because A is positively correlated with B does not mean that A caused B, even when that difference is statistically significant. Correlational evidence is never sufficient grounds, all by itself, to infer causation. We may have perfect correlation, yet resist making a causal inference. For example, despite the perfect correlation between wind blowing on PEI and the lack of crop failure due to stampeding elephants, the causal prediction that winds prevent crop-destroying elephant stampedes is unwarranted. Likewise, every time you come to the university you may brush your teeth, but it hardly follows from that that your brushing your teeth causes you to come to the university.

To avoid confusing correlation with causation, it is helpful to realize that correlation is a *symmetrical* relation, while causation is *asymmetrical*. If A is correlated with B, B is likewise correlated with A. But this symmetry does not exist with causal relations. If A caused B, B did *not* cause A.

11.2.2 Causal Laws and the Problem of Induction

The striking feature about causation is that it asserts a *law*. If A caused B, then under similar circumstances, A will *always* cause B. What we witnessed when A caused B was an *instance* of a general LAW that such circumstances (A) are always accompanied by such phenomena (B).

So how do we tell correlation from cause? We test it. We set up or observe identical situations to see if in the presence of A, B occurs. If B does not occur, and *everything else was the same*, then the presence of B occurring with A in previous encounters was merely *coincidence*. When we speak of "cause" we speak of a *causal law*.

Ok, so what? We can tell when something is merely coincidental if under similar circumstances B does not occur with A. But how can we ever be confident enough to make the claim that A in fact caused B? If we are speaking of causation, then it must be the case that under similar circumstances B will always occur after A. But how can we check this out? Like all inductive arguments, the causal relation is not a purely logical or demonstrative relation. It cannot be discovered by any *a priori* reasoning. Causal laws can only be discovered by an appeal to experience. But our experiences are always of particular circumstances. Even if all observations we make show us that B follows A, how do we conclude that it is a law that B follows A? How do we know that after we die, B will not follow A? Or that B follows A only when we look, but not otherwise? Or simply that it is a coincidence that whenever we have looked B follows A, but many times, although unknown to us, B did not follow A? Deductively, our observations can only show us that in some cases B follows A, or that in the cases we have observed, B follows A.

This problem was noted by David Hume (1711–1776). We refer to it as *the Problem of Induction*. It raises the question, How are we to get from particular evidence that B follows A to the general proposition that B always follows A, which is what is required if we want to claim that A caused B? Plainly, we cannot resolve this deep philosophical skepticism. Still, we cannot operate in the world without the belief in causation. Although our past inability to fly cannot count as indubitable proof that we cannot now fly, we do well to continue to believe that past events provide sufficient predictors of future events. The prospect of passing on one's genes is thereby increased. Still, the problem of induction challenges us to become more reflective about our causal claims. To that end, let us distinguish between different sorts of causal conditions.

11.2.3 Four Causal Conditions

When we assert that A caused B, we have to recognize an *all things being equal* clause. Consider the case where someone strikes a match and fire erupts on the match head. We typically say that striking the match caused the fire. Although striking the match *usually* causes fire, it will not if the match is wet. This shows that events do not just happen, but occur *only under certain conditions*. There are four causal conditions we should observe: necessary, sufficient, contributing, and catalytic.

i. Necessary Condition. A necessary condition is a circumstance in whose absence the event cannot take place. Since fire can occur without a match (lightning, electrical shortage, lighters, etc.), striking a match is not a necessary condition for fire. The presence of oxygen, however, is a necessary condition for fire, since without oxygen, there could be no fire.

ii. Sufficient Condition. A sufficient condition is a circumstance in whose presence the event will normally occur. Striking a match, under normal circumstances, is a sufficient condition for fire, since this is one way in which fires can be started. Oxygen, by itself, however, is not a sufficient condition for fire. There is oxygen in this room right now, for example, and yet no fire.

If our goal is to *prevent* something from happening, we will do well to seek out one of the necessary conditions for that occurrence and eliminate or prevent it. If our goal is to produce something, then we will do well to ensure the presence of a sufficient condition for its occurrence.

iii. Contributing Condition.   Most often when we speak of X causing Y in normal discourse, we mean something different than either sufficient and/or necessary conditions. We mean something like X was one of the *contributing* causes of Y. When we say X caused Y, we normally mean it is this thing X, in the presence of other conditions normally occurring, which produced the effect Y. Rarely is X a sufficient condition, and often X isn't even a necessary condition, but we still think of X as a contributing condition, and we are often interested in that.

Why do we introduce this third condition? Consider: we have already shown that striking a match is not a necessary condition for fire. It is not even a necessary condition for that match being on fire, since we could stick the match into a fire already lit. Above we recklessly claimed that striking a match is a sufficient condition for fire, but is this true? Not if the match is wet! Not if there is no more of that sandpaper stuff on the package. Not if the match has lost its sulphur head. Not if there is no oxygen in the room at the time. Striking the match, all by itself, then, is neither a sufficient condition of fire, nor a necessary condition of fire. But we do, nevertheless want to say it was the striking of the match that caused the fire. So what's going on?

We can see that a sufficient condition is rarely going to be a single thing. *Most causal relations depend on a multiplicity of factors.* Now, many of these factors normally occur anyway (normally the match is dry, normally there is oxygen in the room ...). If the match doesn't have its sulphur head we call it a defective match, and when we speak of matches we mean to speak of working matches, and not defective matches, etc.

iv. Catalytic Condition.   Calling the match merely a "contributing" condition seems to undermine the special role the match played. When we want to highlight a special contributing factor, we call it the *catalytic condition*. Identifying the catalytic condition enables us to single out the match. Against the backdrop of normal conditions it points its finger at the *main difference* between no fire and fire, in this case, the striking of the match.

Contributing factors of a person's striking the match may have been his going to the store to buy matches, or its being cold in the room and his wanting to get warm, and hence wanting to light a fire. We can always single out a number of contributing causes, but typically there will be no ambiguity concerning what the catalytic cause is. If a police officer asks us what was the cause of the accident, presumably she is asking for our interpretation of the *catalytic condition*, and not a long list of contributing factors. In fact, most often when we hear the word "cause" it is meant in this fashion. Asking, "Why is that vase broken?" is not meant (normally) to elicit dissertations on gravity or on the fragility of certain types of vases. The question is (normally) to be understood as asking: "*Ignoring the normal background conditions*, what is the catalytic cause of this vase being broken?"*

Sometimes, however, the catalytic cause will depend on *context*. For example, we know that protecting our king is *necessary* to win a chess game, since if we don't protect our king, we lose, whereas checkmating our opponent's king is *sufficient* to win a chess game, but not necessary, since our opponent might resign prior to that and we still win. But what is the catalytic cause of one's losing a chess game? Catalytic causes depend very much on context and background information. If someone asks Kasparov why he lost the chess game, and Kasparov knows that she doesn't play chess herself, Kasparov might respond, "I was checkmated. See, my king is under attack where it sits and I cannot move my king anywhere, and that constitutes the end of the game." The catalytic cause is deemed to be the final move of Kasparov's opponent. On the other hand, if Kasparov knows the questioner plays chess, he can assume that she won't be satisfied by his telling her he was checkmated. She can see that. That can't be what she is interested in. She is looking for what led to such an ignominious defeat. Consequently, Kasparov might reply, "I doubled up my pawn structure early in the game and that cost me in the end game." In this case, he has singled out the catalytic condition as occurring in the twelfth move, rather than the forty-seventh. The difference is borne out by context and intent.

---

* Sometimes people use the interrogative "What?" when they really mean "Why?" The police officer might ask the car thief "What are you doing in the car?" when he really means "Why are you in this car?" Responding "I'm trying to see if I can start the car without the key" is not really answering the intended question.

Exercise 11.1

For the following, state whether the first event (Event A) is necessary, sufficient, both necessary and sufficient, or neither necessary nor sufficient for the second event (Event B). Where needed, indicate the contributing conditions you're assuming. (Answers to selected questions provided in Appendix 1.)

	Event A	*Event B*
☞ 1	lying	telling a falsehood
☞ 2	shooting	killing
☞ 3	hitting a home run	hitting a grand slam
☞ 4	rain falling	the ground getting wet
5	being older than twenty	being sixty years old
6	being a dog	being an animal
7	knowing someone	loving someone
8	touching the baseball	being charged with an error
9	being a bachelor	being an unmarried adult male
10	dynamiting the building	destroying the building
11	sinking the putt	getting a birdie
☞ 12	dancing	having a partner
☞ 13	cracking eggs	frying eggs
☞ 14	being a parking lot attendant	having a job
☞ 15	breathing	being alive
16	golfing	relaxing
17	being hungry	stealing bread
18	being literate	reading
19	exercising	reducing calories
20	watching a comedy	laughing

11.2.4 Three Fallacies of Causal Thinking

In order to assess causal inferences we will do well to pay attention to three common errors in causal claims: coincidence, reverse order, and 3rd variable.

i. Coincidence   People seem psychologically unwilling to accept coincidence as an explanation (see section 11.3.3 below). We cannot rule out the possibility that two events occur together, even with some degree of regularity, for reasons none other than chance. Consider the following causal claims:

1   A strong direct correlation holds between the birthrate in Holland and the number of storks nesting in chimneys.
2   A man cancelled his flight to Egypt, and the flight he would have been on

crashed, killing everyone aboard. He took his last minute jitters as a psychic premonition that saved his life.

Concerning 1, there is, of course, the theory that babies come from storks, but this is not backed by scientific evidence. It doesn't fit with the rest of our understanding of how babies come about. For the lack of any other explanation, the correlation just seems weird, and it is not imprudent to simply ignore it rather than make any claims about it.

Concerning 2, we have to pay attention to what the probability of flight cancellation is prior to any flight. Let's estimate there to be about a 5 per cent cancellation rate. Though this is low, it does mean we can predict, for every plane that takes off, 5 per cent of the people decided not to get on it for one reason or another. Since every plane that crashed is also a plane that took off, we can predict 5 per cent of the people decided not to get on that particular flight, lucky for them. The coincidence is explained by probability alone. Appeals to simple math show the man's fortune is due to chance, not fate.

ii Reverse-Order Errors   Reverse-order fallacies, as the name suggests, get the causal ordering backward. Rather than A's causing B, it may well be the reverse. Consider the following claims:

1 The more fire trucks there are in a given area, the more fires there are. Therefore, we should put less money into the fire station, not more.
2 The more passes thrown in the fourth quarter of a football game, the less chance of winning. This suggests that, in order to win, teams should run with the ball in the fourth quarter.
3 We should have capital punishment in Canada. Capital punishment instills a horror of murder in a way that no other form of punishment can, and thus will be an effective deterrent.

All commit the causal error of reverse-order. In 1, the reason there are more fire trucks is *because* there are more fires, not the reverse.

In 2, closer examination reveals that when a team is losing, it is more likely to gamble by throwing more passes late in the game. The asserted causal connection is, again, backwards. They do not lose *because* they throw long passes in the fourth quarter; rather they throw long passes in the last quarter *because* they're losing.

In 3, if there is a causal relationship at all (the evidence does not support it), it seems to be reversed here. Our horror of murder causes us to think it requires a severe punishment. Otherwise we could say, "Let's make premarital sex an offence meriting capital punishment, since that would instill a horror of premarital sex." The absurdity noted here is due to the fact that we do not share the same degree of horror toward premarital sex as we do toward murder. This shows the horror is the reason for thinking of capital punishment, and not that horror is instilled in us *because* or *only if* we have capital punishment. It is more likely, of course, that capital punishment does not deter murder. People are generally deterred from murder in Canada, yet there is no capital punishment here. As Jeffrey Reiman notes, the assumption that the greater the punishment, the greater the deterrence effect cannot be unlimited. Spending eternity in hell is worse than spending 1000 years in hell, but both are equally sufficient deterrents. Chopping off two limbs is severe, but the threat of having one limb chopped off may be a sufficient deterrent to some action. This shows that it is not necessarily the case that the greater the punishment the greater the deterrent. (Reiman, "Common sense, the Deterrent Effect of the Death penalty, and the Best Bet Argument," 102–7)

iii. 3rd Variable Errors In 3rd variable errors, there is likely an alternative hypothesis that can explain the correlation between A and B without reference to the belief that A caused B or B caused A. Consider the following causal claims:

1 A survey of nearly 900 rural families in Ohio found that 60 per cent of the residents regularly locked their doors and yet were burglarized more often than residents who did not lock their doors. Therefore there is no evidence to support the claim that locking doors helps prevent burglaries.
2 Cameron argues that homosexuality ought to be discouraged and "cured" by invasive psychotherapies on the basis that studies show that homosexuals are less happy and less trusting than heterosexuals. (Paul Cameron, "A Case Against Homosexuality," 341–9)
3 Religion is the cause of sin. The more churches there are in a given area, the more crimes exist.

The reason none of the above arguments sounds convincing is that they each commit the 3rd variable offence. In 1, a third factor is likely to be involved. The richer you are, the more likely you will lock your doors to protect your possessions. The poorer you are, the less likely you will lock your doors. Since burglars are after riches, not poverty, they will tend to target richer homes (that also happen to lock their doors). In this case, we might also wonder if a reverse-order causal fallacy has occurred. It is not that burglars target only houses that have locked their doors. Rather, families are more inclined to lock their doors in areas where burglaries occur more often.

In 2, there is again a 3rd variable lurking. People in society, by and large, discriminate against homosexuals, kick them out of public offices, spit upon them, call them names, etc. Surely *this* is the cause of their unhappiness and lack of trust, not their homosexuality. So, if we want homosexuals to be happier and more trusting, we should create a more tolerant society, not further discourage homosexuals. (In this particular study, there is a further problem concerning the sample. See 11.3.3 below.)

In 3, the third variable is likely to be population size. The greater the population density the greater of everything: churches and crime, but also bakeries and taxis.

Exercise 11.2

The following arguments all commit causal errors. Explain which one and why. (Answers to selected questions are provided in Appendix 1.)

☞ 1 Due to increasing population in China, there exist government restrictions on the number of children couples may have. This motivated many studies in birth control. One such study discovered a correlation between fewer children and owning a toaster. Should we adopt the toaster method for birth control?

2 Gas produced by cows' digestion causes the atmosphere to warm up. There are more cows than ever before, and there's global warming, and scientists have discovered that cows produce methane gas, a gas known to trap heat in the atmosphere.

3 It's the thirteenth today and our air plane took off from gate 13. No wonder we're experiencing so much turbulence.

4 The prevalence of violence in the media causes people to be violent on the street.

☞ 5 Don't sit too close to your computer. The only people I know who sit really close to their computer screen have bad eyesight.

☞ 6 Children who are not fed breakfast do poorly in school. Therefore poor nutrition contributes to poor grades.

☞ 7 Children who have positive attitudes about themselves are more likely than others to receive positive evaluations from adults around them. Therefore, children's positive views of themselves derive from positive evaluations by adults around them.

8 Sixty-five per cent of rapists use pornography: therefore, we have grounds to stamp out pornography.

9 Zoe is irritable because she can't sleep properly.

10 More young people are attending high schools than ever before, yet there is more juvenile delinquency than ever before. What are they teaching in schools these days?

11.2.5 Assessing Causal Relations

Causal relations hold between two events or conditions. "Striking the match caused it to light" asserts a causal connection between striking the match and having the match burn. "The patient's fever caused his pallor" asserts a causal connection between the patient's fever and the patient's pallor. Under the same conditions, the same cause will induce the same effect *always*. If B doesn't follow A in one case, then either A didn't cause

B, or some necessary condition is absent in that one case. By recognizing this law of causation, we can develop four ways of assessing causal claims: temporality, regularity, variation, and coherence.

i. Temporality   *If A causes B, A must precede B in time.*

Not only does the cause/effect relation hold between events or conditions but, whenever the cause/effect relation holds, the cause *temporally precedes* the effect. We do not say the disease caused the germs to appear. No, it was the other way around. The germs were there first, and their presence caused the disease.

By focussing on temporality conditions, we should reduce the chances of committing reverse-order errors.

ii. Regularity   *If A causes B, A must regularly precede B in time.*

In the cause/effect relation, the relation holds between events or conditions, the cause temporarily precedes the effect, and the relation involves a *regularity*. If we say *X* caused *Y*, we should expect that *whenever X* occurs within the appropriate circumstances, *Y* occurs. If *Y* occurs only sometimes after *X* is present, we cannot say *X* caused *Y*.

The condition of regularity will help reduce the chances of mistaking coincidence for causation. For example, if I was thinking of my brother and then he phoned, we cannot conclude that my thinking of my brother, which occurred before the phone call, caused my brother's phoning me unless it is always the case that when I think of my brother, he phones me. Even then, we may not want to attribute a causal relation to this event until we rule out 3rd variables.

iii. Variation

If A causes B, A must regularly precede B in time under all circumstances.

Mere regularity is not sufficient to make causal claims. That I regularly brush my teeth before I leave the house is not evidence that brushing my teeth is the cause of my leaving the house. This shows the difference between *causation* and *correlation*. Two events are correlated when they occur together with a certain degree of regularity, but mere correlation is not sufficient grounds to assume causation.

To avoid 3rd variable errors, we need to vary the circumstances that precede the effect. For example, if I can leave the house *without* brushing my teeth, or brush my teeth *without* leaving the house, we can avoid committing the 3rd variable error. Variation will help distinguish contributing factors from non-contributing factors, as well as hone in on the catalytic condition.

iv. Coherence

The proposed causal relation must not contradict known laws of physics.

Does the proposed causal explanation fit within our current general understanding of how the world works? If not, this should count against the causal claim.

It is possible, of course, that our general understanding of how the world works is mistaken. In such cases, our new causal account may replace the old view. But such a revision is not to be taken lightly. Here is how Richard Dawkins, professor of zoology at Oxford university puts it:

> There have been times in the history of science when the whole of orthodox science has been rightly thrown over because of a single awkward fact. It would be arrogant to assert that such overthrows will never happen again. But we naturally, and rightly, demand a higher standard of authentication before accepting a fact that would turn a major and successful scientific edifice upside down, than accepting a fact which, even if surprising, is readily accommodated by existing science. For a plesiosaur in Loch Ness, I would accept the evidence of my own eyes. If I saw a man levitating himself, before rejecting the whole of physics I would suspect that I was the victim of a hallucination or a conjuring trick. There is a continuum, from theories that probably are not true but easily could be, to theories that could only be true at the cost of overthrowing large edifices of successful orthodox science. (Dawkins, *The Blind Watchmaker*, 292–3)

A Contradiction?

Earlier we argued that causal relations involve *laws*. Nevertheless, causal inferences are a form of inductive reasoning that can never be *certain*. Have we contradicted ourselves? Recall the *Law of the Excluded Middle* (9.3.1) from our discussion of logic, that a proposition must be true or false. Nothing can be partially true. Nothing can be more true than something else. Still, it doesn't follow that we know whether it is true or not. Our degree of conviction about the proposition being true or false will vary. We shouldn't confuse these things. It is the same with causation. If A caused B in circumstance C, then it must be the case that any A will cause any B in any circumstance C. In other words, we are claiming that there exists a causal relation. If that is true, it is a law. But *is* it true? That is where we can only assert with varying degrees of confidence. Our confidence should be greater if the claim has passed the four criteria above; weaker otherwise.

The greater the number of observed instances, the higher the probability that the correlation is lawful rather than fortuitous. Still, it is important to remember that causal inferences are never deductive.

The media often report studies showing that two events are "linked" or "associated." Frequently, the coverage is presented as if there is evidence of a causal link, although it may not say that directly. In such cases, ask whether there is evidence to assume causation, or merely correlation.

Often there is much debate about whether the relation between two events is correlational or causal. A striking correlation between smoking and lung cancer was vigorously denounced as merely correlational, and not causal, by the tobacco industry. Is a similar ploy being used by the Americans to squelch the Kyoto accord for environmental protection? The following article highlights the debate:

> George W. Bush will be met by a searing blast of indignation from European Union leaders in Stockholm tomorrow over his dismissal of the 1997 Kyoto Protocol and his country's alleged disregard for global warming. Last week, the National Academy of Sciences released a report apparently finding that greenhouse gases such as carbon dioxide are accumulating in the atmosphere because of industrialization. As a result, surface air temperatures and subsurface ocean temperatures are rising. Many people hailed the NAS report as decisively proving global warming is real and would get worse without the implementation of the Kyoto Protocol to reduce greenhouse-gas emissions. On Monday, the EU affirmed its commitment to Kyoto by cutting emissions by 8% by 2012 from 1990 levels. Canada is also on board. "We disagree with the Americans," said David Anderson, Canada's Minister of Environment. "We would have preferred the Americans stay in the Kyoto process, which, after all, is the only one around at the moment." A few hours after the EU announcement, Mr. Bush set out his views clearly. Calling the Kyoto Protocol "fatally flawed in fundamental ways," he acknowledged a correlation between emissions and global warming, but refused to concede a firm causal relationship between the two. ["Because of the large and still uncertain level of natural variability inherent in the climate record and the uncertainties in the time histories of the various forcing agents ... a causal linkage between the buildup of greenhouse gases in the atmosphere and the observed climate changes in the 20th century cannot be unequivocally established." In short, just because the 20th century was a little warmer "does not constitute proof" that there's a link to greenhouse gases. (Terence Corcoran, "The Kyoto accord finally flames out," *National Post*, 8 June 2001,14)] Instead, he laid out the guidelines of an alternative policy. This would include more research to determine the degree of causality. (Alexander Rose, "Global thinking crushes Kyoto," *National Post*, 13 June 2001, A10)

Recap
To determine whether A caused B, ask the following:

1 Does A actually precede B?
2 How many observations of As preceding Bs have there been? The more the better; the fewer, the worse.
3 Are there any counter-examples (where A did not precede B, or where despite A's occurrence, B was nowhere to be found)?
4 Does the proposed causal relation cohere with our general scientific understanding of the world?

11.3 Probabilistic Reasoning

11.3.1 Probability

Many relationships in nature are probabilistic, rather than universal. When we say, "men are taller than women," we mean that, on the whole, or statistically, men are taller than women. We do not mean that *all* men are taller than *all* women. When we say someone dies every second, or a woman gives birth every seven seconds, we do not mean that a single person keeps dying over and over again or that a single woman is giving birth every seven seconds. Probabilistic trends and laws do not claim that the relationship holds true in every single case. In fact, probability is the science of predicting the behaviour of large groups of individuals.

Virtually every fact and relationship uncovered by the sciences is stated in terms of probabilities rather than certainties. Probabilistic relationships, however, are not well understood by the population at large.

Formulas for determining probabilities will vary depending on what sort of events we're investigating. An event may be comprised of a single outcome, a conjunction of outcomes, or a disjunction of outcomes. In each case, there is a specific outcome (x) which we are measuring against a background of possible outcomes (n). The general formula for determining the probability of an outcome A $(p(A))$, is simply x/n. For example, the probability of rolling a three on a die is $1/6$, or .167. The probability of rolling two threes on two dice, however, is the probability of rolling a three on one die multiplied by the probability of rolling a three on the second die $(.167 \times .167 = .028)$. The odds of rolling a three on at least one die in two throws is $.167 + .167 = .334$. That is, despite the basic formula, slight variations in calculation occur depending on whether we are looking at events comprising *single outcomes*, a *conjunction of outcomes*, or a *disjunction of outcomes*.

1 Probability of a single outcome = x/n
2 Probability of a conjunction of independent outcomes = $x_1/n_1 \times x_2/n_2 \times ... x_n/n_n$
3 Probability of a disjunction of independent outcomes = $x_1/n_1 + x_2/n_2 + ... + x_n/n_n$

In the case of *single events*, we might wonder what the probability is of pulling from a deck of cards the queen of hearts. The x in this case is the event where pulling the queen of hearts occurs. The background number of possible cases of pulling a card equals the number of cards in a deck. Hence, the probability of pulling the queen of hearts is 152, or .019. There is approximately a 2 per cent chance of succeeding.

In the case of a *conjunction of independent events*, we might wonder what the probability is of tossing two fair coins and both landing heads? In this case, the probability of the first coin landing heads up is 1/2, and the probability of the second coin landing heads up is also 1/2. The second coin's landing heads is *independent* of whatever the first coin did, and vice versa. (To fail to appreciate this is to commit the *Gambler's Fallacy*, see 11.3.4.) Therefore, to determine the probability of the event of both coins landing heads we multiply 1/2 x 1/2, which equals 1/4. That is, its probability is .25. We'd also use this formula to determine the likelihood of two separate single events occurring together, for example, throwing a heads with one coin and a six with one die. The probability of such an event is x_1/n_1 x x_2/n_2 = 1/2 x 1/6 (or .5 x .167) = .084. We'd have about an 8 per cent chance of success.

In the case of a *disjunction of independent outcomes*, we might wonder what the probability is of tossing three coins at once and obtaining two heads and one tail. The probability of coin one landing heads, coin two landing heads, and coin three landing tails is 1/2 x 1/2 x 1/2 = 1/8. But this doesn't exhaust the permutations of there being two heads and one tail. Another permutation is when coin one lands heads, coin two lands tails, and coin three lands heads. The odds of this is 1/2 x 1/2 x 1/2 = 1/8. Another permutation is also possible, however, where coin one lands tails, coin two lands heads, and coin three lands heads. The odds of this occurrence is, again, 1/2 x 1/2 x 1/2 = 1/8. To determine the probability of any permutation of two heads and one tail in a throw of three coins, therefore, is to add the odds of the separate permutations together. Hence, 1/8 + 1/8 + 1/8 = 3/8, or 0.375.

Notice that whenever any two events, A and B, are mutually exclusive, the probability of both A and B occurring simultaneously is 0. In the toss of two coins, let A represent the outcome event of there being two tails, and let B represent the outcome event of there being exactly one head. These two events are mutually exclusive, the probability of both A and B occurring is zero. Notice, however, that the probability of the disjunct of two mutually exclusive events A *or* B will not necessarily add up to 1. In this case, the probability of A (two tails) *or* B (exactly one head) equals 1/4 + 1/2 = 3/4.

Exercise 11.3

Determine the probabilities for the following, using the formula for determining the probability of single events, conjunction of events, or disjunction of events. In all cases assume the games in question are "fair." (Answers to selected questions provided in Appendix 1.)

☞ 1 There are two jars. Jar A contains three black, four white, and three red marbles. Jar B contains eight green, three white, and two black marbles. Assume the marbles in both jars are randomly mixed. If you blindly reach into both jars at once and pull out one marble from each jar, what is the probability that both marbles drawn will be black?

2 There are two jars. Jar A contains three black, four white, and three red marbles. Jar B contains eight green, three white, and two black marbles. Assume the marbles in both jars are randomly mixed. If you blindly reach into both jars at once and pull out one marble from each jar, what is the probability that at least one marble will be white?

☞ 3 What is the probability of throwing eight dice at once and none of them yielding a three?

4 Four decks of cards are in front of you. If you randomly draw one card from each deck, what is the probability that all cards will be red?

5 What is the probability that four dice thrown together will all turn up an even number?

6 Sally asks Tom to bring in her two cats from the garden. Tom discovers there are five cats in the garden. Assuming Tom cannot recognize Sally's cats and can capture any two – but only two – cats, what are the odds of Tom's grabbing both of Sally's cats? What are the odds he gets at least one of Sally's cats?

☞ 7 Imagine you are given a standard deck of fifty-two playing cards and invited to participate in a charity-based draw. Drawing the queen of any suit wins $25.00, and drawing the queen of hearts wins $100.00. Calculate the probability of winning $25.00 in one draw.

8 As in the above game, you will win $25.00 by drawing the queen of any suit, and $100.00 by drawing the queen of hearts. Calculate the probability of winning $ 25.00 in three draws. Assume you are replacing the previously drawn card, and that the deck is reshuffled before each draw.

9 Imagine you are given a standard deck of fifty-two playing cards and invited to participate in a charity-based draw. Drawing the queen of any suit wins $25.00, and drawing the queen of hearts wins $100.00. Calculate the probability of winning $100.00 in one draw.

☞10 Assuming a woman has given birth to three children, what is the probability two are girls and one is a boy?

11 A barrel contains one hundred balls, forty-four of which are green, fourteen of which are blue, and forty-two of which are red. A single ball is drawn at random. What is the probability a blue or red ball is chosen?

12 In a class of forty students, evenly divided between male and female, the instructor is to assign male-female dyads for two group projects, assuring only that the same dyads won't be repeated. You especially want to be paired with one person in particular on either occasion. What are the odds your wish will come true?

13 If we throw two coins, we (now) know the probability of having exactly one head is .5. Likewise the probability of exactly one tail. What is the probability of having one head and one tail?

14 On Sundays, the odds of Dennis practising batting is .85. The odds of
Dennis hitting a baseball with a bat is .2. When Dennis hits the ball,
it goes to the right with odds of .3. Assuming Dennis hits the ball to
the right, the odds of the ball hitting the west wall of Mr. Wilson's
house is .25. One quarter of the west wall of Mr. Wilson's house is
composed of windows. The odds of a baseball hit by Dennis's bat
breaking glass is .9. Whenever Dennis breaks a window while practising batting, he stops practising. Given the above, what are the odds
of Dennis breaking one of Mr. Wilson's windows on any given Sunday?

Sampling without Replacement

A slight complication is required in cases where sampling *without replacement* occurs. The odds of pulling an ace from a deck of cards is determined
by the formula for single events x/n. That is, 4/52, or .077. The odds of
pulling an ace in two tries depends on whether we are replacing the first
card in the deck (and reshuffling), or not. If we replace the first card we've
drawn and reshuffle the deck, we determine the odds of pulling an ace
from a deck of cards in two tries by the formula for a disjunct of mutually
exclusive events: $x_1/n_1 + x_2/n_2 + ... + x_n/n_n$. In this case, that would be .077
+ .077 = .154. But if we *do not* replace the card, the odds should be slightly
better. Pulling an ace in the first try = 4/52. Pulling an ace in the second
try assumes, first, that an ace wasn't pulled in the first try. Therefore, there
are still four aces in the deck. But the deck is slightly smaller. It excludes
the card we've pulled first. Therefore, the odds of the second try will be
4/51. The odds, therefore, of pulling an ace in two tries when we do not
replace the first card is 4/52 + 4/51 = .077 + .078 = .155. Not much better,
admittedly, but better.

The issue of replacement also affects the probability of a conjunction of
independent outcomes $(x_1/n_1 \times x_2/n_2 \times ... x_n/n_n)$. The odds of pulling two
aces in two tries without replacement is slightly *worse* than the odds of
pulling two aces in two tries with replacement. That is, if the event of
pulling one ace in the first try is satisfied, the number of aces in the deck
diminishes for the second try. The odds of the first outcome being satisfied
is 4/52 (.077). The odds of the second is 3/51 (.059). The odds of pulling
two aces from the deck in two tries *with* replacement is 4/52 x 4/52 =
.0059. The odds of pulling two aces from the deck in two tries *without*
replacement is 4/52 x 3/51 = .0045.

The formula for determining this is as follows:

(4) Probability of a conjunction of outcomes *without replacement* = x_1/n_1 x
x_2/n_{n-1} ...

(5) Probability of a disjunction of outcomes *without replacement* = x_1/n_1 +
x_2/n_{n-1} ...

Practice 2

What is the probability of drawing any two cards in a deck and both being spades?

Answer:

Unlike the case of tossing coins, the probability of the second card being a spade is *dependent* on what the previous card was. If the probability of the first card being a spade is 13/52 (since there are 13 spades (x) in a deck of 52 cards (n)), the probability of the second card being a spade cannot *also* be 13/52, but rather 12/51. Using the formula for a conjunction of events without replacement yields the following: x_1/n_n x x_2/n_{n-1} = 13/52 x 12/51 (or .25 x .235) = .059. Your odds are about 6 per cent of succeeding.

Now you try.

Exercise 11.4

Determine the probabilities for the following, using the formulae for determining the probability of single events, conjunction of events with replacement, disjunction of events with replacement, or events where sampling is done without replacement. In all cases assume the games in question are "fair." (Answers to selected questions provided in Appendix 1.)

☞ 1 You have a jar containing three black, four white, and three red marbles, randomly mixed. You have two blind draws without replacement. What is the probability that both marbles drawn will be black?

2 After cutting a deck of cards, you randomly, but blindly, draw four cards without replacement. What is the probability that all cards will be red?

☞ 3 What is the probability of throwing eight dice at once and each die showing either a five or a six?

4 What is the probability that three dice thrown together will each turn up an odd number or a six?

☞ 5 What is the probability of pulling three cards from a deck without replacement and each sharing the same suit?

6 Imagine you are given a standard deck of fifty-two playing cards and offered to participate in a charity-based draw. Drawing the queen of any suit wins $25.00, and drawing the queen of hearts wins $100.00. Calculate the probability of winning $ 25.00 in three draws. Assume you are not replacing the drawn cards.

☞ 7 Imagine you are given a standard deck of fifty-two playing cards and invited to participate in a charity-based draw. Drawing the queen of any suit wins $25.00, and drawing the queen of hearts wins $100.00. Calculate the probability of winning $100.00 in three draws. Assume you are not replacing the drawn cards.

8 A barrel contains forty-five balls, eighteen of which are green, twenty-four of which are blue, and three of which are red. Assume the balls are randomly mixed. Two balls are drawn at random without replacement. What is the probability a blue or red ball is chosen?

9 A barrel contains forty-five balls, eighteen of which are green, twenty-four of which are blue, and three of which are red. Assume the balls are randomly mixed. Two balls are drawn at random without replacement. What is the probability a blue and green ball is chosen?

11.3.2 Maximizing Expected Utility

John von Neuman and Oskar Morgenstern provided a theory of probability reasoning according to the principle of *maximizing expected utility*. (*Theory of Games and Economic Behavior*) *Utility* is a measurement of an individual person's preferences or values. "Utility" in this sense is subjectively relative. If Nebojsa likes mushrooms and Malcolm does not, eating mushrooms would count as a positive utility for Nebojsa but a negative utility for Malcolm. We cannot specify what the utility of mushrooms is, *simpliciter*. We can only do so *relative* to a particular subject. A feature of being rational is preferring more utility rather than less, other things being equal. The key, though, is determining the concept of one's *expected* utility.

Utility has to be understood as a *net* measurement, not a *gross* measurement. For example, suppose that winning at poker will earn us $650. But to win we need not merely the right cards relative to our competitor's cards, we also have to throw in our ante. Let's say in this high-stake game we bet $150. If we win, our *gross* winning is $650, but our *net* winning is $500. Still, the decision to play is not simply decided by subtracting $150 from $650 and seeing that that value is greater than the 0 we'd get by not playing. What's missing is the probability of winning and the probability of losing. Often, the probability of losing is simply 1 minus the probability of winning. But sometimes one may also break even. Let's imagine in this case that the odds of winning are .15, the odds of breaking even .25, and the odds of losing .6. Given these odds, not playing is a better deal for us. To see why, multiply the net winnings ($500) with the probability of winning (.15) and add the product of the probability of losing and the cost (-$150). We get $[(.15)($500) + (.6)(-$150)]$ = an expected *loss* of $15.*

Given the above calculations, it is not in our interest to play this game of poker *assuming dollar amounts capture our subjective utility*. This assumption is not always (and perhaps never) met, however. For example, the thrill of the gamble itself may be worth more to us than the $15.00 we stand to lose. If so, it is in our interest to play this game. For our purposes,

---

* Adding a negative cost may seem a cumbersome way of saying "subtract the cost," but understanding probability in its general form is easier if we always sum the entire series of products of any p_i m_i.

however, the example is sufficient to illustrate the formula for calculating expected utility.

Expected utility $(E(u)) = \Sigma p_i \mu_i$,

where p_i refers to the probability of a particular event, μ_i refers to the net utility of a given outcome, and $\Sigma p_i \mu_i$, indicates the sum of the function for each instance of $p_i \mu_i$ ($p_1 \mu_1 + p_2 \mu_2 + ... + p_n \mu_n$). In English, we may say, *Expected utility is the odds of winning multiplied by the amount to be won plus the cost of playing.*

The cost of playing is generally negative. As the saying goes, nothing is free. Whether we're buying a lottery ticket, where the cost is fixed, or playing poker, where the cost varies depending on our bet, the formula for determining the expected payoff is the same. Let's say the winner of a lottery gets $500, the ticket costs 75¢, and the odds of winning are .001. In this case outcome 1 (μ_1) is the *net* winnings ($500 -$0.75 = $499.25). The probability of that outcome (p_1) is 0.001. Hence $p_1 \mu_1 = (.001)($499.25) = 0.50$. Outcome 2 in this case is -$0.75. The probability that outcome 2 will occur is .999. The product of $p_2 \mu_2$ is $(.999)(-$0.75) = -0.75. The sum of $p_1 \mu_1 + p_2 \mu_2 = -0.25. That is, we stand to lose 25¢ by playing this lottery.

Consider the following scenario. Inside a drawer are ten socks, seven of which are red, and three are yellow. We now know that the odds of blindly pulling out a yellow sock is only .3. Consider the following choice:

"I'll give you (A) $10.00 or (B) the chance of winning $50 if you blindly pull from the drawer a yellow sock in one try."

Assuming the dollar amounts match our subjective utility, which should we choose: A or B?

Most people when confronted with this choice opt for A rather than B. They surmise that at least A offers a sure bet. A bird in the hand is worth more than two in the bush, they might say. A offers 100% chance of winning compared with only 30% chance in B. With B, our odds of losing are far greater. They choose unwisely, though, at least according to the theory of maximizing expected utility.

Using the formula $(E(u) = \Sigma p_i \mu_i)$, we need to multiply the payoffs with the odds of winning. More technically, the *expected value* of each bet is equal to the probability of winning multiplied by the amount to be won. The expected utility for A is $10. $(1($10) + 0(0))$. The expected value for B is $15. $(.3($50) + .7($0))$ In other words, probability reasoning tells us to choose B. At least, the formula for maximizing expected utility would tell us to choose B if the lottery offered was a series of games, not a single game. The expected value is the long-term average winnings, not a prediction of what we will win on any given try. If this is a single game, seventy per cent of the time we'd do better choosing A.

In the sock lottery, there is no risk of our losing anything in any of the gambles. In real life this is rare. Do we maximize our expected utility when we buy a lottery ticket? Let's say the ticket costs a measly $1.00. If we win, we will receive (gross) $2,000,000. The odds of that jackpot, let's say, are one in a million. Should we buy the lottery ticket? Our expected payoff will be negative $0.80. The cost of the dollar is not offset by the (gross) gain of 20¢. Again, to see how we get that, we use the formula, $E(u) = \Sigma p_i\,\mu_i$. We get (.0000001 x $1,999,999) + (.999999 x -$1.00)]. When our expected utility is negative, our advice is, don't take the bet.

A slight improvement occurs if we add to the lottery above various consolation prizes. Perhaps at an odd of 1 in 10,000 we may win $1,000, and at an odd of 1 in 1,000 we stand to win $100, and at an odd of 1 in 100, we stand to get $2.00 back, and 1 in 50, we get another ticket (which has about a 20¢ value, but which people mistakenly think has a value equal to the dollar they paid). What is our expected utility in this bet? Well, we may expect to lose 77¢. ((2,000,000 x .0000001) + ($1,000 x .00001) + ($100 x .0001) + ($2 x .001) + ($0.20 x .02) + (-$1.00 x 1]. But look at all the chances of winning! Look at how much we can win! Think of all we could do if we won the lottery! Don't we know someone who won? These are the considerations that beguile the unwary.

Practice 3

Which among the following lotteries (if any) should you choose?

   (A) You have a .25 probability of winning $16.00 but a .75 probability of losing $5.00.
   (B) You have a .85 probability of winning $4.00 but a .15 probability of losing $12.00.
   (C) You have a .05 probability of winning $100.00 but a .95 probability of losing $7.50.

Answer:
Using the formula for expected utility, $(E(u) = \Sigma p_i\,\mu_i)$, the expected utility for each gamble is determined by summing each instance of the product of the probability with the expected outcomes. Another way of thinking of this is to multiply the probability of winning by the amount to be won and then subtracting the product of the probability of losing and the amount to be lost. The expected utilities for the gambles above are as follows:

   (A) .25($16) + .75(-$5) = $0.25
   (B) .85($4.00) + .15(-$12.00) = $1.60
   (C) .05(100) + .95(-$7.50) = -$2.13

Assuming your utility matches the dollar amounts, to maximize your expected utility, choose (B). At any rate, avoid (C).

Casinos

Why do casinos stay in business? The answer must be that the expected payoff for every gamble a patron makes is negative. Consider the roulette wheel. An ivory ball is set in motion on a spinning wheel. The wheel contains thirty-eight compartments. Eighteen of the compartments are black, eighteen red, one is labelled "zero," and one is labelled "double zero."* These last two are neither red nor black. Let's assume we place a $1.00 bet on the ivory ball landing on a black square. If the ball lands on black, we get $2.00. Otherwise, nothing. Our expected payoff is [(18/38)(2.00) + -$1.00] = -$0.06. But if everyone stands to lose, why would people keep playing? The answer is that the loss is small enough not to outweigh the subjective utility of playing. Of course, why one would derive subjective utility from a game where the expected payoff is negative may itself be worth exploring.

Exercise 11.5

Provide the expected payoff for the following. (Answers to selected questions are provided in Appendix 1.)

☞ 1 All things considered equal, should you take a bet where you have an 85 per cent chance of winning $35.00, but a 15 per cent chance of losing $175.00?

2 You are given a choice to write a final paper or to write a final exam. Your record indicates that the mark in your final paper is on average 95 per cent of your mid-term paper in the course. Your mark in a final exam is on average 85 per cent of your mark on the mid-term of the same course. In this course you've written both a mid-term and a paper already. Your mark on the mid-term was 83. Your mark on the paper was 77. Assuming you want the highest overall grade possible, which should you choose: paper or exam?

☞ 3 In front of you are four shells. Under one shell is a marble. If you select the shell with the marble, you win $7.00. If you're wrong, you owe $2.50. Assuming the game is fair, is this a good gamble?

4 Lottery A gives you a 40 per cent chance of winning $10.00, a 40 per cent chance of breaking even, and a 20 per cent chance of losing $15.00. Lottery B gives you a 70 per cent chance of winning $5.00, a 10 per cent chance of breaking even, and a 20 per cent chance of losing $2.00. Assuming lottery A costs you $1.00 to enter, and lottery B costs you $3.00, and that dollars equal your subjective utility in this case, which lottery, if any, should you choose?

---

* Without zeros, a patron can divide her money on both black and red in a bet, thus guaranteeing to break even. Patrons breaking even mean casino owners make no profit (excluding tobacco and alcohol sales and any cover charges).

5 Five thousand raffle tickets are sold for $1.00 each. One first prize of $1000, two second prizes of $500.00 each, and five third prizes of $100 each are to be awarded. The third-place winners are drawn first, then second-place winners, and last, the grand-prize winner. What is your expected payoff if you bought five tickets?

6 Imagine you are given a standard deck of fifty-two playing cards and invited to participate in a charity-based draw. You have the option of purchasing one draw at $4.00 or one package of three draws at $11.00. Drawing the queen of any suit wins $25.00, and drawing the queen of hearts wins $100.00. Without replacing the drawn cards, calculate the expected payoff if

   ☞ (a) you buy one single draw.
     (b) you buy one package of three draws.
     (c) you buy one single draw and one package of three draws.

7 Imagine you are the organizer of the above-mentioned, charity-based, draw. You estimate that 500 people will purchase the draws. Your hope is to generate $1,000.00 for the charity. What is the probability of generating that amount given that

     (a) 250 people buy $4.00 tickets and 250 people buy $11.00 tickets
     (b) 300 people buy $4.00 tickets and 200 people buy $11.00 tickets
     (c) 400 people buy $4.00 tickets and 100 people buy $11.00 tickets

8 A game consists of rolling a single die and the payoffs are as follows: $3.00 for a six, $2.00 for a five, $1.00 for a four, nothing for a three, -$1.00 for a two, and -$2.00 for a one. How much should the organizers charge to play this game in order to break even?

Pascal's Wager

In the *Pensées*, Blaise Pascal (1623–1662) argued that faith in the Judeo-Christian God is a reasonable bet. If the Judeo-Christian God exists, then if we believe in Him, there will be great return for our investment. Sure we'll have to go to church and help out our neighbour and not swear, but the rewards of heaven surely outweigh all those inconveniences. Of course, if God doesn't exist, then we don't get any reward. We may incur the costs of going to church and being nice for nothing. But surely the rewards of heaven far outshine the paltry and ephemeral rewards of earth. Meanwhile, if God exists and we remain a skeptic or atheist, well, the penalty for that is hell. That's really bad. If God doesn't exist there's no punishment for being an atheist, and there may even be some gain in terms of earthly delight, but that gain can't compare to the gain of heaven, and the risk in being an atheist is huge. The following table illustrates the various outcomes:

	Believe in God	Don't
God Exists	heaven	hell
God doesn't exist	wasted time	earthly pleasure

Attaching numerical values to the outcomes is difficult, but to press Pascal's point we need to. Assuming a scale from -100 to +100, we can easily assign +100 to heaven and -100 to hell. Calculating the utility for "wasted time" is contentious, since some may argue that there is psychological benefit in having even false faith, and many philosophers argue that earthly pleasure alone has a net loss. For immediate purposes, however, this debate won't matter. Let's say wasted time = -25, and earthly pleasure = 25. Giving these (admittedly arbitrary) utilities still shows Pascal's point: one will maximize one's expected utility by believing in God.

	Believe in God	Don't
God Exists	100	-100
God doesn't exist	-25	25
TOTAL	75	-75

Believing in God yields an expected utility of 75, which is greater than the expected utility afforded by not believing in God (-75).

Pascal was excommunicated for this argument. The church felt that believing in God for such self-serving reasons was not the right approach. Pascal actually responded to that charge, but the response was ignored. The real problem with Pascal's wager, however, is something else. Let's compare the structure of his argument with the following table on purchasing a lottery ticket

	Buy a lottery ticket	Don't
Win	$999,999.00	$0
Lose	-$1.00	$0
TOTAL	$999,998	$0

According to the above table, it is stupid *not* to buy a lottery ticket. Obviously, what's missing is taking probability into account. Since God either exists or doesn't, Pascal assumed the odds of God's existence is 50 per cent. But the mere fact that one will win the lottery or not doesn't mean the odds of winning equal the odds of losing. What odds we should give to God's existence is, of course, not to be answered here. All we need highlight is that atheists, precisely the audience Pascal has in mind, clearly won't concede to very high odds at all. Theists need to convince atheists first that the odds of God's existence are sufficiently high before Pascal's wager can get off the ground, but since Pascal's wager is used precisely to do this very thing, the argument is hopeless.*

11.3.3 Person-Who Fallacy

Failing to understand the mathematical formulae for probability reasoning may be excusable. Our inability to comprehend probability goes deeper than a mere failure of mathematics, however, as the *Person-Who Fallacy* amply demonstrates. Person-who fallacies entail a misconstrual of statistics. Consider the absurdity of the following claim: "Since every third child in New York is a Catholic, Protestant families should have no more than two children." Few would make such a mistake, since when we utter statistical claims like "Every third child in New York is a Catholic," we don't mean this *literally*. Nor do we mean it *literally* when we say a woman gives birth every seven seconds. Person-who fallacies can be understood as making precisely this sort of error, however. When we say, "smoking causes lung cancer" most of us understand that smoking vastly increases the probability of getting lung cancer compared to not smoking. Science can tell us that most people who smoke will get lung cancer. What science cannot tell us, however, is *which* individuals will get lung cancer. Why? Because the relationship is probabilistic. It does not hold in every case. We are all aware of this ... *aren't we?*

How often have we seen a smoker argue for his continuing smoking on the grounds that "I know a *person who* has smoked all his life and never got lung cancer"? The obvious implication one is supposed to draw from these "person-who" testimonials is that, because it did not happen in these particular cases, the statistics are somehow faulty. This shows a complete misunderstanding of probabilistic reasoning. A single instance does not refute a probabilistic law or trend. Citing these "person-who" claims reflects a failure to understand statistical laws.

A single opinion given to a subject, face-to-face, is more effective in changing attitudes than much more accurate and reliable statistical information. The problem is, it shouldn't be. A 1980 study by Hamill, Wilson, and Nisbett showed a taped interview with a prison guard to volunteer participants. ("Insensitivity to sample bias," 578–89) For half the participants, the guard was portrayed as extremely humane and agreeable. For the others, the guard was portrayed as extremely inhumane and disagreeable. For each group, half the participants were told that this guard was typical of

---

* A defence is available to Pascal. We assigned a finite value to heaven and hell. Pascal did not. He thought both the rewards of heaven and the punishments of hell were infinite. If so, assigning even a probability of .0000000001 to God's existence will still work out in Pascal's favour. If the atheist tolerates the assignation of infinity to heaven, her only recourse is to claim the probability of God's existence is 0.

the prison guard population. The other half was told this guard was atypical of the prison guard population. What we have, then, are four different conditions: (1) A group of volunteer participants viewed a tape of a *humane* prison guard, while being told that the prison guard being shown was *atypical.* (2) A group of volunteer participants viewed a tape of a *humane* prison guard, while being told that the prison guard being shown was *typical.* (3) A group of volunteer participants viewed a tape of an *inhumane* prison guard, while being told that the prison guard shown was *atypical.* (4) A group of volunteer participants viewed a tape of an *inhumane* prison guard, while being told that the prison guard shown was *typical.* Afterwards, all participants were asked what they thought of prison guards in general. What might we predict?

What occurred was that the statistical information was ignored. The people who saw the humane guard thought that guards were on the whole pretty good. Those who saw the inhumane guard thought guards were on the whole pretty bad. Whether they were told that the guards they viewed were typical or atypical had no effect on their judgment.

Research like this shows the dangerously alluring characteristics of testimonials or anecdotal evidence. Person-who fallacies have deep-rooted psychological sources and are not easily eradicated. Nevertheless, they offer extremely inadequate empirical justifications for any claim. Anecdotal evidence is vastly overweighted in decision-making, something of which advertisers and political parties are well aware.

A single instance does not refute a probabilistic law or trend. Citing these "person-who" claims reflects a failure to understand statistical laws. (For more on person-who fallacies, see 14.3.2.)

11.3.4 The Gambler's Fallacy

Overemphasizing anecdotal evidence and underrating the base-rate information is also the culprit in the *Gambler's Fallacy.* How much would we bet on a fair coin coming up tails in a single throw? Apart from how much disposable money we have, our answer will take into account the odds of winning being 50 per cent. We know this. Now, would we raise our bet if we learned that in a previous series, the coin came up heads five times in a row?

If we say "Yes," we are probably thinking along the following lines: "Hmm, the chances of a coin coming up heads five times in a row is 0.5 x 0.5 x 0.5 x 0.5 x 0.5 = 0.03. Now the probability of it coming up heads again is 0.03 x 0.5 = 0.02. Since that is obviously unlikely, I should bet tails."

The math is fine, the reasoning is not. The problem with this reasoning may best be seen by asking: "What, you expect the probability of the coin coming up tails in the next throw is 98 per cent?!" Surely, something's gone wrong.

What is wrong is somehow believing that the next throw is causally related to previous throws. This confusion happens so often it has war-

ranted the name *The Gambler's Fallacy*. The gambler's fallacy is the tendency to see links between events that are really independent. Two outcomes are independent when the occurrence of one does not affect the
probability of the other. The number that comes up on the roulette wheel
is independent of the outcome that preceded it. There are an equal number of red and black squares on a roulette wheel, so the probability of its
coming up red in a turn is about 47 per cent. Nevertheless, after five turns
in a row in which the roulette wheel comes up red, many bettors switch
their bets to black. Since which colour came up last is independent of
which will come up next, it is a fallacy of reasoning by the gamblers. A better understanding of probability will lessen the odds of our committing the
person-who and gambler's fallacies.

11.3.5 Chance and Coincidence

i. Chance   Many things that happen in nature are a complex result of systematic, explainable factors, and *chance*. For example, we know that smoking greatly increases the probability of lung cancer. Still, some people
never do get lung cancer from smoking. This may well be due to chance.

The appeal to chance is not understood as an admission that something
is left unexplained. Perhaps we are lucky enough to win the lottery. Do we
need an explanation for such fortune beyond an appeal to chance? No.
Our winning the lottery is due to chance. We needn't ask, "Well, yes, but
why was I so lucky?" Nor is it sensible to interpret our winning the lottery
by chance as an admission that there is something left unexplained.
Chance *is* the explanation.

Claiming that *X* happened by chance is not a very alluring explanation
to most people. We seem psychologically motivated to have answers at the
same time that we seem mentally unprepared to believe that chance *counts*
as an answer. In any event, it is common for people to reject chance as an
adequate explanation and instead to postulate a premature theory to pur-
posely explain away chance.

The philosopher Stephen Toulmin asks us to consider a "family all
who died on their birthdays. When, after the first two children have died
on their birthdays, the third does also, you may well be surprised; but
the fact that it happens is one to be accepted, not to be explained."
("The Logic of Moral Reasoning," 156) Importantly, it is not the case
that science is *unable* to explain the phenomenon. The explanation is
that it's due to chance. The fact that we're not happy with the answer
reveals our own foibles and superstitions. Consider, again, a parallel case
of winning a lottery. To ask *why* did Billy win the lottery is senseless. We
might point out that Billy bought a ticket and that Billy's winning is consistent with the odds of winning, but beyond that there isn't any further
answer. It isn't quite right to say science *can't* go further, since this allows
room to believe there *is* somewhere further to go but that science is too

anal-retentive to get there. There *is* no further place to go. The answer is complete.

This is why what Toulmin says next is misleading: "[T]here is a point up to which science can take you, but beyond that point it cannot go." Science cannot go beyond that because there is no beyond that. Toulmin presents the case as if science were limited: that there is much more to the world than science can speak about. To conclude from the fact that science can say only "chance" to explain why all the children of a family died on their birthdays that there is something else that can explain it is to have misunderstood.

Unlike pseudo-science, science is not loathe to admit chance as a viable explanation. We can also make predictions based on chance. The odds of flipping a fair coin so that it comes up heads five times in a row is .03. If we flip a coin the requisite number of times so that there are one hundred series of five throws, we can predict there will be about three occasions where the condition is met. (Question: How many throws are needed to make a hundred series of five throws? Notice that ten throws yields six series of five tosses. Can you see why?)

Before accepting a complicated explanation, consider what part chance might play in the occurrence. Scientists are not reluctant to claim that chance factors were involved in the lack of perfect conformity of their data to their theories. Non-scientific claims, however, will try to account for every little quirk. This ties into why pseudo-science is non-falsifiable in a way that science purports not to be.

O.J. Simpson's lawyer, Alan Derschowitz, used a variety of tactics on Simpson's behalf. One such tactic was his pointing out the extremely low odds that someone who batters his wife also murders his wife. Evidently this is 1 in 1,000. Thomas Hazlett noted the inanity of such a defence:

> The 1–in-1,000 probability is nonsense, because it tosses out the most important and least disputed fact of the entire trial: Nicole Brown Simpson has been murdered. Instead of predicting what the chances are that a battered wife will be slain, we have two pieces of evidence and ponder a third: Given that Nicole was battered and that she was murdered, what are the chances the crime was committed by the ex- who battered her? Of the 2,000 such victims per year, one would think an overwhelming proportion – 90 percent? 99 percent? – are murdered by those who abused them. (Thomas Hazlett, *Reason*, February 1995)

Design or Evolution?

We have a psychological need to impose meaningless theories on random data even when, or especially when, there is no systematic explanation currently available. Because the claim that all of life, as we know, originated by chance is displeasing, people have been quick to invoke a Designer. Design *seems* to be a better explanation than evolution. The impetus behind the theory of evolution is chance. People commonly wonder, though, how *chance* can explain all this. It seems especially unlikely, and we ought not bet on the unlikely, so we are moved (by disjunctive syllogism, as long as we aren't committing the fallacy of false dichotomy) to the theory that the world was designed. And who is capable of such a task but a deity, after all?

Consider the immaculate fit. The earth is perfectly distanced from the sun. Further away, and we'd freeze; closer, and we'd burn up. More, the moon is itself the right number and the right size. Either bigger or smaller, more or less, and the earth would flip off its axis so that it would no longer turn. Without alternating night and day, one half of the earth would be eternal day, and we'd burn up; the other half, eternal night, and we'd freeze. Consider, too, our neighbouring planets. They have a role in our survival. There is evidence of a horrific meteor shower that would have devastated our little planet had it not been for the larger inert masses surrounding us taking much of the brunt. What are the odds of our planet being so perfectly situated? Pretty low. Hence, a better bet is that everything was placed with purpose.

This conclusion misses the role of chance. If we ask, what are the odds of our winning the lottery, we know the answer is going to be slim. But if we ask, what are the odds of *someone*'s winning, the ratio (if the lottery isn't fixed) is 1:1 – a guarantee. Similarly, if we ask what are the odds of this little planet having all the right conditions to produce life, the answer is slim. But if we ask what are the odds of *some* planet having all these conditions, the odds have vastly increased in direct proportion to the number of suns and planets and moons in the universe.

The discussion need not end there. Some speak about the intricacies of life here on earth. Everything has such immaculate fit. Trees give off oxygen and drink up carbon monoxide; while we do the reverse. The complexities of the eco-system, as environmentalists and biologists like to remind us, are awe-inspiring. The mere working of the eye is so immaculately complex that to imagine all this came about by chance is too farfetched to contemplate seriously.

Such an argument misunderstands the explanation of chance. It treats "chance" as a cop-out, an "I dunno" sort of response. Even so, it hardly follows that, on the basis of our inability to explain the origin of something, we ought to accept the first theory that is forced upon us. (Such an inference commits the *fallacy of ignorance*. See 14.3.3.) In this case, however, chance provides a much better account of the intricate "design" than the theory of design itself. The survival of the fittest claims that the things that can survive in an environment do so; those that can't, don't. What can we expect from this? Those that will survive are those that fit in best. We are left with only those things that fit, and not any of those things that don't fit. Consequently, looking at the fit as evidence of design rather than chance is not warranted.

Moreover, if the design theory were right, we wouldn't expect many things to have been designed that wouldn't fit. If the design theory were true, what we have should be pretty much what was designed. Whereas for the evolutionary theory, what we have should be a mere fraction of what there has been and will be. Alas, fossil evidence supports the latter theory and counts against the first theory. Evidence has it that the species existing today are less than 1 per cent of the species *known* to have existed. It seems a poor design if only 1 per cent of it survives.

Admittedly, chance cannot well account for how anything got started in the first place, and this leaves the door open for religious discourse. The point here is not to speak against religion, but to speak in favour of chance as a viable scientific account.

A Caveat

"Chance" may be a legitimately poor explanation. Don't take us to be denying that. For example, one kind of fruit fly (Drosophila) took over a population of other fruit flies. The other strains died off. Why did this happen? Saying "Chance," is too general an answer. We can do better. We can pinpoint what gene altered and why that alteration proved a good thing for the carrier of that gene. It turns out a chromosome inversion produced a thicker thorax in the Drosophila and that extra thickness better enabled them to survive over the cold winter. There is no appeal to "chance" in that explanation. But sometimes we ask, "Yes, but *why* did the chromosome inversion take place? Did it happen *in order* to produce a thicker thorax in the fruit fly? Did it happen *in order* for the fruit fly population to better withstand the winter?" These questions are the senseless questions, to which, if we respond at all, the answer "chance" is perfectly apt.

ii. Coincidence Coincidence also needs no special explanation. Calling events coincidences is all the explanation they warrant. A coincidence is simply the coinciding of two events, nothing remarkable in and of itself. The term tends to be used in ways more narrow than this, however. It is used when the conjunction of events for some reason *ought not to have happened*. Of course, the proper understanding of this normative ought-claim is that the probability of its happening was low. Typically, it is the recognition of the very low probability of the coincidence that seems to drive people into looking for some *other* explanation for its occurrence.

But don't forget, something's having a low probability of occurring doesn't mean it will not occur. In fact, given enough instances, we can guarantee its occurrence. Recall our five heads in a row, and someone's winning the lottery. Something's having a low probability means that we should not *count* on its occurring in *this* instance. But once it does occur, we should not think it miraculous, or evidence of some otherworldly influence. Mere mathematical probability is all the otherworldly influence needed to account for it.

But people tend to think of "coincidences" as meaning something totally different. We hear them saying "My goodness, what a coincidence. I wonder *why* that happened." Most people who seek to understand coincidences *ignore* the role of chance. They overlook chance as an explanation.

Rare events do happen, purely by chance. No other explanation is necessary. Still, when people utter things like "Hey, there was one in a million chances of that happening, and it *did*," such an utterance belies the belief in an unexplained force. Saying that something has a one in a million chance of happening is not saying that there is *no* chance of it happening. Rather, given a million occurrences, it will probably happen once. Which is exactly what did occur. So what's the big mystery?

In fact, the laws of probability guarantee that as the number of events increases, the probability that *some* coincidence will occur gets very high. The probability of flipping a coin and its coming up heads five times in a row is 1/32 or .03. So that is an unlikely event. But if you flipped five coins at once 100 times, the probability of at least one of those trials coming up all five heads is .96. That is, in one hundred trials it is *very likely* that this rare event, this coincidence, will happen. What people tend to forget is the base-rate information, that the number of occurrences in which coincidences might occur is itself very large.

Coincidences in one's own life are very memorable. This helps to distort their importance. An uninteresting day is not very memorable. We more easily recount many of the remarkable coincidences that happened to us, and tend to forget the mundane events. Thinking of so-and-so and her phoning, being late for the bus and thereby meeting the person we ended up marrying, etc. These cases stick in our minds. The very much more common events get forgotten. How many times did we miss a bus and nothing happened? How many people did we meet whom we didn't marry? When we compare the remarkable coincidences in our lives that we remember with the unremarkable events that we tend to forget, it is not surprising the former seem much more prevalent or salient. This is due to distortion in memory. We tend to forget or ignore the base-rate information.

Let's say we define "coincidence" as the unlikely, perhaps unexplainable conjunction of events. Perhaps we have a dream about an aunt and the next day she phones. Perhaps we are thinking salacious thoughts and the next thing a crow smashes into the windshield of our car. Let's further suppose we remember six or seven such weird coincidences over the last ten years. Should we contemplate the possibility of otherworldly influences in our lives, or can a better understanding of chance be all the explanation we need?

Let's imagine that in a single day, one hundred events occurred. This is excessively conservative. "Event" is pretty much open-ended. Think of turning off our alarm without knocking it to the floor, having a shower without the water fluctuating between scalding and freezing, opening our drawer and finding the socks we put there, brushing our teeth and not having toothpaste get all over our fingers, answering the phone and it's not a wrong number, etc., etc. A coincidence, neutrally understood, is the conjunction of two events. If there are merely a hundred events in our day, there are 4,950 different pairings of events possible in a typical day. This is true 365 days of the year. So our six or seven remembered coincidences must be considered against the background information of the pool of non-weird coincidences over that same period. That is 4,950 pairs per day x 365 days per year x 10 years, or 18,067,500.

In short, six coincidences happened to us in 10 years, while 18 million coincidences that weren't salient or memorable for us also happened. The probability of a *weird* coincidence happening in our life is .00000033. It hardly seems strange that six out of 18 million conjunctions of events in our life should be odd. What makes them notable is precisely that they are odd. Odd things do happen. In fact, chance guarantees it.

Exercise 11.6

Discuss the merits of the following causal arguments. Avail yourself of the information given in the entire chapter. (Answers to selected questions are provided in Appendix 1.)

☞ 1 Marriage is the chief cause of divorce.
   2 Harry's university degree helped him get a high-paying job the year after he graduated.
   3 Although Smith ran the red light and crashed into Jones, Jones was not wearing her seatbelt, and so Smith's lawyer argued Smith should pay only 50 per cent of Jones's injuries.
☞ 4 Greenpeace must brainwash its members to get them to actually chain themselves together in the face of bulldozers and chainsaws. You wouldn't catch me doing that.
   5 A storm is coming, because the birds are sheltering down.
   6 Explain why dreams that seem to accurately predict future events are no big deal.
☞ 7 The Statistics Canada report found 16% of older children who had never or rarely participated in organized sports outside school reported low self-esteem, four times higher than those who played sports. Among 12- to 15-year-olds, 42% of those who did not join athletic teams or rarely got involved were unhappy with their looks, compared to 24% of those who participated ... Dr. Dan Offord, director of Canadian Studies for Children at Risk at McMaster University, who has studied the link between activity outside school and behaviour among children, said yesterday's report suggests children who participate are better balanced. "It suggests children who have the opportunity [to play sports and join clubs] are better off, have raised

self-esteem, are healthier, do better in school." (Julie Smyth, "Too many activities can be bad: study," *National Post*, 31 May 2001, A12)

8 A daily glass of red wine has been shown to help stave off heart disease and even cancer, but a new Danish study said the salutary effects may be due to imbibers' sense of well-being. The study of nearly 700 Danish adults aged 29 to 34 drew comparisons between wine drinkers and beer and liquor consumers. Wine drinkers tended to have a higher socioeconomic status and to score higher on intelligence tests than beer or liquor drinkers, which the study speculated had ramifications for physical health. "Our results suggest wine drinking is associated with optimal social, intellectual and personality functioning," study author Erik Mortensen of the Danish Epistemology Science Center in Copenhagen wrote in the *Archives of Internal Medicine*. In the Danish study, beer-drinking men scored poorly on personality disorder tests for anxiety and neuroticism compared with wine drinkers. ("Hypochondriac's corner: Healthy wine drinkers," *National Post*, 20 August 2001, D2)

☞ 9 Arthur Jensen claims there exists a positive correlation (0.25) between height and IQ score. (*The g Factor: The Science of Mental Ability*) Does this indicate a direct causal relationship, or is there a third variable involved?

10 Polygamy should not be permitted in a constitutional democracy. No polygamous society has such a government, and no constitutional democracy has ever been anything but monogamous. This is because, in a polygamous society, the rich gain greater social control over the less well-to-do by attracting greater numbers of mates to their wealth and then isolating them, frustrating the men and encouraging them to become violent. Also, polygamy encourages people to think of women as chattel, rather than as human beings, and this is inimical to a democracy. Therefore, it should not become the general social model. Furthermore, humans are, by nature, slightly inclined to polygamy; therefore, it should not be permitted at all, lest the social fabric of constitutional democracy become compromised. (Adapted from Tom Flanagan, "Democracy, polygamy, and the sexual constitution." *National Post*, 23 May 2001, A14)

11 When Medicare was introduced in the US, the proportion of the Gross Domestic Product spent on medicine and health care increased. Obviously, people developed an insatiable hunger for free medicine, and therefore socialized medicine is doomed.

12 Women outnumber men as students at the University of Prince Edward Island by about six to four. Imagine if you and a friend are drinking coffee and watching students pass. You notice that over the last ten minutes, ten women have passed, and no men. Your friend also notices this and so offers you a wager: "I'll bet you $10 that the next person to pass will be a man." Assuming you can afford to lose,

and there is no trickery involved, should you accept the bet? Why or why not?

13 Jones stayed home from work on September 11. She worked at the World Trade Center in New York. She was not sick. She just felt something which, after the fact, she interpreted as a premonition. As a result, she is alive today. Mere chance seems too facile an explanation to satisfy most people. How would you attempt to convince naysayers her survival is due to chance?

☞14 Most car accidents occur near one's home. Why shouldn't we be surprised by this?

15 Apart from any charity associated with lotteries, is buying a lottery ticket rationally justifiable?

16 A remarkable fact is that many of the great scientists and mathematicians in history have had a deep interest in music. Einstein, for example, was a devoted violinist and Newton is said to have been fascinated by the mathematical structure of musical compositions. If you want your child to pursue a career in science, you would be well advised to do everything you can to develop his or her interest in music. (Carey, *A Beginner's Guide to Scientific Method*, 133)

17 Horoscopes have even helped people stay in good health. Mary Kelly credits astrology with saving her from an operation on her legs that would have left her crippled. "My doctor decided an operation was needed, and told me to check into the hospital Friday for the operation on Monday. I consulted my astrologer. He told me to have the operation changed to Wednesday. I did this, and on Tuesday the doctor suddenly discovered a blood clot was causing the trouble. Had he performed the operation on Friday's symptoms, I probably would never have walked again." (American Astrological Association ad in *Glamour*.)

$$\frac{12}{\sqrt{5}}$$

Science

The Scientific Method
Science and Its Critics

12.1 The Scientific Method

Science is the discipline best suited to test causal claims. It has developed the experimental method, which promises rigour and predictive results unparalleled in human history. Clearly, the scientific method begins with a general question, "What Causes Y?" From this, we form an hypothesis: "X causes Y." We need to test the hypothesis. If X causes Y, then in the presence of X, Y will occur, *and* in the absence of X, Y will not occur. If either of these conditions is not met, we must reject our hypothesis that X causes Y.

If X is pornography, and Y is rape, then we might be wondering whether pornography causes rape. It is not enough that some rapists have read pornography. If some rapists have not read pornography, then pornography cannot be the cause. Perhaps a large percentage of rapists have read pornography. Still, this is not enough. We also have to see the percentage of those who have read pornography who are not rapists. If 90 per cent of the population has read pornography, yet 30 per cent are rapists, the hypothesis that pornography causes rape will be undermined.

If our hypothesis is that X causes Y, we refer to X as the *independent variable* and Y as the *dependent variable*. If our hypothesis is correct, X is *dependent* on Y. Both are variables because they are subject to change. We may refer to a variable as that which may be manipulated. The experimenter cannot manipulate a person's height, but she may select participants in her experiment *by* height. Perhaps she is testing whether prestige jobs are more likely to be awarded to taller people. Thus height would be an independent variable. Height may even be a dependent variable in a long-term study. Does smoking while pregnant stunt growth in fetuses? In such a study, smoking while pregnant is the independent variable and the eventual height of the child is the dependent variable.

Variables may be *discrete* or *continuous*. Being pregnant is discrete. One is either pregnant or not. Discrete variables have (typically) two conditions, or *values*: absence or presence. If the independent variable is being pregnant, there are only two values: yes or no. Binary systems, like electrical circuits, are discrete. A light is either on or off. Height, however, is continuous. It isn't the case that children either have height or no height. Rather, there is a continuous range of heights between tall and short. Noise is also a continuous variable. Perhaps we want to study the effects of background noise on study habits. We cannot have a condition of zero noise. Noise is not either on or off. The variable of noise is continuous, not discrete. Perhaps there is an optimal level of background noise that is conducive to retention of material studied. In this case, too little noise may yield poor results, and too much noise may also yield poor results. In the case of pornography, we might measure whether participants have or have not viewed pornography. In such a case, pornography is a discrete variable. Conversely we might group *amounts* or *frequency* of pornography viewed. We could divide participants into a variety of groups: those who have never viewed pornography, those who have viewed a little, those who have viewed quite a bit, and those who have viewed a lot. Furthermore, the *type* of pornography may itself be demarcated, from soft porn to hard porn, child pornography, pornography with violence, and a host of ranges in between. The variable of pornography is continuous.

Whether discrete or continuous, variables can be separated into at least two values. In the case of discrete variables, the two values will be understood in terms of absence or presence. In terms of continuous variables, the values will be demarcated in terms of more or less. The different values represent the different *conditions* of the experiment. In all scientific experiments, there must be at least two conditions. If we think X causes Y, we must see what happens when X is present *and* when X is absent, or when there is *more* of X, versus when there is *less* of X. In the latter case, our hypothesis will predict that when there is more of X, there will be more of Y, and when there is less of X, there will be less of Y. In such a case, we would predict that a *positive relation* holds between X and Y. Conversely, we might predict a *negative relation*. In this case, the more of X, the less of Y, and the less of X, the more of Y. Consider, for example, the negative relation in sports psychology between being tense and performing well. The more tense we are, the poorer we tend to do. Conversely, the more relaxed we are, the better we do. (The drawback is that knowing this does not seem to help. Our motive to relax is *in order* to do well, an incoherence.)

Different values determine the different experimental groups. We may have a variety of experimental groups, or, with discrete variables, an *experimental group* contrasted with a *control group*. In such a case, the experimental group is one in which our hypothesized independent variable is present. Our control group is one in which our hypothesized independent variable is absent.

Consider the following experiment. Introducing a new product at a discount price seems like a reasonable way to elicit long-term sales. People may not be interested in buying the product unless it's on sale. Once they buy it, and it really is good, they may then become loyal to it. Such reasoning runs counter to other social-psychological studies concerning liking behaviour, however. It turns out we are more apt to like something the greater the obstacles are to achieving the thing in question. The benefits of playing hard to get in the dating ritual, for example, has empirical backing. Might this tendency also play a role in business?

Doob et al. hypothesized that offering new products at discount prices would not increase sales. In such a case, the independent variable was price. Price is a continuous variable. The conditions or values in this particular experiment were sale price and regular price. In one experiment, a new brand of mouthwash was offered on sale for 25¢ a quart in the experimental condition, and at its regular price of 39¢ a quart in the control group. Nine days later the price was raised to 39¢ per quart in all stores. The dependent variable was the number of sales recorded by the buyers as they replenished their stock. Doob et al. found, as they predicted, that in subsequent weeks more mouthwash was sold in the stores that had not used the introductory low price offer. ("Effect of initial selling price on subsequent sales")

12.1.1 Random and Systematic Errors

Anything that affects the dependent variable other than the independent variable is a source of error. There are two kinds of errors that can contaminate our causal inference: *random and systematic.* Random errors affect both (or all) conditions equally. Systematic errors affect the experimental conditions unequally. Of the two, systematic errors are more problematic.

Random error refers to extraneous variables not controlled by the experimenter but whose average influence on the outcome is the same in both (or all) conditions. Random errors may come from outside sources – sudden noises in the hallway, perhaps – or from the participants themselves. Participants in the study vary in a wide range of ways, and these differences may affect the outcome. People differ in degrees of intelligence, confidence, skill, maturity, experience, upbringing, religion, class, culture, race, sex, and these differences may impact their responses in ways that can obscure the effect of the independent variable. But as long as these difference are equally divided between both (or all) conditions, we can expect that they will not affect the differences in the dependent variable for the experimental and control conditions. But even when random errors are evenly divided between all conditions, they may create sufficient background noise to mask real differences between the conditions. Analogously, background noise may prevent us from discriminating whether a flute is played in the distance. Perhaps the TV is too loud, the neighbours are fighting again, the lawnmower is going, or dogs are barking. All these things can prevent our hearing the flute. The background noise is the random error. It does not affect whether or not the flute is being played, but the background noise may be enough to prevent us from knowing whether the flute is being played. Similarly, random error may prevent us from claiming that a true hypothesis is supported. Random error may cause us to mistakenly reject our hypothesis.

Mistakenly rejecting a true hypothesis is referred to as a *Type I Error*. Among errors this is tolerable, for if there is a real difference, other studies may eventually find this out. A *Type II Error*, on the other hand, is to mistakenly think a false hypothesis is true. A Type II error is more heinous than a Type I error, for once we adopt a false belief, it is often difficult to eradicate it. False beliefs have a tendency to breed further false beliefs. We are being led down the wrong track and our failure to recognize it leads us further astray. Systematic errors are more likely to create Type II errors.

Systematic errors are unplanned contaminations in the design that affect only members of one condition, or differentially affect the members of the different conditions. It is something about these contaminations that causes the dependent variable to occur, and not the hypothesized independent variable. Failing to notice the systematic error will lead the researcher to erroneously conclude that her hypothesis is supported, a Type II error.

Let's return to Doob et al.'s study mentioned above. Location of stores may dictate the volume of sales, or traffic. How might this affect the study? If the mouthwash with the reduced price was at stores that had, in general, less traffic than the stores where the mouthwash was being offered at regular price, the dependent variable (stock replacement) could not be attributed to the independent variable (original price). If the discount condition always occurred at the low-traffic stores, then this would be a case of systematic error. If there were no attempt at pairing the stores, so that the two conditions had equal numbers of low- and high-traffic stores, the study may have committed a Type II error. Conversely, if the difference in volume between the different stores was larger than the real effects of the independent variable, we may not expect a difference between the two conditions to be noticeable. This would be a case of a random error. Doob et al. avoided both errors by, first, pairing off stores in terms of traffic, and then randomly assigning the stores to the different conditions.

Another worry was avoided by Doob et al. The dependent variable was not measured in terms of dollars, for that would contaminate the study. The same number of sales will yield a higher number of dollars to the higher-priced item. The dependent variable was measured in terms of stock replacement. Studies must be carefully designed to avoid random and systematic errors.

Recall from chapter 4 another case of systematic bias contaminating the results. A number of studies found that males perform better than females on cognitive spatial-orientation tasks. For example, males were found to be superior to females in distinguishing whether a line is vertical absent any horizontal reference. (Of course, even if true, why this should matter is a separate worry.) To remove the horizontal reference, the standard ploy was to place participants in a darkened room, and to shine a light beam on a wall. The male experimenter would seat the subject on a chair, turn off the light, and adjust a light beam on the far wall, asking participants to push a button when the light beam reached the absolute vertical. Can you detect what could be problematic with such a design?

The answer is this: The design entails placing a person in a darkened room with a strange male. Such a design feature will likely affect men and women differently. Women may feel uncomfortable, if not downright fearful, given the horrors of rape and sexual harassment in our society. If so, they will likely be willing to push the little button more readily if that's what it takes to get out of the fearful situation. To test this theory, the experimental methodology was altered. Now, participants performed for a female experimenter, sat in a brightly lit, white room (still absent horizontal markers), and were shown black lines on a screen. Under these conditions, men and women performed equally. (Fausto-Sterling, *Myths of Gender*, 32)

The original design suffered from systematic error. A contaminant affected one group and not another. This leads us to our next section, how to avoid error in experimental design.

12.1.2 Evaluation

To evaluate inductive generalizations, we ask three things: (i) Is the sample size large enough for the target population? (ii) Is the sample varied enough? and (iii) Has potential bias been reduced as much as is feasible?

i. Sample Size We can avoid, or at least lessen, the possibility of random error by increasing our sample size. Consider the following scenario:

> A certain town is served by two hospitals. In the large hospital, about forty-five babies are born each day. In the smaller hospital about fifteen babies are born each day. About 50 per cent of all babies born are boys. Of course, the exact percentage varies from day to day. Sometimes it may be higher than 50 per cent, sometimes lower. For a period of one year, each hospital recorded the days on which more than 60 per cent of the babies born were boys. Which hospital do you think recorded more such days?
> a. The larger hospital.   b. The smaller hospital.   c. About the same.

Approximately 50 per cent of respondents answer (c), about the same. People not choosing this answer pick either (a) or (b) with about the same frequency. The correct answer is (b), the smaller hospital. Thus, about 75 per cent of people answer this question incorrectly.

Incorrect answers result from an inability to recognize the importance of sample size in the problem. Other things being equal, *a larger sample size always more accurately estimates a population value.* Thus, we should expect greater deviation from the norm in *smaller* samples compared to larger samples. That is why the small hospital will likely record greater deviations in birth rates than the larger hospital.

The sample size refers to the size of the sample. This may seem obvious, but it is often overlooked. A sample is a smaller subset of a larger population. A sample must always be understood in reference to this larger population. Of course, a sample need not represent *all* populations. Its goal is to be representative of the *target population.* The target population is the group we really want to speak about. Our sample has to be representative of that target population. If the target population is large, a larger sample may be required. If the target population is itself small, a smaller sample will suffice.

In the claim, "People tend to under-appreciate the importance of sample size," the target population is the entire class of people. This is fairly large. The speaker's claim will be stronger in proportion to the number of people surveyed. If her claim is based on two individuals she happens to know who under-appreciate sample size, we may accuse the speaker of under-appreciating sample size. *Hasty Generalization* is the crime of generalizing from an insufficient sample.

One's sample size may be too small, resulting in insufficient power to generalize. On the other hand, the sample size may be too large. Sometimes we see studies with 25,000 participants or some other enormous number. If we accept the basic, unqualified claim that larger is better, this would lead us to the conclusion that a study with 25,000 participants is more generalizable than a study with 500 participants. Remarkably, this isn't so. With a sufficient sample size, accurate statistical claims can be generated. So, increasing the sample size beyond this happy median will simply waste time and resources. Worse, a great number of participants will increase the background noise from random error.

Generally, the greater the variability in the target population, the larger the sample that is needed to represent it. But once we find a sufficient sample size to represent the variability in our target population, we have no need to increase it beyond that. Studies that do may therefore seem suspicious. There are mathematical formulae to determine correct sample size, but we shall leave this discussion to classes in statistics.

ii. Sample Selection   Is the sample varied enough? From our last point, we should see that the real issue about sampling is not how large the sample is, but whether it is sufficiently representative of our target population. Generally, the greater the size of our sample, the greater the chances of representation, but this is not necessarily so. Imagine that we are concerned about what proportion of the population is in favour of reinstating capital punishment. We approach a group of protestors carrying placards outside the court house. Let's suppose 80 per cent of our respondents are in favour of reinstating capital punishment. Assuming our sample size is large enough, can we now safely generalize that 80 per cent of Canadians are in favour of capital punishment? What could be wrong with such a strategy?

It obviously depends on what the placards say. If the protestors are there precisely to advocate the reinstatement of capital punishment, they are unrepresentative of the population at large. The people sampled are a *self-selected* group. Those who are against capital punishment certainly wouldn't join a rally in favour of capital punishment. Polling only those joining a rally in favour of capital punishment will obviously miss the population who are opposed to capital punishment. The results of the study would be skewed. The risk of a Type II error is increased if the sample size is not varied enough between the experimental conditions. By paying attention to sampling selection, we can avoid or minimize systematic error.

The general strategy for ensuring unbiased sampling is to generate a randomizing device in the selection of samples, or participants. If the selection of our samples is random, we can expect the participants will better represent the heterogeneity (or variability) within our target population. A fair representation of the mixed population in our sample is necessary if our goal is to generalize to the target population at large. That is, our sample should be a fair representation of our target population.

Recall from 11.2.4, the following argument: "Cameron argues that homosexuality ought to be discouraged and cured by invasive psychotherapies on the basis that studies show that homosexuals are less happy and less trusting than heterosexuals." We said this commits the 3rd variable error. This means that the mere truth of the premises does not support the conclusion. We may also wonder whether the premises are themselves true. If one is gay, presumably one would be happier accepting one's orientation than trying to repress it. It also turned out that the sample selection for this study was flawed. The sample for the study was taken from persons in mental institutions. Consequently the finding of unhappiness may have little to do with their being gay, but more to do with the psychological conditions which drove them to the psychiatric wards in the first place.

Stratification

If the population is not known to be reasonably uniform, the sample should be large enough to reflect the likely variety within the population. Otherwise the sample must be *stratified* in order to be representative of the target population. Stratification involves manipulating the sample to help ensure that it will be representative of the target population. If we're interested in random sampling, stratification seems to go against this. Its justification is that it provides a more representative sampling than we can expect from random selection. If we want a policy to accommodate the health interests of students, and 10 per cent of the student population is native and 5 per cent are disabled, a purely random sample may not capture either enough native or disabled participants. But, then, generalizing from a homogenous population cannot address the health concerns of these populations. Thus, we might wish to ensure that 10 per cent of our sample is native and 5 per cent are disabled. To do this, we can't rely on mere chance. Still, it is crucial to select a random population from within our stratified groups. Insofar as it reflects the proportions of the relevant subgroups within the population, the stratified sample has a relatively good chance of fairly representing the target population.

iii. Bias   Despite having a suitable size of well-represented participants, there may be other forms of interference that could contaminate the test results. These may stem from *Demand Effects* and *Experimenter Bias*. These are cases of unintentional bias. We will look at ways in which intentional bias acts to impinge on scientific results in section 12.2.

Demand Effects

Perhaps we wish to improve worker productivity. One suggestion is that lighting may have an influence. To test whether worker productivity would increase by altered lighting, one study was conducted in the following manner. Experimenters went into a factory, changed the light bulbs, and stood around recording the worker's reactions. They found that with dimmer lights, productivity increased. Next, they changed the lights to brighter lights and found that productivity also increased. In either case, productivity increased from the time before the experiment began.* What went wrong?

For those sufficiently familiar with the drudgery of factory work, the answer will likely seem obvious: the mere presence of the experimenters affected productivity and had nothing to do with the experimental hypothesis being tested.

Other forms of demand effects occur when the participants wish to "please" the researcher. Even when told, "There are no right answers," few really believe this. The researchers must be looking for *something*, and participants are often willing to provide it. Don't forget, most participants are *voluntarily* recruited. This means experimental participants are a *self-selected* group, and are thereby, at the outset, unrepresentative of the population at large. Given their voluntarism, they may be more willing than others to

---

* This is referred to as the *Hawthorne Effect*, since the study was conducted at the Hawthorne plant of Western Electric company in Illinois. See F.J. Roethlisberger and W.J. Dickson, *Management and the Worker.*

placate researchers. So the prospect of participants saying what they think the researcher wants to hear cannot be ignored.

In fact, there is a host of experimental results pertaining to the docility and cooperativeness of participants in experimental situations. Orne attempted to find a set of operations that would lead participants to refuse to cooperate. (Orne, "On the social psychology of the psychological experiment.") No matter how noxious, meaningless, or boring the tasks were, participants continued for protracted periods of time, with little error, little decrement in speed, and relatively little indication of hostility. Some tasks included performing a page of mundane addition problems, followed by the experimenter's instructions to tear up their answer sheets into thirty-two pieces. After this task was accomplished, they were to begin afresh on the next page of mundane addition problems with the same instructions to tear the answers up once they finished. They were asked to continue this process for several hours. None of the participants showed any disinclination to continue the clearly pointless activity.

Although participants' ready compliance raises an ethical issue, our concern is that such compliancy may unwittingly contaminate results. Consider the well-documented *Placebo Effect*. A placebo is a non-medicinal pill presented as if it were a real pill. About 33 per cent of patients taking placebos report improvement in their conditions. (Beecher, "Generalization from pain," 267–8.)* The same occurs with placebo hallucinogenics: people report experiences akin to hallucinogenic effects.

There are likely two distinct motives behind demand effects. Participants want to adjust their behaviour to what is normal, good, healthy, or intelligent. (Aronson and VanHoose, "The cooperative subject," 1–10) Alternatively, participants wish to help the experimenter confirm her hypothesis. (Rosenberg, "The conditions and consequences of evaluation apprehension")

One way to avoid or lessen demand effects is to invoke a certain amount of deception in one's design. When participants are provided with false information, they may be less likely to contaminate the study. Since deception is generally an immoral act, alternative ways of avoiding demand characteristics which do not involve deception are preferable.

Experimenter Effects

There was a horse named *Clever Hans*, who responded to math questions with an appropriate number of hoof stomps. The horse would be asked "How much is five plus two?" and Clever Hans would stomp on the ground seven times. To rule out the prospect that he stomped seven times to any question, the questions were varied. "What is four minus two?" Hans would

---

* Some variations occur depending on the type of illness. Placebos had less effect on asthma, quite a pronounced effect on headache relief (H. Haas, H. Fink, and G. Hartfelder, "Das Placeboproblem.")

stomp two times and stop. An alternative explanation to the horse under-standing English and math was eventually discovered. It turned out the horse was a complete dolt when his master was not present. There was no trickery involved; his master sincerely believed the horse could do math, but it turned out, instead, that the horse could pick up subtle cues. His trainer would nod his head (unintentionally) to each hoof stomp, and would stop nodding his head when the horse reached the magic number. By playing with variations in this nodding, it was discovered the horse stomped as long as the trainer nodded, and stopped when he stopped nod-ding, irrespective of the correct math answer. Of course this is a pretty clever feat in its own right, but what this case revealed was that participants can respond to subtle, often unintentional, cues of experimenters. The case of Clever Hans has incited research into the phenomenon known as *Experimenter Effect*.

To test the extent to which experimenter effects affect scientific experi-ments with human participants, a series of experiments was conducted putatively to test learning in rats. In these experiments, different experi-menters were randomly assigned a rat after being told that the animal had been specifically bred for brightness or dullness. When the results were tabulated, it was found that the so-called bright rats learned more quickly than the so-called dull rats. Yet there was no difference between the rats. The only difference, the real independent variable, was having a group of experimenters *believe* that they were observing the smart rats, while the other group *believed* they were observing the dull rats. (Rosenthal and Fode, "Three Experiments in experimenter bias," and Rosenthal and Law-son, "A longitudinal study of the effects of experimenter bias on the oper-ant learning of laboratory rats")

Experimenter bias is a tendency for experimenters to see in neutral data what they want to see – a clear danger to the scientific method.

12.1.3 Presentation of Statistics

Sometimes statistical results are offered as a way to convince us to accept a conclusion or product. Who are we to challenge statistics, we might feel. If the expectation is that we will be impressed by graphs and statistics with-out knowing what they're about, or how they were produced, then their use is simply an appeal to authority. The implicit idea is that we ought to defer our judgment to the impressive results of statistics.

There is much to know about the statistics before we should accept them, however. Consider the following oft-heard claim:

Four out of five dentists recommend Crest.

This looks suitably impressive, but as we've discovered, three important factors need to be considered before any conclusion can be drawn.

How large is the sample? Were there only five dentists checked? Twenty-five? The smaller the number, the less robust the result. If we're really sceptical, we might recognize that such a claim is consistent with 80 per cent of the people disagreeing, as long as somewhere in a series of five dentists surveyed, four of them recommended Crest. Of course, we are supposed to interpret the four-out-of-five claim as a proportion of a significantly larger number, but nothing impels us to make such an assumption, and we should be wary of doing so.

How biased is the sample? Which dentists were checked? Was it a national survey, or did the surveyors go to their friends? Were there side payments to the dentists interviewed that might have biased the results? The more biased, the less generalizable the results.

Recall, from chapter 4, the Tylenol ads boasting that hospitals dispensed more Tylenol than any other leading brand, while while forgetting to tell us that they supplied the hospitals with the Tylenol to dispense. Appealing to those hospitals who were provided free Tylenol to see whether they would dispense Tylenol is to introduce bias. Are we unreasonable to suspect Crest may have used a similar ploy?

What is the methodology? Is it at all plausible that four out of five dentists said yes to the question: "Would you recommend Crest above all other toothpastes?" Given the acceptability of the other toothpastes on the market, it would seem hard to believe that four-fifths of respondents actually answered "yes" to this. It would seem a lesser miracle to believe that the wording of the question has something to do with the results than to believe dentists really recommend Crest over all other brands with similar ingredients. Imagine, for example, if the question were worded this way:

"Would you recommend that people brush their teeth using toothpaste such as Crest?"

Four out of five saying "Yes," to this seems plausible, but it hardly warrants Crest's grand claim that four out of five dentists recommend Crest. What is more interesting, perhaps, is that one out of five dentists would not recommend toothpaste at all. Since one of the ingredients in toothpaste is sugar, this may not be that surprising.

Similarly, we might hear the claim:

Ninety per cent of Prince Edward Islanders surveyed are against the legalization of abortion.

This will probably strike us as impressive, if not appalling. But, as above, we need to know a bit more information, primarily concerning sampling and method. Concerning sampling, we need to know two things: *(1)* What was the size of the sample? The fewer the numbers, the less generalizable to the whole population *(2)* Was the sample biased in any untoward way? Are these respondents from a mail-in survey from the *Catholic Reform Newsletter?* If so, we'd be more puzzled about that 10 per cent. Another worry concerning mail-in surveys is that they tend to create two groups: those who mail them in and those who don't. There is a particular problem when those who don't outnumber those who do. If this is the case, we should naturally wonder whether the sort of people who mail in these surveys are unrepresentative of the population at large. Those who mail them in may be a self-selected group.

Consider an analogy. Suppose we want to know what proportion of the population finds phone surveys annoying. Those who find phone surveys annoying are likely not to volunteer to take the survey. Those who don't are more likely to take the survey. Should we be impressed if such a method discovers that people by and large don't mind phone surveys?

Our other worry is methodology. Surveys can be worded in ways that are leading. How would we answer the following question? "Would you be in favour of killing babies whose only crime was not yet being born?" Or perhaps we responded "No" to the following question: "Do you think a woman should have an abortion for the sole reason that she wants a male child, but her fetus is female?" But can we interpret the "No" to this question as a more general "No" to abortion? Presumably not.

Consider the following article relying on an impressive statistic.

> Private career colleges have a long tradition of working closely with the business community to develop programs based on employers' needs. That attention to detail often brings with it an impressive success rate, with the number of employed graduates approaching 100 per cent in many cases. (Tom Mason, Special Advertising Feature, "Private career colleges chart the way," *Chronicle-Herald,* 22 May 2001, A13)

The statistic is misleading, however, because it doesn't tell us if the graduates are actually employed in their area of study. They could all be working at McDonald's, flipping burgers.

Here is a case where a reader correctly notes that numbers alone don't tell us enough.

> You write that "the (B.C.) Liberals argue that four million student days have been lost to labour disputes in the education system over the last decade." (Education to be Essential Service in B.C., Aug.15). Shocking. What a horrifying number. Until one realizes that this statistic is a very small piece of the puzzle and a clever way of playing with numbers to foment public anger while rationalizing the declaration of education as an essential service. Just how many billions of days, in total, did students spend in schools during that decade? Doesn't the lost time for job action add up to less than 1% of all time spent in school? Isn't it likely that the common cold, the flu, other illnesses, orthodontist appointments or even truancy were responsible for a much

greater loss of student learning time than labour unrest? The number four million might as well be four gazillion, in schoolyard hyperbole, in terms of its
power to create furor. Thanks to the *National Post* for providing me with a fine
example of bias to use as a teaching tool in my senior English classes. (M.E.
Plommer, letter to the editor, *National Post*, 20 August 2001, A15)

Graphs

Statistical claims are often made with pictorial graphs. They provide a
quick, visual representation. Sometimes they may be creative and colour-
ful. Perhaps bright red cars are piled on top of each other to represent the
number of cars sold by a large-car manufacturer. Beside this stack is a
much smaller one of dull brown cars representing the sales of its rival. A
danger lurks. What we're interested in is whether the differences in sales
is *significant.* When studies reveal no significant difference, it does not
mean there is no difference. It simply means the differences that exist are
due to chance. Thus, showing us visual representation of differences is
beside the point. Mere graphic representation cannot distinguish significance.

Imagine a chart showing differential widget production between two
plants, A and B. The fact that A produced more widgets than B may well
be clearly shown in the graph, a fact we shall further assume is true. But
what the graph by itself cannot show is whether this difference is significant. A common ploy to be wary of is the failure of graphs to show the zero
point. A difference of $1000 may seem huge or quite petty if the compari-
son is between millions of dollars. If the comparison starts at 0 dollars, the
results will seem less interesting; but if the graph begins after the first million, a difference of $1000 will *appear* significant.

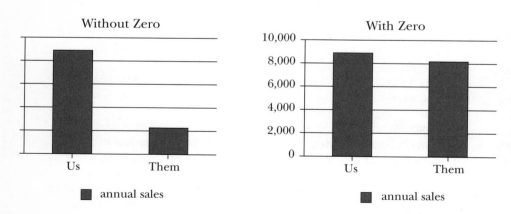

Consider next a graph in which the monetary units are distorted. Without paying attention to this, the graph on the left looks far worse than the
(admittedly bad) reality pictured in the graph on the right. The graphs are

highlighting the fact that while federal transfer payments to universities has decreased over the years, tuition fees have increased. The graph on the left appeared in posters throughout Canadian universities in 2000. It distorts matters. The graph on the right is the more accurate picture.

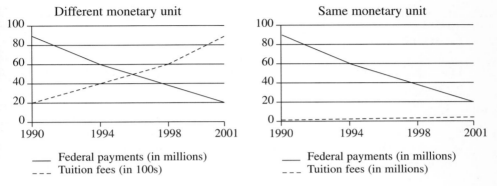

____ Federal payments (in millions)	____ Federal payments (in millions)
_ _ _ Tuition fees (in 100s)	_ _ _ Tuition fees (in millions)

Meaningless Statistics

Another concern is the bantering about of empty statistics. "With new and improved Dawn, dishes are 43% cleaner!" is an odd claim. Not only do we not know what the 43 per cent is being compared to (other brands, the previous brand, doing dishes without any detergent at all?), we may wonder how they come up with this measurement. President's Choice Reduced Fat Tuxedo crackers are advertised as being 44 per cent reduced in fat compared to their regular Tuxedo crackers. Here, at least, they provide the comparison. Without the comparison, the statistic is meaningless. But even with the comparison, the statistic seems far too exact for what it's measuring. It sounds like a huge reduction. The fat content of regular Tuxedo crackers is only 3.6 grams. A 44 per cent reduction means that the amount in Reduced Fat Tuxedo crackers is 2 grams. Is telling us about a 44 per cent reduction rather than a reduction of 1.6 grams fair?

Percentages by themselves are relatively useless. We need background information to know whether they are significant, or likely to be significant. After installation of the new 911 number, fires are down 32 per cent this year. Before we see how successful 911 has been, we might want to know how many fires we are talking about. If there were fifteen fires last year, and ten this year, this is a reduction by a little more than 32 per cent. But such fluctuations in fires may not be significant. Consider the following argument:

> The strip bar opened downtown, and we've had an increase in murders by 12 per cent. You tell me whether we shouldn't kick out the strippers!

Well, it depends on whether an increase by 12 per cent of murders is due to chance or not. If there aren't many murders to begin with, say eight, an increase of 12 per cent is an increase of one.

Imagine buying stock, and after it rises we sell and earn a 50 per cent gain. Encouraged, we buy stock again. This time, it drops, so we sell, and take a 33 per cent loss. We might think that, overall, we still came out ahead. Is it possible we in fact lost money? Absolutely. It depends on how much we invested. A 50 per cent gain of $100 is $50. A 33 per cent loss of $500 is $165. After the two transactions, we're down $115.

Exercise 12.1

Highlight what is problematic with the following. (Answers to select questions are provided in Appendix 1.)

1 Everyone knows that Egyptian mummies have remained remarkably well preserved for thousands of years. The reason, claim some people, is that the mummies were entombed in pyramid-shaped structures, and in some way not yet understood, that shape focuses a mysterious form of energy on objects housed within it. Advocates of pyramid power claim, for example, that organic matter of just about any sort can be preserved if housed under something with the shape of a pyramid. (Carey, *A Beginner's guide to Scientific Method*, 107)

☞ 2 A happy marriage and a good education point the way to living to a ripe old age, according to a Harvard Medical School study. Researchers say longevity may be a matter of personal choice and found there were seven ways to increase the chance of living to 80. They are a stable marriage, moderate alcohol use, no smoking, exercise, appropriate weight, positive coping mechanisms and no depressive illness. Depression was the only factor beyond individual control, according to the research, which began in 1940 and is the longest continuous study of mental and physical health in the world ... The study tracked the health of 724 white American men for 60 years, from 1940 until last year. The researchers compared the mental and physical health status of two groups of men: 268 Harvard sophomores and 456 disadvantaged inner-city youths ... The researchers based their research on participants' regular psychosocial and physical examinations. They say their conclusions also apply to Canadians, including women.(Mary Vallis, "60-year study finds 7 keys to long life," *National Post*, 1 June 2001, A1, A12)

3 Seven out of 10 women wear the wrong size bra, according to surveys by Playtex, a bra manufacturer ... this statistic was based on women who came to Playtex bra-fitting clinics. (*The Windsor Star*, 24 October 1995.)

☞ 4 Skydiving is really much less dangerous than soccer. Last year in Canada there were fewer than 100 serious injuries from skydiving, and more than 300 serious injuries from playing soccer.

5 Attendance at the Atlantic Region Philosophers' Association was up 32 per cent from last year.

☞ 6 In 1983 and 1984, the Reagan administration attempted to convince the public that educational quality is not linked to teacher salary levels. One finding was proudly displayed: California students did significantly worse on Scholastic Aptitude Test (SAT) scores than students from Mississippi. Since teacher salaries were significantly higher in California than in Mississippi, this statistical trend was much applauded by the Reagan administration. Consider two other factors. 1. Not all students take SAT scores; only those intending to go to university. 2. Significantly more California students intend to go to university than do students from Mississippi. How do these two bits of information weaken the claims made by the Reagan administration? (Adapted from Keith Stanovich, *How to Think Straight About Psychology*, 60–1)

7 The number of abandoned refugee claims is considered by some to be a barometer of illegal immigration. In 1989, 44 claims were abandoned. By 1998, the number had risen to more than 4,000 a year. Between 1989 and 2000, more than 25,000 claims were abandoned. The number of refugee claims denied can also be a window into how many illegal immigrants live here. In 1989, 84 per cent of the people who claimed refugee status in Canada were approved. By 1997, the approval rate had fallen to 40 per cent. (Peter Cheney, C. Freeze, "Tracking illegal migrants difficult," *Globe and Mail*, 26 May 2001, A8)

☞ 8 Our weather predictions are done either by computers or by humans. Computers are used to predict long-range forecasts, while humans do short-range forecasts. It turns out that computers have a worse track record for predictions than do humans. On the basis of a two-month study, they concluded that computers therefore are worse weather predictors than humans. This is important given the backdrop of the meteorologists' ongoing complaints that they're being replaced by computers. Conclusions from the study suggest they stop investing in the computers and hire more people. (CBC Radio 2, 6 July 2002)

9 More than a generation ago, psychiatrist Robert Spitzer helped millions of Americans get instantly well. In 1973 Spitzer, a professor at Columbia University, led the charge to have homosexuality removed from diagnostic manuals as a mental disorder. In a stroke, a segment of the population once considered sexually deviant was declared mentally sound. Last week Dr. Spitzer appeared to take a troubling step away from that clean bill of health. In a study presented at the convention of the American Psychiatric Association, he argued that some "highly motivated" homosexuals may be able to turn themselves into heterosexuals. The APA quickly distanced itself from the study, and gay-rights groups condemned it. In the days since, the work has sparked a firestorm in the psychological community, one that may say more about questionable science than it could ever

about sexual orientation. The biggest problem with Spitzer's study is the way he conducted it. Relying on telephone surveys, he interviewed 143 men and 57 women who had sought help – in some cases through religious groups that openly oppose homosexuality – to change their sexual orientation. His surveys convinced him that 66% of the men and 44% of the women had indeed achieved "good heterosexual functioning." These are surprising numbers – until you consider the sample group. Drawing conclusions about homosexuality from gays trying to go straight is like surveying public opinion about one religion by polling people converting to another. Spitzer argues that since the goal of his work was simply to show that heterosexual conversion is possible, contacting people working to make the change was the only sensible method. The question wasn't "Does *everybody* change?" he says. "The question was, does *anyone?*" Fair enough, but did anyone? Spitzer measured his "good heterosexual functioning" with decidedly subjective standards – asking the respondents if their heterosexual experiences were satisfying. More rigorous studies might have looked for signs of physical arousal in the presence of various visual stimuli. What's more, his work has not yet been published or peer reviewed, two basic stripes that studies usually must earn to be taken seriously. Spitzer is clearly the same researcher he was in 1973, and nothing in his study suggests that he believes homosexuality has any place in a manual of disorders. The new work, however, does feel oddly out of step with mainstream thinking. Most scientists stress that everything from brain architecture to environment help determine sexuality. While gays may be able to swear off one kind of sex and grimly slog away at another, that doesn't alter their basic orientation. "It's possible to change almost any human behaviour," says geneticist Dean Hamer of the National Institute of Health. "But changing the underlying mechanism is a different matter." A study presented at the same convention addressed the same topic and found that of 202 homosexuals who sought to change, 178 failed. Spitzer stands by his findings and insists they should never be used to justify coercive or discriminatory treatment of gays. In a culture in which homosexuals already face so much of both, however, his work certainly doesn't help. (Jeffrey Kluger, "Can gays switch sides?" *Time* (Canadian edition), 21 May 2001, 52)

10 Comparisons in sales before and after the introduction of the new red packaging indicates the colour red sells. Sales in one month prior to the introduction of the red packaging was $130,000. Afterwards, it was $135,000. That's $5000 per month, a great payoff compared to the nominal additional cost in packaging.

☞11 Small children may be the world's biggest sexists. A U.S. study released yesterday shows that anyone trying to change the world's gender relations may be fighting a losing battle because even children as young as

3 fall under the sway of their peers and quickly learn what it means to be a girl or a boy. "Peers may play the role of gender 'enforcers', who monitor and maintain gender boundaries by conveying information about the correct behaviour for girls and boys and about the consequences likely to occur if gender boundaries are violated," Carol Lynn Martin and Richard Fabes of Arizona State University write in Developmental Psychology, a journal of the American Psychological Association. The findings come as no surprise to Jacqui Strachan, a Toronto mother of two boys, aged 8 and 5. "You can influence your children to be positive toward the opposite sex – I don't think you can force them to be the opposite sex," she said, explaining that she has not been able to convince her boys that playing with dolls is great fun. "It surprises and amazes me as a feminist to think that I was so wrong. You can't change them. Boys are boys and girls are girls." Even where teachers have been encouraged to promote gender equality, same-sex segregation remains pervasive, the study's authors report. Dr. Martin and Dr. Fabes spent six months watching 28 boys and 33 girls. The children, aged 3 to 6, played at an unidentified university daycare facility in the southwestern United States. In the beginning of the school year, the boys and girls behaved in similar ways. By spring, the differences were noticeable. More than 80 per cent of the children showed clear preferences to play with children of the same sex. The study also found: While one girl played with boys as much as 40 per cent of the time, about half of the girls played almost exclusively with other girls. About 35 per cent of the boys played exclusively with boys, while about 11 per cent (three boys) played with girls more than with boys. The more that boys played with boys, the more likely they were to be rougher, more aggressive and more active in their play by the spring; For girls, playing with one another seemed to contribute to calmer, less aggressive play. On one hand, this wasn't a bad thing, the researchers reported. For instance, the more that boys played with boys, the more positive emotions they expressed over time. (Boys who don't like aggressive play tend to withdraw from playing with other boys and may be rejected by other boys.) As boys played together, they tended to spend less time playing near adults, which the researchers believe may contribute to the increasingly aggressive and active nature of their play. On the other hand, the researchers believe that there may be long-term consequences to the sex segregation small children seem naturally to favour. "These different styles of play socialize boys and girls to behave in ways the other sex likely finds increasingly unattractive and uninteresting." But Ms. Strachan said that parents should not be alarmed. "It's almost like an evolution. They start off finding their boy-dom and once they're comfortable with that they can move on to expand their relationships with girls." (Sean Fine, "Scientists prove boys will be boys," *Globe and Mail,* 23 May 2001)

12.2 Science and Its Critics

12.2.1 Science and Pseudo-Science

The scientist's task is to discover general truths. Scientists strive to understand the world and search for natural laws and the underlying principles that govern those laws. They seek not merely to know what the facts are, but to explain them. Toward this end, they devise theories.

A common misconception of science is that science offers nothing but the facts. Such a supposition is very peculiar. It erroneously assumes that the whole is not more than the sum of its parts. Such an error in reasoning is called *the fallacy of composition* (see 12.3.5). Scientific theories are more than just a jumble of disorganized facts. The facts must be organized, and it is the basis on which they are organized that creates heated debates within scientific circles. In general, the organized pattern that wins out is the one that has the best predictive power.

Understanding the purpose of science helps us to distinguish scientific theories from nonscientific theories. Nonscientific theories tend to be dogmatic, and the appeal tends to be to authority or popularity. Scientific theories are (ideally) non-dogmatic, always open to refutation and modification, and the appeal is to the evidence, even if it goes against popular conceptions of the time.

These two differences can be made clearer by pointing out the fundamental difference between scientific and nonscientific explanations for events in the world. It is the essence of a scientific explanation or hypothesis to be empirically *testable*.

12.2.2 Quine's Criteria

W.V. Quine presented four criteria for distinguishing scientific claims from pseudoscientific claims. They are relevance, coherence, predictive power, and simplicity. ("Ontological Relativity")

i. Relevance   No hypothesis is proposed for its own sake, but is always intended as an explanation of some fact or other. Therefore it must be relevant to the fact it is intended to explain: i.e., the fact in question must be *deducible* from the proposed hypothesis. That a butterfly flaps its wings in Taiwan is not clearly relevant to the causes of a hurricane in Brazil, despite recognition of a tightly woven ecosystem.

ii. Coherence   A theory should generally be coherent or compatible with the network of accepted scientific theories already in vogue. To the extent that it isn't, the burden of proof lies with the new theory.

This does not mean that a new theory will never gain acceptance at the price of an old system of beliefs. This has happened many times in the history of science. Copernicus, Galileo, Einstein all managed scientific revolutions or paradigm shifts. Simply, if a new theory supplants an old theory, the new theory must cohere with observable data better than the old theory. That is, the new theory must not merely provide a better explanation of empirical data, but also promise better predictive power than the old theory. For example, new theories should also explain a number of quirks that the old theories could not adequately account for.

The message here is that the *totality* of hypotheses accepted at any one time must be consistent or compatible with each other. One's network of beliefs must cohere.

iii. Predictive or Explanatory Power   The predictive or explanatory power concerns the *range* of observable facts that can be derived from the theory. The greater the predictive power, the more it explains. The more a theory explains and the more accurately it can predict future outcomes, the better the theory is.

If the theory predicts something that does not happen, we count this as evidence against the theory. If the test was well conducted, we call the disconfirming result a case of *falsifying* the theory (see the discussion of non-falsifiability in 7.4.3, as well as that which is to come in 12.2.3). Pseudoscience can provide an explanation after the fact. Peasants blaming the deluge on God's wrath is a case in point. Although the theory that bad things are due to God's wrath offers an explanation of events, it cannot hope to provide any predictive guidance. If illness, for example, is due to poor hygiene, blaming the patient for sinning is hardly helpful in finding a preventative cure. Science promises pragmatic results in ways that pseudoscience cannot. This is the importance of a theory's having predictive power.

iv. Simplicity   Another criterion for a good scientific hypothesis or theory concerns simplicity. By this, Quine did not mean that a simpler *theory* is better than a more complicated theory. Rather, the theory that pictures the *world* as being simpler is to be preferred to a theory that describes the world as being more complicated. Quine is not original in this. The principle of simplicity may be traced back to William of Ockham (1300–1349). The principle of simplicity is often referred to as *Ockham's Razor*, evocative of lopping off unnecessary appendages.

The principle of simplicity, or Ockham's Razor, may seem arbitrary. If a true theory pictures a complicated world, and a false theory describes the world as being inordinately simple, we should not opt for the simple theory. Of course that presupposes that we know which one is true and which false. Quine's point is that as long as *other things are equal*, opt for simplicity. Everything we witness in nature *does* seem to operate on the principle of simplicity. Water takes the path of least resistance, for example.

As long as two theories have equal predictive power, are equally compatible, and are each relevant, then the simpler one of the two is chosen.

12.2.3 Critics of Science

Science is not without its critics. The idea that science is *testable*, whereas pseudoscience is not, has met serious challenge. The objections focus on problems of verification, problems of falsification, and other insidious biases that contaminate the program of science.

i. Verifiability Let's say our theory is that people are by nature immoral. In other words, we're only moral because of external sanctions and the presence of police. Well, how can we test this? One possibility is to invite participants to take part in an experiment where we provide them with a mundane task. Perhaps we tell them to proofread various pages of script. While we walk the participants into the room to show them the scripts they'll have to proofread, we notice a five-dollar bill lying on the table. "Oh, that must belong to the last participant. I saw him going into the washroom. Do you mind chasing him down and returning it to him? I'll wait for you here, and when you get back we'll get started." All this is a ruse, of course. There is no participant who lost five dollars. We're interested to see how many participants will come back and confess that they did not find the other participant who lost the five dollars. Such a study would have difficulty passing an ethical review, for we are deceiving the participants, and when we deceive participants, we need to inform them afterward about the deception in kind, gentle ways so they don't feel bad. But in this case, if any participants have indeed pocketed the money, no amount of "debriefing" will likely make them feel better. For them, it may be best simply not to tell them. But then, should the real nature of the study be imparted to them, the risk is even greater. For our purposes, let's ignore the ethical constraints and proceed anyway. Imagine that the result of the study is that fifty of fifty participants walked away with the $5. Have we verified our theory?

The answer is "No." Even if no participant returned the money to the researcher, we cannot conclude that our theory has been verified. This is so for two reasons (1) The old claim was that scientific theories can be proven true by empirical investigation. This is false. We cannot conclusively prove a general law true from even a million observations that cohere with the theory. The claim that all swans are white is not proven to be true by observing one million white swans. After all, this is the deciding feature between deductive and inductive arguments. Inductive arguments can only give good odds, they can never "verify." Verification is a term appropriate only for deductive arguments. Alas, science deals in induction, not deduction.

(2) Perhaps worse is that the very structure of verifiability commits the fallacy of *affirming the consequent* (see 10.5.1). Consider

If everyone is a crook, these participants will take the five dollars.
These participants took the five dollars.
Therefore, everyone is a crook.

1 C ⊃ T   p
2 T   p
3 C   ???   1,2 AC Invalid!

ii. Falsifiability We cannot verify theories, but, on the other hand, we can disconfirm a hypothesis by falsifying it. Recall *modus tollens*:

1 A ⊃ B
2 ~B
3 ~A   1,2 m.t.

So if the claim is that most people will grab unguarded money, we do not prove the hypothesis true if fifty participants in a row grab money left unguarded. On the other hand, we do prove that hypothesis *false* if more than half of the participants do not grab the money, by *modus tollens*.

This move to *falsifiability* as the pivotal distinction between scientific theories and nonscientific theories was defended by Sir Karl Popper (1902–1994). A scientific hypothesis should be testable. Since it cannot properly be verified, Popper suggested scientific theories can at least be falsified. That is, we should know what will disprove the theory. If a theory is put in such a way that it is impossible to even conceive a way to show it to be wrong, it is not a scientific hypothesis. (*The Logic of Scientific Discovery*)

The falsifiability criterion is one of the means we can use to distinguish pseudoscience from real science. The claims of ESP, religion, miracle diets, communication with spirits, numerology, horoscopes, and Freudian psychoanalysis are non-falsifiable. Let's look at Freudian psychoanalysis. Freud is generally credited with being the father of psychology. He proposed a complicated conceptual structure to explain human behaviour after the fact but not to predict behaviour. The theory could explain everything, but it is precisely this property that makes it scientifically vacuous. The theory makes no specific predictions. Its adherents spent much time and effort getting it to explain every known human event, from individual quirks of behaviour to large-scale social phenomena, but their success at making it a rich source of after-the-fact explanation has robbed it of any scientific utility.

For example, how can we test the hypothesis that Joan has developed a rash because she has repressed a sexual desire for her father. If she says, "Yeah, I do have sexual fantasies about my father, how did you know?" we have confirming evidence. If, instead, she claims she never had this sexual desire, the response is "See: you've repressed it, and that's why it has come out as a rash." Precisely because everything can be accounted for in this way, the theory is empty.

Horoscopes are also non-falsifiable. They are carefully worded to make vacuous predictions which almost any event would count as satisfying and, with enough weasel words thrown in, no event can count as disconfirming. Scientific theories, on the other hand, go out on a limb. Scientists boldly claim that a theory will be proven false if very specific sorts of events happen. Without clear, falsifiable predictions, the theory is not testable. If it is not testable, it cannot count as science – or so Popper argued.

The notion of falsifiability has not gone without criticism, however. The shift to falsifiability suggests that scientists are ready to reject their own theories at the drop of a hat. Scientists are people, however, and are as much subject to bias and vested interest as the rest of us. Since reputation often hinges on the success of the research, it is unlikely scientists will be willing to simply discard it after their theory has been deemed false. Scientists may be impurely motivated. We have heard of scientists cooking their data. They may be motivated to get grant money; they may have invested years of their lives; their advancement, their careers may be on the line. To think they will simply discard their theory over a single contradictory result is naive.

Besides improper motivation, there may be other very legitimate reasons why scientists will be loathe to reject their theories merely on the grounds of falsification. The methodology itself may have been flawed. If so, it would be too quick to assume the theory is wrong. It is prudent to first wonder whether the experiment itself was contaminated in unknown ways.

Consider again our experiment about people's moral motives. Let's imagine that most people returned the money. (This is in fact the case in similar studies. Most empirical studies find that people are, by and large, moral, not immoral.) Does this show that people are intrinsically moral, moral even when it counts against their self-interest? Not necessarily. (1) Recall the problem with demand characteristics. Here is a case where the self-selection of volunteer participants may have introduced systematic bias. Only the nice are apt to volunteer in the first place. (2) Even if some of these volunteers were prone to theft, some other factors of the design may have discouraged it. Perhaps the participants suspected something. What we have learned from Clever Hans is that participants can pick up subtle cues. It is conceivable that the experimenter gave cues enough to alert the participant that something was suspect. (3) Besides, if the other participant did return for the money (the impossibility of this is not known to the participants), the theft would be discovered. So it is not quite a case of free money as they had hoped. (4) Perhaps wary of psychological studies, the participants considered the possibility of hidden cameras or one-way mirrors. (5) Perhaps word got out, somehow, of the true intent of the study. (6) Perhaps $5.00 was too measly a price to risk social sanction. If we increase the money to $20, or $50, or $100, perhaps the temptation would be greater. Before we jump to the conclusion that our theory is wrong, we would have to rule out these and other possible 3rd variables that might have contaminated our results.

Let's say we quiz those participants who didn't take the money. Perhaps they invariably reply "No, I didn't suspect anyone was guarding it. Yes, I would have done the same with $20. No, I had no reason to believe the student was going to come back for it." Have we now disproved our theory that everyone will take unguarded money? Only if we also assume the participants are telling us a psychological truth. (1) They may be lying. (2) They may be anxious to get on with their lives and out of the experiment. (3) They may be saying what they think the experimenter wants to hear. (4) Having volunteered, they may be a self-selected bunch of do-gooders and not representative of the population as a whole. Or any number of other possibilities.

How do we rule out these alternative explanations? The answer should be obvious: by doing more studies, not by abandoning one's hypothesis. And it is this frank admission that undermines the claim that science, unlike pseudoscience, is falsifiable.

The falsifiability criterion claims that, although we cannot verify theories, we can at least prove a theory false by a single disconfirming bit of information. We have seen that there are many exceptions to this rule. Because of the imperfections in many experimental situations, people complain that science isn't any more open to refutation and testability than the dogmatic, nonscientific explanations they are intended to replace.

Further Difficulties with the Non-Falsifiability Criterion
More needs to be said, admittedly. Here are three difficulties.

(i)   Is the non-falsifiability theory itself falsifiable?
(ii) Although Universal Affirmative statements (All As are Bs) are falsified by Particular Negative statements (Some A is not a B), and Universal Negative ones (No As are Bs) are falsified by Particular Affirmatives (Some A is a B), are the particular statements themselves falsifiable? After all, "There is one apple that is rotten" is not falsified by "Here are a bunch of non-rotten apples," since the two propositions are perfectly compatible. And finding a rotten apple concerns *verification*, not falsification.
(iii) Are probability statements falsifiable? Take flipping a fair coin. We say it has a 50 per cent chance of landing heads. But on any actual trial of even one thousand throws, we wouldn't actually bet on exactly 500 heads coming up. If we did, we'd commit the Gambler's Fallacy. So is the probability claim of .5 odds non-falsifiable?

The discussion doesn't end here, but we shall.

iii. Political and Corporate Influences   A further objection is commonly made. Bias can creep in well before the running of the experiment. Studies need to be funded. In order to get funding, researchers may apply to government or corporate agencies. Which researchers are most likely to get funding? Not surprisingly, those that cohere with the current political agenda or corporate interests. Although culturally isolated science may be neutral, no science is culturally neutral. Particularly, political and corporate-funded science is not.

Further, once a study is funded and the experiment complete, the results need to be published. Journals and publishers may themselves have agendas which determine the selection criteria. Studies which find their way into the public domain may themselves suffer the problem of being self-selected.

12.2.4 Science Is Social

So, should we throw science out? Should we demote science to the status of voodooism, tea-leaf reading, seance, rain dance, and religious doctrine? That would be a little hasty. Science tends toward reaching for a clearer understanding of the world. That it is still susceptible to error is no reason, by itself, to throw it out. Surely science is less susceptible to error than non-scientific explanations. Claiming that everyone is biased to some extent does nothing to prevent us from distinguishing *degrees of bias*. Bias is not a discreet variable.

There is a further aspect of science that moves toward eliminating the problems of collecting and interpreting data – the public domain of science. Scientific thinking is a general pattern of reasoning from evidence to conclusions that can be tested by experience. That it can be tested means more than being tested by personal opinion. *Science is social.* By this we mean that it should be publicized so that others may test the theory themselves. Any testing of a theory should be public and repeatable. This helps maintain the objective characteristic of science. It avoids, or at least reduces, the chances of subjective bias creeping in. That it is public and open to others to test reduces the possibility of everyone missing an alternative hypothesis. Importantly, the openness of its testability allows those with contrary biases to test it out as well. If, despite all these tests by people differently motivated, the results are similar, this stands in the theory's favour.

By public repeatability, we hope to better ensure that hidden assumptions and biases are brought out into the open and scrutinized. Future experiments may be run with the detected biases contained, removed, or countered.

Arguments by Analogy

*Analogical Reasoning • Analogical Argument
Form • Appraising Analogical Arguments
Refutation by Logical Analogy*

13.1 Analogical Reasoning

Analogy is the linking one thing with another by noting similarities. If often takes the form of simile or metaphor. Consider some of Shakespeare's metaphors, for example. "How sharper than a serpent's tooth it is to have a thankless child" (*King Lear,* I, iv, 310). "But I will wear my heart upon my sleeve for dawes to peck at" (*Othello,* I, i, 64). Or the haunting metaphor in Ezra Pound's "In A Station of the Metro":

The apparition of these faces in a crowd;
Petals on a wet, black bough.

Analogy helps liven boring prose and conversation. It can better reveal the peculiar phenomenological sensations of the writer when literal renditions are too bland. Comparing one thing to another is also a helpful device when we are trying to explain something. The audience can understand a new concept if it can be likened to a familiar one. For example,

The expanding universe is sort of like a raisin muffin in an oven. The raisins grow further apart from each other as the dough rises. Similarly, the stars and galaxies grow further apart from each other as the universe expands.

Plato availed himself of a variety of analogies in his writing. He believed that perception was not a true account of reality, that reality was something totally removed from what the senses could provide, and that reality was accessible only by pure thought, not by observation. He admitted this was a bit tricky to understand, so shackled are we by our perceptions. So he offered the following *Analogy of the Cave.*

> Consider being shackled in a cave all your life. Your head is chained so that you stare ahead at a wall. There are images on the wall and you develop a language to describe them: a "tree," a "dog," a "canoe." These images, unbeknownst to you, are really shadows cast upon the wall by firelight, situated behind you. More, it is not the case that a tree, a dog, a canoe passes in front of the fire. Rather, there are wooden cut-outs of trees, dogs, canoes that persons carry back and forth between the fire and your shackled back. So what you see as real are only shadows of cut-out images of reality. You would have to break out of the shackles, and escape the cave to finally see the reality as it really is. Likewise, what we perceive is far removed from what is real. (Paraphrased from Plato, *Republic*, 7.514a-516b)

Plato is not giving an argument here. He is merely trying to illustrate the import of his claim. The argument for his position occurs elsewhere.

So far, we have seen analogy used to *describe* things. The purpose is not to establish a conclusion. Consider the following:

> If Paul Martin were a tailor, he wouldn't just make your pants with belt and suspenders. He'd probably equip them with buttons, Velcro, hooks and safety pins to boot – and dub all these devices the proper measure of prudence against the risk of a sudden surge of gravity. The federal finance minister is famous for fitting his budget forecasts with airbags – fluffy contingency cushions to ensure the actual bottom line will never be worse, and usually better, than the forecast. Indeed, critics charge him with prudence overkill – of understating the true scope for tax cuts or new spending. ("Pants pinned on prudence," *Chronicle-Herald*, 19, May 2001, C3)

As put, no argument is given. A simple analogy is made between Paul Martin's conservative budget and a somewhat paranoid tailor. We may certainly read into this an unstated claim that Paul Martin's budget is unreasonable, or as unreasonable as such a tailor, but the analogy is used here to *illustrate* the degree to which the author thinks Martin's budget is excessive. No reasons other than the illustration are provided, and we cannot take the illustration to *count* as a reason, any more than we should take what happens to muffins as a *reason* for our belief in an expanding universe.

When analogy is used in an argument, something more is being done with it than describing, illustrating, or explaining. If the author is attempting to establish the truth of a proposition on the basis of an analogy, the passage is argumentative. This is done when the premises assert, first that two (or more) things are similar in one (or more) respects, and second that, since one (or more) of those things also possesses a certain characteristic, it is *concluded* that the other thing *also* has that characteristic. This is the form of an argument by analogy.

In fact, most of our everyday inferences are by analogy. Because it happened a certain way in the past, it will probably happen that way again in the future. We reason from past experience to what the future will probably hold. For example, whenever I drink too much, I always feel bad the next day. Therefore if I drink too much tonight, I will probably feel bad tomorrow. Notice that this argument uses the word "probably." This is because no argument from analogy is deductive. The conclusion is not 100 per cent guaranteed. Rather, it is a probabilistic prediction.

The purpose of analogical reasoning is to *extend our knowledge of the world* by making comparisons between things that are familiar to us and things that are not so familiar.

The following are words that are *Analogy Indicators*:

same as	resembles	similar(ly)	in like manner
in comparison	as (in)	like	by the same token
alike	analogously	akin to	just as ...

13.2 Analogical Argument Form

13.2.1 Terms

Every analogical inference proceeds from the similarity of two or more things in one or more respects to the similarity of those things in some further respect. We cite a number of *Analogues* which share in common with the *Primary Subject* a number of *Shared Attributes*. Because these analogues also have the *Target Attribute*, we conclude the primary subject also has the target attribute.

Such an argument takes the following form:

1 Entities a, b, c, and d have attributes P and Q.
2 Entities a, b, and c have attribute R.
3 Therefore, entity d probably has attribute R

where,

Analogue(s) = Entities a, b, and c
Primary Subject = Entity d
Shared attribute(s) = P and Q
Target Attribute = R

Consider, for example, the following analogical argument:

1 John, his brother Sam, and their parents smoked two packs of cigarettes a day since they were teenagers, and ate a diet rich in fatty foods.
2 John's parents and Sam all died prematurely of heart attacks.
3 Therefore, probably John will die of a heart attack also. (Adapted from Freeman, *Thinking Logically*, 320)

In this argument, the primary subject (the subject of the conclusion) is John. The target attribute (the predicate of the conclusion) is dying of a heart attack. The analogues (the items being compared to our primary subject) are the brother, the mother, and the father. The shared attributes (the things that the primary subject has in common with the analogues) are eating fatty foods and smoking since teenage-hood.

It is important to note that an argument by analogy is not restricted to four entities (a, b, c, and d) and three attributes (P, Q, and R).

Here is an argument by analogy with only one analogue and one shared attribute.

1 John and Bill each have a car.
2 Bill crashed his car.
3 Therefore John will probably crash his car too.

This example illustrates the general rule that the more analogues and the more shared attributes we have, the stronger the argument. The fewer analogues, and the fewer shared attributes, the weaker the argument.

Consider another example:

I bought three pairs of shoes from Supershoes. All were a good price and lasted a long time and looked great. I'm going to buy another pair of shoes at Supershoes. I have them picked out already. They too look great and they too are a great price. I expect that they also will last a long time.

In this case, the fourth pair of shoes is being predicted to last a long time. This is the conclusion. To understand the components of analogical arguments, it is helpful to single out the conclusion. Once we have the conclusion, we can now distinguish the primary subject (in this case shoe 4), and the target attribute (lasting a long time), merely by understanding what is the subject of the conclusion (the primary subject), and what is the predicate (the target attribute). Now, we pair off the primary subject with the analogues, the things the primary subject is being compared to. In this case, that's shoe 1, shoe 2, and shoe 3. What do all shoes listed have in common? That will give us the shared attributes. In this case, it is that they all have a good price and look great. There is one more attribute that is not explicitly stated, but which we are entitled to add: they all come from the same store, Supershoes. Hence,

Primary subject = shoe 4
Target attribute = last a long time
Analogues = shoe 1, shoe 2, shoe 3.
Shared attributes = good price, looks great, Supershoes.

One more. This is a rendition of Paley's *Argument by Design* for the existence of God.

A watch could not assemble itself. The complex arrangements of parts into a working watch is possible only because there is a craftsman who designs and constructs the watch. In just the same way, the complicated parts of the world could not arrange themselves into the natural order. So there must be a designer of the world, and that is God. (William Paley, *Natural Theology*, 1805.)

In this case, the conclusion is that the world must be designed. Therefore, the primary subject is the "world," and the target attribute is "being designed." The analogue is that to which the world is being compared, in this case, a watch. What do the world and watches have in common? That is, what is the shared attribute? In this case it's the complex arrangement of all its parts. The shared attribute, therefore is "complex arrangements of parts." We'll assess this argument at the end of 13.3.

13.2.2 Suppressed Conclusions

Sometimes we encounter an argument from analogy in which no conclusion is stated. How then can we tell whether this is meant to be an argument rather than a description or explanation? The answer is that, if it is an argument from analogy, there will be two premises required: one asserting what the analogues and primary subject have in common, and one asserting what extra ingredient the analogues share. Given these premises, the conclusion is forced upon us.
    Consider the following:

Jones, Smith, Santayana, and Phillips all voted for the Libertarian Party and have been married more than once. Moreover, Smith, Santayana and Phillips have been charged with fraud.

However poor an analogy it may be, we can infer that the intended conclusion is the likelihood of Jones being convicted of fraud as well.

Exercise 13.1

Are the following analogical arguments? For those that are, dissect them into the proper analogical components: primary subject, target attribute, analogues, shared attributes. (Answers to selected questions provided in Appendix 1.)

☞ 1 Racists violate the principle of equality by giving greater weight to the interests of members of their own race when there is a clash between their interests and the interests of those of another race. Sexists violate the principle of equality by favouring the interests of their own sex. Similarly, speciesists allow the interests of their own species to override the greater interests of members of other species. The pattern is identical in each case. (Hint: A suppressed conclusion lurks here). (Singer, *Animal Liberation*, 2nd ed., 9)

2 The best reason for thinking that BSE – mad cow disease – will not infect people is that scrapie – mad sheep disease – never has. Scrapie is BSE, except that it appears in a different species and has been around for at least 250 years. In all that time sheep-eaters exposed to scrapie have been no more demented than the rest of the population. Thus cow-eaters exposed to BSE, the argument goes, will also remain healthy. ("Science and Technology," *The Economist*, 28 July 1990, 69)

☞ 3 Competitive sports are by definition cruel and elitist; they do not tolerate weakness and they are not subject to compassionate intervention. Casey Martin is a good golfer who lacks one key aspect of success at the pro game; in this way, he is not unlike a decent pitcher who lacks a curve ball. The fact that Martin's condition is officially a disability rather than the result of an injury or sheer lack of talent is not relevant in the truly impartial court of physical achievement. (Mark Kingwell, "The cart ruling: one golfer gets a free ride," *National Post*, 30 May 2001, A14)

4 While he was attending a group of drug addicts at a sanitarium in Berlin in 1927, it occurred to Dr. Manfred Sakel to try insulin on them. This hormone promotes the utilization of sugar in the body, and on theoretical grounds he believed its effect should relieve the paradox by which a slave of the drug habit requires larger and larger doses of what is essentially a poison. He hoped that, through the insulin, he might free the victim of dependence on morphine. Some of the men reacted to the insulin with convulsions, but most of them broke into perspiration and lapsed into deep sleep. When they came out of their seizure, or were awakened after a few hours of coma, their conduct surprised the doctor. He noticed that the morbid fears and anxieties which habitually oppress addicts had diminished and odd notions of persecution, jumpy nerves, and other psychotic symptoms were gone. This unexpected outcome set Dr. Sakel to thinking. If insulin improved the mental climate of the drug-crazed men, what would it do for the frankly insane? (George W. Gray, *The Advancing Front of Medicine*.)

☞ 5 I infer that others have minds as I do, despite the fact that I cannot see their minds. Whenever I am in pain, I tend to hold the injured part, scream, and claim to the world that I am in pain. When I see others hold their injured limb, scream, and profess to the world their pain, I make the conclusion that they too have mental states. (Bertrand Russell, *Human Knowledge: Its Scope and Limits*, 482–6)

6 The Middle East has entered a feedback loop sometimes described as a vicious circle. Ariel Sharon says, "This strategy will continue until the violence stops." I am reminded of the rather dense manager who insisted, "The beatings will continue until the morale improves." (R. Nathan Pila, letter to the editor, *Globe and Mail*, 12 May 2001, A12)

☞ 7 The moral relativist might argue that our language should be reformed. We should talk differently. At one time people used to talk and act as if the world were flat. Now they don't. The relativist could suggest that we can change our ethical language in the same way. But consider how radical the relativists' response is. Since most, if not all, cultures speak and act as if there were universal moral principles, the relativist can be right only if almost everyone else is wrong. How plausible is that? (Bowie, "Relativism and the Moral Obligations of Multinational Corporations," 539)

8 If American millionaire Dennis Tito wants to pay millions to stay at the universe's most expensive hotel, the International Space Station [April 30], the partners who own the place should take the money! Is it any more "distasteful" to accept millions of dollars to take visitors to the real McCoy than it is for NASA to charge a steep admission for visitors to gawk at the boringly earth-bound Kennedy space center? NASA may be missing the boat on pocketing well-needed research money for something that will become common-place in the future: paid space visits. All the best to Mr. Tito. Enjoy your flight, and send us some pictures! (Dan Herauf, letter to the editor, *Time* (Canadian edition), 21 May 2001, p 8)

9 Creativity resembles humour, as E.B. White described it: You can dissect humour, as you can dissect a frog, but in the process you kill it. (Robert Fulford, "Whose bright idea was this?" *National Post*, 30 May 2001, A14)

10 The worst part of this kind of government initiative, however, is that it presumes that people want or need highspeed Internet access – which not everyone does. Some people are probably more than happy to be without it, in the same way that some people are quite happy to live without cable television. Why not pour billions of dollars into ensuring that every Canadian has access to gourmet coffee, or that every rural resident can afford to buy a new truck once a year? That $2-billion could be spent on better roads, or even upgrading the regular old rural telephone system. (Matthew Ingram, "Ottawa's broadband plan is dumb and expensive," *Globe and Mail*, 20 June 2001, B14)

☞11 One wonders how the Anglicans and the other religious denomina-
     tions that participated in this sorry episode would feel if the shoe
     were on the other foot. Imagine the furor if Christian children had
     been kidnapped, taken deep into the bush, taught to hunt and trap
     and had the hell whipped out of them if they tried to have a Christ-
     ian church service or speak English. (William E. McLeod, letter to
     the editor, *Globe and Mail*, 28 June 2001, A14)

  12 If the privatization of water testing led to the tragedy in Walkerton,
     Ont., where will the privatization of driver testing (Ontario privatizes
     driver testing – June 1) lead? (Rachel Evans, letter to the editor, *Globe
     and Mail*, 4 June 2001, A14)

  13 At hearings in 1986, President Reagan apparently was unable to
     remember whether he had approved a 1985 shipment of arms by
     Israel to Iran. Supporters of the President tried to defend him
     against claims that he was either lying or becoming senile. One such
     argument claimed that since few people could remember what they
     had for lunch on the first day of September 1985, it was not reason-
     able to expect President Reagan to remember whether he had
     approved the arms shipment in 1985. (Adapted from Seech, *Logic in
     Everyday Life: Practical Reasoning Skills*, 89)

☞14 Among the seven children who went to Roger's birthday party, Ellen,
     Katie, and Paul got lice, while Roger, Kevin, Rebecca, and Emma did
     not. At that party, only Ellen, Katie, and Paul wore birthday hats
     rented from Gus's Party Favour Rental Shop. We may conclude from
     this that the lice came from Gus's Party Favour Rental Shop.

  15 The atomic model which emerged from the work of Rutherford and
     others resembled a planetary system, for the force which binds plan-
     ets to the sun obeys the same general form of law as the force which
     binds electrons to the nucleus. Both gravity and electricity decrease
     in strength with the square of distance. From this it follows that the
     particle-electron, attracted by the positive electricity of the nucleus,
     should move around it in the same way that a planet moves around
     the sun. (Barbara Lovett Cline, *Men Who Made a New Physics.*)

13.3 Appraising Analogical Arguments

Analogical arguments may be good or bad. They can be assessed as establishing their conclusions with more or less probability. We assess them by
applying the following six *prima facie* criteria.

"*Prima facie*" means "at first face," or "at face value," or "all else being
equal." As in the case of acceptability conditions and inference indicators,
the following criteria provide guidelines. Familiarity with them should
sound little bells in our heads, telling us to pay closer attention. That the
criteria are *prima facie* tells us that a good analogical argument may violate
some. Nevertheless no good analogical argument will violate all of these

criteria. Nor will an analogical argument that satisfies all of these criteria likely be bad.

13.3.1 Number of Analogues

The more analogues the better. The fewer the analogues the worse.
    Imagine this argument:

> Some of the components for nuclear power plants are built by G. E. Westing-house, which also manufactures toasters. Toasters frequently break down. So we can be practically certain that nuclear power plants will break down also. (Adapted from *Informal Logic Newsletter*, Examples Supplement, 1980)

How many analogues are there here? The answer is one: toaster. Westinghouse makes toasters and nuclear power plant parts. Nuclear power plant parts is the target item, so we don't include it as itself an analogue.
    Of course, toasters frequently break down. So can we think of toaster 1, toaster 2, toaster 3, etc., as we did above with shoes? We could if the target item were another toaster. But it isn't. So the whole class of toasters counts as only one comparison entity.

13.3.2 Number of Shared Attributes

The more shared attributes cited, the better. The fewer shared attributes, the worse.
    If the number of respects in which the things involved are said to be analogous is greater, the more likely it is that they will also share the attribute claimed in the conclusion. In our language, this means that the more shared attributes there are between the comparison entity and the primary subject, the more likely the primary subject will also share the target attribute.
    In the nuclear toaster example, how many shared attributes are there? One: both toasters and certain nuclear power plant parts are made by Westinghouse. Again, not very strong. The greater the number of shared attributes, the stronger the argument.

13.3.3 Variety among the Analogues

The less similar the analogues are to each other, the better.
    The less similar the analogues are to each other, the less likely that all of them are dissimilar to the primary subject. The more alike the analogues are to each other, and the less they are similar to the primary subject, the less likely they will share the target attribute.
    But if they share attributes and are nevertheless dissimilar in other respects, then the dissimilarities between the entities are less likely to be

relevant. Polling a fraternity house about drinking habits may not be generalizable to the population at large. The analogues are too homogeneous, or too dissimilar to the population at large. Polling Playboy subscribers about whether they think pornography is demeaning to women will also likely fail the demand for variety among the analogues, if we hope to generalize from this group to the population at large.

Consider the following information. Suppose your highschool classmates Alicia, Bill, Candace, Doug, and Elizabeth all did well in logic at university. Can you conclude you should do well in logic in university as well? You might reply: "It depends." Your expectation of doing well does, indeed, depend on some other information. Imagine that Alicia, Bill, Candace, Doug, and Elizabeth each had a high school average in the 90s. If so, chances are that it is not merely being classmates that increases their logic skills, but that either having good grades increases logic skills, or the reverse, that logic skills are requisite for good grades. If you did not happen to have a high school average in the 90s, merely being a classmate of people who did will not likely be sufficient.

The more varied the analogues are among themselves, the greater chance the shared attributes are the relevant causal factor in our predicting that the primary subject has the target attribute.

A poll finds that one hundred people are going to vote for the Liberal candidate. We can generalize from this to the population at large if these one hundred people are a random sample. If they are a random sample, then we would expect a lot of differences between them, differences in education, race, sex, age, etc. Only then can we better generalize from this statement.

What if the one hundred people canvassed were at a Liberal Party convention? Then here is a similarity among them. Thus, we cannot generalize from this sample size to the population at large. Why? Because the analogues are not dissimilar. The connection to the target attribute and the primary subject is cut, since the analogues all share something in common (attending a Liberal convention) that the primary subject (Canadian voters in general) do not.

Similarly, if ten students who took a critical thinking course all became experts in their field, can we conclude that you too will become an expert in your field? Well, the prediction will be stronger if these ten people all came from different backgrounds. If so, it is more likely the case that the critical thinking course is what made them successful, rather than something else. If all ten people happened to have had A+ averages throughout their university education, then it is not necessarily the case that the critical thinking course had anything to do with their success. Thus, the mere fact that you are taking a critical thinking course will not guarantee your success. The problem is that the ten analogues were all similar in some other respect. If they are dissimilar in many respects other than the shared attributes, then it is something about those shared attributes rather than anything else that makes us willing to bet on the primary subject having the target attribute.

We can see that the variety-among-the-analogues criterion links to our discussion about variability in sample selection discussed in both chapters 11 and 12. We wish to rule out *3rd variable errors*.

13.3.4 Strength of the Conclusion

The stronger the conclusion, the weaker the argument. Conversely, the weaker the conclusion, the stronger the argument.

What does this mean, and why should we believe it? "An argument is stronger the less susceptible it is to refutation." This makes sense, right? If we say, "You seem to be right, I can't think of anything to refute that," we aren't saying the argument is weak, are we? We're saying that it is a strong argument.

When we're saying the argument is weak, we are saying, "Hey, wait a minute, here's a counter-example that refutes or seriously challenges your claim, at least as put." What do we mean, "as put"? Well, generally, what we're doing when we assess arguments is checking to see if the conclusion is warranted from the premises. So the strength of the conclusion must match the strength of the premises. If the conclusion is put more strongly than the premises warrant, we are entitled to complain.

We can put things strongly, for example:

"There is no way Jones will get elected."

Compare the weaker conclusion:

"It is unlikely that Jones will get elected."

Pointing out that Jones got elected refutes the first strong claim, but not the weaker claim, since something's being unlikely does not prevent it from occurring.

So, the stronger the conclusion, the more susceptible it is to being shown false. The weaker the conclusion, the less susceptible it is to being shown false. And the less likely an argument is to be shown to be false, the stronger it is. The more likely an argument is to be shown false, the weaker it is. Hence, the stronger the conclusion, the weaker the argument. And the weaker the conclusion, the stronger the argument.

In the nuclear toaster example, the conclusion was "We can be practically certain ... " This is pretty strong. As a result, the argument is weaker. In the shoe example, the conclusion was "I expect that they also will last a long time." This is a weaker claim than being "practically certain." Still, it is fairly strong. There isn't any mincing about his expectations. The tone is one of confidence.

Of course, sometimes a strong conclusion is warranted. If so, it is only because it matches the strength of the premises. The argument will always be stronger if the conclusion is weaker. Valid deductive arguments are entitled to use extremely strong conclusions. The strength of the conclusion in inductive arguments (of which analogical arguments are a type) must vary in proportion to the merit of the premises.

A danger exists. A very weak conclusion often makes the argument wishy-washy, or pedestrian. A claim such as "It is possible that some people, anyway, might feel that capital punishment should be at least considered in very, very bad offences," will have lost the audience before the end of the sentence. Strunk and White's classic *The Elements of Style* puts it succinctly:

> *Rather, very, little, pretty* – these are the leeches that infest the pond of prose, sucking the blood of words. The constant use of the adjective *little* (except to indicate size) is particularly debilitating; we should all try to do a little better, we should all be very watchful of this rule, for it is a rather important one and we are pretty sure to violate it now and then. (3rd ed., 73)

Let us suggest, then, the following rule: *Match the strength of the conclusion to the strength of the premises.*

13.3.5 The Number of Disanalogies

For most things, however many similarities we could cite, we can probably cite more differences. Even if we give five analogues and five shared attributes, if we can likewise cite a hundred dissimilarities between the target item and the analogues, it seems more probable that the primary subject does not share the target attribute. Thus, the fewer the number of disanalogies between the target and the analogues, the better the analogical argument.

There seems to be a good number of disanalogies between the toaster manufacture and the nuclear power plant parts manufacture, and so this argument is pretty weak. For example, we wouldn't expect the same workers to be building both toasters and nuclear power plant parts, since, presumably, the amount of education, training, and skill required to construct a toaster will be lower than the amount of education, training, and skill to construct nuclear power plant components. On the other hand, there are few disanalogies in the shoe example, and so this argument is fairly strong.

Justice demands treating like cases alike, and different cases differently. When we are pointing out relevant differences between cases, we are using the criterion concerning the number of disanalogies. Consider the following complaint by a student to his teacher.

"Sue handed in her assignment one day late and was not penalized. I handed in my assignment one day late, and therefore ought not be penalized either."

A professor's task, if she is to avoid the charge of unfairness, is to find a relevant difference. The professor might respond, "Yes, but Sue checked with me about that first, and you did not; therefore these are not like cases, and so different treatment is justified." Or perhaps she will reply, "Yes, but this is the third time you've handed in your assignments late, whereas this is the first time for Sue." The professor's defence is an appeal to a relevant disanalogy.

Consider, next, the following.

Those of us trying to find new ways to end the Atlantic provinces' dependence on federal transfers have seen great promise in the newly developing offshore oil and gas industry. Major deposits are being exploited in Nova Scotia and Newfoundland, and more may be forthcoming. We've been arguing that equalization treats that natural resource endowment inequitably, and retards its development by making the federal government, rather than the provinces, the chief beneficiary of the revenue generated. Mr. [Mike] Harris says Nova Scotia and Newfoundland keeping the royalty revenues generated by the offshore oil and gas industry without reduction in equalization payments is like a welfare recipient winning the lottery and wanting to keep his benefits. The analogy doesn't hold up. The welfare recipient who wins the lottery has something he didn't have before: his lottery winnings. Ken Boessenkool, a national policy analyst, argues in a recent paper that when the Atlantic provinces get their royalty revenues from the sale of offshore oil and gas, they are merely converting an asset they already essentially control – petroleum resources – to a different form, cash. No net new wealth has been created, but a non-renewable resource is depleted. If equalization claws back that revenue, Ottawa is in effect seizing the province's capital, not reducing the federal contribution to the province's annual income. (Brian Lee Crowley, "Harris aims at the wrong target," *National Post*, 23 July 2001, A14)

Mike Harris makes an analogical argument to show why we need not continue federal transfer of payments to Newfoundland and Nova Scotia. After all, they earn royalties on offshore oil and gas industries. And this would be like continuing to give welfare payments to someone who just won a million dollars in the lottery. Crowley argues that the analogy is flawed. There is a disanalogy between welfare recipients winning a lottery and the Atlantic provinces receiving federal transfer payments.

13.3.6 Relevance

An analogical argument can meet all of the above five requirements and still be a poor argument if the comparison attributes are *irrelevant* to the target attribute.

> I think I will get a good grade in this course because I have red hair and my
> last name starts with a consonant and my student number has five digits in it,
> and I like cats, and I've noticed that five red-haired people with last names
> that start with a consonant and student numbers that have five digits who like
> cats, and yet who were dissimilar to each other in other respects, have taken
> this course and did well.

This argument meets all the first five criteria but fails rather miserably in
showing a relevant connection between these characteristics and doing
well in this course. It may be mere coincidence. Notice, also, how some of
the similarities are simply uninformative. It would be like saying "Wait, we
both have noses; let's date!"

An argument based on a single relevant analogy connected with a single
comparison entity will be more cogent than one that points out a dozen
irrelevant points of resemblance between the primary subject and the analogues. The relevance criteria is probably the most crucial of criteria. It,
unlike the others, is clearly a necessary ingredient for a good analogical
argument. Relevance is also important for assessing whether there are any
dissimilarities. The dissimilarities must be relevant dissimilarities to count
against the analogical argument.

Recall the professor's defence of unequal treatment concerning late
assignments. Her defence was that, although she treated the cases differently, the cases themselves were different, and so she is acting within the
bounds of justice. Imagine, however, if she replied to your complaint about
differential treatment "Well, I like Sue; I don't care for you much," or "Sue
is a woman, whereas you are a man," or "Sue is attractive, whereas, you are
plain, at best," or "Sue is white, whereas you are not." These may all be real
differences, but whether they are relevant differences is another thing altogether!

What counts as relevant? The relevant analogies are those that deal with
causally related attributes or circumstances. To find out what counts as
causal connection, please refer back to chapter 11.

Practice

Let us use our new-found skills in assessing Paley's *argument by design*.

> A watch could not assemble itself. The complex arrangements of parts into a
> working watch is possible only because there is a craftsman who designs and
> constructs the watch. In just the same way, the complicated parts of the world
> could not arrange themselves into the natural order. So there must be a
> designer of the world, and that is God.

Recall that there is one analogue, a watch, which is being compared
to the world. The fewer the number of analogues, the worse the argu-

ment. Of course, a watch is simply *an example*. We could cite many such examples. Notice, though, that we cannot cite *natural* examples, such as eyes and ecosystems, since whether they are designed is what the conclusion is trying to establish. The only type of analogue we could cite is something made by humans. So really, the analogue is between human-made articles and nature. Although a watch is merely one example of human-made article, like the number of toasters, it still constitutes only one analogue.

The number of shared attributes is one: things have perfect fit. One shared attribute is not a lot to work with – especially when we have already seen alternative explanations for such fit (11.3.5). After all, we might note that things made by humans require many prototypes; break down in any event; are by and large poorly designed; are made by teamwork; and are often made not for the things themselves, but so that they may serve our ends. Thus, perhaps we should conclude that many botched worlds have occurred prior to this one; that this world is destined to break down, is poorly designed, is made by a team of gods, not a single God; and that we, part of the world, are mere tools of the designer deities. Picking on only one shared attribute over others leaves us open for such *reductio ad absurdum* arguments, as David Hume noted in *Dialogues Concerning Natural Religion*.

With only one analogue there is no variety among analogues, and the conclusion is presented quite strongly. So far, the argument by design isn't doing well. Things get worse.

We can conceive of a number of relevant disanalogies. Watches are crafted on an assembly line or in a jeweller's shop. But much of what we see in nature is birthed, or hatched, or grows from seeds. This seems to be a relevant disanalogy when we are linking one very peculiar part of the world to account for the whole. If we pick another part of the world, say the birthing of a calf, we might conclude the world was not designed, but birthed.

Exercise 13.2

Assess whether the additions to the argument below strengthen, weaken, or leave unaffected the original argument. State which rule justifies your decision. (Number of Analogues, Number of Shared Attributes, Variety Among the Analogues, Strength of the Conclusion, Number of Disanalogies, and Relevance.) (Answers to selected questions are provided in Appendix 1.)

1 The par 3 fourth hole at Avondale golf course was 155 yards over water. The last three times Annika played, she used an eight iron and came up short. This time she decided to use more club, figuring that the hole really played 165 yards.

a. Suppose she came up short only the last time she played.

b. Suppose the last times she came up short, the wind was in her face, but this time, there was no wind.

c. Suppose the last times she came up short, the wind was in her face, and the wind was in her face this time as well.

d. Suppose she had taken lessons since the last time she played, and has been hitting the ball better as a result.

☞ 2 Heartened by their university's football team winning their last four games, Bert and Ernie decide to bet their money that their team will win the next game too.

a. Suppose that, since the last game, their university team's star running back was injured in practice and will be out for the remainder of the season.

b. Suppose that two of the last four games were played away and that two were home games.

Suppose that, just before the game, it is announced that a member of the university's Chemistry Department has been awarded a Nobel Prize.

d. Suppose that their university team had won their last six games instead of only four.

e. Suppose that it has rained hard during each of the four preceding games, and rain is in the forecast for the next game too.

f. Suppose that Bert and Ernie decide to bet that their team will win by a margin of twenty-eight points. (Adapted from Copi and Burgess-Jackson, *Informal Logic*, 201)

3 An investor has purchased one hundred shares of oil stock every December for the past five years. In every case the value of the stock has appreciated about 15 per cent a year, and it has paid regular dividends of about 8 per cent a year on the price at which she bought it. This December she decides to buy another hundred shares of oil stock, reasoning that she will probably receive modest earnings while watching the value of her new purchase increase over the years.

a. Suppose that she had always purchased stock in eastern oil companies before and plans to purchase stock in an eastern oil company this year too.

b. Suppose that she had purchased oil stocks every December for the past fifteen years instead of only five.

c. Suppose that her previous purchases of oil stock had been in Arabian, Texan, and Albertan oil companies.

d. Suppose that she learns of a new and vast discovery of oil off of Newfoundland.

4 Penelope did poorly in three previous exams. Consequently, she went into her next exam confident she would do poorly again.

a. Suppose that her previous three exams were in sciences, and this exam was in English.

b. Suppose that she did poorly in her high school exams as well.

c. Suppose her previous exams were in biology, psychology, and English, and the next exam was in philosophy.

d. Suppose that, rather than being confident she would do poorly, she merely suspected she would do poorly.

e. Suppose it rained on the days of the previous exams, and rained the day of her next exam as well.

f. Suppose that her previous exams occurred during a term when she had been extremely ill and had missed many classes and readings, but that this next exam was in a new term during which time she was 100 per cent better.

☞ 5 Although she was bored by the last few foreign films she saw, Charlene agrees to see another one this evening fully expecting to be bored again.

a. Suppose that Charlene also was bored by the last few American movies she saw.

b. Suppose that the star of this evening's film (married to another popular actor) has recently been caught with a prostitute.

c. Suppose that the last few foreign films were by an Italian director, and that tonight's film is also by an Italian director.

d. Suppose that Charlene ate peanut butter during the last movies and fell asleep, but this night refuses to eat peanut butter.

e. Suppose that tonight's foreign film is in English, whereas the previous films were subtitled.

f. Suppose that the previous movies were Italian, Polish, and Swedish, and tonight's film is German.

g. Suppose she went to the previous films with boring dates, but tonight's film is with her friends. (Copi and Burgess-Jackson, *Informal Logic*, 201)

6 William needed to make a five-foot putt to win the club championship. On the basis that William has won the last two club championships in a row, Martin bets that William will indeed sink the putt.

a. Suppose that the previous year's club championships had not been televised, whereas this year's club championship is.

b. Suppose that William's eyesight had deteriorated over the last year and he has not gotten a new prescription.

c. Suppose he has made every putt inside eight feet so far today.

d. Suppose William won the previous championships despite three-putting the last green.

e. Suppose William had won only one club championship, rather than two.

f. Suppose the two previous club championships had been won at the nine-hole Vista Bay course with a different field. This year's club championship is at Glen Abbey.

☞ 7 Kirby's father was scheduled for surgery on Monday. "Don't worry, Dad," Kirby told him, "I've known three people who have undergone surgery and everything turned out great."

a. Suppose the three surgeries to which Kirby alluded were for gall bladder, kidney stone, and knee surgery, whereas his father was undergoing open-heart surgery.

b. Suppose the three surgeries to which Kirby referred were performed by Dr. Quimby, and that she was also performing the surgery on his father.

c. Suppose that Kirby knew of only one other person who had surgery.

d. Suppose that the other surgeries were performed on Wednesday.

e. Suppose that the three surgeries were performed by different surgeons.

f. Suppose that the three surgeries to which Kirby referred, as well as the surgery Kirby's father was to undergo, were all for prostate cancer.

Exercise 13.3

Assess the arguments below using our six criteria. (Number of Analogues, Number of Shared Attributes, Strength of the Conclusion, Number of Disanalogies, Variety Among the Analogues, and Relevance.) (Answers to selected questions provided in appendix 1.)

1 At hearings in 1986, President Reagan apparently was unable to remember whether he had approved a 1985 shipment of arms by Israel to Iran. Supporters of the president tried to defend him against claims that he was either lying or becoming senile. One such argument claimed that since few people could remember what they had for lunch on the first day of September 1985, it was not reasonable to expect President Reagan to remember whether he had approved the arms shipment in 1985.

☞ 2 Racists violate the principle of equality by giving greater weight to the interests of members of their own race when there is a clash between their interests and the interests of those of another race. Sexists violate the principle of equality by favouring the interests of their own sex. Similarly, speciesists allow the interests of their own species to override the greater interests of members of other species. The pattern is identical in each case.

3 It is as wrong to force a woman to go full term against her wishes as it is to force a patient to undergo surgery – even if the surgery, say a liver transplant, can save the life of someone else – say a famous violinist. (Adapted from Thompson, "A Defense of Abortion").

4 While he was attending a group of drug addicts at a sanitarium in Berlin in 1927, it occurred to Dr. Manfred Sakel to try insulin on them. This hormone promotes the utilization of sugar in the body, and on theoretical grounds he believed its effect should relieve the paradox by which a slave of the drug habit requires larger and larger doses of what is essentially a poison. He hoped that, through the insulin, he might free the victim of dependence on morphine. Some of the men reacted to the insulin with convulsions, but most of them broke into perspiration and lapsed into deep sleep. When they came out of their seizure, or were awakened after a few hours of coma, their conduct surprised the doctor. He noticed that the morbid fears and anxieties which habitually oppress addicts had diminished and odd notions of persecution, jumpy nerves, and other psychotic symptoms were gone. This unexpected outcome set Dr. Sakel to thinking. If insulin improved the mental climate of the drug-crazed men, what would it do for the frankly insane? (George W. Gray, *The Advancing Front of Medicine.*)

☞ 5 The libertarians would grant each of us the liberty to pursue our own interests without interference. I don't know what liberty we can pursue if homeless, hungry, and cold. It's like they're telling us no one should interfere with the runners of a race. Absolutely, we applaud that, but they forget the racers aren't starting on equal terms. A fair race is one in which everyone begins at the starting line, not scattered all over the race by a lottery of fortune. The role of egalitarianism is to right this injustice, to have everyone begin at the same place, with truly an equal opportunity.

6 Egalitarians would have us believe that if we don't get an equal share of the resources, we have a right to cry foul. They picture the allocation of resources being due to a central distributer, like a giant cake cutter. A cake cutter, in doling out pieces of the cake to children at a birthday party, ensures that every child gets an equal piece. And since we deem that the model of fairness for birthday parties, we should also deem it a model of fairness for world resources. The problem is goods are not distributed in terms of a central distributer. (Nozick, *Anarchy, State, and Utopia*, 149)

☞ 7 Re: bill to remove cap on electrical rates ... This past sitting of the house should have passed a bill removing the amount that landlords can raise residential rents, because they are dealing with the same costs as Maritime Electric. I would think it would be unfair not to give them the same benefit. (Wolf Smith, letter to the editor, *Guardian*, 17 May 2001, A7)

8 Can you imagine what the reaction would be if governments started advertising, "You should drink more before you drive." Or, "Light up another one before you go." But that's what they do with gambling, isn't it? Pump some more money into the abyss. The very least we could do is to take some of these ill-gotten gains and use them to help some of the people who have been wounded by the VLTs. (Peter Gzowski, "Luck is not a lady when it comes to VLTs," *Globe and Mail*, 19 May 2001, F3)

9 The union [Canadian Auto Workers, in defence of bus drivers in Vancouver who have been on strike for four months] also claims part-time workers are less professional in their attitude toward their work, and provide a lower quality of service. When I raised this line of reasoning with friends who are part-time doctors, nurses, teachers and lawyers, their scorn was instantaneous and blistering. We entrust other important jobs in society to part-timers; there is no reason why operating a public vehicle should be excluded. (Anne Giardini, "Driving need for part-time work," *National Post*, 24 July 2001, B1)

☞10 Brigitte Boisselier, director of the biotech company Clonaid, said there is a demand for cloning, especially among infertile and gay couples, as well as middle-aged single women who want to have a baby. The real issue is freedom of choice, she argues. "Today, nobody will tell you that you shouldn't mix your genes with this person or that person, you have the right to choose," Ms. Boisselier said in a phone interview. "So if you choose not to mix your genes but have a baby with only your genes because you're a 45-year old single woman, why should people tell you not to do that?" (Michelle MacAfee, "Cloning worries 88.9% of Canadians, poll finds," *National Post*, 20 August 2001, A4)

11 Among the seven children who went to Roger's birthday party, Ellen, Katie, and Paul, got lice, while Roger, Kevin, Rebecca, and Emma did not. At that party, only Ellen, Katie, and Paul wore birthday hats rented from Gus's Party Favour Rental Shop. We may conclude from this that the lice came from Gus's Party Favour Rental Shop.

☞12 University students should not be required to attend class in order to pass a course. When you enroll in a class and pay your tuition, that gives you the right to attend the class. But it doesn't mean you should be required to attend class. It's like buying a season ticket to watch the symphony. When you buy the ticket, that gives you the right to attend every concert if you so wish; but it certainly doesn't give the symphony the right to require you to attend every performance. Likewise, paying your tuition for a class gives you the right to attend, but it doesn't give your professor the right to require you to attend.

13 The Supreme Court has decided that it is a constitutional right for a doctor to terminate medical treatment that prolongs the life of a terminally ill or brain-dead person, as long as the doctor acts according

to the wishes of that person (*Curzan vs. Director, Missouri Department of Health*, 497 U.S. 261). Therefore, the Supreme Court should decide that assisting someone to commit suicide, someone who is terminally ill or in great suffering, as Dr. Kevorkian does, is a constitutionally protected right (*Compassion in Dying vs. State of Washington*).

14 Taxation of earnings from labor is on par with forced labor. Some persons find this claim obviously true; taking the earnings of n hours of labor is like taking n hours from the person; it is like forcing the person to work n hours for another's purpose. Others find the claim absurd. But even these, if they object to forced labor, would oppose forcing unemployed hippies to work for the benefit of the needy.

    ... The man who chooses to work longer to gain an income more than sufficient for his basic needs prefers some extra goods or services to the leisure and activities he could perform during those possible non-working hours; whereas the man who chooses not to work the extra time prefers the leisure activities to the extra goods or services he could acquire by working more. Given this, if it would be illegitimate for a tax system to seize some of a man's leisure (forced labor) for the purpose of serving the needy, how can it be legitimate for a tax system to seize some of a man's goods for that purpose? (Nozick, *Anarchy, State and Utopia*, 169–70)

15 The concept of responsibility is particularly weak when behavior is traced to genetic determiners. We may admire beauty, grace and sensitivity, but we do not blame a person because he is ugly, spastic, or color blind. Less conspicuous forms of genetic endowment nevertheless cause trouble. Individuals presumably differ, as species differ, in the extent to which they respond aggressively or are reinforced when they effect aggressive damage or are affected by sexual reinforcement. Are they, therefore, equally responsible for controlling their aggressive or sexual behavior, and is it fair to punish them to the same extent? If we do not punish a person for a club foot, should we punish him for being quick to anger or highly susceptible to sexual reinforcement? The issue has recently been raised by the possibility that many criminals show an anomaly in their chromosomes. The concept of responsibility offers little help. The issue is controllability. We cannot change genetic defects by punishment; we can work only through genetic measures which operate on a much longer time scale. What must be changed is not the responsibility of autonomous man but the conditions, environmental or genetic, of which a person's behavior is a function. (Skinner, *Beyond Freedom and Dignity*, 75)

16 By what conceivable standard can the policy of price-fixing be a crime, when practiced by businessmen, but a public benefit, when practiced by the government? There are many industries in peacetime – trucking, for instance – whose prices are fixed by the government. If price-fixing is harmful to competition, to industry, to pro-

duction, to consumers, to the whole economy and to the "public interest" – as the advocates of the antitrust laws have claimed – then how can that same harmful policy become beneficial in the hands of the government? Since there is no rational answer to this question, I suggest that you question the economic knowledge, the purpose and the motives of the champions of antitrust. (Rand, *Capitalism: The Unknown Ideal*, 52)

17 President Truman, regarding the cessation of atmospheric testing of nuclear weapons, stated: "We should never have stopped it. Where would we be today if Thomas Edison had been forced to stop his experiments with the electric bulb?" (Engel, *Analyzing Informal Fallacies*, 120)

13.4 Refutation by Logical Analogy

13.4.1 Form

We have been examining the uses of analogical arguments. From known similarities, we conclude an extra similarity is to be expected. But there is another use of analogy, and it concerns *refutation*.

We successfully refute an argument if we can demonstrate that the conclusion does not follow from the stated premises. We can do this by giving an argument *of exactly the same form* as the target argument, but whose premises are known to be true and yet whose conclusion is known to be false or absurd. *By analogy*, we have shown that the original argument, since it shares the same form, is thereby also to be rejected.

Imagine that Jones utters the following argument:

> If we allow strip clubs, we will allow women the freedom of choice to elect alternative means of supporting themselves. Surely we don't want to forbid women the opportunity of supporting themselves. That's why I'm in favour of allowing strip clubs.

We could respond to such a person that she has committed the fallacy of affirming the consequent, or, worse, "That's an A.C.!" Chances are this revelation won't work, since we would have to explain what's up with A.C.s. A more effective rebuttal is to illustrate the loopiness of A.C.s by giving an argument that takes the same form, but switch the content so that it is an obvious case of true premises and an absurd conclusion.

For example,

> "That's just like saying, 'If I'm pregnant, then I'm a woman. Look, I'm a woman (or you don't want to deny me the right of being a woman, do you?). Therefore I'm pregnant'."

The above works to highlight what's wrong with A.C.s, but may be too far removed from the original case in Jones's opinion. Therefore, it is preferable to find a refutation by logical analogy that more closely approximates the argument we wish to refute. For example, we might reply to Jones with the following:

> Your argument takes the same form as the following: "If we legalize hired assassinations, this will increase legalized employment figures. Surely you're not against increasing employment figures are you? That's why I'm in favour of legalized assassinations."

The discussion wouldn't end there, presumably. Jones will likely point out a relevant disanalogy. Stripping, Jones might argue, doesn't harm anyone the way assassination does. If so, would the refutation by logical analogy fail? That's debatable. The original argument pointed out, roughly, that legalizing something would increase the number of legal activities. This is trivially true, so uninformative. Jones's second argument focuses on the reasons for legal sanctions, and claims that while assassination fits those criteria, stripping does not. The refutation by logical analogy helped prompt Jones to this better form of argument. The original version is to be abandoned.

Typically, when we are confronted with a refutation by logical analogy, we will generally see the following sort of phrases:

> You might just as well say ...
> The same argument proves ...
> This is about as logical as arguing that ...
> I could use the same reasoning to claim that ...
> Using the same logic, one might conclude that ...
> The same methodology would lead to the conclusion that ...

13.4.2 Assessment

Refutation by logical argument is successful if and only if

1 The two arguments actually have the same form
2 The refuting argument has true premises and a false conclusion.

Consider the following argument written as a letter to the editor in 1999 over the Supreme Court ruling on native fishing and the subsequent retaliation of non-native fishers:

> Precisely because the natives have been bullied by non-natives to the point where violence seems immanent, Dhaliwal suggests to the natives that they

"voluntarily" stop fishing, despite the supreme court's ruling. Without "voluntary" withdrawal, Dhaliwal will close the native fishery on the basis of "public safety." This is similar to the recommendation that you "voluntarily" hand muggers your money, since the muggers may get nasty if you continue to refuse. Canadians are ready to fly to other countries to show how little we tolerate such bullying tactics. Why do we condone it here?

The argument being refuted takes the following form: "Refusing to comply with the non-native demands makes the non-natives cranky, hence comply with non-native demands." The refuting argument takes the identical form: "Refusing to comply with muggers makes the muggers nasty, hence comply with muggers." Since the conclusion in the second is ludicrous, logical consistency has it that it must likewise be ludicrous in the first form.

Ann Landers well understands the structure of refutation by logical analogy

Dear Ann: I live in North Carolina and I sure wish you would quit trying to put the tobacco industry out of business. A lot of folks down here depend on it for a living. Don't you know tobacco is a gift from God? He gave us the plant to be used and enjoyed. So lay off, lady. You are getting to be a real bore. – *Raleigh Reader*

Dear Raleigh: Your argument is ridiculous. God also gave us poison ivy. – Ann Landers (*Honolulu Advertiser*, 24 July 1986, C4)

Exercise 13.4

Are the following refutations by logical analogy good or bad? Do they have the same form? Are the premises unequivocally true yet the conclusion ludicrously false? (Answers to selected questions provided in Appendix 1.)

☞ 1 The creationists frequently stress that we cannot explain everything. This comes oddly from a group that many conclude can explain nothing. It would be as foolish to discard evolutionary theory today because it cannot explain everything as it would be to disband the medical establishment because it cannot cure the common cold. (John A. Moore, "Countering the Creationists," 16)

2 Until 1909, no one in Lower Binfield believed that human beings would ever learn to fly. The official doctrine was that if God had meant us to fly He'd have given us wings. Uncle Ezekiel couldn't help retorting that if God had meant us to ride He'd have given us wheels. (George Orwell, *Coming up for Air.*)

☞ 3 In your thought-provoking cover story about nuclear warfare ... you said, "Deterrence has worked for 38 years." Has it? I could use the same reasoning to claim that my house has never been struck by lightning because I painted a face on the roof that frightens the lightning away. If something has never happened, we have no way of knowing what prevents it from happening. It is dangerous to award nuclear buildup a credit it may not deserve. (George M. Hieber, letter to the editor, *Newsweek*, 19 December 1983, 7)

4 You claim we should not legalize marijuana, since most cocaine users started off taking marijuana. We could just as easily conclude that we should make milk illegal, since most cocaine users started off drinking milk.

5 I can't prove that God *doesn't* exist, but to think I should therefore embrace the belief that God *does* exist is as inane as believing that an invisible monster with magical powers of avoiding detection lives under my bed merely on the grounds that I can't prove otherwise.

☞ 6 Q: Hypothetically, would it be unethical to place a security firm's lawn signs around my front yard even though I have not installed its security system? These fake "caveats" would discourage intruders, and the security firm would get free advertising for its product. So who's hurt?

A: I do consider this unethical. The same dubious "who loses?" justification can be trotted out by anyone who, for example, vaults the subway turnstile or hooks into cable TV without paying ... If everyone followed your free-ride example and refrained from paying, there'd be no money to finance subway service – plus, my imaginary Aunt Minna would injure herself severely trying to hurdle the turnstile in heels and a demure suit in a nice cotton-poly blend. (Randy Cohen, "Everyday ethics – Fake guard signs hurt home-security industry," *Chronicle-Herald*, 16 June 2001, E6)

7 Suppose that by paying 250 dollars you could go into the largest and most exclusive department store in town and pick out and take home anything you could carry away with you. You would have access to the finest silks, precious jewels, handworked bracelets of gold and platinum, fabulous clothes by the best designers in the world. It would be foolish to the point of imbecility if you paid your money, walked in, and picked out a piece of bubble gum. Well, that's what many college students do, in effect. They pay a nominal amount of money, and by doing so they gain access to some of the greatest treasures of the intellect in the world. Merely by asking, they can discover things that people laboured for years to find out. Just by going to class, they can receive the outcome of years of thought and effort of the most outstanding thinkers and scientists the human race has produced. Do they take advantage of this? Often they do not. They merely want to know which courses are the easiest ones, which don't have to be taken, and what are the minimum requirements for graduation. For their money they are offered a fortune, but they choose a piece of mental bubble gum. (Munson, *The Way of Words: An Informal Logic*, 357)

8 In a courtroom in Provo, Utah, Tom Green is on trial for polygamy. The husband of five and father of 29 has been charged with four counts of bigamy and one count of criminal nonsupport ... But it is hard to believe that any jury will send a man to prison because his family arrangements are – to use the current term – nontraditional. This is 2001, even in Utah, and if there is one thing modern Americans are supposed to be clear on by now, it is that we do not punish people because their household doesn't resemble Ozzie and Harriet's ... Some children have only one parent at home, Samson [Cindi Samson, director of the elementary division] explained to a reporter. "There may be two fathers, two mothers, the mother may not have custody, it could be a grandmother." By now, everybody knows that Heather has two mommies. There are not many precincts left where anyone would refuse to recognize them as a genuine family. Why should the reaction be any different if Heather's friend has five mommies and a daddy? ... [The American Civil Liberties Union] believes that the state must not interfere with the intimate union of consenting adults. What difference does it make if these adults are two gay men or a "fundamentalist" Mormon and his five wives? ... No one who supports same-sex marriages can logically oppose the legalization of polygamy. If it is bigotry to insist that marriage be restricted to people of the opposite sex, it must be bigotry to insist that it be restricted to two people. In some ways, the case for plural marriage is even stronger than the case for same-sex marriage: In much of the world, after all, polygamy is both lawful and common. (Jeff Jacoby, "Why should the state have the right to punish polygamy?" *Chronicle-Herald*, 19 May 2001, C3)

9 If the Olympic selection committee were to favour Beijing – Beijing, for heaven's sake! – over Toronto because of Lastman's joke, we ought to conclude that the world has gone truly mad. It would be like parents sending their daughter to a boarding school run by Jack the Ripper, because of their concern that a boarding school run by Jerry Lee Lewis might be a bad influence on her. (George Jonas, "Milosevic heading to wrong court," *Guardian*, 29 June 2001, A6)

10 Scientists, testing a hypothesis, watch for two types of errors: In the first case, of rejecting a true statement as false, and in the second, of accepting (or failing to reject) a false statement as true. To use a real world example, suppose a company, seeking to deter employee theft, subjects its entire workforce to a lie detector test. The lie detector is, let us imagine, accurate 90% of the time, meaning it has a one in 10 chance either of mistaking an honest answer for a lie (Type II), or of failing to identify a lie when it is told one (Type I). But if even 10% of workers are stealing from the company, then the odds are that as many honest employees will fail that test as thieves. User fees are intended to pose much the same kind of test: In place of "Are you a

thief?" they ask, in effect, "Are you a hypochondriac?" But, like the lie detector, they are prone to the two types of errors. That some are willing to pay a fee to see their doctor does not prove they are truly sick; that others are unwilling or unable to pay does not mean that they aren't. (Andrew Coyne, "User fees are an error, of a type," *National Post*, 25 June 2001, A15)

☞11 Reagan's Strategic Defence Initiative was an "act of folly," a "dream" that "cannot be achieved." Worse, the whole scam was a "telling commentary on his Presidential style," according to Philip Geyelin in *The Washington Post* in 1984: "Reagan had no proposal worked out when he first floated the idea almost casually ... He had only a fatuous, personal vision of a nuclear-free world." Just as President Kennedy had no proposal worked out, only a fatuous personal vision of putting a man on the moon within the decade. (Mark Steyn, "Missile defence is hardly pie in the sky," *National Post*, 30 July 2001, A14)

12 Is the American government supposed to be in the business of designing computer operating systems? Should every complaint from a company like Kodak – which said Microsoft was giving its own image software precedence over the film company's version – result in a press conference by some senator speculating about the antitrust implications? That appears to be the kind of never-never land we're in at the moment. Maybe U.S. legislators should broaden their reach a bit: Perhaps they should entertain complaints from Samsung or Mitsubishi about how their car stereos aren't being included in vehicles from General Motors as often as they should be, or Starbucks could lodge some kind of grievance with the U.S. Justice Department about how their Venti cups don't fit into the cup holders in the new Extinction SUV. Shouldn't the car maker be forced to provide standard cup holders that fit everyone else's cups? That's absurd, obviously. And yet to some, it seems perfectly sane to police the placement of specific icons on the Windows desktop – icons that are, after all, simply shortcuts to software programs or devices. Putting an AOL icon on the desktop does not mean users automatically have access to the on-line service, just as the MSN logo on the desktop does nothing to force anyone to use Microsoft's service. (Matthew Ingram, "Mom! Microsoft's oppressing me again!" *Globe and Mail*, 15 August 2001, B7)

☞13 Some of the most damaging testimony about the day-to-day workings of the witch-hunter is provided by a German Jesuit who had himself assisted the Inquisition but later turned against it. Friedrich von Spee's *Cautio Criminalis (Precautions for Prosecutors)*, published in 1631, was a major attempt to oppose the therapeutic program of the Church against alleged heretics. Spee, who had acted as confessor to hundreds of witches burned at the stake, writes: "Previously I never thought of doubting that there were many witches in the world; now,

however, when I examine the public record, I find myself believing
that there are hardly any." As to the use of confessions, Father Spee
remarks: "... the result is the same whether she [the accused] confesses or not. If she confesses, her guilt is clear: she is executed. All
recantation is in vain. If she does not confess, the torture is repeated
– twice, thrice, four times ... She can never clear herself. The investigating body would feel disgraced if it acquitted a woman; once
arrested and in chains, she has to be guilty, by fair means or foul."
The person accused of mental illness is in much the same position. If
he admits to the signs and symptoms of mental illness imputed to
him by his denouncers, it proves that he is mentally ill: he recognizes
the gravity of his illness and the need for its treatment in a mental
institution. If he denies the "illness," it only proves that he lacks
"insight" into his condition; this, even more than confession of illness, is thought to justify involuntary confinement and treatment.
The basic similarity between the two situations is that the accusers
can do no wrong, and the accused can do no right. For the victim,
admission and denial of both witchcraft and mental illness lead to
the same destructive end. As for the authorities, their attitude is illustrated by Father Spee's observation that "If the prisoner dies under
so much torture, they say the Devil broke his neck." Just so with the
hospitalized mental patient today. If he regresses in the mental hospital, it is because he suffers from "incurable" chronic schizophrenia;
if his back is broken by convulsions induced by electroshock, it is
because "there is no medical treatment without risk." (Szasz, *The
Manufacture of Madness*, 30–1)

14 Oh, what on earth is Allan Rock on about now? Banishing "mild" and
"light" descriptions from cigarette packages, as if looming photographs of diseased lung tissue and discoloured teeth hadn't got the
bloody point across already. This is such a bizarre and protracted
campaign, for a government that has it within its power to just ban
the stupid things and be done with it. I can't even imagine a compa-
rable scenario in the history of free enterprise and public health. "All
right, you can sell chicken with salmonella, but we get to tax it, and
you have to festoon the package with pictures of people vomiting."
"Go ahead, sell angel dust at the corner store, but we want warning
labels on it about psychotic derangement and criminal violence." "Of
course you can distribute bottled water filled with ant poison, but we
absolutely must insist that you depict people clutching their stom-
achs in agony on the label. And we get to tax it." (Patricia Pearson,
"Don't take the war on cigarettes lightly," *National Post*, 15 August
2001, A14)

15 Compare this to morphine. We don't allow morphine on the street
but we permit it in the doctor's arsenal for the treatment of pain.

Imagine the uproar if we made morphine illegal. There is no logic in treating marijuana differently. (Ellen Goodman, "Blow some of that smoke down here," *National Post*, 8 August 2001, A15)

☞ 16 You observe that "the marijuana industry is alive and well in Canada. Despite decades of judicial effort to stamp it out, marijuana is perhaps more readily available than ever." This is true. Of course, theft is also alive and well in Canada, despite judicial efforts to stamp it out. As is murder. Is this a reasonable argument to legalize theft and murder? If not, then why is it relevant to whether or not marijuana should be legalized? (Paul Ward, letter to the editor, *National Post*, 17 August 2001, A15)

17 [Background: Trusler has accused Blake of believing that malevolence has no cause. Trusler's retort is that malevolence does have a cause: envy. Blake refutes Trusler's argument using an analogy. Claiming envy is the cause of malevolence is like arguing that poverty is the cause of theft. In actual fact, though, poverty *can't* be the *cause* of theft, because many people live in poverty without engaging in theft.] But Want of Money & the Distress of A Thief can never be alleged as the Cause of his Thieving, for many honest people endure greater hardships with Fortitude. We must therefore seek the Cause elsewhere than in want of Money, for that is the Miser's passion, not the Thief's. (William Blake, in a letter to Dr John Trusler, August 23rd, 1799)

18 Much as the moon influences the tides and sunspot activity can disturb radio transmissions, so do the positions of the planets have an important influence on formation of the human personality. Modern science is constantly confirming the interconnectedness of all things. Is it any surprise that distant events, such as the movement of the planets and the decisions people make, should be connected? (Carey, *A Beginner's Guide to Scientific Method*, 120)

19 The problem of the winner losing and the loser winning in a democratic political system is a profound one. Professor Paul Freund of the Harvard Law School aptly summed up this problem when he testified: "The one objective that any democratic electoral system must achieve is to avoid the election of a candidate who secures fewer popular votes than an opposing candidate. The electoral college system offers no assurance of this, and in fact three times in our history the election went to a candidate other than the winner in the popular count. It has been said that this record is a good one, showing that in 93 percent of our elections the popular winner was the actual winner. This is like boasting that 93 percent of the planes leaving Washington airport arrive at their destination." (Longley and Braun, *The Politics of Electoral College Reform*, 20–1)

Exercise 13.5

Examine the following arguments. Now provide a refutation by logical analogy. To be successful, you need to provide an argument with the same form, with true premises and an obviously false or absurd conclusion. (Sample answers to select questions are provide in Appendix 1.)

 1 Sixty-five per cent of rapists view pornography. Therefore we must abolish pornography.
☞ 2 Breast enlargements are unnatural and therefore unattractive.
 3 Unlike the Bible, Shakespeare's works are not divine. Therefore nothing in them can have any worth.
☞ 4 We've always used pesticides, so there's no reason we should stop.
 5 Abortion is wrong. Take responsibility for your actions. Don't whine to me if you got pregnant. One consents to pregnancy because one had sex.
☞ 6 Teachers who go on strike are just plain wrong. The reason can be put in five words: It is against the law.
 7 A ban on handguns won't deter crime. After all, making drugs illegal doesn't work.
 8 If we prevent the scientific advances in genetic research, we might as well ban the scientific advances of medicine.
☞ 9 Just as alcohol and tobacco are legal, we should legalize the use of marijuana.
 10 Don't believe what your teacher says. Keegstra taught students in Alberta that the Holocaust never happened.

Part Six

Fallacies

Fallacies

Problems with Premises • Problems with Relevance • Problems with Sufficiency

Despite wide variety of content, argument structure itself is fairly limited. For this reason we can begin to see problematic argument forms more readily. This chapter will offer a catalogue of problematic argument forms, called *fallacies*. Fallacies are common ways in which our reasoning patterns go astray.

Our focus in this chapter will be on *informal fallacies*, as opposed to *formal fallacies*. *Formal fallacies* are violations of logic. We have already been introduced (10.5) to affirming the consequent, denying the antecedent, and the disjunctive fallacy. Whether an argument is valid or invalid concerns merely the *logic* of the argument, and not the *truth* of the premises and conclusion, that is, *soundness* of the argument. If an argument is invalid, a fallacy has been committed. This type of fallacy, then, is what we mean by "formal fallacies."

The fallacies we will look at in this chapter, however, are called *informal fallacies*. They are mistakes that people commonly make. But it is important to realize that their occurrence does not mean the argument is invalid. Nor, for that matter, does the commission of these fallacies necessarily mean the argument is to be rejected. Simply, they should act as warning signs. They give us reason to challenge the argument. Although they will often provide sufficient reason to reject the argument, further reflection may deem the argument worth accepting. Just as inference indicators were neither sufficient nor necessary to alert us to the fact than an argument was present, the detection of the following fallacies is neither sufficient nor necessary to show that we should reject the argument. They tell us to investigate further, or to pass the burden of proof back to the arguer.

One last word of caution should be raised: Sometimes the use of these fallacies is a very effective part of persuasion or rhetoric. Advertisers, lawyers, and politicians are adept at using them to their advantage. And in certain contexts, it seems perfectly legitimate to do so! Our goal is to become familiar with them so that we can avoid committing them unawares, avoid being misled by them, and, less often and always with caution, see when it suits our purpose to use them.

We shall divide our list of fallacies into three groups: *problems with premises, problems with relevance,* and *problems with sufficiency.* Problems with premises will be fallacies that have more to do with the premises themselves. These shall be distinguished from the unacceptability conditions introduced in chapter 7. Problems with relevance will be common argument forms that detract from the issue at hand. They will often concern rebuttals, or arguments aimed at defeating another argument. If these rebuttals are themselves irrelevant to the merits or demerits of the targeted argument, we have grounds to reject the rebuttal. Problems with sufficiency will focus on argument patterns that fail to provide enough support to warrant the conclusion.

Fallacies of the first sort will include *equivocation, question begging, leading questions, false dichotomy,* and *slippery slope.* Fallacies of the second sort will include *red herring, ad hominem, emotional appeals, bandwagon,* and *straw man.* Fallacies of the third group include *false cause, person-who, appeal to ignorance, genetic fallacy,* and *composition and division.*

These groupings are approximations. Certain fallacies may fit another group equally well. We shall point out some of these cases as we go. The important point is not the grouping itself, but our ability to recognize when these fallacies occur in arguments.

14.1 Problems with Premises

We have seen problems with premises in chapter 6. We have reason to dismiss claims based on improper appeals to authority and poor testimony. Likewise we have reason to dismiss arguments that contain internally inconsistent premises, or premises that are *a priori* false, or premises that are as contentious as the conclusion itself, or arguments that rely on contentious assumptions. Having become more familiar with the logical structure of propositions themselves – for example, conditional and disjunctive statements – we can introduce a few other problems with premises. We shall examine *equivocation, question begging, leading questions, false dichotomy,* and *slippery slope* fallacies.

14.1.1 Equivocation

Most words have more than one meaning. This fact may cause ambiguity in our arguments. There is a form of fallacious reasoning that indiscriminately uses both senses of an ambiguous term. It is called *equivocation.* When we confuse the different meanings of a single word or phrase, and use it in different senses in the same context, we are using that word or phrase or concept equivocally.

An argument that suffers from equivocation will look like a valid argument, *but only when mistranslated.* When properly translated, arguments suffering from equivocation will take the form of an invalid argument because of disjointed inferences.

Consider, for example, the following:

1 Only man is rational
2 No woman is a man
3 Therefore no woman is rational

Here, "man" in premise 1 refers to *Homo sapiens*. The "man" in the second premise is really a different concept altogether; it refers to male. Because the symbol "man" is really a different word in each premise, there can be no logical connection between the two premises. Hence the conclusion cannot logically follow from the premises, and failing to see this is committing the fallacy of equivocation.

Whenever you see the same word or phrase repeated in different senses, be on guard for equivocation. Nevertheless, equivocation may occur without repeating the actual word, phrase or concept. Consider this one line joke:

Have you ever seen a house fly?

If we answer yes, we are assumed strange for seeing houses move on their own through the air. If we answer no, we are equally regarded as strange for never having encountered one of the most common insects.

Also, the word "it" or "that" may refer back to the term being used equivocally. So merely finding no term or phrase repeated is not evidence by itself that equivocation isn't taking place. Consider this rather common philosophic argument.

We have rights to property
I have no property
Therefore society is obliged to give it to me

In this argument, "property" occurs twice, and the pronoun in the conclusion refers to property as well, but there is no equivocation on property. One might think of property as land and one might also think of having property claims on objects, for example a book, or a car. In essence, though, both are instances of the general term property, and thus we cannot complain of equivocation on this point. There is equivocation here, however, and it is on "rights."

There are two sorts of rights: positive and negative. A negative right is to not have your possessions taken from you. Property rights and liberty rights and the right not to be killed or harmed are negative rights in this sense. No one has a right to kill you, harm you, or take what is yours. Positive rights, however, are things that are to be given to you if you don't have them. The right to vote, for example is a positive right under certain political structures. I have the right to be supplied a vote. In Canada, access to free health care is also deemed a positive right, although constantly at threat of erosion.

Now, if we lend the plausibility of a right to basic needs by recognizing that we certainly have a negative right to these needs, it doesn't follow that we also have a positive right, so the equivocation occurs in confusing the different senses of "right."

By the way, rights and obligations go hand in hand. If you have a right to x, someone has a duty or obligation concerning x (to leave it alone or to give it to you). Thus, when the conclusion speaks of the *obligation* of society, this is where the equivocation on right occurs.

Since the conclusion is that society must give the proponent his basic needs, he is understanding his right to basic needs in a positive sense. Since the credibility of the first premise comes from only considering his right to property only in the negative sense, he equivocates on these different senses of right.

Some may, of course, argue that we do in fact have positive rights to property. If so, then no equivocation is taking place. Rather, a different informal fallacy occurs, namely, the fallacy of *begging the question*, which we'll look at in section 14.1.2.

Why Equivocation Is a Fallacy

Recall the argument above:

> Only men are rational.
> Women are not men.
> Therefore women are not rational.

We could translate this into categorical form and test its validity using the Venn diagram method (chapter 8). If we are not careful, we might translate the above in the following manner:

> All R are M (recall how to translate "only")
> No W are M (recall how to translate "All ... are not ... ")
> No W are R

As translated, the argument is valid. The difficulty, though, is that it is a poor translation. We have treated the two different senses of the term "men" the same. If we recognize the equivocation on "man," however, we should properly denote each with separate letters. The acceptability of the first premise is predicated on our translating "man" here as "*Homo sapiens.*"

The acceptability of the second premise is predicated on our translating "man" here as "male." Given this new translation scheme, we get the following argument:

All R are H
No W are M
No W are R

We now have a categorical syllogism with *four* terms, rather than the requisite three. If we draw four overlapping circles (our standard three with one at the top) and follow our Venn diagramming method, we will discover that after diagramming the first two premises, the conclusion is no longer forced upon us (the subset W-H-R will still be open, indicating the possibility that some W are R).

Alternatively, we could translate the above into propositional form (chapter 9). If so, we will get the following translation:

If you are rational you are a man
If you are a man you are not a woman
Therefore, if you are a woman you are not rational.

Failing to detect the equivocation would tempt us to translate the argument as

R ⊃ M
M ⊃ ~ W
Therefore, R ⊃ ~ W

As translated, the argument is a valid hypothetical syllogism. Pointing out the equivocation, however, shows that the two instances of M in the translation above is inaccurate. If we translate the first "man" as "human" and the second "man" as "male," we can see that the argument takes on this form:

R ⊃ H
M ⊃ ~ W
Therefore, R ⊃ ~ C

We should see that this no longer fits the hypothetical syllogism, and would be deemed invalid. Here is another example of equivocation in action:

Electricity is power.
Power corrupts.
Therefore, electricity corrupts.

Invalid reasoning encourages us to draw a false conclusion from true premises. The argument above tempts us to do so. It is true to say "Electricity is power" and it may well be accepted that "Power corrupts," but we should realize that we are using the word "power" in two distinct senses. In terms of syllogistic reasoning, we are not using three classes of objects; instead, we are using four classes of objects (electricity, things that corrupt, electrically-effected power, social and political dimensions of power).

When the terms have been properly translated, we see that equivocation is really a case of irrelevance; thus we might be tempted to categorize the fallacy of equivocation in our second grouping. When properly translated, we see that the premises are irrelevant to the conclusion. We include equivocation as a problem with premises, not because we think the premises themselves are problematic, but because *detection* of this fallacy is through paying attention to the premises themselves.

14.1.2 Question-Begging

A *Friends* episode revolved around Ross's refusal to divorce or annul his marriage with Rachel. He didn't want to be divorced for a third time and assumed it would make no difference to Rachel. After all, it merely involved checking a different box on her tax form. Since this failed to convince her, he appealed to her *as his wife*. This is a classic case of begging the question, since whether she wanted to be his wife was the real issue.

To beg the question is to sneak the conclusion in as one of the premises. As put, then, the simple form of a question-begging argument is this:

P, therefore P.

Such a claim is valid. It may be offered as the paradigm of validity, for if P did not follow from P, what would? To accuse someone of begging the question, then, is not to accuse them of invalidity. It is, rather, to accuse them of uttering something *uninteresting*. For although "P therefore P" is the paradigm of validity, it is also the epitome of tedium. Still, it has great success in misleading the unwary.

In arguments, recall, our task is to give reasons for accepting the conclusion. If our reason for accepting the conclusion is itself the conclusion, we have not given any reasons at all; we have simply reiterated the conclusion. This does not mean the conclusion is wrong; it simply means no argument was actually given for it. And that's precisely what happens in a question-begging argument.

Perhaps I claim that I should have the last cookie. Understandably, you ask why. Is it an adequate answer to reply, "Because I should have the last cookie"? Clearly it is not. I have not answered the question. Instead, I have begged the question. I have simply repeated myself. I have offered nothing new to support my claim. (Of course, I might have at the same time raised my voice, or showed my fist, or divulged a few incriminating pictures of you, but that's another matter.) That is what question begging does. In this simple form, we should see why it is an unconvincing method of argumentation.

An argument begs the question when it assumes the truth (or falsity) of the very claim it is trying to prove (or disprove). Consider, for example, this rather typical reply: "Surely you're not an atheist: don't you know what God can do to you?"

This little remark commits three fallacies. Let us leave aside the fallacies of *Leading Question* (section 14.1.3) and *Appeal to Fear* (14.2.3) and focus instead on how it commits the fallacy of begging the question. What the speaker assumes true (that God exists) is precisely the proposition the intended audience rejects. The argument has force only if we presuppose the conclusion, but whether we should presuppose the conclusion is presumably what the argument is intended to support.

Recall the distinction between sentences and propositions. It is possible to state the same proposition over and over with a variety of different sentences. Confusing sentences for propositions is often what causes purported arguments to collapse into mere exercises in question begging.

Consider the following student responses to philosophical relativism:

1 This is philosophical relativism and it is a bad argument because it cannot be proven to be correct. If all people believe something different, they cannot all be correct since there can only be one right answer.
2 Truth is not relative. Truth is based on fact. If the facts for Smith are false, then the facts must be questionable. X cannot be true for one and false for another, it must be either both true or false. The truth is the truth and not subject to change, that's why it's called truth.

In both cases, nothing has been said other than a repetition that truth is not relative. Every other statement asserts nothing new. Recall that the contradiction of "All T are R" is that "Some T are not R" (8.3). Asserting, instead, that No T are R is merely asserting the contrary. Asserting the contrary is not a demonstration of anything. On the other hand, if we could demonstrate that at least one T is not an R, then we have done something. Although the two examples above both look like arguments, neither is. Both merely use the conclusion as one of the premises. We should see question-begging arguments for what they are.

Evidence should be independent of and supportive of the conclusion for which it is presented. It would not be evidence for inflicting capital punishment on convicted drug dealers to state that capital punishment should be meted out to all convicted drug dealers. Nor for that matter would it be evidence in favour of capital punishment that the Diesel engine is named after Dr. Rudolf Diesel. The first begs the question since it is not independent of the conclusion. The second is simply irrelevant.

Let us look again at the rights to property argument presented in our discussion of equivocation (14.1.1):

1 We have rights to property
2 I have no property.
3 Therefore society is obliged to give it to me.

If the rights in the first premise are negative and the rights in the conclusion are positive, the argument commits the fallacy of equivocation. If the rights in the first premise are meant as positive, then I claimed the argument begs the question. We are now in a position to explain why this is so.

Notice what the conclusion is "Society is obligated to give me property." Since obligation and rights are understood in tandem, this can be translated as saying I have a positive right to property, but that's what the first premise is claimed to have already said if it is to avoid the charge of equivocation. The argument fails in either case.

Four Forms of Question Begging

Question begging occurs when one sneaks the conclusion into one of the premises. It "supports" the conclusion with the conclusion itself. Since propositions and sentences are not the same, the conclusion being supported by itself is often not apparent at first glance. Here are four common ways in which question begging can occur.

i. Synonyms.   Using synonymous terms in the premise and conclusion may obscure the fact that the propositions are identical. For example,

Theft is immoral because it is wrong.
Of course hydrogen burns, it's combustible isn't it?

Astute readers will not be duped. "Immoral" and "wrong" are synonymous, so there is no more than one proposition here, and the word "because" is misapplied. Likewise, "things that burn" is synonymous with "things that are combustible," so no new proposition has been uttered in support of the conclusion.

ii. General-Particular.   In some arguments a more general form of the conclusion is assumed as a premise. Although this can dupe the unwary, it commits the fallacy of begging the question. For example,

Smoking marijuana is wrong because taking drugs is wrong.

In this case, "drugs" is a general term, while "marijuana" is a particular subset of the general order of drugs. Since marijuana is itself a drug, the discussion hasn't advanced very far. Notice that marijuana isn't synonymous with drugs, since marijuana is a particular kind of drug, but the putative "argument" begs the question just the same.

iii. Extended Circularity.

As with circular definitions, sometimes question-begging arguments are revealed only after a series of arguments. Consider this often-heard question-begging argument:

> God exists because it says so in the Bible and the Bible is authoritative because it is the revealed word of God.

The premises have to be less controversial than the conclusion in an argument, otherwise they cannot support the conclusion. For this argument to be successful, the listener must accept the existence of God first. But since that is the very aim of the argument, it doesn't get off the ground.

Question-begging arguments assert only what was already asserted in the premises, and hence the argument is utterly incapable of establishing the truth of its conclusion. An argument that uses some form of its own conclusion as part of the evidence offered to support that very conclusion commits the fallacy of begging the question. Consider the following discussion:

> "People can't help doing what they do."
> "Really, Why not?"
> "Because they always follow the strongest motive."
> "But what is the strongest motive? How do we tell?"
> "It is, of course, the one that people follow."

As you can see, the explanation for why people can't help doing what they do begs the question. It is important to note that the question-begging patterns of reasoning are circular. Our discussion of circular definitions, then, is similar to our discussion of question begging. Consider the following dialogue:

> Sarah: "No true Canadian would support free trade."
> Will: "Adams, a Canadian, supports free trade."
> Sarah: "That just goes to show that Adams isn't a true Canadian."

By redefining what she means by "true Canadian" as one who supports free trade, Sarah has ensured that her original claim is true. Will's response to this should be "You have redefined the word 'Canadian' to suit your purposes and so have used a question-begging definition."

iv. Negating the Contradiction.

Sometimes people argue against a claim by asserting its contradiction (or worse, contrary or sub-contrary, see discussion in 8.3). But the contradiction cannot merely be asserted, it must be supported. If I assert "X" and you say I'm wrong, and then proceed to "support" that by claiming "Not-X," you have simply begged the question. A commonly used strategy of refuting someone else's argument is to incorporate in the premises the negation of the contradiction of one's conclusion. In simplistic terms, this is like saying

Not non-P: therefore P.

Depending on how we define a non-P, this may not be a tautology at all. For example, if I am not someone's ex-husband, it doesn't follow I am her husband. Or if I am not an ex-smoker, it doesn't follow that I am a smoker. The tautology only works if our non-P is itself a simple negation of P. For example, I am her husband if I am not not her husband, and I am a smoker if I am not not a smoker. Consider again the following two examples:

Truth is not relative. Truth is based on fact. If the facts for Smith are false, then the facts must be questionable. X cannot be true for one and false for another, it must be either both true or false. The truth is the truth and not subject to change, that's why it's called truth.
Surely you're not an atheist: don't you know what God can do to you?

We know both commit the fallacy of begging the question, since we've already discussed these. There is no argument here at all, since the conclusion has been inserted into the premises. Notice, however, that both try to conceal (perhaps unwittingly) this fact by incorporating into the premises the negation of the contradiction of the conclusion, not the conclusion *per se*. If truth is relative, then truth is not based on fact. Therefore, "Truth is not relative" and "Truth is based on fact" are equivalent propositions. Likewise, since being an atheist means not believing in God, saying "You're wrong" to an atheist is the same as saying "God exists." One does not support the other, since it is in fact merely the negation of the contradiction of the other; i.e., they are identical propositions.

Colloquial Uses of Question Begging
People often say, "That begs the question ... " and mean merely that a particular premise requires support. We mean something more technical than this. For us, someone has begged the question if and only if the conclusion is itself one of the premises. Consider the following argument:

Smoking marijuana is wrong because it's self-destruction, and self-destruction is wrong.

We could imagine someone's complaining about either or both premises. Perhaps they reject the notion that self-destruction is wrong. Perhaps they reject the notion that smoking marijuana is a case of self-destruction. In doing either, people are prone to utter, "that begs the question ... " Technically, if they utter this, they should continue the sentence to include the question begged, and stopping short is failing to speak grammatically. When they utter this, they mean that at least one premise requires support. This use of the phrase "begging the question" may fit better than our use, but the point here is that it is not what philosophers mean when they use the phrase "begging the question." For us, a fallacy counts as begging the question only when the conclusion is inserted as one of the premises. Whatever other fault the above argument possesses, it is not a case of begging the question. (Granted, there *may* be a question-begging fallacy lurking. The speaker may continue, "and self-destruction is wrong because it's forbidden." Here, we can point out that for all intents and purposes something forbidden is synonymous with something being wrong. It is bad form, however, to assume the speaker *will* commit a fallacy; we can only assess what's there or what is logically required given what's there.)

14.1.3 Leading Question

In courts of law leading questions are questions that presuppose the guilt of the suspect and are, for that reason, to be disallowed. Leading questions in arguments are similarly problematic.

Consider the following question: "Are you still obsessed with Pat?" How should you answer this? If you answer "No," you implicitly admit you *were* obsessed with Pat. If this seems inaccurate, perhaps you will answer "Yes." Ah ha!, then you admit you are *still* obsessed with Pat! Something has gone wrong: you've been placed into a damned-if-you-do and damned-if-you-don't situation. And that's precisely the intent of leading questions.

The following are all examples of leading questions.

Have you stopped beating your wife?
When did you leave the scene of the crime?
Why did you rob Andrews?
Will agriculture benefit by the increased prices which will follow the increase of taxes on imported foods?
Why are the Conservatives in favour of slave labour?
Why are the NDP committed to ruining this country's economic future?

In order to answer each of these questions, you must *presuppose* some other statement is true. What's worse, it is precisely this presupposition you may find faulty. You cannot have stopped beating your wife without admitting you have beaten your wife, a claim that may be false. Giving a time you left the scene of the crime presupposes you were there. Answering *why* you robbed Andrews comes after our being settled on the fact that you *did* rob Andrews.

Leading questions are fallacious because the mere fact that a statement is presupposed by a question is not good evidence that the statement is true. To assume it is true merely on these grounds is to make a dubious assumption. Wondering about the benefits to agriculture as a result of increased prices presupposes that there will be increased prices as a result of increased taxes on imported foods, a supposition we might want to challenge. We may disagree with the proposition that Conservatives are in favour of slave labour, and so answering *why* they are is moot. Likewise, we may disagree that the NDP's intent is to ruin the country, whether that's what their policies do in fact.

Our point is that a leading question forces us into assuming something we might wish to reject.

14.1.4 False Dichotomy

A false dichotomy is a disjunctive proposition that we have independent reasons to reject. Recall that a disjunctive proposition takes the form: A or B. Disjunctive propositions claim that at least one of these proposition units is true. If both are false, then the disjunctive proposition is false. A false dichotomy is simply one in which this condition is met. The fourth line of the truth table for disjunctive propositions (9.3.1) shows such cases.

In an argument, a false dichotomy will likely occur in a disjunctive syllogism. Recall that the disjunctive syllogism is in the following form:

A v B
~A
Therefore B.

Now this argument, although always valid, will only be cogent as long as the original premise, ("A v B") is true (or acceptable). But for the premise "A v B" to be true or acceptable, it must be the case that at least one of the clauses (either A or B) is true. If both are false, then showing that one is false does not show that the other is true, since it may be false as well.

For example,

"Either you love me or you hate me."
"Well, I don't hate you."
"Oh good, you love me."

It is possible that I do not love you, even though it is also true that I do not hate you. I may be indifferent, frankly. The problem is the assumption that there are no other alternatives. For one last example, detect the false dichotomy lurking in the following:

The only real choice humans face is whether to adopt a leftist type scheme of nationalized health insurance, or the more reasonable system of everyone being responsible for his or her own debts, whether they are medical or otherwise.

Not every disjunctive proposition is to be rejected. Many are true. Still, whenever we are faced with disjunctive propositions, we should ask ourselves whether a false dichotomy is lurking. That is, whenever we are presented with a disjunctive ultimatum in this form, we should be wary.

14.1.5 Slippery Slope

The fallacy of a slippery slope is so named because of its analogy with stepping on the top of a slippery slope. If we take the first step, we'll inevitably tumble to the bottom. On the presupposition that we don't want to tumble to the bottom, we ought not take the first step. A slippery slope argument usually takes the form of a hypothetical syllogism or a series of hypothetical syllogisms conjoined with a modus tollens (see 10.1 if these are unfamiliar terms). That is, they take the following structure:

If A, then B
And if B, then C
C is a heinous place to be
Therefore we should not allow A

It says roughly that if one thing happens, something else will happen, and if that other thing happens, some final disaster will occur, and that, since we don't want that final disaster, we ought not want the first step.

Since hypothetical syllogisms and *modus tollens* are valid forms, we cannot say that a slippery slope is invalid. It is not a formal fallacy. The fallacy is instead understood in terms of challenging one of the conditional premises. The claim "If A, then B" may itself be challenged if we believe the occurrence of A does not necessarily yield B. Or perhaps we might grant that, but doubt that B yields C.

Phrases that are suggestive of a slippery slope fallacy include, but are not exhausted by, the following:

But that just leads to ...
But what you've proposed will result in ...
Next you'll be saying ...

Here are three slippery slope arguments in action:

(1) There is no question in my mind that the government is seeking an all-out prohibition on cigarettes. And once we've let them achieve their goal

they'll be free to pursue other targets. They'll go for liquor and fast food and buttermilk and who knows what else. There's a line of dominoes a mile long.

(2) The young man standing next to him asked, "What time is it?" The old man refused to reply. The young man moved on. The old man's friend, sensing something was wrong, asked, "Why were you so discourteous to the young man asking for the time?" The old man answered, "If I had given him the time of day, next he would want to know where I'm going. Then we might talk about our interests. If we did that, he might invite himself to my house for dinner. If he did, he would meet my lovely daughter. If he met her, they would fall in love. I don't want my daughter marrying someone who can't afford a watch." (Engel, *Analyzing Informal Fallacies*, 94)

(3) If you continue to lie then you'll surely begin to steal. All those who steal end up in jail, and if you're imprisoned then you are on the sure road to committing a serious crime. And, of course, if you committed a serious crime then you'd get executed.

Even if an act leads to bad consequences, it is debatable whether it should therefore be forbidden. After all, some might say (Immanuel Kant, for example), an act should be deemed right or wrong *independently* of its consequences. To think otherwise is to believe the ends may justify the means.

There are two ways to defend against a slippery slope. The first is to show that the alleged undesirable consequences are not the inevitable result of the proposal. The second is to accept that the result does follow, but deny that it is undesirable.

Concerning the first, we ask, Is it really the case that one thing will inevitably follow the other? A slippery slope often depends on assuming similarities between cases. To deny that the slippery slope ensues is to point out relevant differences between the cases. For example, a common argument against active euthanasia is that it will lead to genocide, and the Nazis' use of both euthanasia and genocide are often pointed to as an illustration of how this slippery slope occurs. Proponents of active euthanasia point out that active euthanasia is permissible *only if* the person, or a relevant proxy, has provided informed, competent, not unduly influenced, voluntary consent. In the case of genocide, this condition is not satisfied. Pointing this out defuses the slippery slope.

Alternatively, we can challenge a slippery slope by suggesting that the bottom of the hill in the particular case is not so dire. For example, if someone were to complain that the legalization of marijuana would lead next to the legalization of hashish and cocaine, one might reply, "So? I think that's right, too."

Another way of looking at slippery slopes is to see them as chains of predictions, each of which may be uncontentious, but the chain as a whole is weak. For example, if a company argues that it cannot afford a 1 per cent increase in wages this year, because then the union will ask for another 1 per cent increase next year, and another the following year, etc, we are on a slippery slope: the company can make it appear much riskier than it actually is. This form of the slippery slope may be referred to as the *fallacy of the heap*. If one grain of sand does not a heap make, and the addition of one grain of sand does not make a heap, then we can never get a heap. Similarly, we ought not mind gaining fifty pounds, since we don't mind gaining one ounce, and thereby don't mind gaining another ounce, and thereby don't mind gaining … until we've hefted up a good fifty pounds. Somewhere along this chain, we may not be sure exactly where, we mind gaining the extra weight.

When we challenge conditionals, we are suggesting that even if the antecedent is true, the conditional does not follow. As a result, we're challenging the premise of slippery slope arguments, and not the form of slippery slopes. Since we're challenging the conditional premise, we might refer to the fallacy as simply a case of a *false conditional*, to associate it more closely with the fallacy of *false dichotomy*. After all, we know by *implication* (see 10.4.5) that any conditional may be converted into a disjunctive. Therefore, if the problem of a slippery slope is a false conditional, then slippery slopes are really instances of false dichotomies. Consider the active euthanasia argument:

If we allow active euthanasia, then we'll tolerate genocide,

becomes

Either we don't allow active euthanasia or we'll tolerate genocide.

Either form of the premise is problematic. It is for this reason we place the fallacy of slippery slopes among problems with premises.

As with all informal fallacies, however, arguments that take these forms are not necessarily bad. Simply, warning bells should ring in our heads whenever we see the structure of an informal fallacy, and we should then take a closer look. After reflection, we may decide the slippery slope is warranted, although calling it a slippery slope at that point may be misleading.

Exercise 14.1

Identify the fallacy connected to problems with premises (*equivocation, begging the question, leading question, false dichotomy,* or *slippery slope*). (Answers to selected questions provided in Appendix 1.)

☞ 1 I am entitled to smoke in public places since it is a right.
 2 I take it you're not going to continue engaging in the morally obnoxious practice of eating veal?

☞ 3 Let's stop at Sleep Easy Motel, since I haven't been able to sleep well since the tax auditors came to our door.

4 Pornography causes harm to women, since men who read pornography treat women as sex objects and in doing so cause harm to the women they encounter.

5 Surely you don't believe in having women remove their shirts in public and undermining the fabric of human decency and morality?

☞ 6 First off, we would like to say how beautiful Prince Edward Island is. Why would you want to destroy it with Sunday shopping? (Tony Lohnes and Peter Hare, letter to the editor, *Guardian*, 1 December 2001, A7)

7 Legalizing abortion for first-trimester pregnancies is just one step away from slaughtering orphans, so abortion should not be legalized.

8 In every situation, it's either you or the other person who's going to come out on top, so you might as well be an ethical egoist.

9 Monarchy is obviously the only right choice, because democracy is a leftist philosophy.

☞10 Monarchy is wrong because democracy is right, since having any decision dictated by a single, hereditary ruler is wrong and undemocratic.

☞11 No good can ever come from abolishing the monarchy. Once a Canadian head of state is recognized, it's only a matter of time before the dollar collapses; Quebec, BC, Alberta, and the Maritimes secede; utilities, welfare, health care, and infrastructure become privatized; gun control laws are repealed; and caribou are driven to extinction. Once all that happens, it's only a hop and a skip to all-out Communism.

12 With regard to Martin-Robbin's 'With these names, I thee wed', I wonder what will happen if the children of this mixed-names couple decide to be as 'romantic' when they get married, and become Martin-Robbins-Jones-Smith. And what about their grandchildren? They will have eight last names! Where will it end? You can call the practice of women changing their names on marriage traditional, but I'll call it practical. (Joe Fox, letter to the editor, *Maclean's*, 14 May 2001, 6)

☞13 Bunny: What should I do: Marry Jim and become a housewife, or finish my education and have a career, like you? (J.F. Lawton, *Cannibal Women of the Avocado Jungle of Death*, Movie, 1988)

14 Free speech is to ideas what free trade is to commerce. The only way to discover the truth is to let everybody express an opinion, including tobacco companies. The free flow of information is more efficient for the consumer than regulation of information by the state. Indeed, the main problem with tobacco advertising bans is that manufacturers are incapable of communicating new information to consumers. (Pierre Lemieux, "Label ban a smokescreen for government agenda," *National Post*, 17 August 2001, C15)

15 Kent Brockman: "Once cat burglary starts, can mass murder be far behind?" (Matt Groening, *The Simpsons*, Episode 1F09)

☞16 No, I'm not going to buy an electric jigsaw. If I did, you would want a circular saw, and then a power drill, and soon you would want a whole workshop. We can't afford all that.

17 What does not destroy me, makes me stronger. (Nietzsche, *Twilight of the Idols*)

18 There are only two kinds of people in this world: winners or losers.

☞19 We can become independent of Arab oil only by ruining our environment. (Engel, *Analyzing Informal Fallacies*, 53)

20 The Good is that at which all things aim. Therefore we ought to pursue the good and shun evil. (Aristotle, *Nichomachean Ethics*)

☞21 According to Freud, we are often frustrated because our sex drives are blocked, and they become blocked apparently because we are thwarted in our desires. (Engel, *Analyzing Informal Fallacies*, 123)

22 I was dismayed to read (May 24) that a U.S. organization has changed the name of the jewfish to the goliath grouper. What's next? Will botanists wake up with a new name for the wandering Jew? What about the jew's-harp? Somebody had better warn Norman Jewison. (Russell Silverstein, "Name-dropping," *Globe and Mail*, 26 May 2001, A14)

23 The crime this man committed is the result of his childhood environment; for all such crimes are rooted in childhood environment, as this man's case proves. (Engel, *Analyzing Informal Fallacies*, 62)

24 Child: I don't believe in Santa Claus.
   Mother: You'd better, or he won't bring you any presents. (Ibid., 163)

25 Either you major in history or remain culturally ignorant for the rest of your life.

14.2 Problems with Relevance

Evidence should be independent of and supportive of the conclusion for which it is presented. It would not be evidence for the reinstatement of capital punishment if we were to claim that the butternut tree is a close relative of the walnut. The premise is simply irrelevant. Irrelevant premises are referred to as *non sequiturs*. A *non sequitur* is an argument that gives completely irrelevant reasons for its conclusion. That is to say, there is nothing in the premises that relates in the relevant sense to the conclusion.

Consider the following example:

A man explains his failure to become pregnant during the past year on the ground that he has regularly consumed his wife's birth control pills, and that any man who regularly takes oral contraceptives will avoid getting pregnant.

It would be a mistake to say that this man's explanation is unacceptable – after all, he may well have consumed his wife's birth control pills, and it is true that any man who takes oral contraceptives will avoid getting pregnant. The problem, in this case, is that of relevance. What difference does it make that he took or did not take his wife's birth control pills? There is no difference whatsoever; he does not stand a chance of getting pregnant anyway. His explanation is irrelevant.

We should be aware that relevance is a matter of degree, and that relevance is context dependent. For example, the fact that someone's fingers are yellow from smoking tobacco is obviously irrelevant to judging that person's computer skills. At the same time, the former can be quite relevant in assessing that same person's risk of lung cancer.

We shall examine five common types of errors of irrelevance: *red herring, ad hominem, emotional appeals, bandwagon,* and *straw man.*

14.2.1 Red Herring

"I don't care if you don't like your spinach. Don't you know there are people starving in Afghanistan?" We always knew something was wrong with this sort of argument. Now we can put a name to it: *red herring.*

In preparing for fox hunts, it was a practice to drag a dead and smelly fish (a red herring, typically) about the fields. The idea was that less well-trained dogs would scamper after this false trail, and thereby be misled from the intended trail of the fox.

Logical red herrings do the same. To avoid discussing a problematic point, people often divert the audience's attention by a discussion of some other point. When a teenager comes home late and speaks about anything other than the reasons for her lateness, she is attempting to throw her parents off the trail. It is a classic case of red herring. When Calvin commiserates with Ms. Wormwood about the disparity between monetary remuneration and the real value of teachers, he is attempting to throw Ms. Wormwood off the trail of discovering that Calvin did not do his homework: a red herring. Likewise, sibling communication is often rife with red herrings:

"I'm telling! Mom said you are not allowed in my room!"
"Yeah? Well, you've got a big butt!"

(Notice that this "argument" employs an abusive ad hominem fallacy as well, see 14.2.2.)

Siblings are not alone in using red herrings. Advertisers and politicians often avail themselves of this ploy:

Here's an attractive model. Look at her. Look at her long, slender legs. Look at her full, red lips. Buy a Mazda!

Here's a bunch of snowboarders in the Rockies. Buy Canadian beer.
Stockwell Day: "Mr. Prime Minister, you claimed you were going to cut out the
GST. Did you?"
Jean Chretien: "Since I've been in office, unemployment has dropped, we've
lowered our national debt, and we've been on the forefront of international trade
and peace."

Red herrings usually indicate an inability of the speaker to adequately address the original issue. An irrelevant issue is being introduced to divert attention from the point being discussed. For one last example, consider the following letter to the editor. It concerns Commodore Eric Lerhe's voluntary confession, and subsequent dismissal, that he surfed the net for porn. He confessed after he was asked to participate in the prosecution of a fellow seaman for surfing the net for porn on company equipment.

Geraldine Glattstein of Women Against Violence Against Women claims that
men who surf porn shouldn't be supervising women in the workplace. But I
say Commodore Eric Lerhe deserves a promotion, not dismissal. This princi-
pled officer has put his career at risk because he refused to participate in the
prosecution of someone guilty of a "crime" he himself has committed. Would
you have as much courage, Ms. Glattstein? (Eric Sparling, letter to the editor,
Globe and Mail, 20 June 2001, A14)

Good critical thinkers will see a red herring for what it is and direct the discussion back on track. Sometimes, of course, depending on the circumstances, one ought to be magnanimous and simply let the issue drop.

Politicking

It may be unfair to pick on politicians as standard users of red herrings. The impression that they are may be partly due to the media. News coverage is highly competitive, and to cram as many newsworthy items as possible into an ever decreasing time slot, news editors are going to be selective. As we've already seen in chapter 4, this selection process is prone to bias, but that is not our concern here. Rather, news shows are not going to show a picture of a politician with his head down. They want a full-face picture. So politicians are trained to enter into the fray of reporters with their heads down. A host of questions will be fired at them, none of which they can clearly hear anyway, since the questions are asked almost simultaneously. Some of them have no bearing on the discussions with which the politicians have been most recently engaged. Standing with one's face in the camera in shock at such a barrage will make one look worried, shifty, and evasive. The solution? Keep one's head down until ready. Savvy politicians will have a prepared statement (it doesn't matter if it's a response to any question raised) and when ready (or when a question bears on their pre-prepared statement), they merely lift their heads, stare into the camera, and deliver their speech.

News editors will not show the scene prior to that, because who wants to look at the top of somebody's head? As a result, the question most recently asked, or loudest, will be cut out. All viewers will see is a confident politician delivering his statement amidst the pandemonium of reporters. Viewers at home won't appreciate the red herring.

Conversational Red Herrings?

Of course, in conversation, it is common for topics to shift in mid-stream, and an indication of a good conversant is the ability to move with that flow at ease, like a good dancer. Persons who constantly bring the discussion back to some previous point are tiresome. The more insipid, the less chance of being invited back. The difference here, of course, is whether the point of the discussion is an argument or a friendly conversation. We cannot overemphasize that we are talking about skills in *arguments* only; not all communications count as arguments. That is, our task is to reject red herrings in arguments, but perhaps accept them in friendly conversation.

14.2.2 Ad Hominem

To commit *ad hominem* fallacies is to do two things: (i) attack the arguer and not her argument, and (ii) conclude *as a result* of the diatribe that her argument should be rejected.

Defined this way, an ad hominem argument is always fallacious. Recent textbooks on critical thinking would not make such a claim, but this is due to their defining ad hominems only by the first condition. Admittedly there are periodically legitimate reasons to criticize the arguer herself, so this ploy cannot be deemed a fallacy. It is a fallacy, however, when the defect of the speaker is attributed to the argument without further ado. The fact that the arguer has been insulted is irrelevant to our assessment of the argument. The argument should stand or fall on its own merits.

Earlier we claimed that reasons should be independent of the conclusion, otherwise the argument begs the question. Evidence should also be supportive of the conclusion for which it is presented. It would not be evidence for capital punishment that the butternut tree is a close relative of the walnut. Such a remark is clearly irrelevant. The point is, most ad hominem attacks are equally irrelevant to the merit of the argument.

If the argument is bad, this should be detectable on the basis of the argument itself. That the arguer has bad breath does not magically make an otherwise sound argument into one that is unsound. This should seem obvious; nevertheless, ad hominems are one of the most common fallacies. There is a variety of ad hominems. All focus on the speaker rather than the argument. They are *abusive, tu quoque, irrationality, hypocrisy*, and *vested interests*.

i. Abusive In *abusive ad hominems,* we simply abuse the speaker for one reason or another, and thereby hope to turn the audience against the speaker's argument. For example, a typical strategy in the defence of rape is to attack the woman, to discredit her character, as if this proves that the rapist is innocent. Here is another example:

> "Here's an interesting letter to the editor arguing against the use of genetically modified foods."
> "It's all rot, the guy's gay."

Well, perhaps it's all rot and perhaps the writer is gay, but it would be a grave error of reasoning to suppose that it is all rot because he is gay. Consider next

> "Victor claims that genetically altered foods pose no health risks to humans, but I happen to know he's been cheating on his wife."

Perhaps Victor has been cheating on his wife, and we are certainly free to frown upon him for that, but it hardly shows that his argument is faulty, or that genetically altered foods pose no health risk to humans.

> "Heidegger was a Nazi: therefore his philosophy should be burned."

It happens to be true that Heidegger was a Nazi, and some believe his philosophy should be burned, but it does not follow that his philosophy should be burned because he was a Nazi. In each of the above examples the arguments should stand or fall on their own merits, not on the basis of who said them. Consequently any abuse the arguer receives (justifiably or not) should be irrelevant.

One more example from our politicians:

> [T]o those who criticized the spending of between $2-billion and $4-billion to extend broadband Internet access to the smallest communities in Canada, [Federal Industry Minister Brian Tobin] offered this measured response. "I think that kind of pompous, arrogant, misguided, shortsighted thinking has no place in a modern, contemporary Canada ... " ("The Tobin tack," *Globe and Mail*, 28 June 2001, A14)

Abusive ad hominems are irrelevant to the issue at hand.

ii. Tu Quoque *Tu quoque* means "you're another." Typically this is a defensive manoeuvre to ward off rebuttal to one's own position. It occurs as a response to a criticism of one's argument. The tactic is to accuse the critic of an unrelated crime or error, rather than to respond to the criticism itself.

Consider asking your roommate to please rinse the dishes. You point out how gucky un-rinsed dishes get, and how much more difficult it is to clean them as a result. Moreover, you show how little time it takes to rinse them. Your argument seems reasonable. What can your roommate say in reply? One too often heard strategy is something like the following:

> Yeah, well you never close the toilet seat.

Your roommate has engaged in an ad hominem fallacy called tu quoque.

Tu quoques shift the attention away from the weakness of one's own argument. Political platforms are rife with tu quoques: each political party accuses the other of some atrocity or oversight without responding to any of the charges laid against them. Their strategy is, "I may not be worth voting for, but neither is my opponent" followed by, "Now vote for me."

Tu quoques are a special form of red herrings. There is still the diversionary tactic being employed, as with red herrings, but they take the specific form of saying, Yeah, well you're bad too. Consider

> Stockwell Day: "Mr. Prime Minister, you claimed you were going to cut out the GST. Did you?"
> Jean Chrétien: "Your political platform, Mr. Day, is to reinstitute capital punishment and abortion and to legislate the discrimination of homosexuals. It is only fair that our voters know this, rather than try to hide it from them."

Chrétien may have a point. Our complaint is not with that. It is that Chrétien's response avoids answering Day's challenge. It is thereby irrelevant to the issue at hand.

iii. Irrationality   The ad hominem fallacy of irrationality points out a case where the speaker gave an irrational argument, and concludes that we should therefore reject the present argument. Offhand, this doesn't seem to be in any obvious sense a fallacy. After all, to show that someone is irrational is to look at her arguments, so it doesn't seem to fall under our ad hominem heading. Moreover, we are clearly not wrong to reject any argument found to be irrational.

There is a fallacy here, however. Because the speaker made some logical flaw in an unrelated argument, it does not follow that her current argument is fallacious as well. Nothing of the sort follows.

Our beliefs are many and varied. We have a vast network of beliefs, and a full catalogue would likely reveal that some of our beliefs are inconsistent with others. Likewise, we make many arguments. Some of these we may later reject. But merely on the grounds that we've rejected some of our earlier arguments, it would be fallacious to conclude we must now reject all of our arguments. (If so, shouldn't we then reject the argument we made to reject our earlier argument? If so, then our earlier argument still stands, so we are now entitled to make further arguments. But, wait, if so, we can now reject the rejection of our rejection, but then the rejection of the reinstated argument still stands, so we are inconsistent, which undermines that rejection of the rejection of the rejection; but that opens the door up, again for ... etc., etc., *ad nauseam.*)

The point is this: Maintaining problematic arguments in one sphere does not mean one is incapable of presenting cogent arguments. To think otherwise is the ad hominem irrationality fallacy.

The following argument may be accused of committing the ad hominem irrational fallacy.

> Dr. Pojman committed the fallacy of ignorance in his argument against capital punishment. You can see therefore that we should also reject his argument against active euthanasia.

The fact that Dr. Pojman's argument for capital punishment was weak does not show that his argument against active euthanasia is weak. Admittedly, the fact that the arguer has a track record of providing poor arguments should cause us to examine the present argument with a certain modicum of suspicion. But it is a fallacy to assume that Pojman's present argument is to be rejected on the mere grounds that Pojman's previous argument is to be rejected. Arguments will stand or fall on their own merits. If the present argument is to be rejected, we can point to relevant reasons within the argument itself.

iv. Hypocrisy   Calling someone a hypocrite is an insult of sorts, although it is conceivable that it is justified. The claim that someone is a hypocrite is not by itself a fallacy. Charging someone with hypocrisy is simply claiming that the arguer does not abide in practice by his own argument. Consider for example, this rather typical manouevre in the political arena:

> Mr. MacDonald left not a dry eye at his party's convention as he described his sister's death from smoking-induced lung cancer. Yet, Mr. MacDonald failed to mention that for some years following her death, his family continued to grow tobacco, and that he continued to accept campaign money from tobacco interests.

True, there is something we may wonder about Mr. MacDonald, but there is a fallacy in rejecting Mr. MacDonald's argument on the mere grounds that he himself doesn't abide by it. The argument he gives should stand or fall on its own merits, and the mere fact that the speaker himself doesn't abide by it is irrelevant to whether we should. Consider, as well,

> Religious people never do what they preach. Therefore I'm an atheist.

Presumably, God's existence is independent of whether people believe in Him or not, let alone how well they behave on earth. The fact that some, maybe many, theists are hypocritical is therefore irrelevant to whether we should believe in God. Consider the following examples.

> I find it ironic that an American representative is urging both sides in Northern Ireland to disarm, and saying that "guns have no place in the democratic process." Especially since a significant faction of Americans' own governing coalition believes that their Constitution gives them the right to attempt the armed overthrow of their government when it becomes, in their own estimation, "tyrannical." (Stephen DeGrace, letter to the editor, *Globe and Mail*, 4 July 2001, A12)

Despite the hypocrisy, disarmament may be a good thing. One more:

> "[Environmental lobbies are] great at coming out with objections to development in certain areas, but they never seem to come out with an alternative," [McGuigan] says. "You take resource extraction – they might fly up in a jet and burn 10,000 lb. of fuel to get here, to tell you to use wind power. You've never seen them sailing up in a sailboat." (Ken MacQueen, "Down but not out," *Maclean's*, 9 July 2001, 22–3.)

Such strategies are to be seen for what they are, irrelevant distractions from the issues at hand.

An Exception?

One exception to this rule is worth noting. It may be the case that it is impossible to practice what is being preached. Then the hypocrisy of the speaker is not itself the issue; rather it is that no one can follow such advice. For example, if moral theories yield duties that exceed what we are psychologically capable perhaps this will count against the theory. Alternatively, we ought to psychologically adapt.

v. Vested Interests   To accuse an arguer of having vested interests is to accuse him of being improperly motivated in making a particular argument. That is to say, we claim we are entitled to reject the argument on the grounds that the speaker will benefit from our accepting it. If a doctor says, "Oh, you had better come for more tests," we might wonder whether we should, if it is revealed that his sole motivation is to milk you or the governmental health plan for all it's worth.

On the other hand, the fact that the doctor may benefit from your long-term care does not by itself undermine the possibility that you do in fact require long-term care. It is this observation that reveals why it is a fallacy to reject an argument on the sole basis of vested interests.

Granted, vested interests may make us cautious, but an argument should stand or fall on its own terms, and whether the speaker benefits from our accepting her argument should be irrelevant to that assessment.

Here are some examples:

> Of course he thinks spanking is a legitimate form of punishment; he doesn't want to relinquish his power.
> Sure she says that the beauty industry is manipulative, but look at her: she will benefit if she can prevent others from looking attractive!
> Of course he thinks you need a new alternator; how do you think mechanics make their money?
> One cannot believe the arguments of conscientious objectors, since they are obviously trying to escape the draft.
> The Chrétien government, as you would expect, is hostile to any federal regulations against PWCS [personal watercraft]. Not because Ottawa lacks jurisdiction, since navigable waterways fall under federal law, but because the Chrétien government is, for all intents and purposes, composed of Honourable Members from Bombardier. (Jeffrey Simpson, "Two solitudes: jet-ski riders and jet-ski haters," *Globe and Mail*, 11 July 2001. A13)

It is important to recall that the ad hominem fallacy, in any of its forms, occurs only when, from the alleged fact of irrationality, hypocrisy, greed, or some other objectionable characteristic, one infers that the person's argument is defective. The fallacy consists in transferring the defect in the person to the argument without further ado.

14.2.3 Emotional Appeals

Often, acting from emotion is precisely the right thing to do, but sometimes it is not, and we should be aware of the difference. Emotional language may be very effective in motivating people to act in ways we want them to. However, the reverse holds; we may be motivated to act in ways we would not act had we the foresight to consider the situation unemotionally.

Clearly, we should act in ways for which we have good reasons. Emotional appeals sometimes cloud the fact that no good reasons are to be had. In fact, strongly felt emotions can prevent thinking. An emotion may so overwhelm us that we fail to realize that there is *no* argument present! We are being caused to move rather than given a reason to act.

The distinction raised in chapter 4 between emotive terms and cognitive terms applies here as well. By tweaking our emotions, effective rhetoric may cajole us into believing we are confronted with a good argument, when no argument is present at all. Let us consider two common appeals to emotion: *pity* and *fear*.

i. Fear   Fear is a powerful motivator. If we fear something, let's say X, we have reason to avoid it. Likewise, if in order to avoid X, we must do Y, we are motivated by fear to do *Y*. People can play on this emotion for their own ends, and our task is to be wary.

The fallacy occurs if we can point out that we needn't do *Y* in order to avoid *X*. If we can show this, we have discovered that the argument to do *Y* to avoid *X* is a fallacious appeal to fear. If we can avoid *X* without doing *Y*, *Y* is irrelevant to our fear about *X*.

Threats are an extreme form of an appeal to fear. If you don't do (or if you do) *Y*, I will cause a very unpleasant thing *X* to happen to you. Such coercion usually does not allow one to stay at one's status quo. That is, if I happen to be alive and have my wallet in my pocket, my status quo is being alive and having my wallet in my pocket. If a mugger demands I hand over my wallet or lose my life, my status quo is not an option. Denying the status quo as a viable option is an operational definition of coercion.

We might be in a position to threaten without altering the individual's status quo. For example, a voter may threaten a politician not to cut a program or suffer the consequence of losing a vote. Perhaps the voter is a member of a larger group, all eager to vote against the politician if she cuts the designated program. The fact that the voter or the group of voters is not obligated to vote for the politician shows that the threat does not undermine the politician's status quo. Her status quo is that the voters may voluntarily vote for her or not for *any* reason. So their threat to not vote for her cannot constitute an immoral sort of threat. But it is a threat. It is an appeal to fear.

Appeals to fear are more problematic when the prophesied bad event is itself highly suspect. We ought not cheat at cards. Let us take this as a given. Still, imagine claiming that one ought not cheat at cards because doing so will cause karmic reaction and something bad will happen to us as a result. This plays on our fear of bad things happening to us. We don't want that. But, surely something bad will likely happen to us at some point in our life *whether or not we cheat at cards*. Thus the threat seems unconnected, irrelevant.

Advertisements play on our fears. For example, home security companies instill fear of robbery in their prospective customers, to be cured by purchasing their product. The same is true of cosmetics. They first instill fear in us that we'll have bad breath, or smelly armpits, or wrinkled skin, or cellulite, and then inform us that their product will deliver us from this fear. Insurance companies prey on our extant fears as well.

ii. Pity   In the privacy of our own home through the wonderful avenue of television, a celebrity may show us pictures of a some impoverished children. Their faces, too will be the epitome of pity (and condemnation of anyone dour enough not to share such pity). These techniques are often strong motivation for us to send money.

Seeing that a child is living in poor conditions does not tell us the *prevalence* of poverty, or to what extent our money will actually help this particular child. Still, if we are moved to pity someone, this may well count as strong motivation to do things to relieve their suffering. No practical logician can possibly complain about this. We are certainly free to be so moved. Some may condemn us for failure to be so moved. Still, we may not fully recognize how much our sentiment of pity was targeted, and this is an issue of concern.

Lawyers and politicians, for example, sometimes appeal to pity to advance their own cause. Also, students often come to their professors and appeal for higher grades based on mere pity. "Look, they'll kick me out of the program if you don't raise my grade." Being moved to pity alone would be unfair to others, and is therefore inappropriate. Consider the following advertisement for corn oil margarine:

Should an 8-year-old worry about cholesterol? (Engel, 147)

The answer is presumably no. But does answering no mean we should buy corn oil margarine?

Other Emotions?

There are other emotions that arguments may appeal to, for example nationalism, loyalty, love, hate, etc. We might hear the following sort of irrelevant rally cry:

You love your country, right? Well, then let's burn down abortion clinics!

In all cases of the fallacy of emotional appeal, it is not the emotions *per se* that are bad, but rather that there is no necessary link between the associated emotion and the proposed action. Advertisements are excellent examples of this. If you buy this product, you'll be as beautiful as this model. If you buy this aftershave lotion a life of adventure and romance will finally be yours. If you drink this beer, anorexic, silicone-injected women will love you for who you are and not what you look like.

14.2.4 Bandwagon

The bandwagon fallacy is driven by the psychological need to conform. The appeal to "jump on the bandwagon" is to get us to do or believe whatever it is the masses are doing or believing. Such an appeal has a strong psychological tug. General assent to a claim does not prove it to be true, however. The fact that there are only a few of product x left is not sufficient reason for us to buy product x.

Of course, if everyone is doing x, perhaps that should give us some indication that x may be worth our doing. There is nothing wrong in such a supposition. Simply, we can't on the basis of bandwagon appeals conclude we ought to jump on the bandwagon. The fact that many are doing so is presumably not simply because others were doing so. If there is a reason to jump on the bandwagon, then, it has to be something *other* than the mere fact that people are jumping on the bandwagon. We are encouraged to check out that reason. There may even be a very good reason; it should be *that* reason that motivates us to concur, and not the mere fact that others are doing so.

Advertisements are rife with bandwagon appeals. "Look: billions of people are buying our product. You should too." If people are buying the product for a good reason, why not just tell us that reason? They can't be buying the product because others are buying the product, for this couldn't explain why the first persons bought the product. Since we assume advertisers want to give us the strongest claim possible, noting that they don't tell us the reason, but only the fact that other people are buying it, might lead us to wonder what other reasons could motivate such a rush? Are equal numbers buying the competitor's brand? Does this product hold a monopoly, so that consumers don't have a choice?

The fallacy of the bandwagon appeal is nevertheless a very powerful motivator. We have an innate drive to be like everyone else, to fit in, to belong. Of course, we also have an innate drive to assert our uniqueness, which shows to what extent schizophrenia is the norm.

The power of the bandwagon fallacy can be readily seen in mobs. People do things in mobs that they would never dream about doing on their own. Our drive to conform is found not only in the Nazi party members whose defence was that they were merely following orders, it is present in all cultures in all times.

Take, for example, elevator travel. Normally when we get on an elevator, we turn and face the door. There is nothing necessary about this, yet there is a strong feeling of stepping out of line if we attempt to deviate from this practice. This feeling is particularly germane when we get on elevators with two sets of doors, one at the front and one at the back. Which way to stand? Which way will it open? How embarrassing it is when the door opens behind us and people witness our indiscretion.

Following the work of Solomon Asch, social-psychological experiments have been conducted with elevators and conformity. Confederates stand on an elevator facing the back wall and clandestinely note how many people who enter the elevator also face the back wall. Most do. Beware the power of the bandwagon appeal. Consider this bandwagon appeal:

One custom that has never changed: a friendly social drink. (Engel, 139)

Change "social drink" to "owning slaves" or "not having women vote" or "sacrificing virgins" and we can see that the mere fact that something has been done is not a sufficient reason to continue to do it.

14.2.5 Straw Man

A figure made of nothing but straw is easily knocked down. Likewise, poorly constructed arguments are easily refuted. Just as one's virility is not proven by defeating an effigy made of straw, one's position is not strengthened by defeating a misrepresentation of a counter argument. The pretense of doing so is called a *straw man argument*.

A straw man fallacy occurs when our objective is to refute our opponent's claim. We give a poor rendition of her argument, and then proceed to show where all the holes are. This is a fallacy if the holes are due to *our* construction of her argument, and not the original argument itself. This fallacy consists in misrepresenting an opponent's point of view or argument, usually, for the purpose of making it easier to attack.

Quite often, what happens is that the opponent's argument is given in an *extreme* form. Imagine Jones says

"Under certain conditions, like life-threatening situations to the mother, or forced rape, I believe abortion should not be ruled out."

Next imagine Smith attacks Jones by saying

"Jones says killing of innocent babies is legitimate. He should be locked up!"

Smith has taken Jones's argument *out of context*. As a result, we can condemn Smith's argument as a straw man.

For another illustration, consider the following:

Concerned citizen: It would be a good idea to ban advertising beer and wine on radio and television. These ads encourage teenagers to drink, often with disastrous consequences.
Alcohol industry representative: You cannot get people to give up drinking, they've been doing it for thousands of years. (CBS News with Dan Rather, 24 December 1984)

The alcohol industry obviously has a vested interest in arguing against any restrictions on their business, but the above response commits the straw man fallacy, since the concerned citizen didn't say anything about forbidding drinking.

Given the misconstrual inherent in the refutation, the straw man argument is irrelevant to our assessment of the original argument.

A Worry
One worry about straw man arguments is that we often do not have the luxury or luck of knowing whether a critique is misconstruing the original

argument. We may be privy only to the critique, and not the argument that is being criticized. Consequently, we may not know whether the critique is a straw man or not. On the grounds that most people are reasonable, any time we see an argument easily refuted, we should feel free to at least suspect a straw man. As with all these informal fallacies, the potentiality of a straw man should set an alarm bell ringing in our ears. If we deem the issue of sufficient import, we may be motivated to check out the original argument to see if the critic has fairly represented it.

Exercise 14.2

Identify the fallacies of relevance in the following arguments: red herring, ad hominem (abusive, tu quoque, irrationality, hypocrisy, vested interest), emotional appeal (fear, pity), bandwagon, and straw man. (Answers to selected questions provided in appendix 1.)

☞ 1 My opponent in this election wants to know about my record on social issues. But what I want to know is what she thinks about defence spending.

☞ 2 Materialism, the view that humans are just machines, is simply false.

3 However, it matters very little now what the King of England either says or does; he hath wickedly broken through every moral and human obligation, trampled nature and conscience beneath his feet, and by a steady and constitutional spirit of insolence and cruelty procured for himself an universal hatred.

☞ 4 How can you not like McDonald's? They've served over a billion customers!

5 Fader Security Systems: when you don't want your home invaded!

6 As he fights for a different way to tackle drugs, the Governor [of New Mexico] insists this is an issue that belongs to Republicans. He points to the traditional Republican idea that people should take responsibility for their own actions and the party's disdain for the nanny state. Republicans believe smokers have no right to sue tobacco companies because only an idiot would not realize smoking is harmful. They feel guns do not kill people; people kill people. But the party is hooked on the anti-drug war, enthusiastically building prisons and passing ever harsher drug-sentencing laws. (Jan Cienski, "Pot's U.S. poster boy," *National Post*, 30 May 2001, A13)

7 So why is the Sierra Club going to war to defend the rights of dandelions? The main reason is that, on the whole, dandelions are good, human beings suck. It simply irritates Green activists to their core that many people, maybe most, have a penchant for order and think green grass is aesthetically pleasing. It's a sign of human intelligence and achievement. Neat, tended and orderly ground space is evidence of human beings enjoying themselves. (Terence Corcoran,

"Dandelions are good. Human beings suck," *National Post*, 25 May 2001, A18)

☞ 8 [The following letter was written in response to the court ruling that operators of B&Bs cannot deny service to gay people.] While not particularly religious myself, I was under the impression that in our country the separation of state and religion was inviolable. For the operator to be deprived of a livelihood by the state's flagrant intrusion on a person's religious beliefs on behalf of political correctness, is to me, and I am sure to many Islanders, abhorrent. (Donald W. Smith, letter to the editor, *Guardian*, 31 May 2001, 7)

9 Global Exchange [a human rights organization] said Nike has failed to eliminate child labor, involve non-governmental organizations in monitoring and ensure factories pay a living wage. In a telephone interview, Nike's director of corporate responsibility, Dusty Kidd, said the report as described to him failed to recognize the sporting goods giant's recent willingness to reveal sensitive findings about violence and intimidation at the factories. (Shu Shin Luh, "Intimidation cited at Nike Indonesian plants," *Globe and Mail*, 18 May 2001, M2)

☞ 10 The American Society of Newspaper Editors turned aside White House pleas to tone down the McVeigh coverage, saying the media doesn't need a civics lesson from a President who presided over 131 executions during the five years he was governor of Texas. (Robert Sheppard, "Anatomy of an Execution," *Maclean's*, 14 May 2001, 43)

11 Diana was a wonderful princess who died tragically. Now we must preserve the throne so that her son William has an opportunity to participate in the institution. To abolish it now would be to defile her memory.

☞ 12 Many people of my generation consider the campaign against spanking to be faintly ridiculous. Spanking used to be such a common practice, including in schools – with an inanimate object, no less: the ubiquitous "strap." (Ian Hunter, "When it comes to spanking, let's keep an open mind," *Globe and Mail*, 26 July 2001, A15)

13 Ms. Mella [Prince Edward Island Treasurer], your government and that of others in Canada should be thankful there isn't a history of revolution here. Yet. (Stephen Nowell, letter to the editor, *Guardian*, 17 May 2001, A7)

☞ 14 In a way, it all started with that first hokey press conference, when the new leader [Stockwell Day] came roaring up on his personal watercraft. I do not know of a single Canadian with an IQ in three figures who does not think that those noisy machines are an abomination, the playthings of the obnoxious and the cretinous. Right away, one wondered if Stockwell Day understood the world around him. Or was his the world of the two-figured IQ, the obnoxious, and the cretinous? (Michael Bliss, "He never stopped shrinking," *National Post*, 9 July 2001, A1)

15 The successful opposition to extending a no-smoking policy into public spaces is due to all the smokers in the legislature.

☞16 Stockwell Day's plea to Progressive Conservatives to join him under a new right-wing banner has been derided by Tory leader Joe Clark and some Canadian Alliance members as a transparent attempt to divert attention from his leadership woes. (Campbell Clark and Brina Laghi, "Day 'desperate' Clark says," *Globe and Mail*, 15 June 2001, A1)

17 I was surprised Mr. Gee saw fit to demean our judicial system. For his information, there are more than one billion Muslims who believe that the Koran is the sacred word of God and that punishments specified in the Koran are binding for all time. They resent attacks on their religion, even when they come under the guise of "human rights." Many cultures around the world believe in capital punishment and corporal punishment. Amnesty begs to differ, and we, the majority of the human race, beg to differ with Amnesty. (Mohammed R. Hussen, letter to the editor, *Globe and Mail*, 15 June 2001, A14)

☞18 [The following letter to the editor concerns Commodore Eric Lerhe's voluntary confession, and subsequent dismissal, that he surfed the net for porn, when asked to participate in the prosecution of a fellow seaman for surfing the net for porn on company equipment.] Commodore Eric Lerhe's censure for looking at pornography on his DND laptop in his spare time is another example of the "straight bashing" that has come to characterize our feminist culture. How do men defend the country when they are condemned for having testosterone? (Henry Makow, letter to the editor, *Globe and Mail*, 20 June 2001, A14)

19 It's time to do a survey of the educational choices certain politicians and columnists make in their own lives. How many of these apparently passionate defenders of the public system have sent their own children to private schools? (Penna, Pav, Letter to the Editor – "Student exodus not new," *The Globe and Mail*, May 18, 2001, A12)

☞20 [The Amistad Committee] calls for [Yale] university to acknowledge how it has benefited from the profits of slave trade, and to consider reparations to those whose ancestors suffered under slavery ... In its response, the university noted its progressive policies toward blacks and the study of slavery. Yale says it was the first to grant a doctoral degree to a black student in 1876. (Kate Zernike, "The taint of slavery," *National Post*, 14 August 2001, A11)

21 Your reviewer charges me with bad taste in using Dr. Josef Mengele, late of Auschwitz, as the villain of my novel *The Boys from Brazil* (February 23). I must concede that what I have done is almost on a par with putting a would-be assassin on the cover of a national magazine or publishing a list of dead presidents' rumored mistresses. (Engel, 133)

22 An attorney says a sixty-two-year-old man accused of bilking several

members of the Seventh Day Adventist Church out of thousands of dollars could suffer a fatal attack if compelled to stand trial. (Engel, 148)

23 I believe I do deserve a 75 in this course, because if I don't get a 75, I'll lose my scholarship, and I can't afford to attend university if I lose my scholarship.

14.3 Problems with Sufficiency

A good argument needs to provide enough evidence in order to compel us to accept its conclusion. But how much evidence is enough? This question is the essence of our last criterion of fallacies: problems with *sufficiency*.

Problems with sufficiency include *false cause, person-who, appeals to ignorance, genetic fallacy*, and *composition and division*.

14.3.1 False Cause

The fallacy of false cause is to mistakenly assume a causal relation where there isn't one. The mere fact of a correlation between two or more events does not by itself establish a causal relation. People are in the habit of brushing their teeth before leaving the house, but we cannot assume brushing one's teeth *causes* people to leave the house. This should strike even the most obtuse as fairly obvious, but remarkably it is often overlooked. Consider, for example the debate about pornography. Perhaps pornography is despicable, and predicated on sexism, but does it *cause* harm to women in general? People have cited statistical trends such as 68 per cent of rapists use pornography. Rape is bad and one should never discount this, but if more than 68 per cent of men use pornography, while less than 68 per cent of men rape, this statistic is a red herring.

Belief in ESP may well be linked to fallacious use of causal reasoning. That I happened to be thinking of you when you phoned does not mean there is a causal connection here. How many times have you phoned when I wasn't thinking of you? How many times was I thinking of you when you didn't phone? These are relevant considerations that are often ignored in our urgency to make causal claims.

Even if event A has often happened with or prior to event B, it is no guarantee that A caused B. For example, the fact that those in Japan who have toasters also have lower birth rates does not mean toasters are a good method of contraception. There may be a mediating factor causing both low birth rate and the purchase of toasters. Education is presumably linked to higher income brackets (or the reverse), which in turn is linked to affording toasters.

Our point: Correlation (even regular correlation) of two events does not mean one event caused the other. Be wary of claims that do not provide further evidence than temporal succession.

The fallacy of false cause may be divided into three types: *coincidence, reverse order,* and *3rd variable* (a more thorough discussion of these errors is provided in 11.2.4).

i. Chance   There is a strong direct correlation between the birthrate in Holland and the number of storks nesting in chimneys. What should we make of this? There is of course the theory that babies come from storks, but this is not backed by scientific evidence. Perhaps storks nest in chimneys that are heated. Perhaps there is some further correlation between warmer houses and larger families. Another explanation is the correlation came about by chance: it's simply a fluke.

Causal fallacies that ignore the role of chance are often called *hasty generalizations.* We generalize without good cause. Consider the following examples of hasty generalizations:

> I was so sick after I ate those green apples, I swear I'll never eat another.
> Tortoises live for over a hundred years: therefore if you move slowly, you will live long.
> Pop singer Brandy eats an exorbitant amount of salmon, and her skin is beautiful. There must be something in salmon that is good for skin.

ii. Reverse-Order Errors   Reverse-order causal errors get the causal relation backward. Sometimes we conclude that Y is caused by X when in reality X may be causing Y. Consider, for example,

> Twenty-five years after graduation, alumni of Harvard have an average income five times that of people of the same age who have no college education. If a person wants to be wealthy, he or she should enroll at Harvard.

Another possibility, of course, is that the wealthy tend to go to Harvard. That is, the causal connection was backwards.

Consider two more cases of the reverse-order causal fallacy:

> Night is the cause of the extinction of the sun, for as evening comes on, the shadows arise from the valleys and blot out the sunlight. (Early Greek Physics)
> Isn't it true that students who get As study hard? So if you want me to study hard, give me an A.

iii. 3rd Variable Errors   Third variable errors see a well documented correlation between two events but ignore the possibility that a third variable is the cause of both. Even in cases where A regularly precedes B, it is conceivable that the relation between A and B is through a third variable, C, that causes both.

Consider the following:

> I think his daughter's marriage must have worried him dreadfully. She was his only child, you know. He never talked about her but I noticed that his hair began to turn white after the wedding.

Before we jump to that conclusion, we might notice that another event occurred since the wedding: age. For another example of the 3rd variable error, consider this correlation:

> Studies show that prisoners who serve their full term are twice as likely to re-offend as prisoners who are released early. If we want to keep crime down, keep people out of prisons.

What else could be a factor? Presumably prisoners aren't randomly released early. Rather, those less likely to re-offend are better candidates for early release. The hasty conclusion from an insufficient correlation has committed the 3rd variable causal error. Consider the following testimonial for a facial cream:

> That cream cleared up her complexion within two months!

Should we be confident that the cream is the cause of her improved complexion, or might a third factor be the culprit?

One thing we should note with 3rd variable errors: to cite them as the problem requires us to supply what the likely 3rd variable is. The following report, for example, does not merely claim that a 3rd variable is more likely the cause, but explicates what that variable is likely to be.

> Researchers at the University of Michigan who studied the effects of the increase in the drinking age found that states on average reduced drinking among high school seniors 13.3%. The change also contributed to a 58% drop in alcohol-related deaths among 15- to 20-year-olds since 1982 ... Skeptics believe it [the drop in traffic fatalities] may have less to do with changing the drinking age than with the new mores about drinking and driving and the more aggressive enforcement of DUI laws. (Jeffrey Kluger, "How to manage teen drinking (the smart way)," *Time* (Canadian edition), 18 June 2001, 35)

14.3.2 Person-Who Fallacies

Person-who fallacies entail a misconstrual of statistics (see also 11.3.3). Consider the absurdity of the following claim: "Since every third child in NewYork is a Catholic, Protestant families should have no more than two children." (Engel, 22) Few would make such a mistake, since when we utter statistical claims like "Every third child in New York is a Catholic," we don't mean this literally. Nor do we mean it literally when we say a woman gives birth every seven seconds. Person-who fallacies can be understood as making precisely this sort of error, however.

When we say, "smoking causes lung cancer," most of us understand that smoking vastly increases the probability of getting lung cancer compared to not smoking. Science can tell us that most people who smoke will get lung cancer. What science cannot tell us, however, is *which* ones will get lung cancer. Why? Because the relationship is probabilistic. It does not hold in every case. We are all aware of this: *or are we?*

How often have we seen a smoker argue for his continuing smoking on the grounds that "My uncle Leroy smoked all his life and never got lung cancer." The obvious implication one is supposed to draw from these person-who testimonials is that because it did not happen in these particular cases, it won't, or is less likely to, happen in mine.

This shows a complete misunderstanding of probabilistic reasoning. A single instance does not refute a probabilistic law or trend. Citing these person-who claims reflects a failure to understand statistical laws. Consider the following person-who claims:

> "You say job opportunities are lessening for white males in philosophy? I say, no way. I know a white male who just got a job in Red Deer."
>
> "You say children tend to adopt the religious beliefs of their parents. Well I say, no way! My friend was raised as a Mennonite and now he's a Roman catholic!
>
> "I am tired of reading in the popular press, and other so-called enlightened journals, that abused children grow up to become abusers of their own or other people's children ... It appears that certain psychologists who function as 20th century prophets, seers, or sages – operating as if they talked with the Supreme Being himself/herself – assure us that the young abused are predestined to become adult abusers. According to this Pavlovian theory, it is all mechanistically and automatically determined: the abused child will grow up to become an abuser of the next generation." (My Turn, *Newsweek*, 25 June 1984)

Concerning this last illustration, notice that there is much ad hominem here, as well as a straw man argument. But the main error is misunderstanding probabilistic reasoning. The scientific report did not say abused children will grow up to be abusers. Rather, the probability was high. Thus the complaint of "predestination," "mechanistically and automatically determined" is simply false.

14.3.3 Appeal to Ignorance

To appeal to ignorance is to claim that a conclusion should be accepted as true on the basis that its negation has not yet been proven. Imagine if a child cries out at night in fear. You, the doting parent, answer her call and run into her room. "There's a monster under the bed," she cries. Parental strategies at this point differ, but perhaps you venture onto your ailing knees and report back to the child that you see no monster. "But the monster is invisible," she cries. Perhaps you get her hockey stick out of the closet and swipe it under the bed. You report back your findings: "The stick didn't hit anything, visible or invisible." "The monster can shrink to the size of a flea at will!"screams your child. However patient you are as a parent, there will come a limit. Perhaps you have reached it by now. "Look," you might say to your child, "there is no monster. Now go back to sleep." "No," says your child, who at a very early age became adept at appealing to ignorance, "Your not finding a monster is not proof that it isn't there: therefore, I shall maintain my belief that it is."

Children do not talk this way, but we can be pretty sure the fallacy of ignorance captures their reasoning process. One would hope that they grow out of it, but, alas, the appeal to ignorance is pretty well-entrenched in adults too. A classic appeal to ignorance often occurs when a theist criticizes an atheist on the following grounds:

Do you know what created life, the earth, and the universe? No? Well, then it must be God.

Translated, this simply says "Because you don't know the answer, I posit God," which really shouldn't be that convincing. If you prefer, the fallacy of ignorance may be construed as a translation error. The theist's argument above, can be presented as follows:

1 Either God created the earth or something else did.
2 You can't show that something else did.
3 Therefore we conclude God did.

The problem focuses on how we ought to translate the second premise. If the first premise is translated as G v S, is the second premise properly understood as ~S? Assuming so is committing the fallacy of ignorance. Here is another example of an appeal to ignorance:

I believe in astrology and always read my horoscope in the paper every day. I can't actually prove that it is true but nobody can disprove it.

Here is another case of the fallacy of ignorance in action:

[A]t present, we must conclude that we lack strong statistical evidence that capital punishment deters. But this should not be construed as evidence against the deterrence thesis. There is no such evidence for nondeterrence either. (Pojman, "Deterrence and the Death Penalty")

If the evidence does not support capital punishment, then this should be construed as evidence against the deterrence effect. To think otherwise is to commit the fallacy of ignorance.

Burden of Proof

The fallacy of ignorance can be construed as mistaking which side has the burden of proof. Because we can't *prove* conclusively that aliens have never landed on earth does not mean the status quo is to believe aliens *have* landed on earth. The task is to prove that they *have* landed, and failing that proof is good reason to stick with the status quo belief that they haven't.

The criterion for deciding who properly has the burden of proof is itself open for debate, however. One might argue that the person arguing for the *presence* of something always has the burden of proof over someone arguing for the *absence* of something. Thus, the child has the burden of proof in arguing for the existence of the monster, not the mother in arguing for its non-existence. On the other hand, if someone comes up and says, "See that chair that you're sitting on, well it doesn't really exist," you might want to say (if you're polite), "Why do you say such a thing?" It hardly seems fair if he replies: "No, it's up to you to prove that it's there, because you have the burden of proof, not me."

Consequently, some feel that the burden of proof belongs to the person making a claim that goes against common evidence. Common evidence supports the absence of monsters under the bed and the presence of chairs under our seats.

Does this definition help decide who has the burden of proof between the atheist and theist? Not clearly. The atheist will claim common evidence supports her side, that is, theists admit we can't see God, or hear God, or touch God, like other stuff, so it's up to the theist to prove his point. The theist, on the other hand, points to the general majority of persons who believe in a God (although the Judeo-Christian God is not the only God persons believe in) to support the interpretation that the burden of proof resides with common knowledge, not common evidence, strictly speaking. If so, it is up to the atheist to prove her point: a difficult task. It is difficult to prove the absence of something when the absence of evidence is not counted as supporting evidence!

How does this tie back into our discussion of the fallacy of ignorance? If the burden of proof resides with proving A, and this fails, we are justified in believing ~A *without committing the fallacy of ignorance*. Conversely, if ~A has the burden of proof, and that argument fails, then we are justified in believing A, *without committing the fallacy of ignorance*. This is very helpful, particularly in cases where we must act absent full information. Absent sufficient information supporting A, we may reasonably conclude ~A. But notice, this is a reasonable inference only if it is the case that A has the burden of proof. If ~A has the burden of proof, it commits the fallacy of ignorance. Consequently, a proper understanding of the fallacy of ignorance requires our understanding who has the burden of proof.

A Slight Variant

Sometimes people reject an argument on the grounds that they don't understand it. This seems consistent with our talk on language and clarity. If we can't understand an argument, we don't know how to begin to assess it. Also, the fault may well lie in the argument: it may have been poorly written, vague, ambiguous, cluttered, irrelevant, etc. But it would be a mistake to conclude that the argument thereby holds no weight, or, worse, that the conclusion is thereby wrong. Simply, we must admit we can't make heads or tails of it. Recall, though, the possibility remains that it's our problem, not the argument's.

Because *we* don't know anything about it, or can't understand the argument, it doesn't follow that the conclusion must be wrong. The strategy with this variant of the fallacy of ignorance is *If we are ignorant of it, ignore it.* This should be seen for what it is: fallacious reasoning.

14.3.4 Genetic Fallacy

To commit a genetic fallacy is to attack a thesis, institution, or idea by condemning its background or origin. Consider, for example, the following two arguments:

> The concept of God was first formulated by those who were uneducated, weak, powerless, fearful, and superstitious. To think we should maintain that barbaric belief now is absurd.
> America will never settle down, look at the rabble-rousers who founded it.

Both arguments commit the genetic fallacy. Because an idea came from shaky beginnings, they assume the idea is false. Conversely, because an idea originated from good motives, or good sources, its current incarnation must be good. Nothing of the sort follows. Take, for instance, the first airplane. It was crude, short-flighted, and dangerous. To conclude that therefore any plane today is crude, short-flighted, and dangerous is obviously to make some sort of induction error. We now have a name for the error: the genetic fallacy.

To show why the structure of genetic fallacies is problematic, it might help to reduce the form of the argument to something completely absurd. Consider: "When you were young you required a wet nurse to wipe your nose and change your diaper; therefore you still do." Clearly something's gone amiss, and it is the genetic fallacy rearing its head once more.

A similar error could be made in reverse: Because the origin of the idea was good, the result must be good. This too doesn't follow, and the adage "Hell is filled with the well-intended" is a recognition that good beginnings aren't sufficient to justify good ends. Marxism may be challenged, but the motive for Marxism is certainly good. Or, to return to America, the NRA may be understood as committing a genetic fallacy:

> Guns were a necessary feature in the making of America: hence they still are!

14.3.5 Division and Composition

The fallacies of division and composition make the mistake of forgetting that the whole is not the sum of its parts. The fallacy of division assumes what is true of the whole is also true of the parts. It is a case of dividing the whole, and thinking no damage has been done. The fallacy of composition does the opposite: it assumes what is true of the parts must be true of the whole. Neither inference follows.

i. Division We commit the fallacy of division if we assume that what is true of the whole is true of the parts. The whole is typically more than the mere sum of its parts: it is an *organized collection of parts*. For example, a wall is not merely a pile of bricks; a pile of bricks is a pile of bricks. A wall is an organized arrangement of bricks. Likewise, humans think, feel, and see, but that does not mean that their brain thinks, or their skin feels, or their eyes see. Similarly, although the Nazi army was brutal, it does not follow that a particular Nazi soldier was brutal or inhuman.

Consider the case of division that occurs in the following:

> The B.C. government will restrict the right of teachers to strike by declaring education an essential service ... Teachers and labour leaders reacted angrily ... But Mr. Bruce [Labour Minister Graham Bruce] said the bill is widely supported by voters, who gave the Liberals an overwhelming mandate for change. The party won 77 of 79 seats. (Kim Lunman, "B.C. legislation enrages teachers," *Globe and Mail*, 15 August 2001, A6)

Mr. Bruce's argument is that since the teachers voted for the Liberals, they agree to every policy the Liberals decree. This hardly follows. Mr. Bruce has committed the fallacy of division. What is true of the whole is not necessarily true of the parts.

Here is another case of committing the fallacy of division.

> It is absurd to say that poverty is a problem for Americans. America is the wealthiest nation in the history of the world. (Adapted from James Freeman, *Thinking Logically*, 278)

ii. Composition The fallacy of composition is the opposite of the fallacy of division. Here, the fallacy occurs when someone mistakenly assumes that the whole always possesses the characteristics of its parts.

Having good people in society does not make the society good. Explaining the function of various parts of an organism does not necessarily lead to any conclusion about the function of the organism as a whole.

The argument from design was originated by St. Thomas Aquinas. The intent was to prove the existence of God through reason. William Paley's version goes something like this:

1 Many things on earth work because they are so designed to work. Think of a watch, for example.
2 Thus, things in nature that work must be designed as well.
3 Thus the whole of the earth and the universe is designed.
4 Wherever there is a design, there is a designer.
5 We call that designer God.

Now, the move from 1 to 2 is by analogy. It is a problematic move in its own right, and we have seen why in chapter 13. The move from 4 to 5 is also unfounded. The theory of evolution offers an alternative account for why something that looks designed could occur by mere chance. We have seen such arguments in 11.3.5. But let us focus here on the supposed connection between propositions 2 and 3. It says, roughly, because the parts of the world or universe have evidence of design, the whole world or universe must also be designed.

This is a fallacy of composition. It assumes what is true of the parts is necessarily true of the whole. It is as fallacious as the following argument: Since books are made of paper, the library, a collection of books, is made of paper.

John Stuart Mill committed the fallacy of composition in his defence of Utilitarianism. Utilitarianism offers the moral theory that right action is whatever furthers the happiness of the society as a whole. Mill argued,

No reason can be given why the general happiness is desirable except that each person, so far as he believes it to be attainable, desires his own happiness. (J.S. Mill, *Utilitarianism*, 50)

Something seems sensible here, and there is even a moral intuition that the statement supports; roughly the argument we should take care of others when they are in need. Despite its pleasant conclusion, it is fallacious. That we each strive after our own happiness hardly shows that we therefore strive after everyone's happiness. This is an example of the fallacy of composition. It presumes what is true of the parts (individuals desiring their own happiness) is also true of the whole (individuals desiring the happiness of the group). It follows no more than assuming because computer chips that make up computers are small, computers are small.

Mill was not alone. Here's Aristotle's fallacy of composition:

> Should we not assume that just as the eye, the hand, the foot, and in general each part of the body clearly has its own proper function, so man too has some function over and above the function of his parts? (Aristotle, *Nichomachean Ethics*, 1, 7, 942)

Recall the fallacy of the heap? We could also understand this as committing the fallacy of composition. Consider

> One grain of sand does not make a heap. A second grain of sand added to the first does not make a heap. Indeed each and every grain of sand, when added to the others, does not make a heap which was not a heap before. Therefore, all the grains of sand in existence can still not a heap make.

In this case, we assume what is true of the parts (that an addition of a single grain of sand cannot make a heap), is true of the whole (therefore the whole can never amount to a heap).

Exercise 14.3

For the following arguments, identify the fallacy concerning sufficiency most likely committed: false cause (chance, reverse-order, 3rd variable); person-who; appeals to ignorance; genetic fallacy; and composition & division. (Answers to select questions are provided in appendix 1.)

☞ 1 There are no known natural causes to explain the visage of Mary appearing over Napoli; therefore it is divine.
2 Hemingway is no great writer. Look at his sentence structure. Every single sentence is a simple sentence.
3 Don't give beggars any money. I've seen a number take it to the bar.
☞ 4 You're eating mushrooms? Don't you know they grow out of cow's dung?
5 At the time of women's emancipation, women started to suffer from bulimia and anorexia. Eating disorders are a further tactic of men intent on keeping women in subordinate positions.
☞ 6 People say we should maintain the monarchy because it represents a tradition of peace. In actual fact, the monarchy represents the 'tradition' of the corporate police state and the doctrine of genetic superiority – the two underpinnings of the feudal system. This simply isn't acceptable in a modern society.
7 More young people are attending high schools, colleges, and universities than ever before, yet there is more juvenile delinquency than ever before. This makes it clear that to eliminate delinquency among the youth we must abolish the schools.(Copi and Burgess-Jackson, *Informal Logic*, 126)

☞ 8 One hopes that Canadians will not succumb to the current fashion for republicanism which is filling the globe with presidencies, many of which have dubious democratic credentials and poor human rights records. (J.K. Malone, "The monarchy: a necessary tradition for a stable democracy," *Guardian*, 24 May 2001, A7)

9 As P.M. Zamprelli of Edmonton can easily find out from the book *The New Canada*, Preston Manning carefully considered the premature deaths of all other Western-based populist movements. His knowledge of their history led him to create the Canadian Alliance. Unfortunately for Mr. Zamprelli, but fortunately for Canada, no amount of wishful thinking on his part will make us go away. The Alliance is hardly a Western protest party: I am nearly as far away from the West as it is possible to be in Canada, yet I am a strong supporter. (A. Banks, "Prescience," *National Post*, 23 July 2001, A15)

☞ 10 I can find no better reason to end the monarchy in Canada than the story about The Earl of Derby, Never Been to a Game (June 1). Apparently Sir Edward Richard William John Stanley, who is the great-great-grandson of the revered Lord Stanley, has never been to a hockey game and was not even familiar with the details of his great-great-grandfather donating the cup. Why are we Canadians so caught up with our tradition of being subservient to people who do not consider Canada's history as part of their tradition? Long live the Republic of Canada. (V. Narusevicius, "Our game," *National Post*, 6 June 2001, A15)

11 We have not established the absence of any health risks from the ingestion of genetically modified foods, and we therefore have sufficient grounds to reject GM foods.

12 When you've got a better theory, you can criticize mine.

☞ 13 It is not going to help the energy crisis to have people ride buses instead of cars. Buses use more gas than cars.

14 If not God, you tell me how the world came about.

☞ 15 To press forward with a properly ordered wage structure in each industry is the first condition for curbing competitive bargaining; but there is no reason why the process should stop there. What is good for each industry can hardly be bad for the economy as a whole. (Allen Flanders et al., *Twentieth Century Socialism: The Economy of Tomorrow*, 73)

16 When the natives sacrificed virgins to the volcano, they were assured a good crop.

☞ 17 Cheering in a hockey arena can boost the home team's morale to win. But such an effect is possible only if the cheering is loud enough. No single cheer can make a difference, therefore, cheering is not a rational strategy.

18 The chances of winning the grand prize of a lottery ticket are dismal. Therefore the chance of anyone winning the grand prize is dismal.

☞19 A child fell out of a boat upstream of Niagara Falls. She drifted past in plain sight of thousands of holiday spectators, yet no one saved her. This shows that the modern age has corrupted our moral sense.

20 I've had two women bosses in my lifetime and both of them have been incompetent. Women should stay out of management positions.

21 While General Grant was winning battles in the West, President Lincoln received many complaints about Grant's being a drunkard. When a delegation told him one day that Grant was hopelessly addicted to whiskey, the President is said to have replied: "I wish General Grant would send a barrel of his whiskey to each of my other Generals!" (Copi and Burgess-Jackson, *Informal Logic*, 126)

☞22 Salt is not poisonous, so neither of the elements of which it is composed – sodium and chlorine – is poisonous either. (Engel, *Analyzing Informal Fallacies*, 23.)

23 DEAR ABBY: You said that most male doctors do not get turned on by an attractive female patient. You're all wet! My ex-wife had a thing going with her doctor for a long time before I caught on. I didn't prosecute because I figured the poor guy had enough trouble being emotionally involved with my wife. During the last five years I paid enough doctor bills to put another Cadillac in his garage. Sweetie, you may know a lot about teenagers, but you had better do a little more research on doctors. (Cited in Engel, 45.)

☞24 On the Senate floor in 1950, Joe McCarthy announced that he had penetrated "Truman's iron curtain of secrecy." He had 81 case histories of persons who he considered to be Communists in the State Department. Of case 40, he said, "I do not have much information on this except the general statement of the agency that there is nothing in the files to disprove his Communist connections." (Ibid., 157.)

25 There is no way that scientists will ever be able to examine all the planets around all the stars in billions of galaxies. It is simply impossible to show that there are no intelligent beings existing elsewhere. So it seems altogether clear that there are intelligent beings in the universe besides us. (MacKinnon, *Basic Reasoning*, 287)

Exercise 14.4

Identify the fallacy most likely committed in the following arguments. Avail yourselves of the entire set of fallacies learned in this chapter: I. equivocation, question-begging, leading question, false dichotomy, slippery slope; II. red herring, ad hominem (abusive, tu quoque, hypocrisy, inconsistency, vested interests), emotional appeals (pity, fear), bandwagon, straw man; III. false cause (chance, reverse-order, 3rd variable), person-who, genetic fallacy, composition & division. (Answers to selected questions are provided in Appendix 1.)

☞ 1 You can gargle with Scope or have bad breath.

2 Aren't your kids worth Crest?

☞ 3 Most liberals say that the death penalty does not deter murderers. I don't know why. There is not a single case where a killer who has been executed has killed again. It certainly deters him.

☞ 4 We must accept the traditions of the men of old who affirm themselves the offspring of the gods – that is what they say – and they must surely have known their own ancestors. How can we doubt the word of the children of the gods? (Plato, *Timaeus*)

☞ 5 No one has yet stepped in and told us that we've been mistreating our workers, and we've been in business since long before you've been born, so I can't see any merit to your charge of negligence or exploitation.

6 Ford trucks outsell Chevy trucks, so buy a Ford.

7 It hasn't been proven that fetuses are not persons in the relevant moral sense, and so we must treat fetuses as persons with full rights.

8 Jones criticizes me for being a meat-eater, claiming that it is morally wrong to do so since it is a clear violation of animal rights, but I notice that Jones is wearing a leather belt which necessitated killing an animal.

☞ 9 There must be a God. Belief in God has been a feature of every society at every time in human history. How could all those people be wrong?

10 "Our paper certainly deserves the support of every German. We shall continue to forward copies of it to you, and hope that you will not want to expose yourself to unfortunate consequences in the case of cancellation." (Nazi notice to German readers who let their subscriptions lapse).

☞ 11 The reluctance to extend protection of rape laws to married women is attributable to the feelings of self-preservation on the part of married male legislators. (Margaret Gordon & Stephanie Riger, *The Social Cost of Rape*, 1991)

12 Why is private enterprise so much more efficient than any government control of industry?

13 If Quebec is allowed to secede, it's only a matter of time before Alberta follows, and then British Columbia, and then the Maritimes, and next thing we know there won't any longer be a Canada. If you want to remain Canadian, you cannot allow Quebec to separate.

14 Capital punishment is wrong. I witnessed Frederick Manning being given several lethal injections and he was in obvious pain until death finally occurred. It was horrible.

15 Aren't you glad you use Dial?

☞ 16 Yes, yes, I heard Smith's argument about how deer hunting helps strengthens the herd, but he's just wrong. It's false to suppose that deer don't mind being killed. Every organism, human and animal alike, strives to continue living.

17 Immigration and Naturalization service district director Ronald Chandler says he could find no "compelling" reasons to stop Salvadoran refugee Vince Quezada from deportation. Perhaps he should have looked into the eyes of four children and a wife who likely now will be forced to accept welfare subsidies. (Karen Kutach, letter to the editor, *Dallas Morning News*, 9 October 1989)

☞18 People who believe they have a duty to help those who are less fortunate than themselves almost always get pleasure from their unselfish actions. This just proves that it is the expectation of pleasure which causes people to act morally or to adopt their moral beliefs.

19 Marijuana can't be all that bad. Everyone knows about barroom brawls, but marijuana makes people peaceful.

☞20 I still think that I am wasting my tax money paying for a party that cannot even agree within themselves [sic]. Its [sic] sad to see that a guy like Day is not getting the drift. The man is an absolute looser [sic] and very incompetent. I cannot believe that he was the financial minister for Alberta. No wonder Klein wanted to get rid of the man. (Guy Larabie, "CNEWS – Your View," 8 June 2001, http://www.canoe.ca/CNEWS/yourview.html)

21 The world was not created by God, for matter has always existed and therefore the world must have always existed.

☞22 I see that our courts are being asked to rule on the propriety of outlawing video games as a "waste of time and money." It seems that we may be onto something here. A favourable ruling would open the door to new laws eliminating show business, spectator sports, cocktail lounges, the state of Nevada, public education, and of course, the entire federal bureaucracy.

23 Free speech is to ideas what free trade is to commerce. The only way to discover the truth is to let everybody express an opinion, including tobacco companies. The free flow of information is more efficient for the consumer than regulation of information by the state. Indeed, the main problem with tobacco advertising bans is that manufacturers are incapable of communicating new information to consumers. (Pierre Lemieux, "Label ban a smokescreen for government agenda," *National Post*, 17 August 2001, C15)

☞24 We should defer to the wisdom of the ages. If it was fine for them, who are we to disagree?

25 Why do all Muslims hate the freedom that America represents?

26 Not all of us can be famous because it's impossible for all of us to be well-known.

☞27 [The following letter to the editor concerns Commodore Eric

Lerhe's voluntary confession, and subsequent dismissal, that he surfed the net for porn using company equipment, when asked to participate in the prosecution of a fellow seaman for surfing the net for porn on company equipment.] To even suggest that visiting soft-porn sites using your own Internet account should be grounds for a fine in the neighbourhood of $300,000 (unofficial promotion freeze with subsequent pension implications, even if there is not official punishment resulting from the charges brought to date) and public humiliation is ludicrous. Would all senior officers, men and women, who have not visited a strip club during their career please step forward? Hmm ... small crowd. (Lewis MacKenzie, "No sex please – we're Canadian soldiers," *Globe and Mail*, 20 June 2001, A13)

28 [The following letter to the editor concerns previous letters about Commodore Eric Lerhe's voluntary confession, and subsequent dismissal, that he surfed the net for porn, when asked to participate in the prosecution of a fellow seaman for surfing the net for porn on company equipment.] For all of you morons (letters – June 20) who think that a little porn on the side is nothing to ballyhoo about, listen up: Web porn is spoon-feeding porn addictions at an alarming rate. At least 6 per cent of the population is addicted. Marriages break up and jobs are lost because of it. Porn is a huge industry and a problem. Just because you have testosterone doesn't mean you shouldn't get a real hobby. (Gay Isber, letter to the editor, *Globe and Mail*, 21, June 2001, A18)

29 Mel Lastman makes a stupid and insensitive remark. This outrage is enough to tilt the Olympic committee away from Toronto. The anti-democratic, autocratic government of China slaughters countless numbers of its own citizens, eliminates all human rights, muffles the press, threatens their neighbours and they are the beneficiary of Mel's travesty of words. Is there anybody who doesn't get the logic of this besides me? If a simple slur is enough to cost you the Games you would think China wouldn't even be eligible for consideration. Welcome to the wonderland of international bodies. (James Podesta, letter to the editor, *National Post*, 22 June 2001, A15)

☞30 A press release from the National Education Association (NEA) distributed in November begins with the following statement: "America's teachers see smaller classes as the most critical element in doing a better job, a survey by the NEA indicates ... " But the NEA, of course, is interested in having as many teachers in the school as possible. For example, in a 3,000-pupil school system with 30 pupils assigned to each class, the teaching staff would be approximately 100. But if class size were changed to 25 the total number of teachers would rise to 120. And in time of shrinking enrollments, that is a way to keep teachers on the public payroll. It is unfortunate that an organization with the professional reputation the National Education Association enjoys should be so self-serving. (Cynthia Parson, *Christian Science Monitor* Service, February 1976.)

31 It is strange that you should think it inhumane of me to take so much pleasure in hunting; you don't seem to mind feeding on the flesh of harmless animals.

☞32 Don't worry; your husband has received many injuries, true, but none of them is serious when considered individually.

33 All people should be free, for liberty is the universal right of humanity.

☞34 In some ways, the case for plural marriage is even stronger than the case for same-sex marriage: In much of the world, after all, polygamy is both lawful and common. (Jeff Jacoby, "Why should the state have the right to punish polygamy?" *Chronicle-Herald*, 19 May 2001, C3)

35 I enjoy reading only good books. If they're not good, I don't enjoy them. (Engel, 60)

36 Why is the US intent on destroying the autonomy of every Arab state?

☞37 Diamonds are seldom found in this country, so you better not mislay your engagement ring. (Engel, 16)

38 Everything that happens has a cause; for if something should occur without a cause, it would have been caused by itself. But this is impossible. (Aquinas, *Summa Theologica*, Part I, 3rd article)

39 Can you prove, beyond a shadow of a doubt, that a monarchical government *won't* lead Canada to dominate the world economic scene in 2025? No? Then why are you talking about repatriating the head of state?

☞40 "Experience is already showing how a tragic coarsening of consciences accompanies the assault on innocent human life in the womb," [Pope John Paul] said. This could lead "to accommodation and acquiescence in the face of other related evils such as euthanasia, infanticide and, most recently, proposals for the creation for research purposes of human embryos destined to destruction in the process." (Anton La Guardia, "Pope takes Bush by the hand, literally," *National Post*, 24 July 2001, A14)

41 Modern chicken farming is inhumane and therefore immoral.

☞42 Many of the entries for the *Oxford English Dictionary* were written by a man in an insane asylum. No wonder the English language is so screwed up.

43 Supposedly Canadian children are putting on weight. This certainly isn't true with my kids, nor their friends. It makes you wonder where they get these statistics from.

☞44 A recent study by social psychologists at the University of Waterloo, after a $450,000 grant, claimed to have discovered that people tend to like each other more with increased contact. I don't know which takes more gall: wasting taxpayers' money, or making clearly fallacious claims. The problem I have with my neighbour is not that we don't come in contact with each other enough, it's because we come into contact with each other *too* much.

45 Order is indispensable to justice because justice can be achieved only by means of a social and legal order. (Ernest van den Haag, *Punishing Criminals.*)

☞46 Reagan's Strategic Defence Initiative was an "act of folly," a "dream" that "cannot be achieved." Worse, the whole scam was a "telling commentary on his Presidential style," according to Philip Geyelin in *The Washington Post* in 1984: "Reagan had no proposal worked out when he first floated the idea almost casually ... He had only a fatuous, personal vision of a nuclear-free world." Just as President Kennedy had no proposal worked out, only a fatuous personal vision of putting a man on the moon within the decade. (Mark Steyn, "Missile defence is hardly pie in the sky," *National Post*, 30 July 2001, A14)

47 Cheers all around for this Jackie Robinson of golf (Golfer wins a ride and sparks disability debate – May 30). No longer will I have to deal with the systematic barriers that have prohibited me from achieving my full potential on the professional golfing circuit. For years, I have been convinced that I could challenge golf's greats if the barriers to golf weren't so prejudicial. The door is finally open. Now, with my team of psychologists (I believe that my difficulty in concentrating on the golf course is probably due to some childhood trauma) at my side, a pinch hitter at the tee (I've had a kink in my arm for the past few years; can't really explain the nature of the injury, but it seems to make my drives deviate quite a bit from the freeway), and an automatic putting device (a new invention I'm envisioning that would deal with these constant shakes that are obviously neuromuscular in origin), I'm ready to tackle the PGA and start earning what is rightfully mine. (Garry Guitor, letter to the editor, *Globe and Mail*, 1 June 2001, A12)

48 [I]t is only when it is believed that I could have acted otherwise that I am held to be morally responsible for what I have done. For a man is not thought to be morally responsible for an action that it was not in his power to avoid. (Alfred J. Ayer, "Freedom and Necessity," *Polemic*, No. 5, 1946.)

49 She says that she loves me and she must be telling the truth, because she certainly wouldn't lie to someone she loves. (Copi and Burgess-Jackson, *Informal Logic*, 127)

50 Miracles are impossible, for they cannot happen. (Engel, 56)

51 Honesty is praiseworthy because it deserves the approval of all. (Ibid., 121)

52 Zsa Zsa Gabor was told in front of millions of television viewers last night she is vain, untalented and a complete non-event ... The incident took place on a late-night celebrity program, "The Eamonn Andrews Show." Zsa Zsa's outspoken fellow guest was comedian Peter Cook ... "You cannot be very talented yourself otherwise you would recognize talent in others and you would not have said I was untalented," bit back Miss Gabor (in response to Cook's criticism). ("Zsa Zsa Told She's Untalented Non-Event," Reuters News Service, *Miami News*, 10 January 1969, 5A)

53 Your ideas are immaterial. But whatever is immaterial does not matter. Therefore, your ideas do not matter. (Leo A. Groarke et al., *Good Reasoning Matters!* 128)

54 With millions of college grads seeking employment, it should not be hard to replace dissatisfied teachers who feel the urge to strike. (Engel, 163)

55 Rome tolerated, and even praised, homosexuality. This led to the collapse of the Roman Empire. Now America is beginning to tolerate homosexuality; in San Francisco, it's a regular way of life. If we continue in this path, it will surely lead to the collapse of our country. (MacKinnon, *Basic Reasoning*, 287.)

56 The witness is wearing a miniskirt in court. Her hair is obviously bleached. She's decked out with cheap perfume and junk jewelry. So, there is certainly no good reason to believe her account of how the accident happened. (Ibid., 289.)

57 [T]he universe is spherical in form ... because all the constituent parts of the universe, that is the sun, moon, and the planets appear in this form. (Nicolas Copernicus, "The New Idea of the Universe")

☞58 I am concerned by the recent letters to the editor which portray the Women's Health Care Centre as an abortion clinic. I would like to point out that the Women's Health Care Centre provides many valuable services ... pregnancy non-stress testing; colposcopy clinic; lactation consultant (breast feeding support); counselling and information on a wide range of health issues of concern to women and their families; workshops concerning PMS, menopause, body image, living alone, and many others. (Letter to the editor, *Peterborough Examiner*, May 20, 1992, reported in Groarke et al., *Good Reasoning Matters!* 214–15)

59 Here's a bad apple in the bushel. They all must be bad.

60 I was glad to see obscenity receive another great blow with the banning of December's *Penthouse* magazine. What shall we ban next? Libraries? We could stop a lot of book thefts by banning libraries. (Letter to the Editor, *Toronto Star*, Nov. 21, 1984, reported in Groarke et al., *Good Reasoning Matters!* 260)

Summary

Problems with ...

I. PREMISES	II. RELEVANCE	III. SUFFICIENCY
equivocation	ad hominem	false cause
begging the question	abusive	chance
leading question	tu quoque	reverse-order
false dichotomy	hypocrisy	3rd variable
slippery slope	inconsistency	person-who
	vested interests	appeal to ignorance
	emotional appeals	genetic fallacy
	pity	composition & division
	fear	
	bandwagon	
	straw man	
	red herring	

Appendices

Appendix One

Answers to Selected Questions

Chapter One: Overview

Exercise 1.1

1 The premises are fine – they pass the acceptability condition – but the logic is suspect. None of the reasons are sufficient to warrant the inference to the stated conclusion.

4 The acceptability condition is violated here. The first premise is precisely the sort of thing we may challenge. Some hard-nosed free market Libertarian types may also challenge the second premise. Even if we accept that drugs harm, it doesn't follow that we ought to do anything about it. Mere facts can't justify oughts in so simple a way.

5 The first premise occurs as part of the first sentence, after the word "because." And this premise may be challenged in terms of clarity (what is meant by "unnatural"), or in terms of acceptability. We might say it isn't unnatural (depending on how we define what's natural). The second premise is also problematic. We can cast doubt on this claim merely by pointing out something that is unnatural that we don't believe should be banned, for example, prosthetic limbs. The third premise, meanwhile, is at least contentious. Lastly, we could complain about the grounds condition. That X is unnatural is not sufficient reason to infer that X is immoral.

7 Acceptability condition is violated. Assuming the line has to be drawn anywhere at all is a bit presumptuous, but even if we accept that the line has to be drawn, why need we draw it there? A grounds worry is also present. Merely because X is the law doesn't entail that X is a *good* law. And the issue seems to be focussing precisely on whether the law ought to be changed, so pointing out what the law *is*, in this case, is hardly relevant to what the law *ought to be*.

12 A grounds problem. This is an interesting "reason." Is it the case that declining to celebrate the Queen's 50th anniversary is sufficient

grounds to decline declaring Nelson Mandela an honorary Canadian citizen?

15 Sometimes it's difficult to make out the argument at all. In this case, let's highlight the premise that rodeo is part of our heritage. This is sort of like saying that, because we did it in the past, we should continue to do it now. As put, this should seem a rather weak connection. After all, merely because my parents smoked doesn't mean I ought to as well. Grounds condition is violated.

17 Acceptability problem. Well, what if? Can mere speculation prove a case?

19 The grounds condition is met. How about the acceptability conditions? Premises 1 and 3 seem uncontroversial, but what about 2 and 4? Looking only at 2, we might ask whether suffering is necessarily caused by craving. If, while walking through a park, a tree falls on me and breaks my back, is my suffering due to my craving? Was it my craving to walk through a park? Or perhaps my craving to walk through a park without being assaulted by falling trees? Even if that was my craving, is the suffering because I had that craving? Alternatively, we might suggest that the pain in my back is felt merely because I interpret it as pain and suffering. If I didn't do that, then it wouldn't be pain and suffering to me ... To assess 4, we'd need more information.

Chapter Two: Argument Components

Exercise 2.1

1 Yes, this is an argument. The main conclusion is that schools do not prepare children for their future learning styles. The main support concerns the lack of group work.

3 This is not an argument. Despite the *decoy* "because," it is simply an explanation. We are not in doubt that accidents occur in the workplace. What we might want an argument about is whether this explanation is accurate.

5 This is not an argument. It is simply an explanation. We are not asked to accept any inference. We might expect an argument that drug use among young people is increasing, but the author is simply presupposing this. If we treated it as an argument, the next line, that drug use tends to increase when people go to college, cannot support the inference that drug use among youth is on the *increase*, since, presumably young people have been going to college for quite some time.

7 Whether we treat this prose as an argument or an explanation depends on how likely we are to accept the first line, that supermarkets try to increase sales. As long as we are prone to accept this without argument, the rest is simply an interesting *account* or *explanation* of how supermarkets manage to do this. As long as we are unlikely to accept this first

claim by itself, *and* are willing to take the subsequent lines as *more obvious* than the first line, then we may call this an argument. We can guess that the former interpretation is more common than the latter.

8 This is an explanation, despite the decoy "because."

10 The quoted passage is an argument. The conclusion is the attention should be given to those adjacent areas around the park that have potential to be developed. Notice the inference indicator, "since," that begins the argument. By the way, one may be inclined to say this is an explanation only, because it is an account *of* an argument, and not itself an argument. That is to say, although Garreth provides an argument, Gauthier, the journalist, does not.

Exercise 2.2

2 "Hence" in the last line is a conclusion indicator. What follows it is the main conclusion of the argument. That is, it is not reasonable for women to consent to non-communicative sex. The first two sentences approximate the two premises used to support the conclusion. Notice that the two premises must work in tandem to support the conclusion; they do not support the conclusion independently from each other. In chapter 3 we will pay more attention to this.

4 The conclusion is that computers cannot cheat. This is inferred on the basis that they cannot break rules. The phrase "we should be able to see, then" acts as a conclusion indicator here.

6 The inference indicator "for" tells us that what follows is the premise. Therefore the conclusion is not that God is love, which we might expect, but that he that loveth not, knoweth not God.

8 Let's highlight the inference indicators in this argument. "That today's parents are under an increasing strain in bringing up children *is shown by* the rapid and horrible rise in the incidence of child abuse. Obviously the government must provide substantial help to the family, *which means* there should be a broad system of day-care centres for children of working parents. The number of working mothers is constantly increasing, *so* certainly small children will be even more neglected unless there are day-care centres. Moreover, we now know how important it is for children to be stimulated and given the chance to learn at the earliest ages, and this need can best be filled by such centres." What this shows is that some conclusions act as premises to further conclusions. So what's the main conclusion, or the main point of the argument? As presented, we must say the main conclusion is that there should be a broad system of day-care centres for children of working parents. Now, we might want to qualify this by asserting that these should be government-supported, and not merely private. Unfortunately, the "which means" prevents us from claiming that. It claims, rightly or wrongly, that the need for governments to provide substan-

tial help to the family is a *premise* which leads to the need of daycares. One might suggest the relation ought to go in the reverse direction.

11 The conclusion is the first line. There are no inference indicators.

Exercise 2.3

2 There is a missing premise and a missing conclusion here. The missing premise is "We ought not (or don't prefer to) sell ourselves into slavery." The missing conclusion is "We ought not favour the anti-terrorist bill."

6 The missing proposition is quickly gleaned by asking the following question: is a fetal stem cell an "innocent human life"? The arguer here presumes the answer is "yes," and it is here we may challenge her.

9 The assumption here is that the anti-gun legislation, anti-smoking legislation, and de-criminalization of marijuana use are all "wrongs."

Chapter Three: Mapping an Argument

Exercise 3.1

1 (1) [Surrogacy is really another form of prostitution]. (2) [Prostitutes "rent" out their bodies and are renumerated]. (3) [So too do surrogates]. ((Since)) (4) [prostitution is outlawed], (5) [surrogacy should be outlawed, too]. Notice that the "so" in proposition 3 is a *decoy* indicator. It's more like an "also" in this case. Also notice that we did not break the disjunct (2) into two propositions. To do so, we would need to link the two conjuncts. Notice also that we demarcated the last sentence into two propositions. The premise indicator "since" tells us that what's coming next is a premise, but it doesn't follow that the whole thing is a premise. Rather, it is on the basis of (4) that (5) is being claimed. Here is the diagram.

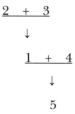

4 (1) [The signers of the Declaration of Independence did not intend to claim that men and women should be considered equal]. For one thing, (2) [they used the word *men* in the statement, "All men are created equal."] For another, (3) [it is a historical fact that men and

women were not considered equal in 1776]. (4) [Women were not even guaranteed the right to vote in the United States until 1920].

6 (1) [Desert mountaintops make good sites for astronomy]. (2) [Being high], (3) [they sit above a portion of the atmosphere], (4) [enabling a star's light to reach a telescope without having to swim through the entire depth of the atmosphere.] (5) [Being dry], (6) [the desert is also relatively cloud-free]. (7) [The merest veil of haze or cloud can render a sky useless for many astronomical measures].

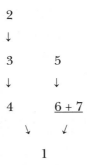

To distinguish whether one proposition leads to another or vice versa, it is wise to ask, "why that?" One proposition should stand out. For example, if we ask "why are deserts cloud free?" the answer will be "Because they're dry." Or, if we ask "Why do they sit above a portion of the atmosphere?" the answer will be "Because they're high." One may also question why (3) leads to (4) when (6) is conjoined with (7). The answer is that's how the argument is worded. If we ask why a star's light reaches a telescope without having to swim through the entire depth of the atmosphere, we have the answer, because it sits above a chunk of the atmosphere, whereas if we ask why the merest veil of haze renders a sky useless for astronomical gazing, we do *not* get the answer that the desert is relatively cloud free. Still, the basic structure of the argument may be understood in the following simpler manner: (1) [Desert mountaintops make good sites for astronomy]. (2) [Being high, they sit above a portion of the atmosphere, enabling a star's light to reach a telescope without having to swim through the entire depth of the atmosphere]. (3) Being dry, the desert is also relatively cloud-free]. (4) [The merest veil of haze or cloud can render a sky useless for many astronomical measures].

9 (1) [Don't go to the hospital unless you have absolutely no choice]. (2) [The director of the Centre for Disease Control says] (3) [two million of the people who enter hospitals each year catch infections unrelated to their original conditions]. (4) [Eighty thousand die from these infections]. (5) [This makes hospitals more lethal than highways], (6) [and that's not even counting victims of botched surgery].

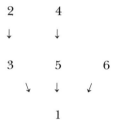

We might quibble about the standardization. Many will treat (2) and (3) as one proposition. Alternatively some may skip over the content indicated by (2) entirely. But we are given a reason for (3) here. For example, someone might say, "Why should I believe you about (3)?" And the answer is provided: a pretty good authority has said so. The reason for breaking up (5) and (6) is that it strikes us that these are different things. Admittedly the author mentions (6) tangentially, but it clearly acts as an independent reason on its own, and so should not be ignored.

Conversely, we may quibble about the diagram. Look again at (3) and (4). Students generally see that they should distinguish these, but is this the best mapping of them? Aren't (4) and (3) related to each other in some closer connection than shown here? Do they not instead converge on (5)? The answer is No, since (5) speaks about fatalities, whereas (3) speaks about illnesses only. So (3) cannot by itself lead to (5). Granted, some will say, but doesn't this merely show that (3) is thereby *linked* with (4) to yield (5)? Clearly the deaths indicated in (4) are *integrally connected* to (3). Perhaps this is precisely as the author intended. Still, we may wonder, isn't getting an unrelated illness *itself* a reason not to go to the hospital? If so, (3) provides independent support for (1). And notice, neither can we maintain that (3) leads to (4) (which leads to (5)). For we do not answer "why (4)?" with (3). That people get sick does not mean they will die.

11 (1) [If you give people a monetary incentive to return the bottles, then they will]. But (2) [if people return the bottles, then they will not be discarded as litter]. But (3) [a monetary incentive is precisely what the bottle bill provides]. ((Hence)) (4) [the bottle bill would remove a major source of litter].

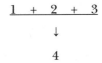

Notice, first, how many lines were superfluous to the argument. Notice, next the odd use of the negative conjunction "but." Usually "but" indicates that what's coming next is negatively relevant to what came before, whereas, here, they are all positively connected. Also, conjunctions, as we've noted, tend to be indicators of *convergent* arguments, whereas here the argument is clearly linked. In the next chapter we'll focus on the importance of clarity. If part of our intent is to convince someone of something, we should also help them understand what it is they should be convinced about!

13 (1) [A strong case can be made for amending the sanctions [on Iraq]]. First, (2) [as with most embargoes, they leak like a sieve] (3) [Smuggled oil is pouring across Iraq's borders, most notably into Turkey, Syria and Jordan]. Second, (4) [the sanctions clearly worsen the plight of Iraq's 22 million captive people, notwithstanding the 1997 oil-for-food program, which allows the regime to sell a portion of its oil output to buy food, medicine and other humanitarian goods]. Third, (5) [the sanctions provide Baghdad with its most powerful ammunition in portraying itself as a victim of Western aggression]

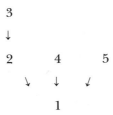

Notice we are ignoring, here, the "notwithstanding" clause. We'll deal with those sort of propositions in 3.5.

16 "We think (1) [the current slump in the telecom sector will be prolonged], ((due to)) (2) [a decline in telecom operator spending], (3)

[a glut of network capacity], and (4) [the absence of compelling new network technologies]," agreed analysts at UBS Warburg.

Exercise 3.2

1 (1) [To date, diplomacy isn't doing the job]. (2) [The Iraqis won't evacuate Kuwait because the United Nations' secretary-general – or even the garrulous Jesse Jackson – lays on the unction of sweet reason]. (3) [If Saddam Hussein were reasonable, he wouldn't have invaded Kuwait in the first place]. (H4) Saddam Hussein invaded Kuwait. ((Therefore)) (H5) [Saddam Hussein is not reasonable].

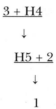

4 (1) [You are inconsistent]. (2) [You argue against capital punishment by saying you are opposed to the taking of human life]. Yet (3) [you argue for a pro-choice stand on abortion]. (H4) [A pro-choice stand on abortion entails the taking of human life].

7 (1) [The administration's economic program is unwise], ((because)) (2) [it takes significant benefits away from the poor]. ((Furthermore)), (3) [Its environmental impact is enormous]. (4) [12 million hectares of environmentally sensitive swamp lands are zoned for a silicone parkland]. (H5) [Taking benefits away from the poor is unwise]. (H6) [Negatively impacting the environment is unwise].

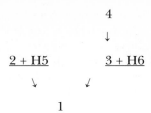

10 (1) [The claim that family-planning programs have contributed to the decline of sexual mores is not supported by the evidence]. (2) [Family planning first came onto the scene in the 70s]. (3) [In the 50s and 60s, more than half of all teenage women entering marriage were pregnant], and (4) [many others who became pregnant escaped notice by obtaining illegal abortions]. ((Therefore)) (H5) [teenagers demonstrated a collapse of sexual mores prior to the 70s].

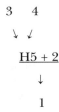

Exercise 3.3

1 A second argument (1) [[for vegetarianism]] concerns (2) [the suffering inflicted on animals by modern factory farming] ... (3) [Sometimes suffering is justified by later benefits], ((but)) (4) [here the benefits are morally trivial]. (5) [Unlike wolves or lions, we humans don't need meat for a healthy diet]. And (6) [the pleasures of the table surely don't justify torturing animals throughout their lives].

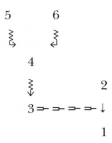

2 (1) [The National Rifle Association (NRA) argues that having guns in the home will lessen violent attacks in the home]. ((Even if this were true, it is not to the point)). (2) [A substantial majority of the nation's gun victims are felled by relatives or friends, not by criminals, often in the heat of anger or passion, using readily available handguns]. (3) [If a gun were not so handy, it is possible a less deadly weapon would suffice to release the momentary surge of aggression].

$$\underline{2 + 3}$$
$$\wr\downarrow$$
$$1$$

4 (1) [The Ontario Ministry of the Environment is not criminally responsible for allowing dangerous pollutants to flow from an abandoned mine into a tiny village's water] ((because)) (2) [the government was working to fix the problem], a judge ruled yesterday. Justice Celynne Dorval ((conceded)) (3) [ministry officials allowed some liquid contaminated with metals to flow into the water surrounding Deloro, Ont.], ((but)) said the government is not at fault ((because)) (4) [it had taken significant steps to remedy the discharge]. Notice that "the government is not at fault" is the same proposition already numbered (1). Therefore, we have simply skipped over it. The diagram is

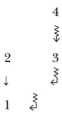

In this case, although (3) is a counter-consideration to (1), (4) is a counter-consideration to (3). The idea is that two negatives cancel each other out.

7 (1) [The report does not deny the accomplishments for which Yale presumably chose its honorees – prominent politicians, philosophers and inventors]. ((It objects, however, to)) (2) [Yale, even now, making no mention of these men's more questionable positions and activities in support of slavery], which might have made them more controversial choices when the campus's most prominent honorees were named ... (3) ["Yale is far from being the only or the worst in this regard]," said Gerald Horne, a professor of African and Afro-American studies at the University of North Carolina, "((but on the other hand)), (4) [Yale purports to be, and is, a leading force in higher education in the

United States], and (5) [it's important for Yale to set an example]."
(H6) [Yale erred.] Here we need to add the missing conclusion: something like "Boo on Yale." The diagram proceeds thus

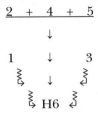

Chapter Four: Language Use

Exercise 4.1

3 This one was commented upon in the *National Post.* "Read that again
slowly: China has a 'legitimate' right to target Los Angeles without the
Americans being so unsporting as to put up defences that would 'nullify' them" (Mark Steyn, "Missile defence is hardly pie in the sky,"
National Post, 30 July 2001, A11).

5 Here, the author is relying more heavily on emotive rhetoric than argument, and good critical thinkers should be able to detect that fairly
quickly. First off, the first line associates the use of genetically altered
foods with "crimes of ignorance and greed beset upon us by our own
government." This is a pretty bold statement and requires argumentation – we can't simply accept it as true, just because it is stated in nice
rhetoric. Calling genetically modified foods "Franken-foods" is another
way to appeal to our ready-built emotions, rather than providing an
argument. Frankenstein is, of course, a case where science went amok,
so it's fitting to the extent that this is what the speaker wants us to conclude, but again what we want is a demonstration that the parallel is
apt, and not merely an assertion that it is so. That it "may" cause
"unnamed" defects is consistent with the possibility that it "may not"
which, on closer inspection, is not really the sort of damning evidence
that can legitimate the previous emotive rhetoric. Really, what looks
like an argument is just a barrage of emotive language. We may agree
with the conclusion, but we can't possibly agree with the reasons given.

7 Bias against the natives is revealed in at least three ways here. First, the
natives are associated with other wild beasts: deer, alligators, and
turkeys. So displacing the natives shouldn't upset us any more than
displacing alligators. Second, notice the inclusion of the Corn Dance.
This has nothing to do with the story, so we must ask ourselves, why is
this included? The answer seems to be, that at least there's one difference between the natives and wild turkeys: the natives are somehow

sillier. Third, the concept of intrusion only counts for any "eventual resident." Clearly the current residents just don't count.

10 The emphasis on what the two women politicians were wearing seems
innocuous enough by itself, but do we find such details in journalistic
reports about male politicians? What does the fact that we don't reveal
about this report? Of course, the colouring is supposed to make us
think that MacPhail and Kwan will be docile, hardly the desired dispo-
sition of the opposition, but is their clothing the only evidence that
we're offered for this judgment? Emphasizing women's clothing seems
apt in a report of the Oscars, perhaps, but when it is done in a report
of the throne speech, it seems that the author is confused about what
to make of women politicians at all.

12 This is not to say, by any means, that Cheerios isn't a healthy part of a
complete breakfast. But, one would certainly wonder if the writers of
the blurb knew the meaning of the word "endorsement," since this
clearly is one. In any event, the most interesting element is the statement, on the one hand, that "Cheerios financially supports Health
Check," and then later, that "Cheerios is proud to be the first cereal in
Canada to participate" in the program. This in no way undermines the
meaning of the Health Check emblem, but it's something that must be
kept in mind.

Also consider the line, "Emphasizing grain products such as cereals
and increasing fibre intake are components of healthy eating." We may
accept this without knowing to what degree this "component" constitutes healthy eating, or to what degree we can accommodate this component without Cheerios.

15 The use of quotation marks indicates innuendo in this case, particularly against the backdrop of what follows.

17 Notice that the author mentions why parents and critics welcome the
move, but says nothing about why teachers and school boards are
opposed. Are we to assume that the teachers' motives are purely self-
interested? This is a case of slanting by omission.

20 A use of a weasel word lurks here. Notice that they *could* be relocated. Of
course this is consistent with a plan to simply continue to ignore them.

23 We may accuse the speaker of obfuscation. Afraid to reveal our ignorance of Latin, we may be duped into believing a sound argument lurks
here somewhere.

25 A weasel word lurks here. That there is a *potential* is not by itself sufficient justification for the existence of a separate epistemology for
women.

Exercise 4.2

1 This is a verbal disagreement. The dispute stems from their disagreeing on what counts as "free will." Huck defines it in the normal sense,

as having no immediate external forces acting upon Injun Joe. Tom, on the other hand, interprets free will in a grand, metaphysical sense, which ignores the distinction between being bound and gagged and not being bound and gagged. Tom's sense is what makes some people complain that many of the so-called philosophical problems are caused by the weird way philosophers tend to define their terms, and many of their problems dissolve when we revert to ordinary language. Once Tom and Huck decide what they mean by free will for the case at hand, we can expect agreement.

3 This is a verbal disagreement. It may strike one as a factual dispute, since the subject of the debate is hard-core numbers. But paying closer attention reveals that they define "unemployed" in different senses. Scary Spice computes her figures in a way that is not consistent with what we normally mean by "the unemployed." She takes the total number of persons working subtracted by the total population. The problem is this will include children and the retired. Normally we define unemployed as those *who are capable* of working yet who are not. This will not include children and the infirm. It's all a matter of definition.

5 This is an attitudinal debate. There is nothing factual we can appeal to here in order to resolve the issue, nor are the disputants disagreeing about what sex means, presumably.

7 There are two arguments here. The first is verbal, the second factual. In the first dispute, Alice understands free speech as having no boundaries whatsoever, whereas this is rejected by the queen. Generally a right entails a duty in someone else to uphold that right. If we are to have equal rights, then, our rights will automatically be curtailed by our duties to uphold others' like rights. A common limitation on the right to free speech is that we are not allowed to yell "FIRE" in a crowded public domain merely because we think it would be fun.

The second debate is factual. Whether or not violence in the media causes harm is an empirical matter. It is not resolved by redefining our terms or revealing our attitudes.

Chapter Five: Definitions

Exercise 5.1

A: 3 and 8 are semantic ambiguities. The others are syntactic ambiguities.

Exercise 5.2

2 "Academic *ability*" is vague. It includes basing the hiring on proven record, obviously, but also includes basing the decision on mere *potentiality* – almost *despite* the record. Before this vagueness is settled, the claim is empty.

3 Ambiguous. On the one hand, if we go over to visit a professor, this may indeed be boring. But a "visiting professor" is also a noun indicating a *type* of professor; one who holds a position at University A, while she teaches for a term at University B. These people may be boring.

7 Syntactic ambiguity. *Who* can't go to the game? Kevin or James?

13 Both vague and ambiguous. Vague: What counts as a "mature" person is unspecified. There exist mature eight-year-olds. Ambiguous concerns "home deliveries." Do the applicants need to be midwives, or do they need merely to toss a Sears catalogue into the mailbox?

14 Vague. Don't we all strive for excellence? But what constitutes "excellence"? Also what constitutes a "quality" product? Another vague term. Typical buzz words that convey nothing.

17 Vague. "Streamlining" is not sufficiently specified for us to know what this means. Also, being "more responsible" is vague, not merely concerning what constitutes "responsibility," but also concerning the term "more." More compared to what?

22 Syntactic ambiguity. Presumably she isn't better *because* she was thrown off the building, in the manner of "that'll teach her."

27 Syntactic ambiguity. Actually, as put, there's no ambiguity. Grammatically it is the woman who must have curved legs and large drawers, and not the desk, but presumably such predicates belong to the desk and not to the woman for whom the desk is suitable. The ambiguity, thereby, resides between the grammar and the intent.

Exercise 5.3

1 Stipulative.

3 Emotively persuasive.

5 Lexical. At least this is the intention of Jonas. We may complain about Jonas's rendition, however. To think that stereotypes grant us "the power to guess the unseen from the seen" is to imagine an objective reality behind all stereotypes that is unwarranted from Jonas's other claims.

7 Emotively persuasive. Notice the word "true."

8 Both stipulative and emotively persuasive.

Exercise 5.4

1 Example: Intension: four-legged canine, often used as pets. Extension: Lassie, Snoopy, Fido, Asta. Conversely, one might list a variety of breeds of dogs: German Shepherds, Collies ...

7 Example: Intension: a humourous drawing, often accompanied with captions. Extension: Calvin & Hobbes, Charlie Brown, The Simpsons, The Far Side, Bizarro, the Mad Milkman.

Exercise 5.5

1 Too narrow. Democracy needn't involve complete martyrdom, one would hope.

4 Too narrow. Sneezing often involves audible emission of wind through the mouth, not the nose. Too broad. Heavy sighs (audible emission of wind through the nose) would count as sneezing.

7 Circular. Basically amounts to "Freedom of choice: the ability to choose freely."

8 Emotively persuasive.

11 Too narrow. We can have a true belief without knowing that we do. For example, I form a belief which, by fluke, happens to be true. Usually we must qualify Plato's definition by throwing the word "justified" into the mix, although there may be occasions where even justified true belief may not constitute knowledge. An example following Gettier is as follows: I borrow my neighbour's red Volvo, because my red Honda is in the shop. You see me get out of the neighbour's car and form the not unreasonable belief that I drive a red car. Your belief is true, and it is justified to the extent that it is based on evidence. Unfortunately, the evidence was not sufficient for you to formulate your belief, so despite it being justified true belief, we may not wish to claim that you *know* my car is red.

15 Narrow. One needn't desire sex with *any* other woman to be a lesbian.

18 Much criticism and debate have revolved around this definition. As put, it is excessively broad. Very few would count as being healthy in this full, robust sense. The World Health Organization defends this as an ideal toward which nations should aspire. Fine, but what are the implications? Citizens of developing nations who are starving and diseased are no more unhealthy than the overfed citizens of industrial nations.

20 Vague. This is so open-ended it's a tautology. By such a definition, *every* act is self-interested. If so, the charge of too broad is apt. Heroic altruism, for example, constitutes a self-interested act.

23 A suppressed definition is lurking here. Basically the author defines the concept of "liberty" as committed to pure freedom: anything goes, without restrictions. This is too narrow, since it excludes understanding the concept of liberty as being curtailed by the like liberty of others. Theft and murder are clearly bad acts by the principle of liberty, and any definition that pretends otherwise simply misconstrues "liberty" for "pure freedom."

26 Emotively persuasive and too narrow. Compare, though, Oscar Wilde's comment on opera: "Some say opera is not what it used to be and that's the problem. I say it is what it used to be and that's the problem."

28 Too narrow. This rules out the possibility of heterosexual female protagonists, although it may well be viewed as a negative commentary on precisely that point.

32 Too narrow. Good friends meet at places other than Cheers. Too broad. Other people meet at Cheers who aren't good friends.

35 "Properly speaking," eh? This is a tell-tale emotively persuasive indicator. Also too narrow if we're trying to capture common usage.

36 Too broad. Many things may be deemed useful that aren't particularly moral. It's useful to me to take your money. It's useful to us if a particular group became our slaves, etc. Too vague. What precisely is meant by "useful"? Who constitutes "us"?

38 "Making community use a prerequisite of creativity carries a whiff of totalitarianism," claims Fulford. In other words, it is too narrow. The definition excludes creativity that has no such community "use." We may also complain about vagueness. As Fulford states, "The passage is pure bureaucratese, all-inclusive and useless."

39 Too broad. Knowledge can't be assessed merely by the internal mental state. Believing something sincerely doesn't make it true. Also too narrow. We may know something without making such a big deal about it. "This is a piece of lint." It's something I know, but am I going to be as emphatic about it as the definition alludes? Hardly, though we may wonder about the definition of "sincere" and "strong," in which case this raises a vagueness issue.

41 Too broad. A sunset has aesthetic value, but isn't what we mean by art. Possibly too narrow, since some things we may recognize as art don't have aesthetic value *to us* anyway. And the fact that we may wonder whether we should add "to us" or not shows the definition also suffers from being too vague.

44 Obscure and vague.

47 Vague and too broad. Is it "practising" or doing? It may be practising for something, but that is not typically referred to as self-abuse. Besides, self-abuse comes in many flavours, not all of which are considered masturbation. The problem with this definition stems from the fear of offending fragile readers; thus the OED relies on euphemism.

Chapter Six: Acceptability Conditions

Exercise 6.1 A

2 *A priori* true. This may strike one as odd. Notice that what is *a priori* true is the *relation* between continued identity and the soul, and not that one survives after death. Consider: "If this is an incline, then it's also a decline." Surely this is true, but nothing about the truth of this commits us to believe either that it is an incline or that it is a decline.

5 The premise is clearly appealing to an authority. Whether this is an acceptable or faulty appeal depends on what sort of therapist this is. Is she a financial advisor, a sports therapist, or a marriage counsellor? Only if she were the latter would we have grounds to accept the

premise. Even then, this would be so only as long as most marriage counsellors don't disagree. Another strong reason cited is sexual incompatibility, for example. In this case, we might accept the premise *provisionally.*

9 This may be accepted due to textual support. We know where to look, at least, if we doubt it.

Exercise 6.1 B

3 This is acceptable testimony. Again, one may be surprised about this, but the task is to assess the merits of the *premise*, and not the merits of the argument as a whole. It is a poor argument, admittedly. Merely seeing a cat without a tail does not provide sufficient proof that the cat's tail was hacked off by an axe. As far as Wally's testimony goes, however, we have no reason to reject it. Recall, the default is acceptance of testimony. We change our minds only as long as evidence points to one of our four criteria being violated. But without further information about Wally's moral character, or position when witnessing the event, the testament is a report, not an interpretation, and the claim is plausible: there do exist cats without tails. Therefore, we can accept the claim by the criterion of adequate testimony.

4 This fails the condition of adequate testimony. That she was standing right there covers our position condition, but it is clearly an interpretation, not a report.

5 On what basis are we asked to accept the claim that Chrétien will support getting rid of the sexist language in Canada's national anthem? The answer is a statement made by the wife of one of Chrétien's advisors. This smacks of a faulty appeal to authority.

6 The testimony is plausible, and there is little reason for us to doubt it, but did you notice the source of this report? Knowing that the *National Inquirer* has a poor reputation for honest reporting, we have grounds to doubt the claim.

Exercise 6.2

1 Internal inconsistency. The first premise claims, "None are ...," the second admits "Some are ... "

3 Premise is less certain than the conclusion. That I'm having troubled dreams is possible, but that it's because of *that* reason is less so.

8 An unacceptable assumption lurks here. It assumes that if stores are open seven days a week, workers will be forced to work seven days a week. But workers don't work six days a week merely because stores are open six days, and workers don't work twenty-four hours a day merely because stores are open twenty-four hours a day.

10 Here is a case of appealing to a faulty assumption. In this case, the argu-

ment rests on not having the right not to allow homosexuals into one's own home. For that matter, we have a right to not allow anyone into our own home. This is what is meant by it's being our own home: we have exclusionary rights. But в&вs are businesses, not private homes in this sense.

13 Non-falsifiable. What would show that the Irish had really rejected the Nice Treaty?

15 Premises less certain than the conclusion. Whether Canada is recognized as one of the world's leaders is itself questionable, but certainly that is more acceptable than the reason cited.

Chapter Seven: Categorical Logic

Exercise 7.1

1 All D are F

5 Some P are not T (Here we used T to stand for "pretty," since P already stands for prostitute.)

7 Some F are W (Some flies are things that found their way into a flybottle.)

9 We'll do this in two steps. First we translate the name as a universal. Hence, All J are not D. This is not in proper categorical form. So we need to translate this as No J are D. No things that are identical to Jones are things that could get dates.

12 We'll do this one in two steps. First, All W are not J. But this is not in proper categorical form. So now we need to translate this into No W are J: No white boys are things that can jump.

15 Some L are P. (Admittedly, this says less than the original claim, but for logical purposes, it will suffice.)

17 All C are H. (H stands for "going to the homeopath down the street in the old Gym.")

18 All A are Q. (Note the reversal of subject and predicate?)

23 All S are T. (S stands for the average salary of professional baseball players and T stands for the two million plus.)

Exercise 7.2

1 1 All euthanasia is murder.
  2 All murder is wrong.
  3 All euthanasia is wrong

    1 All E are M
    2 All M are W
    3 All E are W

3 1 Some GM foods are products which may be dangerous.
2 All products which may be dangerous are products which should be labelled.
3 Therefore Some GM foods are products which should be labelled.

   1 Some G are D
   2 All D are L
   3 Some G are L

There's often no way to tell in advance whether a certain product poses a risk. So, one might be justified in declaring that the first line should be translated as a universal, rather than a particular.

Hence, 1. All GM foods are products which may be dangerous. (All G are D)
This is fine, as long as we don't confuse "... are D" with being a translation for "... are dangerous." Instead, it is to read as "... are products which may be dangerous." Whether *any* genetically modified food product actually *is* dangerous is impossible to tell without extensive testing, and therefore it must be assumed that all of them *may* pose a risk. So the deduction could reasonably be framed as

   1. All G are D
   2. All D are L
   3. All G are L

6 The conclusion is that students should not pay the deficit. That students are paying too much already is an extra proposition that does no work. That I'm paying too much already doesn't necessarily mean I don't owe anything further. The second line, "The problem with the deficit is the politician's not the students," is saying minimally that students are not responsible for the deficit. This is idle unless we insert an assumption. Consider: if you pass someone drowning, do you have a duty to save the person if you can without danger to yourself? Most will answer yes. But imagine if someone claimed: "Yeah, but I didn't cause his drowning: I'm not responsible for his drowning," we would find the utterance odd, if not immoral. This shows that the line asserting that the students are not responsible for the deficit will add to the argument only if we insert the assumption that "Only those responsible for the deficit should pay." Thus we get the gist of the argument.

   Only those responsible for the deficit should pay.
   Students are not responsible for the deficit.
   Therefore students should not pay.

This, in turn, is translated so:

1 All P are R
2 No S are R
3 No S are P

7 1 All fruits and vegetables prevent cancer.   = 1 All F are P
   2 All fruits and vegetables contain vitamin C. = 2 All F are C
   3 Therefore, all vitamin C prevents cancer.   = 3 All C are P

Exercise 7.3

1 All clowns are scary.   C 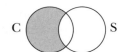 S

3 No hockey players are underpaid.   H  U

4 Some lawyers are trustworthy.   L  T

6 Some television shows are not boring.   T  B

7 All teletubbies are creepy.   T 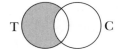 C

8 Some classes never end.   C  N

10 Some jokes are not funny.   J  F

12 All things that cry are babies.   C  B

16 Some guests are things that became sick.   G 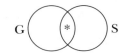 S

21 No things identical to you can castle in this case.

24 Some tooth fairies are things that visited my pillow.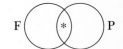

28 No killers are things that should be executed.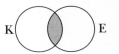

Chapter Eight: Categorical Logic: Validity

Exercise 8.1 A

1 All Ontarians are Canadians.
  Some Ontarians are not sports fans.
  Therefore, some Canadians are not sports fans.

All O are C
Some O are not S
Some C are not S

Valid

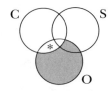

2 No Canadians want Quebec to separate.
  All Quebecers want Quebec to separate.
  Therefore no Quebecer is Canadian.

No C are S
All Q are S
No Q are C
{S = things that want Quebec to separate}   Valid

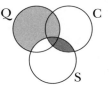

4 All coyotes are animals that love to howl at the moon.
  All kids are animals that love to howl at the moon.
  Hence all kids are coyotes.

All C are M
All K are M
All K are C
{M = things that love to howl at the moon}

Invalid

5 No ministers are cigarette smokers.
  Some cigarette smokers are persons who will succumb to cancer.
  Therefore, some ministers are not persons who will succumb to cancer.

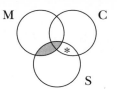

No M are S
Some S are C
Some M are C
    invalid {need an asterisk in M}

9 No True islander was in favour of the Bridge.
  Some Islanders were in favour of the bridge.
  Some Islanders are not true islanders.

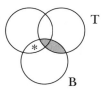

No T are B
Some I are B
Some I are not T
{B = things in favour of the bridge}   valid

Exercise 8.1 B

2 All R are H.
  No F are H.
  No R are F.

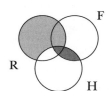

        valid

3 No T are A.
  No A are N
  No N are T.

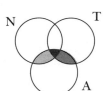

        invalid

7 All Z are M
  All M are V
  All Z are V

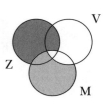

        valid

8 No E are O
   Some O are U
   Some U are not E

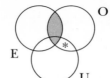

valid

Exercise 8.2

1 All V are T
   Some T are not C
   Some C are not V

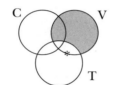

invalid {on the line}

2 No M are D
   Some M are not H
   Some H are D

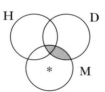

{H = things found in heroic tales}   invalid

3 Some J are D
   All J are T
   Some T are D

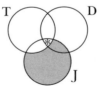

{T = two-dimensional}   valid   {hint: do universals first}

4 Some C are not A
   All C are H
   Some H are not A

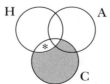

valid

5 All M are G
   All G are T
   Some M are T

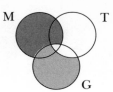

invalid {null set problem}

Exercise 8.3

1 Argument 1.
   1 All J are P.
   2 No P are A.
   3 {Therefore No J are A}

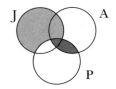

Valid

Argument 2.
   3 {No J are A.}
   4 All M are A
   5 Therefore No J are M

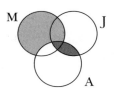

Valid

All steps are valid, so the argument as a whole is valid.

3 Argument 1.
   1 Some K are not F.
   2 All H are F.
   3 Therefore {Some K are not H.}

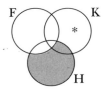

Valid

Argument 2.
   3 {Some K are not H.}
   4 All K are P.
   5 Therefore Some P are not H.

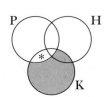

Valid

Since each syllogism is valid, the entire argument is valid.

6 Argument 1
    1 All F are G.
    2 No G are P.
    3 Therefore {No F are P.}

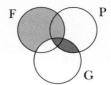

Valid

Argument 2.
    3 {No F are P.}
    4 Some P are L.
    5 Therefore {Some L are not F.}

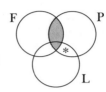

Valid

Argument 3.
    5 {Some L are not F.}
    6 All L are O
    7 Therefore {Some O are not F}

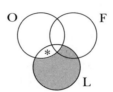

Valid

Argument 4.
    7 {Some O are not F}
    8 All O are M
    9 Therefore Some M are not F.

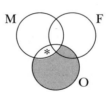

Valid

Since each separate syllogism (arguments 1–4) is valid, the whole argument is valid.

Exercise 8.4 A

1 a. It is false that some loitering is allowed. {rule of contradiction}
5 c. It is false that some tasty foods are non-fattening. {This is determined by two steps. 1. rule of contraposition (All tasty foods are fattening). 2. rule of contradiction (It is false that some tasty foods are non-fattening.}

Exercise 8.4 B

The answers are the last line given. The preceding line(s) show the steps to get there. The rules are given in {brackets}.

1 People who are going to be punished are immoral.
    1 All P are not M
    2 No P are M   {obversion}
2 Not all professors are impRactical
    1 Not all P are not R
    2 Some P are not non-R   {"not all" rule}
    3 Some P are C   {contraposition}
  {Note: "1. Not all P are I" is fine, as long as all moral things are treated as "not I"}
3 The only thing we have to Fear is fear Itself.
    1 Only F are I
    2 All I are F   {"only" rule}
4 Man is the only creature that consumes without producing.
    1 Only M are C
    2 All C are M   {"only" rule}
5 Any product that is not better than any other like product is not worth buying if it costs more than another similar brand.
    B = products that are better than any other like product.
    W = things not worth buying if it costs more than another similar brand.
    1 All non-B are not W
    2 All W are B   {contraposition}

7 All lonely people are prone to exploitation by others.
    All L are E
8 Every dog has his day.
    All D are Y
13 It is false that all white boys can't jump.
    1 ~[All W are not J]
    2 ~[No W are J]   {obversion}
    3 Some W are J   {rule of contradiction}
15. It's absolutely wrong to suppose that some non-persons are not non-fetuses.
    1. ~[Some non-P are not non-F]
    2. ~[Some F are not P]   {contraposition}
    3. All F are P   {rule of contradiction}
21 No shoes, no service. This is a good one. Let's treat shoes as S, and service as V. We could translate this as "No S are non-V." This doesn't fit our proper categorical form. But with obversion, we get, "All S are V." Hence,

1 No S are non-V
2 All S are V   {obversion}

That is, all things with shoes are serviced. But you might notice this is an odd translation of the original message, which is clearly placed in the negative. Let's examine this more closely. "No shoes, no service" claims that if one has no shoes, one will not receive service. So all shoeless people will not get service. Assuming shoeless persons are S and receiving service is V, we may translate this first step as All non-S are not V. This is not in proper categorical form, but the rule of contraposition tells us we can translate this as No S are V. Hence,

1 All Non-S are not V
2 All V are S   {contraposition}

This claims that all serviced things are things with shoes.

"All S are V" and "All V are S" are not equivalent, as we know. Since we may think of other conditions that might disqualify one from service, the best translation is the second: "All V are S."

Exercise 8.4 C

1 All S are P
   All E are S
   All E are P

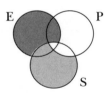

Valid

3 No V are F
   All D are not F
        = No D are F
   All D are V

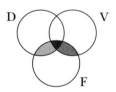

invalid

6 Some D are not N
   All N are W
   Some D are not W

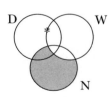

invalid {on the line}

10 All E are C
    Some C are N
    All E are N

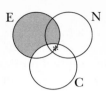

                    invalid {on the line}

12 Some non-T are not non-P
        = Some P are T {contraposition}
    All non-P are not H
        = All H are P {contraposition}

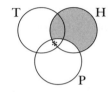

    No T are H   invalid {on the line}

13 Only non-F are non-S
        = All non S are non F {"only"}
        = All F are S {contraposition}
    All S are not G
        = No S are G {obversion}

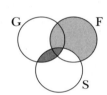

    Some G are not F   invalid {null set}

14 ~[Some E are not F]
        = No E are F {contradiction}
    ~[Some F are M]
        = No F are M {contradiction}
    All M are not E

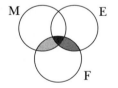

        = No M are E {obversion}   invalid

15 {H = things identical with Harry; S = things that love Sally; L = things
    that love Lucy}
    All H are S
    All S are not L
        = No S are L {obversion}
    All H are not L

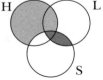

        = No H are L {obversion}   valid

Exercise 8.5

The numbers to the right of the translations indicate the rule numbers. A
✔ represents satisfaction with the rule, whereas an ✘ indicates violation of

the rule. In cases where rules are inapplicable, as when the first condition is not met, we will treat this as satisfaction with the rule. When any ✘ occurs in any rule, the argument as a whole is invalid.

1 Some B are S   #1. ✔
   All S are M   #2. ✔
   Some B are M   #3. ✔
                           #4. ✔
                           #5. ✔   Valid

2 No V are R   #1. ✔
   Some R are not D   #2. ✔
   Some D are not V   #3. ✘
                           #4. ✔
                           #5. ✔   Invalid

4 No M are S   #1. ✔
   Some F are not M   #2. ✔
   Some F are S   #3. ✘
                           #4. ✘
                           #5. ✔   Invalid

8 Some P are not T   #1. ✔
   All T are R   #2. ✘
   Some P are not R   #3. ✔
                           #4. ✔
                           #5. ✔   Invalid

11 All M are G   #1. ✔
   All G are T   #2. ✔
   Some M are T   #3. ✔
                           #4. ✔
                           #5. ✘   Invalid

14 All C are F   #1. ✔
   No F are A   #2. ✔
   No C are A   #3. ✔
                           #4. ✔
                           #5. ✔   Valid

17 All S are P   #1. ✔
   All E are S   #2. ✔
   All E are P   #3. ✔
                           #4. ✔
                           #5. ✔   Valid

19 No V are F   #1. ✔
    {All D are not F}   #2. ✔
        = No D are F   #3. ✘
    All D are V   #4. ✘
                                  #5. ✔   Invalid

21 Some T are E   #1. ✘
    {Some E are not non-B}   #2. ✔
        = Some E are B   #3. ✔
    Some T are B   #4. ✔
                                  #5. ✔   Invalid

24 {Not all S are D}   #1. ✘
        = Some S are not D   #2. ✔
    Some S are H   #3. ✔
    Some H are D   #4. ✘
                                  #5. ✔   Invalid

Chapter Nine: Propositional Logic: Translation

Exercise 9.1

1 A ⊃ ~L
4 T ⊃ ~C {Really we want "If the test is NOT cancelled ...": hence, ~C ⊃ ...
   But C in this case stands for having a chance. But if the test is
   not cancelled, then this is equivalent to the test occurring, hence T.
   Alternatively, we can designate "having a chance" as F for fortune, in
   which case "Unless the test is cancelled, I don't have a chance"
   becomes ~C ⊃ ~F.}
7 E ⊃ ~P
10 I • F
13 T ⊃ S
16 W ⊃ F
19 ~E ⊃ ~P

Exercise 9.2 A

1 ~(A v S)	5 M v ~O	9 ~(C ⊃ J)
c. ~A • ~ S	c. ~(~M • O)	b. ~(~J ⊃ ~C)
3 ~Y ⊃ Q	6 ~D • N	12 Z • ~G
a. ~Q ⊃ Y	b. ~(D v ~N)	d. ~(~Z v G)

Exercise 9.2 B

1 ~(~C ⊃ S). "S" represents survive death. We could instead say ~D, for not dying.

4 P • [(F v S) • ~C]. P = playoffs. F = first round. S = second round. C = winning the Stanley Cup.

7 ~(F v V) ⊃ G. Alternatively we could say: (~F • ~V) ⊃ G.

9 ~L

13 E ⊃ S. E = Sometimes readers of Homer experience events in their lives that coincide with Ulysses' plight. S = A case of serendipity.

15 ~(M v L) ⊃ D. Alternatively, (~M • ~L) ⊃ D. These are equivalent by DeMorgan's Law.

Exercise 9.3

(1)
1 ~B v B
2 ~B ⊃ ~K
3 B

(4)
1 R ⊃ ~C
2 C
3 ~R

(8)
1 A ⊃ I
2 I ⊃ H
3 ~H
4 ~A
{or 3 ~H • ~I,
or 3 ~(H v I)}

(11)
1 ~(L • D) ⊃ B
2 B
3 ~(L • D)

(13)
1 (L • D) ⊃ ~B
2 ~(L • D)
3 B

(15)
1 R ⊃ U
2 ~U
3 ~R

(18)
1 R v ~U
2 U
3 R

Exercise 9.4

1	F	R	~F	F v R	(F v R) ⊃ ~F
	T	T	F	T	F
	T	F	F	T	F
	F	T	T	T	T
	F	F	T	F	T

2	T	E	T • E	(T • E) ⊃ T
	T	T	T	T
	T	F	F	T
	F	T	F	T
	F	F	F	T

When a truth table has all T's in it like this, we are confronted with a tautology, or an *a priori* truth. The truth table for P ⊃ P, would be another example, as would P v ~P. When a truth table reveals all F's we are confronted with an *a priori falsehood*. The truth table for P • ~P would be such an example. Notice that P ⊃ ~P would *not* yield Fs in every row. This is because whenever the antecedent is F, the conditional statement is T. This condition is met in the second row of the two-row truth table for P ⊃ ~P:

P	~P	P ⊃ ~P
T	F	F
F	T	T

3

G	W	~W	G • ~W	~(G • ~W)	~(G • ~W) v W
T	T	F	F	T	T
T	F	T	T	F	F
F	T	F	F	T	T
F	F	T	F	T	T

8

J	L	~J	~L	(J • ~L)	(J • ~L) v ~J
T	T	F	F	F	F
T	F	F	T	T	T
F	T	T	F	F	T
F	F	T	T	F	T

9

F	H	~F	(H • ~F)	F v (H • ~F)
T	T	F	F	T
T	F	F	F	T
F	T	T	T	T
F	F	T	F	F

12

O	G	~O	(~O v O)	(~O v O) ⊃ G
T	T	F	T	T
T	F	F	T	F
F	T	T	T	T
F	F	T	T	F

Exercise 9.5

1 1 M ⊃ P
   2 P
   3 M

c	p	p	
M	P	M ⊃ P	
T	T	T	Invalid.
T	F	F	Premises true while
F*	**T***	**T***	conclusion false.
F	F	F	

3 1 K ⊃ T
   2 ~T
   3 ~K

	K	T	c ~K	p ~T	p K ⊃ T	
	T	T	F	F	T	Valid
	T	F	F	T	F	Conclusion true in all
	F	T	T	F	T	cases where all premises
	F	F	**T***	**T***	**T***	are true.

5 1 R v T
   2 T ⊃ K
   3 ~R
   4 K

	R	T	c K	p ~R	p R v T	p T ⊃ K	
	T	T	T	F	T	T	
	T	T	F	F	T	F	
	T	F	T	F	T	T	Valid.
	T	F	F	F	T	T	Conclusion true in
	F	T	**T***	**T***	**T***	**T***	all cases where all
	F	T	F	T	T	F	premises are true.
	F	F	T	T	F	T	
	F	F	F	T	F	T	

7

H	O	W	(H • W)	(O ⊃ W)	c H • (O ⊃ W)	p (H • O) ⊃ W
T	T	T	T	T	T	T
T	T	F	T	F	F	F
T	F	T	F	T	T	T
T	F	F	F	T	T	T
F	T	T	F	T	F*	T*
F	T	F	F	F	F	T
F	F	T	F	T	F	T
F	F	F	F	T	F	T

Invalid. Premises true while conclusion false.

Exercise 10.1 A

1 1 F ⊃ ~R   p
   2 R   p
   3 ~F   1,2 m.t.

Notice that the US's imposing limitations is a case of another country imposing restrictions. Hence the second line is a negation of the consequent of the first line.

3 1 K v H   p
   2 ~K   p
   3 H   1,3 d.s.

We treat the second line as simply the denial that it is Kant.

6 1 L ⊃ I   p
   2 I ⊃ C   p
   3 L ⊃ C   1,2, h.s.

8 1 S   p
   2 S ⊃ T   p
   3 T   1,2 m.p.

"Mystics are typically very sincere about their religious experiences."
This is translated as S. "A true belief is simply that which is sincerely
held" is translated in reverse: if it is sincerely held, the belief is true.
Hence S ⊃ T. Since something's being "veridical" means that it is true,
the conclusion is the consequent of the conditional presented on the
second line: T. The second premise is false, by the way, but the argument is valid.

10 1 S v B   p
    2 ~B   p
    3 S   1,2 d.s.

14 1 R v ~U   p
    2 U   p
    3 R   1,2 d.s.

Exercise 10.1 B

1 There is a missing premise and conclusion here. The missing premise
   is "Mr. Milosevic is the only government leader on trial." The missing
   conclusion is "The tribunal in The Hague is not honest."

3 The missing premise is "If tests turn up nothing, reasonable terms
   should be negotiated." Given this, we can now add the missing conclusion: "More reasonable terms should be negotiated." (Or "Their anxiety is not unfounded.")

6 The conclusion is not stated here. It is "If private companies get
   involved, then quality goes down."

9 To make this a case of *modus tollens*, we may note that Saddam Hussein
   did invade Kuwait, and therefore Saddam Hussein is *not* reasonable.

12 To make this into a *modus ponens*, we need to add the missing conditional proposition "If something is there for a reason, it deserves to be
   treated with respect." Then we can interpret the case of the crow as
   merely an instance of the general proposition that *everything* (or at least

of things created by God) is there for a purpose. Of course, we should also make this explicit, i.e, that a crow is one of God's creations. For present purposes, we'll let that go, since it would bring in too many propositions for a *modus ponens* argument. As far as challenging this argument goes, we are certainly entitled to doubt God's existence (and thereby his creating crows for a purpose). More germane, however, is whether the missing conditional proposition is acceptable. After all, terrorist activity certainly has a purpose, but it might stretch our tolerance to thereby respect it. Some purposes may be good or bad, and we might reserve our respect to only those purposes that are good.

Exercise 10.2

2	1 R ⊃ ~I	p
	2 ~I ⊃ ~T	p
	3 ~T ⊃ M	p
	4 R	p
	5 R ⊃ ~T	1,2 h.s.
	6 R ⊃ M	3,5 h.s.
	7 M	4,6 m.p.
		Or
	5 ~I	1,4 m.p.
	6 ~T	2,5 m.p.
	7 M	3,6 m.p.

7	1 H ⊃ F	p
	2 L	p
	3 F ⊃ ~L	p
	4 H v ~M	p
	5 H ⊃ ~L	1,3 h.s.
	6 ~H	2,5 m.t.
	7 ~M	4,6 d.s.

3	1 I v E	p
	2 E ⊃ J	p
	3 ~J	p
	4 ~E	2,3 m.t.
	5 I	1,4 d.s.

8	1 O ⊃ (P v ~E)	p
	2 Y ⊃ O	p
	3 E	p
	4 Y	p
	5 O	2,4 mp
	6 P v ~E	1,5 mp
	7 P	3,6 ds
	Or	
	5 Y ⊃ (P v ~E)	1,2, hs
	6 P v ~E	4,5 mp
	7 P	3,6 d.s.

10	1 S	p
	2 W ⊃ ~T	p
	3 D v T	p
	4 S ⊃ ~D	p
	5 ~D	1,4 m.p.
	6 T	3,5 d.s.
	7 ~W	2,6 m.t.

Exercise 10.3

1	1 R • A	p
	2 R	1, simp
	3 R v Z	2, add

2	1 ~(C ⊃ J)	p
	2 ~(~C v J)	1, imp
	3 C • ~J	2, dem
	4 C	3, simp

3 1 K   p
   2 K v ~B   1, add
   3 ~K ⊃ ~B   2, imp
   4 B ⊃ K   3, tran

5 1 K ⊃ ~G   p
   2 ~K v ~G   1, imp
   3 ~(K • G)   2, dem

8 1 ~N   p
   2 ~N v ~M   1, add
   3 ~(N • M)   2, dem

10 1 H • ~O   p
   2 H   1, simp
   3 H v ~L   2, add
   4 ~H ⊃ ~L   3, imp
   5 L ⊃ H   4, tran

Exercise 10.4

1 1 (W • F) ⊃ C   p
   2 R ⊃ W   p
   3 R   p
   4 F   p
   5 W   2,3 m.p.
   6 W • F   4,5 conj
   7 C   1,6 m.p.

4 1 (~J ⊃ ~P) ⊃ M p
   2 P ⊃ J   p
   3 ~M v L   p
   4 ~J ⊃ ~P   2, tran
   5 M   1,4 m.p.
   6 L   3,5 d.s.

8 1 (D ⊃ C) • (~E ⊃ ~C) • (~E v G)   p
   2 D ⊃ C   1, simp
   3 ~E ⊃ ~C   1, simp
   4 ~E v G   1, simp
   5 ~C ⊃ ~D   2, trans
   6 ~E ⊃ ~D   3,5 h.s.
   5 E ⊃ G   4, imp
   7 ~G ⊃ ~E   5, trans
   8 ~G ⊃ ~D   6,7 h.s.
   9 G v ~D   8, imp

9 1 (F • ~Q) ⊃ V   p
   2 ~V   p
   3 (~F v Q) ⊃ W   p
   4 ~(F • ~Q)   1,2 m.t.
   5 ~F v Q   4, dem
   6 W   3,5 m.p.

12 1 (M ⊃ D) ⊃ O   p
   2 ~O v N   p
   3 D   p
   4 D v ~M   3, add
   5 ~D ⊃ ~M   4, imp
   6 M ⊃ D   5, trans
   7 O   1,6 m.p.
   8 N   2,7 d.s.

10 1 A v R   p
   2 R ⊃ L   p
   3 W ⊃ ~L   p
   4 ~A ⊃ R   1, imp
   5 ~A ⊃ L   2,4 h.s.
   6 L ⊃ ~W   3, trans
   7 ~A ⊃ ~W   5,6 h.s.

14 1 (G • ~N) ⊃ ~Y   p
    2 (O v G) • ~F   p
    3 {(K ⊃ L) v ~[I• (L v ~A)]} ⊃ ~O   p
    4 N ⊃ F   p
    5 S v ~J   p
    6 S ⊃ {(K ⊃ L) v ~[I • (L v ~A)]}   p
    7 J • ~K   p
    8 J   7, simp
    9 ~K   7, simp
   11 ~F   2, simp
   12 O v G   2, simp
   13 ~N   4,11 m.t.
   14 S ⊃ ~O   3,6 h.s.
   15 S   5,8 d.s.
   16 ~O   14,15 m.p.
   17 G   12,16 d.s.
   18 G • ~N   13,17 conj
   19 ~Y   1,18 m.p.

Exercise 10.5

2 1 ~(L • D) ⊃ B   p
   2 B   p
   3 ~(L • D)   ??? 1,2 AC invalid

4 1 (L • D) ⊃ ~B   p
   2 ~(L • D)   p
   3 B   ??? 1,2 DA invalid

10 1 ~R v U   p
   2 ~R   p
   3 ~U   ??? 1,2 DF invalid

13 1 R ⊃ ~P   p
   2 ~R   p
   3 P ??? 1,2 DA invalid
   Her period being three days late
   is *not* being *regular*, hence ~R.

15 1 (C v S) ⊃ ~E   p
   2 ~E   p
   3 C v S   ???, 1,2 AC invalid
   Opposing expansion = ~E. Voting
   against weapons systems
   = opposing expansion (~E)

17 1 A v B   p
   2 ~B ⊃ C   p
   3 D v ~C   p
   4 ~D   p
   5 ~C   3,4 d.s.
   6 B   2,5 m.t.
   7 ~A   ??? 1,6 DF invalid

18 1 P • M   p
   2 L ⊃ ~Y   p
   3 O v L   p
   4 ~Y ⊃ ~ (P • M)   p
   5 Y   1,4 m.t.
   6 ~L   2,5 m.t.
   7 O   3,6 d.s.

21 1 (F ⊃ G) v D   p
   2 ~S ⊃ ~F   p
   3 ~G ⊃ ~S   p
   4 ~G ⊃ ~F   2,3 hs
   5 F ⊃ G   4, tran
   6 ~D   ???   1,5 DF
   invalid

23 1 Y • R   p
    2 V ⊃ (~Y v ~R)   p
    3 ~(~Y v ~R)   1, dem
    4 ~V   2,3 m.t.

25 1 ~E ⊃ ~R   p
    2 E ⊃ ~K   p
    3 (L • ~Y) v F   p
    4 (~Y ⊃ K) • ~F   p
    5 K ⊃ ~E   2,trans
    6 K ⊃ ~R   1,5 h.s.
    7 ~Y ⊃ K   4, simp
    8 ~Y ⊃ ~R   6,7 h.s.
    9 ~F   4, simp
   10 L • ~Y   3,9 d.s.
   11 ~Y   10, simp
   12 ~R   8,11 m.p.

29 1 B • (G ⊃ ~R)   p
    2 F ⊃ ~R   p
    3 F ⊃ ~B   p
    4 B   1, simp
    5 G ⊃ ~R   1, simp
    6 ~F   3,4 m.t.
    7 R   ? 2,6 DA invalid
    8 ~G   5,7 m.t.
                  Or
    7 R ⊃ ~F   2, trans
    8 R   ? 6,7 AC invalid
    9 ~G   5,8 m.t.

30 1 A v B   p
    2 ~B   p
    3 A ⊃ C   p
    4 ~D ⊃ C   p
    5 A   1,2 d.s.
    6 C   3,5 m.p.
    7 ~D   ??? 4,6 AC invalid

33 1 M ⊃ G   p
    2 (I v ~E) ⊃ ~H   p
    3 ~T v H   p
    4 G ⊃ T   p
    5 M   p
    6 M ⊃ T   1,4 h.s.
    7 T ⊃ H   3, imp
    8 M ⊃ H   6,7 h.s.
    9 H   5,8 m.p.
   10 ~(I v ~E)   2,9 m.t.
   11 ~I • E   10, dem
   12 E   11, simp

Note, there may be other ways of proving the validity or invalidity than the ways shown here. You're right as long as each step fits one of our four logical forms or one of our six logical inferences; wrong otherwise.

Chapter Eleven: Causation and Probability

EXERCISE 11.1

1 Normally understood, lying is sufficient, but not necessary, for telling a falsehood. One may tell a falsehood unintentionally. Lying constitutes the intentional telling of a falsehood. Admittedly, one may lie yet not tell a falsehood. For example, perhaps ~P is true. If I mistakenly believe P, but for some reason want you to believe ~P, my telling you ~P is a lie, yet not a falsehood. In such cases, lying would be neither sufficient nor

necessary for telling a falsehood. This reflection may be challenged if we rigorously maintain a lie does necessarily entail telling a *real* falsehood, as opposed to merely an *intended* falsehood.

2 Shooting normally is sufficient for killing, but not necessary for killing, since there are countless other ways of killing: poisoning, drowning, hanging, etc. But this supposes a few contributing conditions: for example, one is a good aim, one is shooting bullets as opposed to peas or water, etc. Taking these other considerations into account, we could say shooting is not even sufficient for killing.

3 Hitting a home run is necessary for hitting a grand slam, but not sufficient for hitting a grand slam. A grand slam in baseball is the case where a home run is hit when all the bases are loaded. If a home run is hit without all the bases loaded, this does not constitute a grand slam.

4 Rain falling under normal conditions is sufficient, but not necessary, for the ground getting wet. The ground may become wet for other reasons than rain falling: flood from melting snow, watering the yard, pool fights, young children or pets urinating, etc. Depending on what ground we're talking about, we can imagine rain falling without getting a *particular* bit of ground wet, for example the ground under the house or the tent.

11 Sinking a putt is not sufficient for getting a birdie, since the putt may be for a par or bogey or worse. Normally, sinking the putt is necessary for getting the birdie, for merely having a birdie putt does not guarantee one will make the putt. But one may have chipped in and got a birdie that way, in which case sinking a putt is not a necessary condition for getting a birdie. Plus, in match play, one's partner may have granted a gimme, thus constituting a birdie without actually having sunk the putt. Given these last conditions, sinking a putt is neither necessary nor sufficient for getting a birdie.

12 Dancing may be done without a partner. One may have a partner and not dance. Therefore dancing is neither sufficient nor necessary for having a partner.

13 Cracking eggs is necessary for frying eggs. It is not sufficient, however. We also need a frying pan and a heat source of some kind

14 Being a parking lot attendant, as long as it is not voluntary, is sufficient for having a job. It is not necessary for having a job.

15 For mammals, anyway, breathing is both necessary and sufficient for being alive. If you breathe, you are alive: hence it is sufficient. If you're alive, you're breathing: hence it is necessary. Plants and amoebas are alive without breathing, however, so for non-mammals, breathing is not necessary for being alive, unless we define breathing more broadly.

Exercise 11.2

1 Third variable problem. Those with lower numbers of offspring and those with toasters have something else in common: education and

wealth. It is conceivable that it is education and wealth, which themselves tend to go hand in hand, that increase the chances of owning a toaster and understanding contraception. One may either need wealth to get the education, or else one may have the education which tends to increase the chances for better careers which increases the chances for wealth.

5 Reverse-order problem. The individuals in question may sit close to their computers *because* they have bad eyesight.

6 Third variable. Children who are not fed breakfast may also be suffering from parental neglect. This is not to underestimate the importance of diet, but it may not be diet alone that is the culprit.

7 Reverse-order. At least this is conceivable. It is possible that people respond more positively to those who have a positive self-image, and not the reverse.

Exercise 11.3

1 We need to discover the probability of a conjunction of independent outcomes = x_1/n_1 x x_2/n_2. The odds of pulling a black marble from jar A is 3/10. The odds of pulling a black marble from Jar B is 2/13. The odds of holding two black marbles is 3/10 x 2/13 (or .3 x .154) = .046, or about 5%.

3 This is a case of a conjunction of independent outcomes = x_1/n_1 x x_2/n_2 x ... x_n/n_n. The probability of throwing a single die and *not* getting a three is 5/6. Hence, the probability of throwing eight dice and not getting a three is 5/6 x 5/6 x 5/6 x 5/6 x 5/6 x 5/6 x 5/6 x 5/6 = 390,625/1,679,616. In other words, the odds of the event happening is .232, or about 23%. Not bad.

7 The odds of winning $25 means you've drawn a queen of any suit, *but not the queen of hearts*. Had you drawn the queen of hearts, that would mean you won $100, not $25. We are examining a single event where *n* is the number of cards in the deck (52) and *x* the event under question will be three of those cards, the queen of diamonds, the queen of spades, and the queen of clubs. In other words, the odds are 3/52, or .058.

10 Here we are examining the probability of a disjunction of mutually exclusive alternative events. A variety of different outcomes may satisfy this event, and so we are examining the probability of a disjunction of these possible states. Child 1 may be a boy or a girl, likewise child 2, likewise child 3. The combination of the children being boys or girls needs to be *added*, not multiplied. Using the terms C for child, B for boy, and G for girl, we get the following:

clb = 1/2 x c2g = 1/2 x c3g = 1/2 = 1/8
clg = 1/2 x c2g = 1/2 x c3b = 1/2 = 1/8
clg = 1/2 x c2b = 1/2 x c3g = 1/2 = 1/8.
= 1/8 + 1/8 + 1/8 = 3/8 =.375

In other words, the odds of the stipulated event occurring are 37.5%.

Exercise 11.4

1 We need the formula for determining probability of a conjunction of outcomes without replacement: $x_1 n_n$ x $x_2 n_{n-1}$. Hence, $3/10$ x $2/9$ = $6/90$, or .067.

3 This is a case of a conjunction of independent events = x_1/n_1 x x_2/n_2. The probability of throwing a single die and getting a 5 or a 6 is $1/6$ + $1/6$ or $2/6$. Hence, the probability of throwing eight dice and getting only 5s or 6s is $2/6$ x $2/6$ x $2/6$ x $2/6$ x $2/6$ x $2/6$ x $2/6$ x $2/6$ = .00014.

5 There are four permutations of outcomes which satisfy this event: the case where all three cards are hearts, the case where they are all clubs, the case where they are all spades, and the case where they are all diamonds. The odds that one of these permutations is satisfied is determined by the probability formula concerning conjunction without replacement: x_1/n_n x x_2/n_{n-1}. Taking the first possibility, the odds that the first card is a heart is $13/52$. The odds that the second card is a heart is $12/51$. The odds of the third being a heart is $11/50$. The odds of all three being a heart, therefore is $13/52$ x $12/51$ x $11/50$ = .016. We determine the probability of this event by adding the probability of each permutation. Since the probability of each permutation is the same and there are four such permutations, the probability for this event is .016 + .016 + .016 + .016 = .064.

7 If you win $100, you've drawn the queen of hearts, lucky you, but notice that you *haven't* drawn any of the other queens in your three tries, since the winnings would be greater than $100. Notice that the probability of drawing the queen of hearts in three tries without replacing the cards is greater than the probability of drawing the queen of hearts in one try. That is, we are dealing with mutually exclusive alternative events. We are not examining the *conjunction* of dependent events. (We would be if we asked what is the odds of pulling *two* queens from the deck in three tries without replacing the cards. If you use the formula for the conjunction of dependent events $(x_1/n_n$ x $x_2/n_{n-1})$, the odds of drawing the queen of hearts in three tries will be less than the odds of drawing the queen of hearts on one try. That can't be right.) Rather, we are dealing with mutually exclusive but dependent events. In this case, that means $1/52$ + $1/51$ + $1/50$. That is, .019 + .0196 + .02 = .059, a little less than 6% chance.

Exercise 11.5

1 Yes. The formula is $E(u) = \Sigma p_i \mu_i$. Your expected payoff is $[(.85$ x $35)$ + $(.15$ x -$175)]$ = $3.50. That's $3.50 more than you would expect by declining the bet. Perhaps, an expected payoff of $3.50 cannot outweigh the subjective disutility in risking losing $175 however, even at .15 odds.

3 The odds of selecting the right marble is .25. The odds of failing to select the right marble is .75. The odds of winning $7.00, then is .25,

the odds of giving up \$2.50 is .75. The formula for expected utility is $E(u) = \Sigma p_i \, \mu_i$. In this case, $0.25(\$7.00) + 0.75(-\$2.50) = -\$0.125$. That is, you can expect to lose about 13 cents per gamble.

6 (a) In this case we need to assess the probability of winning anything (either \$25 or \$100) while subtracting the cost of the ticket. The formula for determining expected utility is the odds of winning multiplied by the amount to be won subtracting the cost of playing. To assess the odds of winning either \$25 or \$100 in this case is to appeal to the probability formula for single events (*xn*) 4/52. That is, the odds of winning *something* will be .077. But notice, the odds of winning \$25 is 3/52 (or .058), since if one draws the queen of hearts, one will win \$100, not \$25. Since there is only a single draw in this case, the odds of drawing the \$100 queen is 1/52 (or .019). (Notice that $3/52 + 1/52 = 4/52$.) To get the expected value we need to multiply the winnings with the odds of winning. Hence, $1/52(100) + 3/52(25) = 1.93 + 1.44 = 3.37$. Now we subtract the price of the ticket, \$4.00. (Or using the more general formula, we add the probability of the outcome of losing multiplied by the probability of losing, which in this case equals precisely the cost of the ticket.) As a result, the expected payoff of this gamble is -\$0.63. That is, you stand to lose 63 cents by playing this game.

Exercise 11.6

1 Of course one cannot get a divorce without being married, so marriage will be perfectly correlated with divorce. But as long as we can be married without divorce, we cannot call marriage the *cause* of divorce. A third variable is more likely, and this will vary depending on circumstances.

4 This is a person-who problem. The fact that we know someone who wouldn't do it voluntarily hardly shows that *no one* would.

7 Reverse-order. It's possible that it's not sports which give children self-esteem, etc. but that children with better self-esteem, etc. are more likely to take part in sports.

9 Third Variable error. Here is Stephen Jay Gould's response: "Is it not more likely that height vs. brain size represents the primary causal correlation for the obvious reason that tall people tend to have large body parts? Brain size would then be an imperfect measure of height, and IQ might correlate with it (at the low value of 0.3) for the primarily environmental reason that poverty and poor nutrition can lead both to reduced stature and poor IQ scores. The third variable is wealth, which provides both better nutrition (greater growth of entire body, and hence brain, as well as better ability to concentrate) as well as better education (both of which correspond to higher IQ scores)." (Stephen Jay Gould, *The Mismeasure of Man*, 108–9)

14 Pay attention to the base-rate information. Most of our driving is done closer to our home than anywhere else, since wherever we go, we must

start from our house and return to our house. Therefore, the number of occasions for accidents is largest there.

Chapter Twelve: Science

Exercise 12.1

2 It seems a little bit suspect that they only studied white men but assume that their results can apply to women as well. The same can be said for racial differences. A long-standing problem in medicine has been that studies do not include women, but assume results are just as valid for them, which is not always the case. Factors causing heart problems are different for men and women, and, only recently, it has been determined that asthma affects women very differently than it does men.

4 Sample size and base-rate issue. Presumably soccer players far outnumber skydives. This is mainly the problem, but some may also point out that serious injuries with skydiving likely result in death, whereas this isn't likely to be the case in soccer.

6 The problem is a combination of self-selection and sample size. Since fewer aspire to go to university in Mississippi than in California, those who take the SAT scores in Mississippi are likely to be already exceptional students. Where going to university is more the norm, as it is in California, there will be a wider range of students taking the SAT scores, from which we can predict a lower average.

8 There is a poor comparison here. Humans doing *short-term* predictions are being compared to computers doing *long-term* predictions. That would be like saying golfers hit the ball further than baseball players. There is nothing generalizable about that.

11 A letter to the editor, appearing the following day, provides an adequate response: "Scientists Prove Boys Will Be Boys (May 23) relies on questionable science and ridiculous testimony to 'prove' its point. The findings of these 'scientists,' who studied a grand total of one daycare centre, point more to the ongoing decay of the social sciences than to a convincing revision of gender theory. Buttressed as it is with the musings of one mother of two, I must say the article has me convinced – convinced that the neurotic obsession with alienating the sexes is itself a psychological phenomenon worthy of investigation." (Dee Sparling, letter to the editor, *Globe and Mail*, 24 May 2001)

Chapter Thirteen: Arguments by Analogy

Exercise 13.1

1 Primary subject = speciesism. Target attribute = is immoral. This was a suppressed conclusion, but clearly the intent. Analogues =

racism and sexism. Shared attribute = unequal treatment between groups.

3 Primary subject = Casey Martin (or a golfer). Target attribute = not entitled to a break (despite court ruling). Analogue = pitcher. Shared attributes = competitive athlete, lacking a key aspect for success (no curve ball for the pitcher, no good leg to walk upon for Casey Martin).

5 Primary subject = other people. Target attribute = having a mind. Analogue = me. Shared attribute = pain behaviour.

7 This is not an analogical argument. The analogy to the times when we believed the world was flat is simply an illustration, to help the description. An argument occurs here, but not an analogical argument.

11 Primary subject = Christians. Target attribute = not standing for such treatment of their children. Analogue (suppressed, but gathered from the headline) = Natives. Shared attributes [imagined] = being kidnapped, taught a different culture (hunting, trapping, living in the bush), religion, and language, and being beaten otherwise.

14 Primary subject = The lice. Target attribute = came from Gus's Party Favour Rental shop. Analogues = hats. Shared attribute = on Ellen, Katie's, and Paul's heads only.

Exercise 13.2

2 (a) This weakens the argument by relevant disanalogy. (b) Strengthens by variety of the analogues. (c) Irrelevant. Neither strengthens nor weakens the merit of Bert and Ernie's bet. (d) Strengthens by number of analogues. (e) Strengthens by number of shared attributes. (f) Weakens by strength of the conclusion. To win by exactly twenty-eight points is a stronger claim than the premises warrant. Therefore, there is less chance that this will occur.

5. (a) Strengthens by number of analogues. (b) A variety of answers is possible depending on Charlene's character. For many people, this will be irrelevant to the merits of the film itself. Not all think this, though. Some may be so incensed about what they take to be the actor's immorality that it will affect their enjoyment of the film. Others may find the film thereby more interesting. In the first case, we could say, irrelevant, no change. In the third case, we can say, weaken, relevant disanalogy. The second case is peculiar. It will likely mean she will not enjoy the movie, but it doesn't follow that she will be "bored." Therefore, like the third case, it would actually weaken the argument by relevant disanalogy. (c) Strengthens by number of shared attributes. (d) Weakens by relevant disanalogy. (e) Weakens by relevant disanalogy. (f) Strengthens by variety among the analogues. (g) Weakens by relevant disanalogy.

7 (a) At face value, one might say "strengthen by variety among the analogues," but when we take the relevant differences into account, we can

see that open-heart surgery is far more risky than the others. So this weakens by relevant disanalogy. (b) Strengthens by shared attributes. (c) Weakens by number of analogues. (d) Irrelevant. One might argue that surgeons perform worse on Mondays than Wednesdays, perhaps being annoyed they have to come back to work after the weekend, but evidence would need to be forthcoming first. (e) Strengthen by variety among the analogues. (f) Strengthen by number of shared attributes.

Exercise 13.3

2 There are only two analogues and one shared attribute. This may be too few to generalize fully. An obvious disanalogy, of course, is that both racism and sexism may be wrong for their poor treatment of *people*, whereas the primary subject is a group of non-humans. Whether this disanalogy is *relevant* requires further discussion. Minimally, the mere fact of differential treatment is not what makes something immoral, since it is just to treat different cases differently.

5 There is a problem with relevant disanalogy. Life is not really like a foot race. A race is a zero-sum game. That is, there is one winner and all also-rans are losers. Only one person gets the prize. The others don't. Market transactions and human relations, on the other hand, are understood as offering the prospect of *mutual benefit*. That is, in negotiations, all can come out ahead. Admittedly, the gains need not be equal, but as long as each participant stands to gain in terms they accept, the analogy to a zero-sum foot race is misplaced.

7 There is a cap on electricity rates and rental rates. The House of Commons removed the cap for the electric company, so it should also remove the cap for landlords. Presumably, the author is suggesting that if the electrical company raises its rates, this will affect the landlords who pay electrical bills for tenants. But if the landlords can't raise their rent rates to cover the increase in the electrical bill, it would be unfair. The argument as given doesn't get there, though. For one, to remove a cap is certainly different from raising the cap. To cover a ten cent increase, it will hardly do to raise the rent by twenty-five dollars.

10 The analogy is that if it's ok to mix your genes with the genes of different people, it should be ok not to mix your genes with other people. This is very poorly thought-out. There is a relevant disanalogy between mixing one's genes and *not* mixing one's genes, and that is the little word "not." It's as senseless as the following pronouncement: "If it's ok not to kill someone, then it should be ok to kill someone." Perhaps, by the way, it is ok to procreate by cloning, and our worry may be mere superstition, but the analogical argument given here hardly justifies it.

12 This is pretty good, on the whole. A relevant disanalogy lies in the fact that teachers are paid to "teach" and this is less likely to be successful if people aren't present. Also teaching is not simply entertainment. We

may also speak of grades. We can pass or fail a course, but audience members don't pass or fail a symphony performance. Something along these lines.

Exercise 13.4

1 The creationists reject the theory of evolution because it cannot account for everything. Modern medicine does not account for everything, but we don't reject that. Ergo, it can't count as a reason to reject the theory of evolution. The arguments have the same form and the refuting argument offers what most take to be a ludicrous conclusion. The argument works. For the creationists to press the point, they would have to say that evolution can't account for most things, not merely some things.

3 The refuting argument has the same form as the refuted argument, and yields an inane conclusion. It is thereby successful. One might note, however, that at least nuclear build-up is *relevant* to the lack of nuclear war, in a way that we know painting a happy face on one's barn is not relevant to lightning strikes.

6 This doesn't work. The two arguments are not the same form. The first states that a fake security system sign can ward off intruders, plus provide advertising. The second compares this to vaulting subway turnstiles and getting free cable hookup. What is needed is the added supposition that if everyone put up fake security signs, the security business would go under, for no one would pay for their services, thus eventually rendering the fake sign idea useless, since all up-to-date crooks would know about the ruse. This may be compared to the supposition that if everyone jumped the turnstile, the subway would go out of business. But the two aren't entirely the same, and this isn't merely to highlight the problem that the homeowner isn't advocating that *everyone* do this. Rather, it isn't the case that the homeowner gets the security system without paying, like getting the cable without paying. The homeowner only has a sign. (The sign-makers would stay in business.) Rather, analogously, the homeowner would get a fake satellite dish, or a fake subway ticket that cannot actually be used. The fact that the aunt will injure herself jumping over a turnstile is also wildly irrelevant.

11 Mark Steyn is criticizing the claim that, merely on the grounds that the missile defence system began as a dream, it is therefore impossible, by pointing out other dreams that in fact ended up becoming reality. We might counter that presumably more dreams ended up not coming to fruition; still, the basic structure is good.

13 Szasz identifies modern psychiatry with the old witch hunt. On the basis that the witch hunt is immoral, so too, he concludes, is much of modern treatment of mental illness. Consider the following similari-

ties: (1) Anyone who behaves unpredictably or eccentrically, or challenges dominant social values, is identified as "mentally ill" or "heretic." (2) Once so identified, denial is taken as just as much a sign of guilt as is confession. (3) Anyone who denies the objective existence of mental illness clearly, himself, suffers from mental illness – just as the denial of witchcraft was considered as heretical as practising witchcraft, and branded one as a witch sympathizer. (4) Once a sufficient body of indicting "evidence" is collected, it can be used to impose a sentence of confinement (or in the case of witches, execution) without trial. (5) The authorities responsible for identifying, apprehending, and containing the mentally ill consider it a mission of benevolence, both for society at large and for the mental patient himself. Likewise, the Inquisitor sincerely believed that, not only was he strengthening the Holy Church's social power, he was also saving the heretic's soul by extracting a confession and allowing the possibility of redemption. (6) Any harm that befalls the accused in the course of assessment or treatment of "mental illness" or "witchcraft" is considered to be a direct result of the condition itself, rather than of the intervention itself – or else is a necessary danger that must be tolerated in the quest for a cure. (7) Unlike private counsellors or clinical psychologists, and also unlike medical doctors, institutional psychiatrists and Inquisitors are under the employ of powerful political organizations, and are not bound by many of the constitutional restrictions that the former face. They are also assessed in terms of the number of patients they can identify and "treat." (8) The greater one's desire to treat all mental illness, the more one comes to see *everyone* as being mentally ill to some capacity; likewise, the greater one's desire to deliver all sinners, the more one comes to see *everyone* as being heretical to some extent.

16 This is a good refutation by logical analogy. The two arguments, the original and the refuting, are in identical form, and the conclusion is absurd in the latter, and thereby the conclusion must be seen as similarly absurd in the former. That is, the argument to legalize marijuana cannot be made on *these* grounds.

Exercise 13.5

These are suggested answers. A wide range is possible, as long as you have the identical form with an absurd conclusion.

2 The Mona Lisa and the Taj Mahal are both unnatural, and therefore unattractive.

4 At the time of slavery, the same could be said: We've always had slaves, so there's no reason to stop. In fact, the same argument was used to keep women from voting. "We never had women vote, and we did just fine." "We" in this case is men, obviously.

6 Failing to turn in Jews to the Nazis is wrong, because it (was) against the law. Or, helping slaves escape is wrong, because it (was) against the law, etc.

9 Two possibilities are "Just as boxing in a ring is legal, assault should be legal," or "Just as it's legal for me to drive a car, I should be able to drive an F16 fighter jet." One may argue that both fail. The refutations *presuppose* that marijuana is far more dangerous than tobacco and alcohol, whereas proponents of the original argument may deny precisely this. Still, you get the idea.

Chapter Fourteen: Fallacies

Exercise 14.1

1 Begging the question. "Rights" and "Entitled to" are synonymous.

3 Equivocation. Naming the motel "Sleep Easy" does not mean one will sleep easy there.

6 Leading question. Presupposes (1) that we do want to destroy PEI, and (2) that instituting Sunday shopping is a good way to destroy PEI. We may wish to reject both assumptions.

10 Begging the question. This occurs in two ways: (1) by negating the contradiction, X is wrong because not-X is right, and (2) synonyms. "Monarchy" and "a single, hereditary ruler" are the same. And of course, something's being undemocratic is bad only if we presuppose that democracy is right.

11 Slippery slope.

13 False dichotomy. One would think that, even in 1988, a woman could marry someone and still have a career.

16 Slippery slope.

19 This may be identified as either a false dichotomy or a slippery slope (a false conditional). To emphasize the false dichotomy is to recognize that we're presented a choice between being independent of Arab oil and ruining our environment. Our complaint is that we might be able to be independent of Arab oil without ruining our environment. The slippery slope component, understood here as a false conditional, is to complain about the same issue, namely that ruining our environment is not conditional upon accepting Arab oil.

21 Question begging. The explanation presupposes the very claim it was trying to demonstrate.

Exercise 14.2

1 Ad hominem: tu quoque.

2 Straw man. Materialism does not say that we are simply machines. It says instead that our minds may be defined solely in material terms.

4 Bandwagon.
8 Straw man fallacy. We can be pretty sure the decision was made based on human rights and not on political correctness.
10 Ad hominem: hypocrisy.
12 Bandwagon.
14 Ad hominem: abusive.
16 Ad hominem: vested interests.
18 Straw man. The reason for censoring Commodore Lerhe was certainly not that he had testosterone.
20 Red herring. That it granted a doctoral degree to a black student does not show that Yale did not benefit from the slave trade.

Exercise 14.3

1 Appeal to ignorance.
4 Genetic fallacy. The unpalatable origins of mushrooms do not show that mushrooms are unpalatable.
6 Genetic fallacy.
8 False cause: 3rd variable. Is it likely that some countries have dubious democratic credentials and poor human rights records *because* they don't have a monarchy, or even because they have a president?
10 Person-who. Narusevicius bases his generalization of the English on the basis of one anecdotal report.
13 Fallacy of composition. Buses may use more gas than cars, but not more gas than the number of cars that would be used by passengers of buses if they did not use the bus. What is true of the parts (buses) is not necessarily true of the whole (automobile pollution).
15 Composition.
17 Composition. Although no single cheer can matter, it doesn't follow that a group's cheering will not matter.
19 False cause: 3rd variable. It is possible that everyone would have loved to save the child, but were simply unable to do so.
22 Fallacy of division.
24 Fallacy of ignorance. Here is a clear case of misplaced burden of proof. The burden of proof ought not fall on the accused, but the prosecution.

Exercise 14.4

1 False dichotomy.
3 Equivocation. "Deters" is normally understood as "deters others from doing the same," and not, as this author interprets it, "deters the culprit from repeating the crime."
4 Begging the question.
5 Appeal to ignorance.

 9 Bandwagon.

11 Ad hominem: vested interests.

16 Straw man.

18 Question begging. It presupposes what it set out to demonstrate.

20 Ad hominem: abusive. We won't comment on the grammatical errors, save to point out how they tend to reduce the likelihood that one will be taken seriously.

22 Slippery slope.

24 Question begging.

27 Straw man. The grounds for the fine were not that Eric Lerhe had visited soft-porn sites, but that he had visited these sites using a business computer, which was against DND regulations.

30 Ad hominem: vested interests.

32 Composition. Hardly placating, is it? Note: some might suggest "Division" instead, but this would get the intent backwards. The intent (we would argue) is "Since the parts are not bad taken individually, they cannot be bad taken as a whole."

34 Bandwagon. The appeal is to straightforward numbers.

37 Equivocation on "finding." The first concerns original extraction of diamonds from the earth, the second is the mundane rediscovery of the temporarily misplaced.

40 Slippery slope.

42 Genetic fallacy. The premise is true, by the way. Dr William Chester Minor, an American surgeon from New Haven, Connecticut, submitted nearly ten thousand entries to be used in the dictionary, all while incarcerated in a hospital for the criminally insane.

44 Person-who. We might also complain about a false dichotomy, but the bigger culprit here is a failure to understand statistical claims.

46 Genetic fallacy. That something starts out as a dream does not mean it cannot ever reach reality.

48 Straw man or red herring. The author is responding to the charge that the Women's Centre is an abortion clinic. Saying that it is *more* than an abortion clinic does not say that it is not an abortion clinic. It would be an appropriate response if the charge was that the Women's Centre was *only* an abortion clinic.

Appendix Two

A Bad Essay

Criticize the following essay. Use any relevant material from the entire course.* Not all material covered in this course will necessarily apply, mind you. Note all problems paragraph by paragraph. Show where the errors occur and briefly explain them.

Vegetarianism and Moral Duty

We all have a moral duty to become vegetarians and those not seeing this are like slave owners of the past, too petty and mean-spirited to look past their vicious interests to the world as it is. They refuse to see the moral obligation to be vegetarians, partly due to their obvious taste for blood that they don't want to give up. We should come out of the dark ages of heathens and advance toward a morally superior society! Imagine: a small baby lamb mewing placidly, and someone coming up and viciously hacking it to pieces with an axe, against its weak cries for help. No one can claim with a clear conscience that this is permissible. Ask yourself: Do you really want to persist in the morally obnoxious practice of eating meat?

My cousin lives near a pig farm and says she sees how pigs are treated when she drives by on the highway. Don't imagine it's a pretty sight. She claims they are maliciously beaten and prodded for no other reason than the workers find enjoyment out of the suffering of innocents. And that's ignoring the killing. Anyone with half a brain can realize that eating meat necessitates being insensitive to killing animals, but what is little understood is that it is not a far cry to start becoming insensitive to killing humans. Look at the violence shown on TV and in the movies. We

---

* Note: Do not attempt to diagram any part of this essay. Nor ought you to attempt to formalize any part of the argument into propositional or categorical logic, unless doing so reveals errors of logic.

find it entertaining. We must stop killing, period; and that necessitates vegetarianism.

Part of the difficulty in recognizing the moral duty to being vegetarians is due to the scientific fact that meat-eating makes one more stupid. According to Dr. Rizzaro, a leading physicist, meat-eating dulls one's intellectual capabilities. The human brain is composed of myriad ganglion cells, and there are interconnections between these. Meat-eating slows the connections between these ganglion cells by 27%. 80% of meat-eaters surveyed had slowed ganglion transmissions. So, the mere fact that meat-eaters have become too dim-witted to realize that meat-eating is wrong should hardly be surprising. Of course, some meat-eaters recognize it is wrong, but are too weak-willed to do anything about it. Some say that the protein from meat increases one's chances of health more than protein from vegetables. But I know a vegetarian who is extremely healthy and runs marathons. More, my brother is a meat-eater, and suffers heart problems.

But meat-eating is not wrong merely because it makes us dim-witted or unhealthy. Dr. Rudolph Hamill, a veterinarian, argues that animals are not merely able to feel pain, they can suffer psychological distress as well from being cooped up in barns or pens or stalls, although cruel meat-eating proponents, who merely want to justify their own vicious habits, argue that other veterinarians have resisted Dr. Hamill's important finding. These so-called veterinarians, by the very fact of furthering the despicable practice of meat-eating, cannot be true veterinarians. So citing their concerns is like polling rapists about whether they think rape is wrong and deciding the matter based on their biased report.

It is obvious: be a vegetarian or happily take part in butchering young calves. No true human, properly speaking, when confronted with such a choice, would hesitate in choosing the moral alternative of vegetarianism. Look me in the face and tell me animals don't feel pain, or don't have rights equal with ours. No one can say such a thing, and this proves, deep down, that animals do have rights equal to us.

If it is wrong to eat humans, it is wrong to eat cows and pigs. Continuing this despicable practice is cannibalism straight and simple. Since God put man here to protect the animals and plants of the world, we're clearly disobeying God's will if we eat the very creatures we were sent to protect. Of course, meat-eaters argue that animals like cows and pigs are bred to be eaten, and so come to like being eaten, and like to be stuffed in small cages. It is beneath me to respond to such a depraved argument. It is further evidence of the slowed ganglion cell emissions of meat-eaters.

Although meat-eaters tend to be less intelligent than vegetarians, and hence are less able to realize the force of these arguments, I do recognize their reluctance to change their habits so drastically. The reason we find meat-eating to be acceptable today is partly driven by the fact that we have in the past found it acceptable. But if we continue to accept the practice of meat-eating, we can never break out of the circle. Even if we approve of meat-eating now, we will produce future generations of meat-eaters, and this obviously should be curtailed.

For these reasons, as well as others that I could cite which are just as convincing, if not more so, we have a clear, unequivocal moral duty not to eat meat. My argument can be summed up in the following: Vegetarianism is the moral choice because it is right. Period.

Appendix Three

Hints for Writing Philosophy Papers

Before Writing

1 Explore the arguments on all sides – pro and con.
2 Be fair to the opposing side – don't misrepresent.
3 Be aware of any *assumptions* you may be making. Can these assumptions be supported?
4 Audience. You are always writing with someone in mind. Choose as your audience an intelligent, fairly knowledgeable person, who nevertheless holds a position contradictory to your own. Your task is to convince her about the merit of your position. To do so, your tone matters.

Organization

1 **Introduction**. Clearly explain the issue you are addressing and where you stand on that issue, and briefly outline how you will attempt to defend that stand. It isn't a detective novel, where the reader must wait until the end to see who did it. Be upfront, be bold.
2 **Body**. The body consists of a development of the issue you're addressing, the argumentation for your position, the main objections to your argument, and your replies to those objections. You may also require a reply to the reply of your reply to the objections! The organization of these components can vary. Note: first and second year undergraduate papers are not long. A few well-developed arguments are better than many only sketched. Readers tend to recall only your *worst* argument and forget the rest. So make sure your worst argument is still adequate. If not, delete it. Also, the more arguments you present, the greater the chance of introducing inconsistency.
3 **Conclusion**. Here you sum up what your basic conclusions are. Note: readers assess how well the arguments support that stated conclusion, so don't try to hoodwink your reader by pretending a grander conclusion than that supported by your arguments.

Writing

1 Use **clear, concrete language**. People tend to think that if they don't understand something, or have no good argument to give, an extra use of large words and never-ending sentences will conceal this from the reader. As Goethe remarked about human nature, when an idea is wanting, a word can always be found to take its place. Remember who your audience is, though: one who is not so easily swayed.

2 **Get to the point quickly**. Don't waste time with fluff. Say, "In this paper I am arguing against the existence of God," or better, "God does not exist," rather than, "Philosophers for centuries have debated about the existence of God ... " Your reader has already fallen asleep. She knows this already (recall who your audience is). Plus, you frankly don't have the space. The more superfluous words and phrases, the less space for good argument. **A note about "I."** It is common to be told not to use "I." Often it is redundant. "I think that ..." is entirely unnecessary. If you didn't think it, you wouldn't write it. When you're saying, "Hello," you don't say, "I'm saying Hello." But I'd rather you say "In this paper I am arguing that ..." than "This paper is arguing that ..." Papers don't have mental states. Too often when we delete "I" we're leaving a subjectless sentence, and that is a far worse crime.

3 **Fit conclusion to premises**. Don't claim more than you have shown.

4 **References**. Reference all work you've used, even if merely paraphrased. In fact, use quotations sparingly, if at all. Use quotations only if it is an exceptionally wonderful quotation, or you want to comment on the specific wording: even then, quote only the necessary. Page-length quotations are like fingernails on a blackboard. Whether using MLA or APA style, your primary goal is to direct your reader to the exact page(s) of your source.

Rewriting

1 **Be clear!** You may know exactly what you mean to say. Often, however, it is far from clear to anyone else. Check for missing links in your argument. "There is design in the world; therefore God exists" is missing "Anything with design requires there to be a designer." (That God should be the designer requires a yet further link.) Explain the connections between your ideas – even if they seem perfectly obvious to you. Points that *seemed* connected to you may not *really* be connected after all.

2 **Check for grammar**. After you let it sit for a day or two, do you STILL know what you were trying to say? Ask a friend to read it, not for content as much as for clarity. Does your friend understand what you are getting at? If not, assume it is your fault, not your friend's.

3 Check **spelling** and **punctuation**. If this isn't checked, the reader may assume other more important things weren't checked either. The reader

loses confidence in your abilities, and the power to persuade is dissipated. **Common errors**: its-it's; their-they're-there; then-than; to-too; apostrophe use in general; run-on sentences; dangling modifiers; punctuation woes, spell-check-approved inanities ... *Never* feel bad about looking up words or grammatical rules. People think it's a sign of scholarship not to need a dictionary. This is false. It is a sign of scholarship if you use a dictionary (although Shakespeare managed quite well without one).

Bibliography

Adams, Henry. *Mont St. Michel and Chartres*. New York: Penguin Classics, 1986.

Anselm. *Proslogium*. In *St. Anselm: Basic Writings*, translated by S.N. Deane. La Salle, IL: The Open Court Publishing Co., 1988.

Aquinas. *Summa Theologica*. In *Basic Writings of Saint Thomas Aquinas*, edited by Anton. C. Pegis. Indianapolis, IN: Hackett Publishing Company, 1997.

Aristotle. *Nichomachean Ethics*. In *The Basic Works of Aristotle*, edited by Richard McKeon, translated by W. D. Ross. New York: Random House, 1941.

Ayer, Alfred J. "Freedom and Necessity." In *Philosophical Essays*. London: MacMillan, 1954: 271–84.

Beardsley, Monroe C. *Thinking Straight: Principles of Reasoning for Readers and Writers*, 4th ed. Englewood Cliffs, NJ: Prentice Hall, 1975.

Beauchamp, Tom and Norman E. Bowie, eds. *Ethical Theory and Business*, 6th ed. New Jersey: Prentice Hall, 2001.

Beecher, H.K. "Generalization from pain of various types of diverse origins," *Science* 130 (1959): 267–8.

Blackburn, Simon. *Ruling Passions: A Theory of Practical Reasoning*. Oxford: Oxford University Press, 1998.

Boatright, John. *Ethics and the Conduct of Business*. New Jersey: Prentice Hall, 1987.

Bowie, Norman E. "Relativism and the Moral Obligations of Multinational Corporations." In *Ethical Theory and Business*, 6th ed., edited by Tom L. Beauchamp and Norman E. Bowie. New Jersey: Prentice Hall (2001): 533–42.

Cameron, Paul. "A Case Against Homosexuality." In *Contemporary Moral Problems*, 4th ed., edited by James White. St. Paul, MN: West Publishing (1994): 341–9.

Carey, Stephen. *A Beginner's Guide to Scientific Method*. Belmont, CA: Wadsworth, 1983.

Carroll, Lewis. *Mind* 4 (1895): 278–80.

Columbia Journalism Review Editors. *Squad Helps Dog Bite Victim and Other Flubs from the Nation's Press*. Garden City, NY: Doubleday, 1980.

Copi, Irving and Keith Burgess-Jackson. *Informal Logic*, 2nd ed. New York: Macmillan Publishing Company, 1992.

Dawkins, Richard. *The Blind Watchmaker*. London: W.W. Norton, 1986.

Doob, A.N., J.M. Carlsmith, J.L. Freedman, T.K. Landauer, and S. Tom, Jr. "Effect of initial selling price on subsequent sales," *Journal of Personality and Social Psychology* 11 (1969): 345–50.

Dworkin, Andrea. "Intercourse." In *Sex and Gender: A Spectrum of Views*, edited by Philip Devine and Celia Wolf-Devine. Belmont, CA: Wadsworth, 2003.

Engel, S. Morris. *Analyzing Informal Fallacies.* Englewood Cliffs, NJ: Prentice Hall, 1980.

Fausto-Sterling, Anne. *Myths of Gender: Biological Theories About Women and Men*, 2nd ed. New York: Basic Books, 1985.

Flanders, Allen, Rita Hinden, Phyllis Wilmott, Peter Wilmott, and Michael Young. *Twentieth Century Socialism: The Economy of Tomorrow.* Harmondsworth: Penguin, 1956.

Fogelin, Robert J. *Understanding Argument: An Introduction to Informal Logic*, 3rd ed. San Diego: Harcourt Brace Jovanovich Inc., 1987.

Freeman, James. *Thinking Logically: Basic Steps for Reasoning.* Englewood Cliffs, NJ: Prentice Hall, 1988.

Gauthier, David. *Morals By Agreement.* Oxford: Oxford University Press, 1986.

Goldstick, D. "Assessing Utilities," *Mind* 80, 320 (1971): 531–41.

Gordon, Margaret and Stephanie Riger. *The Social Cost of Rape.* Illinois: University of Illinois Press, 1991.

Gould, Stephen Jay. *The Mismeasure of Man.* New York: W.W. Norton & Company, 1981.

Govier, Trudy. *A Practical Study of Argument*, 4th ed. Belmont, CA: Wadsworth Publishing Company, 1997.

Groarke, Leo, Chris Tindale, and Linda Fisher. *Good Reasoning Matters! A Constructive Approach to Critical Thinking*, 2nd ed. Oxford: Oxford University Press, 1996.

Haag, Ernst van den. *Punishing Criminals: Concerning a Very Old and Painful Question.* Lanham, MD: University Press of America, 1991.

Haas, H., H. Fink, and G. Hartfelder. "Das Placeboproblem," *Fortschritte der Arzneimnittleforschung* 1 (1959): 279–454.

Hamill, K., T.D. Wilson, and R.E. Nisbett. "Insensitivity to sample bias: generalizing from atypical cases," *Journal of Personality and Social Psychology* 39: 578–89.

Harding, Sandra. *Feminism and Methodology.* Bloomington: Indiana Press, 1986.

Hume, David. *Dialogues Concerning Natural Religion.* Edited by Norman Kemp Smith. New York: MacMillan Publishing Company, 1947.

– *Enquiries Concerning Human Understanding*, 3rd ed. Edited by L.A. Selby-Bigge. Oxford: Clarendon Press, 1989.

Hurka, Thomas. *Principles: Short Essays on Ethics.* Orlando, FL: Harcourt Brace, 1993.

Jensen, Arthur. *The g Factor: The Science of Mental Ability.* Westport, KT: Praeger Publishers, 1998.

Kant, Immanuel. *The Critique of Judgement.* Translated by J.C. Meredith. Oxford: Clarendon Press, 1961.

– *The Critique of Pure Reason.* Translated by Norman Kemp Smith. New York: St. Martin's Press, 1929.

Keynes, J.M. *Scope and Methodology of Political Economy,* 4th ed. New York: A.M. Kelley, 1917.

Longley, Lawrence and Alan Braun. *The Politics of Electoral College Reform.* New Haven, CT: Yale University Press, 1972.

MacKinnon, Edward. *Basic Reasoning.* Englewood Cliffs, NJ: Prentice Hall, 1985.

Moore, G.E. "A Defense of Common Sense." In *Contemporary British Philosophy,* edited by J.H. Muirhead. London: Allen and Unwin, 1925.

Moore, John A. "Countering the Creationists," *Academe* 68 (1982): 13–17.

Munson, Ronald. *The Way of Words: An Informal Logic.* Boston: Houghton Mifflin, 1976.

Neumann, John von and Oskar Morgenstern. *Theory of Games and Economic Behaviour.* New York: Wiley, 1944.

Nozick, Robert. *Anarchy, State and Utopia.* New York: Basic Books, 1974.

Orne, M. "On the social psychology of the psychological experiment," *American Psychologist* 17 (1962): 776–83.

Paley, William. *Natural Theology.* Whitefish, MT: Kessinger Publishing, 2003.

Pascal, Blaise. *Pensées.* Translated by W.F. Trotter. New York: Dutton, 1958.

Perry, John and Michael Bateman, eds. *Introduction to Philosophy: Classical and Contemporary Readings,* 2nd ed. Oxford: Oxford University Press, 1993.

Pineau, Lois. "Date Rape: A Feminist Analysis," *Law and Philosophy* 8, no.2 (August 1989): 217–43.

Plato: The Collected Dialogues. Edited by Edith Hamilton and Huntington Cairns. Princeton: Princeton University Press, 1961.

Pojman, Louis. "Deterrence and the Death Penalty." In *The Death Penalty: For and Against,* edited by Louis Pojman and Jeffrey Reiman. Lanham, MD: Rowan and Littlefield (1998): 37–41.

Popper, Karl. *The Logic of Scientific Discovery.* New York: Harper and Row, 1959.

Quine, W.V.O. "Ontological Relativity." In *Ontological Relativity and Other Essays.* New York: Columbia University Press, 1969.

Rand, Ayn. *Capitalism: The Unknown Ideal.* New York: NAL, 1966.

Reiman, Jeffrey. "Common Sense, the Deterrent Effect of the Death Penalty, and the Best Bet Argument." In *The Death Penalty: For and Against,* edited by Louis Pojman and Jeffrey Reiman. Lanham, MD: Rowan and Littlefield (1998): 102–7.

Roethelisberger, F.J. and W.J. Dickson. *Management and the Worker.* Cambridge, MA: Harvard University Press, 1939.

Rosenberg, M.J. "The Conditions and Consequences of Evaluation Apprehension." In *Artifact in Behavioural Research,* edited by R. Rosenthal and R. Rosnow. New York: Academic Press (1969): 279–349.

Rosenthal, R. and K.L. Fode. "Three experiments in experimenter bias," *Psychological Reports* 12 (1963): 491–511.

Rosenthal, R. and R. Lawson. "A longitudinal study of the effects of experimenter bias on operant learning of laboratory rats," *Journal of Psychiatric Research* 2 (1964): 61–72.

Russell, Bertrand. *Human Knowledge: Its Scope and Limits.* New York: Simon and Schuster, 1948.

Saul, John Ralston. *The Unconscious Civilization.* Toronto: House of Anansi Press, Ltd, 1995.

Schlesinger, William, J.F. Reynolds, G.L. Cunningham, L.F. Huenneke, W.M. Jerrell, R.A. Virginia, and W.G. Whitford. "Biological feedbacks in global desertification," *Science* 247, 2 (March 1990): 1043–8.

Seech, Zachary. *Logic in Everyday Life: Practical Reasoning Skills.* Belmont, CA: Wadsworth Publishing Company, 1987.

Sigall, H., E. Aronson and T. VanHoose. "The cooperative subject: Myth or reality?" *Journal of Experimental Psychology* 61 (1970):1–10.

Singer, Peter. *Animal Liberation,* 2nd ed. New York: New York Review of Books, 1990.

Skinner, B.F. *Beyond Freedom and Dignity.* New York: Knopf, 1971.

Sober, Elliott. *Philosophy of Biology.* Boulder, CO: Westview, 1993.

Stanovich, Keith. *How to Think Straight about Psychology.* Glenview, IL: Scott, Foresman and Company, 1986.

Steinberg, David. "The Roots of Pornography." In *Gender Basics: Feminist Perspectives on Women and Men,* edited by Anne Minas. Belmont, CA: Wadsworth, 1993.

Strunk, William and E.B. White. *The Elements of Style,* 3rd ed. London: Collier Macmillan, 1979.

Szasz, Thomas. *Heresies.* New York: Doubleday, 1976.

– *The Manufacture of Madness.* New York: Dell, 1970.

Thompson, Judith Jarvis. "A defense of abortion," *Philosophy and Public Affairs* 1, 1(1979): 173–87.

Toulmin, Stephen. "The Logic of Moral Reasoning." In *The Place of Reason in Ethics.* New York: Cambridge University Press (1970): 144–65.

Tversky, A. and D. Kahneman. "Extensional versus intuitive reasoning: The conjunction fallacy in probability judgement," *Psychological Bulletin* 90 (1983): 293–315.

Velasquez, Manuel. *Business Ethics: Concepts and Cases,* 4th ed. Upper Saddle River, NJ: Prentice Hall, 1998.

Wiggins, David. *Needs, Values, Truth.* Oxford: Oxford University Press, 1998.

Winchester, Simon. *The Professor and the Madman, a Tale of Murder, Insanity, and the Making of the Oxford English Dictionary.* New York: Harper Collins, 1988.

Wittgenstein, Ludwig. *Philosophical Investigations.* Oxford: Blackwell, 2001.

Index